T0178526

Lecture Notes in Computer Science 14219

Founding Editors

Gerhard Goos
Juris Hartmanis

The series Lecture Notes in Computer Science (LNCS), including its subseries Lecture Notes in Artificial Intelligence (LNAI) and Lecture Notes in Bioinformatics (LNBI), has established itself as a medium for the publication of new developments in computer science and information technology research, teaching, and education.

LNCS enjoys close cooperation with the computer science R & D community, the series counts many renowned academics among its volume editors and paper authors, and collaborates with prestigious societies. Its mission is to serve this international community by providing an invaluable service, mainly focused on the publication of conference and workshop proceedings and postproceedings. LNCS commenced publication in 1973.

Lucio Tommaso De Paolis · Pasquale Arpaia ·
Marco Sacco

Editors

Extended Reality

International Conference, XR Salento 2023
Lecce, Italy, September 6–9, 2023
Proceedings, Part II

 Springer

Editors
Lucio Tommaso De Paolis 🆔
University of Salento
Lecce, Italy

Pasquale Arpaia 🆔
University of Naples Federico II
Naples, Italy

Marco Sacco 🆔
CNR-STIIMA
Lecco, Italy

ISSN 0302-9743   ISSN 1611-3349 (electronic)
Lecture Notes in Computer Science
ISBN 978-3-031-43403-7   ISBN 978-3-031-43404-4 (eBook)
https://doi.org/10.1007/978-3-031-43404-4

This Springer imprint is published by the registered company Springer Nature Switzerland AG
The registered company address is: Gewerbestrasse 11, 6330 Cham, Switzerland

Paper in this product is recyclable.

Preface

In recent years, there has been a huge research interest in Virtual Reality (VR), Augmented Reality (AR), and Mixed Reality (MR) technologies that now play a very important role in various fields of application such as medicine, industry, cultural heritage, and education. The boundary between the virtual and real worlds continues to blur, and the constant and rapid spread of applications of these technologies makes it possible to create shortcuts that facilitate the interaction between humans and their environment and to encourage and facilitate the process of recognition and learning.

Virtual Reality technology enables the creation of realistic-looking worlds and enables the user to completely isolate himself from the reality around him, entering a new digitally created world. User inputs are used to modify the digital environment in real time and this interactivity contributes to the feeling of being part of the virtual world. Augmented Reality and Mixed Reality technologies, on the other hand, allow the real-time fusion of digital content into the real world to enhance perception by visualizing information that the user cannot directly detect with his/her senses. Applications of AR and MR technologies complement reality rather than replacing it completely and the user has the impression that virtual and real objects coexist in the same space.

eXtended Reality (XR) is an umbrella term encapsulating Virtual Reality, Augmented Reality, and Mixed Reality technologies.

Thanks to the increase in features that allow us to extend our real world and combine it with virtual elements, eXtended Reality is progressively expanding the boundaries of how we live, work, and relate.

The potential of XR technology is amazing and can transform consumers' everyday experiences and generate benefits in many market sectors, from industrial manufacturing to healthcare, education, cultural heritage, and retail.

This book contains the contributions to the International Conference on eXtended Reality (XR SALENTO 2023) held on 6–9 September 2023 in Lecce (Italy) and organized by the Augmented and Virtual Reality Laboratory (AVR Lab) at University of Salento (Italy). To accommodate many situations, XR Salento 2023 has been scheduled as a hybrid conference with the option of attending and presenting the paper in-person or following the scheduled activities remotely.

The goal of XR SALENTO 2023 is to create a unique opportunity for discussion and debate among scientists, engineers, educators, and students and allows them to connect with fellow entrepreneurs and companies operating in the same sector, thus experiencing applications of these emerging technologies.

XR SALENTO is an evolution of previous editions of the International Conference on Augmented Reality, Virtual Reality and Computer Graphics (SALENTO AVR), which had united the AR/VR community since 2014.

To cope with the growing demand for applications of eXtended Reality combined with other technologies, XR SALENTO 2023 also considered applications based on Digital Twins, Artificial Intelligence, and Data Mining technologies and realized to create a digital representation, collect and store data in real time, simulate the future state, and facilitate optimization.

We would like to sincerely thank the keynote speakers who gladly accepted our invitation and shared their expertise through enlightening speeches, helping us to fully meet the conference objectives. We were honored to have the following invited speakers:

- **Mariano Luis Alcañiz Raya** - Universitat Politècnica de València, Spain
- **Antonella Guidazzoli** - CINECA, Italy
- **Fabrizio Lamberti** - Politecnico di Torino, Italy

We cordially invite you to visit the XR SALENTO 2023 website (www.xrsalento.it) where you can find all relevant information about this event.

We are very grateful to the members of the Program Committee for their support and time spent in reviewing and discussing the submitted papers and doing so in a timely and professional manner. The received submissions were reviewed considering originality, significance, technical soundness, and clarity of exposition.

Based on the reviewing scores and critiques, 70 papers were selected for oral and poster presentation and publication in these proceedings.

We hope the readers will find in these pages interesting material and fruitful ideas for their future work.

July 2023   Lucio Tommaso De Paolis
                                                 Pasquale Arpaia
                                                 Marco Sacco

Organization

Conference Chair

Lucio Tommaso De Paolis   University of Salento, Italy

General Chairs

Pasquale Arpaia   University of Naples Federico II, Italy
Marco Sacco   STIIMA-CNR, Italy

Steering Committee

Andres Bustillo   University of Burgos, Spain
Antonio Lanzotti   University of Naples Federico II, Italy
Salvatore Livatino   University of Hertfordshire, UK
Roberto Pierdicca   Polytechnic University of Marche, Italy
Paolo Proietti   Leonardo SpA, Italy
Antonio Emmanuele Uva   Polytechnic University of Bari, Italy

Scientific Program Committee

Andrea Francesco Abate   University of Salerno, Italy
Sara Arlati   STIIMA-CNR, Italy
Álvar Arnaiz-González   Universidad de Burgos, Spain
Selim Balcisoy   Sabancı University, Turkey
Fabio Bello   Leonardo SpA, Italy
Marco Biagini   Italian Ministry of Defence, Italy
Monica Bordegoni   Polytechnic University of Milan, Italy
Davide Borra   No Real Interactive, Italy
Andrea Bottino   Polytechnic University of Turin, Italy
Andres Bustillo   University of Burgos, Spain
Massimo Cafaro   University of Salento, Italy
Maria Concetta Carruba   Università Telematica Pegaso, Italy
Marina Carulli   Politecnico di Milano, Italy
Laura Cercenelli   University of Bologna, Italy

Lucia Cimmino	University of Salerno, Italy
Laura Corchia	University of Salento, Italy
David Checa Cruz	University of Burgos, Spain
Rita Cucchiara	University of Modena, Italy
Yevgeniya Daineko	International Information Technology University, Kazakhstan
Egidio De Benedetto	University of Naples Federico II, Italy
Mariolino De Cecco	University of Trento, Italy
Valerio De Luca	University of Salento, Italy
Aida de Haro-García	Universidad de Cordoba, Spain
Giovanni D'Errico	Polytechnic University of Turin, Italy
Giuseppe Di Gironimo	University of Naples Federico II, Italy
Italo Epicoco	University of Salento, Italy
Aldo Franco Dragoni	Polytechnic University of Marche, Italy
Ben Falchuk	Peraton Labs, USA
Emanuele Frontoni	Polytechnic University of Marche, Italy
Maria Cristina Gaeta	Suor Orsola Benincasa University of Naples, Italy
Luigi Gallo	ICAR/CNR, Italy
Carola Gatto	University of Salento, Italy
Antonella Guidazzoli	CINECA Interuniversity Consortium, Italy
Leo Joskowicz	Hebrew University of Jerusalem, Israel
Tomas Krilavičius	Vytautas Magnus University, Lithuania
Vladimir Kuts	Tallinn University of Technology, Estonia
Fabrizio Lamberti	Polytechnic University of Turin, Italy
Mariangela Lazoi	University of Salento, Italy
Silvia Liaci	University of Basilicata, Italy
Salvatore Livatino	University of Hertfordshire, UK
Antonella Longo	University of Salento, Italy
Luca Mainetti	University of Salento, Italy
Eva Savina Malinverni	Polytechnic University of Marche, Italy
Federico Manuri	Politecnico di Torino, Italy
Matija Marolt	University of Ljubljana, Slovenia
Kim Martínez García	University of Burgos, Spain
Nicola Masini	CNR – Institute of Cultural Heritage Sciences, Italy
Nicola Moccaldi	University of Naples Federico II, Italy
Fabrizio Nunnari	German Research Center for Artificial Intelligence (DFKI), Germany
Üyesi Yasin Ortakci	Karabük University, Turkey
Miguel A. Padilla Castañeda	Universidad Nacional Autónoma de México, Mexico
Volker Paelke	Bremen University of Applied Sciences, Germany

Roberto Paiano	University of Salento, Italy
Giorgos Papadourakis	Hellenic Mediterranean University, Greece
Luigi Patrono	University of Salento, Italy
Giulia Pellegrino	University of Salento, Italy
Eduard Petlenkov	Tallinn University of Technology, Estonia
Roberto Pierdicca	Polytechnic University of Marche, Italy
Paolo Proietti	Leonardo SpA, Italy
Marco Pulimeno	University of Salento, Italy
Mario Covarrubias Rodriguez	Politecnico di Milano, Italy
Luis Javier Sánchez Aparicio	Higher Polytechnic School of Madrid, Spain
Andrea Sanna	Polytechnic University of Turin, Italy
Jaume Segura Garcia	Universitat de València, Spain
Huseyin Seker	Birmingham City University, UK
Italo Spada	CETMA, Italy
Elena Spadoni	Politecnico di Milano, Italy
Aleksei Tepljakov	Tallinn University of Technology, Estonia
Walter Terkaj	STIIMA-CNR, Italy
Stefano Triberti	Università Telematica Pegaso, Italy
Antonio Emmanuele Uva	Polytechnic University of Bari, Italy
Kristina Vassiljeva	Tallinn University of Technology, Estonia
Roberto Vergallo	University of Salento, Italy
Krzysztof Walczak	Poznań University of Economics and Business, Poland

Award Committee

Pasquale Arpaia	University of Naples Federico II, Italy
Lucio Tommaso De Paolis	University of Salento, Italy
Paolo Proietti	Leonardo SpA, Italy

Exhibit and Sponsor Committee

Pasquale Arpaia	University of Naples Federico II, Italy
Lucio Tommaso De Paolis	University of Salento, Italy

Local Organizing Committee

Silke Miss	XRtechnology srl, Italy
Maria Cristina Barba	University of Salento, Italy

Keynote Speakers

From Reality to Extended-Social Reality: Conceptualizing XR As a Bridge Between Mirror Worlds

Mariano Alcañiz

Polytechnic University of Valencia, Spain

Mariano Alcañiz, Ph.D., is the founding director of the Immersive Neurotechnologies Lab (LabLENI) at UPV and a Full Professor of Biomedical Engineering at the Polytechnic University of Valencia. His general research interests hover around a better understanding and enhancement of human cognition, combining insights and methods from computer science, psychology, and neuroscience. His work is centered on using empirical, behavioral science methodologies to explore people as they interact in these digital worlds. Still, he also researches to develop new ways to produce Extended Reality (XR) simulations. Towards this end, he has been involved in clinical psychology, neurodevelopmental disorders, consumer neuroscience, organizational neuroscience, education and training projects.

He has published more than 350 academic papers in interdisciplinary journals such as Scientific Reports and PLoS One and domain-specific journals in biomedical engineering, computer science, psychology, marketing, management, psychology, and education. The Spanish Research Agency and the European Commission have continuously funded his work for 30 years.

He is the coordinator of several national and European R&D programs of excellence. He has been the National Program Coordinator of the Information Society Technology (IST) of the Ministry of Science and Innovation of Spain (2015–2019) and the Spanish representative for ICT area at the Horizon 2020 European Research Program Committee. He is also Vice-President for Academic and Scientific Issues of the European Association for Extended Reality (EURO-XR).

Transforming Cultural Heritage Preservation and Valorization: The Contribution of Supercomputing, Artificial Intelligence, and the Digital Twin Paradigm

Antonella Guidazzoli

CINECA, Italy

Antonella Guidazzoli graduated with honors in Electronics and History from the University of Bologna. Since 2007, she has been the head of the Visual Information Technology Laboratory (VISIT Lab - http://visitlab.cineca.it) at CINECA (www.cineca.it/en), one of the most important Supercomputing centers internationally. The Visit Lab is responsible for activities on advanced visualization methods ranging from scientific visualization to real-time 3D graphics and XR applications.

She is also a lecturer and course director of the CINECA Summer School on Computer Graphics for Cultural Heritage. Antonella has published several papers in major international conferences such as the ACM SIGGRAPH conference and won awards for projects in the field of e-Culture and Digital Heritage. In addition, Antonella is an evangelist of Quantum computing.

eXtended Reality for Education and Training

Fabrizio Lamberti

Politecnico di Torino, Italy

Fabrizio Lamberti received his MSc and PhD degrees in Computer Engineering from Politecnico di Torino, Italy in 2000 and 2005 respectively. Currently, he is a Full Professor at the Department of Control and Computer Engineering, Politecnico di Torino, where he leads the "Graphics and Intelligent Systems" research laboratory and is responsible for the hub of VR@POLITO, the "Virtual Reality" initiative of Politecnico di Torino. Since October 2021, he is the Chair of the PhD Programme of Politecnico di Torino in "Computer and Control Engineering". Fabrizio Lamberti has authored/co-authored more than 250 technical papers in the areas of computer graphics and vision, human-machine interaction, intelligent computing, and educational technologies. Since 2002, he is a Senior Member of IEEE. He is currently a Member of the Board of Governors (Elected Member at Large 2021–2023) of IEEE Consumer Technology Society (CTSoc). He also serves as Vice President for Technical Activities of CTSoc. He currently serves as an Associate Editor for IEEE Transactions on Computers, IEEE Transactions on Learning Technologies, IEEE Transactions on Consumer Electronics, and IEEE Consumer Electronics Magazine.

Contents – Part II

eXtended Reality in Health and Medicine

Contents – Part I

Digital Twin

Artificial Intelligence

User Experience in eXtended Reality

**Virtual Reality for Neurofeedback, Biofeedback and Emotion
Recognition**

eXtended Reality in Education

Google Earth in VR, for Students with Special Needs

Maria Concetta Carruba[2] , Alessandra Calcagno[1], and Mario Covarrubias[1(✉)]

[1] Mechanical Engineering Department, Politecnico di Milano, Milan, Italy
mario.covarrubias@polimi.it
[2] Universita' Telematica Pegaso, Milan, Italy

Abstract. Virtual Reality (VR) is one of the major technology trends right now and will increase much more in the future. This technology promotes a new way of interaction, communication, and productivity. This paper aims to allow students with special needs to work and interact with Google Earth using VR. The theoretical framework used, the International Classification of Functioning, Disability, and Health (ICF) perspective and checklists, allows us to identify the best way to propose an interactive and funny learning process for students with Special Educational Needs (SEN). By means of ICF, the definition of the proper technological tools and of the main steps in which the learning process can be divided is possible. This approach, indeed, leads to the translation of cognitive tasks that can result too complex for students with cognitive fragilities into concrete experiences more easily to do for all, promoting inclusion and equity in our modern digital society. In the present work, the inclusive VR-based technology is tested on a group of 10 students with SEN in Google Earth environment, and the final outcomes in terms of system usability are presented.

Keywords: Extended Reality · Training · Special Education · Neurodevelopmental Disorder · Down Syndrome · Autism · Inclusive Education · Special Educational Needs

1 Introduction

This paper is the result of an experimental activity carried out with students with different types of disabilities, such as Down syndrome, Autism Spectrum Disorder, and intellectual fragility, who belong to the Italian association on cognitive enhancement (ASPOC) [1] based in Lecco, Italy. The group of students, aged 19 to 35, are in that stalemate phase from the conclusion of the compulsory education and training to the early stages of entering the work environment. Families of such young adults often receive poor assistance both in managing their children in everyday life and, more importantly, in enhancing or at least maintaining their residual motor and cognitive skills. ASPOC College was created to overcome these limits and become a bridge between the end of the standard education path and the working world. Specifically, among the various skills

L. T. De Paolis et al. (Eds.): XR Salento 2023, LNCS 14219, pp. 3–14, 2023.
https://doi.org/10.1007/978-3-031-43404-4_1

being coached in the ASPOC College (such as autonomy and decision-making), students are being ferried to the development of digital skills, now fundamental in our society. Increasingly, it is essential to build educational curricula that on the one hand promote inclusion and respect for everyone, and on the other, promote active engagement, motivation, and curiosity in students [2]. Learning is a natural process which requires effort, both for healthy students and, even more, for those students whose learning process is more complex because of their diagnostic framework. Nowadays, the market offers technologies that could promote, or at least support, the teaching and learning processes. Given the attraction that young adults generally feel to digital, the use of alternative technological means could also enhance students' involvement and, therefore, learning outcomes. For this reason, it's important not only to design proper and accessible technology, but also to promote the pleasure of learning. In this context, Virtual Reality (VR) is an example of emerging technology promising in promoting a new immersive and interactive way of learning. The present work aimed to develop a VR-based module able to involve ASPOC students in different activities with various digital tools. The main idea was to implement and test a new learning technology that could cheer the learning processes without ever losing the goal of empowerment. In the next sections, we will introduce the approaches and instruments used in order to adopt the VR-based computing module as an inclusive and versatile learning mean for students with cognitive difficulties. Finally, we will describe one of the several activities carried out with the enrolled subjects thanks to this technology: exploration of the world with Google Earth.

1.1 Virtual Reality in Education

In a society of constant connection and mobile devices, we have witnessed not only the exponential growth of the phenomena of access to (and possession of) digital devices but, at the same time, the proliferation of new opportunities for innovation on various levels: from those of production to those of innovative methodologies in education. Today, Europe and the logic of internationalization are more and more asking schools to train students with expendable digital skills, in order to prepare them to the near future, which is going to be increasingly digitized. To avoid that this innovation process brings to the generation of new forms of exclusion, it is incumbent upon us to extend an innovative and digital educational proposal to each one. The new educational challenge, also recorded by the research trajectories in this field (horizon 2030), experience technology and digital as a real support for learning. Artificial Intelligence (AI), VR, Extended Reality (ER), and Augmented Reality (AR) can be considered real facilitators based on the ICF [3] perspective by WHO (explored further in the next section, 1.4 Paraghaph). In this paper, we will focus on the evaluation of VR as an instrument to support inclusive education. VR, indeed, has particular potentialities that make it an adequate technology for this purpose. First of all, VR seems to be associated to an increase in students' engagement and to promote optimal learning and student satisfaction [4]. Secondly, VR is able to fill the gap between theory and practice, which is effective for every learner, especially for students with cognitive fragility. In the third instance, VR allows high degrees of personalization and differentiation [5], and this allows to design learning processes tailored to each learner. Therefore, basing on the previous users' experiences and research results in this area, the student will be able to personalize his or her experience with the tools. Nowadays, we are still far from the complete introduction of these new technologies in the learning processes, which still represents a challenge. Nevertheless, recent research shows that such teaching revolution is both an effective choice in terms of learning outcomes and almost a dutiful act to respond to the challenges our society imposes on us. Moreover, it promotes well-being and rediscover the pleasure of learning. According to Wells [6], education can be seen as "a process by which entities transmit value sets, information, and expertise to others, whereas, learning could well be the process of obtaining, expanding on, and sustaining new knowledge, value sets, and skills". Nothing could be more relevant today. According to Wells [6], the learning process can be the conscious or unintentional response to education or an unintended situational stimulus, if education is considered a purposeful collection of activities developed and conducted with the intention of provoking change in a learner. As they engage, observe, and manipulate objects in their environment, learners can learn concepts, construct knowledge, gain experience, and understand situations using these stimuli from planned or unplanned settings [6,7]. Based on the aforementioned concepts, it is clear that chances for education and learning exist outside of mainstream or formal contexts, including training facilities, the workplace, and other settings [8,9]. In recent years, a noticeable increase in the need for accountability in educational procedures that are intended to encourage learning occurred. Specifically, it is necessary to shed light on the connections between implemented processes and expected learning results. Educational and learning managers implemented several strategies to guarantee accountability for educational results and enhance performance effectiveness in order to meet the accountability and learning outcomes needs. Virtual reality (VR) integration into teaching and learning is one of such strategies [10]. The main idea is to bring the learning activities in rich and authentic contexts, even if virtual, so that students can experience in a realistic way the phenomena being studied [11] [12] [13]. In order to focus on specialized or targeted core learning units, content designers and managers can redirect, redistribute, or scale cognitive efforts that would have been invested in attempting to situate complexity through VR programming [11] [10] [14] [7]. Moreover, VR makes learning increasingly concrete and enjoyable for students and, therefore, can effectively meet the specific needs of SEN students, whose cognitive frailties could make difficult the process of abstraction and necessary the practice to support the theoretical learning process. In the literature emerges that the usage of VR in general education opens new learning possibilities [12]. For instance, teaching astronomy by using VR tile, virtual 3D modeling package, web camera, projector, and a whiteboard to overtake traditional methods based on books. VR can be used to visualize abstract concepts like airflow, magnetic field, molecules, and so on but also can be used to create VR games that enhance students' engagement. A group of student learned to collect data on simulated radiation values on their campus which was hypothetically near a Nuclear Power Plant by means of an Android tablet. Moreover, in [13] the beneficial use of such technology as a means of visualizing abstract concepts, phenomena that are too small, large, fast, or slow to be seen with human eyes, was demonstrated. To summarize the key points obtained from the examples presented, VR could enable (i) learning content in 3D, (ii) collaborative learning; (iii) learners' senses of presence, immediacy, and immersion, (iv) visualizing the invisible, and (v) bridging formal and informal learning. VR can also enhance students' knowledge with practical skills that are difficult to obtain with the traditional learning method. The main difference is that VR gives a new sense of learning to the students, enhancing their interest in the topic by immersing them directly inside it, and improving spatial and psycho-motor cognitive skills. These aspects are confirmed by Matt Bower et al. [15] during their research. They pointed out some of the pedagogic aspects that AR can support: (1) constructivist learning: AR makes students more interested in the topic and engaged on a deeper level of concepts, (2) situated learning: AR enables to bring the real world directly inside classrooms, (3) game-based learning: the use of a game-based interface facilitates students in learning some specific topics, like the examples provided in [12], (4) inquiry-based learning based on electronically gather data for future analysis. In the case of the group of students who were involved in the present work, it is shown with a clear table all the advantages of AR [10] [13]in the educational setting: learning outcomes, pedagogical contributions, interaction, and others.

1.2   Case Study. ASPOC Association: The Sample

This work involved 10 young adults with special needs, who are also part of the Association for the Development of Cognitive Potential named ASPOC. This association was founded in 2004 in Lecco (Lombardy, Italy) by a group of parents of kids with cognitive problems. This Association organizes training activities with the aim of promoting inclusiveness for its students not only in the classroom, but also in society at large. One of the first goals for ASPOC families is to improve how the cultural and social environment supports people with disabilities and their parents. Specifically, the idea is to boost cognitive development and carry on improving residual skills to prepare SEN participants to work experiences. The ASPOC project takes place in the three contexts of family, health, and school where SENs are needed to participate regularly. The parents are invited to recognize the significant roles of educators, rehabilitation specialists, siblings, healthcare professionals, and institutions as part of the mediated learning process. The importance of context, the procedures, and the caliber of mediated learning processes, according to ASPOC, play a crucial part in the growth of each. Based on scientific evidence that people's neural architecture can change if exposed to enough and effective stimuli (i.e., neural plasticity), the association tries to identify innovative and attracting learning activities able to exploit this physiological mechanism and promote cognitive improvements in its students. For this reason, the association closely coordinates its activities with the resources and facilities offered in Italy. In particular, ASPOC also collaborates with Politecnico di Milano in order to identify the best technology-based practices for rehabilitation pathways. Among the different identified activities, ASPOC with Politecnico di Milano tested the Computing Module as learning tool on the 10 enrolled students (age range 19–35). Involved subjects are affected by different kind of disabilities, such as Down syndrome, Autism Spectrum Disorder, neurodevelopmental disorder, and cognitive fragility. In addition to employing both the technological and instructional approaches, we are determining the ideal rehabilitation sets to enable cognitive enhancement for these students.

1.3   The Inclusive Approach

The design process of the teaching activity, supported by the pedagogical approach, allowed students to break down the task executed with the Computing Module into multiple steps that they could more easily pursue. This approach makes the learning process more concrete and promotes digital skills and process generalization. Based on the appropriate set of exercises, this technology can meet the cognitive enhancement needs of students by allowing them to create an appropriate context, work on motivation, making the process enjoyable.
The design process is structured on these phases:

1. observation based on the ICF (further explored in 1.4 Paraghaph) check list of each individual student to identify specific characteristics;
2. analysis of the educational potential of the set of exercises on the platform;
3. identification of a set of exercises for each student;
4. design of a monitoring tool;
5. data collection;
6. data analysis;
7. dissemination and sharing;
8. project design open to a larger sample.

   The adequate sets work to improve cognitive skills and respect the social-emotional skills. The analysis of the adequate sets, will be based on ICF, by WHO, approach: the health condition is a result of activities and participation. The ICF framework includes the contexts as facilitators or barriers.

1.4   Theoretical Framework. The ICF for the Design of Inclusive Activities

To identify students' strengths and weaknesses, impediments, and facilitators needed to support them throughout proposed activities, these latter were conducted after a preliminary observation of students based on a checklist on the ICF (International Classification of Functioning) by WHO model. Explaining functionality, capacity, and performance using terms and tests that are commonplace is crucial. In order to accomplish this goal, the WHO created the International Classification of Functioning, Disability, and Health (ICF) as an addendum to the International Classification of Diseases (ICD). The World Health Organization (WHO) approved ICF as a systematic classification of health and health-related domains in 2001 [16] [17], covering biological structures and functions, activity, participation, and environmental factors (Fig. 1).

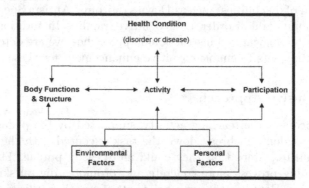

Fig. 1. Contextual factors and Health Conditions

The United Nations also recommended ICF as a good tool for defending the rights of people with disabilities. ICF stands for the holistic, biopsychosocial understanding of functioning as opposed to the conventional biomedical approach. According to the biological perspective, a person's functional restriction is a static trait that can be altered by treating a disease or damage [18,19]. The functional difficulty is defined as a mismatch between a person's health status and the demands placed on him by his actual living circumstances by the biopsychosocial model [20]. We were able to start from a solid understanding of the kids and develop activities that were manageable for them by setting the activities from an ICF perspective. Checklist observation is crucial. The ability to tailor and differentiate the pathway based on the student's abilities is made possible by this particular observation, which is based on the ICF checklist. In the ICF paradimg, an important distinction must be done between performance and capacity, since the former identifies what the student has already completed while the latter defines potential empowering scenarios that are feasible for the student.

2   Tools and Technologies Used to Promote Inclusion

2.1   Google Earth VR

Google Earth VR [21] allows to explore the world from totally new perspectives in virtual reality. This virtual reality app allows to see the world's cities, landmarks, and natural wonders. It is possible to fly over a city, stand at the top of the highest peaks, and even soar into space. Earth VR comes with cinematic tours and hand-picked destinations that send the user to the Amazon River, the Manhattan skyline, the Grand Canyon, the Swiss Alps, and more.

Figure 2 shows some places that can be selected from the user while he/she is using the Google Earth VR application.

Fig. 2. Google Earth in Virtual Reality

2.2 Oculus Quest 2 Setup: Create Your Virtual Playspace

The Oculus Quest 2 is a fully standalone system, this allows to run the applications on the go without fear of tangled cables. The Quest 2 is characterized by a per-eye resolution of $1,832 \times 1,920$ pixels with 6GB of RAM and a 90 Hz refresh rate.

A calibration procedure is performed by the educator, before using the Google Earth VR application, which is necessary in order to guarantee the proper safety distances while the user interacts in the Virtual Environment.

- The guardian boundary for the Oculus Quest 2. The user'll be greeted by a colorless view of the real world space around him/her. This is called passthrough and merges the real world with virtual elements. Here the user'll use the controller to draw the playspace boundaries. This virtual barrier prevents the user from running into walls or breaking the TV during an intense game activity.
- If the user plays VR in multiple rooms throughout the house/school, the user'll be pleased to know that these boundaries are persistent. This allow to walk in and out of boundaries without having to redraw the space every time. Leaving an area to see a floating untouched playspace tows the line between futuristic and eerie.
- Oculus prevent from recording when setting up the boundary for safety reasons.

2.3   Visiting a Place Thorough Google Earth VR

This activity involved 10 ASPOC students. They have learned how to use the Quest 2 controllers for:

- Select the place (city, parks, ecc)
- Navigate in the Virtual Reality Environment
- Use the tele-transportation approach
- Use the street view option as well

This activity involves 15 min of training before using Google Earth in VR with the help of 10 volunteer students from Politecnico di Milano. These students are part of the university Leadership Program.

Figure 3 shows some of the training sessions with the volunteer students helping the ASPOC students in the VR activities.

Fig. 3. ASPOC students while using Google Earth VR supported by Polimi Volunteer Students

2.4   System Usability Scale (SUS)

The System Usability Scale (SUS) proposed by John Brooke in 1986 [22] was applied. This tool consists of a 10-item questionnaire with five response options; from strongly agree to strongly disagree. It allows the evaluation of a wide variety of products and services, including applications. In this case, to have a better learning outcome for the ASPOC students, it was decided to introduce the application first with the help of a projector guiding students to understand all the important aspects of the process. Then participants had the possibility to use the Google Earth VR individually. Some ASPOC students had difficulties associating their answer with the traditional scale of the SUS which is based on a

5-point Likert Scale from strongly disagree to strongly agree. To simplify this relation, the scale has been modified using a 5-smiley representation as shown in Fig. 4. In addition, the questionnaire was administered orally by the educators to students, both to better explain the unclear questions and to clearly identify the students' responses on the scale. In addition, spontaneous comments during and after the interaction with the Google Earth VR application have been used to best understand their experience.

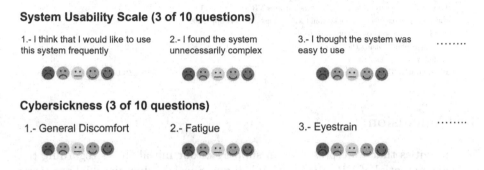

System Usability Scale (3 of 10 questions)

1.- I think that I would like to use this system frequently

2.- I found the system unnecessarily complex

3.- I thought the system was easy to use

Cybersickness (3 of 10 questions)

1.- General Discomfort   2.- Fatigue   3.- Eyestrain

Fig. 4. ASPOC SUS and Cybersickness questionnaires.

To obtain the final score as number out of 100, the 5-smiley scale has been converted to the classical numerical scale from 1 to 5. Then, the answers have been normalized: for each of the odd numbered questions, subtract 1 from the score, for each of the even numbered questions, subtract their value from 5. These values have been added up and multiplied by 2.5. Final results are summarized in Table 1.

From the SUS questionnaires and the comments collected during the activity, we can conclude that Google Earth VR experience was, on average, very engaging for the ASPOC students, who showed enthusiasm in visiting and exploring many places around the world. All students were excited about the possibility of seeing and interact with the virtual application that clearly is not a common activity. The Cybersicknes result shows that ASPOC Students can wear without problems the Quest 2 device. The approach adopted in this activity allow the ASPOC Student to explore in first person the Virtual Place (who wears the Quest 2) while the classmates assist to the virtual path in third person through the use of a streaming screen. This is however an inclusive approach in order to allow all students to explore the virtual places.

Table 1. SUS questionnaire results for the Google Earth VR based application. Mean values ranges from 0 to 4 and negatively worded items have been normalized. The system obtain 73/100

	Statement	Likert Scale (1:5)	Normal Mean (0:4)	Std. Dev
1	I think that I would like to use this VR app frequently	4.00	3.00	1.26
2	I found the VR app unnecessarily complex	2.45	2.55	1.44
3	I thought the system was easy to use	4.09	3.09	0.94
4	I think that I would need the support of a technical person	3.27	1.73	1.42
5	I found the various functions in this VR app were well integrated	4.27	3.27	0.90
6	I thought there was too much inconsistency in this VR app	1.82	3.18	1.08
7	I would imagine that most people would learn to use this VR app	4.00	3.00	0.63
8	I found the VR app very cumbersome to use	2.36	2.64	1.29
9	I felt very confident using the VR app	3.82	2.82	1.08
10	I needed to learn a lot of things before	2.27	2.73	0.79
	Total (Sum*2.5)		**73.00**	**18.5**

3 Conclusion

The activities that were presented in support of our initial thesis regarding the inclusive potential of VR in Education [23] and Special Education [24] processes are tangible examples of how technologies can be designed for educational and inclusive purposes at the same time and how, with a multidisciplinary (technical and pedagogical) approach, ethical and inclusive use of technology can be promoted. Virtual reality enabled students to train in the following educational skills:

– Knowledge of technologies and, in this specific case, VR tools and learning how to use them;
– Decision-making skills (which country do I want to visit?) and problem-solving skills (how do I organize the activity to learn about this city?);
– Awareness of proprioception and proximity within group contexts;
– The distinction between real and virtual;
– Metacognition to reframe the lived experience.

These promising results, let us hypothesize that VR-based learning activities of this kind could become functional and repeatable models, that promote digital innovation and the development of an equitable and inclusive society, which fits well for all and promotes well-being.

References

1. Aspoc association (2023). http://www.aspoc.it/
2. Faruk, M., M, I.M.S.U., Syafi'i, I., Mukhidin, Sukirman, D., Ali, M., Alias, N.: The role of using virtual reality in learning in an education environment. In: Proceedings of the Unima International Conference on Social Sciences and Humanities (UNICSSH 2022), pp. 1234–1238. Atlantis Press (2023). https://doi.org/10.2991/978-2-494069-35-0_148

3. Organization, W.H.: International Classification of Functioning. Disability and Health. World Health Organization, Geneva, Switzerland (2001)
4. Di Paolo, A., Beatini, V., Di Tore, S., Todino, M.: How serious game can promote inclusion, history and cultural heritage through the virtual reality. J. Inclusive Methodol. Technol. Learn. Teach. **3** (2023)
5. Tomlinson, C.A., Sousa, D.A.: Differentiation and the Brain: How Neuroscience supports the Learner-Friendly Classroom. Solution Tree, 1st edn. (2010)
6. Wells, G.: Dialogic Inquiry: Towards a Socio-cultural Practice and Theory of Education. Learning in Doing: Social, Cognitive and Computational Perspectives, Cambridge University Press (1999). https://doi.org/10.1017/CBO9780511605895
7. Tzanavari, A., Tsapatsoulis, N.: Affective, interactive and cognitive methods for E-Learning design: creating an optimal education experience. IGI Global (2010). https://doi.org/10.4018/978-1-60566-940-3
8. Bandura, A.: Social Learning Theory. Prentice Hall, Englewood Cliffs (1977)
9. Bandura, A.: Social Fundations of Though and Action. Prentice-Hall, Michigan (1986)
10. Akçayir, M., Akçayir, G.: Advantages and challenges associated with augmented reality for education: a systematic review of the literature. Educ. Res. Rev. **20**, 1–11 (2017). https://doi.org/10.1016/j.edurev.2016.11.002. https://www.sciencedirect.com/science/article/pii/S1747938X16300616
11. Christou, C.: Virtual Reality in Education. Affective, Interactive and Cognitive Methods for E-Learning Design: Creating an Optimal Education Experience. IGI Global. https://doi.org/10.4018/978-1-60566-940-3
12. Wu, H.K., Lee, S.W.Y., Chang, H.Y., Liang, J.C.: Current status, opportunities and challenges of augmented reality in education. Comput. Educ. **62**, 41–49 (2013). https://doi.org/10.1016/j.compedu.2012.10.024. https://www.sciencedirect.com/science/article/pii/S0360131512002527
13. Saidin, N.F., Halim, N.D.A., Yahaya, N.: A review of research on augmented reality in education: advantages and applications. Int. Educ. Stud. **8**(13) (2015). https://doi.org/10.1016/j.edurev.2016.11.002. https://www.sciencedirect.com/science/article/pii/S1747938X16300616
14. Frederiksen, J.G., Sørensen, S.M.D., Konge, L., Svendsen, M.B.S., Nobel-Jørgensen, M., Bjerrum, F., Andersen, S.A.W.: Cognitive load and performance in immersive virtual reality versus conventional virtual reality simulation training of laparoscopic surgery: a randomized trial. Surg. Endosc. **34**, 1244–1252 (2020)
15. Bower, M., Howe, C., McCredie, N., Robinson, A., Grover, D.: Augmented reality in education - cases, places and potentials. Educ. Media Int. **51**(1), 1–15 (2014). https://doi.org/10.1080/09523987.2014.889400
16. Yaruss, J.S., Quesal, R.W.: Overall assessment of the speaker's experience of stuttering (oases): documenting multiple outcomes in stuttering treatment. J. Fluency Disord. **31**(2), 90–115 (2006)
17. Organization, W.H.: International Classification of Functioning, Disability, and Health: Children & Youth Version: ICF-CY. World Health Organization (2007)
18. Barnes, C., Mercer, G.: Competing models and approaches. Exploring disability, pp. 14–42 (2010)
19. Peterson, D.B.: International classification of functioning, disability and health: an introduction for rehabilitation psychologists. Rehabil. Psychol. **50**(2), 105 (2005)
20. Schuntermann, M.F.: The implementation of the international classification of functioning, disability and health in germany: experiences and problems. Int. J. Rehabil. Res. **28**(2), 93–102 (2005)

21. Google earth vr (2023). https://arvr.google.com/earth/
22. Brooke, J., et al.: Sus-a quick and dirty usability scale. Usability Eval. Ind. **189**(194), 4–7 (1996)
23. Rojas-Sánchez, M.A., Palos-Sánchez, P.R., Folgado-Fernández, J.A.: Systematic literature review and bibliometric analysis on virtual reality and education. Educ. Inf. Technol. **28**(1), 155–192 (2023)
24. Lorenzo, G.G., Newbutt, N.N., Lorenzo-Lledo, A.A.: Design concepts for solution and solid-state emitters-a modern viewpoint on classical and non-classical approaches. Education and information technologies (2023)

A Systematic Literature Review of Mixed Reality Learning Approaches

Benedikt Hensen$^{(\boxtimes)}$ (iD)

Chair of Computer Science 5, RWTH Aachen University, Aachen, Germany
hensen@dbis.rwth-aachen.de

Abstract. Mixed reality provides a high potential to support learning activities. There are many individual case studies in the literature which investigate mixed reality learning in a specific use case. The research process has been expedited by recent mixed reality innovations like developments in mobile augmented reality and headsets. In this systematic literature study, the cross connections between these existing case studies were investigated in detail by inspecting how researchers used mixed reality technology to support learning and teaching in formal and informal education by comparing similar results and same encountered challenges. 80 publications were analyzed to gain insights into the used technology, learning methods, integration in educational processes, the use cases, the target audience, the evaluation setups and common results in 19 categories of this set of publications. Based on the results, a mixed reality learning cube for classifying the approaches was developed in a co-evolutionary process. Each cell of the mixed reality learning cube describes a possible way of integrating mixed reality in education, based on the learning design, technology approach and integration point in the process. The assignment of publications to cells of the cube also highlights where future research is required. A technology landscape emerged to classify the mixed reality devices regarding their characteristics. The elaborated mixed reality learning cube enables a systematic approach to integrate mixed reality in formal and informal education.

Keywords: Mixed Reality · Augmented Reality · Virtual Reality · Technology-Enhanced Learning

1 Introduction

Digital solutions for education are on the rise, e.g. as a consequence of the necessity for remote teaching, especially during the COVID-19 pandemic. Even before the pandemic, institutions integrated solutions in the realm of virtual learning

I thank the German Federal Ministry of Education and Research for their support within the project "Personalisierte Kompetenzentwicklung und hybrides KI-Mentoring" (tech4compKI; id: 16DHB2213).

L. T. De Paolis et al. (Eds.): XR Salento 2023, LNCS 14219, pp. 15–34, 2023.
https://doi.org/10.1007/978-3-031-43404-4_2

environments into their curriculum. An emerging opportunity for digital learning is provided by mixed reality. During the last six years, mixed reality made a leap with regard to technology and enables researchers to further explore the possibilities to integrate it into educational settings. Utilizing available hardware like the Microsoft HoloLens or smartphone-based augmented reality, educators are able to realize new learning experiences for formal and informal education and make them accessible to a larger number of students. The potential beneficial effects of mixed reality on learning outcomes were already proven [15]. Research is currently producing mixed reality (MR) learning studies for specific use cases in order to explore and evaluate different approaches and solutions with regard to their effectiveness for learning. Hence, an extensive literature survey was conducted with the goal to provide detailed insights and analyses regarding the common results and differences that were found by the previous research. The main contributions of this paper are a detailed analysis of a large dataset extracted from representative literature in the field of mixed reality-enhanced learning an MR learning cube that formalizes the research field regarding the combinations of learning design with mixed reality technology and its integration point in education, a technology landscape that gives insights into the different characteristics of available devices to realize mixed reality learning prototypes and the identification of overall results, as well as gaps in the research field.

The paper is structured as follows: Sect. 2 shows previous literature studies about similar content. Section 3 highlights our methodology for querying the literature. After that, Sect. 4 gives a detailed insight into the various results that were collected from the literature, e.g. regarding the learning design, used technology, use cases, target audience, etc. In Sect. 5, the discovered results are discussed and the paper concludes with Sect. 6.

2   Related Work

This paper focuses on learning with MR. As there are several definitions and understandings in research about what MR entails and encompasses [77], this paper refers to the wide-spread definition of MR which was first proposed by Milgram and Kishino [57]. They define MR as a spectrum of all degrees of mixtures between real-world elements and virtual views, including the technologies of augmented reality (AR), augmented virtuality and virtual reality (VR).

In the related work, there are existing overviews about MR learning which cover different time periods or focus on particular sub-topics. Pellas et al. [64] inspect 21 studies where MR is applied for K12 learning between the years of 2002 and 2018. Similarly, Suryodiningrat et al. [80] focus on MR research for schools and training scenarios in their systematic literature review of 41 publications between 2011 and 2021. Moreover, a study of 68 papers up to 2019 focuses on VR in classroom education [19]. Another literature study by González Vargas et al. [29] inspected 84 studies published between 2009 and 2019 with the particular focus on AR applied for the field of cultural heritage. A broader study was conducted by Annafi et al. [4] who give an overview of MR in all levels of education, including special needs education. Their results are based on 30 studies from 2009 to 2019.

These studies collect valuable insights about approaches to augment learning with earlier MR technologies. Most of the literature studies, however, end in the last decade and do not fully cover the surge in new research publications which was enabled by the publications of the two Microsoft HoloLens generations in 2016 and 2019, as well as advancements for mobile AR technologies with the releases of the libraries ARCore and ARKit in 2018 and 2017. In the years following these breakthroughs, novel research was released which was also influenced by the new relevance of e-learning and remote teaching due to the COVID-19 pandemic. For these reasons, it was decided to conduct a research study which spans the years 2017 to 2022 and to inspect studies where MR is applied in higher education, K12 and professional training scenarios.

3 Methodology

For this literature study, papers were collected which apply MR technologies in a learning context. Queries for publications use the search engines of Springer Link, IEEE Xplore, ACM Digital Library and dblp. A query schema was constructed as shown in Fig. 1 based on keywords from MR and learning. For MR, the process searches for the terminology, hardware and software names. In the learning field, keywords include common terminology and educational approaches. The final set of queries is created with the Cartesian product of the lists with MR and learning termini to combine both fields and to account for variety in the naming.

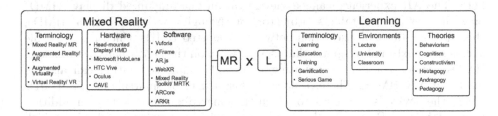

Fig. 1. Query Schema for Combining Keywords

These query combinations yielded a raw set of 4,716 publications. To collect comparable research studies, the publications were filtered according to the following criteria: The publication needs to present a study that applies MR in a learning use case. Moreover, it needs to conduct a user study with the given MR intervention. Only English papers were included. Based on this, the papers were filtered in a semi-automatic process. In a first pass, the titles and abstracts of the selected papers were extracted and based on the title, papers were filtered out which are not about the combination of MR and learning. This excluded publications with similar terminology but about different topics like machine learning for MR. As a result, 2,170 publications were left. Next, papers were flagged which already state in the abstracts that they conducted a user study. The rest was manually screened to exclude those without an evaluation like research proposals and extended abstracts. In the next manual pass, the papers were rated from one to five based on quality criteria such as evaluation setup, sample size, expressiveness of results and innovative ideas. The top 80 publications were included for the detailed data extraction and analysis.

4 Literature Analysis

Out of the 80 papers, 41 cover AR, 30 are aboutVR and nine publications combine AR and VR. In the use cases, medicine is predominant with 18 publications, followed by six studies about general education, five MR systems applied in museums, four construction training scenarios and three industrial use cases.

4.1 Technology Analysis

After viewing and extracting the data about the specific hardware components that the literature describes, I developed an overview of the AR and VR hardware landscape. It is depicted in the Euler diagram of Fig. 2a.

The landscape depicts classes of AR and VR hardware. On the AR side, it is split into marker-based and markerless tracking approaches. In the marker-based approach, the system searches for cards with specific patterns and reconstructs the viewing perspective from the distortion of the pattern. In markerless tracking, the system is able to track the user's position and movement without external help. The AR experience can be viewed on an head-mounted display (HMD) or with smartphones, tablets, projectors or through a webcam. For the HMDs, there is an additional distinction between supported HMDs which require cable access to an external computer that is, e.g., worn on the belt, whereas standalone HMDs are self-contained computing units. The same separation can also be made for VR HMDs. There, a special class exists of smartphone VR HMDs where the device is a casing into which the smartphone is inserted. In addition to the HMDs, VR can also be experienced with a stereoscopic display which can either be screens or projections. A special case is the CAVE [22], a room-size installation where the walls are displays. Figure 2b shows the distributed devices of the studies onto the technology landscape. The results show that supported VR HMDs are most prevalent with 29 cases. 21 of these instances use the HTC Vive. This is followed by 21 publications with marker-based AR implementations on the smartphone. 16 of them are created using the marker-tracking library Vuforia. The third most used technology class are markerless standalone AR HMDs with 11 publications whose systems were created with the Microsoft HoloLens. Regarding the software, the most used development tool is the Unity 3D engine with 56 instances. This is followed by 22 studies which apply the Vuforia library, six which developed their system with SteamVR and five were built with Microsoft's Mixed Reality Toolkit.

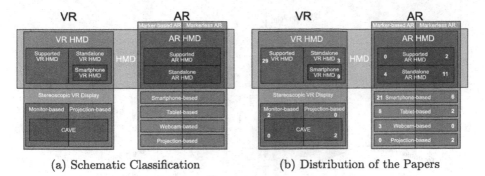

(a) Schematic Classification   (b) Distribution of the Papers

Fig. 2. Mixed Reality Technology Landscape

4.2   Approach Classification

Based on the studies in the literature, I identified recurring approaches. They can be structured on three axes: The learning design determines how knowledge is conveyed and how students interact with the system. Moreover, the integration point specifies how the MR application is applied in the educational process, e.g., during lectures or in group work. The third dimension regards the technological approach on how the system was realized using the available MR hardware. For each axis, four recognizable classes were identified which were present in the literature. In the learning design, four categories are predominantly applied. They concern the application of individual modules where the application is a general framework which can be configured to work with content from any fields of study. An example is a system which lets the user upload own 3D models from any domain and then provides the tools to set up a learning experience on this 3D model. Many systems also apply gamification or game-based learning to enhance the motivation of students. One common approach for learning is also to simulate real scenarios in AR or VR to prepare students. Another learning approach utilizes the 3D space of MR to organize the learning content spatially.

A research approach is then classified as a combination of cells in the resulting MR learning cube visualized in Fig. 3 by identifying the approaches for each axis. For instance, a MR learning intervention which runs on the Microsoft HoloLens which provides quests, badges and leaderboards to motivate group work in the MR environment can be classified as the highlighted cell in Fig. 3. An MR learning application can also cover multiple cells as the classes on an axis do not exclude each. It is also possible to combine the approaches to a composite application. In the technology approach, applications can be cross-platform compatible and provide versions for HMDs and smartphones which would cover immersive AR & VR technologies and markerless non-immersive AR. Similarly, an application can target multiple integration points as it can, e.g., target collaboration between students and also allow for interactions between tutors and their students. In the same way, learning designs can also be combined, e.g., by gamifying simulations. Overall, the MR learning cube allows for a systematic

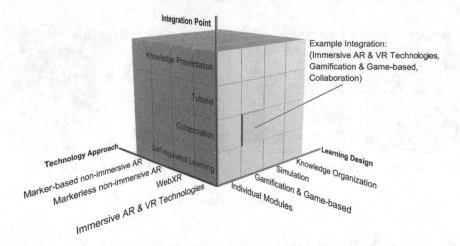

Fig. 3. MR Learning Cube to Classify MR Education Approaches

categorization of integrations of MR into educational processes, e.g., at university and practical trainings. It can highlight possible combinations, as well as under-researched cells onto which future work can focus.

Figure 4 illustrates a view of the MR learning cube sliced into its planes based on the integration point and assigned the studies to each cell. Approaches can appear in multiple cells as techniques, learning designs and targeted use cases can overlap. Hence, the sum of the cells is larger than 80 papers. The result shows the most explored and least investigated approaches to MR-enhanced learning. The most covered cell regards learning systems with 11 publications which use immersive AR and VR technologies to simulate scenarios for self-regulated learning. With 10 instances each, the two learning designs of individual modules and simulation with immersive AR and VR technologies in knowledge presentation such as lectures are also prevalent. Generally, the immersive MR technologies with native apps are most dominant in the inspected papers with 53 instances. In contrast to this, there were only two examples which apply WebXR to build their learning application. Moreover, in the learning design, only two studies inspected knowledge organisation where the spatial nature of MR is used to structure knowledge visually in the space, e.g., in the Method of Loci. There are only seven approaches for markerless non-immersive AR which is likely due to the fact that it requires high-end smartphones and tablets. In the integration points, 33 systems target knowledge presentation use cases, 31 are for self-regulated learning, 18 cover tutorials and 14 involve collaboration. The cells with few instances highlight onto which aspects future work can focus.

4.3   Common Results and Differences Based on the Evaluations

I identified 19 areas to which researchers made statements and then compared the common results and differences.

Self-regulated Learning

	Individual Modules	Gamification & Game-based	Simulation	Knowledge Organization
Marker-based non-immersive AR	2	3	2	0
Markerless non-immersive AR	0	0	0	0
WebXR	0	0	0	0
Immersive AR & VR Technologies	6	9	11	2

Collaboration

	Individual Modules	Gamification & Game-based	Simulation	Knowledge Organization
Marker-based non-immersive AR	0	1	2	0
Markerless non-immersive AR	1	1	2	0
WebXR	0	0	0	0
Immersive AR & VR Technologies	4	2	4	0

Tutorial

	Individual Modules	Gamification & Game-based	Simulation	Knowledge Organization
Marker-based non-immersive AR	1	0	2	0
Markerless non-immersive AR	0	0	1	0
WebXR	0	0	0	0
Immersive AR & VR Technologies	6	2	7	0

Knowledge Presentation

	Individual Modules	Gamification & Game-based	Simulation	Knowledge Organization
Marker-based non-immersive AR	8	2	2	0
Markerless non-immersive AR	1	0	1	0
WebXR	1	0	1	0
Immersive AR & VR Technologies	10	3	10	0

Fig. 4. Sliced MR Learning Cube with the Distribution of Publications

Accessibility. The main point raised about accessibility is the expensive price of the hardware, e.g., of the Microsoft HoloLens and Oculus HMD [24,36]. This is also due to the high requirements of the hardware, meaning that only high-end smartphones are available as alternatives to HMDs [70,79]. However, it was also argued that possible alternatives which provide the same experience are also expensive like training in the real world with real props [24,86]. This is especially true for the medical field where MR helps train without real equipment, as well as without real patients or corpses [3,67]. Moreover, some scenarios cannot realistically be trained in real-life like behavior during earthquakes [50], tornado drills [20] or special training on offshore platforms [78]. For marker-based applications, it is also feasible to use the surface of a unique object as the marker pattern, e.g., for antique coins displayed in a museum [45].

Agents. MR agents where a computer controls a virtual entity are applied in the literature to convey practical instructions. Here, the literature showed that agents are preferred over text manuals [30]. However, results also show that in teaching scenarios, they do not fully substitute the role of a teacher [59] but are an additional tool which can, e.g. help students in self-determined learning. For instance, the agents are always accessible and students do not have to book appointments or adjust their schedules accordingly [84]. Apart from these uses, the literature also suggest it as an intuitive user interface with which students can interact [43]. An important design factor is to avoid the uncanny valley where the agents appear awkward if they are do not appear fully realistic [34].

Audio. The literature sees audio as an essential component for the learning experience [32]. Many MR applications included audio, e.g., to improve the realism [78]. For the audio design, the volume and speed should be fine-tuned to avoid that it is distracting [10] but should also avoid monotony [2]. Nevertheless, study results also showed that the audio needs to complement the visual actions [10,60]. A well-designed soundscape can improve the immersion in VR since it shuts out noise from the real world [9].

Avatar. In contrast to the computer-controlled agents, avatars are representations of real users in the shared MR space [74]. Such an avatar is seen as beneficial for the learning experience [49] and an instructor in the form of an avatar is preferred by students over texts [16]. An important factor for integrating avatars concerns their customization options [87]. In studies, users voiced their preference to select the gender [16] and visual appearance of the avatar [74]. One publication noted that the visualization should be kept realistic to avoid distracting avatar representations [25]. Studies also indicated that it is beneficial if the avatar adjusts to the real height of the user [9,32,83]. The system must track the movements of users and apply them to the avatars to achieve a feeling of embodiment [16,50].

Collaboration. Collaborative spaces have been found beneficial for learning as it increases the fun factor [41,63,70], e.g., with role play [71]. A study also indicated that the collaboration improves the learning performance [70] since students can help each other in the collaborative MR space and evokes interactions between the students [66,87]. However, the collaboration design needs to actively encourage shy students to also participate [54]. Despite this raised level of interactions, the collaboration does not interrupt learning activities [13]. The effect of collaboration is high in co-located AR as the users can see each other, their facial expressions and body language [66,73]. At the same time, there is a risk of collisions if users are not aware of each other [66]. This is more prominent in VR if multiple users wear HMDs with cables that might entangle themselves [63]. In the shared environment, it is important to synchronize the content and application state for all users so that everyone can refer to the same objects in the MR space [13]. For remote usage, voice chat was also regarded as a useful feature [1].

Cybersickness. Cybersickness consists of various symptoms like nausea, dizziness or vertigo. The effect was mainly prevalent in VR but less in AR. This also depends on the used hardware. For instance, in one evaluation, users only experienced dizziness in a CAVE but not with an HTC Vive [23]. In other studies, there were also cybersickness symptoms with various VR HMDs [10,50,87]. The usage of VR for a short time for children between 8 and 10 showed no cybersickness [43]. Two studies hinted at a correlation between cybersickness and wearing glasses or contact lenses as this affects the ability to focus on the screens [28,44].

Development Process. An interdisciplinary development process is seen as beneficial since it combines the knowledge about MR with expertise about the particular field of study [5,72]. As such, a co-design with an expert or the target audience can be applied to tailor the application towards the use case [78]. MR learning applications integrated 3D models for the learning material. One mentioned challenge concerns the limited accessibility of free 3D models online with a good quality [79]. A requirement for the 3D models is their realistic appearance [3]. The support infrastructure for MR learning applications has to be set up to help users overcome the novelty and to provide long-term maintenance [6]. To gain insights how the application is used by students, eye tracking can be applied [50]. For marker-based MR software, the surface finish of the markers needs to be matte to avoid reflections that interfere with the tracking [11].

Gamification. Gamification was regarded as beneficial since it enhances the fun and keeps the students motivated to finish the learning tasks [27,63,68,76,87]. However, in two evaluations, gamification also possessed negative impacts as learners started focusing on maximizing their scores instead of the learning content [5,52]. Nevertheless, it was observed that gamification can reduce the stress while learning [61]. A study collected the feedback that participants preferred an gamified environment without competition [41].

Haptics. Haptic feedback was regarded as important and multiple publications stated that the haptics were missing in their implementation [3,9,11,50]. When included, they were considered as a benefit, especially if they imitate the weight and shape of real objects [8,40,67]. Haptic feedback is a key component to immerse users in the experience [72]. One publication presented a positive effect of haptics during collaboration to be aware of the other user's actions [88].

Immersion. Immersion is seen as an important positive factor for the learning effect [50,63]. High immersion can cause a feeling of presence [9] which is helpful when the learning application conveys a remote environment [32]. Even observers of an MR application who do not wear an HMD themselves can feel immersed, e.g., during remote evaluations [76].

Learning Performance. One of the main benefits in the learning performance according to a multitude of literature was the improved spatial understanding [11,13,21,43,52,82]. With MR, learners gained a deeper understanding about 3D models [36,70]. The spatial understanding also involved that users were able to estimate their own position and velocity better [83]. A study also came to the conclusion that the additional movement while examining learning content enhanced the learning transfer in AR [63]. Comparative studies for both AR and VR to traditional learning have shown a higher level of performance for the group that used mixed reality technology [89]. In VR, better results were achieved compared to the traditional course layout [44], informing via slide-based presentations [48] or video instructions [74]. For AR, improvements were registered compared to self-learning with material like PDF files [2], flashcards [39] or an instructional video [74]. The improvements with mixed reality training manifest in measurements like less errors that were made during tests [47,48,52,81]. Two publications concluded that tasks were completed quicker in MR [14,48].

One study noted that there is a connection between reduced task completion times in VR and previous experiences with the VR technology [10]. VR was also considered to be more time efficient than AR [48]. One study concluded that MR learning increases creativity [18]. Applications that allowed students to design learning activities themselves also helped to increase their own understanding of the knowledge that they conveyed [42,75]. Long-term memorization was also improved by MR [42,50]. Participating in MR simulations also increases the confidence of the learner as the unknown situation can be trained repeatedly [38]. Similarly, systems which display instructions also help novice trainees [51].

Learning Design. The success of an application depends on its learning design. For instance, course creators must be aware of the previous knowledge that students provide [76,83]. Although one application did not require previous knowledge [62], another study concluded that it is an important factor that can lead to better learning results [55]. Moreover, applications can be constructed to offer feedback to the learners while performing their tasks [3,27,33,67,78]. Too static tasks were deemed to be limiting as they only allow for predefined ways of solving the given problem [23] and do not let students explore additional information [52]. The conveyed content gives students the opportunity to connect theory and practice as it provides conceptual information on real-life scenarios [49,58]. For example, it can display virtual replicas of real-life objects in their true scale, thereby giving students an accurate impression [36,74]. However, there is no need to display objects in their natural size but instead, operations that would not be possible in reality, e.g. scaling objects up or down, can be offered to the learner [36]. Similarly, one study overlaid virtual information over real book content to add new information [17] and another project augmented presentation slides with 3D models [37]. Researchers also argued that it is not sufficient to only model best case scenarios in the simulation but it should incorporate failures and random errors [67]. Authors of two papers faced the challenge that participants were more interested in the mixed reality technology and due to this did not pay close attention to the learning content [83,87]. With the involvement of smartphone-based applications they can also cause distractions because of incoming push notifications, messages or calls [54]. A study recommended that teachers should be trained with the novel MR technologies [5]. Additional help should also be provided regarding the pedagogical integration in courses to maximize the learning effect for the students [6]. It was suggested to integrate MR with smartphones and tablets in traditional lectures [12]. A visual-design problem-based pedagogy approach has a positive influence on the learning outcomes, as it encourages students to creatively look for own solutions [7]. So, the MR application rewards critical thinking and is designed in a way that students do not just repeat task demonstrations [5]. Creative thinking can also be supported by applying the Method of Loci as it allows students to visualize thoughts and associate them with places in the real world to remember them [39]. An important feature of a MR lesson is that it is constant and reproducible. This means that no matter at which time or by which teacher the lesson is held [67], the content and the way how it is conveyed stays the same [24,28,36].

Motivation. Studies stated that the MR technology itself already increases the motivation because of its novelty [26,31,43]. As an example, a high level of motivation was determined in a VR application [44]. This is also due to a general positive opinion about these innovations [28,46]. Publications saw a correlation between the AR application's design and the motivation [90]. For instance, a pedagogical approach that includes problem-based tasks with an emphasis on visual design can enhance the motivation and general engagement of the learners [7].

Pandemic. Five of the analyzed papers which were published in 2020 highlight the benefits of MR for remote learning in the context of the COVID-19 pandemic, e.g. for home schooling and online courses [28,46,65,74,76]. As it was recommended or even mandated that people do not meet in person, MR learning environments offer a safe alternative [74].

Personalization. MR with HMDs or smartphones provide the chance to view content individually. Therefore, the learning design can be adaptive to tailor the MR experience to individual students [13,49,67] This allows learning applications to adapt to their choice of goals and tasks [6]. An individual level offers students to learn according to their time schedule and understanding of the topics [5,12,36]. Because of this flexibility, 3D models can be positioned optimally for each student [13]. In VR, the homes of students can be 3D modeled and integrated into simulations so that they can e.g. train emergency situations directly in a familiar and real surrounding [50]. In AR, this connection automatically exists since the students are always able to see their surroundings and therefore their own room.

Privacy. The personal nature of MR also grants privacy. For personal devices like HMDs, the content that is viewed is only visible to the wearer but not to bystanders unless the view is explicitly shared [63]. In collaborative environments, filters are necessary to protect the communication and shown virtual content from unauthorized views in the shared space [85].

Safety. The literature also discovered benefits of MR regarding safety. Dangerous experiments, e.g. in Chemistry [24], can realistically be simulated in virtuality. This way, the advantages of experiment-based teaching can be combined with a low risk environment for students [53]. Especially medical procedures can be trained in a safe way without the risk of harm for patients [24]. Therefore, there is also no need to supervise students as they are not operating in a dangerous location [63]. Nevertheless, the simulations can be used to train students to recognize dangers in the working environment and to respond in the right way to them [38,50,74]. One study shows that such repeated training can actually reduce the dangers that a real-life working environment, e.g. on an offshore platform, can pose because of the realistic preparation [78].

Technical Challenges. A commonly mentioned issue about the hardware is its limited field of view when wearing an HMD [33,44,63,76]. In a simulation, this also changes the user's behavior as they cannot glance to the sides with their eyes but actively need to rotate their head to observe the peripheral view [50]. With smartphones for AR applications, a similar issue was identified because of the small screen size which is unable to show a large portion of the environment at once [54]. This can, however, be improved by applying tablets which feature a larger screen [70]. Regarding the technical usability of the systems, it was noted that users should get an introduction to the technology prior to their first experience with the learning application [69].

Usability. The usability was also found to be affected by inexperience with VR technology [28]. Authors also observed that the VR application was more difficult to control [87]. Nevertheless, the interactions can be enhanced by gestures that become possible with the help of VR controllers that track the user's hand movements [62]. In VR, one publication described problems with text input as it was regarded to be too cumbersome to type with controllers on a virtual keyboard [62]. A similar result was found for AR typing in mid-air using gestures [35]. Therefore, it was suggested to use a physical keyboard for text input [62]. Attention must also be paid to the scale of the text so that it is large enough to be read on the MR displays and it should stay legible against differently colored background in the virtual and real world [10]. Some usage scenarios also demand additional equipment, e.g. printed markers that have to be brought in order to interact with the application [2].

5 Discussion

One limitation concerns the comparability of the various studies since they differ in evaluation setups. For instance, the evaluation time span ranges from single sessions with a couple of minutes [43] to long-term studies [18]. In addition, some evaluations contained multiple settings and analyzed target groups in varying use cases [51]. Some prototypes were evaluated with the designated target group of the learning setting, e.g. by paramedic students [11]. However, some prototypes did not require previous knowledge and so it was possible to evaluate them with non-experts [86]. These factors also influence the novelty effect which can affect the results of MR studies if inexperienced users are directly provided with new applications and interaction methods [56]. Depending on the initial research question, a portion of evaluations invited single groups [8] whereas other researchers conducted the evaluation with a between-groups experimental setup [48]. Another aspect regards the feedback during the development process. Some prototypes were implemented with the help of a domain expert, e.g. an offshore worker, who could give exact requirements and the necessary expertise about the final use cases [78]. The analysis of the results showed that researchers agree on many results and can be transferred to other use cases.

6 Conclusion

The growing demand for digital learning solutions and recent innovations in the field of mixed reality has led to a rising research interest in MR-enhanced learning. To gain insights about the benefits and challenges of integrating mixed reality in education, researchers have explored specific use cases in studies with MR learning applications. In this paper, I presented a comprehensive overview of these MR learning approaches. 80 publications have been thoroughly examined and the relevant data were extracted, as well as categorized. As a result of mapping the technology approaches, this paper presents a developed MR technology landscape which shows the different characteristics of technology that can be chosen to realize a MR learning application. Concerning the integration points of the MR applications in formal and informal education, most authors focused on applications that support self-regulated learning. The analysis in this paper shows connections between the learning design with the technology approach and the integration point. They were formalized in a mixed reality learning cube that describes the different possibilities and approaches how MR and learning can be combined. With this MR learning cube, it is possible to map out the approaches of the 80 papers, assign them to the set of applicable cells and point out approaches which can be investigated in future research.

References

1. Ahmed, N., Lataifeh, M., Alhamarna, A.F., Alnahdi, M.M., Almansori, S.T.: LeARn: a collaborative learning environment using augmented reality. In: 2021 IEEE 2nd International Conference on Human-Machine Systems (ICHMS), pp. 1–4. IEEE (2021). https://doi.org/10.1109/ICHMS53169.2021.9582643
2. Akhmalludin, H., Ayu, M.A.: Mobile based augmented reality to improve learning of volcanology for high school students. In: 2019 5th International Conference on Computing Engineering and Design (ICCED), pp. 1–6. IEEE (2019). https://doi.org/10.1109/ICCED46541.2019.9161130
3. Andersson, H.B., Børresen, T., Prasolova-Førland, E., McCallum, S., Estrada, J.G.: Developing an AR application for neurosurgical training: lessons learned for medical specialist education. In: 2020 IEEE Conference on Virtual Reality and 3D User Interfaces Workshops, pp. 407–412. IEEE, Piscataway (2020). https://doi.org/10.1109/VRW50115.2020.00087
4. Annafi, A., Hakim, D.L., Rohendi, D.: Impact of using augmented reality applications in the educational environment. J. Phys. Conf. Ser. **1375**(1), 012080 (2019). https://doi.org/10.1088/1742-6596/1375/1/012080
5. Back, R., Plecher, D.A., Wenrich, R., Dorner, B., Klinker, G.: Mixed reality in art education. In: Teather, R., Itoh, Y., Gabbard, J. (eds.) Proceedings, 26th IEEE Conference on Virtual Reality and 3D User Interfaces, pp. 1583–1587. IEEE, Piscataway (2019). https://doi.org/10.1109/VR.2019.8798101
6. Banerjee, G., Walunj, S.: Exploring in-service teachers' acceptance of augmented reality. In: 2019 IEEE Tenth International Conference on Technology for Education (T4E), pp. 186–192. IEEE (2019). https://doi.org/10.1109/T4E.2019.00043

7. Banic, A., Gamboa, R.: Visual design problem-based learning in a virtual environment improves computational thinking and programming knowledge. In: Teather, R., Itoh, Y., Gabbard, J. (eds.) Proceedings, 26th IEEE Conference on Virtual Reality and 3D User Interfaces, pp. 1588–1593. IEEE, Piscataway (2019). https://doi.org/10.1109/VR.2019.8798013

8. Barmpoutis, A., Faris, R., Garcia, L., Gruber, L., Li, J., Peralta, F., Zhang, M.: Assessing the role of virtual reality with passive haptics in music conductor education: a pilot study. In: Chen, J.Y.C., Fragomeni, G. (eds.) HCII 2020. LNCS, vol. 12190, pp. 275–285. Springer, Cham (2020). https://doi.org/10.1007/978-3-030-49695-1_18

9. Battisti, F., Di Stefano, C.: Virtual Reality meets Degas: an immersive framework for art exploration and learning. In: 2018 7th European Workshop on Visual Information Processing (EUVIP), pp. 1–5. IEEE (2018). https://doi.org/10.1109/EUVIP.2018.8611753

10. Besoain, F., Jego, L., Arenas-Salinas, M.: Implementation of a gamified puzzle based on pro-origami protein structure cartoons: an experience in virtual reality. In: 2018 IEEE Biennial Congress of Argentina (ARGENCON), pp. 1–7. IEEE (2018). https://doi.org/10.1109/ARGENCON.2018.8646202

11. Birt, J., Moore, E., Cowling, M.A.: Piloting mobile mixed reality simulation in paramedic distance education. In: 2017 IEEE 5th International Conference on Serious Games and Applications for Health (SeGAH), pp. 1–8. IEEE (2017). https://doi.org/10.1109/SeGAH.2017.7939270

12. Birt, J., Stromberga, Z., Cowling, M., Moro, C.: Mobile mixed reality for experiential learning and simulation in medical and health sciences education. Information 9(2), 31 (2018). https://doi.org/10.3390/info9020031

13. Bork, F., Lehner, A., Kugelmann, D., Eck, U., Waschke, J., Navab, N.: VesARlius: an augmented reality system for large-group co-located anatomy learning. In: Adjunct proceedings of the 2019 IEEE International Symposium on Mixed and Augmented Reality, pp. 122–123. IEEE Computer Society, Conference Publishing Services, Los Alamitos, California (2019). https://doi.org/10.1109/ISMAR-Adjunct.2019.00-66

14. Cabanillas-Carbonell, M., Canchaya-Ramos, A., Gomez-Osorio, R.: Mobile application with augmented reality as a tool to reinforce learning in pre-Inca cultures. In: 2020 IEEE Engineering International Research Conference (EIRCON), pp. 1–4. IEEE (2020). https://doi.org/10.1109/EIRCON51178.2020.9254018

15. Cabero-Almenara, J., Fernández-Batanero, J.M., Barroso-Osuna, J.: Adoption of augmented reality technology by university students. Heliyon 5(5), e01597 (2019). https://doi.org/10.1016/j.heliyon.2019.e01597

16. Caserman, P., Zhang, H., Zinnacker, J., Gobel, S.: Development of a directed teleport function for immersive training in virtual reality. In: 2019 11th International Conference on Virtual Worlds and Games for Serious Applications (VS-Games), pp. 1–8. IEEE (2019). https://doi.org/10.1109/VS-Games.2019.8864599

17. Casteleiro-Pitrez, J.: Augmented reality textbook: a classroom quasi-experimental study. IEEE Revista Iberoamericana de Tecnologias del Aprendizaje 16(3), 258–266 (2021). https://doi.org/10.1109/RITA.2021.3122887

18. Chamba-Eras, L., Aguilar, J.: Augmented reality in a smart classroom-case study: SaCI. IEEE Revista Iberoamericana de Tecnologias del Aprendizaje 12(4), 165–172 (2017). https://doi.org/10.1109/RITA.2017.2776419

19. Checa, D., Bustillo, A.: A review of immersive virtual reality serious games to enhance learning and training. Multimed. Tools Appl. 79(9), 5501–5527 (2020). https://doi.org/10.1007/s11042-019-08348-9

20. Chiou, Y.M., Shen, C.C.: Collaborative learning with augmented reality tornado simulator. In: 2022 IEEE Conference on Virtual Reality and 3D User Interfaces Abstracts and Workshops (VRW), pp. 293–298. IEEE (2022). https://doi.org/10.1109/VRW55335.2022.00066
21. Collins, J., Regenbrecht, H., Lanalotz, T.: Back to the future: constructivist learning in virtual reality. In: 2018 IEEE International Symposium on Mixed and Augmented Reality Adjunct (ISMAR-Adjunct). pp. 45–46. IEEE (2018). https://doi.org/10.1109/ISMAR-Adjunct.2018.00030
22. Cruz-Neira, C., Sandin, D.J., DeFanti, T.A.: Surround-Screen Projection-Based Virtual Reality. In: Whitton, M.C. (ed.) Proceedings of the 20th Annual Conference on Computer Graphics and Interactive Techniques - SIGGRAPH '93, pp. 135–142. ACM Press, New York (1993). https://doi.org/10.1145/166117.166134
23. Delamarre, A., Lisetti, C., Buche, C.: A cross-platform classroom training simulator: interaction design and evaluation. In: 2020 International Conference on Cyberworlds (CW), pp. 86–93. IEEE (2020). https://doi.org/10.1109/CW49994.2020.00020
24. Duan, X., Kang, S.J., in Choi, J., Kim, S.K.: Mixed reality system for virtual chemistry lab. KSII Trans. Internet Inf. Syst. **14**(4) (2020). https://doi.org/10.3837/tiis.2020.04.014
25. Gao, H., Bozkir, E., Hasenbein, L., Hahn, J.U., Göllner, R., Kasneci, E.: Digital Transformations of Classrooms in Virtual Reality. In: Kitamura, Y., Quigley, A., Isbister, K., Igarashi, T., Bjørn, P., Drucker, S. (eds.) Proceedings of the 2021 CHI Conference on Human Factors in Computing Systems, pp. 1–10. ACM, New York (2021). https://doi.org/10.1145/3411764.3445596
26. Garzon, J., Baldiris, S., Acevedo, J., Pavon, J.: Augmented Reality-based application to foster sustainable agriculture in the context of aquaponics. In: 2020 IEEE 20th International Conference on Advanced Learning Technologies (ICALT), pp. 316–318. IEEE (2020). https://doi.org/10.1109/ICALT49669.2020.00101
27. Gonzalez, D.C., Garnique, L.V.: Development of a simulator with HTC Vive using gamification to improve the learning experience in medical students. In: 2018 Congreso Internacional de Innovación y Tendencias en Ingeniería (CONIITI) pp. 1–6. IEEE (2018). https://doi.org/10.1109/CONIITI.2018.8587058,
28. González Izard, S., Vivo Vicent, C., Juanes Méndez, J.A., Palau, R.: Virtual reality in higher education: an experience with medical students. In: García-Peñalvo, F.J., García-Holgado, A. (eds.) Eighth International Conference on Technological Ecosystems for Enhancing Multiculturality. pp. 414–421. ACM, New York (2020). https://doi.org/10.1145/3434780.3436539
29. González Vargas, J.C., Fabregat, R., Carrillo-Ramos, A., Jové, T.: Survey: using augmented reality to improve learning motivation in cultural heritage studies. Appl. Sci. **10**(3), 897 (2020). https://doi.org/10.3390/app10030897
30. Gupta, A., Cecil, J., Pirela-Cruz, M.: A virtual reality enhanced cyber physical framework to support simulation based training of orthopedic surgical procedures. In: 2018 IEEE 14th International Conference on Automation Science and Engineering (CASE), pp. 433–438. IEEE (2018). https://doi.org/10.1109/COASE.2018.8560602
31. Han, P.F., Zhao, F.K., Zhao, G.: Using augmented reality to improve learning efficacy in a mechanical assembly course. IEEE Trans. Learn. Technol. **15**(2), 279–289 (2022). https://doi.org/10.1109/TLT.2022.3166556

32. Han, P.H., Chen, Y.S., Liu, I.S., Jang, Y.P., Tsai, L., Chang, A., Hung, Y.P.: A compelling virtual tour of the Dunhuang cave with an immersive head-mounted display. IEEE Comput. Graphics Appl. **40**(1), 40–55 (2020). https://doi.org/10.1109/MCG.2019.2936753

33. Han, P.H., Chen, Y.S., Zhong, Y., Wang, H.L., Hung, Y.P.: My Tai-Chi coaches. In: Mistry, P., Maes, P., Seigneur, J.M., Nanayakkara, S., Paradiso, J. (eds.) Proceedings of the 8th Augmented Human International Conference, pp. 1–4. ACM, New York (2017). https://doi.org/10.1145/3041164.3041194

34. Hensen, B., Bekhter, D., Blehm, D., Meinberger, S., Klamma, R.: Mixed reality agents for automated mentoring processes. In: de Paolis, L.T., Arpaia, P., Sacco, M. (eds.) Extended Reality. LNCS, vol. 13446, pp. 3–16. Springer, Cham (2022). https://doi.org/10.1007/978-3-031-15553-6_1

35. Hensen, B., Klamma, R.: 3D skill trees in mixed reality for creating and visualizing learning plans. In: 2022 International Conference on Advanced Learning Technologies (ICALT), pp. 309–313. IEEE (2022). https://doi.org/10.1109/ICALT55010.2022.00099

36. Hensen, B., Koren, I., Klamma, R.: Gamification support for learning in spatial computing environments. J. Univ. Comput. Sci. **2019**(25), 1644–1665 (2019). https://doi.org/10.3217/jucs-025-12-1644, http://www.jucs.org/jucs_25_12/gamification_support_for_learning

37. Hensen, B., Liß, L., Klamma, R.: ImPres: an immersive 3D presentation framework for mixed reality enhanced learning. In: Zhou, W., Mu, Y. (eds.) ICWL 2021. LNCS, vol. 13103, pp. 28–39. Springer, Cham (2021). https://doi.org/10.1007/978-3-030-90785-3_3

38. Hoang, T., Greuter, S., Taylor, S., Aranda, G., Mulvany, G.T.: An evaluation of virtual reality for fear arousal safety training in the construction industry. In: An XRI Mixed-Reality Internet-of-Things Architectural Framework Toward Immersive and Adaptive Smart Environments, pp. 177–182. IEEE (2021). https://doi.org/10.1109/ISMAR-Adjunct54149.2021.00044

39. Ibrahim, A., Huynh, B., Downey, J., Hollerer, T., Chun, D., O'Donovan, J.: ARbis pictus: a study of vocabulary learning with augmented reality. IEEE Trans. Visual Comput. Graphics **24**(11), 2867–2874 (2018). https://doi.org/10.1109/TVCG.2018.2868568

40. Ipsita, A., et al.: Towards modeling of virtual reality welding simulators to promote accessible and scalable training. In: Barbosa, S., Lampe, C., Appert, C., Shamma, D.A., Drucker, S., Williamson, J., Yatani, K. (eds.) CHI Conference on Human Factors in Computing Systems, pp. 1–21. ACM, New York (2022). https://doi.org/10.1145/3491102.3517696

41. Irie, K., Al Sada, M., Yamada, Y., Gushima, K., Nakajima, T.: Pervasive HoloMoL. In: Pardede, E., Haghighi, P.D., Salvadori, I.L., Steinbauer, M., Khalil, I., Anderst-Kotsis, G. (eds.) Proceedings of the 15th International Conference on Advances in Mobile Computing & Multimedia - MoMM2017, pp. 141–145. ACM Press, New York (2017). https://doi.org/10.1145/3151848.3151869

42. Jailungka, P., Charoenseang, S., Thammatinno, C.: Augmented reality and microbit for project-based learning. In: Chen, J.Y.C., Fragomeni, G. (eds.) HCII 2020. LNCS, vol. 12191, pp. 219–235. Springer, Cham (2020). https://doi.org/10.1007/978-3-030-49698-2_15

43. Jia, T., Liu, Y.: Words in kitchen: an instance of leveraging virtual reality technology to learn vocabulary. In: Adjunct Proceedings of the 2019 IEEE International Symposium on Mixed and Augmented Reality, pp. 150–155. IEEE Computer Society, Conference Publishing Services, Los Alamitos, California (2019). https://doi.org/10.1109/ISMAR-Adjunct.2019.00-59

44. Jiménez, E., Mariscal, G., Heredia, M., Castilla, G.: Virtual reality versus master class. In: García-Peñalvo, F.J. (ed.) Proceedings of the Sixth International Conference on Technological Ecosystems for Enhancing Multiculturality - TEEM'18, pp. 568–573. ACM Press, New York (2018). https://doi.org/10.1145/3284179.3284276
45. Juan, M.C., Loachamin-Valencia, M., Garcia-Garcia, I., Melchor, J.M., Benedito, J.: ARCoins. an augmented reality app for learning about numismatics. In: 2017 IEEE 17th International Conference on Advanced Learning Technologies (ICALT), pp. 466–468. IEEE (2017). https://doi.org/10.1109/ICALT.2017.27
46. Jung, K., Nguyen, V.T., Piscarac, D., Yoo, S.C.: Meet the Virtual Jeju Dol Harubang-The Mixed VR/AR Application for Cultural Immersion in Korea's Main Heritage. ISPRS Int. J. Geo Inf. 9(6), 367 (2020). https://doi.org/10.3390/ijgi9060367
47. Kim, J., Olsen, D., Renfroe, J.: Construction workforce training assisted with augmented reality. In: 2022 8th International Conference of the Immersive Learning Research Network (iLRN), pp. 1–6. IEEE (2022). https://doi.org/10.23919/iLRN55037.2022.9815960
48. Koutitas, G., Smith, K.S., Lawrence, G., Metsis, V., Stamper, C., Trahan, M., Lehr, T.: A virtual and augmented reality platform for the training of first responders of the ambulance bus. In: Makedon, F. (ed.) Proceedings of the 12th ACM International Conference on PErvasive Technologies Related to Assistive Environments, pp. 299–302. ACM, New York (2019). https://doi.org/10.1145/3316782.3321542
49. Lang, Y., Wei, L., Xu, F., Zhao, Y., Yu, L.F.: Synthesizing personalized training programs for improving driving habits via virtual reality. In: 2018 IEEE Conference on Virtual Reality and 3D User Interfaces (VR), pp. 297–304. IEEE (2018). https://doi.org/10.1109/VR.2018.8448290
50. Li, C., Liang, W., Quigley, C., Zhao, Y., Yu, L.F.: Earthquake safety training through virtual drills. IEEE Trans. Visual Comput. Graphics 23(4), 1275–1284 (2017). https://doi.org/10.1109/TVCG.2017.2656958
51. Limbu, B., Vovk, A., Jarodzka, H., Klemke, R., Wild, F., Specht, M.: WEKIT.One: a sensor-based augmented reality system for experience capture and re-enactment. In: Scheffel, M., Broisin, J., Pammer-Schindler, V., Ioannou, A., Schneider, J. (eds.) EC-TEL 2019. LNCS, vol. 11722, pp. 158–171. Springer, Cham (2019). https://doi.org/10.1007/978-3-030-29736-7_12
52. Liu, C., Chen, X., Liu, S., Zhang, X., Ding, S., Long, Y., Zhou, D.: The exploration on interacting teaching mode of augmented reality based on hololens. In: Cheung, S.K.S., Jiao, J., Lee, L.-K., Zhang, X., Li, K.C., Zhan, Z. (eds.) ICTE 2019. CCIS, vol. 1048, pp. 91–102. Springer, Singapore (2019). https://doi.org/10.1007/978-981-13-9895-7_9
53. Lucas, P., Vaca, D., Dominguez, F., Ochoa, X.: Virtual Circuits: An Augmented Reality Circuit Simulator for Engineering Students. In: 2018 IEEE 18th International Conference on Advanced Learning Technologies (ICALT), pp. 380–384. IEEE (2018). https://doi.org/10.1109/ICALT.2018.00097
54. Mei, B., Yang, S.: Nurturing Environmental Education at the Tertiary Education Level in China: Can Mobile Augmented Reality and Gamification Help? Sustainability 11(16) (2019). https://doi.org/10.3390/su11164292
55. Meyer, O.A., Omdahl, M.K., Makransky, G.: Investigating the effect of pre-training when learning through immersive virtual reality and video: a media and methods experiment. Comput. Educ. 140, 103603 (2019). https://doi.org/10.1016/j.compedu.2019.103603

56. Miguel-Alonso, I., Rodriguez-Garcia, B., Checa, D., Bustillo, A.: Countering the novelty effect: a tutorial for immersive virtual reality learning environments. Appl. Sci. **13**(1), 593 (2023). https://doi.org/10.3390/app13010593
57. Milgram, P., Kishino, F.: A Taxonomy of Mixed Reality Visual Displays. IEICE Trans. Inf. Syst. **E77-D**(12), 1321–1329 (1994)
58. Murrell, S., Wang, F., Aldrich, E., Xu, X.: MeteorologyAR: a mobile AR app to increase student engagement and promote active learning in a large lecture class. In: 2020 IEEE Conference on Virtual Reality and 3D User Interfaces Workshops, pp. 848–849. IEEE, Piscataway (2020). https://doi.org/10.1109/VRW50115.2020.00275
59. Mystakidis, S., Cachafeiro, E., Hatzilygeroudis, I.: Enter the serious E-scape room: a cost-effective serious game model for deep and meaningful E-learning. In: 2019 10th International Conference on Information, Intelligence, Systems and Applications (IISA), pp. 1–6. IEEE (2019). https://doi.org/10.1109/IISA.2019.8900673
60. Nguyen, V.T., Jung, K., Yoo, S., Kim, S., Park, S., Currie, M.: Civil war battlefield experience: historical event simulation using augmented reality technology. In: 2019 IEEE International Conference on Artificial Intelligence and Virtual Reality (AIVR), pp. 294–2943. IEEE (2019). https://doi.org/10.1109/AIVR46125.2019.00068
61. Nicola, S., Stoicu-Tivadar, L.: Mixed reality supporting modern medical education. Stud. Health Technol. Inform. **255**, 242–246 (2018)
62. Oberdörfer, S., Heidrich, D., Latoschik, M.E.: Usability of gamified knowledge learning in VR and Desktop-3D. In: Proceedings of the 2019 CHI Conference on Human Factors in Computing Systems, CHI 2019, pp. 1–13. ACM, New York (2019). https://doi.org/10.1145/3290605.3300405
63. Oh, S., So, H.J., Gaydos, M.: Hybrid augmented reality for participatory learning: the hidden efficacy of multi-user game-based simulation. IEEE Trans. Learn. Technol. **11**(1), 115–127 (2018). https://doi.org/10.1109/TLT.2017.2750673
64. Pellas, N., Kazanidis, I., Palaigeorgiou, G.: A systematic literature review of mixed reality environments in K-12 education. Educ. Inf. Technol. **7**(1), 54 (2019). https://doi.org/10.1007/s10639-019-10076-4
65. Puspasari, S., Suhandi, N., Iman, J.N.: Augmented reality development for supporting cultural education role in SMB II museum during Covid-19 pandemic. In: 2020 Fifth International Conference on Informatics and Computing (ICIC), pp. 1–6. IEEE (2020). https://doi.org/10.1109/ICIC50835.2020.9288619
66. Reinoso, M., Hoang, T.N., Vetere, F., Tanin, E.: Annotating animated AR objects for Co-located learning. In: 2018 IEEE International Conference on Teaching, Assessment, and Learning for Engineering (TALE), pp. 470–477. IEEE (2018). https://doi.org/10.1109/TALE.2018.8615452
67. Richards, J.P., Done, A.J., Barber, S.R., Jain, S., Son, Y.J., Chang, E.H.: Virtual coach: the next tool in functional endoscopic sinus surgery education. Int. Forum Allergy Rhinology **10**(1), 97–102 (2020). https://doi.org/10.1002/alr.22452
68. Rifa'i, A., Kusumawati, T.I.J., Purnomo, M.H.: Mobile serious game using augmented reality for increasing quality of learning. In: 2021 6th International Conference on New Media Studies (CONMEDIA), pp. 7–11. IEEE (2021). https://doi.org/10.1109/CONMEDIA53104.2021.9617176
69. Sankaran, N.K., et al.: Efficacy Study on Interactive Mixed Reality (IMR) software with sepsis prevention medical education. In: Teather, R., Itoh, Y., Gabbard, J. (eds.) Proceedings, 26th IEEE Conference on Virtual Reality and 3D User Interfaces, pp. 664–670. IEEE, Piscataway (2019). https://doi.org/10.1109/VR.2019.8798089

70. Sarkar, P., Pillai, J.S., Gupta, A.: ScholAR: a collaborative learning experience for rural schools using augmented reality application. In: 2018 IEEE Tenth International Conference on Technology for Education (T4E), pp. 8–15. IEEE (2018). https://doi.org/10.1109/T4E.2018.00010

71. Schiffeler, N., Stehling, V., Haberstroh, M., Isenhardt, I.: Collaborative augmented reality in engineering education. In: Auer, M.E., Ram B., K. (eds.) REV2019 2019. LNNS, vol. 80, pp. 719–732. Springer, Cham (2020). https://doi.org/10.1007/978-3-030-23162-0_65

72. Schild, J., Elsenbast, C., Carbonell, G.: ViTAWiN - developing multiprofessional medical emergency training with mixed reality. In: 2021 IEEE 9th International Conference on Serious Games and Applications for Health (SeGAH), pp. 1–9. IEEE (2021). https://doi.org/10.1109/SEGAH52098.2021.9551890

73. Schott, D., et al.: A VR/AR environment for multi-user liver anatomy education. In: 2021 IEEE Virtual Reality and 3D User Interfaces (VR), pp. 296–305. IEEE (2021). https://doi.org/10.1109/VR50410.2021.00052

74. Sepasgozar, S.M.: Digital twin and web-based virtual gaming technologies for online education: a case of construction management and engineering. Appl. Sci. **10**(13) (2020). https://doi.org/10.3390/app10134678

75. Southgate, E., Grant, S., Ostrowski, S., Norwood, A., Williams, M., Tafazoli, D.: School students creating a virtual reality learning resource for children. In: 2022 IEEE Conference on Virtual Reality and 3D User Interfaces Abstracts and Workshops (VRW), pp. 01–06. IEEE (2022). https://doi.org/10.1109/VRW55335.2022.00060

76. Souza, V., Maciel, A., Nedel, L., Kopper, R., Loges, K., Schlemmer, E.: The effect of virtual reality on knowledge transfer and retention in collaborative group-based learning for neuroanatomy students. In: 2020 22nd Symposium on Virtual and Augmented Reality (SVR), pp. 92–101. IEEE (2020). https://doi.org/10.1109/SVR51698.2020.00028

77. Speicher, M., Hall, B.D., Nebeling, M.: What is mixed reality? In: Proceedings of the 2019 CHI Conference on Human Factors in Computing Systems, CHI 2019, pp. 1–15. ACM, New York (2019). https://doi.org/10.1145/3290605.3300767

78. Sulaiman, S.b., Ali, S.S.A., Adil, S.H., Ebrahim, M., Raza, K.: Virtual reality training and skill enhancement for offshore workers. In: 2020 International Conference on Computational Intelligence (ICCI), pp. 287–292. IEEE (2020). https://doi.org/10.1109/ICCI51257.2020.9247819

79. Sunil, S., Kumaran Nair, S.S.: An educational augmented reality app to facilitate learning experience. In: 2017 International Conference on Computer and Applications (ICCA), pp. 279–282. IEEE (2017). https://doi.org/10.1109/COMAPP.2017.8079771

80. Suryodiningrat, S.P., Prabowo, H., Meyliana, Hidayanto, A.N.: Mixed reality system for teaching and learning: a systematic literature review. In: 2021 IEEE 5th International Conference on Information Technology, Information Systems and Electrical Engineering (ICITISEE), pp. 387–392. IEEE (2021). https://doi.org/10.1109/ICITISEE53823.2021.9655922

81. Suselo, T., Wünsche, B.C., Luxton-Reilly, A.: Using mobile augmented reality for teaching 3D transformations. In: Sherriff, M., Merkle, L.D., Cutter, P., Monge, A., Sheard, J. (eds.) Proceedings of the 52nd ACM Technical Symposium on Computer Science Education, pp. 872–878. ACM, New York (2021). https://doi.org/10.1145/3408877.3432401

82. Swamy, K.L,N., Chavan, P.S., Murthy, S.: StereoChem: augmented reality 3D molecular model visualization app for teaching and learning stereochemistry. In: 2018 IEEE 18th International Conference on Advanced Learning Technologies (ICALT), pp. 252–256. IEEE (2018). https://doi.org/10.1109/ICALT.2018.00065

83. Tamaddon, K., Stiefs, D.: Embodied experiment of levitation in microgravity in a simulated virtual reality environment for science learning. In: 2017 IEEE Virtual Reality Workshop on K-12 Embodied Learning through Virtual & Augmented Reality (KELVAR), pp. 1–5. IEEE (2017). https://doi.org/10.1109/KELVAR.2017.7961560

84. Torres, C., Figueroa, P.: Learning how to play a guitar with the HoloLens: a case study. In: 2018 XLIV Latin American Computer Conference (CLEI), pp. 606–611. IEEE (2018). https://doi.org/10.1109/CLEI.2018.00078

85. Tran, L.A., Hensen, B., Klamma, R., Chantaraskul, S.: Privacy and security in mixed reality learning environments by input and user/bot interaction protection. In: 2022 4th Asia Pacific Information Technology Conference, pp. 63–71. ACM, New York (2022). https://doi.org/10.1145/3512353.3512363

86. Trujano, F., Khan, M., Maes, P.: ARPiano efficient music learning using augmented reality. In: Wu, T.-T., Huang, Y.-M., Shadieva, R., Lin, L., Starčič, A.I. (eds.) ICITL 2018. LNCS, vol. 11003, pp. 3–17. Springer, Cham (2018). https://doi.org/10.1007/978-3-319-99737-7_1

87. Vasilevski, N., Birt, J.: Analysing construction student experiences of mobile mixed reality enhanced learning in virtual and augmented reality environments. Res. Learn. Technol. **28** (2020). https://doi.org/10.25304/rlt.v28.2329

88. Villanueva, A., Zhu, Z., Liu, Z., Wang, F., Chidambaram, S., Ramani, K.: ColabAR: a toolkit for remote collaboration in tangible augmented reality laboratories. Proceedings of the ACM on Human-Computer Interaction **6**(CSCW1), 1–22 (2022). https://doi.org/10.1145/3512928

89. Wijewickrema, S., et al.: Development and validation of a virtual reality tutor to teach clinically oriented surgical anatomy of the ear. In: 2018 IEEE 31st International Symposium on Computer-Based Medical Systems (CBMS), pp. 12–17. IEEE (2018). https://doi.org/10.1109/CBMS.2018.00010

90. Xiao, J., Cai, S., Li, X., Qiao, H.: Assessing the effectiveness of augmented reality courseware "Eight Planets in the Solar System". In: 2018 9th International Conference on Information Technology in Medicine and Education (ITME), pp. 388–392. IEEE (2018). https://doi.org/10.1109/ITME.2018.00093

Multi-label Generalized Zero-Shot Learning Using Identifiable Variational Autoencoders

Muqaddas Gull[(✉)] [iD] and Omar Arif [iD]

School of Electrical Engineering and Computer Science, National University of
Sciences and Technology (NUST), Islamabad 44000, Pakistan
{mgull.dphd18seecs,omar.arif}@seecs.edu.pk

Abstract. Multi-label Zero-Shot Learning (ZSL) is an extension of traditional single-label ZSL, where the objective is to accurately classify
images containing multiple unseen classes that are not available during training. Current techniques depends on attention mechanisms and
Generative Adversarial Networks (GAN) to address multi-label ZSL and
Generalized Zero-Shot Learning (GZSL) challenge. However, generating
features for both multi-label ZSL and GZSL in the context of disentangled representation learning remains unexplored. In this paper, we
propose an identifiable Variational Autoencoder (iVAE) based generative framework for multi-label ZSL and GZSL. The main idea of our
proposed approach is to learn disentangled representations for generating semantically consistent multi-label features using an attribute-level
feature fusion technique. We perform comprehensive experiments on two
benchmark datasets, NUS-WIDE and MS COCO, for both multi-label
ZSL and GZSL. Furthermore, disentangled representation learning for
both multi-label ZSL and GZSL on standard datasets achieves commendable performance as compared to existing methods.

Keywords: Attribute-Level Feature Fusion · Zero-Shot Learning ·
Disentangled Representation Learning · Generalized Zero-Shot
Learning

1 Introduction

In this modern age, deep learning models have achieved remarkable success in
numerous computer vision applications, such as medical imaging [38], image
classification [18,20], object detection [50,54], autonomous vehicles [14], and
agriculture [27]. Among others, single-label classification, which involves identifying a single object in an image, has been extensively studied in the field of
image classification. A significant amount of data has been gathered for this purpose, including ImageNet 21K [51] and ImageNet 1K [8]. pagebreak However,

---

Supported by National University of Sciences and Technology (NUST).

L. T. De Paolis et al. (Eds.): XR Salento 2023, LNCS 14219, pp. 35–50, 2023.
https://doi.org/10.1007/978-3-031-43404-4_3

natural images often contain multiple concepts and objects, which underscores the significance of multi-label classification [5,9,11,15,56,58,66,70], where the task involves classifying multiple objects independently.

Significant progress has been made in the field of multi-label classification by leveraging recurrent neural networks [44,58,67], attention mechanisms [68,69], and label correlation [9,60]. However, the challenge of multi-label zero-shot classification remains unsolved using these approaches. This task involves classifying images into novel categories during testing without any visual examples available during training [59,62]. Multi-label Zero-Shot Learning (ZSL) extends the concept of multi-label classification. In contrast to conventional multi-label ZSL, GZSL is another setting where the test image can belong to either unseen or seen classes, making it more practical. In this study, we tackle the complex task of multi-label ZSL and GZSL.

In contrast to the multi-label classification scenario, considerable attention has been directed towards single-label Zero-Shot Learning (ZSL) and Generalized Zero-Shot Learning (GZSL), where an image is associated with only one category label [10,13,25,36,53,61–63]. These methods rely on VAE [31] and GAN [16] to generate novel features for classes not encountered during training. Generative approaches have become the prevailing method for single-label ZSL and GZSL [10,36,61,63] as they can generate features for unseen classes by learning the underlying feature distribution from only seen classes. However, limited research has been conducted on developing a feature generator for the multi-label ZSL and GZSL paradigms, as current frameworks for ZSL and GZSL can only produce single-label features.

In recent years, there has been a growing interest in disentangled representation learning as a means to improve the quality of generated data [26,41,46]. Disentangled representation learning involves defining data based on latent variables that account for its variations, with VAE being the most commonly used model for learning such representations. To learn these latent variables, VAE aims to approximate the distribution of observed data. However, learning these true latent representations of data is only possible once the model is identifiable [39]. Early research on identifiability of latent variables primarily focused on linear models, such as linear Independent Component Analysis (ICA) [22] and identifying these latent variables in general is challenging because they are not directly observable, and it is impossible to learn their true values without proper inductive biases [24]. Recently, a non-linear ICA-based framework for an iVAE has been introduced [28], which shows that having an auxiliary observed variable with the data helps to identify the distribution of the latent space and the joint data.

In this study, we introduce a generative model that addresses the challenges of multi-label Zero-Shot Learning (ZSL) and Generalized Zero-Shot Learning (GZSL) by leveraging the iVAE framework for disentangled representation learning. To the best of our knowledge, disentangled representation learning has not yet been explored in the context of multi-label ZSL and GZSL. Building upon the insights from [17], our proposed generative model incorporates an attribute-level feature fusion technique to generate semantically consistent multi-label visual features using corresponding semantic information. Once trained, our model is capable of generating visual features for all unseen classes, providing us with features for both unseen and seen classes. Consequently, this multi-label ZSL and GZSL problem can be approached as a supervised learning problem, where the generated features enable us to employ supervised learning techn

2   Related Work

We will review the literature of multi-label ZSL, GZSL and disentangled representation learning.

2.1   Multi-label ZSL and GZSL

Multi-label classification is a complicated task that requires classifying multiple objects or concepts within a single image, that is difficult than standard single-label classification. The most commonly used method for multi-label classifications is to train a binary classifier for each label present in the training data [49,57]. Along with this, to capture label correlation, there are also a few graph based [5,35,37] and structure based learning techniques [15,58,72]. Recently, vision transformer-based methods have gained significant interest due to their exceptional ability to capture global dependencies [6,34,42].

However, despite their success in multi-label classification, they struggle to deal with unseen classes, which limits their real-world use. ZSL generally uses class semantic information, i.e., class attributes, to identify unseen classes as it was first introduced by [33], where they have performed attribute-based classification. Additionally, [12,64] aimed to learn a function that performed mapping between semantic and visual features space to perform conventional ZSL where the search space is restricted to unseen classes only. In GZSL, which is a more practical scenario than conventional ZSL, the test image can be either from unseen or seen classes. Various GZSL approaches also learn a function to perform mapping between semantic and visual features [12,47]. GZSL has been treated as a missing data problem, and to address this, recent methods uses GAN [16] and VAE [31] as generative models for visual feature generation [10,61,63]. However, these ZSL and GZSL frameworks are limited to single-label classification and cannot handle multi-label ZSL and GZSL.

Multi-label ZSL and GZSL can be considered an extension of multi-label classification, which involves the alignment of an image visual embedding with its corresponding label embedding and determining the relationship between seen and unseen labels. Studies such as [4,20,55] concentrate on finding label correlations to perform classification by identifying relationships among labels. To accommodate semantic diversity between labels and images, SDL [2] identifies an image principal embedding vectors by upweighting the sample with the highest semantic diversity. While LESA [21] and BiAM [45] on the other hand use attention modules for multi-label classification by locating each label in an image. GMLZL [17] suggests a GAN-based generative model to leverage multi-class semantic information for multi-label feature synthesis.

2.2 Disentangled Representation Learning

Disentangled representation learning aims to identify the independent and generative factors of variation in data. Various techniques based on VAE have been developed to achieve this goal. For instance, [19] proposed an unsupervised VAE-based learning method that extracts a factorized latent representation from the data. This approach incorporates a flexible hyperparameter that balances the trade-off between independent latent factors and accurate data reconstruction. [3] introduced another variant of VAE that focuses on detecting overall correlations among latent variables to uncover independent sources of variation in the data. To penalize total correlation, [29] employed adversarial training, using a discriminator to differentiate between inputs derived from the product of marginal distributions and inputs derived from the marginal distribution itself. [39] suggested a flow-based model capable of restoring the joint distribution between observed and latent variables, with the primary objective of achieving disentangled representations without compromising reconstruction quality.

In this study, we propose a generative method for multi-label ZSL and GZSL that leverages disentangled representations to enhance the quality of generated data. Our approach incorporates a cross-level feature fusion technique [17] to generate semantically consistent multi-label visual features for all unseen classes. By learning disentangled representations, our method aims to improve the performance and applicability of multi-label ZSL and GZSL.

3 Methodology

In our section, we start by investigating the baseline model for disentangled latent space learning. We then proceed to describe the attribute-level feature fusion module, which plays a crucial role in generating semantically consistent multi-label visual features for all unseen classes. This module ensures that the generated features maintain semantic coherence across multiple labels, thereby enhancing the performance of our proposed method in multi-label ZSL and GZSL.

3.1 Preliminary

The problem formulation for multi-label ZSL and GZSL is as follows. We have a set Y that denotes the class labels, is split into two sets as $Y = Y^s \cup Y^u$ and $Y^s \cap Y^u = \phi$, where Y^s represents seen class labels presents in training data and Y^u represents unseen class labels. Here, $x \in X^s$ is the set of encoded features of multi-label images and $y \in \{0,1\}^s$ the corresponding multi-hot labels from seen classes labels set Y^s with p positive classes present in the image. The category specific class level embedding are used as side information in our case and it is represented as $a(k) = \{a(k_j), \forall j : y[j] = 1\}$ where $|a(k)| = p$. Given U and S, the goal of multi-label ZSL and GZSL is to learn a classifier $f_{zsl} : X \rightarrow \{0,1\}^U$ and $f_{gzsl} : X \rightarrow \{0,1\}^{S+U}$ respectively, where for ZSL the exploration domain is limited to unseen classes only, whereas for GZSL the exploration domain encompasses both seen and unseen classes.

3.2   Disentangled Latent Space Learning

Our proposed model, built upon the framework of VAE, is specifically designed to generate visual features for all unseen classes in the context of multi-label ZSL and GZSL. The core concept of disentangled representation learning is based on the notion that real-world data is influenced by a small number of latent factors that account for its variations. Therefore, our model focuses on learning these latent factors by approximating the underlying distribution of the observed data. The VAE based generative model, given the latent variable z and observed data x, is as follows:

$$p_\theta(x, z) = p_\theta(x|z)p_\theta(z), \tag{1}$$

The model parameters are denoted by θ, and the prior probability distribution for the latent variables is represented as $p_\theta(z)$. One of the main challenges faced by the generative model in Eq. (1) is the lack of identifiability. Identifiability refers to the ability to uncover the underlying factors that generate the observed data [39]. However, models with unconditional latent priors are not identifiable [28]. On the other hand, non-linear ICA always aims for identifiability by extracting independent components while assuming strong conditional independence [23]. Therefore, the key requirement for achieving identifiability involves a factorized prior distribution of the latent variables, with the presence of an additional observed variable denoted as a, as proposed in [28]:

$$p_\theta(x, z|a(y)) = p_\theta(x|z)p_\theta(z|a(y)), \tag{2}$$

In our proposed model, we introduce an additional observed variable denoted as $a(y)$, which represents the class semantic information along with the visual features x. These variables play a crucial role in enabling the learning of disentangled representations and enhancing the quality of the generated data using the identifiable generative model described in Eq. (2). The Variational Autoencoder (VAE) approximates a proxy posterior distribution $q_\phi(z|x, a(y))$ and aims to uncover the true posterior distribution $p_\theta(z|x, a(y))$ by minimizing the discrepancy between them through the variational lower bound constraint:

$$L(\theta, \phi) := E_{q_\phi(z|x,a(y))}[\log p_\theta(x|z)] - D_{KL}(q_\phi(z|x, a(y))||p_\theta(z|a(y))), \tag{3}$$

as the first term in (3) represent the reconstruction error and the second term, denoted as D_{KL}, corresponds to the Kullback-Leibler (KL) divergence between the inference model $q_\phi(z|x, a(y))$ and the conditionally factorized prior distribution $p_\theta(z|a(y))$ of the latent variables. We model the prior distribution using a Gaussian location-scale family, represented as $p_\theta(z|a(y))$.

3.3   Multi-label Feature Generator

We utilize the attribute-level feature fusion approach [17] as represented in Fig. 1. In the attribute-level feature fusion approach, the goal is to generate fused multi-label visual features for unseen classes while considering the inter dependencies among the image labels. This approach takes into account the class semantic information associated with various labels present in the image. To derive a comprehensive image-level global visual feature, the attribute-level feature fusion method combines the individual class semantic information. This fusion process involves aggregating the semantic information associated with positive labels found in the image. One way to achieve this is by averaging the individual class semantic information, denoted as $a(y)$, and the global image-level embedding a_μ is defined as:

$$a_\mu = \frac{1}{n} \sum_{j:y[j]=1} a(y), \tag{4}$$

We then integrate this attribute-level feature fusion module to train our proposed generative model. After training of the proposed generative model, this global image-level embedding a_μ along with the noise vector z is responsible for generating fused image-level features for unseen classes i.e., $\tilde{x} = G(z, a_\mu)$.

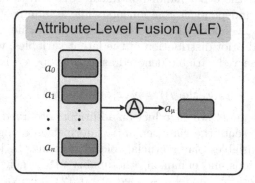

Fig. 1. Overview of the attribute-level feature fusion process to generate global image-level embedding.

3.4 The Proposed Model

To acquire a disentangled representation for generating visual features, we suggest using iVAE for multi-label ZSL and GZSL, as depicted in Fig. 2. The proposed model combines iVAE with two VAE networks that aims to minimize the subsequent loss function:

$$L_{iVAE(\theta,\phi_1)} := E_{(q_{\phi_1}(z_1|x,a(y)))}[\log p_\theta(x|z_1)] - D_{KL}(q_{\phi_1}(z_1|x,a(y))\|p_\theta(z_1|a(y))), \tag{5}$$

as in Eq. (5), the first term on the right-hand side represents the reconstruction error, which measures the dissimilarity between the reconstructed visual features $\tilde{x}$ and the real visual features x. The goal is to minimize this reconstruction error to ensure that the generated features closely resemble the original

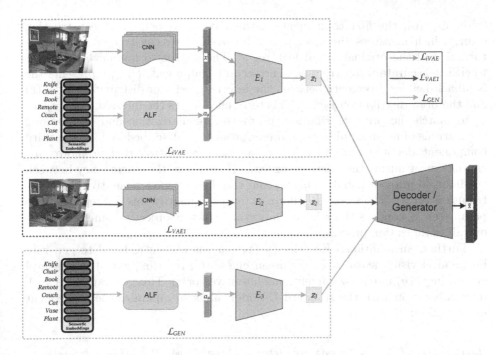

Fig. 2. The overall framework of our proposed generative model for Multi-label ZSL and GZSL.

ones. The second term, D_{KL}, corresponds to the Kullback-Leibler (KL) divergence between the prior distribution $p_\theta(z_1|a(y))$ and the approximate posterior distribution $q_\phi(z_1|x, a(y))$. The probabilistic encoder $q_\phi(z_1|x, a(y))$ takes both the image-level features x and the attribute-level feature fusion $a(y)$ as inputs and maps them to the latent space z_1. On the other hand, the probabilistic decoder $p_\theta(z_1|a(y))$ utilizes the latent vector z_1 conditioned on the image-level embedding $a(y)$ to reconstruct the visual features $\tilde{x}$. By conditioning the latent prior $p_\theta(z_1|a(y))$ on the image-level embedding $a(y)$, the model aims to achieve a disentangled representation of the latent space z_1. This means that different components of z_1 capture distinct factors of variation in the data that are independent of each other. By disentangling the latent space, the model can learn and generate visual features that are more interpretable and semantically meaningful.

The second Encoder, $q_\phi(z_2|x)$, as in $VAE1$ maps the input image x, to a latent vector z_2 while the Decoder, on the other hand, is responsible for reconstructing the image x with the primary objective is to diminish the following loss function:

$$L_{VAE1(\theta,\phi_2)} := E_{q_{\phi_2}(z_2|x)}[\log p_\theta(x|z_2)] - D_{KL}(q_{\phi_2}(z_2|x)||p_\theta(z_2)) - \lambda_1 D(q_{\phi_2}(z_2)||p_\theta(z_2)), \quad (6)$$

in Eq. (6), the first component on the RHS represents the reconstruction error, which measures the discrepancy between the reconstructed visual features $\tilde{x}$ and the original visual features x. The goal is to minimize this error to ensure accurate reconstruction. The second component, D_{KL}, represents the Kullback-Leibler divergence between the inferred posterior distribution $q_\phi(z_2|x)$ and the prior distribution $p_\theta(z_2)$. This term encourages the inferred latent space z_2 to match the prior distribution, promoting regularization and encouraging the learning of meaningful latent representations. As described in [32], the third component, denoted as D, functions as an extra regularizer that promotes disentanglement during the inference process. It measures the discrepancy between the inferred prior distribution $q_\phi(z_2)$ and the disentangled generative prior distribution $p_\theta(z_2)$. The squared l_2 norm is used to quantify this discrepancy. The parameter λ_1 controls the relative importance of this objective function in the overall optimization process.

Further, an additional Encoder $q_{\phi_3}(z_3|a(y))$ is also introduced to generate image-level visual features $\tilde{x}$ for unseen classes U, by using global image-level embedding $a(y)$ into a low-dimensional latent vector z_3. This generative network in collaboration with the standard Decoder, aims to minimize the subsequent loss function:

$$L_{GEN(\theta,\phi_3)} := E_{q_{\phi_3}(z_3|x)}[\log p_\theta(x|z_3)] - D_{KL}(q_{\phi_3}(z_3|a(y))\|p_\theta(z_3)) - \lambda_2 D(q_{\phi_3}(z_3)\|p_\theta(z_3)),$$
(7)

in Eq. (7), the first component on the RHS represents the reconstruction error, which measures the discrepancy between the reconstructed visual features $\tilde{x}$ and the original visual features x. The goal is to minimize this error to ensure accurate reconstruction. The second component, D_{KL}, represents the Kullback-Leibler divergence between the inferred posterior distribution $q_\phi(z_3|x)$ and the prior distribution $p_\theta(z_3)$. This term encourages the inferred latent space z_3 to match the prior distribution, promoting regularization and encouraging the learning of meaningful latent representations. As described in [32], the third component, denoted as D, functions as an extra regularizer that promotes disentanglement during the inference process. It measures the discrepancy between the inferred prior distribution $q_\phi(z_3)$ and the disentangled generative prior distribution $p_\theta(z_3)$. The squared l_2 norm is used to quantify this discrepancy. The parameter λ_2 controls the relative importance of this objective function in the overall optimization process.

Consequently, (8) illustrates the overall loss of the proposed generative model as:

$$L_{Total} = L_{iVAE(\theta,\phi_1)} + L_{VAE1(\theta,\phi_2)} + L_{GEN(\theta,\phi_3)}.$$
(8)

So, the primary objective is to train the model in a way that brings the latent spaces closer together. Once the generative model is trained, it becomes possible to generate multi-label visual features $\tilde{x}$ for all unseen classes U by using their global image-level semantic information a_μ. After training, we also have the generated features for unobserved categories as $\hat{U} = \{(\tilde{x}, u, a_\mu) | \tilde{x} \in X^u, u \in Y^u, a_\mu \in A\}$ along with the real seen classes features. Based on the task at hand, whether it is ZSL or GZSL, samples from both observed classes S and unobserved classes $\hat{U}$ are utilized to train the final classifier i.e., softmax, along with the binary cross entropy loss $BCE=(f_{zsl}(\tilde{x}), y_u)$ and $BCE=(f_{gzsl}(\tilde{x}), y_{u+s})$ for both multi-label ZSL and GZSL, respectively.

4   Experiments

4.1   Datasets

We assess our proposed approach for multi-label ZSL and GZSL on two benchmark datasets, specifically, for MS COCO [40] and NUS-WIDE [7]. The NUS-WIDE dataset has about 270,000 images classified into 81 categories by human annotators, and 925 labels derived from tags added by Flickr users. Following [21,71], for seen labels we select the 925 labels, and the remaining 81 labels are human-annotated are considered as unseen. The MS COCO dataset has 122,218 images across 80 categories, with a validation set of 40,137 and a training set of 82,081 images. We use this dataset for both multi-label ZSL and GZSL, adopting the same 15 unseen and 65 seen classes split as in [17].

4.2   Evaluation Protocols

To measure the performance of our proposed generative approach, we use F1 score and mean Average Precision (mAP) for both multi-label ZSL and GZSL as in [21,71]. The mAP metric evaluates label retrieval accuracy, reflecting the model ability to rank the correct labels for each image. Conversely, the top-k F1 score measures the model prediction accuracy by considering the top-k most probable labels for each image. This metric also accounts for both precision and recall and is commonly used for multi-class classification tasks.

4.3   Implementation Details

We outline the implementation specifics of our proposed model in this section. We employ the pretrained VGG-19 model [21,71] for multi-label image feature extraction. We use the FC7 layer output, which has 4096 image-level visual features, as input to our proposed model. Our model Encoder and Decoder networks are implemented as feed-forward neural networks with two hidden layers and 4096 hidden units. For both datasets, the latent vector size is 64 for each Encoder. We use Glove vectors [48] for class semantic information and apply the Adam optimizer for all datasets. Both for multi-label ZSL and GZSL, we trained the classifier with the learning rates of $\alpha = 0.001$ for NUS-WIDE and MS COCO. We determine all these parameters exclusively through cross-validation. The regularization parameters λ_1 and λ_1 are set to 10 for both datasets, and for every experiment, we create 300 visual depictions for each unseen category (Fig. 3).

Original Images

banana	person	train*
apple	wine	backpack
orange	cup	person
sandwich*	dining table	handbag
hot dog*	fork*	suitcase*

Fig. 3. Comparison of the prediction on test samples from MS COC datasets. The result represents the Top-5 predictions for Multi-label GZSL. '*' represents the unseen labels, while green text represents True Positive prediction and red text represents the apparently incorrect predictions. (Color figure online)

5   Results

In our comparative analysis, we evaluate the performance of our proposed model against state-of-the-art methods, including attribute-level fusion and feature-level fusion, for multi-label ZSL and GZSL tasks. The results of these evaluations are presented in Table 1 and Table 2. To assess the performance of our model, we consider metrics such as mean Average Precision (mAP) and F1 score for different values of K (top-K predictions), where K is selected from the set 3, 5. Additionally, we provide precision (P) and recall (R) metrics for each F1 score, enabling a comprehensive evaluation of our model's predictive capabilities. Among the compared methods, CONSE [47] utilizes a convex combination of class embedding vectors to associate images with their corresponding semantic embedding space, without requiring additional training. On the other hand, LabelEM [1] proposes an attribute-based classification method that maps each class to its corresponding semantic information. Fast0Tag [71] focuses on determining principal directions in the word vector space to prioritize relevant tags over irrelevant ones. Attention per Label [30] utilizes bilinear attention networks to efficiently leverage vision-language information by identifying bilinear attention distributions. LESA [21] and BiAM [45] both integrate a shared multi-attention mechanism for multi-label ZSL and GZSL classification. This approach enables the recognition of multiple labels, detection of unseen labels within an image, and identification of relevant regions for each label.

Meanwhile, ML-Decoder [52] introduces a new attention-based classification head for various classification tasks, including multi-label ZSL. GMLZSL [17] presents a GAN-based generative model that leverages multi-class semantic information through a cross-level feature fusion technique for visual feature generation. SDL [2] develops a method to encourage semantic diversity among image labels by assigning higher weights to samples exhibiting greater diversity. In contrast to the other methods, ML-ZSL [43] introduces an innovative approach to unbiased multi-label ZSL, which takes into account different class-specific regions

to enhance the training process of the classifier. The key component of this approach is the Pyramid Feature Attention (PFA), which establishes connections
between global and local information within the samples, ensuring a balanced
representation of each class. Lastly, ADDS [65] introduces a framework for multi-
label classification that incorporates a flexible constraint to enhance the alignment of visual and textual features. In this framework, they have introduced
DM-Decoder, an innovative transformer decoder that facilitates the merging of
semantics from dual-modal information sources. The results show that the feature generating method for multi-label ZSL and GZSL outperforms all other
state-of-the-art methods on both datasets.

As for NUS-WIDE dataset, in conventional multi-label ZSL, the proposed
approach achieves improved results over the best existing method ML-Decoder,
with the mAP score of 32.6%. While in terms of F1 score, our proposed approach
also attains the improved results as comapred to ML-ZSL with the score of 37.7%
at K = 3 and 37.8% at K = 5. For GZSL, ML-Decoder outperform all the existing
methods with the mAP score of 19.9% and our proposed method achieves an
improvement with an absolute gain of 1.8% over ML-Decoder. In terms of F1
score, our proposed approach also achieves better performance as compare to
ML-Decoder with the absolute again of 0.8% at K = 3 and 1.6% at K = 5 with
the F1 score of 24.1% and 27.7%, respectively.

For MS COCO, in multi-label ZSL and GZSL our proposed method achieves
improved results with the mAP score of 52.8% and 33.7%, respectively. Similarly,
for conventional multi-label ZSL in terms of F1 score, our proposed methods
achieves an absolute gain of 2.2% at K = 3. While for GZSL, we have achieved
the absolute gain of 0.5% at K = 3 and K = 5 with the F1 score of 44.6% and
43.9%, respectively. Our proposed approach achieves significantly higher results
for multi-label ZSL and GZSL, for both NUS-WIDE and MS COCO datasets,
in terms of mAP and F1 score, as compared to other existing methods.

Table 1. Comparative analysis of State-of-the-art methods for Multi-label ZSL and
GZSL on NUS-WIDE dataset. We present the findings using mAP and F1 score with
$K \in 3, 5$. The best outcomes are highlighted in bold. A dash ('-') signifies that the
respective methods either do not supply their results or do not experiment with the
datasets.

Method	Task	NUS-WIDE													
		ZSL							GZSL						
		K=3			K=5				K=3			K=5			
		P	R	F1	P	R	F1	mAP	P	R	F1	P	R	F1	mAP
Fast0Tag [71]		22.6	36.2	27.8	18.2	48.4	26.4	15.1	18.8	8.3	11.5	15.9	11.7	13.5	3.7
ML-Decoder [52]		-	-	34.1	-	-	30.8	31.1	-	-	23.3	-	-	26.1	19.9
LESA [21]		25.7	41.1	31.6	19.7	52.5	28.7	19.4	23.6	10.4	14.4	19.8	14.6	16.8	5.6
SDL [2]		-	-	30.5	-	-	27.8	25.9	-	-	18.5	-	-	21.0	12.1
Attention per Label [30]		20.9	33.5	25.8	16.2	43.2	23.6	10.4	17.9	7.9	10.9	15.6	11.5	13.2	3.7
GMLZSL [17]		26.6	**42.8**	32.8	20.1	53.6	29.3	25.7	30.9	13.6	18.9	26.0	19.1	22.0	8.9
BiAM [45]		-	-	33.1	-	-	30.7	26.3	-	-	16.1	-	-	19.0	9.3
ML-ZSL [43]		34.0	42.3	**37.7**	26.7	55.3	36.0	28.0	31.2	13.9	19.2	26.4	19.6	22.5	9.3
ADDS [65]		-	-	34.2	-	-	36.0	36.5	-	-	-	-	-	-	-
OURS		**34.3**	41.8	**37.7**	**28.6**	**55.8**	**37.8**	**36.8**	**33.3**	18.9	**24.1**	**29.8**	**25.8**	**27.7**	**21.7**

Table 2. Comparative analysis of State-of-the-art methods for Multi-label ZSL and GZSL on MS COCO dataset. We present the findings using mAP and F1 score with $K \in 3, 5$. The best outcomes are highlighted in bold. A dash ('-') signifies that the respective methods either do not supply their results or do not experiment with the datasets.

Method	Task	MS COCO												
		ZSL						GZSL						
		K=3			K=5				K=3			K=5		
		P	R	F1	P	R	F1	mAP	P	R	F1	P	R	F1	mAP
Fast0Tag [71]		-	-	37.5	-	-	-	43.3	-	-	33.8	-	-	34.6	27.9
LabelEM [1]		-	-	10.3	-	-	-	9.6	-	-	6.7	-	-	7.9	4.0
LESA [21]		-	-	33.6	-	-	-	31.8	-	-	26.7	-	-	28.0	17.7
CONSE [47]		-	-	18.4	-	-	-	13.2	-	-	19.6	-	-	18.9	7.7
GMLZSL [17]		-	-	43.5	-	-	-	52.2	-	-	44.1	-	-	43.4	33.2
OURS		32.1	79.7	**45.7**	25.5	86.6	39.7	**52.8**	45.9	43.4	**44.6**	37.1	53.7	**43.9**	**33.7**

6 Conclusion

We propose a generative framework to learn disentangled representations for multi-label ZSL and GZSL. The proposed generative model employs iVAE along with two VAE networks to learn three distinct latent spaces, for disentangled representation learning, using attribute-level feature fusion technique. VAE is a most commonly employed network for extracting independent aspects of variability within data, with the primary assumption of identifiability for the factored latent prior to achieve disentangled representations. The attribute-level feature fusion technique will integrate semantic embedding against all the labels present in an image to learn global image-level embedding. Further, this global image-level embedding, is used for generating fused multi-label visual features against all unseen classes. Subsequently, we employ a softmax classifier, trained on both seen and unseen classes, to perform classification. Extensive experiments are performed on two standard datasets i.e., NUS-WIDE and MSCOCO, to determine the effectiveness of our proposed generative model for both multi-label ZSL and GZSL.

Acknowledgements. The authors express their heartfelt gratitude to the editors and anonymous reviewers for their insightful feedback. This research was made possible through the support of the National University of Sciences and Technology (NUST) in Islamabad, Pakistan.

References

1. Akata, Z., Perronnin, F., Harchaoui, Z., Schmid, C.: Label-embedding for image classification. IEEE Trans. Pattern Anal. Mach. Intell. **38**(7), 1425–1438 (2015)
2. Ben-Cohen, A., Zamir, N., Ben-Baruch, E., Friedman, I., Zelnik-Manor, L.: Semantic diversity learning for zero-shot multi-label classification. In: Proceedings of the IEEE/CVF International Conference on Computer Vision, pp. 640–650 (2021)

3. Chen, R.T., Li, X., Grosse, R.B., Duvenaud, D.K.: Isolating sources of disentanglement in variational autoencoders. Advances in neural information processing systems 31 (2018)
4. Chen, Z.M., Cui, Q., Wei, X.S., Jin, X., Guo, Y.: Disentangling, embedding and ranking label cues for multi-label image recognition. IEEE Trans. Multimedia **23**, 1827–1840 (2020)
5. Chen, Z.M., Wei, X.S., Wang, P., Guo, Y.: Multi-label image recognition with graph convolutional networks. In: Proceedings of the IEEE/CVF Conference on Computer Vision and Pattern Recognition, pp. 5177–5186 (2019)
6. Cheng, X., Lin, H., Wu, X., Shen, D., Yang, F., Liu, H., Shi, N.: Mltr: Multi-label classification with transformer. In: 2022 IEEE International Conference on Multimedia and Expo (ICME), pp. 1–6. IEEE (2022)
7. Chua, T.S., Tang, J., Hong, R., Li, H., Luo, Z., Zheng, Y.: Nus-wide: a real-world web image database from national university of Singapore. In: Proceedings of the ACM International Conference on Image and Video Retrieval, pp. 1–9 (2009)
8. Deng, J., Dong, W., Socher, R., Li, L.J., Li, K., Fei-Fei, L.: Imagenet: A large-scale hierarchical image database. In: 2009 IEEE Conference on Computer Vision and Pattern Recognition, pp. 248–255. IEEE (2009)
9. Durand, T., Mehrasa, N., Mori, G.: Learning a deep convnet for multi-label classification with partial labels. In: Proceedings of the IEEE/CVF Conference on Computer Vision and Pattern Recognition, pp. 647–657 (2019)
10. Felix, R., Kumar, V.B., Reid, I., Carneiro, G.: Multi-modal cycle-consistent generalized zero-shot learning. In: Proceedings of the European Conference on Computer Vision (ECCV), pp. 21–37 (2018)
11. Feng, L., An, B., He, S.: Collaboration based multi-label learning. In: Proceedings of the AAAI Conference on Artificial Intelligence, vol. 33, pp. 3550–3557 (2019)
12. Frome, A., et al.: Devise: a deep visual-semantic embedding model. In: Advances in Neural Information Processing Systems, pp. 2121–2129 (2013)
13. Fu, Y., Hospedales, T.M., Xiang, T., Gong, S.: Transductive multi-view zero-shot learning. IEEE Trans. Pattern Anal. Mach. Intell. **37**(11), 2332–2345 (2015)
14. Fujiyoshi, H., Hirakawa, T., Yamashita, T.: Deep learning-based image recognition for autonomous driving. IATSS Res. **43**(4), 244–252 (2019)
15. Gong, Y., Jia, Y., Leung, T., Toshev, A., Ioffe, S.: Deep convolutional ranking for multilabel image annotation. arXiv preprint arXiv:1312.4894 (2013)
16. Goodfellow, I., et al.: Generative adversarial nets. In: Advances in neural information processing systems, pp. 2672–2680 (2014)
17. Gupta, A., Narayan, S., Khan, S., Khan, F.S., Shao, L., van de Weijer, J.: Generative multi-label zero-shot learning. arXiv preprint arXiv:2101.11606 (2021)
18. He, K., Zhang, X., Ren, S., Sun, J.: Deep residual learning for image recognition. In: Proceedings of the IEEE Conference on Computer Vision and Pattern Recognition, pp. 770–778 (2016)
19. Higgins, I., et al.: beta-vae: learning basic visual concepts with a constrained variational framework. In: International Conference on Learning Representations (2017)
20. Huang, H., Wang, C., Yu, P.S., Wang, C.D.: Generative dual adversarial network for generalized zero-shot learning. In: Proceedings of the IEEE/CVF Conference on Computer Vision and Pattern Recognition, pp. 801–810 (2019)
21. Huynh, D., Elhamifar, E.: A shared multi-attention framework for multi-label zero-shot learning. In: Proceedings of the IEEE/CVF Conference on Computer Vision and Pattern Recognition, pp. 8776–8786 (2020)

22. Hyvarinen, A., Morioka, H.: Unsupervised feature extraction by time-contrastive learning and nonlinear ICA. In: Advances in Neural Information Processing Systems, pp. 3765–3773 (2016)
23. Hyvarinen, A., Morioka, H.: Nonlinear ICA of temporally dependent stationary sources. In: Artificial Intelligence and Statistics, pp. 460–469. PMLR (2017)
24. Hyvarinen, A., Sasaki, H., Turner, R.: Nonlinear ICA using auxiliary variables and generalized contrastive learning. In: The 22nd International Conference on Artificial Intelligence and Statistics, pp. 859–868 (2019)
25. Jayaraman, D., Grauman, K.: Zero-shot recognition with unreliable attributes. Advances in neural information processing systems 27 (2014)
26. Jeon, I., Lee, W., Kim, G.: Ib-gan: disentangled representation learning with information bottleneck gan (2018)
27. Kamilaris, A., Prenafeta-Boldú, F.X.: Deep learning in agriculture: a survey. Comput. Electron. Agric. **147**, 70–90 (2018)
28. Khemakhem, I., Kingma, D., Monti, R., Hyvarinen, A.: Variational autoencoders and nonlinear ICA: a unifying framework. In: International Conference on Artificial Intelligence and Statistics, pp. 2207–2217 (2020)
29. Kim, H., Mnih, A.: Disentangling by factorising. In: International Conference on Machine Learning, pp. 2649–2658. PMLR (2018)
30. Kim, J.H., Jun, J., Zhang, B.T.: Bilinear attention networks. Advances in neural information processing systems 31 (2018)
31. Kingma, D.P., Welling, M.: Auto-encoding variational bayes. arXiv preprint arXiv:1312.6114 (2013)
32. Kumar, A., Sattigeri, P., Balakrishnan, A.: Variational inference of disentangled latent concepts from unlabeled observations. arXiv preprint arXiv:1711.00848 (2017)
33. Lampert, C.H., Nickisch, H., Harmeling, S.: Learning to detect unseen object classes by between-class attribute transfer. In: 2009 IEEE Conference on Computer Vision and Pattern Recognition, pp. 951–958 (2009). https://doi.org/10.1109/CVPR.2009.5206594
34. Lanchantin, J., Wang, T., Ordonez, V., Qi, Y.: General multi-label image classification with transformers. In: Proceedings of the IEEE/CVF Conference on Computer Vision and Pattern Recognition, pp. 16478–16488 (2021)
35. Lee, C.W., Fang, W., Yeh, C.K., Wang, Y.C.F.: Multi-label zero-shot learning with structured knowledge graphs. In: Proceedings of the IEEE Conference on Computer Vision and Pattern Recognition, pp. 1576–1585 (2018)
36. Li, J., Jing, M., Lu, K., Ding, Z., Zhu, L., Huang, Z.: Leveraging the invariant side of generative zero-shot learning. In: Proceedings of the IEEE/CVF Conference on Computer Vision and Pattern Recognition, pp. 7402–7411 (2019)
37. Li, Q., Qiao, M., Bian, W., Tao, D.: Conditional graphical lasso for multi-label image classification. In: Proceedings of the IEEE Conference on Computer Vision and Pattern Recognition, pp. 2977–2986 (2016)
38. Li, Q., Cai, W., Wang, X., Zhou, Y., Feng, D.D., Chen, M.: Medical image classification with convolutional neural network. In: 2014 13th International Conference on Control Automation Robotics & Vision (ICARCV), pp. 844–848. IEEE (2014)
39. Li, S., Hooi, B., Lee, G.H.: Identifying through flows for recovering latent representations. arXiv preprint arXiv:1909.12555 (2019)
40. Lin, T.-Y., Maire, M., Belongie, S., Hays, J., Perona, P., Ramanan, D., Dollár, P., Zitnick, C.L.: Microsoft COCO: common objects in context. In: Fleet, D., Pajdla, T., Schiele, B., Tuytelaars, T. (eds.) ECCV 2014. LNCS, vol. 8693, pp. 740–755. Springer, Cham (2014). https://doi.org/10.1007/978-3-319-10602-1_48

41. Liu, B., Zhu, Y., Fu, Z., de Melo, G., Elgammal, A.: Oogan: disentangling gan with one-hot sampling and orthogonal regularization. In: AAAI, pp. 4836–4843 (2020)
42. Liu, S., Zhang, L., Yang, X., Su, H., Zhu, J.: Query2label: a simple transformer way to multi-label classification. arXiv preprint arXiv:2107.10834 (2021)
43. Liu, Z., Guo, S., Guo, J., Xu, Y., Huo, F.: Towards unbiased multi-label zero-shot learning with pyramid and semantic attention (2022)
44. Nam, J., Loza Mencía, E., Kim, H.J., Fürnkranz, J.: Maximizing subset accuracy with recurrent neural networks in multi-label classification. Advances in neural information processing systems 30 (2017)
45. Narayan, S., Gupta, A., Khan, S., Khan, F.S., Shao, L., Shah, M.: Discriminative region-based multi-label zero-shot learning. In: Proceedings of the IEEE/CVF International Conference on Computer Vision, pp. 8731–8740 (2021)
46. Nguyen-Phuoc, T., Li, C., Theis, L., Richardt, C., Yang, Y.L.: Hologan: unsupervised learning of 3d representations from natural images. In: Proceedings of the IEEE International Conference on Computer Vision, pp. 7588–7597 (2019)
47. Norouzi, M., et al.: Zero-shot learning by convex combination of semantic embeddings. In: International Conference on Learning Representations (2013)
48. Pennington, J., Socher, R., Manning, C.D.: Glove: global vectors for word representation. In: Proceedings of the 2014 Conference on Empirical Methods in Natural Language Processing (EMNLP), pp. 1532–1543 (2014)
49. Read, J., Pfahringer, B., Holmes, G., Frank, E.: Classifier chains for multi-label classification. Mach. Learn. **85**, 333–359 (2011)
50. Ren, S., He, K., Girshick, R., Sun, J.: Faster R-CNN: towards real-time object detection with region proposal networks. Advances in neural information processing systems 28 (2015)
51. Ridnik, T., Ben-Baruch, E., Noy, A., Zelnik-Manor, L.: Imagenet-21k pretraining for the masses. arXiv preprint arXiv:2104.10972 (2021)
52. Ridnik, T., Sharir, G., Ben-Cohen, A., Ben-Baruch, E., Noy, A.: Ml-decoder: scalable and versatile classification head. In: Proceedings of the IEEE/CVF Winter Conference on Applications of Computer Vision, pp. 32–41 (2023)
53. Romera-Paredes, B., Torr, P.: An embarrassingly simple approach to zero-shot learning. In: International Conference on Machine Learning, pp. 2152–2161 (2015)
54. Shen, Y., Qin, J., Huang, L., Liu, L., Zhu, F., Shao, L.: Invertible zero-shot recognition flows. In: Computer Vision-ECCV 2020: 16th European Conference, Glasgow, UK, August 23–28, 2020, Proceedings, Part XVI 16, pp. 614–631. Springer (2020)
55. Shi, M., Tang, Y., Zhu, X., Liu, J.: Multi-label graph convolutional network representation learning. IEEE Trans. Big Data **8**(5), 1169–1181 (2020)
56. Tsoumakas, G., Katakis, I.: Multi-label classification: An overview international journal of data warehousing and mining. The label powerset algorithm is called PT3 3(3) (2006)
57. Tsoumakas, G., Katakis, I.: Multi-label classification: an overview. Int. J. Data Warehousing Mining (IJDWM) **3**(3), 1–13 (2007)
58. Wang, J., Yang, Y., Mao, J., Huang, Z., Huang, C., Xu, W.: CNN-RNN: a unified framework for multi-label image classification. In: Proceedings of the IEEE Conference on Computer Vision and Pattern Recognition, pp. 2285–2294 (2016)
59. Wang, W., Zheng, V.W., Yu, H., Miao, C.: A survey of zero-shot learning: settings, methods, and applications. ACM Trans. Intell. Syst. Technol. (TIST) **10**(2), 1–37 (2019)
60. Weston, J., Bengio, S., Usunier, N.: Wsabie: scaling up to large vocabulary image annotation (2011)

61. Xian, Y., Lorenz, T., Schiele, B., Akata, Z.: Feature generating networks for zero-shot learning. In: Proceedings of the IEEE Conference on Computer Vision and Pattern Recognition, pp. 5542–5551 (2018)
62. Xian, Y., Schiele, B., Akata, Z.: Zero-shot learning-the good, the bad and the ugly. In: Proceedings of the IEEE Conference on Computer Vision and Pattern Recognition, pp. 4582–4591 (2017)
63. Xian, Y., Sharma, S., Schiele, B., Akata, Z.: f-vaegan-d2: a feature generating framework for any-shot learning. In: Proceedings of the IEEE Conference on Computer Vision and Pattern Recognition, pp. 10275–10284 (2019)
64. Xie, G.S., Liu, L., Jin, X., Zhu, F., Zhang, Z., Qin, J., Yao, Y., Shao, L.: Attentive region embedding network for zero-shot learning. In: 2019 IEEE/CVF Conference on Computer Vision and Pattern Recognition (CVPR), pp. 9376–9385 (2019). https://doi.org/10.1109/CVPR.2019.00961
65. Xu, S., Li, Y., Hsiao, J., Ho, C., Qi, Z.: A dual modality approach for (zero-shot) multi-label classification (2022)
66. Yang, H., Tianyi Zhou, J., Zhang, Y., Gao, B.B., Wu, J., Cai, J.: Exploit bounding box annotations for multi-label object recognition. In: Proceedings of the IEEE Conference on Computer Vision and Pattern Recognition, pp. 280–288 (2016)
67. Yazici, V.O., Gonzalez-Garcia, A., Ramisa, A., Twardowski, B., Weijer, J.v.d.: Orderless recurrent models for multi-label classification. In: Proceedings of the IEEE/CVF Conference on Computer Vision and Pattern Recognition, pp. 13440–13449 (2020)
68. Ye, J., He, J., Peng, X., Wu, W., Qiao, Yu.: Attention-driven dynamic graph convolutional network for multi-label image recognition. In: Vedaldi, A., Bischof, H., Brox, T., Frahm, J.-M. (eds.) ECCV 2020. LNCS, vol. 12366, pp. 649–665. Springer, Cham (2020). https://doi.org/10.1007/978-3-030-58589-1_39
69. You, R., Guo, Z., Cui, L., Long, X., Bao, Y., Wen, S.: Cross-modality attention with semantic graph embedding for multi-label classification. In: Proceedings of the AAAI Conference on Artificial Intelligence, vol. 34, pp. 12709–12716 (2020)
70. Yu, H.F., Jain, P., Kar, P., Dhillon, I.: Large-scale multi-label learning with missing labels. In: International Conference on Machine Learning, pp. 593–601. PMLR (2014)
71. Zhang, Y., Gong, B., Shah, M.: Fast zero-shot image tagging. In: 2016 IEEE Conference on Computer Vision and Pattern Recognition (CVPR), pp. 5985–5994. IEEE (2016)
72. Zhu, F., Li, H., Ouyang, W., Yu, N., Wang, X.: Learning spatial regularization with image-level supervisions for multi-label image classification. In: Proceedings of the IEEE Conference on Computer Vision and Pattern Recognition, pp. 5513–5522 (2017)

A VR-Based "Time-Space" Interactive Map Teaching System for Modern Chinese History

YanXiang Zhang[1](✉), WenBin Hu[1], QiXian Ling[1], ChenXiao Zhao[1], and Yi Song[2]

[1] Department of Communication of Science and Technology,
University of Science and Technology of China, Hefei, Anhui, China
petrel@ustc.edu.cn, {huwb,zhaochx2022}@mail.ustc.edu.cn
[2] College of Marxism, University of Science and Technology of China, Hefei, Anhui, China
imena80@ustc.edu.cn

Abstract. Modern China was an important period in the development and sublimation of patriotism, and studying modern Chinese History is conducive to grasping the essence of patriotism. However, for a long time, teaching modern Chinese History in universities has focused on historical chronology. Still, there is an apparent lack of knowledge of historical space, and the role of maps in history teaching has yet to be fully exploited. In the face of this dilemma, this paper is based on multimodal learning theory and is developed using GEOVIS Earth. With the help of panoramic technology and 3D real-world modeling, we have designed a V.R. teaching tool that can be used in a desktop environment - the VR "Time-Space" interactive map teaching system. Through tests and interviews, we found that this system is more advantageous than the traditional lecture-based teaching method, which allows students to form an overall layout of historical events in their minds and enhances their interest and effectiveness in learning modern Chinese History.

Keywords: VR · Education · History · Maps · Time-Space

1 Introduction

Patriotism is a strong spiritual pillar on which a nation rests and a necessary spiritual motivation that drives a country toward prosperity and strength [1]. Modern China (1840–1949) was a short period, but it transformed China from a traditional society into a modern society in various fields such as politics, economy, society, ideology, and culture. It was not only an all-encompassing and exceptionally complex historical period, but an important period in the development and sublimation of patriotism as well, so studying modern Chinese History is conducive to grasping the essence of patriotism [4]. The Outline of Modern Chinese History, is one of the compulsory courses in the ideological and political theory courses of Chinese universities and is an introductory course for history education and patriotic education [2]. Therefore, how to better educate patriotism in the teaching of modern Chinese History so that students can understand and grasp the characteristics of the development of modern Chinese History is a problem to be solved and a goal to be achieved in Chinese universities.

L. T. De Paolis et al. (Eds.): XR Salento 2023, LNCS 14219, pp. 51–68, 2023.
https://doi.org/10.1007/978-3-031-43404-4_4

To teach History well and develop students' ability to be creative in the subject, it is necessary to pay attention to the spatial concepts [5]. Everything in History happens under specific, concrete conditions of time and space, and it is only within a specific spatial and temporal framework that an accurate understanding of historical events is possible [6]. The concept of time and space is the basis for understanding and appreciating historical facts and is the essence of the discipline of History. [7]. For a long time, the teaching of modern Chinese History in universities has focused on the chronology of History. Still, the perception of historical space is inadequate, so students' historical impressions only include the vertical clues of the past and the present without the horizontal spatial concepts of the upper and lower quadrants [8].

Historical maps visually illustrate the chronological and spatial correlation of the geographical areas of interest [9]. It carries the pedagogical function of permeating the cultivation of spatiotemporal concepts [10]. In history teaching, the use of maps can activate historical processes and stimulate students' spatiotemporal thinking. Through map reading and interpretation, students' core literacy in History can be cultivated in a subtle way [10]. Maps in history education is, therefore, a common practice. For this reason, maps are often used as a teaching tool in history education.

Although maps are often used as a teaching tool in history education, their role in modern Chinese history education in colleges and universities still needs to be stronger. On the one hand, the maps currently used in history education are rich in resources but lack systematic integration. Most of them are presented in static form in books and textbooks, and the presentation needs to be more attractive. On the other hand, students' map-reading skills are weak, and most of them have a poor sense of time and space. Some students only pay attention to the changes in the flow of dynamic maps or the legends and notes and lack an overall sense of the events or phenomena they reflect. They cannot link their knowledge of History, geography, and politics [11]. At the root of this is the tendency to understand 'spatiotemporal concepts' as 'simple linear sequences,' to understand time and space in History as physical time and space, and to give students less guidance in interpreting the continuity and change of History in different spatiotemporal frameworks [12]. This is the case with the map. It is time to change how history maps are presented and improve their status and role in History learning.

Scholars have put forward many ideas to remedy the current shortcomings of historical maps. Sebastien Caquard and William Cartwright refer to the narrative power of maps, and there is a growing recognition of the importance of developing narratives [13]. The storytelling potential of maps is now widely acknowledged [13]. Narrative cartography, a new branch of cartography, combines the strengths of cartography in the representation of spatial information with the strengths of narrative in the representation of temporal information [14]. It combines interactive maps with remote sensing images, audio, and video to help people understand the spatial occurrence and development of events and develop a deeper understanding of the events themselves [15]. This also provides a new type of spatial narrative vehicle for teaching History. Just as French history textbooks combine timelines and maps designed to help students develop a spatial and temporal view of history [16], The narrative map can combine the advantages of cartography and narratology for the representation of spatial and temporal information [17]. The map can combine the advantages of cartography and narrative to represent spatial and temporal information [17]. Combining a general map with a timeline, therefore, helps to enhance the narrative power of the map.

In addition to combining maps with timelines, we can incorporate V.R. technology to harness the narrative power of maps better. V.R. (Virtual Reality) is a computer system that allows the creation and experience of virtual worlds [18]. V.R. has the advantages of interactivity, immersion, and intuitiveness [19]. This makes it uniquely valuable and helpful in the field of education, allowing learners to immerse themselves in a realistic virtual teaching environment and, with the spread of 5G, has laid the technological foundation for the application of the V.R. teaching model [20]. Nowadays, virtual reality technology has received strong support from the government and relevant departments in China's education research and development sector and has become an important technology penetrating the education sector [21].

It is worth noting that different V.R. technologies produce different levels of immersion, depending on the level of realism and how the user interacts with the system. In this way, so-called high-immersion V.R. environments and low-immersion desktop V.R. environments were created [22]. Highly immersive V.R. systems typically use a head-mounted display (HMD-VR) that fills the user's field of view. Auditory and haptic aspects can be added to the environment, allowing users to interact with the system using a joystick, handheld sensors, gloves, or tights. Low-immersion Desktop V.R. systems use conventional computers with monitors, keyboards, and mice, which the user operates to interact with the environment displayed on the screen [22].

Several scholars have done empirical research on the advantages and disadvantages of these two V.R. technologies in teaching and learning applications. In terms of learning performance, Bagher, Mahda M found that while students showed higher levels of reflective thinking in HMD-VR compared to desktop V.R., students gained significant knowledge in both conditions [28]. Yan Feng also found that when people used the more simple desktop V.R. technology was more conducive to conducting research with simple pathfinding tasks [23] Carbonell-Carrera also used empirical research to demonstrate that, unlike HMD-VR environments, students in Desktop V.R. environments did not report fatigue or dizziness, making Desktop V.R. environments an alternative to HMD-VR environments [22]. Moreover, a rapid and drastic fall in prices, a massive leap in computer processing power, the proliferation of the World Wide Web, and the prevalence of broadband connections have aggravated the use of desktop V.R. in schools and colleges [24–26]. Most Chinese universities need more money to purchase enough head-mounted V.R. devices to allow every student to experience it simultaneously; therefore, considering the portability and achievability, Desktop V.R. is more appropriate than HMD-VR in Chinese university classrooms with more students.

2 Related Works

Existing research generally agrees that maps are a good narrative tool, and researchers have made many theoretical and technical efforts to visualize spatiotemporal narratives.

In terms of theory, Sebastien Caquard and William Cartwright outline multiple ways of envisioning the relationship between maps and narrative from a mapmaking perspective, exploring the potential of maps as narratives and the importance of linking them to a complete mapping process through narrative [13]. Wang Shuang proposed a theory of spatiotemporal narrative visualization, establishing a mechanism for mapping textual space to geographical space and realizing a multidimensional visualization of events based on free narrative genres and normative narrative genres [27]. Sun Jian attempts to explore the ways and means to implement the "spatiotemporal concept" in teaching practice through the development of the connotation of "spatiotemporal concept [12]. Tu Mingjiang propose a theoretical model of distributed teaching based on V.R. [20].

In terms of V.R. technology, Zhang Shulin has tried to apply V.R. technology to teaching geography subjects. He wanted to build a geography teaching technology system based on V.R. technology, such as VR-GIS, VR-Google, VR-APP, VR-Drones, etc., which provided technical system support for VR-assisted geography classroom teaching and a new model for geography teaching change [19]. At the same time, Lau Siew Yun and Chen Chwen Jen argue that most of the research studies focus on immersive V.R. that involves expensive and bulky settings, which eventually limit its feasibility to be ubiquitously used. Thus, they look into the potential of non-immersive V.R., also known as desktop V.R., for educational purposes. This alternative low-cost and affordable V.R. technology requires only conventional computer settings. Still, it can present an interactive real-time three-dimensional virtual environment (VE) that the learners can navigate in and interact with.

In terms of map technology, we found that most of the existing research applies geospatial applications to physical geography and mapping, geology, environmental science, etc. Very few people apply geospatial applications to history education. For example, Se´bastien Caquard and William Cartwright proposed a web mapping app to help correctly map the many dimensions of a narrative, including the places of the narrative (geography), the connections between these places (geometry), and the temporal dimension inherent to storytelling [13].

In summary, existing scholars have noted the importance of spatiotemporal cues in map narratives, which is very sensible. Some scholars have also begun to explore the use of V.R. technology to aid classroom teaching, but they have yet to attempt to construct the temporal logic of historical events in the form of interactive maps and timelines and place them in a desktop V.R. environment for learners to experience.

3 System Design

This study has designed an innovative model, the VR "Time-Space" interactive map teaching system, a V.R. teaching tool that can be used in a desktop environment. The user can interact with the environment displayed on the screen using a computer or a mobile device such as a mobile phone. This teaching system is based on multiple sources, such as satellite remote-sensing images, photographs, and historical records. It uses 3D modeling technology and V.R. panoramic technology to interactively present the temporal and spatial clues of the development of historical events, presenting a multi-scale, multi-carrier narrative map of modern Chinese history. This system will bring learners a more intuitive and vivid impression and enhance their learning of modern Chinese history content.

The development tool used for the system is GEOVIS Earth, a similar Google Earth Engine (GEE) tool for interactive 3D content creation [29]. GEOVIS Earth deconstructs the digital map creation process and helps developers to create virtual simulation scenarios and thematic maps [29].

The theoretical basis for this study is the theory of multimodalisation in teaching and learning. Multimodalisation combines different symbolic modalities in a finished communication product or activity [30]. Multimodal teaching and learning theory consider using multiple means and symbolic resources such as the Internet, pictures, and videos to fully engage learners' senses of sight, hearing, and touch [31]. Based on the multimodal teaching theory, this study innovatively supplemented traditional classroom teaching with a "time-space" interactive map teaching system, adding multiple teaching modalities such as spatiotemporal narrative design, visualization design, and interaction design, which work together to enhance students' learning of History.

3.1 Spatio-Temporal Narrative Design

The spatiotemporal narrative steps of the VR "time-space" interactive map teaching system can be divided into collecting information and sorting out temporal and spatial clues.

3.1.1 Collecting Information

GEOVIS Earth provides a wide range of online data as base maps, with the ability to add overlay layers to support the import of personal data such as images, images, and models, and contains a wide range of rich Earth elements that users can choose to use according to their needs [29]. The GEOVIS Earth is a powerful tool for the user.

In addition to the maps, the system also requires images, music, texts, and V.R. panoramas related to History. Most images, music, and texts are obtained from books, official websites, and archives, while the V.R. panoramas are mainly obtained through field photography.

3.1.2 Sorting Out Temporal and Spatial Clues

In terms of narrative, GEOVIS Earth has a full range of macro, meso, and micro-expressions, allowing users to interpret multiple scenes from multiple dimensions and different perspectives, such as geography, History, current affairs, and military [29]. We sort through the timeline of event development, list key time points, and mark the geographical locations corresponding to these points in GEOVIS Earth to form a specific playback sequence. When learners initially enter the VR "Time-Space" interactive map teaching system, the screen will automatically play according to the time trial. When a critical point in time is reached, the frame automatically changes, and the viewpoint animation and style animation are freely matched to show the temporal scene experienced by people, events, and landscapes through the lens, relying on visual footage to describe facts and express emotions, making the images a meaningful narrative discourse. GEOVIS Earth is able to provide users with uninterrupted visual continuity in the process of switching between far - medium - close views, showing the temporal path of historical events [29]. Learners can not only zoom in and out on their own but can also click on crucial points to go to specific scenes to see more details.

3.2   Visual Design

Having sorted out the spatiotemporal narrative design path for the VR "Time-Space" interactive map teaching system, how do you select, process, and place these rich materials so they are logically presented in the VR "Time-Space" interactive map teaching system? We have used the idea of knowledge visualization here.

Knowledge visualization is an emerging research field based on scientific computing visualization, data visualization, and information visualization [32]. It improves knowledge creation and transfers with specific methods, including holistic frameworks, conceptual diagrams, knowledge diagrams, visual metaphors, knowledge maps, etc. [33]. It improves knowledge creation and transfer using holistic frameworks, conceptual diagrams, knowledge diagrams and visual metaphors, knowledge maps, etc. [33]. Based on the object of visualization, this paper illustrates the visualization of knowledge in a VR "Time-Space" interactive map teaching system, taking the Red Army's Long March (1934.10–1936.10) in modern Chinese History as an example (Fig. 1).

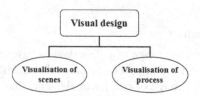

Fig. 1. Visual design of the VR "Time-Space" interactive map teaching system

3.2.1   Visualisation of Scenes

A. Geographical environment. Traditional static maps make combining route diagrams with accurate terrain maps challenging, leaving learners with a sense of fragmentation in the learning process. However, the VR interactive map designed with GEOVIS Earth solves this problem perfectly, allowing the learner's perspective to switch between the big picture and the details. Learners can not only see the whole picture of the course of historical events but also grasp the natural geography of each node and experience every historical moment from all angles. Whether on a distant or close-up scale, the VR "Time-Space" interactive map teaching system uses simple arrows, squares, and text to represent the overall route and distribution of forces of the Red Army's Long March.

For example, learners can observe the shape of the overall route of the Long March from the long-range scale (Fig. 2) and the geography of the "Crafty crossing of the Jinsha River" from the close-range scale (Fig. 3). Switching between scales helps learners to develop a sense of 'from the whole to the local' and helps to develop students' spatial and temporal concepts.

Fig. 2. Representation of the elements of things at a long-range scale. Example: Map of the overall route of the Long March of the Red Army

Fig. 3. Representation of elements of things at mid- and close-up scales. Example: Topographical map of the Jinsha River

B. Entity objects. For different types of entity objects, we can use different visualization tools.

Firstly, using V.R. panoramas to show the site and environment of real historical sites. We use insta360 to capture the panorama and then use A-FRAME, a web framework for building virtual reality (V.R.) experiences, to create a 3D panorama. A-Frame is based on top of HTML, making it A-Frame is not just a 3D scene graph or a markup language; the core is a robust entity-component framework that provides a declarative, extensible, and composable structure to three.js. [34] Therefore, we can easily use A-Frame to convert image footage into V.R. panoramas. Taking the Zunyi Conference, a critical meeting in the History of China's Long March, as an example, we first used insta360 to capture a panoramic view of the old Zunyi Conference site. Then we used A-Frame to transform it into a V.R. panorama. We then inserted the V.R. panorama as a hyperlink to the "Zunyi Conference" node in GEOVIS Earth so that learners could click on the hyperlink to open the corresponding V.R. panorama for roaming (Fig. 4).

Secondly, using 3D modeling to display historical buildings and objects. Because of GEOVIS Earth's powerful mapping capabilities, users can flexibly add points, lines, surfaces, images, models, text, and other mapping elements to a 3D scene, providing a very intuitive and accurate description of the scene in 3D space. This allows developers to use SketchUp and Lumion to build a 3D model of the scene and import it directly into GEOVIS Earth in glb format, allowing the learner to roam inside the model with a finger or mouse click when they reach the critical node. For example, the author's team used SketchUp and Lumion to build a 3D model of the Ruijin Central Revolutionary Base Area Memorial Hall, the starting place of the Red Army (Fig. 5), and imported it into GEOVIS Earth in glb format as Learners can click on the model on the map with

Fig. 4. Panoramic view using insta360 to show existing real-life scenes. Example: the former site of the Zunyi Conference

Fig. 5. Red base scene restored using SketchUp, lumion. Example: Ruijin Central Revolutionary Base Area Memorial Hall

their finger or mouse to access the 3D model of the site and learn about History while roaming around the site.

Thirdly, using historical paintings to showcase specific historical scenes. For example, at the 'Flying over Luding Bridge' node, the author's team inserted an oil painting in jpg format into GEOVIS Earth - 'Flying over Luding Bridge' (Chinese painter Liu Guoshu, 1959), accompanied by a textual introduction to help learners understand the brutality of war (Fig. 6).

Fig. 6. Historical drawings to aid understanding of historical facts. Example: Liu Guoshu The Flying of the Luding Bridge (1959)

C. Abstract objects. Suppose the object is an abstract thing, such as the relationship between elements and changes in data. In that case, we can use essential point, line, and surface graphics such as color blocks, arrows, and curved bar charts to represent them symbolically. For example, in Fig. 7, we have used a red color block to represent the Red Army's sphere of influence.

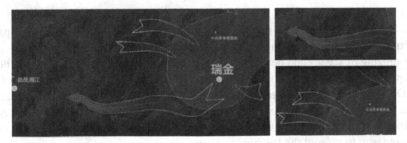

Fig. 7. Different colored blocks and arrows, each representing the sphere of influence and direction of advance of the army. Example: red color blocks represent the Red Army's sphere of influence, red arrows represent the route of the Red Army's Long March, blue arrows represent the Kuomintang attack route (Color figure online)

3.2.2 Visualisation of the Process

Process visualization means visualizing procedural or dynamic content [33]. Especially for long periods, the spatial state of the event and other elements of its properties can be dynamically displayed by visualizing the spatiotemporal dimension. With a wide range of mapping elements available, the scene can be visually and accurately described in 3D space. Thus, we can use different colors and types of arrows to represent the route of the Red Army's Long March and the route of the Nationalist attack (Fig. 7). In addition, GEOVIS Earth enables developers to freely match the perspective and style animations to show the temporal scene experienced by people, events, and landscapes through the lens. For example, at the Four Crossings of Chishui node, the interactive "time-space" map based on GEOVIS Earth dynamically shows the direction, route, and terrain of the Red Army's "four" crossings of Chishui (Fig. 8), allowing learners to follow the direction of the Red Army's advance from a first-hand perspective. In this way, learners know the 'what' and the 'how,' which is impossible with text and static illustrations.

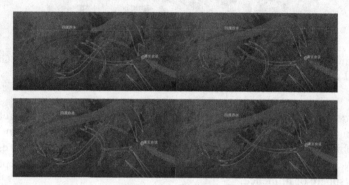

Fig. 8. Dynamic arrows depicting the forward path. Example: Four Crossings of Chishui node

The following table shows methods and examples of how the VR "Time-Space" interactive map teaching system visualizes knowledge (Table 1).

Visualizing of scenes and processes can solve the problem of historical events being too exquisite and the details challenging to understand. In particular, in terms of the visual Design and content arrangement of the VR "Time-Space" interactive map teaching system, we suggest that the overall structure of the historical event should be used as a starting point and that symbols, signs, routes, and transitions should be set up in a reasonable way to present the teaching content.

Table 1. Methods for visualizing knowledge in the VR "Time-Space" interactive map teaching system

	Object	Realization method		Example
Visualisation of scenes	Geography	Realistic terrain with GEOVIS Earth		As in Fig. 2, learners can observe the Long March's overall route from above As shown in Fig. 3 (right), learners can observe the 'Jinsha River's environment in detail from a low altitude
	Entity objects	The site and environment of real historical sites	Use insta360 to capture panoramic data, use A-FRAME to convert it into a V.R. panorama, and then import it as a hyperlink to GEOVIS Earth	As in Fig. 4, a live view of the Zunyi Conference taken with insta360 and made into a V.R panorama using A-Frame, then imported into GEOVIS Earth as a hyperlink
		Historic buildings and objects	Modeled using SketchUp, lumion, and imported into GEOVIS Earth in glb format	As in Fig. 5, the Ruijin Central Revolutionary Base Memorial Hall was restored using SketchUp and lumion and then imported into GEOVIS Earth in glb format
		Specific historical scenes	Use historical paintings for display. Importing them into GEOVIS Earth in jpg format	As in Fig. 6, import the jpg format of Liu Guoshu The Flying of the Luding Bridge (1959)

(continued)

Table 1. (*continued*)

	Object	Realization method	Example
	Abstract objects	Basic graphic representations using colour blocks, arrows, curves, etc	As in Fig. 7, use the red colour block to represent the Red sphere of influence
Visualisation of the process	Distribution of forces	The different coloured blocks, shades and boxes indicate the areas where the forces are present	As in Fig. 7, the red and blue arrows are used to show dynamically the marching routes of the Red Army and the Nationalist army respectively
	Development process	Time-based, with dovetail arrows to present the direction of events geographically	As in Fig. 8, dynamic arrows depict the path of the four crossings of Chishui so that learners are clear about the sequence of the route

4 Experimental Design

To verify whether the multimodal teaching mode based on the VR "Time-Space" interactive map teaching system can stimulate the interest of university students in the course of Modern History compared with other traditional teaching modes based on the teacher's lecture, we recruited 30 first-year undergraduates at the University of Science and Technology of China (USTC), aged 17–19. We conducted the study through quantitative and qualitative methods such as knowledge tests and interviews.

4.1 Subjects of Study

The subjects of this study were 30 freshmen of the University of Science and Technology of China, Class of 2022, 15 were in the experimental group, and 15 were in the control group, a total of 30. The age range of the subjects was 17–19 years old, of which 26 were male, and 4 were female. All study participants were unified to take the 2022 Chinese National College Entrance Examination (NMET). According to the 2022 Chinese NMET rules, in addition to the three compulsory subjects of Language, Mathematics, and English, candidates must choose any three of the six subjects of Politics, History, Geography, Physics, Chemistry, and Biology to take the examination. None of the students of our research took History, so their knowledge was not reinforced by revision for the Chinese NMET. All the subjects came from the same class and were randomly assigned to the significant class by choice. Within the first semester of their enrolment, they all undertook the same primary course with the same lecturers, the same syllabus, the same teaching materials, and the same conditions for the post-test. The two groups are, therefore, equal.

At the end of the first semester of the 30 subjects' enrolment, author administered a test on their knowledge of the History of the Red Army's Long March. This test, known as the 'pre-test,' was designed to check whether the students in the experimental and control groups had similar levels of knowledge about the history of the Long March of the Red Army.

In the second semester of their enrolment, we made subjects all take the course "Outline of Modern Chinese History". The course was taught once a week and consisted of three lessons of 45 min each. On the one hand, we adopted a multimodal teaching mode based on VR interactive maps for the experimental group, i.e., while the class was being taught, the subjects were allowed to personally experience the "Red Army Long March" content through the use of mobile phones, computers, and other terminals using the VR "time-space "The interactive map teaching system. On the other hand, the control group still received the traditional lecture method based on the teacher's explanation.

4.2 Experimental Procedure

Preparation Phase. A "pre-test" was administered to 30 participants at the end of the first semester to assess the level of knowledge of the Red Army Long March in both groups. The test consisted of 20 objective questions (4 points each) and 1 subjective question (20 points each), and was scored out of 100 points. The experimental and control groups were required to complete the same questions within 45 min. The test was marked uniformly by the teachers of Chinese Modern History.

This study is based on the syllabus of Modern Chinese History and produces a VR "time-space" interactive map teaching system with the content of "The Long March of the Red Army." The VR "Time-Space" interactive map teaching system is presented in the form of Desktop VR, which can be opened by the subjects using their mobile phones or computers to begin independent learning.

Prior to the formal experiment, author guided the 30 participants through the basic operations of Desktop V.R. to ensure that they adapted to the new teaching method as soon as possible.

Specific Teaching Steps. Because each lesson consisted of three sessions, one of which lasted 45 min, in the experimental group, the first and second sessions of each lesson began with a brief presentation by the teacher on the content of the lesson, such as an introduction to the relevant historical background, the chronology, general framework and significance of the historical event. In the third session, the teacher projected the QR code of Desktop VR, a time-space interactive map teaching system, on the projection screen in the classroom or sent the link to the WeChat group, which included only the students present. The experimental group could either scan the code on their mobile phones or click on the link on their computers to access Desktop VR for independent study of the Long March content. The duration of each independent study was 45 min, once a week, for a total of 2 weeks.

In the control group, traditional teaching methods were used, with all three sessions of each lesson being dominated by the teacher's narration, and the content learned was the same as in the experimental group. These study subjects were not allowed access to the links or Q.R. codes used in the experimental group.

Experimental Results. Two weeks into the experiment, the author tested the extent to which the two groups had mastered the history of the Red Army Long March. The post-test was conducted using a different set of questions from the pre-test, which also contained 20 objective questions (4 marks each) and 1 subjective question (20 marks each) and was worth 100 marks. The experimental and control groups were required to complete this set of questions within 45 min. The teachers of Modern History uniformly mark the answers.

The experiment compared the test scores of the pre-test with those of the post-test. The test scores were analyzed by SPSS 27.0, and the test results are shown in the following table. Table 2 shows that students in the experimental and control groups had similar levels of knowledge of the Long March before the experiment, with Average of 59.0667 and 60.5333, respectively. After the experiment, the Average of the experimental group was 78.8667, while the control group was 71.0667. The Standard deviation of the experimental group was 8.8226, and the control group was 9.0984, respectively, indicating that the students in the experimental group performed higher than the control group.

Table 2. Experimental results

	Experimental Group Pro-test	Control Group Pre-test	Experimental Group Post-test	Control Group Post-test
Number of Subjects	15	15	15	15
Minimum value	38	38	64	52
Maximum value	72	76	92	84
Average	59.0667	60.5333	78.8667	71.0667
Standard deviation	11.5293	11.9933	8.8226	9.0984

In addition, Fig. 9 illustrates that the experimental group has a significant difference in performance before and after the experiment. Before the experiment, the number of students scoring below 60 was 46.7%, while the number of students scoring above 70 was 20%; after the experiment, the number of students scoring below 60 was 0, while the number of students scoring above 70 was 80%, which fully indicates the overall improvement of student's performance in the experimental group.

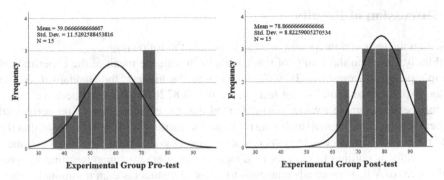

Fig. 9. Frequency distribution of Experimental Group Pro-test and Post-test

The experimental and control groups showed significant differences in their knowledge of the Long March after the experiment, demonstrating the desirability of a multimodal learning environment based on the VR "Time-Space" interactive map teaching system.

4.3 User Feedback

A week after the end of the experiment, the author conducted face-to-face interviews with some of the students in the experimental group. As a supplement to the test, the questions mentioned in the interviews were open-ended, for example: What impressed you most about the new teaching model? What was your favorite point about using the VR "Time-Space" interactive map teaching system? Did you find the system a hindrance to your learning of History? How long did you stay focused for the longest time when using the system? What difficulties or problems did you encounter? Do you have any suggestions or recommendations to improve this VR "Time-Space" interactive map teaching system? Each interviewee's answers were recorded in writing. Through the interviews, I learned that 13 participants (86.7%) in the experimental group indicated that the VR "Time-Space" interactive map system had made them more willing to learn modern History.

The following are some of the User feedback:

"I've never tried learning history in such an interesting way, and using V.R. for the first time made me a little giddy, but after getting used to it, it was like discovering a new world,"

"Learning history in a manipulable map is cool! I can zoom in and out at will, go anywhere I want, learn about any node, giving me a great sense of control."

"I think the VR interactive map teaching system has been beneficial in developing my global perspective."

"There is an extreme wealth of detail hidden under each node, leaving me unsure of which part to read first, which can leave me with cognitive overload."

5 Discussion of Results

Based on the tests and interviews, we can conclude the following:

Firstly, based on the results of the achievement test, the mean of the experimental group's post-test scores was 78.8667, which was the highest; the standard deviation of the experimental group's post-test scores was 8.8226, which was the lowest; and the independent sample t-values also indicated that the experimental group performed higher than the control group under the multimodal learning system. This shows that the VR "time-space" interactive map system helps to improve students' learning outcomes.

Secondly, according to the user feedback, using interactive map teaching systems in the form of V.R. is more advantageous to university students than traditional lecture methods. The interactive, three-dimensional nature of the V.R. "Time-Space" interactive map system allows students to form an overall layout of historical events in their minds, which exercises the learners' logical skills and enhances their motivation for history learning.

The VR "time-space" interactive map teaching system based on multimodal teaching theory can stimulate undergraduates' interest in Modern Chinese History and improve their learning outcomes. However, at the same time, the system's excessive detail may cause information overload for learners, which needs to be considered in future research.

6 Conclusion and Discussion

This paper designs an innovative teaching tool for modern Chinese history education - VR "Time-Space" interactive map teaching system, providing users with a rich interactive experience. Based on multiple sources such as satellite remote sensing images, photographs, and historical records, the system uses V.R. technology and 3D modeling technology to interactively present historical events' temporal and spatial clues and design a multi-scale, multi-carrier narrative map of modern Chinese History. In this model, the user's role changes from that of a passive recipient of information to that of a 'manipulator,' reinforcing the sense of learner participation. This model will give learners a more vivid impression of the content and enhance their learning of Modern Chinese History.

However, developing a VR "time-space" interactive map teaching system is still in the exploratory stage, and there are still certain limitations and difficulties in developing it on a large scale. For example, the development and application of VR are more technically demanding and financially demanding, and it requires close collaboration between technical staff and teaching designers to make the vast amount of historical knowledge look exciting and logical. In the future, the author will need to continue to expand the adequate resources available for teaching and learning, improve the user experience based on learner feedback, and make the VR "time-space" interactive map teaching system more and more perfect.

Acknowledgments. The research was sponsored by The National Social Science Fund of China, project number: 21VSZ1242;

The New Liberal Arts Fund of University of Science and Technology of China, project number: FSSF-A-230311;

The Center for Marxism and Contemporary Chinese Studies, University of Science and Technology of China, project number: 2021YJZX007YB;

The Institute of Party Building and Ideological and Political Work of the University of Science and Technology of China (2021–2022).

References

1. Zhang, P.: Experimenting with patriotic education in teaching modern Chinese History in secondary schools. Jiangxi Soc. Sci. **06**, 169–171 (2003)
2. Li, W.: Correction of controversial issues in teaching Outline of Modern Chinese History. Academic **06**, 121–125 (2008)
3. Zhu, Y., Li, L.: How to carry out classroom discussion in history seminar teaching in higher education: an example of a research-based course on "Topics in Modern Chinese History." History Teach. (College Edn.) **09**, 68–73 (2009)
4. Gong, S.: Learning modern Chinese History and patriotic education. Chin. High. Educ. **10**, 10–11 (1996)
5. Luo, J., Yu, Y.: Teaching spatial concepts of History and the development of disciplinary innovation. Teach. Manage. **18**, 65–66 (2004)
6. People's Education Press, History Curriculum Standards for General High Schools (2017 edition, revised in 2020), p. 5 (2020)
7. Zhou, Y.Z.: Strengthening students' spatial and temporal concepts in preparation for examinations - an example of revising history maps for the GCE. Issues History Teach. **2020**(02), 135–139+156 (2020)
8. Han, B.: Historical Geography of China. Historical Geography of China (1995)
9. Tao, R.: A threefold approach to the conception of time and space based on historical maps. Issues History Teach. **2021**(05), 129–132+122 (2021)
10. Huang, T.: Using historical maps to foster spatial and temporal conceptual literacy. Teach. Manage. **04**, 66–68 (2019)
11. Xing, J.: Research on the application of dynamic maps in high school history under modern information technology. In: 2023 Curriculum Education Exploration Academic Forum. Beijing, China (2023)
12. Tan, X., et al.: The connotation and teaching practice of the "spatiotemporal concept" in History. Issues History Teach. **01**, 115–118 (2018)
13. Caquard, S., Cartwright, W.: Narrative cartography: from mapping stories to the narrative of maps and mapping. Cartograph. J. **51**(2), 101–106 (2014)
14. Caquard, S., Fiset, J.P.: How can we map stories? A cybercartography application for narrative cartography. J. Maps **10**(1), 18–25 (2014)
15. Wojtkowski W., Gregory, W.W.: Storytelling: its role in information visualization. In: European Conference on Systems Science. Emerald Group Publishing Ltd, Crete (2022)
16. Lin, M., Yao, W.: A study of the value construction of French history textbooks for primary education. J. Comparat. Educ. **03**, 164–176 (2021)
17. Zhong, L., et al.: Design and implement an ancient city narrative map based on spatiotemporal knowledge mapping. J. Remote Sens. **25**(12), 2421–2430 (2021)
18. Gao, S.: The application of V.R. technology in high school geography teaching. New Curricul. Stud. (Upper J.) **2016**(07), 117–118 (2016)
19. Zhang, S.: Teaching geography based on V.R. technology. Geography Teach. **2018**(07), 43–46 (2018)
20. Tu, M.J., Liu, Y.B., Wu, N.C.: VR-based distributed teaching: a theoretical model and implementation strategy. Res. Electro-Chem. Educ. **42**(01), 93–99+121 (2021)

21. Zhang, L.: Research on the application of virtual reality technology in teaching art history courses in colleges and universities. Educ. Theory Pract. **41**(24), 61–64 (2021)
22. Carbonell-Carrera, C., Saorin, J.L., Jaeger, A.J.: Navigation tasks in desktop VR environments to improve the spatial orientation skill of building engineers. Buildings **11** (2021). https://doi.org/10.3390/buildings11100492
23. Yan, F.: Do different types of V.R. influence pedestrian route choice behavior? A comparison study of Desktop V.R. and HMD VR. In: Kitamura, Y., et al. (ed.) CHI EA 2021: Extended Abstracts of the 2021 CHI Conference on Human Factors in Computing Systems, 482 (7 pp.) (2021)
24. Lee, E.A.-L., Wong, K.W., Fung, C.C.: Educational Values of Virtual Reality: The Case of Spatial Ability (2009)
25. McArdle, G., et al.: A web-based multimedia virtual reality environment for e-learning. Proc. Eurograph. **4**, 9–13 (2004)
26. Liu, G.-Z., et al.: Handbook of Research on Educational Communications and Technology, 3rd edn (2010)
27. Wang, S.: Research on the theory and method of spatiotemporal narrative visualization. J. Surv. Map. **48**(03), 401 (2019)
28. Han, J.R.: The use of Google Earth in primary education in the United States and its inspiration. Educ. Sci. **29**(02), 92–96 (2013)
29. Planet Map Studio. Planet Map Studio - Interactive 3D Content Creation Tool (2023). https://studiohome.geovisearth.com/
30. Leeuwen, T.M. v. Introducing social semiotics. 2005
31. Zhang, Y.: Exploring multimodal English and American literature teaching based on computer networks. Foreign Lang. e-learn. **02**, 65–68 (2012)
32. Zhao, G.: Analysis and revision of the definition of knowledge visualization 2004. Res. Electro-Chem. Educ. **03**, 15–18 (2009)
33. Sun, F.: Research on information processing strategies of multimedia courseware. China Educ. **2012**(03), 81–84+89 (2012)
34. aframe.io. A-Frame introduction (2023). https://aframe.io/docs/1.4.0/introduction/#getting-started

Evaluating Virtual Reality as Immersive Medium for Enhancing Music Skills

Nejc Hirci, Žiga Lesar(ID), Matija Marolt(ID), and Matevž Pesek(✉)(ID)

Faculty of Computer and Information Science,
University of Ljubljana, Vecna Pot 113, 1000 Ljubljana, Slovenia
{nejc.hirci,ziga.lesar,matija.marolt,matevz.pesek}@fri.uni-lj.si
http://musiclab.si

Abstract. The VR interfaces have become more affordable than ever before. Because of their multimodal interaction capabilities, these interfaces provide a medium to virtually participate in various learning processes that can engage both sensory and motor senses. In this paper, we present an ongoing study to evaluate a VR game designed to enhance four aspects of rhythmic perceptual skills in elementary school children. The game developed is based on a well-known tower defense scenario in which the user controls units with different rhythmic patterns and tempo changes. Currently, 22 students are participating in the study, which shows promising results. We report the preliminary results and discuss possible applications of e-learning in virtual environments in music theory education.

Keywords: Virtual reality · Music theory · E-learning

1 Introduction

Virtual reality environments (VR) are widespread in everyday leisure use, especially among younger users [11]. A key factor in its success is the increasing affordability of VR devices, with Meta (Oculus) Quest leading the way with over 20 million units sold in the last three years[1]. Its popularity could also be due to the new approach of the standalone VR headset, which does not require a computer or other device to use compared to the company's previous models and other manufacturers' devices (such as HTC Vive, PlayStation VR and others). Still, the performance of Meta Quest models is somewhat limited due to the small size and battery power required. However, besides the affordable price, the user's ability to move freely without a cable, the number of supported appli-

---

[1] https://www.theverge.com/2023/2/28/23619730/meta-vr-oculus-ar-glasses-smartwatch-plans.

© The Author(s), under exclusive license to Springer Nature Switzerland AG 2023
L. T. De Paolis et al. (Eds.): XR Salento 2023, LNCS 14219, pp. 69–78, 2023.
https://doi.org/10.1007/978-3-031-43404-4_5

cations, and last but not least, the ability to connect the device to a computer and use it in a similar way as other non-standalone devices have earned Meta Quest devices a leading position in the current VR market[2]

Meta Quest applications are, of course, mainly games, in the majority with modes that allow users to interact and communicate with other users online. While some games focus on more common scenarios transposed into a VR environment, others engage multiple perceptive modalities, such as free movement, hand tracking, and in some cases mixed reality (Beyond this world[3], Demeo[4], and others). The ability to move and track hands in VR also opens up new options for e-learning, which was previously mostly limited to standard web and mobile interfaces, learning management systems [9] and one-way multimedia content such as videos, and specialised e-learning interfaces such as Troubadour [6].

1.1 Motivation

The Troubadour platform is an open source online music theory and ear training platform that includes exercises for melodic, rhythmic, and harmonic dictation. It allows students to receive direct feedback on their performance and personalised, automatically generated and graded exercises guided by the teacher. In its mobile application[5], Troubadour uses special interfaces for user input, as well as audio input via the built-in microphone. It also includes several gamification elements such as levels, badges, leaderboards, and others. Considering the previously evaluated increase in student performance [5,7], a VR immersive experience using motoric input provides a new modality of user input and could further improve user performance through an immersive gamified virtual environment.

In this paper, we present an ongoing study to evaluate a VR game designed to promote four aspects of rhythmic perception skills in elementary school children. The game is based on a well-known tower defense scenario in which the user controls units with different rhythmic patterns and tempo changes by tracking motor movements of the VR unit controllers. The game is connected to the Troubadour platform, which generates rhythmic exercises on five different levels. The exercises are further adapted to fit the VR environment. In the following, we first describe the four rhythmic aspects that we wish to improve for the user/player. We then elaborate on the developed framework of the VR game *Steady the drums!*[6], which we then extended into an educational game for tracking and evaluating user performance. We also present the current results of the ongoing study and conclude the paper with a discussion of the implications of the results for such games in the context of music e-learning and broader issues affecting motoric skills.

---

[2] According to Steam's monthly survey - April 2023, accessed at: https://store.steampowered.com/hwsurvey/Steam-Hardware-Software-Sur-vey-Welcome-to-Steam.
[3] https://www.oculus.com/experiences/quest/4873390506111025/.
[4] https://www.oculus.com/experiences/quest/3634830803298285/.
[5] https://play.google.com/store/apps/details?id=si.trubadur.v2.
[6] https://www.oculus.com/experiences/quest/5470851372933076/.

2   Rhythmic Perception and Performance

In recent years, there has been a growing interest in the potential of virtual reality (VR) and augmented reality (AR) technologies for music education. The study by Serafin et al. [10] explores the considerations on the use of VR and AR in music education, highlighting that VRMIs (Virtual Reality Musical Instruments) have not gained significant attention in the music sphere. This may be due to musicians' reliance on auditory and tactile feedback and interaction with the audience, although calibration could potentially address the first two aspects. The lack of low-cost and portable visualization devices until recent years, such as Oculus Quest 2, could also explain the limited adoption of VRMIs. The study identifies the value of VR in training rhythmical skills, playing together while being apart, addressing stage fear, teaching composition and music production, and developing STEAM skills through programming.

Another study by Keeler [2] examines the impact of video games on rhythmic performance in music education. The research compares non-VR and VR games with pre- and post-test measures of rhythmic achievement and beat competency using Flohr's Rhythm Performance Test Revised (2004) and the Short Flow State Scale-2 for measuring flow, but with a small user study with only 8 participants, which could be the cause for a only small difference in rhythmic achievement between non-VR and VR games. In "Teach me drums" [4], a VR application specifically tailored for hand drums is developed. The study focuses on teaching how to hit the drum and four rhythm patterns, using rhythm accuracy and questionnaires on flow, user-experience, oneness, and presence as evaluation metrics. They used the VR application only in the form of a pre-recorded 360 degree video and did not utilize any visual immersive components.

The design of a VR action observation tool for rhythmic coordination training is presented by Pinkl and Cohen [8]. The study investigates three perspective options, including a prerecorded monoscopic spherical video scene, a first-person point of view scene, and a third option displaying arm and hand movement. The goal is to learn by experiencing the performed gestures of rhythms in the first person and matching the playing of the sticks or hands in the virtual scene or video. A pilot study by Davis et al. [3] examines the impact of training using a commercial immersive VR system on hand-eye coordination and reaction time in young musicians.

In a recent study by Bonacina et al. [1] exploring rhythmic skills in school-age children (ages 5–8 years), researchers investigated the relationships among four rhythmic tasks hypothesized to reflect different clusters of skills. These tasks included drumming to an isochronous beat, remembering rhythmic patterns, drumming to the beat in music, and clapping in time with feedback. The study found no significant relationship between drumming to a beat and remembering rhythmic patterns. However, clapping in time with feedback was found to correlate with performance on the other three rhythm tasks. Moreover, while drumming to a beat of music did not change, the other three rhythm skills improved from Year 1 to Year 2.

These findings suggest that rhythmic skills develop as a global skill early in life and become more specialized later in life. The study also supports the potential use of clapping in time training as a way to affect a broad spectrum of rhythmic abilities that are linked to language and literacy processes. Despite the contributions to understanding the taxonomy and developmental trajectory of rhythmic skills, the study has limitations that require further investigation. Future research could involve following the same population for an extended period, from childhood to adulthood, to better understand the taxonomy of rhythmic skills from a broader developmental perspective.

3   Steady the Drums! Framework

Steady the drums! is a VR game based on a tower defense scenario. The game was developed using the Unity framework and with Unity assets made available through their store. The game works as a mixture of real-time strategy and rhythm game in which the player beats various patterns on the virtual drums with their controllers to perform different actions, such as attack, defense and summoning different types of soldiers. The game was released to the Oculus Lab App platform on November 2, 2022. While the game incorporated users' motoric movements to produce rhythmic sequences, the educational aspect was not the primary goal. Shortly after, we began developing a specialized version more deeply focusing on the game's potential for rhythmic training. Therefore, a modified version was developed, which included four scenarios, interconnected with the four aspects of rhythm [1] (Fig. 1).

3.1   Implementation of Four Scenarios

The modified version of the game included four scenarios: synchronised beating to the downbeat, following the rhythm, beating to alternating tempo (faster/slower), and repeating the rhythmic pattern. We retained the two-drum setup from the original game, which were both marked by a unique color and label. All four scenarios were designed with a visual assistance in mind in the form of a floating panel with appropriate drum labels, which lighten up in-sync with each beat, and a blank drum label representing a pause. The rhythm variations were generated with the help of the online music learning platform Troubadour, which also meant that we could provide increasing levels of difficulty that the platform provides. Similarly the tempo variations were selected with increasing levels of difficulty for both the downbeat and alternating tempo tasks. We construct 5 different levels of difficulty, which are supported by different visual stimuli for the player with varying monsters for each level. If the player correctly plays at least a small section of the task pattern, the knights in his army successfully attack the monsters. After beating all monster waves on a particular stage the player can continue to the next level.

In the first scenario the player must simply follow the downbeat played in the background, without the need to match the appropriate drum. The core of

(a)   (b)

(c)   (d)

Fig. 1. Screenshots of the Steady the drums! game.

the task stays the same for the second scenario, but the the tempo can now alter at the end of the sequence and the player is visually notified of the change by three bar elements representing normal, faster and slower speed. Third scenario requires the player to correctly match the drum labels in a rhythmic pattern in sync with the audio cues in the background. For the final scenario the player must first listen to a rhythmic pattern, which is presented by both the previously mentioned visual assistance and similar audio cues in the background as in the previous task. After the sequence finishes a short countdown begins prompting the player to repeat the sequence only with the help of the visual assistant still present, but without the played audio cues (Fig. 2).

4   Experimental Setup

In this study, we investigate the effect of VR educational game on the development of rhythmic skills in children aged 7–15 years. We gathered 22 participants in total. Their music experience ranges from no musical training to 6+ years of musical training.

We used three separate instruments during the evaluation: the PROMS test, the general questionnaire about the use of games and VR environments, and the user experience questionnaire (UEQ) to assess the game itself. The PROMS test, which was used to assess rhythmic skills before (pre-test) and after (post-test) the use participants' use of the VR device. The test included only the temporal-related parts (rhythm, rhythm-to-melody, accent), relevant to our study. The

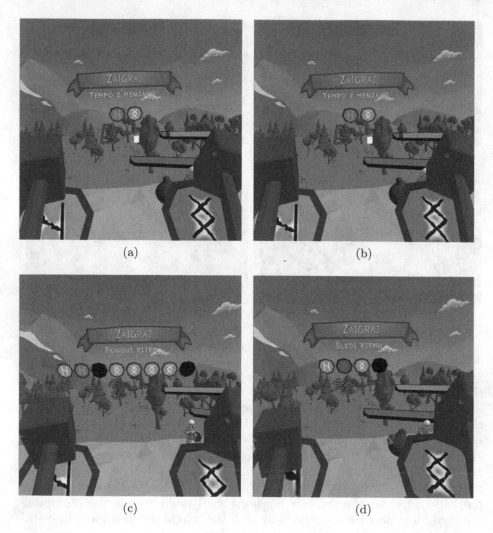

Fig. 2. Screenshots of the Steady the drums! learning modification of the game. Each sub-figure represents one of the four scenarios.

pre-study questionnaire included questions related to the participants' age, music experience and gaming/VR experience. The post-study questionnaire included questions about their game experience (favourite and most difficult scenarios), their overall experience using the virtual reality headset and the UEQ question-naire to evaluate the general user experience.

The experiment is individually conducted for each individual. There are three stages of the experiment as follows:

– First in-person meeting: pre-study questionnaire and PROMS evaluation, getting acquainted with the device (both child and parent)

- 14-day period of using the device in a home environment, approximately 15 min a day
- Second in-person meeting: post-study questionnaire and PROMS evaluation

During the 14-day period, the participants were given a Meta Quest 2 device to use at home. Their parents were given instructions how to manage the device, troubleshoot basic problems (e.g. chromecasting) and administer the device (giving them the account credentials). The participants' in-game actions (controller movements, accuracy of their inputs for an individual exercise) were stored on a server.

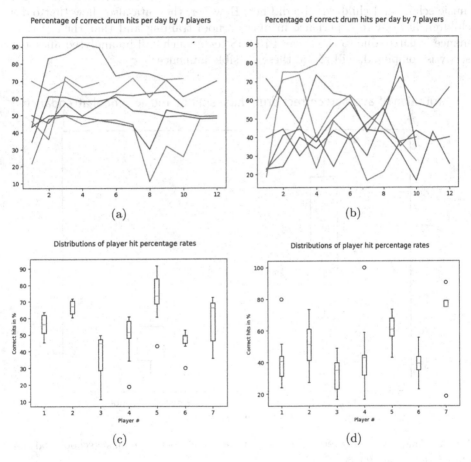

Fig. 3. Percentage of correct drum hits for the currently involved 7 users (top a and b subfigures), and distributions of hit rates per player for players 1–7 (bottom c and d subfigures).

4.1 Preliminary Results

There are 7 children who have currently completed the study and 22 children who are participating in this study; the children range in age from 8 to 15 years old. The children are at different proficiency levels of music education. The preliminary results of the ongoing performance monitoring show a gradual improvement of the children's performance with daily fluctuations. (Fig. 3). Comparing scenarios 1 (drumming to the beat) and 4 (independent repetition of the rhythmic pattern), the difference in performance between users can be attributed to the different difficulty levels of the two scenarios.

Figure 4 shows the difference in outcomes between children who attended music school and children who did not. However, the data also show that older children have more experience in music school training and that their performance is partly due to their age. PROMS test, which will be analysed after the study is completed, will reveal these possible influences.

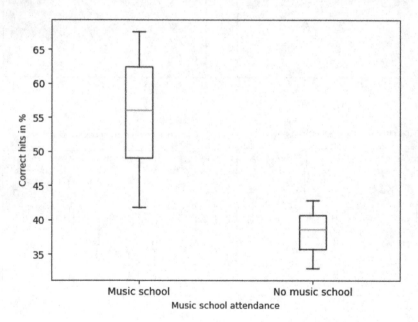

Fig. 4. Comparison of average correct hit rate, split between music-school and no-music-school subgroups.

5   Discussion and Future Work

The use of virtual reality interfaces for music theory and rhythmic ear training holds promising potential. The ongoing study with the adapted VR game

"Steady the drums!" has shown that multimodal interaction through virtual reality environments can provide an engaging and immersive learning experience for elementary school children, regardless of their prior musical knowledge. Designed as a tower-defense scenario, the game allows users to control units with different rhythmic patterns and tempo changes, enhancing four key aspects of rhythmic perceptual skills. The VR game is linked to the Troubadour platform, which generates rhythmic exercises with different levels of difficulty. Incorporating the established platform into the VR game scenarios also opens up new opportunities for incorporating gamification beyond the basic gamification elements such as levels, badges, and leaderboards.

The preliminary results of the ongoing study are encouraging. Children from diverse musical backgrounds have participated in the study, further underscoring the versatility of play as a learning tool. Notably, older children, especially those with music school training, showed higher levels of performance. However, the significant increase in performance among students without music school experience also suggests that VR play may be a fun and useful method for improving rhythmic and perceptual skills. The current study shows that the tracked data over a relatively short period of up to 14 d does not necessarily show a significant impact on user performance. However, the post-test results, which are not yet presented in this study due to the small number of users, indicate improvement in the majority of users currently involved.

Looking to the future, this innovative VR approach to e-learning in music offers a variety of exciting possibilities. As the experiment continues, we will continue to collect and analyze data to understand how the VR game affects user performance over a longer period and across a larger group of users. The game could also be adapted for other areas of music theory, providing a comprehensive, engaging, and immersive learning platform for music education.

While this study is ongoing, its initial results highlight the potential of VR for everyday practice on music-related tasks. This form of immersive learning could change the way teachers view the current conventional approaches in music theory education and provide students with a fun, engaging, and effective way to develop their musical skills. As VR technology continues to advance and becomes more accessible, it is clear that its application in education, especially music theory education, will only become more widespread and beneficial in various scenarios, such as distance learning.

References

1. Bonacina, S., Krizman, J., White-Schwoch, T., Nicol, T., Kraus, N.: How rhythmic skills relate and develop in school-age children. Global Pediatric Health **6** (2019). https://doi.org/10.1177/2333794X19852045
2. Keeler, K.R.: Video games in music education: the impact of video games on rhythmic performance. Visions Res. Music Educ. **37** (2020)
3. Lai, B., et al.: Feasibility of a commercially available virtual reality system to achieve exercise guidelines in youth with spina bifida: Mixed methods case study. JMIR Serious Games **8** (2020). https://doi.org/10.2196/20667

4. Moth-Poulsen, M., Bednarz, T., Kuchelmeister, V., Serafin, S.: Teach me drums: Learning rhythms through the embodiment of a drumming teacher in virtual reality (2019)
5. Pesek, M., Suhadolnik, L., Šavli, P., Marolt, M.: Motivating students for ear-training with a rhythmic dictation application. Appl. Sci. (Switzerland) **10** (2020). https://doi.org/10.3390/app10196781
6. Pesek, M., Vucko, Z., Savli, P., Kavcic, A., Marolt, M.: Troubadour: A gamified e-learning platform for ear training. IEEE Access **8**, 97090–97102 (2020). https://doi.org/10.1109/ACCESS.2020.2994389, https://ieeexplore.ieee.org/document/9093057/
7. Pesek, M., Klavž, F., Šavli, P., Marolt, M.: Online and in-class evaluation of a music theory e-learning platform. Appl. Sci. (Switzerland) **12** (2022). https://doi.org/10.3390/app12147296
8. Pinkl, J., Cohen, M.: Design of a VR action observation tool for rhythmic coordination training (2022). https://doi.org/10.1109/VRW55335.2022.00232
9. Rahim, Y.A., Mohd, O., Sahari, M.A., Safie, N., Rahim, Z.B.A.: A study on the effects of learning material handling procedures towards information integrity in moodle learning management system (lms), pp. 81–85. IEEE (10 2018). https://doi.org/10.1109/ICon-EEI.2018.8784322, https://ieeexplore.ieee.org/document/8784322/
10. Serafin, S., Adjorlu, A., Nilsson, N., Thomsen, L., Nordahl, R.: Considerations on the use of virtual and augmented reality technologies in music education (2017). https://doi.org/10.1109/KELVAR.2017.7961562
11. VR, O.: What is the market for a VR venue? (2023) https://www.octopodvr.com/blog/what-is-market-for-vr-venue-17

MetaLibrary: Towards Social Immersive Environments for Readers

Federico De Lorenzis⬤, Alessandro Visconti(✉)⬤, Alberto Cannavò⬤,
and Fabrizio Lamberti⬤

Department of Control and Computer Engineering, Politecnico di Torino, Turin, Italy
{Federico.Lorenzis,Alessandro.Visconti,
Alberto.Cannavo,Fabrizio.Lamberti}@polito.it

Abstract. The continuous integration of cutting-edge technologies in various fields such as culture and education is leading institutions towards a radical digital evolution. This work studies how one of the key actors of these domains, i.e., libraries, could exploit the digital transformation to reaffirm their position as primary cultural institutions in today's society. Indeed, there is consensus that, among technologies that could be used to modernize libraries and help them to reach a wider audience, there are Artificial Intelligence (AI) and immersive media like Virtual Reality (VR). In particular, VR has been used to create social platforms that users can join from remote, experiencing virtual environments (VEs) where they can share opinions and perform activities together, thus creating a digital community. In this context, MetaLibrary was created, an immersive VE designed to let readers socialize, attend events with authors, and receive suggestions about books to read from an AI-based recommender system. Deployment is in progress in the city of Turin, Italy.

Keywords: virtual reality · metaverse · library · social platform · recommender system

1 Introduction

In the last few years, several fields of the society like, e.g., culture and education, started to face a radical (r)evolution provoked by the continuous integration of cutting-edge technologies in their underlying processes. One of the main factors behind these changes is indeed the progressive development of technologies aimed to digitalization and meant to connect people independent of their location, which contribute at increasing the accessibility and the diffusion of any type of content. As stated in [12], among the contexts that can benefit more from the adoption of new technologies there are libraries, which could embrace this digital transformation to reaffirm their position as institutions for the preservation of culture.

When considering which technology could be leveraged to modernize libraries and help them to reach a wider public in today's society, there is consensus that

L. T. De Paolis et al. (Eds.): XR Salento 2023, LNCS 14219, pp. 79–87, 2023.
https://doi.org/10.1007/978-3-031-43404-4_6

a prominent role will be played by Artificial Intelligence (AI) and immersive media such as Virtual Reality (VR). Notwithstanding, while the use of AI, e.g., for directing readers towards the books they could be interested into [7] is already well known, the potential of immersive technologies in the considered context is still mostly unexplored. In fact, to the best of the authors' knowledge, so far immersive VR has been used mainly as an alternative interface to explore the content of a book[1], but not yet to enhance the library experience as a whole.

As a medium, VR enables the simulation of complex and realistic scenarios [2] that can be enriched by additional features such as guidance systems or evaluation modules suited, e.g., to training applications [4]. Among the advantages offered by this technology, there is the possibility to create virtual scenarios that can be experienced both via VR kits consisting of an Head-Mounted Displays (HMDs) and possibly a pair of hand controllers, or via mouse and keyboard. This way, different levels of experience can be provided to different types of users. Thus, VR has been leveraged to create social platforms in which multiple users can connect from everywhere and join a virtual environment (VE) where they can share opinions and perform various activities together. Nowadays, such applications are generally associated with the concept of "Metaverse" that, as stated in [1], is considered the natural evolution of the Internet and refers to an interconnected VE in which users interact with each other via a VR interface.

The present paper focuses on how to exploit the above concepts to increase the attractiveness of libraries and improve the readers' experience. The work, which was developed in the context of the Reading (&) Machine project, led to the creation of an immersive VR platform, named MetaLibrary, designed to bring libraries in the Metaverse by letting users join a shared virtual library where they can meet other readers, attend authors' presentations, and access a book recommendation system; this system helps the readers in the book-choosing process, by providing a lists of books they might be interested into based on their previous readings or current preferences elicited though a playful interface.

2   Related Works

Advancements in the field of digital technologies are creating the possibility to modernize the user experience in various contexts. This apply also to the domain addressed by this work, as digital technologies could help to change the way in which library spaces are experienced, thus improving their popularity.

As a matter of example, in [14], the authors focused on a case study represented by the Oodi Library in Helsinki and concluded that digital transformation processes can positively impact libraries and reinforce their role as centers of the intellectual life, while also improving the readers' experience and enabling more personalized services. Similar conclusions were reached in [12], where the authors analyzed new criteria to integrate digital technologies in the libraries; the results of the study showed that the design of technologically advanced libraries is very user-oriented, and can also make a positive contribution to urban life with the use of novel architectures.

---

[1] https://casateatroragazzi.it/spettacoli/nel-mezzo-dellinferno/.

Even though the state of the art suggests that libraries can benefit from the integration of new technologies, there are limited instances of digitalized libraries in the literature. One of the most noticeable examples is the Oodi Library, described in [7]; in this work, the authors present an AI-based mobile app integrating a virtual assistant that can recommend books based on users' preferences. The use of this system enriched the overall library experience, making it more engaging and faster than a more traditional one. Notwithstanding, as anticipated, there are no examples of library experiences enhanced by the use of VR.

Immersive technologies, however, are known for being able to offer a series of advantages that could be particularly relevant in this context; moreover, as stated in [15], VR can be used to create immersive social platforms with a great potential in education, which is a field that can be considered as affine to the tackled one. For instance, the authors of [2] leveraged an immersive VR experience as a complementary module to a course teaching practical skills, showing that, by using the devised system, it was possible to improve the overall trainees' preparation. The use of immersive technologies proved successful also in formal education experiences. As a matter of example, in [17], it is shown how VR-based classrooms can provide new learning modalities for educators and enable the creation of useful and engaging experiences for the students. As suggested by works like [3,16], a shared VR experience with a rich representation of the users' avatar (that involves, e.g., animated characters instead of just the 3D models of the headset and the hand controllers, or a detailed representation of facial expressions) can help to enhance the level of collaboration and communication.

Still in this context, immersive technologies can be also used to create social VR experiences where users can meet and share their opinions, play and do other activities together [10]. For instance, in [9], it is discussed how immersive technologies can be leveraged to create a satisfying virtual experience for participating to oral sessions of scientific conferences or attending their poster sessions. In [11], it was shown how immersive VR and mobile technologies could be used together to create asymmetric social applications letting users engage in collaborative and competitive experiences.

For what it concerns the approaches to create such immersive experiences, one of the most common choices is to rely on existing platforms like, e.g., Mozilla Hubs[2] Some examples are given in [6,8,13] in the context of education and of cultural heritage. However, as stated by the authors of [5], these platforms come with a number of technical limitations, which often require to develop new, dedicated tools.

3 VR Application

This section presents MetaLibrary, the VR-based social experience that, as said, has been created to let readers join a shared VE where they can meet other readers and authors, and find books to read. Books can be selected among the

---

[2] https://hubs.mozilla.com/.

most popular ones, by subject, or be recommended by an integrated AI. In fact, VR also serves as a graphics interface to a recommender system that can produce book recommendations either based on a reader's previous reading history or on preferences expressed by interacting with the application. The recommender systems uses data from a real, physical library, where users can find and rent the recommended books. The application was developed targeting primarily the Oculus Quest 2 VR kit. The kit comes with the headset and the hand controllers, which can be used to interact with the VE. Moreover, the possibility to join the VE using mouse and keyboard was added to the application in order to widen the number of possible users. The application was implemented using Unity, and the VR functionalities were handled with the XR Toolkit framework (using the OpenXR library).

Fig. 1. An immersive VR user, controlling his or her hands using the HMD controllers, interacts with a desktop user (a third-person character controlled via mouse and keyboard).

3.1 Multi-User Architecture

The devised application was designed as a social platform, where multiple users can share a VE and socialize. A client-server architecture was adopted and developed using the Mirror package in Unity. In the resulting configuration, a centralized graphical server manages all the connections, whereas each client can be started independently and runs on a separate, personal device, either as an immersive VR application or a desktop one.

During the connection phase, the users can choose the platform type (*Immersive VR* or *Mouse and Keyboard*), and change their virtual avatar (Fig. 1) choosing from a pool of pre-made characters. Then, they can log in as simple *Readers* – by accessing the platform anonymously or with their library credentials – or as *Librarians* (in this case, a special account is required). The users can experience all the public functionalities offered by the platform. Librarians can also take the role of administrators, by moderating the server, banning unwanted users, and elevating users as presenters for the *Conference room.*

Regardless of the chosen platform and role, the users can communicate with each other using VOIP, and have access to simple settings options to mute or unmute themselves. Moreover, they can change the locomotion method by choosing between continuous movement and teleportation.

Fig. 2. Central hub of the devised VE. The users are spawned in the hub, where they can found a map of the environment and can access all the other virtual areas.

3.2   Virtual Environment

The experience takes place in a VE that was designed to mimic the structure of well-known social applications and games mentioned in the previous sections, while keeping the overall feeling of a real library (Fig. 2). The overall environment was created with a low-poly style in order to limit the overall computational load of the application, so that even users with less powerful PCs may be able to run and experience the devised system.

Once logged in, the users are spawned into a central hub where they can find general information about the platform, together with a map of the VE. The VE consists of several virtual areas, each with a specific and unique function, as described below.

- *Room of the day:* in this area, the users can find a list of five books that changes daily and is based on a specific topic that can be chosen by the administrator. The topic is a word or an expression that is extracted from the books descriptions in the library database and can be used as a filter. The appearance of this room changes with the topic; for instance, the walls are decorated by quotes and images of authors associated with the topic.
- *Most-read room:* in this area, the users can find a list of the top-10 most read books, generated by the renting information provided by the library.

– *Conference room:* in this area , the users can attend conferences that are organized by the administrator; in particular, a user who has been explicitly selected by the administrator can assume the role of presenter, share a presentation (a PDF file uploaded to an external server) and talk to the public. The room is organized to mimic a theater or a real conference room, with a central stage dedicated to the presenter and a series of elevated locations from which the users can spectate and watch the presentation.
– *Access to the Community rooms:* from this area, the users can create Community rooms where they can invite other users.
– *Access to the Assisted research rooms:* from this area, the users can access private Assisted research rooms where they can receive book recommendations. These recommendations are based on previously rented books.

3.3 Assisted Research

To receive personalized book recommendations (in the form of scrollable lists of 30 books), the users can provide additional information that can be used by the recommender system to customize the list of suggested books. To enter this information, the users can leverage a custom interface accessible in the Assisted research rooms and follow the three-step procedure reported in the following.

– *Step 1:* the users can specify one or more genres from a set of 20 alternatives (extracted from library database) to drive the recommendation system. Genres are represented by a set of 3D models placed in the scene. Each time a genre is selected, the system reacts by customizing the list of recommended books; multiple genres lead to the recommendation of books characterised by one or more of the chosen genres (e.g., by choosing "fantasy" and "horror" as genres, the system will output fantasy, horror, and fantasy-horror books). After at least one genre is selected, the users can decide to stop the procedure or move to the next step.
– *Step 2:* in the second step, the users can choose a set of keywords to further filter the recommended books. Both the keywords and the books to be filtered are determined by the genres selected during the first step. After at least one keyword is selected, the users can decide to stop the procedure or move to the next step.
– *Step 3:* in the third step, the users can specify a set of emotions (sadness, fear, anger, happiness) to further filter the recommended books (determined by the choices made in the previous steps). Each book was initially associated a set of emotions extracted by the developed AI from the description of the book itself.

At any moment in time, the users can go back to a previous step to influence the recommendation. By moving to a certain step, the choices made for the following ones (if any) are automatically cancelled.

Fig. 3. The user interacts with a book to visualize the corresponding meta-data. Data are placed in the 3D world to be easily accessible both for immersive VR and desktop users.

3.4 Book Recommendations

Recommended books (in the Room of the day, the Most-read room, or produced by the Assisted research) are presented in the form of collections of meta-data that are extracted from the library database end enriched by external databases (in particular, that used by Anobii[3] an independent social network devoted to readers). Overall, the displayed information for each book (Fig. 3) is the following:

- Cover
- Title
- Author(s)
- Genre(s)
- Page number
- Description
- Average user score

4 Conclusions and Future Developments

This paper presents an immersive VR platform aimed to create a shared experience for readers and to increase the attractiveness of physical libraries. In the devised platform, the users can socialize, attend conferences, and receive book recommendations.

The system is being deployed in Turin, Italy with one client installed in the central public library of the city and opened to readers in April 2023. Usage data are being collected, with the aim to investigate the usability of the application, the effectiveness of the recommendation system, and the overall impact of the devised approach on the popularity of libraries.

---

[3] Anobii: https://www.anobii.com/,.

Regarding further developments, a first direction for future research could involve the creation of different versions of the VE, each created by changing some features like the configuration of the rooms or their style (e.g., low-poly vs photo-realistic), in order to study how these changes impact the overall usability, the quality of the experience, and the social aspects of the application. Furthermore, a similar study could be designed by working on the avatars geometries, focusing again on the complexity of the models, but also on the level of embodiment (e.g., with or without arms or legs), the overall style, the quality of the animations, etc.

Other interesting future works could focus on improving the Conference room. For instance, the possibility to record the live virtual events in order to make them accessible at any time could be considered. Another possibility could be train intelligent conversational agents that users could interact with. These agents could support the users during conferences, e.g., answering basic questions, or could mimic authors from the past in order to simulate conferences that would be otherwise impossible (e.g., a conversation with Charles Darwin).

Acknowledgements. This work was developed by VR@POLITO and supported by Fondazione TIM in the context of the 'FacciamolaFacile' initiative and by PON "Ricerca e Innovazione" 2014-2020 - DM 1062/2021 funds.

References

1. Buhalis, D., Leung, D., Lin, M.: Metaverse as a disruptive technology revolutionising tourism management and marketing. Tourism Manage. **97** (2023). https://doi.org/10.1016/j.tourman.2023.104724
2. Calandra, D., De Lorenzis, F., Cannavò, A., Lamberti, F.: Immersive virtual reality and passive haptic interfaces to improve procedural learning in a formal training course for first responders. Virtual Reality, pp. 1–28 (2022). https://doi.org/10.1007/s10055-022-00704-9
3. Calandra, D., Pratticò, F.G., Lupini, G., Lamberti, F.: Impact of Avatar Representation in a Virtual Reality-based Multi-user Tunnel Fire Simulator for Training Purposes, pp. 3–20 (2023). https://doi.org/10.1007/978-3-031-25477-2_1
4. De Lorenzis, F., Pratticò, F.G., Repetto, M., Pons, E., Lamberti, F.: Immersive virtual reality for procedural training: comparing traditional and learning by teaching approaches. Comput. Ind. **144**, 103785 (2023). https://doi.org/10.1016/j.compind.2022.103785
5. Eriksson, T.: Failure and success in using mozilla hubs for online teaching in a movie production course. In: 2021 7th International Conference of the Immersive Learning Research Network (iLRN), pp. 1–8 (2021). https://doi.org/10.23919/iLRN52045.2021.9459321
6. Hagler, J., Lankes, M., Gallist, N.: Behind the curtains: Comparing mozilla hubs with microsoft teams in a guided virtual theatre experience. In: 2022 IEEE Conference on Virtual Reality and 3D User Interfaces Abstracts and Workshops (VRW), pp. 19–22 (2022). https://doi.org/10.1109/VRW55335.2022.00011
7. Hammais, E., Ketamo, H., Koivisto, A.: Virtual information assistants on mobile app to serve visitors at Helsinki Central Library Oodi (2017)

8. Iglesias, M.I., Jenkins, M., Morison, G.: Enhanced low-cost web-based virtual tour experience for prospective students. In: 2021 IEEE Conference on Virtual Reality and 3D User Interfaces Abstracts and Workshops (VRW), pp. 677–678 (2021). https://doi.org/10.1109/VRW52623.2021.00221

9. Le, D.A., MacIntyre, B., Outlaw, J.: Enhancing the experience of virtual conferences in social virtual environments. In: 2020 IEEE Conference on Virtual Reality and 3D User Interfaces Abstracts and Workshops (VRW), pp. 485–494 (2020). https://doi.org/10.1109/VRW50115.2020.00101

10. Manyuru, P., Dobbins, C., Matthews, B., Baumann, O., Dey, A.: Focus group on social virtual reality in social virtual reality: Effects on emotion and self-awareness. In: 2021 IEEE International Symposium on Mixed and Augmented Reality Adjunct (ISMAR-Adjunct), pp. 437–438 (2021). https://doi.org/10.1109/ISMAR-Adjunct54149.2021.00099

11. Nilsson, S., et al.: Fruit golf: An asymmetrical shared space vr/mobile experience. In: Proceedings - SIGGRAPH 2022 Immersive Pavilion (2022). https://doi.org/10.1145/3532834.3536214

12. Nur Şanlı, S., Sirel, A.: The effects of developing information technologies on 21st century library architecture. Proceedings of the International Conference of Contemporary Affairs in Architecture and Urbanism-ICCAUA 5(1), 12–26 (2022). https://doi.org/10.38027/ICCAUA2022EN0035

13. Prasolova-Førland, E., Estrada, J.G.: Towards increasing adoption of online vr in higher education. In: 2021 International Conference on Cyberworlds (CW), pp. 166–173 (2021). https://doi.org/10.1109/CW52790.2021.00036

14. Sirel, A.: Reflection of paradigm changein information technology to library architecture: the helsinki oodi library. Architect. Urban Plann. 17(1), 123–135 (2021). https://doi.org/10.2478/aup-2021-0012

15. Uskali, T., Rautiainen, M., Juntunen, M., Tallavaara, R., Hiljanen, M.: How to use social VR in higher education: Case study of the JYUXR campus in Finland (2022)

16. Visconti, A., Calandra, D., Lamberti, F., et al.: Comparing technologies for conveying emotions through realistic avatars in metaverse-and virtual reality-based experiences. Comput. Animation Virtual Worlds (2023). https://doi.org/10.1002/cav.2188

17. Williams, S., Enatsky, R., Gillcash, H., Murphy, J.J., Gračanin, D.: Immersive technology in the public school classroom: When a class meets. In: 2021 7th International Conference of the Immersive Learning Research Network (iLRN), pp. 1–8 (2021). https://doi.org/10.23919/iLRN52045.2021.9459371

eXtended Reality and Metaverse
in Cultural Heritage

Bringing Back Lost Heritage into Life by 3D Reconstruction in Metaverse and Virtual Environments: The Case Study of Palmyra, Syria

Yara Jamil Alkhatib[1]([✉]), Anna Forte[1], Gabriele Bitelli[1], Roberto Pierdicca[2], and Eva Malinverni[2]

[1] Dipartimento di Ingegneria Civile, Chimica, Ambientale e dei Materiali (DICAM), Alma Mater Studiorum Università degli Studi di Bologna, 40136 Bologna, Italy
{yarajamil.alkhatib,anna.forte3,gabriele.bitelli}@unibo.it
[2] Dipartimento di Ingegneria Civile, Edile e dell'Architettura (DICEA), Università Politecnica delle Marche, 60131 Ancona, Italy
{r.pierdicca,e.s.malinverni}@staff.univpm.it

Abstract. The advent of the metaverse, a large-scale three-dimensional networked virtual environment that combines physical and digital world, has opened new avenues for preserving and experiencing cultural heritage (CH). By integrating technologies such as 3D reconstruction and modelling with virtual reality (VR), the metaverse offers new opportunities to showcase and celebrate cultural heritage that may otherwise have been lost to time or destruction, as in the case of this work. This paper delves into the fascinating world of digital reconstruction and its application in preserving ancient archaeological sites, with a focus on the Palmyra theater in Syria. The theater, dating back to the Roman era, was once a majestic centerpiece of Palmyra's cultural and social life. However, the Syrian conflict caused irreparable harm to the theater's physical structure and historical significance. The goal of the project was to digitally reconstruct the theatre in a virtual environment, providing an immersive experience that allows users to explore the site in its original form. The 3D reconstruction of the theatre was achieved through a comprehensive survey of images, sketches, textual documents, and artifacts conducted by Professor Gabriele Fangi, from *Università Politecnica delle Marche*, Italy, during his visit to Syria in 2010. Metaverse platforms were implemented to allow for exploring the theatre as it once was. The project presented a range of challenges, including optimizing the digital model's complexity for the metaverse, and fine-tuning textures and materials to provide a realistic experience. This paper provides an in-depth analysis of the project's goals, methods, and outcomes highlighting the exciting possibilities of metaverse technologies, allowing multiple users to experience in real time a digitally reconstructed world, demonstrating its importance in the field of CH preservation. For lost heritage, in particular, these technologies may serve as evidence of our duty towards the importance of preserving CH in the face of conflict and destruction.

Keywords: Geomatics techniques · Lost Heritage · Virtual Reality · Metaverse

L. T. De Paolis et al. (Eds.): XR Salento 2023, LNCS 14219, pp. 91–106, 2023.
https://doi.org/10.1007/978-3-031-43404-4_7

1 Introduction

Cultural heritage (CH) sites around the world provide a tangible and intangible link to our past and help us understand the richness and diversity of human history and culture. CH gives a sense of identity and belonging for communities, promotes cross-cultural understanding and appreciation, and contributes to economic growth and sustainable development. Despite its undeniable importance, CH is under threat from a variety of factors, including climate change, urbanization, natural and anthropogenic disasters. Preserving CH is thus a pressing concern and requires a concerted effort from governments, communities, and individuals around the world.

Through historic buildings, we gain a profound understanding of our past and preserve an integral aspect of our CH. When a building is destroyed, it becomes our responsibility to reconstruct it and maintain it as best we can. Unfortunately, the world is currently losing heritage sites at an alarming rate, faster than we can preserve them. However, with advancements in 3D data acquisition and modelling techniques, it is now possible to accurately capture, store, and share the historical memory of built heritage in a digital format. These technological advances provide feasible, portable tools and methodologies that allow for the preservation of heritage sites and the dissemination of cultural knowledge to a wider audience (Fangi 2015).

Research has shown that virtual environments and metaverse platforms have the potential to significantly enhance learning and retention of information (Hedrick et al. 2022; Hwang and Chen 2022; Muenster 2022). By providing an immersive experience, users can explore and interact with a virtual representation of a cultural heritage site to learn about its history and significance in an engaging and memorable way. Furthermore, the use of 3D reconstruction and optimization techniques can enable the recreation of cultural heritage sites that have been destroyed or damaged (Quattrini et al. 2016; Bitelli et al. 2017). This is particularly relevant in areas affected by conflict or natural disasters, where cultural heritage sites are at risk of being lost forever.

1.1 Lost Architectural Heritage

The preservation of the cultural heritage of a society is indeed considered a fundamental human right, and efforts to protect cultural property in the event of armed conflicts have been established since the 1954 Hague Convention. Unfortunately, in recent years, we have witnessed significant and purposeful destruction of cultural heritage. Bamiyan Buddhas in Afghanistan and Palmyra in Syria are two well-known examples of this phenomenon, as reported by UNESCO, which maintains a country-by-country list of world heritage sites (Fig. 1). Palmyra's Roman Theatre serves as a case study for this research. According to UNESCO, in the previous two years more than 100 ancient structures in Iraq and Syria have been destroyed due to vandalism by various terrorist organizations, and around 56 World Heritage sites are currently in danger of being lost.

Despite the digitization not being able to replace physical monuments, it is widely known that digital replicas are the only way to preserve, at least, their memory. Monuments are not only bricks and stones, but rather represent the identity of a country. Faithful 3D models can be a viable solution to save and preserve their memory.

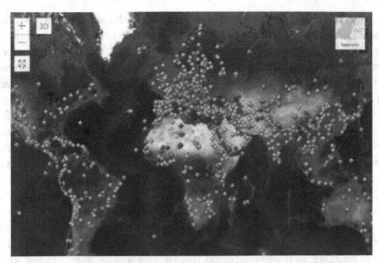

Fig. 1. UNESCO list of world heritage sites map; The red dots represent under threat heritage sites - @UNESCO. (Color figure online)

1.2 Geomatics, Virtual Reality and Metaverse for Lost Cultural Heritage

The use of digital tools has emerged as a major method of preventing the ultimate loss of architectural heritage. Rapid technological developments, from 3D digital modelling by Geomatics techniques to virtual/augmented reality systems to explore the 3D environments are now available and have given history a fresh lease of life in recent years. Despite physical preservation and restoration being the best approach to preserving cultural heritage, digital technologies can indeed be a powerful tool for preserving and sharing lost cultural heritage. They provide immersive and interactive experiences, allowing people to explore ancient architectures and interact with historical sites and artifacts in new ways.

Over the years, there has been major work on the digital reconstruction and visualization of monuments (Remondino et al. 2009; Barazzetti et al. 2010) that may refer to lost sites due to natural or anthropic reasons. In these examples the digital reconstruction was the final goal of the research, as VR technologies were not widely employed yet in the research field in the early 2000's. Later, virtual reality has been used within museums to engage visitors in the storytelling of collections and as a tool to enhance museum educational content (Hutson and Hutson 2023). Of peculiar importance has been, for many years, the role of crowd-sourced images for the 3D reconstruction of sites. In (Wahbeh, W. & Nebiker, S. 2017) the authors make a wise comparison of different source of images for the reconstruction of the lost heritage; unfortunately, this commendable practice never achieved its maturity and the 3D reconstruction is still entrusted on on-site, when possible, and time consuming surveying campaigns.

Examples of exploration of a lost heritage site in VR are also present (yet scarcely) in literature, but they typically employ the VR "standard" configuration, which involves a single user exploring a virtual environment in an individual experience (Chehab & Nakhal 2023). This solo configuration does not allow for an inclusive or collective experience. Additionally, VR devices often come with high costs that are not affordable for all users. The metaverse addresses these two issues associated with traditional VR. Its fundamental principle is precisely the concept of sharing virtual spaces: users meet in an open environment and have a collective experience. Hence, it is theoretically a shared network of virtual events and locations, in which people meet and interact with avatars in a parallel (digital) universe.

More specifically, the word "metaverse" is a combination of the prefix "meta," which means "beyond" or "transcending," and "universe". The concept of the metaverse goes beyond traditional virtual reality and describes a future iteration of the Internet, comprising persistent, shared, 3D virtual spaces linked into a perceived virtual universe. It is seen as the basis for the next version of the Internet, encompassing all virtual worlds (Moneta 2020, Zhang et al. 2022). The Internet provides the necessary infrastructure for the metaverse to exist, allowing connection, data storage, and participation in its economy. Reliable high-speed internet connections are crucial for a seamless and immersive metaverse experience. In the context of this work, the use of the metaverse is proposed in its general meaning, as it was conceived from the theoretical point of view. However, currently the concept of metaverse has not yet materialized, and for now, there are online platforms that guarantee shared virtual experiences and places with other users, but managed by private individuals and companies that may also have commercial purposes; so, the concept of an open and free metaverse that unites people in a unique networked space is not yet present.

Nevertheless, these online shared platforms (which can also be accessed via desktop versions or mobile devices) provide the opportunity to share digital representations of historical sites, artifacts, and cultural landscapes to be experienced and shared in a virtual community, even if they are physically inaccessible or destroyed. Recently, the metaverse has been also employed in the field of education, as mentioned in the introduction, and in the field of architecture, to document and disseminate knowledge about historic buildings in an educational context (Gaafar 2021), although primarily focused on existing heritage sites.

Manovich and Douglas (2021) reported examples of how metaverse platforms can be used for lost cultural heritage, including recreating lost heritage sites, digitizing artifacts, creating interactive and immersive narratives, and enabling collaborative conservation efforts. Metaverse platforms can also facilitate collaborative endeavours to preserve and restore lost cultural heritage sites and artifacts, enabling experts from different parts of the world to collaborate on conservation efforts.

1.3   3D Surveying Methodologies for Virtual Reality Applications

Data acquisition methodologies play a critical role in creating accurate and immersive VR environments. There are several techniques for 3D survey that can be used for VR applications, such as digital photogrammetry or 3D scanning by laser or structured light projection systems. These techniques involve capturing data on the subject's geometry and texture, which are then processed and optimized to create a 3D model suitable for VR.

The instruments employed for a 3D survey are very diverse in their purposes and functions. These include devices that allow to acquire very accurate geometric data designed for small to medium-sized objects, at the micrometre level of accuracy. For large objects or areas other types of instruments are available, such as laser scanners that present long ranges and thus offer the possibility of obtaining geometric information at the architectural level or even over very large areas. The choice of an instrument depends on the needs in terms of precision and accuracy but also on the characteristics of the object to be surveyed from the point of view of size and materials.

1.3.1 Spherical Photogrammetry

The methodology, set up by Prof. Fangi (Università Politecnica delle Marche) and used to create the 3D model subject of this research, is the so-called Spherical Photogrammetry (SP), which represent the metrological foundation of the model used in this research. This method (Fangi 2015) has been tested on several projects, performing the orientation by bundle block adjustment of multiple panoramas (Fig. 2) and finally a manual 3D object reconstruction. The main advantages of this method are the high resolution, the field of view (FOV) up to 360°, the low cost, the completeness of the information, and the high speed of photos acquisition. In contrast, the plotting and the orientation are entirely manual. Nowadays more accurate and efficient tools and instruments are available for CH recording, such as laser scanning and dense multi-view 3D reconstruction. The 3D model of the Palmyra Roman theatre shown in Fig. 3 was created with different workflows using SP and sometimes combining it with other photogrammetric-based technologies.

This method was mainly conceived and designed for cultural and architectural metric documentation. Wireframe and then textured models can be created using the aforementioned technique for Syrian monuments, as done in other places around the world. Starting from the SP orientation, there is the possibility to use 3D modellers to create the 3D models based on the rules of projective geometry with a method called panoramic image-based interactive modelling; this technique is suitable for the architectural survey because it is not a 'point by point' survey of the type that dense multi-view 3D reconstruction produces, and it exploits the geometrical constraints of the architecture's geometry to simplify the 3D modelling process.

Therefore, the surveyor in those techniques must comprehend the geometry of the architecture before modelling it. In this approach, the concept of this methodology is based on the use of texture-mapping techniques in a generic modelling software

Fig. 2. Spherical panorama of Palmyra Roman Theatre Theatre by Professor Gabriele Fangi's team

as the virtual projector of an image and thus used to model an architectural object. If the projection centre and the orientation are fixed in the 3D virtual space, objects could be created, moved, and modified to match the projections. Objects, therefore, take the right shape and location in the virtual space of the surveyed elements. It is an interactive modelling technique because the interaction between the modelled objects and the projection of the images is visible in real-time. Also, the quality of the model is verifiable in various interactive ways.

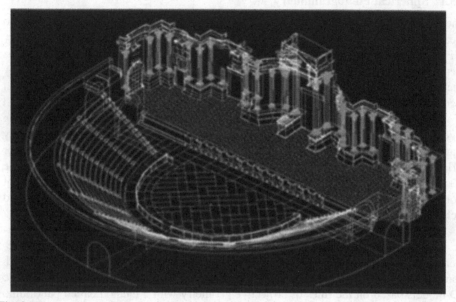

Fig. 3. First version of the theatre 3D model obtained with Spherical photogrammetry (constructed by E. Ministri, Università Politecnica delle Marche)

2   Innovation and Objectives of the Research

Considering the state of the art of the research in the field of Geomatics, VR and metaverse applied to lost heritage (see Sect. 1.2), in the current literature, a discrete number of examples are reported about the sole 3D reconstruction of lost heritage sites with digital technologies. Few examples are instead reported concerning the employment of VR for lost heritage site exploration, and – to the best of our knowledge - no examples are reported about metaverse applied to a lost heritage site reconstructed with a Geomatic based approach.

The innovative component of this work is the employment of a geomatic method for the reconstruction of a lost architecture (spherical photogrammetry, producing metrically accurate 3D models), coupled with an extensive work of 3D modelling to optimize the geometry and the texture of the model, and finally the virtual exploration in the metaverse to exploit the advantages that this technology may bring to the documentation and dissemination to a wide audience. This approach, employing these integrated technologies for a case of lost architecture, represents an innovation in the field of digital techniques applied to the lost CH.

As outlined in the previous paragraphs, architectural and cultural assets are a fundamental part of humanity's heritage, and all necessary actions should be taken to preserve them. Conflicts and wars have caused priceless losses of archaeological and architectural sites around the world. When "physical" maintenance and reconstruction actions cannot take place or are not easy to be accomplished, digital tools and the virtual world can come into play. The motivation behind this work is precisely to try, through digital technologies, to bring back to life architecture that has disappeared due to war and can no longer be visited anywhere but in virtuality.

The 3D model of Palmyra Roman theatre (obtained with a digital photogrammetry approach from Prof. Fangi's team) has been selected as the case study for this experiment. The main objective of this work is to propose a methodology to merge 3D modelling and VR technologies to promote the preservation lost cultural heritage in a digital environment. The following tasks have been fulfilled:

- To optimize the digital model's complexity, texture adjusting for VR and metaverse platforms.
- To explore the optimization challenges involved in accurately reconstructing the theatre in a virtual environment.
- To create an immersive experience for users using VR in a metaverse platform and to evaluate the outcomes of the navigation with a consumer-grade equipment.

3   Case Study: The Roman Theatre of Palmyra

Centrally located in the acropolis of Palmyra are the remains of the ancient city's theatre. The construction of the Roman theatre (Fig. 4) along the colonnaded street began in the second century but was never completed. Besides art performances, political meetings were held here as well. Largely buried under sand until the 1950s, the structure has since been excavated and restored, representing one of the most well-preserved Roman theatres in Syria out-

Fig. 4. The Roman Theatre of Palmyra

side of Bosra. The theatre was constructed in the first half of the second century according to Polish archaeologist Kazimierz Michalowski. It was built in the centre of a semicircular colonnaded plaza that opened to the city's southern gate. The theatre has suffered significant damage due to the war in Syria during which several heritage places have been raided (Fig. 5). The territory of the Republic of Syria continues to maintain the same structure of the "historical apparatus", which, in ancient times included the western region of the Fertile Crescent between the rivers Tigris and Euphrates and the Mediterranean Sea.

Along the centuries, populations left their heritage which nowadays stands as existing monuments and ruins, e.g., Phoenician temples, Greek and Roman theatres, and old cities. Early Christians and Byzantines left remains of churches and monasteries; Crusades raised different defensive fortresses.

Then Islamic civilisation-built mosques and citadels and introduced architectural elements such as a minaret and a madrasah. In the end, the Ottomans allowed modernization of the country and promoted commercial trade with the construction of *souqs* and *khans*. As stated, the last years changed the archaeological situation of the country due to the war, and the fighting reshaped Syria into different control areas. From the human point of view, this can be considered one of the biggest tragedies happened in the latest period. Beyond this tremendous aspect, the conflict is the main threat to the CH that has faced significant damage from military action, clandestine excavations, illegal civil constructions, and acts of vandalism.

Exploiting the work conducted by prof. Fangi about Syrian lost heritage, many photos (almost 17,000) of most of the Syrian CH monuments were taken during his trip in 2010, before the war. This is a priceless database since it is one of the rarest documentations of this heritage. Most of these monuments are included in the Syrian UNESCO heritage list, and many of them were inscribed in the 'List of World Heritage in Danger' in 2014. With the loss of this heritage as a historical and cultural treasure, future generations were deprived of an invaluable inheritance. A chain of humanity, culture, and nature cannot be violated in 21st century without intervening to save it.

Fig. 5. Destructions of the Syrian cultural heritage during the war in Syria: (a,b) Palmyra, @DW/ BBC; (c) Krak des Chevaliers Castel, @BBC; (d) Umayyad mosque – Aleppo @Reuters

For the Roman Theatre of Palmyra, one of the main elements that have been destroyed is the Pediment of the central portico and the central columns, which were highly decorated. According to UNESCO, the stage back-drop, which was adorned with niches for statues and other decorative elements, was destroyed during the conflict in 2015 (Fig. 5).

The actual appearance of the building is therefore lost forever, and it will not be possible for visitors to experience the majesty of this architecture in its original splendour (Fig. 6).

Fig. 6. Orthophotographs of the theatre before and after the attacks @ICONEM

4 Methodology

AEC (Architecture Engineering Construction) professionals have witnessed an epochal change in the previous few years, which has resulted in re-engineering of their daily operations. Simultaneously, VR engines and platforms have provided a completely open logic, allowing for the creation of digital worlds capable of interacting with users via various types of devices using new commands and programming languages, ranging from mobile phones and tablets to the latest generation VR headsets. This section outlines the steps that were taken to achieve the goal of bringing back the lost Syrian heritage through 3D reconstruction in virtual environments, specifically VR and metaverse platforms.

4.1 3D Model of PALmyra's Theatre Description

The 3D model of the Palmyra is depicted in Fig. 7. It was initially optimized by converting it into an all-quad model. This process involved the conversion of all triangular faces into quadrilateral faces, resulting in a more regular and consistent topology.

The advantages of using an all-quad mesh include smoother surface deformations, better support for subdivision surfaces, as well as more predictable shading and surface deformation when animating, which can make the model look smoother and more natural.

4.2 Data Processing – 3D Optimization

In this research project, Blender open-source software was used to optimize the Roman theatre of Palmyra. Through optimization, the number of vertices can be significantly

Fig. 7. All-quad 3D model of the Palmyra's theatre

reduced without sacrificing the overall appearance and quality of the model, leading to faster loading times and smoother performance. Additionally, metaverse platforms often have size limitations for uploaded 3D models, making them easier to upload and share. Overall, the optimization process of 3D models ensures a better user experience, reduces loading times, and can lead to cost savings in terms of storage and bandwidth.

To optimize the Roman theatre of Palmyra model with an *all-quad* mesh in Blender, three different approach/tool were used: the *Decimate modifier*, the *Limited Dissolve tool*, and the *Decimate Geometry*. All the optimization tools were used according to the different types of geometry present in the 3D model, as shown in the Table 1.

Table 1. Optimization tools employed to simplify the theatre's model.

Tool	Description	Object
Decimate Modifier (Planar)	Reducing polygon count	• *Cavea* • Stage
Limited Dissolve tool	Merging the maximum angle between two faces and the maximum distance between two vertices	• Column • Pediment
Decimate Geometry	Create triangles by collapsing edge loops	• Ornate details • Capitals

To optimize other objects in the theatre, a combination of the *Decimate Modifier Planar* and the *Limited Dissolve tool* or *Decimate Geometry* with *Decimate modifier Planar,* were used, which reduces the number of vertices and edges in a mesh. Using these tools together can be effective but was important to use them carefully and review the results to ensure they met the needs and did not compromise the quality or integrity of the geometric model. As a result of these optimization techniques, the model underwent a significant simplification and streamlining process, resulting in a reduction of vertices from 489,779 to 105,221. This reduction was necessary to meet the constraints imposed by the chosen platform-Spatial, which had a mesh vertices limit of 500,000 for the entire environment. However, when uploaded to Unity with the Spatial SDK, the vertex count increased to 250,000 due to differences in optimization settings, compression techniques, and level of detail generation. By implementing these optimization strategies, the theatre model was successfully prepared for efficient uploading and seamless integration within the Spatial platform. A highly optimized model ensures efficient use of system resources, allowing for the creation of larger, more complex, and interactive virtual environments.

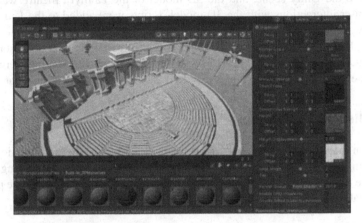

Fig. 8. Unity workflow/ texture adjustment.

4.3 VR Engine – Texture Adjustment

The 3D model of the building was exported in DAE format from *Blender* and imported into the Unity platform. The DAE (COLLADA) format is a 3D asset exchange format that allows seamless and high-fidelity geometry exchange between 3D modelling software. As the photogrammetry process solely captured the geometric information of the model, the next step was to improve its appearance and reliability by adjusting its texture (Fig. 8), This was achieved through a meticulous examination of images captured at the Palmyra theatre and found online. These images served as a reference for making texture adjustments to closely simulate the real texture of the theatre. Tileable textures were employed as a fundamental component to provide visual consistency and efficiency. The objective was to create a more faithful and realistic representation of the site in the virtual space.

4.4 VR Environment – Metaverse Platform

To create experiences for the metaverse using Unity, a range of tools and features within the engine can be used, such as the Unity Editor, which allows designing, building, and testing 3D environments and interactive elements. Unity's scripting tools are also useful for creating custom behaviours and interactions, as well as integrating with other services and platforms, such as blockchain networks, to add new capabilities to the metaverse experiences. There are several platforms and frameworks specifically designed for creating experiences for the metaverse, offering their own tools and features for creating, publishing, and monetizing metaverse experiences. These platforms often have their own communities and ecosystems of developers and users.

For this research, the Spatial Standard Development Kit (SDK) has been used to import the 3D model from Unity into the metaverse platform. To integrate the SDK into Unity, the Spatial SDK was imported into the Unity project. The Spatial object prefab was added to the Unity scene, and the 3D model of the Palmyra theatre was added. To enable user interactions with the 3D model, scripts were added to the Unity scene. The SDK was then configured to ensure that the Unity scene was compatible with the metaverse platform, including setting the appropriate spatial anchors and establishing communication with the Spatial metaverse servers. Testing and debugging were done to ensure that everything was working as expected and to address any issues that arose.

5   Results and Discussions

This section discusses the outcomes of the project, including the optimization of the 3D model in Blender and its integration into Unity, the use of Unity's scripting tools to enhance the user experience, and the publishing of the model in the metaverse platform using Spatial SDK.

5.1   Optimization Output

The project involves creating a highly realistic 3D model of the Palmyra theatre using Blender, which was optimized to reduce the number of vertices (from 489.779 to 105.875) without compromising its appearance (Fig. 9). The model was exported in multiple formats to ensure interoperability with various platforms and software. The optimization also contributed to the scalability of the virtual environment, allowing for the creation of larger and more complex environments while still maintaining realism. Additional objects were added to the environment after optimization to enhance realism.

Fig. 9. Blender Workflow/ the final output of the optimization.

5.2 VR Environment

In this step, the realism of a VR environment in Unity was improved by using high-quality textures with realistic patterns and surfaces, as well as normal and specular maps to create depth and accurate lighting. The VR environment is interoperable, using open standards and protocols for seamless integration with other virtual environments. The use of the Spatial SDK allows for publishing on the metaverse platform, enabling collaboration and data/resource exchange for an interactive user experience.

5.3 Metaverse Platform

The metaverse platform offers social features that enable users to interact and socialize in the virtual environment, enhancing its realism. The virtual reconstruction of the Palmyra theatre is highly ubiquitous, potentially accessible from anywhere in the world through the platform using various devices connected to the internThe compatibility of the platform with a wide range of devices and platforms is ensured through the use of the Spatial SDK, making it highly accessible to all. The navigation of the model in the metaverse platform was tested with *Oculus MetaQuest 2* headset (see Figs. 10 and 11, captured during metaverse navigation in the theatre), which proved effective and suitable for the purposes of this project. Such a simplified model in terms of polygons and the absence of animations and complicated user interactions did not require high-end hardware support, and a consumer grade headset proved sufficient for this first application.

Fig. 10. Final output inside the metaverse platform

Fig. 11. Navigation inside the theatre with an avatar, final output in metaverse platform

6 Conclusions and Future Perspectives

The case study of the Palmyra theatre highlights the potential of 3D reconstruction and metaverse platforms as a tool for bringing back lost heritage. The process of 3D reconstruction, from data acquisition to visualization, is complex and requires interdisciplinary collaboration, but free and/or open-source software can be used to obtain accurate and optimized digital products to be used for similar case studies. Consumer-grade hardware was used to deliver a smooth and immersive experience in the reconstructed virtual environment, ensuring good performance (ensuring that the 3D model is optimized for VR applications as in this case).

This study highlights the importance of exploring and maximizing the use of available resources in virtual reconstruction projects, particularly in a field that faces numerous resource constraints such as lost architectural heritage. The successful application of the methodology presented in this work and the promising results obtained demonstrate the potential for further development and utilization of consumer-grade hardware in lost cultural heritage documentation and dissemination to a wide audience with metaverse platform. This ensures that the tangible and intangible heritage that historic architectures represent is not lost forever, at least in a virtual context.

6.1 Theoretical Implications

This work has raised theoretical considerations about the use of digital and virtual technologies applied to heritage lost due to conflict. First and foremost, ethical aspects have emerged regarding the use of these tools to cases of this nature. The scientific community working in these areas feels a responsibility to preserve cultural heritage through technology, as it carries values that extend beyond their material component. However, the ethical implications of using tools such as the metaverse to disseminate cultural sites have not been explored extensively. These technologies are relatively new and not yet widely used by a broad audience.

Moreover, the platforms on which the metaverse is based are still entrusted on private companies' ownership, having their own rules and policies, even acquiring user data for analytical and commercial purposes. These formal aspects will need to be investigated further by the international scientific community to understand the extent to which these platforms can be used ethically and democratically. Additionally, the potential possibility of platform shutdown presents a drawback when employing metaverse platforms for cultural heritage events, as monetary difficulties, market changes, legal issues, corporate decisions, or technological obstacles may lead to closures. What happens if the virtual platforms adopted for the digital preservation of lost heritage are themselves lost? This raises concerns, and the paradox, about the long-term digital preservation of cultural heritage properties and should be discusses among the scientific community employing such kind of platforms. An interesting discussion was argued in (Hugget J. 2020). NFT (Non-Fungible Token), Blockchain Technologies and cryptocurrencies might be the key to mitigate the risk, even if, nowadays, the attention is more focused on legal and economic aspects of our society, rather than on ethical and societal aspects that lies behind the topic of CH.

6.2 Future Research Opportunities

There are several potential future research opportunities that could be built upon the work carried out in this project:

- The techniques and methodologies employed to digitally reconstruct a destroyed heritage site can be applied to similar case studies of lost heritage.
- Improvements can be made to the accuracy and realism of the 3D model.
- New ways to interact with the virtual environment can be explored for a more immersive experience.

- Comparison between different VR systems (workstation/headset) can be carried out to evaluate the most suitable equipment to guarantee the best virtual experience.
- Experiments may be conducted with a consistent number of people invited to navigate within the theatre in the metaverse space, and their response regarding the experience will be evaluated.
- Further research is needed to fully understand the potential benefits and limitations of virtual environments for education and learning, and to optimize them for educational purposes.
- The role of Non-Fungible Tokens (NFT) in the context of a heritage digital twin in the metaverse should be explored, to evaluate the possibility to "link" the virtual model to the corresponding real object (Cantaluppi & Ceccon 2022).

References

Barazzetti, L., Fangi, G., Remondino, F., Scaioni, M.: Automation in multi-image spherical photogrammetry for 3d architectural reconstructions. VAST: International Symposium on Virtual Reality, p. 7 (2010). https://doi.org/10.2312/PE/VAST/VAST10S/075-081

Bitelli, G., Dellapasqua, M., Girelli, V.A., Sbaraglia, S., Tinia, M.A.: Historical photogrammetry and terrestrial laser scanning for the 3D virtual reconstruction of destroyed structures: a case study in Italy. Int. Arch. Photogram. Remote Sens. Spatial Inform. Sci. **XLII-5/W1**, 113–119 (2017). https://doi.org/10.5194/isprs-archives-XLII-5-W1-113-2017

Chehab, A., Nakhal, B.: Exploring virtual reality as an approach to resurrect destroyed historical buildings - an approach to revive the destroyed 'egg building' through VR. Architect. Plan. J. **28**(3)(Article 17), 1212 (2023). https://doi.org/10.54729/2789-8547

Cantaluppi, E., Ceccon, L.: Defining a metaverse for the cultural heritage. In: CHNT Editorial board. In Proceedings of the 27th International Conference on Cultural Heritage and New Technologies, Vienna, Austria, pp. 10–12 (2022)

Fangi, G.: Documentation of some cultural heritage emergencies in Syria In August 2010 by spherical photrammetry. ISPRS Ann. Photogram. Remote Sens. Spatial Inform. Sci. **II-5/W3**, 401–408 (2015). https://doi.org/10.5194/isprsannals-II-5-W3-401-2015

Gaafar, A.A.: Metaverse in architectural heritage documentation & education. Adv. Ecol. Environ. Res. **6**(10), 66–86 (2021)

Hedrick, E., Harper, M., Oliver, E., Hatch, D.: Teaching & learning in virtual reality: metaverse classroom exploration. In: 2022 Intermountain Engineering, Technology and Computing (IETC), May 2022, pp. 1–5. IEEE, Orem, UT, USA (2022). https://doi.org/10.1109/IETC54973.2022.9796765

Huggett, J.: Virtually real or really virtual: towards a heritage metaverse. Stud. Digital Heritage **4**(1), 1–15 (2020)

Hutson, J., Hutson, P.: Museums and the metaverse: emerging technologies to promote inclusivity and engagement. In: Application of Modern Trends in Museums [Working Title], IntechOpen (2023). https://doi.org/10.5772/intechopen.110044

Hwang, G.J., Chien, S.-Y.: Definition, roles, and potential research issues of the metaverse in education: an artificial intelligence perspective. Comput. Educ. Artific. Intell. **3**, 100082 (2022). https://doi.org/10.1016/j.caeai.2022.100082

Manovich, L., Douglas, J.Y.: Metaverse platforms for cultural heritage: possibilities and challenges. In: Ioannides, M., Arnold, D. (eds.), 3D Research Challenges in Cultural Heritage II, pp. 347–358 (2021)

Moneta, A.: Architecture, heritage, and the metaverse. Tradition. Dwell. Settle. Rev. **32**(1), 37–49 (2020)

Muenster, S.: Digital 3D technologies for humanities research and education: an overview. Appl. Sci. **12**(5), 2426 (2022). https://doi.org/10.3390/app12052426

Quattrini, R., Pierdicca, R., Frontoni, E., Barcaglioni, R.: Virtual reconstruction of lost architectures: from the TLS survey to AR visualization. ISPRS – Int. Arch. Photogram. Remote Sens. Spatial Inform. Sci. **XLI-B5**, 383–390 (2016). https://doi.org/10.5194/isprsarchives-XLI-B5-383-2016

Remondino, F., El-Hakim, S., Girardi, S., Rizzi, A., Benedetti, S., Gonzo, L.: 3D Virtual reconstruction and visualization of complex architectures: The 3D-ARCH project. Int. Arch. Photogramm. Remote Sens. Spatial Inf. Sci. **XXXVIII**(5/W1) (2009). https://doi.org/10.3929/ETHZ-B-000019630

Wahbeh, W., Nebiker, S.: Three dimensional reconstruction workflows for lost cultural heritage monuments exploiting public domain and professional photogrammetric imagery. ISPRS Ann. Photogram. Remote Sens. Spatial Inform. Sci. **4**, 319–325 (2017)

Zhang, X., et al.: Metaverse for cultural heritages. Electronics **11**(22), 3730 (2022)

HerMeS: HERitage sMart Social mEdia aSsistant

A. Bucciero[1] , D. Capaldi[4] , A. Chirivi[1] , M. Codella[3] , M.A. Jaziri[1] ,
L. Leopardi[4] , S.G. Malatesta[4] , I. Muci[1]([✉]) , A. Orlandini[2] ,
A. Palombini[1] , A. Pandurino[1] , E. Panizzi[4] , and A. Umbrico[2]

[1] Digital Heritage Innovation Lab (DHILab), National Research Council—Institute
of Heritage Science in (CNR-ISPC), Lecce, Italy
{alberto.bucciero,augusto.palombini,andrea.pandurino}@cnr.it,
{alessandra.chirivi,mohamedali.jaziri,Irene.muci}@ispc.cnr.it
[2] (CNR-ISTC) National Research Council-Institute for Cognitive Science
and Technology, Rome, Italy
andrea.orlandini@istc.cnr.it, alessandro.umbrico@cnr.it
[3] (CNR-IASI) National Research Council-Institute for Systems Analysis
and Computer, Rome, Italy
marzia.codella@cnr.it
[4] DigiLab -Sapienza University of Rome, Rome, Italy
{donatella.capaldi,laura.leopardi,saveriogiulio.malatesta,panizzi}@uniroma1.it

Abstract. This paper presents the HERitage sMart social mEdia aSsistant (HerMeS) project, funded by Regione Lazio and aimed at offering tools and innovative services to favour the fruition of (tangible and not tangible) Cultural Heritage in the Lazio region through advanced AI and ICT methodologies and technologies. This is the first report to illustrate to the community the newborn tool starting with a survey of the main exploration and sharing of tourist-cultural content Apps to outline its innovative features and its design.

Keywords: cultural heritage · artificial intelligence (AI) · user behaviour · user experience · storytelling · participation in Cultural Heritage

Introduction

The HerMeS (HERitage sMart social mEdia aSsistant) project is developed through the collaboration of Istituto di Scienze del Patrimonio Culturale (ISPC), Istituto per l'Analisi dei Sistemi ed Informatica "Antonio Ruberti" (IASI), Istituto di Scienze e Tecnologie della Cognizione (ISTC), and DigiLab Centro interdipartimentale di Ricerca - Università La Sapienza. The project was elaborate starting from tech specialization mapping edited by Invitalia. All plan is coherent with Horizon 2020, with the Smart Specialisation Strategy or Lazio region and the framework of smart Specialization Platform (S3 Platform), which answers to one of the ex-ante conditionality for the 2014-2020 programming cycle set by the

European Commission in order to achieve the objectives of smart, sustainable and inclusive growth set by the Europe 2020 Strategy.

The idea of creating a social platform where cultural content is generated, described, and uploaded by the same users, according to a paradigm that has been successful in other areas (such as Wikipedia), represents an innovative approach especially when combined with algorithms of artificial intelligence able to propose personalised itineraries in time and space. Within the project, the socialization of the cultural experience is combined with the development of Artificial Intelligence (AI) technologies, which represent the core of the framework. Indeed, AI makes it possible to combine numerous variables to offer tourists and visitors personalized itineraries over time and space, respecting specific needs, needs, and interests.

The HerMeS project aims to build a new application for smartphones with different target users, i.e. tourists, citizens, economic operators, and public administrations. The HerMeS application is designed to meet different needs by pursuing a bottom-up approach: HerMeS provides a collaborative framework where different actors are able to share experiences, feedback, services, and advanced tools. In fact, the planned platform allows registered users to create multimedia content and share information on specific points of interest. At the same time, the identification of visitors' interests and needs permits economic operators to define targeted intervention strategies and the Public Administration to develop solutions for local growth. The project intends to prepare analysis tools to contribute to the sustainable and inclusive development of the territory, according to national and supranational programmatic guidelines.

HerMeS aims to create a prototype of the mobile APP, currently designed and in part developed. In this paper, we present the results achieved so far.

1   Co-Creation Experiences in Tourism Field

A growing number of studies have examined the crucial role of co-creation in the context of tourism. These theoretical and empirical analyses were focused to reveal the foundational elements of active co-creation and interaction with the *Explore* features in shaping the tourist experience.

The touristic sphere encompasses behaviours and psychological aspects associated with experiences before, during, and after travel. The following sections aim to identify and examine the key dimensions that play significant roles in this process.

These dimensions have been identified in the literature and will be discussed in greater detail [3]:

- Pre-travel Stage: This dimension focuses on the activities and decision-making processes that occur before embarking on a trip. Tourists may actively seek out recommendations, read reviews, and engage with online platforms to co-create their travel experiences [2].
- During-travel Stage: This dimension pertains to the actual experience of being a tourist. It involves interactions with the destination, service providers, and

other tourists. Co-creation happens through various activities such as participating in guided tours, engaging in local culture, trying new cuisines, and providing feedback to service providers [18].

– Post-travel Stage: Following the travel experience, tourists engage in reflection and express their experiences through various channels, including social media, travel blogs, and online reviews. This dimension focuses on the post-travel activities of tourists and examines how their actions contribute to the co-creation process by sharing opinions and recommendations with others [9].

Within each dimension, several key factors are expressed in the co-creation process:

– Personal Motivations: Tourists' motivations, needs, and expectations shape their engagement in co-creation activities. Preferences for adventure, cultural immersion, relaxation, social interactions, or educational experiences vary among individuals, influencing their co-creation engagement.
– Social Interactions: Interactions with locals, fellow tourists, and service providers play a crucial role in co-creating tourist experiences. Positive social interactions enhance satisfaction and contribute to the overall travel experience [16].
– Technology and Social Media: The use of technology and social media platforms have revolutionized the co-creation process in tourism. Online platforms enable tourists to access information, share experiences, and engage with others, empowering them to co-create their travel experiences in real-time.
– Cultural and Environmental Factors: Cultural and environmental aspects of a destination influence co-creation. Tourists actively engaging with local culture, traditions, and practices contribute to the co-creation of unique experiences.

These key factors interact within each dimension, shaping the co-creation process and ultimately influencing the quality and satisfaction of the tourist experience.

2 Representing, Learning and Personalizing Touristic Itineraries

In this section, we will introduce a series of components integrated to build the HerMeS core functionalities. In particular, we will present the general concepts considered to implement an AI system realizing the recommendation process for generating personalized touristic itineraries and the basic concepts leveraged to represent the available data about the cultural places that the HerMeS system is supposed to manage.

2.1 Representing Information About Places and Users to Recommend Personalized Itineraries

One of the main objectives of the project is to design and develop a system based on Artificial Intelligence (AI) techniques to propose personalized tourist itineraries to users, tourists and visitors, considering their different needs, preferences and interests. To this aim, when considering a specific area, the AI system will be equipped with a Knowledge Base (KB) that collects information relating to: the **Point of interests**, their history, their characteristics, the touristic services present and all the relevant aspects for their use; the **users**, their interests and preferences and past experiences also considering the possible acquisition of information from their social profiles like, e.g., Facebook, Twitter, etc.

The General Approach. The AI system will therefore leverage this information to feed a recommendation mechanism with the aim of offering to a specific user who wants to visit a certain area a series of points of interest and a *narrative* that connects them, thus proposing an experience that is linked to the user's interests but also proposes characteristic and specific (not necessarily mainstream) elements of the places to visit.

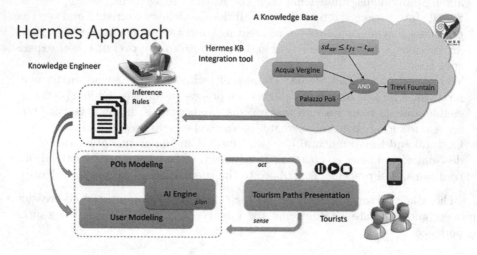

Fig. 1. The AI-based approach to generate personalized touristic itineraries.

The general approach pursued for the AI system is depicted in Fig. 1. A Knowledge Base collects all the information related to points of interest (POIs) and user profiling. Through a set of inference rules and contexts (see more details in Sect. 3) it will be possible to construct a symbolic description of a content recommendation problem considering POIs and a solution generated by the AI system constitutes the personalized path that can be presented to users, e.g., on mobile devices through an APP. The KB was defined considering the works present in the state of the art relating to the representation of information relating to cultural heritage and other tourist aspects. On User Modeling, a user profile mechanism will then be defined with the aim to classify the users characterizing their profiles according to their interests, preferences and needs. This will be implemented considering machine learning techniques applying them to data generated by the users while using the HerMeS system as well as considering information available on social applications. Therefore, the selection of the contents to be considered for the definition of the contents/themes to be presented will constitute the actual algorithm for generating personalized paths.

Temporal Planning Techniques to Synthesize Itineraries. Itineraries are built through AI task planning technology to support the combinatorial reasoning capabilities necessary to take into heterogeneous constraints of a visit (e.g., time, geographic layout, users' interests). In particular, the planning system is able to synthesize itineraries that are coherent with respect to users' interests (personalization) and feasible with respect to the time available for the visit (i.e., the duration of the whole visit and the time estimated for the visit of the single POIs). For this reason, task planning and scheduling capabilities of HerMeS rely on the timeline-based paradigm formalized in [8]. A timeline-based specification consists of a number of *state variables* that describe possible behaviors of domain features to be controlled over time. A state variable is represents states or actions the feature can assume or perform over time; a transition function specifies the valid temporal sequences of values for each single feature; a duration function associates to each value a lower and upper temporal bounds for its execution (i.e., duration bounds of the visit); the specification allows to consider values whose temporal execution is fully *controllable* (i.e., its duration is predictable) and *partially controllable*(i.e., its duration is unpredictable). The above model has been already leveraged to realize intelligent tools for personalized fruition of cultural heritage [7].

In the considered scenario, state variables are organized in a hierarchical way. A high-level goal represents the request of synthesizing a visit for a given user. A goal is enriched with parameters denoting the duration of the whole visit and the topics to be considered while selecting the relevant POIs. A goal is decomposed into a number of *visit actions* targeting selected POIs. The timeline-based model in particular considers different state variables each representing the visit of POIs with different levels of detail and duration. The capability of explicitly representing visit actions with different duration and detail allows the planning systems of making decisions that find a good trade-off between the time available for the visit and the optimal level of detail. The correlation between the high-level goal, the underlying visit actions and the different levels of abstraction are modeled through synchronization rules.

2.2   From Cultural Objects to Cultural Places

A working group at DigiLab - Sapienza University has primarily addressed the conceptual and logical design of Cultural Objects, i.e. the cultural structure of the contents that will be generated by users of the social platform, in order to train and provide indicative parameters to the artificial intelligence envisaged by the project. In order to better define the cultural relations, which are connected with the territorial and economic context, and of possible impact, it was decided to pass from the definition of "Cultural Object", centered on the singularity of the object, to "Cultural Place", a container minimum information in which to decline properties and relationships of an identity object.

Starting points for such definition were: not considering individuals as a basic element, but identity complexes: thus we pass from the concept of single Cultural Object to complexity of the Cultural Place (CP); how to categorize cultural places; definition the territorial/thematic relationships between the different cultural places; keeping in consideration intangible heritage and understand how to integrate something intangible into a defined space; how to define iterations with economic operators; how to manage the intersections with infrastructures, considering transport and the ways of using the routes.

Particular attention was given to the spatial development of the hierarchy, thinking *by places* and no longer *by objects*, in addition to architectural forms, points of interest, landmarks (meeting points, significant traces for the local population) that have shaped it plastically.

Once the CPs were identified, scalar aggregation units of the CPs were established as simple agglomerations, which can be defined as "monumental units", which in turn can be aggregated into scalar macrosystems, capable of expanding the contextual ramifications of the CP in increasingly complex aggregations: monumental complex, topographic unit, topographic complex, territorial unity.

Each aggregation phase, from the micro-conglomerate to the more complex expansion area, is defined by a footprint that characterizes it (e.g., "Monumental unit" = UM_01), and which makes every single step of the CP extension recognizable by the system. However, the survey is not limited to registering the points of interest that make up the CP, or their combination, but inserts information on the productive fabric ("Monumental Complex") and available infrastructures ("Topographical Complex") in the descriptive string.

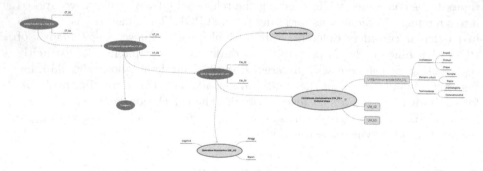

Fig. 2. Hierarchical schema to support the description and evaluation process of Cultural Places.

In Fig. n2, the characteristics of the CP: "Monumental Unit" (UM_01) are depicted. This is the minimum descriptive unit, where information relating to the POI or specific and spatially relevant aspects of the POI is collected. Architecture (palaces, churches, cemeteries, etc.), urban elements (gardens, parks, arches, towers), and testimonies (archaeological, commemorative, etc.) are to be considered

Monumental Units. Elements such as one can be defined as a Complex Monumental unit because the square contains vestiges (fountains, commemorative statues, obelisks, etc.). In the hierarchical and relational process, the aggregation of intangible heritage concerning that place must also be considered (e.g. a procession that starts from that church; the statue of Pasquino with the *pasquinate*): identifiable as PI1, which is integrated into the CP. CP/UM as a "Monumental Complex" (CM_01). Given a series of monumental units, their contextual connection (dialogue) constitutes a more articulated system, which allows the use of their compositional-architectural arrangement and their development according to a precise functionality: this articulation takes the name of "Monumental Complex". The monumental complexes can have a vertical trend. The example is San Clemente church, made up of several layers, all equally usable in their complex division of space, which generates extensive immersive environments that can be identified by stylistic features, frescoes, architectural modules: the 12th century basilica, the lower basilica (IV-XI century) the *mitreum* and the Roman road with *insula* in *opus latericium* and *horrea* from II-III AD. Each of the three layers corresponds to a monumental unit, which generates the monumental complex of San Clemente. It is therefore not the same architectural space in which they are inserted, for example. a Carolingian crypt, a Baroque chapel, or the various interventions over the centuries of an additional or innovative type placed in the same space, without boundaries.

2.3 Topographic Units (UT) and Topographic Complexes (CM)

The monumental complexes constitute a territorial network, therefore the relationships with the urban and territorial context must be considered, including those with the "Economic Operators" (OE) in this series of relationships, thus counting any presences and connections with stakeholders. Several topographical units, coherent and identifying, constitute the topographical complexes, on a larger territorial scale. Once the topographical complexes have been established, it is possible to identify from the mapping the arteries connecting the areas, the transport lines on wheels and on the railway/metro, the stops, and the parking lots, in order to allow the flow of visitors, faster movements, and more articulated and/or scalar itineraries, as envisaged among the functions of artificial intelligence to be developed in the subsequent phases of the project.

2.4 Territorial Unit (TU)

The set of Topographical Complexes corresponds to a system of congruent and narratively assimilable territorial relations. However, there is a macro-structural problem that is always inherent to intangible heritage. It may be useful for the visitor to have a general idea of the extended territory of the main and most famous intangible heritages. For example, if you have "Sabina" as a territorial unit, you might be interested in knowing that the "Festa della Fantasima" takes place in many of its municipalities, and therefore, from this general information linked to the EU, recall the topographical units and monumental complexes where the festival takes place.

2.5   Relationships and Metadata

The hierarchical system and the structure of the database consider values to be assigned to relationships, which can include metadata and categories as well as can be assessed by users.

Therefore, descriptive strings have been devised to facilitate the recognition of the CP and its connections, and at the same time to make the contents in the search easily retrievable. The relationship that binds the different Cultural Places, in all their components and in their scalar development, consists of a string that contains all the identifying acronyms.

Relationships are the basis of the narratives that must be developed in conjunction with the various points, not so much to allow a simple union of POIs within a territorial context, as the offer of a red thread of storytelling, aimed at discovering it, involving the user in a real process of relationship with the territory: this is the radical innovation in the itineraries proposed by HerMeS, the possibility of creating "liquid" cross-country itineraries according to the chosen groupings (one-many) and the temporal measure available at the request of the visitor: 1 h, 3 h, half day, with family, with seniors. Thematic examples can be Archaeological, Architectural/Artistic, Religious, Scientific/educational, and Cultural.

2.6   Taxonomies

In order to identify the relevant taxonomies, a rather wide analysis of the state of the art considering different relationship models based on classification by: Typology (Icomonos)[1], Category (CoE)[2], Sector (France), Object (France, CNRS)[3], georeferenced Buildings (UK), Function (UK, Wall), Main Areas (UNESCO)[4], storytelling main themes(Trans Places).

Scenario 1: UM Thematic/Training CP: Palazzo del Collegio Romano. Given the list of functions of the system of Data Heritage, selecting the voice "Training", a set of related places are shown: college, college building, observatory, museum, library, school, etc.

Scenario 2: CM thematic. Following Wales'map functionalities[5], it joins the CM "Collegio Romano", classified such as Education, adding the principal corresponding voice to the buildings and side streets present. Under Unassigned:

---

[1] https://www.icomos.org/.
[2] http://openarchive.icomos.org/classification.html.
[3] https://www.cnrs.fr/fr.
[4] https://www.unesco.it/.
[5] https://datamap.gov.wales.

Place Name (Piè di Marmo and Gatta); Education:Art Museum (Doria Pamphilji Gallery) and Education:Library (The Biblioteca Casanatense); Civil: Government office (MiC and Police Station); Water supply and drainage: fountain:drinking fountain:Porter Fountain; Religious Ritual and funerary:Shrine: Place of worship:Church (S. Maria in via Lata).

2.7 Evaluations

Parallel to the system of categorisation and taxonomic structuring, the existing methods of analysis and evaluation of Cultural Heritage were analyzed. In this, it was possible to make use of the previous experience of DigiLab Sapienza University of Rome, which houses an "Observatory for Cultural Heritage" and an Observatory for projects for the enhancement of cultural heritage (OsPaC[6]). In collaboration with the museums in the Municipality of Rome, the MUSE360 [4] system was developed, which provides a model of widespread restitution of the entire cultural offer and services of cultural sites, in order to optimize resources and installations. The models for the evaluation are prepared on the basis of a benchmarking of best practices at an international level. The system is modular and scalable, providing for both an expansion of monitoring issues and territorial extensions through agreements with Regions, metropolitan areas or individual cultural institutions. From this project, indications and parameters were extrapolated to analyze: online communication of assets; services for visitors; digital preservation; training; advanced technological applications; social strategies; storytelling/storyliving applied to collections/places.

The parameters for evaluating the "physical" exhibition site and local services, as well as the web presence and digital communication of the cultural institutions themselves, were prepared. The analysis of international museum experiences and specific skills in the field of cultural heritage and digital archives have made it possible to identify a series of useful indicators for an articulated evaluation of cultural institutions online and on site. More in detail, the following were examined: the types of exhibition of the collections; the activation of heritage services (location, tourism, catering, bookshop, press, publishing, job and collaboration opportunities); accessibility, usability and navigability on the web; the innovative use of technologies; Storytelling/storyliving strategies; openness to the dynamics of Web 2.0 and to collaboration with the public for the enhancement of assets; the needs and contributions of the target audience.

Thanks to this parameterize, it was possible to derive a model capable of evaluating the cultural system of the places object of the project, assigning a weight value to each parameter in relation to visitor, educational background, museum entity, relational typology.

3 A Knowledge Base for HerMeS

The Knowledge base of HerMeS should characterize a wide set of information concerning the cultural heritage of a territory. It should characterize geographic

---

[6] https://digilab.uniroma1.it/ricerca/course-projects/ospac-observatory.

and structural features as well as cultural qualities of tangible entities that are part of a specific territory and are relevant from a heritage point of view. However, the objective of HerMeS is not limited to the "semantic indexing" of heritage objects. A key aim of HerMeS is the representation of intangible cultural entities and their correlation with the territory and related tangible entities. A contextual representation of intangible cultural entities and the capability of correlating them to tangible entities are central to unlocking hidden relationships between places, history, religions, food, and local traditions. To characterize such a complex set of information and relationships the knowledge base relies on an ontology formally characterizing concepts and properties [12]. Specifically, we design the HerMeS Ontology as a novel domain ontology [11] extending the ontological model ArCo which was specifically designed for the Cultural Heritage domain [5,6].

3.1   The ARCO Ontology

ArCo is the result of a recent research effort aiming at publishing a knowledge graph (KG) that model the Cultural Heritage domain and a Linked Open Data (LOD) dataset about Italian cultural properties. ArCo KG is available at the MiBAC's official SPARQL endpoint[7]. The endpoint is based on the Open Source version of Virtuoso[8]. Besides the relevance of the produced resource, described in [5], ArCo pushes the state-of-the-art in knowledge graph engineering by sharing its "behind the scenes", i.e. the intellectual and methodological processes performed, the adopted design principles and the lessons learned, all of which constitute are well explained in [6].

The structure of the ArCo ontology is summarized by Fig. 3. The modular network aggregates sever coherent ontological modules that describe cultural objects from different perspectives. The modules `arco` and `core` define top-level concepts and global relations shared among all modules. The `catalogue` module is dedicated to catalogue records especially useful to preserve the provenance and dynamics of the data. The remaining 4 modules (cultural-event, denotative-description, location, context-description) focus on cultural properties and their features.

3.2   The HerMeS Ontology

The modules of the ArCo network support the description of cultural properties and thus constitute a good, ready-to-use, basis for the HerMeS ontology. However, ArCo mainly focuses on `movable` cultural objects and does not provide sufficiently detailed structures to capture the features of `immuvable` cultural properties and `intangible` cultural properties. Intangible cultural properties are in particular a central point of HerMeS to support cross-narratives linking different cultural aspects (e.g., archaeological, social, religious, rituals). HerMeS

---

[7] http://dati.beniculturali.it/sparql.
[8] https://github.com/openlink/virtuoso-opensource.

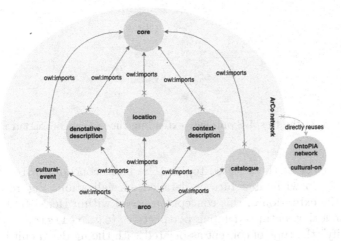

Fig. 3. Overview of the ArCo network of ontology modules from [5].

therefore extends ArCo by defining (and refining) concepts that support the needed level of expressivity. Figure 4 shows an excerpt of the HerMeS ontology pointing out some new concepts and their correlation with ArCo's structures.

HerMeS extends the concept `Immovable Cultural Property` by introducing the concepts `Unita Territoriale` and `Complesso Territoriale`. These concepts support a structured (and layered) description of a territory identifying parts (areas) and sub-parts that are relevant from an heritage perspective. In addition, HerMeS introduces a new type of `Immovable Cultural Property` called `Infrastructural Property` supporting the description of the topological structure of a territory. This concepts generally describe infrastructural entity that connect instances of `Complesso Territoriale` and may represent theirselves cultural properties. In addition to their infrastructural role, streets or square for example could be relevant from an heritage perspective also.

The main extension concerns the structuring of `Intangible` Cultural Property. HerMeS defines a detailed structure of transversal cultural and social properties that are correlated to the `Tangible` Cultural Property (either `movable` or `immovable`) defined into the knowledge. This is the central point correlating tangible with intangible entities that capture the culture, tradition, costumes of a certain territory.

Another central aspect of HerMeS is the capability of indexing modeled cultural properties according to different topics and point of view. With respect to the construction of contextualized narratives [13], the definition of a well-structured taxonomy of topics and themes supports the contextualisation, filtering, and retrieval of (sub-sets of) cultural properties that are relevant and coherent with respect to the selected topics. To define this contextualization, each `Cultural Property` is associated with a non-empty set of `Topic`. Topics are used to "tag" the description/content of a certain cultural entity as rele-

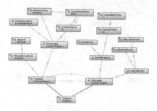

Fig. 4. Excerpt of the HerMeS ontology extending the notions of `CulturalProperty`.

vant with respect to the selected topics. The basic concept `Topic` was already defined in ArCo without a further/detailed specialization. Figure 5 shows an excerpt of the extension of this concept proposed within HerMeS. These topics are taxonomical structures defining perspectives (e.g., `religion`, `social`, `art`) that "classify" the type of content associated with the modeled cultural entities.

4   Generating Personalised Itineraries

4.1   HerMeS Point of View

HerMeS aims to promote the enhancement and enjoyment of Lazio's Cultural Heritage, in its many territorial manifestations and multiple meanings. Through a collaborative and participatory system, stakeholders become an active part of the system by sharing experiences, opinions, services, and tools [17].

There are two main considerations on which the design idea is based:

– **From institutional information to social experiences**: the amount of institutional, promotional and marketing information available and specially

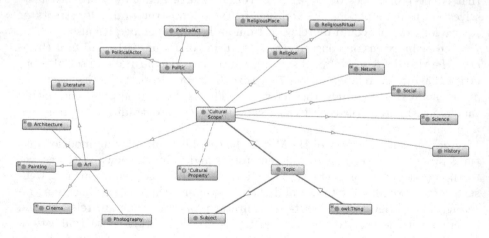

Fig. 5. Excerpt of the taxonomic structure characterizing semantic links between the modeled `CulturalProperty`.

prepared to provide valid support in choosing the places of cultural-tourist interest to visit is so large, it is often considered useless, misleading, and sometimes, even deceptive. On the other hand, we all know that in the moment of embarking on a trip or planning a visit, we rely more on the impressions (reviews, evaluations, stories, etc.) of other visitors and not on the "institutional" or "official" information that describes the place of interest. In other words, we not only trust the "experiences" of those who preceded us, but in many cases, we try to replicate them.
- **From data to information**: in a completely connected world, where information arrives from all over, the common expectation is to have a considerable amount of data precisely at the moment needed, both during the planning of a trip and during its course. Furthermore, this information must have a high "quality" and must be able to respond to particular needs and specific needs of users, linked, for example, to the presence of children, the disabled, etc.

From the first consideration comes the idea of creating a social platform in which content is generated, described and uploaded by the users themselves in the form of multimedia and multichannel *content*, called *PoI Point of Interest* thus proposing an innovative approach in the panorama of tools to support 'Cultural discovery'. On the other hand, for the proposed system to be able to provide valuable information, it must be intelligent. It must understand the expectations, and interests of users and, at the same time, take into account contextual situations (opening hours, availability of places, characteristics of the itinerary, presence of constraints or special needs). The APP must therefore be able to propose personalized paths in time and space. To this end, a study was conducted to evaluate the landscaping of the APP and other social platforms for touristic-cultural content sharing, as well as the current use of AI systems in cultural tourism promotion platforms and their impact in the reference context.

5   The Innovative Tool

The HerMeS project aims to provide a diverse range of tools and advanced services to enhance the enjoyment and exploration of Cultural Heritage, both tangible and intangible, within the Lazio region. These services are designed to cater to the needs of tourists, citizens, businesses, and public administration. HerMeS facilitates the connection of various heterogeneous needs and interests among different stakeholders. Through a bottom-up participation model and leveraging advanced IT technologies, including AI algorithms, personalised itineraries, and valuable information are proposed to tourists and visitors. Simultaneously, the project supports economic operators in defining strategies that align with interventions by the Public Administration. This collaboration fosters the development of sustainable and innovative solutions within the region.

Using AI and machine learning algorithms, the HerMeS APP analyses various variables such as user preferences, historical data, and current trends, to generate personalised itineraries for tourists. The APP recommends specific cultural sites, events or activities based on the individual's interests and preferences.

Furthermore, HerMeS offers real-time information and updates to economic operators, enabling them to make data-driven business decisions. The APP can provide insights on visitor traffic, popular attractions, and emerging trends, empowering operators to tailor their offerings and marketing strategies accordingly.

To support sustainable and innovative growth, the APP integrates a feedback system where users and operators can share their experiences, suggestions, and ideas. The Public Administration can leverage this feedback to identify areas of improvement develop innovative solutions, and prioritise interventions that enhance the cultural heritage landscape.

By combining advanced IT technologies such as AI algorithms, HerMeS can bridge the gap between diverse stakeholders and foster a participatory ecosystem focused on enriching cultural heritage experiences for tourists, citizens, economic operators, and the Public Administration.

6   The Envisaged User Interface

6.1   The Benchmarking Methodology

To achieve the project's objectives, an in-depth analysis and accurate comparison of numerous mobile applications dedicated to the enhancement of tangible and intangible cultural heritage was conducted, adopting the Benchmarking methodology. In project management Benchmarking *"is a process of investigation and learning from the best in a class to get useful information for improving and changing an organisation"* [1]. Its purpose is a kind of evaluation tool which is employed to compare and measure the subject of the project. This tool is essential to detect information or data to reach out for improvement [1]. Benchmarking methodology was applied to the comparative survey which examined the APPs available in the Google Play Store and Apple's App Store. The analysis was also extended to models for the description and representation of information about the resources to be enhanced. An extensive analysis was conducted on 17 platforms for the exploration and sharing of tourist-cultural content, identifying the main features and crossing them with the APPs that were able to support them. The result of this study is outlined in the diagram below:

MOBILE APPS	FUNCTIONALITY															
	Discover	Plan	Create content	Share with app's community	Connect with social platform	Suggested itineraries by geolocation	Audio guide	Feedback	Register itineraries	Share with social platform	Collect all routes as favourites	Share position	User profiling by AI	Download map	Buyticket guided tours	Reserve and buy the stay
Blincoo	✓		✓	✓												
Get Your Guide								✓							✓	
Google Maps				✓								✓		✓		
IDotto						✓	✓							✓		
Izi.TRAVEL	✓	✓	✓			✓	✓			✓	✓					
Komoot	✓	✓		✓	✓	✓			✓	✓	✓	✓		✓		
Loquis			✓	✓			✓									
MapsMe		✓				✓					✓	✓		✓		
Mininube	✓			✓												
MyWoWo	✓						✓	✓	✓							
Roadrippers	✓	✓				✓					✓	✓				✓
Travello	✓		✓	✓	✓			✓			✓	✓				
Trip Case											✓					
Trip Advisor	✓			✓				✓							✓	
Steller	✓		✓	✓	✓											
Yamgu			✓			✓								✓	✓	
Zenzo Fox	✓	✓				✓	✓								✓	

Fig. 6. Survey of the main exploration and sharing of tourist-cultural content Apps

From the analysis of the results of the study, the most common features that arise are:

- *Territory exploration*: 10 out of 17 APPs support the user in the territory exploration phase. It is a must-have feature in tourism apps. For the traveller or the local user, it is useful for discovering hidden places, highlighting a place with details that are usually not noticed, and also creating personalised routes with out-of-the-box paths.
- *Sharing content*: proposing your own lived experiences to other users is the prerogative of the sharing functionality; this functionality is present within 8 out of the 17 APPs.
- *Audio Guide*: from a tool to support culture in museums, galleries, etc., it has made its way to become a function of tourist-cultural applications. In fact, in the study carried out, the number of apps identified with an audio guide is 5 out of 17.
- *Proposal of itineraries through geolocation*: the philosophy of geolocation is also in this case linked to the exploration of new routes and experiences. In this research, 7 out of 17 APPs contain this functionality.

Furthermore, the graph shown in (Fig. n° 7) highlights the lack of a tool to support the tourist who needs to receive information about a PoI around him or to discover or share new content and experiences. From the histogram, it is possible to ascertain that during the research of the state of the art of existing mobile apps, it emerged that there are applications that use artificial intelligence predictive modules but are nevertheless focused on a single functionality. For example, the creation of a new PoI does not take into account during the planning of an itinerary of possible constraints and parameters that instead can be allocated by the HerMeS application.

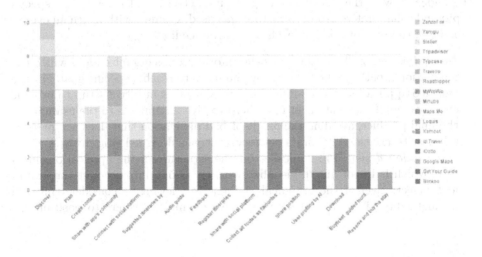

Fig. 7. Histogram representing main APP features

Based on the previous considerations and following User Centre Design [14], the User eXperience was designed focusing on the main features that emerged from the study conducted, such as:

- *Explore*: During the navigation phase, the user can set the reference position and radius in kilometres, enabling them to define their desired search area. A knowledge-based recommendation system comes into play at this point, classifying a subset of Points of Interest (PoI) as potential visiting opportunities based on the user's specified criteria. Factors such as the duration of the PoI visit, expected turnout, and preferred visiting times are taken into consideration by the recommendation system, generating paths that align with the user's indicated preferences and ensuring a tailored experience.
- *Tell*: a crucial step is a creative process that we called "TELL". It allows users to express themselves by creating multimedia and multichannel *content*. These contents give voice to the community's storytelling and provide a platform for people to share interesting content. This encourages interactions among users and fosters relationships based on evaluations of each other's experiences, as explained earlier in the first paragraph of the General Approach.

In the HerMeS application, users can tell their content through a sequence of Points of Interest that can enrich by adding pictures, movies, audio or text descriptions, etc. To ensure a smooth and user-friendly experience, the HerMeS APP was carefully designed with various navigation paths in mind. A collaborative prototyping tool called Figma was used to create an overall plan for the first two design levels. Therefore, *Telling*an experience with the HerMeS application can be done through the flow called *Point of Interest*. Here the user, while moving, can decide to add a new POI to her/his itinerary or to add a description of her/his travel experience, sharing it to the whole community. Concerning these macro functionalities, the various navigational paths were then studied to build the logical flow of the HerMeS concept in its 'activities'. To this end, a special rapid and collaborative prototyping tool was used, Figma[9], with which an overall scheme of the first two design levels were produced:

- *Navigation design*[10]: is about how the information is organized and which the navigational path can be followed by the users to reach a specific goal. For the HerMeS application, the team has set up a dry and intuitive setup to provide effective mobile navigation. It must help to give an impetus to the usability of the final product, avoiding the result of bad navigation that does not prepare the user to use the APP in its entirety as it was designed (Fig. n° 8).
- *Information design* [15]: it focuses on the structure of the application interface, which is important to visualize without taking into account the graphical aspect. Even if the graphical element is relevant to consider, this will be highlighted in a subsequent phase. An example is where to position the

[9] https://www.figma.com.
[10] https://m2.material.io/design/introductiontypes-of-navigation.

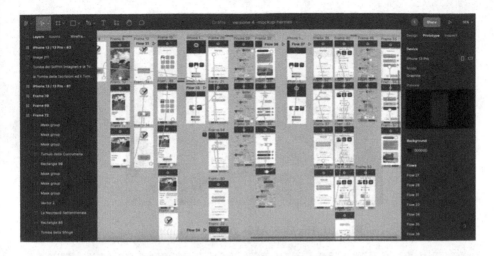

Fig. 8. App navigation design

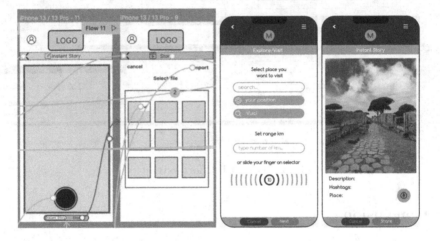

Fig. 9. Left: Information design from Figma and HerMeS APP mockup

button correctly to take a photo or record a video, or prepare a correct selection of content (photos or videos) for the creation of new content(Fig. n° fig:funzionespscrea).

Finally, after the possible graphic skin was produced, allowing the user generated a version of the APP with the graphic design of the HerMeS project (Fig. n° 9). The last step was the creation of a navigable mock-up that allowed us to test the navigational routes, ergonomics, and usability of the HerMeS APP (Fig. n° 10).

Fig. 10. HerMeS APP graphic skinning

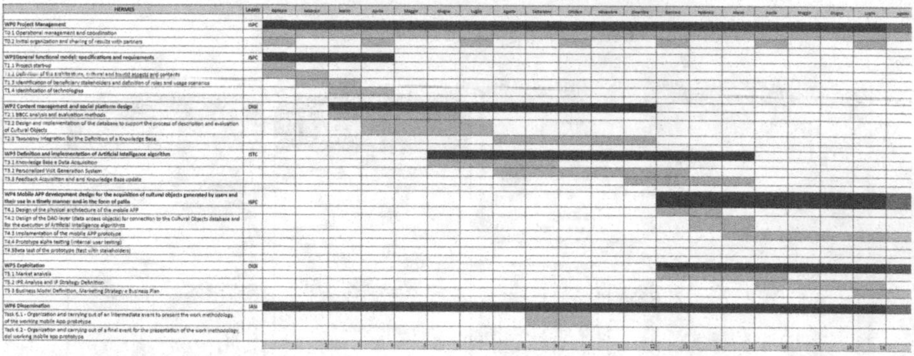

Fig. 11. GANTT Chart extract

7 Conclusion

In this paper, we have introduced HerMeS to the IT and Culture Heritage communities, presenting an innovative and captivating approach to promoting the Cultural Heritage of the Lazio region through advanced AI and ICT methodologies and technologies.

At the time of writing this paper, the mobile application is not currently available for download. The development landscaping is wide and in this paper's section, we illustrated the first steps regarding the user's request and we understood the navigation flow. Each step to follow is based on the Gantt chart [10] (Fig. n° 11) that has been edited to predict the execution phases project on its operating moments.

From the point of view of the software application (APP) industry, over the past decade, it has experienced a notable transformation in software development technologies. Companies of all sizes and across various sectors have shifted from native-platform programming languages to their modern, cross-platform counterparts, often based on open-source technologies, to develop their suite of software products. In fact, the technologies we have used are Open Source. Based on the mock-up and the APP's architecture shown in the last paragraph, the technology that we choose to implement the front-end Hermes layer is the Flutter framework created by Google to create native frames for iOS, Android etc. About Back-end, the layer that handles the application's logic and process typically consists of servers, databases, and application servers that are responsible for managing the application's data and functionality. We choose Node.js (an open-source runtime system multiplatform event oriented to execute JavaScript code) and SQL (an open-source database).

However, adopting these youthful cross-platform technologies also entails certain considerations and trade-offs that require careful evaluation. This first phase of the design and development activities of the project provides an overview of the exciting progress achieved thus far. The potential impact of the HerMeS project is significant, not only for the Lazio region but also for the broader field of Cultural Heritage promotion and preservation.

Acknowledgement. The authors are partially supported by LazioInnova, Regione Lazio ("Gruppi di Ricerca 2020" - POR FESR LAZIO 2014, Ref. G04014).

References

1. Barber, E.: Benchmarking the management of projects: a review of current thinking. Int. J. Project Manage. **22**, 301–307 (2004). https://doi.org/10.1016/j.ijproman.2003.08.001
2. Binkhorst, E., den Dekker, T.: Agenda for co-creation tourism experience research. J. Hospitality Market. Manage. **18**, 311–327 (2009). https://doi.org/10.1080/19368620802594193
3. Campos, A., Mendes, J., Pinto, P., Scott, N.: Co-creation of tourist experiences: a literature review. Current Issues Tourism 21 (2015). https://doi.org/10.1080/13683500.2015.1081158
4. Capaldi, D., Malatesta, S.G., Ilardi, E., Lella, F.: Muse 360: Integrated system of analysis and museum planning. Environ. Sci. Proc. **10**(1) (2021). https://www.mdpi.com/2673-4931/10/1/4
5. Carriero, V.A., et al.: ArCo: the Italian cultural heritage knowledge graph. In: Ghidini, C., et al. (eds.) ISWC 2019. LNCS, vol. 11779, pp. 36–52. Springer, Cham (2019). https://doi.org/10.1007/978-3-030-30796-7_3
6. Carriero, V.A., Gangemi, A., Mancinelli, M.L., Nuzzolese, A.G., Presutti, V., Veninata, C.: Pattern-based design applied to cultural heritage knowledge graphs. Semantic Web **12**(313–357), 2 (2021)
7. Cesta, A.,et al.: Personalizing technology-enhanced learning for cultural visits. In: Adjunct Publication of the 28th ACM Conference on User Modeling, Adaptation and Personalization, pp. 333–339. UMAP '20 Adjunct, Association for Computing Machinery, New York, NY, USA (2020). https://doi.org/10.1145/3386392.3399278
8. Cialdea Mayer, M., Orlandini, A., Umbrico, A.: Planning and execution with flexible timelines: a formal account. Acta Informatica **53**(6–8), 649–680 (2016)
9. Edensor, T.: Staging tourism: tourists as performers. Ann. Tourism Res. **27**, 322–344 (2000)

10. Geraldi, J., Lechter, T.: Gantt charts revisited: A critical analysis of its roots and implications to the management of projects today. Int. J. Manag. Projects Bus. **5**, 389–395 (2012). https://doi.org/10.1108/17538371211268889
11. Guarino, N.: Understanding, building and using ontologies. Int. J. Hum. Comput. Stud. **46**(2), 293–310 (1997)
12. Guarino, N., Oberle, D., Staab, S.: What Is an Ontology?, pp. 1–17. Springer, Berlin Heidelberg, Berlin, Heidelberg (2009)
13. Meghini, C., Bartalesi, V., Metilli, D.: Representing narratives in digital libraries: the narrative ontology. Semantic Web **12**(241–264), 2 (2021)
14. Norman, D.: User centered system design. New perspectives on human-computer interaction (1986)
15. Richard, B.: Information design. Europ. J. Inform. Syst. **20**(4), 375–377 (2011). https://doi.org/10.1057/ejis.2011.22
16. Surra, C.A., Ridley, C.A.: Multiple perspectives on interaction: Participants, peers, and observers. Guilford Press (1991)
17. Varvasovszky, Z., Brugha, R.: A stakeholder analysis. Health Policy Plann. **15**(3), 338–345 (09 2000). https://doi.org/10.1093/heapol/15.3.338
18. Verhoef, P., Lemon, K., Parasuraman, A.P., Roggeveen, A., Tsiros, M., Schlesinger, L.: Customer experience creation: Determinants, dynamics and management strategies. J. Retail. **85**, 31–41 (03 2009). https://doi.org/10.1016/j.jretai.2008.11.001

The Depth Estimation of 2D Content: A New Life for Paintings

Aleksandra Pauls[✉], Roberto Pierdicca, Adriano Mancini,
and Primo Zingaretti

Vision Robotics and Artificial Intelligence (VRAI) lab, Department of Information
Engineering, Marche Polytechnic University, Ancona, Italy
a.pauls@pm.univpm.it

Abstract. The preservation, accessibility, and dissemination of historical artifacts to a wider audience have become increasingly important, and cultural institutions can achieve these goals through the digitization of cultural heritage. In recent years, artificial intelligence (AI) and machine learning (ML) techniques improve the virtualization of cultural artifacts for interactive experiences. In this work, we present a virtualization pipeline for the cultural heritage domain, focusing specifically on paintings, using AI techniques. We outline the basic workflow, including a thorough description of the comparison of various neural network models and their performance metrics. The proposed method creates an immersive experience for viewers to interact with paintings beyond observation. The approach utilizes 2.5D technology by applying depth maps of paintings using deep learning (DL) algorithms. The proof of concept was demonstrated on two real-life paintings of varying complexities, and this innovative approach holds potential for enhancing the appreciation and understanding of cultural heritage in museums and other cultural institutions.

Keywords: cultural heritage · artificial intelligence · monocular depth estimation · immersive experience · paintings · deep learning

1 Introduction

The advancement of new technologies has opened up vast possibilities for the museum and cultural heritage sector, providing innovative solutions to engage visitors and bring artworks to life. The increasing trend towards digitization and the development of 3D technology have changed the way people experience museum visits [26]. While the development of 3D technology has brought about new possibilities for museum visits, it is important to note that traditional 2D content still remains one of the best ways to experience information. From books to images and posters, 2D content provides a simple and straightforward way to present information and allows for easy comprehension. However, the integra-

L. T. De Paolis et al. (Eds.): XR Salento 2023, LNCS 14219, pp. 127–145, 2023.
https://doi.org/10.1007/978-3-031-43404-4_9

tion of new technologies, such as artificial intelligence, has the potential to take 2D content to new heights, transforming it into an immersive and interactive experience that engages visitors on a deeper level.

To make 2D content more engaging, museums can leverage the latest technology to create the feeling that familiar 2D paintings have become three-dimensional [8]. This can be achieved through the use of depth maps and deep learning technology [17]. By generating depth maps of paintings, museums can provide visitors with an immersive 2.5D experience that gives them a sense of depth and volume. This not only enhances the viewing experience but also provides a new level of insight into the artworks on exhibition.

In this paper, we focus on utilizing AI techniques to create a pipeline of 2.5D visualization for paintings in the cultural heritage domain. The paper is structured into several sections. It starts with an introduction, followed by a review of related works and a comparison of different types of content in Sect. 2. Then, in Sect. 3 we describe the methodology, that covers the pipeline used in the monocular depth estimation system, including data acquisition, image pre-processing, depth map extraction, and evaluation metrics. Preliminary results and case studies are presented in Sect. 4, and the paper concludes with a summary and future research directions.

2   Related Works

Cultural heritage objects offer a connection to our past and our sense of identity, but they are vulnerable to natural disasters and human-made threats [10]. Preservation, protection, and accessibility strategies are crucial to ensure their long-term survival, especially in times of crisis. Historic areas are highly susceptible to earthquake damage due to several factors, including the presence of residents and visitors and tangible or intangible heritage assets [25]. Italy has made significant contributions to cultural heritage preservation, particularly in the planned preventive conservation of architectural heritage [28].

Through digital replication of cultural heritage objects, their long-term conservation can be ensured while simultaneously making them available also for educational purposes to a broader audience, irrespective of location or travel accessibility. Virtual museums provide interactive learning environments [2], as they offer ease of use and accessibility to individuals who may not have the opportunity to visit physical sites.

2.1   3D Representation of Artworks and Cultural Heritage Sites

The use of 3D representation in artworks and cultural heritage sites is becoming increasingly popular for a variety of purposes. Classical techniques such as mosaics and bas-reliefs have been used for centuries to create 3D representations of paintings, while modern techniques such as photogrammetry or laser-scanner [11] can create highly detailed and accurate 3D models of artworks. These 3D models can be used for various purposes such as creating 3D printed models for the visually impaired to experience, analyzing the state of the painting [6], or even restoring hidden or damaged parts through photo manipulation [20]. Additionally, 3D models can be used to create virtual reality experiences of cultural heritage sites [13], allowing people to explore and learn about them from anywhere in the world. Overall, the use of 3D representation in artworks and cultural heritage sites has numerous potential applications for both preservation and accessibility.

2.2   AI Application for Artworks

The use of AI in the field of art is rapidly expanding. Generative Adversarial Networks (GANs) are a type of AI algorithm that can learn to create images that resemble existing artworks or even produce entirely new ones [33].In addition to GANs, AI is also used for stylization, which involves creating new images that mimic the style of other artists or artistic movements [19]. AI applications in art employ inpainting as a method to fill in missing or damaged portions of artwork using surrounding content. Segmentation is also a significant tool for analyzing art, allowing AI algorithms to detect objects on paintings or determine the author through style analysis or brushstroke analysis [22]. Additionally, AI can be utilized to create 3D models of artworks by extracting monocular depth maps from 2D images [16]. These models can then be applied in virtual reality experiences for cultural heritage preservation and educational purposes, allowing viewers a unique way for viewers to interact and learn about art.

2.3   Monocular Depth Estimation

The task of estimating depth for a single image has been a popular topic in the fields of computer graphics and computer vision, receiving significant attention from researchers and practitioners. In the last ten years, there has been considerable progress in the field of monocular depth estimation.

In [4] was proposed a structure-aware architecture with spatial attention blocks. Several research studies have a lot of details and new approaches, related to normals [34], semantic constraints [3,4,30], innovative architectures [7,12,14], and new loss functions [18,23,31], to enhance the precision of the overall depth output or certain regions. The authors of [36] have trained their depth prediction model on a combination of data sources, such as high-quality LiDAR sensor data [37] and lower-quality web stereo data [23,29,32]. In this work, we propose the workflow of atomizing the process of obtaining 2.5D visualization in the Cultural Heritage domain for paintings by using Monocular Depth Estimation. We are comparing different neural networks in two case studies to evaluate the hypothesis of applying the 2.5D format to pictures in virtual space.

In various applications, understanding 3D scene geometry relies heavily on monocular depth estimation. Throughout history, artists have used various techniques to create the impression of depth on a flat canvas. Machine learning models trained on realistic photo or video data can analyze these paintings for depth prediction, offering insight into the differences between human and machine perception. Researchers in a recent study [1] explored how these models interpreted art history images and found that they performed well despite the differences from the training data. An open-source visualization[1] was created for further exploration of these findings.

In this article [5], five monocular depth estimation methods based on deep learning are compared, with a focus on their generalization capabilities rather than quantitative evaluation on a specific dataset. The study reveals that these methods perform well on images resembling the training data, but may produce errors when applied to images beyond the training distribution. The methods are assessed using images with atypical perspectives or artistic renderings, and readers are invited to submit their own images for the assessment using an online demo[2] Also, this article [15] examines the use of Deep Learning approaches to estimate monocular depth from RGB images, exploring 13 state-of-the-art techniques and providing an overview of the relevant datasets. It emphasizes the significance of depth estimation in various applications and suggests areas for future research in this field.

2.4   Comparison Different Types of Content

Virtual museums provide their visitors with access to artworks and cultural heritage objects in the form of two-dimensional or three-dimensional representations. In addition to displaying these objects, virtual museums also use pop-ups and links to provide additional information and context to visitors [27]. In the study conducted in reference [9], experiments were conducted to investigate the impact of 3D digital replicas presented in point clouds on users' perception of physical details and spatial awareness of complex shapes. The results of the study provided valuable insights into how individuals perceive artifacts in the absence of physical touch or interaction. However, this type of content also has some disadvantages.

The criteria and the comparison of 3D and 2D content for cultural heritage objects:

1. **Realism.** This criterion concerns how accurately the content represents the physical features of the object and its surroundings. The advantages of 2D content include the ability to be easily stylized or abstracted for artistic purposes but may not represent the physical characteristics of the object and its environment due to its limited dimensions. In the meantime, the 3D content can provide an accurate and detailed representation of the physical characteristics of the object and its environment, but a high level of realism in 3D content can require significant time, effort, and specialized expertise.
2. **Interactivity.** This criterion refers to the user's capacity to interact with the object or its surroundings. The 2D content can be interactive, allowing users

---

to navigate through different views or layers of the image. However, it cannot provide a high level of interactivity, such as allowing users to manipulate the object or its environment while the 3D content can provide a highly interactive experience for the user, but it can be limited by technical and hardware constraints.

3. **Accessibility.** This criterion relates to the ease of access and experience for the users. The 2D content is easier to create, read, and translate, and it is widely accessible through different devices and platforms, but on the other hand, 3D content is more immersive and engaging, but requires more time and resources to create, can be challenging for certain disabilities, and may require more powerful technology.

4. **Flexibility.** This criterion assesses the capacity to customize and manipulate the content. The 2D content is more lightweight and easier to manipulate than 3D content, allowing for quick changes to be made, but it's less flexible compared to 3D content which allows for a wide range of customization and manipulation. At the same time, the customization of 3D content can be quite time-consuming.

5. **Immersion.** This criterion relates to the degree to which the content can engage the user and create a sense of presence. The 2D content may be more suitable for some types of content, such as historical documents or photographs, but may not be as immersive as 3D content due to its limited representation of space and environment. The 3D objects can provide a highly immersive experience for the user, creating a strong sense of presence and allowing users to explore the object and its environment.

6. **Technical requirements.** This criterion examines the hardware and software requirements needed to view and access the content. The 2D requires less powerful hardware and software to access and view, but 3D can take full advantage of more powerful hardware and software, resulting in a more visually impressive experience.

7. **Data acquisition and processing.** This criterion concerns the methods used to acquire and process information about cultural heritage objects. The 2D is generally less complex and time-consuming, but may not provide the same level of detailed information as 3D content, which can provide highly detailed information about cultural heritage and objects, allowing for more accurate representation.

The utilization of 2.5D content can serve as a trade-off between 2D and 3D content for cultural heritage objects, in particular paintings, this type of content incorporates a limited, but some level of interactivity. In [21] paper, the authors proposed a 2.5D scene reconstruction for using in VR. This type of content can offer a more immersive experience than pure 2D content while being less technically demanding and less expensive to produce than full 3D content. Nevertheless, the interactivity and customization potential of 2.5D content may be less than that of 3D, and the overall experience may be less immersive and realistic. Nonetheless, 2.5D can be a reasonable compromise between the two extremes, providing a more engaging and informative experience without the high expenses and technical requirements linked with complete 3D content.

3   Methodology

3.1   Terminology

A *depth map* is a 2D image that contains information about the distance of objects in a scene. It is used in computer vision and graphics applications to create 3D models of the scene or enable depth-based effects. Depth maps can be obtained using *stereo* or *monocular* methods. Stereo involves using two or more cameras, while monocular methods use various visual cues or specialized cameras.

3.2   Pipeline

In this section, we describe the following method to automate the process of creating 2.5D visualization of artwork. The work process was divided into stages, such as Data acquisition, Data pre-processing, Extraction of the depth map, Data post-processing, and 3D visualization. The flowchart of the workflow is shown in Fig. 1.

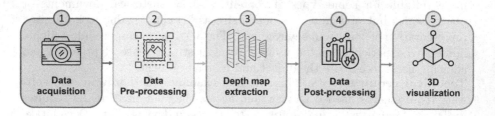

Fig. 1. The workflow of creating 2.5D visualization of artwork

Data Acquisition. Preserving and digitizing historical heritage is essential for ensuring that future generations can appreciate and learn from previous generations' rich cultural and historical legacy. The Marche region in Italy has significant cultural treasures, but it is threatened by earthquakes, the most recent destructive events having occurred in 1997 and 2016. The loss of historical buildings, paintings, and artifacts underscores the importance of preserving and digitizing these treasures to guarantee their survival for future generations.

One crucial aspect of this preservation process is capturing high-quality digital images of paintings. In our study, we utilized this method to acquire high-resolution images of eight ancient paintings from six different historical locations in the Marche region. By capturing the artwork frame-by-frame we achieved high-quality images that can be post-processed using image processing algorithms.

Image Pre-Processing. In the acquisition of digital images for cultural heritage preservation, image pre-processing is an essential step. For our study, image stitching was performed using specialized software called PTGui[3] typically used for panoramic image stitching. Proper alignment during the merging process is critical to avoid distortions in the final image. After obtaining the stitched paintings, adjusting brightness, contrast, and color balance was done to reveal hidden details and restore the original colors of the artwork. This technique is essential to produce a realistic and accurate representation of the artwork.

Extraction of the Depth Map. To extract depth maps from paintings, we utilized two approaches: the MiDaS neural network [23] and the LeReS neural network [36].

We selected the MiDaS and LeReS neural networks over state-of-the-art techniques for various reasons. One is that both networks offer open-source code, which facilitates their accessibility and implementation, promoting replicability and further research development. Also, these models require minimal manual input, making them convenient for large-scale digitization projects. Additionally, they have demonstrated their effectiveness and reliability in several state-of-the-art papers as [23,36], confirming their suitability for our approach. Furthermore, these networks proved to outperform other models in terms of accuracy, precision, and computational efficiency, confirming their superiority for our proposed methodology.

Ranftl et al. [23] developed a technique to estimate depth in disparity space that considers unknown shifts and scales. They aligned the estimated disparity and ground truth using least-squares optimization during training and added a second term to account for imperfect ground truth in available datasets. This second term aligned the estimation and ground truth to have zero translation and unit scale, which improved the robustness of the training process.

The MiDaS network was trained using 12 different datasets, and the authors developed new loss functions that were invariant to dataset incompatibilities. The MiDaS network outperformed state-of-the-art methods in various settings and was subsequently upgraded to the MiDaS v3.0 DPT version [24], which uses the Dense Prediction Transform model. The final loss of the neural network included a multiscale, scale-invariant gradient matching term that made discontinuities sharp and coincided with the discontinuities in the ground truth. This term was applied in the disparity space.

Due to the varying depth ranges and unknown depth scales and shifts in the web stereo datasets, the authors developed an Image-Level Normalized Regression (ILNR) loss to address this issue. They also proposed a Pair-Wise Normal Regression (PWN) loss to enhance local geometric features, incorporating both planes and edges in their sampling approach. The surface normal was derived from the reconstructed 3D point cloud through local least squares fitting [35], with predicted depth aligned to ground truth depth through least squares fitting and a scale and shift factor [23]. The authors sampled paired points on both

---

[3] PTGui official website: https://ptgui.com/.

sides of edges, and on the same plane if planar regions were present, leading to an average of 100,000 paired points per training sample. Additionally, they utilized a structure-guided ranking loss inspired by [32] to refine edge sharpness.

Using these two solutions we get a depth map in the form of an image.

Data Post-Processing. We evaluated the performance of MiDaS and LeReS networks in creating depth maps of pictures using various metrics. More detailed information will be provided in the following Sect. 3.4. Since there is no truth data for the paintings, we compared the results obtained with these approaches to the manually generated sample.

Visualization. As a means of visualization, we used a Web tool (Depth player[4] which takes as input the original image and a depth map. The 3D model is produced through central/perspective projection, using the camera center as the projection center and the focal length as the distance between the image plane and the camera center. A ray is traced from the camera center through each 2D point in the reference image to determine the 3D points, with their position along the ray determined by the depth map. Knowledge of the near and far planes along the principal axis, which goes through the camera and image center, as well as the focal length, is necessary to scale the model accurately. The 3D scene is contained within a pyramid whose four side edges pass through the camera center and a corner of the reference image. Depth Player provides three display modes: Solid, Point Cloud, and Wireframe. There are several adjustable parameters such as Focal Distance, Near Plane, Far Plane, Smooth Mesh, Quad Size, Point Size, and Downsampling. For the 3D scene to be as realistic as possible, the focal distance, near plane, and far plane must be adjusted correctly.

3.3 Paintings and Digitizing Process Features

When it comes to the digitizing process of paintings, there are several peculiarities to consider. Firstly, paintings are 2D images, which means that they don't inherently contain depth information. Secondly, paintings can be made in different styles, such as impressionism or cubism, which can distort the perspective, shape, and size of objects within the image, also because of the artist's worldview. All these factors can make it a challenge to extract an accurate depth map from the image.

Furthermore, digitizing a painting often involves using photographic equipment to capture the image. This introduces additional challenges, as the lighting and angle of the photograph can impact the quality and accuracy of the digitized image. For instance, if the photograph is taken at an angle, it may distort the perspective within the painting, making it more difficult for the correct extraction of the information.

---

[4] Depth Player official website: https://bit.ly/3nMJsk7),.

3.4   Evaluation Metrics

These are the commonly used metrics to evaluate the quality of depth maps. The metrics are divided into two categories: errors and accuracy. The error metrics include Root Mean Squared Error (RMSE), Average Log10 Error (LOG10), and Root Mean Squared Log Error (RMSEL), while the accuracy metrics include Accuracy with δ, Accuracy with δ^2, and Accuracy with δ^3. These metrics are widely used in computer vision and image processing applications to measure the performance of depth estimation algorithms. The equations of metrics are presented as follows:

$$RMSE = \sqrt{\frac{1}{N} \sum_{i=1}^{N} (\hat{y}_i - y_i)^2} \tag{1}$$

where N is the total number of pixels in the depth map, $\hat{y}_i$ is the predicted value, and y_i is the observed value.

$$LOG10 = \frac{1}{N} \sum_{i=1}^{N} |\log_{10} D_i - \log_{10} \hat{D}_i| \tag{2}$$

$$RMSEL = \sqrt{\frac{1}{N} \sum_{i=1}^{N} \left(\log_{10} D_i - \log_{10} \hat{D}_i \right)^2} \tag{3}$$

where N is the total number of pixels in the depth map, $\hat{D}_i$ is the predicted value, and D_i is the observed value.

$$\delta = \max \left(\frac{d_i}{\hat{d}_i}, \frac{\hat{d}_i}{d_i} \right) < 1.25^\tau, here, \tau \in (1, 2, 3) \tag{4}$$

where δ, δ^2, and δ^3 are threshold values that determine the acceptable error margin between the predicted and ground truth depth maps. d_i and $\hat{d}_i$ are ground truth and predicted value for the pixel ι, respectively.

RMSE measures the difference between predicted and actual values, and LOG10 measures the error in predicting the depth value. RMSEL is a combination of RMSE and LOG10, which provides a more complete measure of model performance. Threshold metrics estimate the percentage of pixels with an error below a certain threshold, which helps assess the network's ability to capture fine detail and subtle variations in depth.

Using these metrics, we were able to carefully evaluate the performance of the MiDaS and LeReS networks in creating depth maps of pictures. We chose the most appropriate approach for each picture based on its complexity and texture.

4   Preliminary Results

In this section, we present the results obtained by applying the described method. The approach was applied to two real-world pictures of different levels of complexity: low and high. They differ in the number of details, the overall composition, and the type of framing. The main difficulty for both paintings was the absence of the ground truth. To solve this problem, we used a manually made image based on the source as the ground truth. In the following subsections, we present the results of applying the method described in this article to two real-world pictures with different complexity and provide a table comparing the value of the metrics when using two different neural networks.

4.1   Case Study - Crivelli

"La Madonna Adorante il Bambino con angeli musicanti" is a masterpiece painted by Vittore Crivelli (Fig. 2), a renowned Renaissance artist from Marche. It has been a treasured possession of the Sarnano Municipal Art Gallery for a long time. The painting was created towards the end of the 15th century and is known for its ornate style, particularly in the Madonna's praying robe, which features a distinct design of a multi-petal rose with pomegranate, and the intricate patterns on the salmon-colored vestment that is trimmed with gold. While Cavalcaselle and Testi evaluated the work as modest, Luigi Serra referred to it as "one of Vittore Crivelli's most delicate and sumptuous works."

Fig. 2. The artwork "La Madonna Adorante il Bambino con angeli musicanti" by Vittore Crivelli (The image was obtained by processing data from our research team).

The outcomes of depth map extraction are presented here utilizing two neural networks, namely LeReS and MiDaS. Since there were no ground truth images

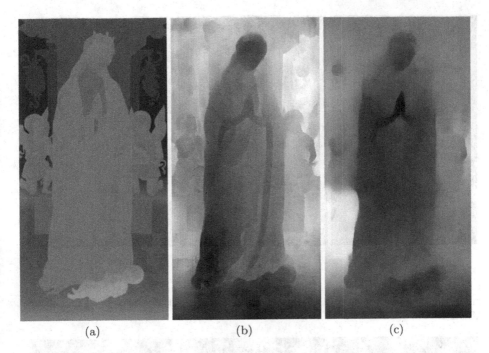

(a)   (b)   (c)

Fig. 3. Obtained the depth maps, where Fig. 3(a) is the baseline (manually made), Fig. 3(b) is the depth map by LeRes, and Fig. 3(c) is the depth map by MiDaS.

available for the pictures, it was determined that they would be created manually (as shown in Fig. 3(a)). However, it contains textures, which are not necessary to understand the spatial relationship between objects. Figures 3(b) and 3(c) display the resulting depth maps obtained using LeReS and MiDaS correspondingly. According to the current findings, it can be inferred that the depth map acquired with LeReS portrays a more detailed image, whereas the one obtained with MiDaS appears to be more blurred.

Typically, a depth map depicts the spatial relationships between objects in a 3D scene, with brighter objects indicating closer proximity, as illustrated in Fig. 3(a). However, to visualize the depth map correctly, it is necessary to invert the image, as demonstrated in Fig. 3(b) and 3(c).

Subsequently, the depth maps were employed in the 3D visualization process, which is demonstrated in Fig. 4. Even in the complete rendering view, there are noticeable incorrect distortions. One such distortion is evident in the enlarged images 5 where the hands appear distorted, thereby influencing the user's perception of the visualization. We aim to enhance the quality of the depth map, as it has a direct impact on the quality of the 3D visualization.

Table 1 presents the results of the depth map evaluation using the metrics described in the previous sections. The results of depth map estimation were evaluated using metrics including RMSE, LOG10, RMSEL, δ, δ^2, and δ^3 for LeReS and MiDaS. MiDaS outperformed LeReS in RMSE, RMSEL, LOG10, and δ. Both LeReS and MiDaS have similar performances in terms of δ^2 and

Fig. 4. 3D visualizations of the artwork, where Fig. 4(a) was obtained by the manually made depth map, Fig. 4(b) was obtained by LeReS, and Fig. 4(c) was obtained by MiDaS

Fig. 5. The enlarged view of 3D visualizations, where Fig. 5(a) was obtained by the manually made depth map, Fig. 5(b) was obtained by LeReS, and Fig. 5(c) was obtained by MiDaS

δ^3. It's worth noting that while the metrics show that MiDaS performed better than LeReS in most areas, in the meantime, the visualization of the depth maps generated by LeReS may look better than those generated by MiDaS, despite the metrics scores.

Table 1. Evaluation of the depth maps of LeReS and MiDaS

Metrics	LeReS	MiDaS
RMSE	0.343	**0.288**
LOG10	0.310	**0.308**
RMSEL	0.236	**0.207**
δ	1.119	**1.133**
δ^2	**1.254**	1.212
δ^3	**1.411**	1.407

4.2   Case Study - Monte San Martino

The "Polittico of Monte San Martino" is a tempera and gold painting on panel by Carlo and Vittore Crivelli, dating from around 1477–1480 and preserved in the church of San Martino Bishop in Monte San Martino, in the province of Macerata. The work was previously attributed to Vittore alone but later critics, including Cavalcaselle and Morelli, suggested that the work could have been a collaboration between the two brothers. The "Polittico" consists of two registers and a dais, with the lower register showing the Madonna and Child and four full-figure saints, and the upper register showing Christ supported by angels and four half-figure saints. The dais depicts the Redeemer among the apostles in small, arched panels that imitate a continuous loggia. The painting is presented in Fig. 6.

Fig. 6. The artwork "Polittico of Monte San Martino" by Carlo and Vittore Crivelli (The image was obtained by processing data from our research team).

The "Polittico of Monte San Martino" is an extraordinary painting that exhibits a remarkable level of complexity. This masterpiece is not only characterized by its intricate and detailed artwork but also by its ornate and complex frame, which adds a layer of intricacy to the piece. Due to the high level of complexity of both the painting and its frame, we decided to focus on the central part of the artwork to showcase the process of depth map extraction on a painting with such intricate details. The central part of the artwork is presented in Fig. 7.

          (a)   (b)

Fig. 7. The central part of the artwork "Polittico of Monte San Martino" by Carlo and Vittore Crivelli, where Fig. 7(a) is a full view of this part, Fig. 7(b) is the view without frame.

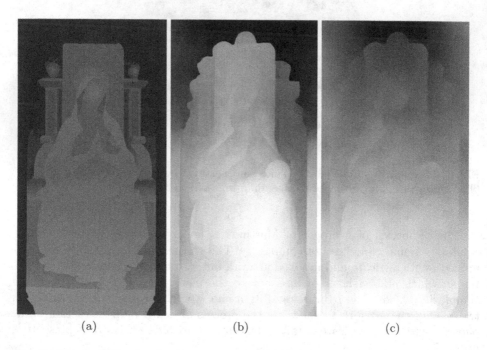

      (a)   (b)   (c)

Fig. 8. Obtained the depth maps, where Fig. 8(a) is the baseline (manually made), Fig. 8(b) is the depth map by LeRes, and Fig. 8(c) is the depth map by MiDaS.

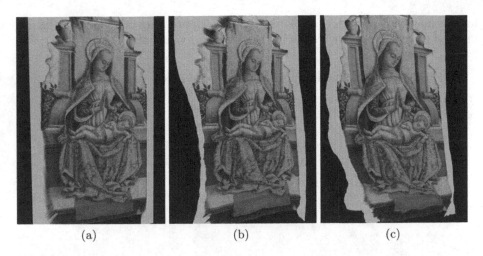

(a)   (b)   (c)

Fig. 9. 3D visualizations of the artwork, where Fig. 9(a) was obtained by the baseline (manually made) depth map, Fig. 9(b) was obtained by LeReS, and Fig. 9(c) was obtained by MiDaS

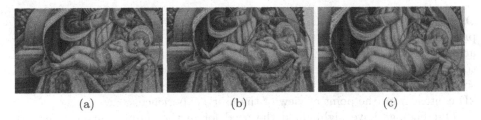

(a)   (b)   (c)

Fig. 10. The enlarged view of 3D visualizations, where Fig. 10(a) was obtained by the baseline (manually made) depth map, Fig. 10(b) was obtained by LeReS, and Fig. 10(c) was obtained by MiDaS

The painting has a high complexity with many details and a highly detailed frame, which can negatively affect image quality. To improve the outcome, it was decided to remove the frame before extracting the depth map and evaluating the results obtained. The artwork without the frame is presented in the Fig. 7(b). This approach can result in a clearer and more accurate depth map.

Table 2 presents the results of the depth map evaluation. For a second case we applied the same method, we obtained the depth maps which are presented in the Fig. 8, and 3D visualizations (Fig. 9). The resulting values for the evaluation metrics are similar to the values presented earlier.

Based on the given metrics and the enlarged portion of the visualization shown in Fig. 10, it can be inferred that the deep learning-based method employed in the context of visual arts may require further improvement. The metrics may suggest that the method is performing reasonably well, but the visualization reveals areas where the method may not be effective enough. Therefore, it may be necessary to explore alternative approaches or refine the current method to achieve better results in the context of visual arts.

Table 2. Evaluation of the depth maps of LeReS and MiDaS

Metrics	LeReS	MiDaS
RMSE	0.345	**0.275**
LOG10	0.275	**0.239**
RMSEL	0.218	**0.180**
δ	1.123	**1.127**
δ^2	**1.382**	1.325
δ^3	**1.603**	1.438

5   Discussion and Conclusion

Our research aims to enhance the experience of museum visits by presenting paintings in an innovative and immersive manner in 2.5D visualization. To achieve this, we have developed a novel method utilizing AI technologies applied to the digital copy of historical paintings, which allows for fast and automated solutions. We assume that it is a good compromise between using purely 3D or 2D content from the point of view of the user's experience.

Our findings have highlighted the need for further improvement in neural networks, and our future research will be guided by the latest technological advancements and the specific requirements of visitors and museums. Our ultimate objective is to simplify the process of obtaining 2.5D visualization, providing individuals with a fresh and unique way to interact with the artwork. In order to further improve the virtualization pipeline for paintings, there are two main areas of future research. Firstly, it would be beneficial to perform a usability study comparing our proposed AI-based method with established techniques such as, for example, anaglyph, to identify strengths and limitations and potential areas for improvement.

Secondly, it is important to investigate the impact of different visualization techniques, including high-resolution displays, auto-stereoscopic visualization, or VR, on the perception and interaction with cultural heritage artifacts in virtual environments. By exploring these different techniques, we can gain a better understanding of viewer perception and enhance the overall virtualization experience, making cultural heritage more accessible and engaging for a wider audience.

References

1. Depth predictions in art. https://storage.googleapis.com/art/history/depth/data/demo/index.html
2. Altınbay, R., Gümüş, N.: Social studies teachers' views on the virtual tour applications. J. Innov. Res. Teacher Educ. **1**(1), 60–71 (2020). https://doi.org/10.29329/jirte.2020.321.5
3. Chen, P.Y., Liu, A.H., Liu, Y.C., Wang, Y.C.F.: Towards scene understanding: unsupervised monocular depth estimation with semantic-aware representation. In: 2019 IEEE/CVF Conference on Computer Vision and Pattern Recognition (CVPR), pp. 2619–2627 (2019). https://doi.org/10.1109/CVPR.2019.00273
4. Chen, T., An, S., Zhang, Y., Ma, C., Wang, H., Guo, X., Zheng, W.: Improving monocular depth estimation by leveraging structural awareness and complementary datasets. CoRR abs/2007.11256 (2020). https://arxiv.org/abs/2007.11256
5. Ehret, T.: Monocular depth estimation: a review of the 2022 state of the art. Image Processing On Line **13**, 38–56 (2023). https://doi.org/10.5201/ipol.2023.459
6. Elkhuizen, W.S., et al.: Comparison of three 3D scanning techniques for paintings, as applied to Vermeer's 'Girl with a Pearl Earring'. Heritage Sci. **7**(1), 1–22 (2019). https://doi.org/10.1186/s40494-019-0331-5
7. Fang, Z., Chen, X., Chen, Y., Van Gool, L.: Towards good practice for CNN-based monocular depth estimation. In: 2020 IEEE Winter Conference on Applications of Computer Vision (WACV), pp. 1080–1089 (2020). https://doi.org/10.1109/WACV45572.2020.9093334
8. Furferi, R., Governi, L., Volpe, Y., Puggelli, L., Vanni, N., Carfagni, M.: From 2D to 2.5D i.e. from painting to tactile model. Graph Models **76**(6), 706–723 (2014). https://doi.org/10.1016/j.gmod.2014.10.001
9. Galeazzi, F., Franco, P.D.G.D., Matthews, J.L.: Comparing 2D pictures with 3D replicas for the digital preservation and analysis of tangible heritage. Museum Manage. Curatorship **30**(5), 462–483 (2015). https://doi.org/10.1080/09647775.2015.1042515
10. Giuliani, F., De Paoli, R., Di Miceli, E.: A risk-reduction framework for urban cultural heritage: a comparative study on Italian historic centres. J. Cultural Heritage Manage. Sustain. Dev. **11**(4), 499–515 (2021). https://doi.org/10.1108/JCHMSD-07-2020-0099
11. Guarneri, M., De Collibus, M.F., Francucci, M., Ciaffi, M.: The importance of artworks 3D digitalization at the time of Covid epidemy: case studies by the use of a multi-wavelengths technique. In: 2020 IEEE 5th International Conference on Image, Vision and Computing (ICIVC), pp. 113–117 (2020). https://doi.org/10.1109/ICIVC50857.2020.9177443
12. Huynh, L., Nguyen-Ha, P., Matas, J., Rahtu, E., Heikkilä, J.: Guiding monocular depth estimation using depth-attention volume. In: Vedaldi, A., Bischof, H., Brox, T., Frahm, J.-M. (eds.) ECCV 2020. LNCS, vol. 12371, pp. 581–597. Springer, Cham (2020). https://doi.org/10.1007/978-3-030-58574-7_35
13. Jin, S., Fan, M., Wang, Y., Liu, Q.: Reconstructing traditional Chinese paintings with immersive virtual reality. In: Extended Abstracts of the 2020 CHI Conference on Human Factors in Computing Systems, pp. 1–8. CHI EA '20, Association for Computing Machinery, New York, NY, USA (2020). https://doi.org/10.1145/3334480.3382934
14. Johnston, A., Carneiro, G.: Self-supervised monocular trained depth estimation using self-attention and discrete disparity volume, pp. 4755–4764 (2020). https://doi.org/10.1109/CVPR42600.2020.00481

15. Khan, F., Salahuddin, S., Javidnia, H.: Deep learning-based monocular depth esti-
    mation methods-a state-of-the-art review. Sensors **20**(8) (2020). https://doi.org/
    10.3390/s20082272, https://www.mdpi.com/1424-8220/20/8/2272
16. Kim, J.H., Ko, K.L., Le Ha, T., Jung, S.W.: Monocular depth estimation of old pho-
    tos via collaboration of monocular and stereo networks. IEEE Access **11**, 11675–
    11684 (2023). https://doi.org/10.1109/ACCESS.2023.3241348
17. Lee, J.H., Kim, C.S.: Single-image depth estimation using relative depths. J.
    Vis. Commun. Image Representation **84**, 103459 (2022). https://doi.org/10.1016/
    j.jvcir.2022.103459
18. Lee, J., Kim, C.S.: Multi-loss rebalancing algorithm for monocular depth estima-
    tion, pp. 785–801 (2020). https://doi.org/10.1007/978-3-030-58520-4_46
19. Liu, Z.S., Wang, L.W., Siu, W.C., Kalogeiton, V.: Name your style: an arbitrary
    artist-aware image style transfer (2022)
20. Pan, J., Li, L., Yamaguchi, H., Hasegawa, K., Thufail, F.I., Brahmantara,
    Tanaka, S.: 3D reconstruction of Borobudur reliefs from 2D monocular pho-
    tographs based on soft-edge enhanced deep learning. ISPRS J. Photogram.
    Remote Sens. **183**, 439–450 (2022). https://doi.org/10.1016/j.isprsjprs.2021.11.
    007, https://www.sciencedirect.com/science/article/pii/S0924271621003051
21. Park, S., Chon, S., Lee, T., Kim, J.: Toward the experiential VR Gallery using
    2.5-D. EasyChair Preprint no. 1091 (EasyChair, 2019)
22. Poornapushpakala, S., Barani, S., Subramoniam, M., Vijayashree, T.: Restoration
    of Tanjore paintings using segmentation and in-painting techniques. Heritage Sci.
    10(1), 1–6 (2022). https://doi.org/10.1186/s40494-022-00661-1
23. Ranftl, R., Lasinger, K., Hafner, D., Schindler, K., Koltun, V.: Towards robust
    monocular depth estimation: mixing datasets for zero-shot cross-dataset transfer.
    44, 1623–1637 (2022). https://doi.org/10.1109/TPAMI.2020.3019967
24. Ranftl, R., Bochkovskiy, A., Koltun, V.: Vision transformers for dense prediction
    (2021). https://doi.org/10.48550/ARXIV.2103.13413
25. Romão, X., Paupério, E.: An indicator for post-disaster economic loss valuation of
    impacts on cultural heritage. Int. J. Architect. Heritage, 1–20 (2019). https://doi.
    org/10.1080/15583058.2019.1643948
26. Skamantzari, M., Georgopoulos, A.: 3D visualization for virtual museum devel-
    opment. Int. Arch. Photogramm. Remote Sens. Spatial Inf. Sci. XLI-B5, 961–968
    (2016). https://doi.org/10.5194/isprs-archives-XLI-B5-961-2016
27. Tatlı, Z., Çelenk, G., Altınışık, D.: Analysis of virtual museums in terms of design
    and perception of presence. Educ. Inf. Technol. (2023). https://doi.org/10.1007/
    s10639-022-11561-z
28. Torre, S.D.: Italian perspective on the planned preventive conservation of archi-
    tectural heritage. Front. Architect. Res. **10**(1), 108–116 (2021). https://doi.org/
    10.1016/j.foar.2020.07.008
29. Wang, C., Lucey, S., Perazzi, F., Wang, O.: Web stereo video supervision for depth
    prediction from dynamic scenes (2019). https://doi.org/10.48550/arxiv.1904.11112
30. Wang, L., Zhang, J., Wang, O., Lin, Z., Lu, H.: SDC-Depth: semantic divide-and-
    conquer network for monocular depth estimation. In: 2020 IEEE/CVF Confer-
    ence on Computer Vision and Pattern Recognition (CVPR), pp. 538–547 (2020).
    https://doi.org/10.1109/CVPR42600.2020.00062
31. Wang, L., Zhang, J., Wang, Y., Lu, H., Ruan, X.: CLIFFNet for monocular depth
    estimation with hierarchical embedding loss, pp. 316–331 (10 2020). https://doi.
    org/10.1007/978-3-030-58558-7_19

32. Xian, K., Zhang, J., Wang, O., Mai, L., Lin, Z., Cao, Z.: Structure-guided ranking loss for single image depth prediction. In: The IEEE/CVF Conference on Computer Vision and Pattern Recognition (CVPR) (2020)
33. Xue, A.: End-to-end Chinese landscape painting creation using generative adversarial networks (2020)
34. Yin, W., Liu, Y., Shen, C., Yan, Y.: Enforcing geometric constraints of virtual normal for depth prediction, pp. 5683–5692 (10 2019). https://doi.org/10.1109/ICCV.2019.00578
35. Yin, W., Liu, Y., Shen, C., Yan, Y.: Enforcing geometric constraints of virtual normal for depth prediction (2019). https://doi.org/10.48550/ARXIV.1907.12209
36. Yin, W., et al.: Learning to recover 3D scene shape from a single image (2020). https://doi.org/10.48550/arxiv.2012.09365
37. Zamir, A., Sax, A., Shen, W., Guibas, L., Malik, J., Savarese, S.: Taskonomy: disentangling task transfer learning (2018). https://doi.org/10.48550/arxiv.1804.08328

Enhancing Accessibility of Cultural Heritage: Extended Reality and Tactile Prints for an Inclusive Experience of the Madonna Dell'Itri Church in Nociglia

Carola Gatto[1]([✉])(iD), Sofia Chiarello[1](iD), Federica Faggiano[1](iD),
Benito Luigi Nuzzo[1](iD), Ileana Riera Panaro[1], Giada Sumerano[2](iD),
and Lucio Tommaso De Paolis[1](iD)

[1] Department of Engeneering for Innovation, University of Salento, 73100 Lecce, Italy
{carola.gatto,sofia.chiarello,federica.faggiano,
benitoluigi.nuzzo,lucio.depaolis,giada.sumerano}@unisalento.it,
ileana.rierapanaro@studenti.unisalento.it
[2] Department of Humanities, University of Salento, 73100 Lecce, Italy

Abstract. This paper presents the partial development and implementation results of an ongoing project aimed at enhancing the accessibility of the Madonna dell'Itri Church in Nociglia (Italy), by means of different smart fruition tools. Thanks to a collaboration between the Department of Engineering for Innovation and the Department of Cultural Heritage of the University of Salento, along with the Municipality of Nociglia, the project aims to study and monitor the conservation status of the cultural asset, to enhance a smart fruition by means of eXtended Reality (XR) technologies and to improve accessibility of the site. This paper specifically focuses on the XR applications developed to achieve these goals, showcasing their potential to provide accessible solutions and improve the overall visitor experience, especially for individuals with special needs.

Keywords: Extended Reality · Accessibility · Virtual Restoration · Digital Cultural Heritage

1 Introduction

The digital revolution we have witnessed in recent decades has completely changed the paradigms of perception and enjoyment of cultural heritage. Technologies such as eXtended Reality (XR) are spreading ever more in contexts as museums, galleries and archaeological sites, so that visitors are learning how to use these new tools, in relation of their own needs. In addition, a multidisciplinary approach is required for designing and developing technological solutions that take into account specific needs for the fruition and the storytelling of cultural heritage, as the one that is described in this contribution. This is not a loss of authenticity, but rather an enrichment for each discipline that can multiply its own potential. The process that outlines the forms and methodologies behind this new approach to cultural heritage is known as digital transformation. The drive to utilize various forms of digital transformation in the cultural heritage (CH) sector can be traced back several decades. In fact, European Commission policies have explicitly emphasized the need to democratize resources of universal value by means of digitization, accessibility, and interoperability. This ensures the sharing of information and responsibilities to safeguard cultural identity and promote awareness. Digitization plays a pivotal role in disseminating knowledge, while the incorporation of immersive reality technologies presents an exciting opportunity to enhance accessibility to cultural heritage in a captivating and innovative manner [4]. Technological development has introduced substantial innovations that affect the faculties of accessing information and content. In cultural tourism, where the communication of tangible and intangible cultural assets has always been of primary importance, the new media and innovative technologies, often mutated from other fields, open up interesting scenarios of investigation. The topic related to XR technology in the sphere of cultural heritage fruition intersects the huge theme of physical accessibility to heritage places on the one hand, since XR can restores the sense of presence, and the theme of sensory and cognitive accessibility, on the other hand. Visitors have the opportunity to explore protected natural or archaeological sites that could not be visited otherwise, to learn about places that no longer exist, or even to immerse themselves in a context that they could not personally visit, due to contingencies and limitations related to their personal sphere. Thus, technology is able to "break down" accessibility barriers for elderly travelers or those with motor, cognitive and sensory limitations. Several studies demonstrated the benefits of providing accessible solutions of fruition of cultural heritage, by means of XR technologies, for people with special needs [11]. This work presents the design and the first step of implementation of a project that is still in progress, called "Intra l'Itri". The project aims at enhancing and developing the accessibility of the Madonna dell'Itri Church in Nociglia (Italy). This Church has a very ancient pictorial palimpsest, the first layers of which are either unreadable or extremely lacunar, as well as the multiple structural alterations that attest to the alternate historical events to which the church has been subjected. The project, funded by the Salento Interprovincial University Consortium (Cuis), involves the Department of Engineering for Innovation and the Department of Cultural Heritage of the University of Salento, along with the Municipality of Nociglia (Lecce, Italy). The project aims to study and monitor the conservation status of frescoes and structure of the Church, enhance smart fruition of the cultural asset, improve accessibility in terms of visitor experience, and promote the local identity through dissemination activities. This paper is focused on the smart fruition and accessible set-up for the Church, in particular on XR applications developed to achieve these goals. The paper is structured as follows: Sect. 2 provides a brief overview of the state of the art in XR (eXtended Reality) and accessibility for cultural heritage, Sect. 3 provides a detailed description of the project's objectives and design, Sect. 4 describes the implementation status of Augmented Reality (AR) and Virtual Reality (VR) applications developed for the Church, Sect. 5 describes the tactile setup based on 3D printing of the digital model for visually impaired accessibility, and finally, Sect. 6 outlines the conclusions and future developments of the project.

2 Related Work

Nowadays, the discussion about the dissemination of information related to cultural heritage digitally reconstructed is increasing, enabling the development of immersive and interactive virtual experiences with the incorporation of cultural and art-historical identity values thanks to eXtended Reality methods [14,16,19]. The eXtended Reality refers to a group of technologies that includes Augmented Reality, Virtual Reality, and Mixed Reality. These technologies enable the creation of interactive experiences by combining real-world elements with digital content [13]. Augmented Reality overlays digital information into the real world, Virtual Reality creates a completely immersive environment, and Mixed Reality blends digital content with the real world, allowing interaction between the two. An innovative Mixed Reality application concerns the use of Virtual Portals, a technological medium that allows the transition from reality to virtuality, from present to past [10]. These technologies are increasingly being used both in the medical field [1,2,12] and in education [5], as well as in the cultural heritage sector to enhance the way people experience and engage with art, historical sites, museums, and other aspects of cultural heritage [6,9]. In this project we focus on the use of this technologies with the purpose of cultural enhancement and accessibility, specifically the use of photogrammetry for the virtual reconstruction of the Byzantine Church of Madonna dell'Itri in Nociglia. This virtual reconstruction gives us the possibility to develop the Augmented Reality application to enjoy and ensure a greater understanding of the pictorial apparatus inside the Church. Connected to the concept of virtual reconstruction, is the word 'digital anastylosis': anastylosis refers to the technique of restoring an artwork of historical significance, such as a fresco or a statue, by recomposing the original pieces of the work itself. Digital technologies come to meet the difficulty usually encountered by experts in reassembling parts of an artwork that may be degraded or mixed with other destroyed heritage items. One approach to digital anastylosis has been carried out in recent years by the SAFFO project for the 2D recomposition of frescoes, using the SIFT (Scale Invariant Feature Transform) method from a series of fragments [3]. A coeval case study can be considered the reconstruction of the frescoes of the Cathedral of San Venanzio in Fabriano [23], which involved 3D laser scanning, photogrammetry and 360 panoramic photos that provided the basis for the subsequent virtual reconstruction analysis. Thanks to this research work just mentioned, the possibilities on the part of Virtual and Augmented Reality to improve the specific visualization of frescoes are reconfirmed, whose details, symbols and allegories can best be visualized by the user thanks to the simplicity of a device, whether mobile or wearable, contributing to a quick understanding and easy enjoyment of what is being viewed. Less recent but no less important was the reconstruction of the frescoes of Etruscan tombs dating back to the 7th-4th centuries B.C., carried out by the Kessler Foundation with the "Etruscans in 3D", brought back restored in a virtual environment: surveying and 3D modeling work was carried out with the aim of digitally documenting and safeguarding Etruscan heritage sites through eXtended Reality techniques [18] [17]. The process of overlaying images before the degradation of a fresco, carried out for the recognition of the Saints painted in the concerned Byzantine Church, is comparable with the case study of digital restoration related to Antonio Palomino's frescoes made for the vault of the central nave of the Church of the Santos Juanes in the city of Valencia (Spain), which were partially lost due to a fire during the Spanish Civil War. A restoration simulation was proposed from the overlay of two black-and-white photographs before the fire, subsequently straightened and georeferenced, so as to lay the foundation for recognition of how the fresco originally looked [21]. Beyond the degree of immersiveness that Virtual Reality provides in order to bring to life a certain inaccessible heritage asset that no longer exists or needs to be safeguarded, Augmented Reality can also be employed for these purposes, and even better to provide a certain amount of information through a mobile device that is more accessible than a Virtual Reality headset. In the same direction as the AR application of this project is the AR application for the fruition of the Roman mosaic in Savignano sul Panaro, Modena. Not only mosaic floor ornaments but also murals, in this case frescoes, have been digitally implemented in their missing portions through 2D reconstructions, particularly geometric patterns [22]. The concept of virtual reconstruction is one of the cornerstones of our case study that follows the desire to ensure a greater understanding, even in 2D and through two-dimensional lines and colors digitally overlaid on the ancient frescoes of the Byzantine Church. By definition, we can certify that virtual reconstruction aims to enhance and disseminate the cultural asset, reinforcing its meanings and functions. According to the Seville Principles, Virtual Reconstruction is a digital process that uses "a virtual model to visually recover a man-made building or object at some point in the past from the available physical evidence of such buildings or objects, from scientifically reasonable comparative inferences, and, in general, from all studies conducted by archaeologists and other experts in relation to the archaeological and historical sciences" [20]. Similar to the process of identifying figurative elements that was carried out for the two-dimensional reconstruction of the frescoed Saints in the Bizantine Church, there is the research and virtual reconstruction of figurative elements of the proscenium of the Farnese Theater in Parma. In this case, the same procedure of digital scanning, outline delineation and definition of the color appearance of the elements was performed [24]. The desire to facilitate and improve the fruition and interpretation of frescoes through Augmented Reality is the basis of an AR application created for the Basilica of St. Catherine of Alexandria in Galatina: through a smartphone or tablet, the user will be able to interact with the frescoes through clickable points of interest, frame the frescoes and receive musical and artistic information related to the framed portion of the fresco [7].

3   The "Intra L'Itri" Project

3.1   Aim and Methodology

The Byzantine Church of Madonna dell'Itri in Nociglia is a small building probably built between the 10th and 11th centuries. The monument's history is linked
to the broader and more complex history of the Terra d'Otranto, which between
the 15th and 16th centuries was the protagonist of important historical events
with the East, such as the taking of Otranto and the Battle of Lepanto. This
historical interweaving is visible on the pictorial palimpsest of the Church walls,
which counts up to six layers of frescoes that are difficult to read and dated
from the mid 11th century to the 16th century. Moreover, direct evidence of the
historical events that affected the building can also be found in the architectural structure of the Church, which has been altered by interventions over the
centuries that have modified its original structure. Therefore, the project aims
to improve the interpretation of the Church's interior paintings and the original
structure of the building by exploiting new technologies for the valorisation of
cultural heritage and based on a solid foundation of scientific data. The objective
is to narrate the historical phases of the building, highlighting its history and
historical-artistic relevance through a smart fruition involving not only the local
community but also the visitor and occasional tourist. Furthermore, the project
pays special attention to accessibility, through the adoption of specific measures
and technological solutions to guarantee an inclusive experience for users with
disabilities. In order to face these challenges, the project intends to decline into
the following specific objectives:

- Deepening knowledge of the building through a series of actions aimed at
  enhancing awareness of the structure and its decorative elements;
- Monitoring the state of conservation of the Church and its frescoes over time,
  identifying any changes or deterioration at both a structural and pictorial
  level. This allows timely intervention to preserve the building and prevent
  further damage;
- Enhancement of the building for a smart fruition through the use of new
  technologies at the service of eXtended Reality, in order to be also disability-
  inclusive.
- Promotion of the territorial identity and the historical and artistic context
  linked to the building through the interaction with the associations operating
  in the area.

In the first instance, starting from a historical, architectural and artistic analysis of the building and a dedicated monographic study, it has been possible to
study the layers of the pictorial cycle and to recreate a three-dimensional model
of the structure through the technique of photogrammetry. Photogrammetry
is a discipline that uses photographs to measure and create three-dimensional
representations of objects or places. It is based on the technique of analyzing
images from different perspectives in order to extract accurate geometric information [15]. The digitisation of the model has a threefold purpose: on the one

hand, the creation of a virtual environment for the Virtual Reality application usable with the Meta Quest 2 headset; on the other hand, the 3D printing of the photogrammetric model obtained, in order to create a tactile equipment for users with partial or total visual disability. Finally, the 3D reproduction of the environment is useful to manage and monitor any collapse or damage to the preparatory layers of the frescoes to be promptly reported to the conservation authorities. In this sense, one of the objectives of the project is to ensure the long-term preservation of the building, maintaining its historical and architectural integrity, but also making it functional and adapted to the needs of all. This ensures that the building continues to play its original role, contributing to the enhancement of cultural heritage and the visitor experience. Two different technological solutions are adopted to provide detailed information about the building and make the visit more engaging, smart and educational. The Augmented Reality application focuses more on the paintings, highlighting the chronological sequences of the layers of frescoes and their iconography. The Virtual Reality application offers a simplified and immersive reading not only of the pictorial cycle but also of the Church's architecture, enriched with historical photos that relate the building to its evolution over time and to other contemporary Churches in the area. In summary, the project is focused on using eXtended Reality technologies in order to study and preserve the building, offer an immersive experience to visitors, and disseminate the history and importance of the Church. The ultimate goal is to create a friendly, educational and inclusive experience that allows people of different ages, backgrounds and abilities to appreciate and understand the beauty and history of the Byzantine Church of Madonna dell'Itri. The next paragraphs will describe in more detail the design of the Augmented and Virtual Reality application experience, the development of both applications, although currently at an early prototyping stage, the tactile equipment with 3D prints of the Church and some details of the sculptures.

3.2   Visitor Experience Design

In order to succeed in opening up the Church of Madonna dell'Itri to the greatest number of visitors and thus improve the experience for all types of public, different dissemination, valorisation and smart-fruition devices have been investigated. The project is based on a strategy that combines XR applications, NFC sensors and tactile set-up. In particular, two panels are to be installed inside the Church that can be suitable for any visitor, ensuring an inclusive visit also for users with different disabilities. Indeed the each text on the panel will be accompanied by a Braille translation and an image with strokes in relief, to enable the visually impaired and blind to understand the shapes described in the text. The panels will be installed at a height that allows them to be consulted by any type of user, whether a child, an adult in a wheelchair or a standing user. Two printed catalogues, carefully studied in their visual design and storytelling, will be placed inside the structure: the first will be an art-historical catalogue in which the pictorial apparatus running along the walls of the Church will be described, accompanying the text with detailed images; the second, on the other hand, will be a tactile catalogue dedicated to the blind or visually impaired, with pages in Braille language and others with relief outlines of the frescoes pertaining to different periods. Both the physical panels and the catalogues will be connected to an Augmented Reality application that is currently under development: this connection will be possible through NFC tags and QR Codes. These two technological tools, once the phone is brought close to the NFC tag or the QR Code is framed with the camera, will activate the audio guides on specific themes and decorative elements, thus allowing for the acquisition of informative and descriptive information also through the sense of hearing. The Augmented Reality application, in fact, has been designed for being accessible and inclusive, giving all the information needed to understand the Church in each of its sections. In this way, both the visually impaired or blind users and the users who want to conduct a real guided tour inside the Church, seeing in front of them what is described in the audio, will be facilitated in accessing the property. Moreover, accessibility, thanks to the mixture of different media, both analogical and digital ones, will be guaranteed for all age groups wishing to visit the site, satisfying all needs and ranging from the most classic tools to the most innovative and technological ones, such as eXtended Reality and NFC sensors.

4   First Implementation: AR and VR Applications

In this section the current state of development of the project is provided, paying attention to the XR applications and the virtual restoration. In order to summarize, a brief overview of tools and software used for the development is now provided. Unity 3D (version 2021.3.8) is the application development engine that the developing team is using in order to implement both the AR and the VR applications. It offers a wide range of features for creating interactive 3D environments, managing user input, and integrating audio and visual elements. It is also compatible with multiple platforms, allowing applications to be developed for mobile devices, VR and AR headsets, and many other platforms. ARFoundation is a framework built into Unity that simplifies the development of cross-platform AR applications. It offers a set of tools and features for managing AR, including detecting and tracking planes, positioning virtual objects in space, and interacting with their surroundings. Using ARFoundation allowed us to develop the AR application more efficiently and with code that can be shared across different platforms. Metashape (formerly known as PhotoScan) is the photogrammetry software used for creating the 3D model of the entire building, starting from a series of photographs. This software processes the images and identifies common points between them to calculate the geometry and position of the points in the three-dimensional model. Blender is the 3D modeling and animation software, used in this work for cleaning up and arranging the model obtained from photogrammetry. The use of these two pieces of software thus led to the three-dimensional reconstruction of the small Church of Madonna dell'Itri, providing an accurate basis for the immersive application and the subsequently printed model. These software and technologies represent an excellent combination for the development of immersive and interactive XR applications.

In the following paragraphs we describe more in detail the Augmented Reality application, the Virtual Realty application and the Virtual Restoration campaign.

4.1 Augmented Reality Application

The first application, based on Augmented Reality, allows visitors to use a mobile device to view overlapping layers on the Church's original fresco. The development makes use of Unity3D as cross platform engine, while AR Foundation 4.2.7 and NFC Plugin 5.1.1 are exploited to handle the Augmented Reality features. In addition to the fruition of the augmented content on the frescoes, the application allows to manage through the scanning of NFC tags and QR Codes the start of audio tracks describing the work that is being observed. The implementation of these technologies is designed to facilitate the understanding and management of audio content for visually impaired and blind individuals. In the AR mode, the application provides a simple slider, that allow the user to switch between different layers, such as:

- Historical archival photos: users can see how the fresco looked before the physical restoration, allowing them to appreciate how it has evolved over time and any changes it has undergone.
- Reconstructed profile of the depicted figure: through AR, it is possible to view a reconstructed digital profile of the figure painted on the fresco, offering a better understanding of the characteristics and details of the subject.
- Digital restoration of the pictorial layer: one of the overlapping layers can represent a digital restoration of the fresco, in which the original colors are restored and damaged or faded parts are digitally reconstructed, restoring the original beauty of the work (Fig. 1).

This makes it possible to "explore" the fresco in a different way and to have a more complete understanding of the artwork.

4.2 Virtual Reality Application

The second application, based on Virtual Reality, offers an immersive virtual tour experience of the Church. Using a VR headset such as the Meta Quest 2, users can explore a photogrammetric reconstruction of the building. As with the AR application, Unity 3D has been chosen for development while XR Interaction Toolkit 2.3.2 and XR Plugin Management 4.2.0 are exploited to manage the virtual reality features. Using Unity XR Interaction Toolkit, it is possible to implement interactions within the virtual environment. In particular, to enable users to interact with buttons that give access to a variety of multimedia content, the application makes use of the Gaze Interactor. This mechanism is based on raycast tracking, which allows the user to interact with visual elements simply by looking at them, without the need to use controllers. Through the Gaze Interactor, users can direct their gaze to a button to activate it and access

Fig. 1. The slider with the digital restoration of the pictorial layer in the AR experience.

related information. This camera direction-based interaction method provides an intuitive and accessible experience without the need to use controllers. In addition, to foster a better understanding of the building's construction phases, users have the option to "go back in time" and see the Church in its original form, devoid of modern additions. As users navigate through the building and interact with the frescoes, they are provided with textual, audio and image information

Fig. 2. The Virtual Restoration of the "Saint Cesarea" fresco, as it can be seen from Meta Quest 2.

describing the works and architectural elements that are still visible but barely decipherable. This provides an immersive learning experience, allowing users to learn about the history and importance of the building. The user, dropped into the historical reconstruction, can move freely within the virtual scenario by teleporting through a series of placeholder footprints scattered along the floor. Interacting with them, in fact, accesses a teleport mechanism that allows the user to shift his point of view in accordance with the frescoes or architectural elements he or she decides to investigate. Once he/she has arrived at the chosen point, he or she can have access to a series of multimedia contents (audio tracks, comparison images and text descriptions) that will be added to that point of interest (Fig. 2).

4.3   Virtual Restoration

In order to proceed with the Virtual Restoration, the first stage of the work was the study of the intricate decorative palimpsest of the walls and the identification of some frescoes of interest. Thanks to Virtual Restoration it is possible to evaluate whether and how to intervene on the art-work without affecting it in any way, thus preserving its current state. The frescoes selected for the digital restoration are: for the Western Wall "Parasceve" (or "Paraskeva") Virgin; for the Northern Wall "Praying Madonna and Child", "Saint Nicholas", "Madonna of the Veil" and "The Holy Face (Mandylion)"; for the Southern Wall "Saint Anthony Abbot (or "Anthony the Great")" and "Saint Cesarea". The choice was considered on the basis of the material that was found for each fresco (bibliographical references and historical photos), the consistency with the storytelling identified by consulting with art historians, the artistic-historical importance, and the best state of preservation that would allow for more reliable integration hypotheses.

All virtual restorations were carried out by hand using the Wacom Intuos tablet. The tablet connects to the computer via the USB cable and its pen allows you to fully use the drawing functions of Photoshop, an Adobe Creative package software specialized in processing digital photos and images. The first step for the production of the Virtual Restoration is the creation of a new Photoshop document with the reference image, obtained from the high resolution photographic mapping and scanning of the stratigraphic reading levels of the pictorial palimpsest. The work was divided into several layers, so that the gradual reconstruction was at the same time ordered and consistent with the original. For this reason, the first level was renamed "Original"; for all the frescoes. For the reconstruction of the original painting has been used the Brush tool, with the Hard Tone mode. The colors used were obtained thanks to the Dropper tool, which allowed the detection of the exact color value of the selected area, in order not to alter the authentic one. In Virtual Restorations, it is very important that the reconstruction respects the original and that, therefore, no elements should be added, because of the historical and artistic inaccuracies that could occur. With this purpose, the intensity of the colors has been increased gradually, so as to respect the pictorial decoration at present but making the final image usable and understandable in the Augmented Reality application. Virtual Restoration is a process that goes step by step, to avoid the loss of continuity with the original. The colour intensity chosen for uploading to the AR application is 70%, which, thanks to the blurred effect, allows the user to read the authentic fresco. Missing parts of mural paintings are all hypothesis of reconstruction, and they are highlighted by brighter colours. For uploading to Augmented and Virtual Reality applications with 3D reconstruction, the images were saved with a .PNG extension, in order to respect transparencies and facilitate the overlap of the virtual reconstructions directly onto the corresponding frescoes.

5   Tactile Equipment and 3D Print

The tactile layout is a very important component of the project, as the accessibility of the content towards the visually impaired is one of the main goals of the project. Therefore, several solutions have been studied and designed to compose the visiting experience of a visually impaired person, thanks to the collaboration with "Centro Italiano Tiflotecnico", in Lecce. In the first instance, the project involves the installation of a model printed through a 3D printer of the entire architectural structure of the Church. This model will be printed in 1:8 scale and in PLA. The printed model will be installed inside the new Church that precedes the entrance to the old building and will allow tactile enjoyment of the architecture. Specifically, the interior walls will present the actual course of the wall texture, with the volumes of plaster and cavities. In addition, the sculptural apparatus composed of the statues of the saints and the altar will be printed. In the second instance, two descriptive panels will be installed inside the Church concerning the structure of the Church in general and the sculptural apparatus respectively, each one containing a brief description also translated into Braille and a reference image with relief-printed profiles. In addition, both panels will be equipped with an NFC sensor and QR Code referring to the audio description. Finally, a tactile catalogue will be printed which will contain only the pictorial apparatus of the Church, with a special focus on the frescoes digitally restored for the project. Each fresco drawing will be printed on paper in microcapsules, allowing the outline of the images to be raised, and supported, like the panels, by a Braille description and a unique NFC sensor and QR Code to launch the audio guide to the catalogue. All these three tools will allow in a complementary way not only a virtual but also a physical fruition of the Church Madonna dell'Itri by anyone with a visual disability, also widening the target of visitors and users of the designed experience.

6   Conclusions and Future Work

This paper presented the partial development and implementation of an ongoing project aimed at enhancing the accessibility of the Madonna dell'Itri Church in Nociglia (Italy). The strategy involved different smart fruition tools, based on the most modern technologies in the field of cultural heritage. Thanks to the collaboration between the Department of Engineering for Innovation and the Department of Cultural Heritage of the University of Salento, along with the Municipality of Nociglia, the project aims at: studying and monitoring the conservation status, improving the accessibility, enhancing a smart fruition by means of eXtended Reality (XR) technologies. In particular, a VR and a AR applications have been partially developed for these purposes, providing 3D contents acquired by means photogrammetry and 2D contents by means the digital restoration of the pictorial cycle. Furthermore, thanks to the tactile equipment, the project aims at improving the accessibility of the information to people with visually impaired people: the project involves the installation of a 3D model of the Church printed in PLA, two descriptive panels concerning the structure of the Church and the sculptural apparatus with Braille translation, relief-printed profiles, NFC sensor and QR Code referring to the audio description, as well as a tactile catalogue with the pictorial apparatus of the Church, with a special focus on the frescoes digitally restored for the project. The adoption of this specific strategy allows to guarantee an inclusive experience for users with disabilities. In order to face these challenges, the next step of the project intends to test the experience, once the development of the applications and the installation of the equipment will be finished. Specifically, we are designing the experimental phase in order to evaluate the efficacy and effectiveness of the applications that we developed. We chose to focus on informal learning, rather than on institutional education: while the latter typically takes place at school, the former leverages intrinsic motivations, such as personal curiosity, which make the whole experience a pleasant activity. We are going to use items taken from SUS (System Usability Scale), NASA-TLX (Task Load Index) and UEQ (User Experience Questionnaire), as in other similar case studies [8]. For the evaluation of the effectiveness of tactile equipment, we are working closely with the "Centro Italiano Tiflotecnico" for the design of the experience, so that at the end of the development, we start to plan and design with them the test phase, according to their evaluation standard.

In this way we will be able to evaluate the experience and to showcase the potential of the strategy in terms of impact on the visitor's awareness and accessibility, especially for individuals with special needs.

Acknowledgments. For the artistic consulting about the Madonna dell'Itri Church, we thank Professor Manuela De Giorgi, from the Department of Cultural Heritage of the University of Salento. Secondly, we would like to thank Professor Beatrice Stasi and Antonella Nisi, from the Department of Humanties from the University of Salento, for the elaboration of textual contents and storytelling. We also thank the Municipality of Nociglia, in particular Vincenzo Vadrucci, Pasquale Sancesario and Stefania Dragone.

References

1. Arpaia, P., D'Errico, G., Paolis, L.T.D., Moccaldi, N., Nuccetelli, F.: A narrative review of mindfulness-based interventions using virtual reality. Mindfulness **13**(3), 556–571 (oct 2021). https://doi.org/10.1007/s12671-021-01783-6

2. Barba, M.C., et al.: BRAVO: a gaming environment for the treatment of ADHD. In: De Paolis, L.T., Bourdot, P. (eds.) AVR 2019. LNCS, vol. 11613, pp. 394–407. Springer, Cham (2019). https://doi.org/10.1007/978-3-030-25965-5_30

3. Barra, P., Barra, S., Nappi, M., Narducci, F.: SAFFO: a SIFT based approach for digital anastylosis for fresco reconstruction. Pattern Recogn. Lett. **138**, 123–129 (2020). https://doi.org/10.1016/j.patrec.2020.07.008

4. Bekele, M., Pierdicca, R., Frontoni, E., Malinverni, E., Gain, J.: A survey of augmented, virtual, and mixed reality for cultural heritage. J. Comput. Cultural Heritage **11**, 1–36 (2018). https://doi.org/10.1145/3145534

5. Checa, D., Gatto, C., Cisternino, D., De Paolis, L.T., Bustillo, A.: A framework for educational and training immersive virtual reality experiences. In: De Paolis, L.T., Bourdot, P. (eds.) AVR 2020. LNCS, vol. 12243, pp. 220–228. Springer, Cham (2020). https://doi.org/10.1007/978-3-030-58468-9_17

6. Cirulis, A., Paolis, L.T.D., Tutberidze, M.: Virtualization of digitalized cultural heritage and use case scenario modeling for sustainability promotion of national identity. Procedia Comput. Sci.**77**, 199–206 (2015). https://doi.org/10.1016/j.procs.2015.12.384, https://www.sciencedirect.com/science/article/pii/S1877050915038946, iCTE in regional Development 2015 Valmiera, Latvia

7. Cisternino, D., et al.: Augmented reality applications to support the promotion of cultural heritage: the case of the basilica of saint catherine of alexandria in Galatina. J. Comput. Cultural Heritage 14 (2021). https://doi.org/10.1145/3460657

8. Cisternino, D., et al.: Augmented reality applications to support the promotion of cultural heritage: the case of the basilica of saint catherine of alexandria in Galatina. J. Comput. Cult. Herit. **14**(4) (2021). https://doi.org/10.1145/3460657

9. Cisternino, D., Gatto, C., De Paolis, L.T.: Augmented reality for the enhancement of Apulian archaeological areas. In: De Paolis, L.T., Bourdot, P. (eds.) AVR 2018. LNCS, vol. 10851, pp. 370–382. Springer, Cham (2018). https://doi.org/10.1007/978-3-319-95282-6_27

10. Cisternino, D., et al.: Virtual portals for a smart fruition of historical and archaeological contexts. In: De Paolis, L.T., Bourdot, P. (eds.) AVR 2019. LNCS, vol. 11614, pp. 264–273. Springer, Cham (2019). https://doi.org/10.1007/978-3-030-25999-0_23

11. De Luca, V., et al.: Virtual reality and spatial augmented reality for social inclusion: the Includiamoci project. Information **14**(1) (2023). https://doi.org/10.3390/info14010038, https://www.mdpi.com/2078-2489/14/1/38

12. Paolis, L.T.: Augmented visualization as surgical support in the treatment of tumors. In: Rojas, I., Ortuño, F. (eds.) IWBBIO 2017. LNCS, vol. 10208, pp. 432–443. Springer, Cham (2017). https://doi.org/10.1007/978-3-319-56148-6_38

13. De Paolis., L.T., Chiarello., S., De Luca., V.: An immersive virtual reality application to preserve the historical memory of tangible and intangible heritage. In: Proceedings of the 18th International Joint Conference on Computer Vision, Imaging and Computer Graphics Theory and Applications (VISIGRAPP 2023) - HUCAPP, pp. 279–286. INSTICC, SciTePress (2023). https://doi.org/10.5220/0011791400003417

14. De Paolis, L.T., Chiarello, S., Gatto, C., Liaci, S., De Luca, V.: Virtual reality for the enhancement of cultural tangible and intangible heritage: The case study of the Castle of Corsano. Digital Appl. Archaeol. Cultural Heritage **27**, e00238 (2022). https://doi.org/10.1016/j.daach.2022.e00238, https://www.sciencedirect.com/science/article/pii/S2212054822000273

15. De Paolis, L.T., De Luca, V., Gatto, C., D'Errico, G., Paladini, G.I.: Photogrammetric 3D reconstruction of small objects for a real-time fruition. In: De Paolis, L.T., Bourdot, P. (eds.) AVR 2020. LNCS, vol. 12242, pp. 375–394. Springer, Cham (2020). https://doi.org/10.1007/978-3-030-58465-8_28

16. De Paolis, L.T., Faggiano, F., Gatto, C., Barba, M.C., De Luca, V.: Immersive virtual reality for the fruition of ancient contexts: the case of the archaeological and Naturalistic Park of Santa Maria d'Agnano in Ostuni. Digital Appl. Archaeol. Cultural Heritage **27**, e00243 (2022). https://doi.org/10.1016/j.daach.2022.e00243, https://www.sciencedirect.com/science/article/pii/S2212054822000327

17. Fernández-Palacios, B.J., Morabito, D., Remondino, F.: Etruscans in 3D - surveying and 3D modeling for a better access and understanding of heritage. Virtual Archaeol. Rev. **4** (11 2015). https://doi.org/10.4995/var.2013.4324

18. Fernández-Palacios, B.J., Morabito, D., Remondino, F.: Access to complex reality-based 3D models using virtual reality solutions. J. Cultural Heritage **23**, 40–48 (2017). https://doi.org/10.1016/j.culher.2016.09.003

19. Gatto, C., D'Errico, G., Nuccetelli, F., De Luca, V., Paladini, G.I., De Paolis, L.T.: XR-based mindfulness and art therapy: facing the psychological impact of Covid-19 emergency. In: De Paolis, L.T., Bourdot, P. (eds.) AVR 2020. LNCS, vol. 12243, pp. 147–155. Springer, Cham (2020). https://doi.org/10.1007/978-3-030-58468-9_11

20. Pietroni, E., Ferdani, D.: Virtual restoration and virtual reconstruction in cultural heritage: terminology, methodologies, visual representation techniques and cognitive models. Information 12 (2021). https://doi.org/10.3390/info12040167

21. Priego, E., Herráez, J., Luis, Denia, J., Navarro, P.: Technical study for restoration of mural paintings through the transfer of a photographic image to the vault of a church. J. Cultural Heritage **58**, 112–121 (2022). https://doi.org/10.1016/j.culher.2022.09.023

22. Santachiara, M., Gherardini, F., Leali, F.: An augmented reality application for the visualization and the pattern analysis of a Roman Mosaic. IOP Conf. Ser.: Mater. Sci. Eng. 364 (2018). https://doi.org/10.1088/1757-899X/364/1/012094

23. Verdiani, G., Charalambous, A., Corsini, F.: Reconstructing the past, enhancing the traces from frescos: the case of the St. Venanzio Cathedral in Fabriano, Italy. i-com **21**(1), 19–32 (2022). https://doi.org/10.1515/icom-2022-0014

24. Zerbi, A., Mikolajewska, S.: Digital technologies for the virtual reconstruction and projection of lost decorations: the case of the proscenium of the Farnese Theatre in Parma. DisegnareCon 14 (2021). https://doi.org/10.20365/disegnarecon.27.2021.5

A Conceptual Framework to Support a New Collaborative Design Process for Immersive Technology Integration in Museum Exhibitions

Elena Spadoni(✉) 🆔, Marina Carulli 🆔, and Monica Bordegoni 🆔

Politecnico di Milano, Milan, Italy
elena.spadoni@polimi.it

Abstract. Immersive technologies are often used in museum visits due to their numerous advantages, including the possibility of enhancing Cultural Heritage dissemination, improving accessibility, and learning activities.

Despite the advantages, museum professionals may be reluctant to integrate immersive technologies during the museum visit due to their potential intrusiveness. In addition, a technology-driven approach is often used, which sometimes leads to scattered results and does not exploit the technological potential to meet the museum's objectives. Moreover, the design process for the creation of immersive exhibition visits is based on a trial-and-error approach rather than on specific guidelines regarding the use of immersive technologies in the museum context. The paper presents a study that investigates the immersive technology-related factors that influence the visitors' experience in museum exhibitions and the immersive technology awareness, benefits, and hindering factors perceived by museum professionals. Specifically, the study focuses on the occurring design process for the integration of immersive technology in museum exhibitions involving multidisciplinary professionals.

It presents mixed methods that include experimental case studies, online surveys, semi-structured interviews, and a participatory action research activity. The result consists of a conceptual framework for a new collaborative design process that aims to facilitate the design of immersive museum exhibitions and, consequently, to help museums achieve their objectives and improve visitors' experience.

Keywords: Immersive technology · Extended Reality · Design process · Museum exhibitions

1 Introduction

Museums serve as reference points for education, enjoyment, and dissemination of knowledge, and cover an important role in society. Nowadays, museums are facing a digital transformation, especially after the Covid pandemic, where different technological means are adopted for many purposes [1, 2]. Concerning museum exhibitions, immersive technologies, also defined as eXtended Reality (XR) technologies, are increasingly

L. T. De Paolis et al. (Eds.): XR Salento 2023, LNCS 14219, pp. 160–178, 2023.
https://doi.org/10.1007/978-3-031-43404-4_11

used to offering benefits for visitors in terms of engagement [3] and interactivity [4]. Several examples illustrate the capability of immersive technologies to enrich the visitor experience in museum exhibitions, as in the case of "The Modigliani VR: The Ochre Atelier" developed as part of the Modigliani exhibition at the Tate Modern Museum in London [5], where the visitor can experience a virtual recreation of the Modigliani's final studio. Another example is offered by The "Mona Lisa: Beyond the Glass" is the Louvre's first Virtual Reality (VR) project [6], which consists of an immersive multi-sensory experience in which the visitor can travel in time. Other successful examples are represented by the VR immersive experience "Dreams of Dalí" which was created by the Salvator Dalì Museum [7], and the Augmented Reality (AR) experience "Re-blink" which was installed at the Art Gallery of Ontario [8]. In addition, the Museo Nazionale della Scienza e della Tecnologia in Milan used AR to create an exhibition called "Leonardo Da Vinci 3D", in which visitors used tablets to explore Da Vinci's drawings and interact with them [9].

However, despite the vast possibilities offered by immersive technologies, given their complex adoption, museum professionals may perceive them as intrusive and face challenges in their introduction. Furthermore, the occurring design process for integrating immersive technology in museums, often involving multidisciplinary professionals, seems typically characterized by a trial-and-error approach, lacking specific guidelines.

This paper presents a study aiming to examine the immersive technology factors that impact museum exhibitions in relation to the museum's objectives and further explores the awareness, benefits, and barriers that museum professionals may perceive in their integration. Additionally, the research investigates the design process currently employed for integrating immersive technology in museum exhibitions. The result of the study consists of a conceptual framework that proposes a new collaborative design process to support museums in achieving their objectives through the integration of immersive technologies, enhancing the experience of museum visitors.

2 Research Context

2.1 Museum's Digital Transformation

Cultural Institutions are defined as organizations within a culture/subculture that work for the preservation and promotion of culture by S. Mariotti [10]. Museums are Cultural Institutions, defined as "not-for-profit, permanent institutions in the service of society that research, collect, conserve, interpret and exhibit tangible and intangible heritage …and operate and communicate ethically, professionally and with the participation of communities, offering varied experiences for education, enjoyment, reflection and knowledge sharing." [11]. This definition provided by the ICOM in 2022 underlines both the cultural and educational objectives of museums, but also their role and their strong relationship with society. In museums, the tangible cultural heritage, which refers to the physical artifacts and sites, and the intangible cultural heritage, which encompasses the practices, representations, expressions, knowledge, and skills [12], is presented to the visitor as traces that witness the culture.

Over the past few decades, museums have been actively embracing innovative methods and tools to enhance communication and knowledge dissemination. Digital and interactive exhibitions have become increasingly common, primarily due to their flexibility and effectiveness in engaging visitors, creating memorable experiences.

The museum's digital transformation has also been accelerated by the Covid pandemic limitations and restrictions. Cultural Institutions use technologies to digitize collections for visual culture for posterity [13], and to pursue their objectives of education, entertainment, accessibility, and exploration [14]. Museums are shifting from places of contemplation to places of representation and interaction, offering new experience modalities. In this context, it also emerges the concept of "Participatory Heritage" [15], in which the visitor becomes an actively involved participant, changing his/her role from a passive spectator to a co-creator of the experience and museum practices [16].

Among the different technologies adopted [17], immersive technologies are becoming increasingly common in the Cultural Heritage context to influence the User Experience, enjoyment, presence, and cognitive, emotional, and behavioral engagement at different levels [18].

2.2 Defining Immersive Technology

Immersive technologies are mainly discussed by scholars in the field of Computer Science, in which are usually identified as Virtual Reality (VR), Augmented Reality (AR) and typically associated with the Virtual Continuum of Milgram and Kishino [19], presented on a Mixed Reality spectrum (MR). Within the Virtual-Continuum framework, AR pertains to the overlay of virtual objects onto the tangible world; VR, on the other hand, encompasses fully displayed content within a virtual environment, and MR encompasses a range of applications that lie between these two ends of the spectrum [20]. Over the past few years, immersive technologies have frequently been linked with the more inclusive concept of Extended Reality (XR) that, according to Zhang [21], encompasses VR, AR, and MR and entails a virtual and fictional reality shaped and expanded by our tangible one. According to Suh [22], XR technologies have the potential to blur the line between the physical and virtual worlds and allow visitors to experience an engaging sense of immersion. Scholars often defined XR technologies by providing specific characteristics, such as sensory involvement [23] and user engagement through interactive real-time simulations [24, 25]. Similarly, many studies related to museums and art galleries emphasize the interactivity and stimulation of multiple human senses [26–28].

2.3 Museum Exhibition Design Processes

Concerning museum exhibition design, numerous studies conducted over the years have recognized the significance of focusing on the design process. For example, Davis [29] has analyzed the production process of an exhibition dividing it into six functional areas, which are: initial idea and development, management and administration, design, and production, understanding and attracting an audience, curatorial functions, and associated program planning. Dean [30] explored the exhibition development process by identifying five design phases: concept, planning and development, production, functional and presenting phase, and assessment stages. Mason and Vavoula [31] created a conceptual framework for the analysis of digital Cultural Heritage design practice along the dimensions of activity, tool mediation, and knowledge production.

In relation to the introduction of immersive technologies in museum exhibitions, a few frameworks have also been proposed. Some focus on User-Centered Design (UCD) methods to support the design process [32, 33], while other researchers have focused more on exhibition development aspects [34, 35]. A different approach is offered by Popoli and Derda [36], that identified a story-driven approach to expose the story through the immersive exhibition, focusing on storytelling. Among these studies, a prevalent approach is to emphasize the involvement of multidisciplinary professionals in collaborative co-design or participatory development processes [37]. In addition, the use of intermediary objects (such as prototypes) has also been pointed out to foster collaboration between professionals who bring different types of skills and socio-cultural backgrounds to the project [38, 39].

2.4 Existing Critical Gaps and Research Questions

While immersive technologies present various advantages for museum visits, they also bring challenges and limitations experienced by heritage professionals [40, 41]. As a result, these technologies are often incorporated into museum exhibitions on a temporary basis [42]. Some museum professionals seem cautious about adopting these new technologies, and as Leoni and Cristofaro [43] reported, some have explicitly declared their intention not to adopt technologies to remain consistent with their intimate relationship with visitors.

It is also frequently underlined the risk that new technologies can favor engagement and enjoyment purposes over educational ones, referring to a "Disneyfication" of the museum's offerings [44–46]. These aspects can be attributed to the prevalent technology-driven approach [47, 48] often adopted, which may not fully leverage the objectives of museums and the needs of museum professionals. As a result, there appears to be a trial-and-error approach in the everyday practice of integrating immersive technologies into museum exhibitions, and the design process sometimes seems to rely on inadequately structured guidelines. In some studies, scholars report innovative co-design processes in which technology is integrated to enhance the museum visitor's experience, as in the Mesch project [49]. However, many technological expedients are considered, not focusing only on immersive experiences. In other studies, where immersive technologies are specifically integrated, the focus seems mainly on technological aspects and rarely on the design process of the User Experience [50].

Starting from the analysis of the identified gaps, this study aims to answer the following research questions (RQ):

1. How do immersive technology factors and modalities impact the experience of museum exhibition visits in relation to the objectives of the museum?
2. What is the level of immersive technology awareness among museum professionals, and what are the perceived benefits and hindering factors associated with integrating immersive technology in museum exhibition visits?
3. What design models and processes are currently being employed for the integration of immersive technology in museum exhibitions?

The final output of the research is a conceptual framework for a new collaborative design process. The following section outlines the research methodology employed to investigate the aforementioned questions.

3 Research Epistemological Approach and Methodology

The research is conducted by adopting a pragmatic epistemological approach, which was defined as "a way of thinking about and making sense of the complexities of the real world" [51], in which the researcher can select the research design and the methodology that are most appropriate to address each research question [52]. The methodology adopted consists of mixed methods, in which elements of qualitative and quantitative research approaches are combined for breadth and depth of understanding and corroboration [53]. This methodology was chosen because the research encompasses aspects that are better suited for investigation through quantitative methods, such as those related to immersive technologies. Additionally, it involves aspects that are more effectively addressed through qualitative approaches, such as understanding the design processes that occur. In the mixed methods, induction, deduction, and abduction are used by researchers [54].

The research started by examining the scientific literature pertaining to museum digital transformation, immersive technology, and design processes for museum exhibitions. A summary of the findings from this literature review was presented in the previous section.

To focus the research, the scope has been narrowed to museums that encompass physical collections, thereby excluding immersive experiences where the technology serves as the experience's primary focus. This exclusion criterion also applies to artistic installations that do not prioritize physical objects as a means of showcasing culture. The rationale behind this exclusion is aligned with the research's objective, which considers immersive technology as a support for delivering culture and education rather than merely emphasizing engagement and entertainment. Then, different methods have been selected to address the three research questions.

Experimental case studies were conducted to investigate the first research question, related to immersive technology factors and modalities in relation to museum objectives. The case studies were tested with end-users through questionnaires for collecting data. The method selected to investigate the second research question, related to immersive technology awareness, perceived benefits, and hindering factors, consisted of an online survey submitted to museum professionals in Italy and abroad. The survey was considered a suitable method since it allows us to investigate and describe the incidence or prevalence of a phenomenon [55].

The third research question, concerning the understanding of the occurring design models and processes, was accessed through semi-structured interviews, organized with museum professionals and company experts in immersive technology exhibition projects. This method was selected as it enables the extraction of perspectives from the interviewee, facilitating the expression of insights regarding opinions, attitudes, beliefs, experiences, processes, and behaviors [56].

In addition, a concurrent participatory action research initiative was undertaken to explore immersive technology awareness and the design process in a real-world context.

This involved active participation in a project centered around the integration of immersive technologies in a science museum, the Museo Astronomico di Brera, Italy. Since the practical implication of the research topic, participatory action research allowed taking practice to legitimate knowledge that influences practice [57].

The activities mentioned so far aim to create a conceptual framework to support a new collaborative process for adopting immersive technologies in museum exhibitions and are described in detail in the next following sections.

4 Immersive Technology Factors that Impact Museum Visits in Relation to Museum Objectives

An initial exploratory approach has been used to explore the immersive technology factors that can influence the museum experience, involving designing and developing a series of experimental cases. In particular, some immersive technology aspects were identified starting from an initial literature review phase and explored in more detail with the implementation of practical experimental cases.

To facilitate a comparative analysis of specific elements, the cases were designed with a common structure but slight variations in certain variables. This approach ensured that the cases remained identical in terms of content and general experience while introducing small differences related to the identified elements for comparison. Two case studies were created, focusing on an immersive experience of the renowned painting "La Nascita di Venere" by Sandro Botticelli, exhibited at the Uffizi Gallery in Florence. The target user for these cases was adults.

The museum's objective concerning User Experience, engagement, and learning outcomes were chosen as the focal point for exploration. Two distinct immersive technologies were compared to examine their effectiveness in achieving this objective. The cases explore semi-immersive, multisensory experience modalities delivered via AR using a smartphone device and VR through a MetaQuest headset. Concerning the AR experience, a 60x90cm reproduction of the painting "La Nascita di Venere" was used to simulate a real museum setting. Notably, these cases do not incorporate collaboration or interaction means.

Starting from the definition of the narrative content regarding the selected painting, a storyboard of the immersive experience was defined and declined for AR and VR technology. Then, experimental case studies were developed using Unity 3D (https://unity.com/), a game engine that allows the development of interactive content in real-time.

4.1 Tests and Results

The experimental study was carried out within a controlled laboratory environment, involving a total of 20 participants (11 female) with ages ranging from 19 to 58 years ($M = 28.45$; $SD = 7.69$). The participants were evenly divided into two groups, with 10 individuals assigned to each group for the respective cases.

Demographic information, technology proficiency, and familiarity with the painting were gathered through a pre-experience questionnaire. Moreover, the initial knowledge related to the painting was accessed through a further questionnaire, presenting open-ended questions on the painting's content. After the experience, the participants were asked to compile two more questionnaires related to User experience/Engagement and learning performances.

The questionnaire on User Experience and engagement was formulated by drawing upon previous studies [58, 59]. It was developed by referencing similar works [60, 61] and integrating elements of Davis's well-established Technology Acceptance Model (TAM) [62].

The questionnaire presents seven sections: quality and engagement of the overall experience, playfulness, self-efficacy, information quality, perceived usefulness, attitude toward use, and behavioral intention. Among these sections, questions using a 7-point Likert scale, semantic differential, and open-ended questions were presented.

The questionnaire on learning performances presented six closed questions that were created based on the narration presented during the experiences.

The data analysis revealed notable outcomes for both cases, with the AR experience receiving higher evaluations in terms of User Experience/engagement, averaging a score of 6.5 out of 7. Additionally, the AR experience proved to be more effective in terms of learning performance, with 53.6% of the presented content retained. These results were derived from the delta value, which represents the difference between pre-experience and post-experience questionnaires assessing participants' knowledge of the painting content.

Considering the User Experience/engagement questionnaire, the VR experience was considered the most satisfying in terms of self-efficacy and perceived ease of use, as shown in Fig. 1.

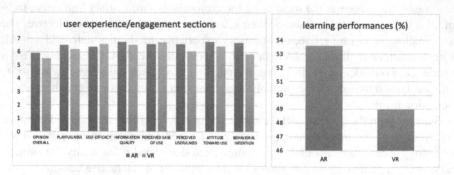

Fig. 1. Results of the two experimental case studies in relation to User Experience/engagement and learning performances.

Through the two experiments, we gained a deeper understanding of immersive technologies, various content representation approaches, and experience modalities in relation to User Experience/engagement and learning activities. These results have helped us define specific technical aspects of the conceptual framework.

5 Immersive Technology Awareness, Perceived Benefits, and Hindering Factors from Museums Professionals' Perspective

To pursue the objective of investigating the technology awareness and perceived benefits of immersive technology adoption, an online survey was administered to 24 museums (21 from Italy and 3 from America/Europe), without discerning the type (e.g., art museum, science museum). The list of museums and museum professionals that responded to the survey is reported in Fig. 2.

The survey included both closed and open questions aimed at understanding the opinion of museum professionals in relation to immersive technology and at identifying the possible hindering factors for their adoption. The questionnaire comprised five sections, starting with demographic questions to gather general information about the interviewees and their roles within the museum. The second section focused on assessing participants' level of technology awareness specifically related to immersive technologies. To avoid possible misunderstandings, immersive technology is expressively referred to as eXtended Reality (XR) technology inside the survey by providing practical examples in the form of pictures to the participants. The third section aimed at understanding if XR technologies were adopted in the museum institution in which participants work. If participants declared that the technologies had not been used, further questions were proposed to explore the possible hindering factors for the lack of adoption in the museum and to express their personal future perspective about a possible integration.

In the initial part of the fourth section, a specific question was included to identify individuals who had participated in projects involving the use of XR technologies to support exhibition visits. If the answer was affirmative, subsequent questions were primarily focused on gathering information about the project, the involved professionals and their respective roles, and the critical aspects of the process. Conversely, if the response was negative, participants were directed to another section of the questionnaire, namely the fifth section, which explored general benefits, hindering factors, and future perspectives regarding the adoption of immersive technologies.

Interesting results concern technology awareness, reporting that 7 people out of 24 "heard about immersive technologies but don't know them well", while 15 participants stated that immersive technologies have never been used in the museum institution in which they work. Participants pointed out the two main causes of the non-adoption, namely the cost and lack of funds and the lack of opportunities to integrate them in the current museum exhibition design. Other listed causes regarded operational difficulties and lack of qualified personnel. Particularly noteworthy is the reason indicated by one participant that declares that immersive technologies have not been adopted because of a "museological choice: no interference in the relationship between observer and objects." This answer reveals a negative perception concerning the adoption of immersive technology, defined as an element of "interference," and confirms one of the existing gaps regarding the reticence of some museum professionals in adopting these new technologies.

Concerning the fourth section, 12 participants declared that they had never taken part in projects in which immersive technologies were adopted. These participants compiled

Museum	Museum location	Professional role
MUSE- Museo della scienza	Trento, Italy	Cultural mediator
Acquario di Genova	Genoa, Italy	Marin Biologist and coordinator
Fondazione MAXII	Rome, Italy	Manager Centro Archivi Architettura
Comune di Palermo	Palermo, Italy	Executive
Opera di Santa Maria del Fiore, Duomo	Florence, Italy	Communication coordinator
Fondazione Musei civici di Venezia	Venice, Italy	Manager Ca' Pesaro
MaMbo-museo arte moderna	Bologna, Italy	Executive secretary
Mic- Galleria Borghese	Rome, Italy	Art historian
Museo di Geologia e Paleontologia-Università degli studi di Firenze	Florence, Italy	Curator
FAI-Fondo per l'ambiente Italiano	Milan, Italy	Responsabile Digital Marketing
Galleria Nazionale delle Marche, Palazzo Ducale	Urbino, Italy	Executive Marketing/communication
Palladio Museum-Centro internazionale di studi di architettura	Vicenza, Italy	Cultural executive
Museo Bagatti Valsecchi	Milan, Italy	Conservator
Muse civici di Varese	Varese, Italy	Communication
MAUTO-Museo Nazionale dell'auto	Turin, Italy	Restorer / Digital services
Fondazione dei Musei civici di Venezia	Venice, Italy	Educational manager
Fondazione M9-Museo del 900	Venice, Italy	Curator
Museo civico di Rieti	Rieti, Italy	Administrative
Museo Egizio di Torino	Turin, Italy	Curator
Labirinto del Masone	Parma, Italy	Museum operator
Sistema Museale di Ateneo-Università degli Studi di Firenze	Florence, Italy	Technical/administrative
The Metropolitan museum of Art	New York, USA	Senior Manager of Digital Product
NEMO science museum	Amsterdam, Netherlands	Project manager/ education developer
The Fine Arts Museums of San Francisco	San Francisco, USA	Manager of Visitor Experience

Fig. 2. List of museums and museum professionals that participated in the survey.

the fifth section of the questionnaire in which they were requested to complete a multiple-choice question to identify the factors commonly perceived as barriers to the adoption of immersive technology in the museum context.

The main causes identified regard a lack of funds (92%), lack of qualified personnel for integrating XR technologies in museums (66%), lack of XR technology knowledge in museums (33%), and lack of design methods for integrating XR in museums (33%).

Regarding this sample, the perception in relation to immersive technology's future adoption was accessed as well. In relation to the question: "Do you think that XR technologies will be used in a pervasive way in museums in the future?" most of the participants reported a positive attitude.

Furthermore, out of the 12 participants, 11 individuals expressed their belief that the integration of XR technologies can enhance the overall museum content experience. Moreover, museum professionals reported the following perceived benefits provided by the integration of XR technologies:

- Improving content offer and cultural heritage approach;
- The benefits depend on the public and content;
- Reconstruction and visualization of environment and artifacts;
- Inclusivity for people with special needs;
- Differentiate the public offer;
- Improving user interactions to approach younger targets;
- Granting success to more understandable content.

Based on these findings, it becomes apparent that while certain museum professionals are in favor of incorporating immersive technologies, the majority of participants have raised concerns and identified challenges in integrating such technologies. Some individuals have even expressed skepticism, showing a preference for more traditional museum visit experiences.

6 Occurring Design Models and Processes for the Integration of Immersive Technology in Museums Exhibitions

To examine the existing design processes and map the multidisciplinary actors involved, a group of 12 participants who had previous experience with projects incorporating immersive technologies were asked additional specific questions through an online survey. Subsequently, some of these participants were contacted for semi-structured interviews to delve deeper into various aspects of the design process. Moreover, professional

Museum	Professional role interviewed	Immersive technology project
Acquario di Genova	Marin Biologist and coordinator	Sala Abissi VR
Galleria Nazionale delle Marche, Palazzo Ducale	Executive Marketing/Communication	Improving experience and accessibility to Galleria Nazionale delle Marche through AR
Fondazione M9-Museo del 900	Curator	Game section with Oculus Rift
The Metropolitan museum of Art	Senior Manager of Digital Product	Chroma: Ancient sculpture in color
NEMO science museum	Project manager/ Education developer	MONA, Museopedagogy and Augmented Reality

Company	Professional role interviewed	Immersive technology project
Bepart	Cultural manager	La visione di Leonardo
Synergique	Designer	The Private World of Rembrandt
Boris Mika Associates	Project director/Architect	Invisible Worlds. AMNH, New York

Fig. 3. Museum and company professionals contacted for the semi-structured interviews.

experts from Companies that address the design and development of immersive technology in the Cultural Heritage field were contacted as well to better investigate the occurring design process. The semi-structured interviews were conducted online with 5 museum professionals and 3 professionals from companies, as reported in Fig. 3.

The questions addressed specific aspects of the design process, such as the duration of the process, the professionals involved, the design phases, and the tools and applications used.

Among the participants interviewed, 3 participated in VR projects, while 5 addressed AR projects. Only 4 interviewees reported previous involvement in other projects that integrated immersive technologies, and 3 claimed to possess a comprehensive understanding of immersive technologies before participating in the project. 4 participants stated that they had only a basic knowledge of immersive technologies, while 1 participant stated having no prior knowledge of them at all.

The design modalities that were identified by 2 museum professionals out of 5 were collaborative, while in the other cases, a non-collaborative/turnkey modality prevailed. Instead, all Company professionals reported that the process was the result of a collaboration among multidisciplinary professionals. The project phases identified by all the respondents can be traced back to 4 typical macro design phases: Research, Design, Develop, and Test. In some cases, a Prototyping phase is identified before the development one, and in other cases, the design and development phases are presented as merged, especially in the turnkey design modality.

All respondents reported one or more review moments in which the design and development progress has been verified by museum professionals. In the collaborative modality, these moments of sharing and definition seem very frequent, while in the turnkey modality, the reviews seem to happen mainly in the final stages of development. An aspect that was identified as of great importance by some participants, and that they would further improve if they were asked to repeat the process, would be greater involvement of the users throughout the process. This aspect was highlighted by many interviewees, even if 4 of them already indicated user involvement during the testing phase of the application, and 2 indicated user involvement throughout the whole design process. In addition, one participant stated that having to repeat the design process would devote more attention to the initial research phase, especially in relation to the definition of the target user and the objectives of the immersive experience.

The design tools adopted in the design phases were also explored during the interviews. The information provided by Bepart and the Metropolitan Museum of Art was of great interest in this sense. In particular, they referred to collaborative design tools such as brainstorming with Mural, writing in shared documents, questionnaires, games, and exercises that aim to create a solid relationship between professionals and increase confidence by creating personal sharing. In addition, the creation of initial prototypes was identified as useful, especially for testing the first solutions with users.

As for the design applications, all participants discussed that they had mainly used databases of online material sharing, such as OneDrive and Google Drive, and specific development or prototyping software, while some have also named collaborative online tools such as Miro.

A mail result of this phase is the identification of several macro-phases and models in the design process, highlighting the significance of collaboration among multidisciplinary professionals. Furthermore, various design tools and applications were mapped as supportive elements for facilitating this collaboration.

7 Participatory Action Research in the MARSS Project

Simultaneously, a practical study was carried out with the Museo Astronomico di Brera (MusAB), with the aim to investigate technology awareness and perception, the design process and tools, and the relationship among multidisciplinary professionals. The participatory action research activity took place within the MARSS (MusAB in Augmented Reality from Science to Society) project. The MARSS project was founded by Fondazione Cariplo and realized by INAF, the leader of the project, in collaboration with the Department of Mechanical Engineering of Politecnico di Milano [63]. The project regarded the design and development of an AR and VR experience to support the museum visit. Specifically, the AR experience provided two distinct narrative paths—one tailored for adults and another for children under 12 years old. The main objective of the AR experience was to facilitate interactive exploration of astronomy, enabling the museum collection to "speak" through the adoption of immersive technology. The design process for the AR experience involved a collaborative effort made by a team of multidisciplinary professionals. This team included astrophysics and science communicators from INAF, university experts specializing in virtual prototyping methods and technologies, external professionals such as a copywriter for storytelling purposes, and a technology provider studio.

The process followed for the design and development of the AR experience was iterative and consisted of four main steps: Research, Design, Develop, and Test. These macro-steps proved to be consistent with the ones emerging from the interviews. The authors played a significant role in the project, primarily focusing on contributing to the design, development, and testing phases of the AR experience. This involvement allowed for direct collaboration with all members of the project team. With the successful achievement of the project objectives, it becomes possible to leverage the collaborative approach employed and provide a critical analysis of key considerations that emerged during the design process. These considerations present interesting points for reflection and further exploration.

Regarding the attitude of the different professionals during the design and development, the following results are presented:

- a slight skepticism in trusting some considerations on aspects of the User Experience and communication modalities while maintaining a privileged view on the purely content aspects.
- difficulty in understanding at an early stage the difference between immersive technologies (e.g., AR, VR) and the associated possibilities of immersion and interaction allowed by the technological tools.
- difficulties in selecting and narrating content in relation to the specific immersive technology adopted, often treated as other technological means not fully exploiting its potential.

- initial attitude towards a less collaborative process, with a slight focus on the development phase, highlighting issues in communication and empathy.

8 Collaborative Design Framework for Integrating Immersive Technology in Museum Exhibitions

Starting from the analysis of the data collected, it was possible to define a first conceptual framework to support a new collaborative design process.

The framework consists of two primary parts. The first part is designed to facilitate the definition of the cultural immersive experience, while the second part is intended to support the overall process, as depicted in Fig. 4.

The upper section of the framework is primarily created on findings derived from the experimental case studies and surveys, while the lower section is more linked to the results of the interviews and the participatory action research conducted.

The *immersive technology* section encompasses:

- museum objectives related to the different target users (A);
- technological tools, which provide different experience modalities created by using different digital resources (B). The experience modalities include factors such as immersion, interaction, sensory stimulation, and collaboration.

The *Process overview* section is composed by:

- professionals involved in the process and their roles/mansions (C)
- characteristics of the design process (D). This section encompasses the various approaches, modalities, models, phases, tools, and applications that are potentially applicable in the design process.

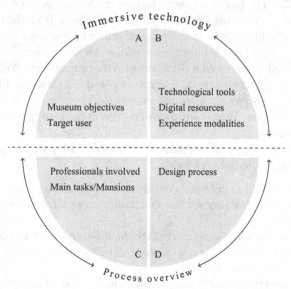

Fig. 4. Framework primary sections related to immersive technology and process. Each quadrant is explained in detail in Fig. 5.

Immersive technology			
A	**Museum objectives**	user experience/engagement learning accessibility exposition/exhibit	▲
	Target audience	adults kids	
B	**Technological tools**	*real environment* ↕ *virtual envoronment*	screen/smartphone/tablet kiosk projection headset
	Digital resources	audio track image/video 3D model/animation odors tactile stimuli	▲
	Experience modalities	**Immersion**	semi-immersive full-immersive
		Sensory stimulation	one sense involved senses involved separately senses involved simultaneously
		Collaboration (H-H)	no collaboration remote collaboration in presence collaboration collaboration human-avatar/AI
		Interaction (H-C)	no interaction basic activation digital gesture realistic gesture

Design Process		
C	**Professionals involved**	project manager/cultural manager expert in the scientific/umanistic field museum archivist/cataloguer museum curator artist designer educational manager marketing/comunication immersive technologies developer academic/researcher users
	Main tasks/mansions	contents production/evaluation user experience technological/technical aspects

Fig. 5. Conceptual framework sections and entailed elements.

D	Design process	Approaches	technology driven
			design driven
		Modalities	collaborative
			non collaborative
		Models	copy of exhisting experience
			focus on museum objectives
			exhibition design
			focus on physical artifacts
		Process phases	research ▲
			design
			development
			review
			test
		Design tools	brainstorming ▲
			workshop
			interview
			questionnaire
			sketching
			prototype
			collaborative games/activities
		Design applicatives	online database
			design software online
			prototyping software
			development software

▲ aspects that can be coexistent

Fig. 5. (*continued*)

The two sections of the framework are interconnected, as depicted in Fig. 5. Each quadrant of the framework represents distinct elements that can be implemented to facilitate the new collaborative process.

The sections presented in the first quadrant (A) allow for setting the objective and target of the experience as first requirements. Based on these considerations, the sections within the second quadrant (B) can be used to establish the immersive technological tools, digital resources, and experience modalities. These elements are grouped together as they often exert mutual influence. For instance, factors like immersion, interaction, sensory stimulation, and collaboration will be facilitated differently depending on the chosen technological tools (e.g., AR smartphones and projections offer distinct possibilities for experience solutions and digital representations). Once the objectives, target audience, and experience characteristics have been defined, the framework can serve as a guide for determining the key professionals involved and their respective tasks (C), as well as the specific attributes of the design process to be adopted (D). As previously mentioned, certain elements within these sections are interconnected, closely influencing each other (e.g., prototyping software can be used for creating prototypes).

Within the same section, certain elements can be chosen individually, being mutually exclusive of one another, while others can coexist simultaneously, as illustrated in Fig. 5.

9 Conclusion and Future Plans

This paper presents a study to investigate the design process for the introduction of immersive technologies to support the museum exhibition visit. Numerous research activities have been undertaken to explore the factors of immersive technology in relation to museum objectives, the perception of museum professionals, potential benefits, and obstacles, as well as the design processes that facilitate their adoption.

To address the first research question (RQ), experimental cases utilizing Augmented Reality (AR) and Virtual Reality (VR) have been used to examine their impact on User Experience, Engagement, and Learning objectives within the museum context. The results showed that both technologies are successful in meeting these objectives, with a slight preference for AR technology in relation to both the User Experience/engagement and Learning objectives. Given the time restriction, this activity presents some limitations that will lead to the future development of further case studies to explore more immersive experience solutions and encompass more museum objectives.

To address the second RQ, the survey results indicate that while most museum professionals have a good understanding of immersive technologies, only a small number of them have been actually implemented, suggesting limited practical experience. This could be attributed to a preference for ready-made solutions during initial adoption attempts. In addition, several obstacles have been identified, including insufficient funding and limitations within the museum infrastructure. Additionally, a lack of technological expertise and integration methods have been cited as well. Although the potential for future introduction is positive, some skepticism is confirmed in the adoption of immersive technologies, also perceived as possible interference during the visit.

In relation to the third RQ, the results from the interviews show mainly two occurring design processes: collaborative or non-collaborative/turnkey. Few collaborative processes offer interesting reflections, mainly concerning activities that aim to create a relationship and establish trust between multidisciplinary professionals.

Starting from the collected data, a conceptual framework, which encompasses both immersive technology and design process aspects, has been designed as a support for a new collaborative process. As future advancements, guidelines will be established using the framework as a basis, aiming to support the collaborative design process. These guidelines will concentrate on specific aspects, primarily intending to:

- Increase the technological positive attitude regarding the possibilities of immersive technologies in relation to museum objectives;
- stimulate the collaboration among the multidisciplinary professionals from the early stages of the project by providing collaborative tools to adopt during the process;
- promote communication among actors by setting a common language on different levels, such as content, User Experience, and technological characteristics.

Subsequently, the experimental tool, based on the framework and guidelines, will be developed and introduced to multidisciplinary professionals through focus groups. This activity will aim to understand the possible improvements to finalize the framework and guidelines and verify their effectiveness in supporting the new collaborative design process in different museum contexts and with multidisciplinary professionals.

Furthermore, the framework and guidelines have the potential to be utilized in the future for the design and development of an actual immersive museum experience, serving as a valuable resource.

References

1. Yuce, A.: Digital transformation-oriented innovation in museum settings via digital engagement: virtual reality. In: Bifulco, F., Tregua, M. (eds.) Handbook of Research on Museum Management in the Digital Era:, pp. 248–264. IGI Global (2022). https://doi.org/10.4018/978-1-7998-9656-2.ch013
2. Kang, Y., Yang, K.C.C.: Framing digital reality technology applications among museums during COVID-19 pandemic: a comparative text mining research. In: Pillai, A.S., Guazzaroni, G. (eds.) Extended Reality Usage During COVID 19 Pandemic, pp. 109–125. Springer International Publishing, Cham (2022). https://doi.org/10.1007/978-3-030-91394-6_8
3. He, Z., Wu, L. and Li, X.: When art meets tech: the role of augmented reality in enhancing museum experiences and purchase intentions. Tour. Manage. (2018)
4. Han, D.-I., tom Dieck, C., Jung, T.: Augmented Reality Smart Glasses (ARSG) visitor adoption in cultural tourism. Leisure Stud. **38**(5), 628–633 (2019)
5. TATE, Modigliani VR: The Ochre Atelier. https://www.tate.org.uk/whats-on/tate-modern/modigliani/modigliani-vr-ochre-atelier. Accessed 1 May 2023
6. Louvre, Mona Lisa: Beyond the Glass. https://www.louvre.fr/en/what-s-on/life-at-the-museum/the-mona-lisa-in-virtual-reality-in-your-own-home. Accessed 1 May 2023
7. The Dalì, Dreams of Dalì. https://thedali.org/dreams-of-dali-2/. Accessed 1 May 2023
8. AGO (Art Gallery Ontario), Reblink. https://ago.ca/exhibitions/reblink. Accessed 1 May 2023
9. Leonardo Da Vinci 3D. Interactive, immersive experience. https://www.arte.it/leonardo/mostra/leonardo-da-vinci-3d-immersive-interactive-experience-60323. Accessed 1 May 2023
10. Mariotti, S.: Gamifying cultural heritage. education, tourism development, and territory promotion: two Italian examples. In: Handbook of Research on Cross-Disciplinary Uses of Gamification in Organizations, pp. 418–444. IGI Global (2022)
11. ICOM (International Council of Museums). https://icom.museum/en/resources/standards-guidelines/museum-definition/. Accessed 1 May 2023
12. UNESCO. Convention for the Safeguarding of the Intangible Cultural Heritage. UNESCO, Paris (2003)
13. Note, M: Managing Image Collections: A Practical Guide. Elsevier (2011)
14. Bekele, M.K., Pierdicca, R., Frontoni, E., Malinverni, E.S., Gain, J.: A survey of augmented, virtual, and mixed reality for cultural heritage. J. Comput. Cultur. Heritage **11**(2), 1–36 (2018)
15. Roued-Cunliffe, H., Copelandis, A.: Introduction: What is Participatory Heritage? Facet Publishing (2017)
16. Bodo, S., Gibbs, K., Sani, M.: Museums as places for intercultural dialogue: selected practices from Europe. MAP for ID group (2009)
17. Hornecker, E., Ciolfi, L.: Human-computer interactions in museums. Synth. Lect. Hum. Centered Inform. **12**(2), i–171 (2019)
18. Verhulst, I., Woods, A., Whittaker, L., Bennett, J., Dalton, P.: Do VR and AR versions of an immersive cultural experience engender different user experiences? Comput. Hum. Behav. **125**, 106951 (2021)
19. Milgram, P., Kishino, F.: A taxonomy of mixed reality visual displays. IEICE Trans. Inf. Syst. **77**(12), 1321–1329 (1994)
20. Lohre, R., Warner, J.J., Athwal, G.S., Goel, D.P.: The evolution of virtual reality in shoulder and elbow surgery. JSES Int. **4**(2), 215–223 (2020)

21. Zhang, C.: The why, what, and how of immersive experience. IEEE Access **8**, 90878–90888
22. Suh, A., Prophet, J.: The state of immersive technology research: a literature analysis. Comput. Hum. Behav. **86**, 77–90 (2018)
23. Hsieh, C.C., Kin, P.S., Hsu, W.C., Wang, J.S., Huang, Y.C., Lim, A.Y., et al.: The effectiveness of a virtual reality-based tai chi exercise on cognitive and physical function in older adults with cognitive impairment. Demen. Geriatr. Cogn. Disord. (2018)
24. Bisson, E., Contant, B., Sveistrup, H., Lajoie, Y.: Functional balance and dual-task reaction times in older adults are improved by virtual reality and biofeedback training. Cyberpsychol. Behav. **10**(1), 16–23 (2007)
25. McCloy, R., Stone, R.: Virtual reality in surgery. BMJ **323** (7318), 912–915 (2001)
26. Obrist, M., Gatti, E., Maggioni, E., Vi, C.T., Velasco, C.: Multisensory experiences in HCI. IEEE Multimedia **24**(2), 9–13 (2017)
27. Marto, A., Gonçalves, A., Melo, M., Bessa, M.: A survey of multisensory VR and AR applications for cultural heritage. Comput. Graph. **102**, 426–440 (2022)
28. Falk, J.H., Dierking, L.D.: The Museum Experience Revisited, vol. 1, 6, pp. 54, 119. Left Coast Press, Walnut Creek, CA (2013)
29. Davies, S.M.: The co-production of temporary museum exhibitions. Museum Manage. Curatorship **25**(3), 305–321 (2010)
30. Dean, D.K.: Planning for success: project management for museum exhibitions. In: The International Handbooks of Museum Studies, pp. 357–378. Wiley-Blackwell, Hoboken (2015)
31. Mason, M., Vavoula, G.: Digital cultural heritage design practice: a conceptual framework. Design J. **24**(3), 405–424 (2021). https://doi.org/10.1080/14606925.2021.1889738
32. Barbieri, L., Bruno, F., Muzzupappa, M.: User-centered design of a virtual reality exhibit for archaeological museums. Int. J. Interact. Des. Manuf. **12**(2), 561–571 (2018)
33. Ruthven, D.I., Hornecker, E.: The MUSETECH model: a comprehensive evaluation framework for museum technology. J. Comput. Cult. Herit. **12**(1), 1–22 (2019)
34. Agudo, D., Paredes, C.B., Parra, O., Granda, M.F.: A methodology to develop extended reality applications for exhibition spaces in museums. In: 2022 XXVIII International Conference on Information, Communication and Automation Technologies (ICAT), pp. 1–6. IEEE (2022)
35. Hajirasouli, A., Banihashemi, S., Kumarasuriyar, A., Talebi, S., Tabadkani, A.: Virtual reality-based digitisation for endangered heritage sites: theoretical framework and application. J. Cult. Herit. **49**, 140–151 (2021)
36. Popoli, Z., Derda, I.: Developing experiences: creative process behind the design and production of immersive exhibitions. Museum Manage. Curatorship **36**(4), 384–402 (2021)
37. Mygind, L., Hällman, A.K., Bentsen, P.: Bridging gaps between intentions and realities: a review of participatory exhibition development in museums. Museum Manage. Curatorship **30**(2), 117–137 (2015)
38. Mason, M.: Prototyping practices supporting interdisciplinary collaboration in digital media design for museums. Museum Manage. Curatorship **30**(5), 394–426 (2015)
39. Vavoula, G., Mason, M.: Digital exhibition design: boundary crossing, intermediary design deliverables and processes of consent. Museum Manage. Curatorship **32**(3), 251–271 (2017)
40. Cerquetti, M.: The importance of being earnest. Enhancing the authentic experience of cultural heritage through the experience-based approach. The Experience Logic as a New Perspective for Marketing Management: From Theory to Practical Applications in Different Sectors, pp. 149–168 (2018)
41. Menegaki, A.N.: New technologies in hotels and museums: supply-side perceptions with education implications for managers and curators. J. Knowl. Econ. 1–22 (2021). https://doi.org/10.1007/s13132-021-00849-z
42. Shehade, M., Stylianou-Lambert, T.: Virtual reality in museums: exploring the experiences of museum professionals. Appl. Sci. **10**(11), 4031 (2020)

43. Leoni, L., Cristofaro, M.: Technology adoption in small Italian museums: an empirical investigation. Il Capitale Culturale **23**, 57–87 (2021)
44. Balloffet, P., Courvoisier, F.H., Lagier, J.: From museum to amusement park: the opportunities and risks of edutainment. Int. J. Arts Manage. **16**(2), 4–18 (2014)
45. Cerquetti, M.: More is better! Current issues and challenges for museum audience development: a literature review. Current issues and challenges for museum audience development: a literature review, J. Cult. Manage. Policy **6**(1) (2016)
46. Bello, R.W., Mohamed, A.S.: Impact of technology on traditional museum collection storage and management. Int. J. Comput. Sci. Mob. Comput. **7**(11), 46–51 (2018)
47. Cameron, F.: Digital Futures I: museum collections, digital technologies, and the cultural construction of knowledge. Curator: Museum J. **46**(3), 325–340 (2003)
48. Trunfio, M., Jung, T., Campana, S.: Mixed reality experiences in museums: exploring the impact of functional elements of the devices on visitors' immersive experiences and post-experience behaviours. Inform. Manage. **59**(8), 103698 (2022)
49. Petrelli, D., Ciolfi, L., Van Dijk, D., Hornecker, E., Not, E., Schmidt, A.: Integrating material and digital: a new way for cultural heritage. Interactions **20**(4), 58–63 (2013)
50. Pescarin, S., d'Annibale, E., Fanini, B., Ferdani, D.: Prototyping on site Virtual Museums: the case study of the co-design approach to the Palatine hill in Rome (Barberini Vineyard) exhibition. In: 2018 3rd Digital Heritage International Congress (DigitalHERITAGE) held jointly with 2018 24th International Conference on Virtual Systems & Multimedia (VSMM 2018), pp. 1–8. IEEE (2018)
51. Patton, M.Q.: Qualitative Research and Evaluation Methods: Integrating Theory and Practice. Sage publications (2014)
52. Kaushik, V., Walsh, C.A.: Pragmatism as a research paradigm and its implications for social work research. Soc. Sci. **8**(9), 255 (2019)
53. Johnson, R.B., Onwuegbuzie, A.J., Turner, L.A.: Toward a definition of mixed methods research. J. Mixed Methods Res. **1**(2), 112–133 (2007)
54. Johnson, R.B., Onwuegbuzie, A.J.: Mixed methods research: a research paradigm whose time has come. Educ. Res. **33**(7), 14–26 (2004)
55. Yin, R.K.: Case Study Research and Applications: Design and Methods. Sage Publication, Los Angeles (2018)
56. Rowley, J.: Conducting research interviews. Manag. Res. Rev. **35**(3/4), 260–271 (2012)
57. Kolb, D.A.: Experiential Learning Experience as the Source of Learning and Development. Englewood Cliffs, NJ Prentice Hall (1984)
58. Spadoni, E., Porro, S., Bordegoni, M., Arosio, I., Barbalini, L., Carulli, M.: Augmented reality to engage visitors of science museums through interactive experiences. Heritage **5**(3), 1370–1394 (2022)
59. Porro, S., Spadoni, E., Bordegoni, M., Carulli, M.: Design of an intrinsically motivating AR experience for environmental awareness. Proc. Design Soc. **2**, 1679–1688 (2022)
60. Mumtaz, K., Iqbal, M.M., Khalid, S., Rafiq, T., Owais, S.M., Al Achhab, M.: An eassessment framework for blended learning with augmented reality to enhance the student learning. Eurasia J. Math. Sci. T **13** (2017)
61. Salloum, S.A., Alhamad, A.Q.M., Al-Emran, M., Monem, A.A., Shaalan, K.: Exploring students' acceptance of e-learning through the development of a comprehensive technology acceptance model. IEEE Access **7**, 128445–128462 (2019)
62. Davis, F.D.: Perceived usefulness, perceived ease of use, and user acceptance of information technology. MIS Q. **13**(3), 319 (1989)
63. Progetto Marss, http://museoastronomico.brera.inaf.it/il-progetto-marss/. Accessed 1 May 2023

Augmented Reality-Based Application to Explore Street Art: Development and Implementation

Juan Garzón[1]([⊠]) [iD], Sebastián Ceballos[1], Esteban Ocampo[2], and Maryam Correa[2]

[1] Universidad Católica de Oriente, Rionegro, Colombia
{fgarzon,sceballos}@uco.edu.co
[2] Centro de la Innovación la agroindustria y la Aviación – Tecnoparque, Rionegro, Colombia
eocampoo@sena.edu.do

Abstract. Augmented reality (AR) has unveiled new possibilities for enhancing how people experience and interact with their surroundings. Similarly, street art has gained popularity as a form of creative expression in urban areas. This study investigates the effects of using an AR-based application to enhance the experience of exploring street art. The application aims to provide users with an interactive and immersive street art experience by overlaying digital information on five murals, such as meaning, historical context, touristic information, and artist information. The study uses a user-centered design approach to develop and evaluate the application's usability and user experience. Findings suggest that the AR-based application is an effective tool for enhancing the exploration and appreciation of street art. The application provides users with a new way to engage with the art and allows for deeper insights into the artist's intention and message. Furthermore, the application promotes cultural tourism, as it facilitates the discovery and exploration of lesser-known street art installations. Overall, using AR-based applications presents exciting opportunities for enriching the exploration and appreciation of art in public spaces.

Keywords: Augmented reality · Street art · Usability · User experience

1 Introduction

Augmented reality (AR) is a technology that overlays digital content on real-world objects, creating an immersive and interactive experience [10]. Street art, on the other hand, is a form of public art typically created on the streets or other public spaces using a variety of materials and techniques [1]. In recent years, these two seemingly unrelated fields have come together to create a new form of art that blends the physical and digital worlds in innovative ways [15]. AR has opened new possibilities for street artists, allowing them to enhance their works with dynamic and interactive digital elements that can be accessed using smartphones or other AR-enabled devices. This combination of traditional street art with cutting-edge technology has created a new and exciting way for artists to engage with their audiences and transform public spaces [7]. In this way, AR

L. T. De Paolis et al. (Eds.): XR Salento 2023, LNCS 14219, pp. 179–193, 2023.
https://doi.org/10.1007/978-3-031-43404-4_12

and street art have become intertwined, paving the way for a new generation of creative expression that pushes the boundaries of what is possible.

Although different technological alternatives exist for complementing the street art experience, AR offers unique affordances allowing for new forms of interaction and engagement between artists, viewers, and public spaces [12, 16, 17]. First, AR can make street art more interactive by allowing users to access additional layers of content and information through their mobile devices. This additional layer of interactivity creates a more immersive and engaging experience for viewers, allowing them to participate in the creation and evolution of the art in new ways. Second, AR can transform physical spaces by allowing artists to create works that exist both in the physical and digital worlds. This allows for new possibilities for creating dynamic, evolving, and interactive public spaces where viewers can engage with the art in new and unexpected ways. Third, AR can encourage collaboration between artists, communities, and audiences. This technology provides an opportunity for artists to work collaboratively with other artists and with members of the community to create works that are interactive, responsive, and participatory. This collaborative approach can lead to a greater sense of ownership and investment in the public spaces where the art is located. Fourth, AR can make street art more accessible to a broader audience. By providing additional layers of information and context, AR can make street art more approachable and understandable to viewers who may not be familiar with the art or its meaning. Fifth, AR can encourage creativity and experimentation by providing artists with new tools and mediums to work with. This can lead to new forms of street art that blend physical and digital elements in innovative ways, pushing the boundaries of what is possible in public art. Overall, the unique affordances of AR on street art offer exciting new possibilities for the future of public art in urban spaces. By enhancing interactivity, transforming physical spaces, encouraging collaboration, enhancing accessibility, and encouraging creativity, AR is unveiling new avenues for artistic expression and engagement in public spaces.

The benefits of using AR to enhance learning outcomes in the field of arts have been widely documented by multiple studies [11, 13, 17]. For example, the study by Garzón and Acevedo [11] measured the impact of AR on students' learning gains. Using Cohen's d effect size [8], the study estimated an effect of 0.82, indicating that AR has a large effect on learning gains in arts education. Additionally, the study pointed out that all the analyzed studies were conducted in formal or semi-formal settings inside academic environments. In this regard, different studies have posed the need to evaluate the effects of using AR technologies on arts outside the academic scenario [5, 13]. This information can help spur innovation and creativity and encourage educators and artists to explore new ways of using these technologies to enhance the learning and creative process.

Based on the previous background, the purpose of this research is twofold. First, we present the development of an AR-based application to explore street art. Second, we implemented the application in the context of a user study on an art route in a town in northwestern Colombia. The objective of the user study was to evaluate the application's usability and the user's experience to identify how users interact with the application and how they feel about that interaction. This evaluation was conducted in a route that comprises five murals closely related to the past and modern history of the town. Twenty-two tourists participating in a tour by the murals were asked to take part in the study voluntarily. The user study results indicate that the tourists found it easy to navigate through the application. Additionally, most of them agreed that they had enjoyed the experience of exploring the murals using the AR application, as it provided them with an enriched panorama of the meaning of each mural and the context of the town.

2   Related Work

AR has been increasingly used in the street art environment to create dynamic and interactive experiences. Some of those experiences have taken place in academic settings and have been documented as academic research. Below, we present some research that has explored the uses of AR in street art, focusing on its potential to enhance the creative process, engage with audiences, and encourage community involvement.

Perhaps one of the most representative projects related to the combination of street art and AR is the Museum of Augmented Urban Art (MAUA)[1]. This open-air gallery was born in Milan, Italy, and includes more than fifty pieces of street art animated by AR technology. Thanks to its positive influence on the city, this project has spread to other Italian cities, such as Torino, Chieri, and Palermo and Waterford in Ireland. The study by Vavassori [31] describes the museum creation process and how the unique characteristics of AR contribute to the accessibility of street art anywhere, anytime. As mentioned in the study, this museum has become an academic and artistic referent for locals and tourists and has inspired similar projects worldwide.

One of the key benefits of AR in street art is its ability to enhance the creative process by allowing artists to explore new dimensions of their work. According to the study by Gwilt and Wilde [18], AR allows artists to experiment with new digital tools and techniques, which can help expand street art's creative possibilities. By overlaying digital elements on physical spaces, artists can create interactive installations that blur the boundaries between the real and virtual worlds and invite audiences to engage with their work in new and exciting ways. The study also noted that AR provides new opportunities for collaboration between artists and communities, enhancing their belonging sense toward the urban spaces.

In addition to enhancing the creative process, AR can engage audiences and encourage community involvement in street art. In a study by Gong et al. [16], participants reported that they felt more connected to their communities when they were able to interact with street art through AR. By providing an interactive and immersive experience, AR helps engage a broader range of audiences, including those who may not typically be interested in street art. Hence, AR becomes an inclusion tool in street art, as it helps create opportunities for participation and collaboration. Furthermore, by allowing people to add their own digital content to a piece of street art, AR can turn a static piece into a dynamic and evolving installation that reflects the community's creativity and diversity.

Street art and AR have also been blended as a mechanism to further activism causes. The study by Skwarek [30] explores several cases, including the use of AR to create virtual memorials for victims of police brutality, to challenge gender stereotypes, and to

---

[1] Https://mauamuseum.com/

visualize the impact of climate change. The study highlights the unique opportunities that AR offers for creating immersive and interactive experiences that engage and educate viewers. However, the author also acknowledges the challenges associated with the use of AR activism, including the need for technical expertise, access to devices, and concerns about the potential for AR to perpetuate inequalities. Overall, the study suggests that AR activism represents an innovative and exciting social and political engagement approach that can potentially reach new audiences and create positive change.

Finally, the study by Chin et al. [6] used an AR-based mobile learning system to teach a liberal arts course following the situated learning approach. To evaluate the system's efficiency, the researchers designed a study where the students were taken outside the traditional classroom. The study results suggested that the AR-based mobile system provided students with a more interactive and engaging learning experience, leading to improved learning outcomes and higher motivation levels.

Overall, the abovementioned studies suggest that AR has the potential to transform the way we engage with and experience street art. By providing new opportunities for interactivity, collaboration, and experimentation, AR is opening new possibilities for street artists and audiences alike. However, although AR technology has already been successfully adopted in formal learning environments, further effort must be made to prove that AR-based systems are excellent educational tools that positively impact alternative educational settings.

3 The Application

We developed an AR-based application to enhance the experience of interacting with the murals in the "full-color memory" art tour. Inspired by the project MAUA, this tour comprehends an artistic and cultural route throughout a municipality in northwestern Colombia. The route consists of five murals, which different expert international street artists painted. The purpose of the application is to introduce viewers to the context of the mural, including information about the techniques implemented, the artists, nature, and the municipality. Thus, it intends to become not only an innovative tool to appreciate art, but also a pedagogical tool to encourage care for the environment and promote tourism in the municipality.

3.1 Description

The application was designed using Unity 2022.1 (the application), Vuforia SDK (AR features), Blender (3D and 2D graphics), and Adobe Premier Pro (video and audio editing). It presents two types of experiences: *field experience* and *home experience*. The field experience is carried out in the abovementioned art route using a mobile device with Android operating system. On the other hand, the home experience can be carried out from any computer device to allow users to live the experience without being in the actual route. The home experience contains information related to the project. We provide a webpage where users can download the application, access images of all the murals, and get instructions on how to use the application.

When executing the application for the first time, it deploys a "welcome" message, including valuable information on the project. At any time, the user can skip this information. The application then presents the five murals for users to select the mural they wish to explore (see Fig. 1-left). After selecting a specific mural, the application deploys three tabs with information on a) How to get there, b) Start the experience, and c) About (see Fig. 1-right). The "How to get there" tab opens the Google Maps application to indicate to the users how to get to the physical location of the mural (in case the user is in a different place). The "Start the experience" tab opens the mobile device's camera so that the user can focus it on the mural. Finally, the "About" tab presents the metadata of the mural, including the date it was painted, the names and countries of the artists, their social media, and the technique implemented.

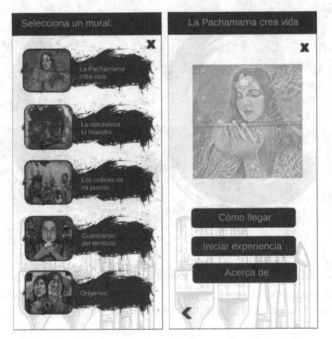

Fig. 1. Sections: Select a mural (left); Select an action (right)

All the murals are related to nature and the aborigines who inhabited the region in the pre-Hispanic era. When users intend to explore a specific mural, the application recommends standing on the other side of the street (on the sidewalk in front of the mural) to avoid accidents with passing vehicles. Then, the user must focus the mural with the mobile device's camera. The mural will serve as the trigger for the augmentation to begin. Figure 2 presents a full photo of each of the five murals. These photos were taken from the sidewalk in front of each mural, giving an idea of their size. The murals are separated about 100 m from each other; therefore, the art route comprises about 500 m.

The augmentation of each mural contains four moments: first, an audio file that explains the meaning of the elements in the mural. Second, the explanation of the message

Fig. 2. The five murals: Guardians of the territory (top-left); The colors of my town (top-right); Nature, your teacher (middle); Origins (bottom-left); Pachamama creates life (bottom-right)

that the mural intends to teach. Third, a story inspired by the mural, and fourth, touristic information about the town, so that the tourists get to know more about the different touristic activities it can offer. Aside from these elements, different parts of each mural, such as the persons' eyes, the leaves, the currents of water, and the animals, have been given movement to improve the interactivity between the users and the murals. Figure 3 (top and bottom) presents an augmented scene in the Guardians of the territory mural. This augmentation consists of a video that promotes some touristic activities that can be carried out in the municipality.

Fig. 3. Augmented scene to promote tourism

4 User Study

4.1 User Study Design

This study intends to evaluate the usability of the application and the users' experience when interacting with it; therefore, we did not include any control group or any pre-measurement before the experimental treatment. In this context, the independent variable (experimental treatment) involves the use of an AR-based application to explore five murals of an art route in a Colombian town and the dependent variables are the usability of the system and the user experience.

The International Organization for Standardization (ISO) [19] defines usability as the degree to which a product, service, or system can be used by its intended users to achieve specific goals effectively, efficiently, and with satisfaction [23]. It measures how easy and intuitive a product or system is to use, how quickly users can learn to use it, and how error-prone it is. In the context of design, usability is one of the essential factors that contribute to the overall quality of a product or system [26, 32]. Therefore, to improve a system's usability, designers strive to create products that are not only visually appealing but also easy to use, intuitive, and accessible to a wide range of users. To measure our application's usability, we used the System Usability Scale (SUS)[2] questionnaire [3]. This instrument has been described as the most widely used questionnaire for evaluating perceived usability [24], due to its excellent reliability ($\alpha > 0.93$) [27]. It consists of ten questions grouped into two scales: learnability, which refers to the ability to learn to use

---

[2] Https://www.usability.gov/

a system efficiently and independently, and usability in a stricter sense. Each question is measured using a five-point Likert scale, where 1 represents "strongly disagree" and 5 "strongly agree."

On the other hand, user experience refers to a person's overall experience when using a product, service, or system [20]. It encompasses all aspects of the user's interaction with the product, including visual design, ease of use, accessibility, and emotional response. The goal of user experience design is to create products that are not only functional but also provide a positive and meaningful experience for the user [2]. To achieve this, user experience designers focus on understanding the needs and behaviors of users, as well as the context in which the product will be used. A good user experience is important for the success of a product or system, as a positive experience can lead to increased user satisfaction, loyalty, and adoption, while a negative experience can lead to frustration and abandonment [26]. Therefore, user experience design is an essential part of the product development process and is increasingly recognized as a key factor in the educational technology context. To evaluate the user experience, we used the User Experience Questionnaire (UEQ)[3] [21]. In addition to providing essential information about the user experience, this instrument compares the quality of the product with that of similar products, making it a tool that encourages improvement in each new educational application [29]. This questionnaire contains 26 items grouped into six scales: attractiveness, perspicuity, efficiency, dependability, stimulation, and novelty. It was evaluated using a seven-point Likert scale, where 1 represents "strongly disagree" and 7 "strongly agree."

4.2 User Study Procedure

We recruited 22 participants, 13 (59%) men and 9 (41%) women, whose ages ranged from 19 to 60 (Mean: 32.59). All the participants were tourists visiting the art route at the time. The participants were taken from a group of 28 tourists; although all the group members were invited to participate, only 22 agreed. Eighteen participants (82%) indicated they had no prior experience using an AR-based system, but all had a smartphone capable of running the application.

The participants were asked to download the application using the public Wi-Fi network provided by the municipality. They then completed a simple questionnaire with basic information such as name, gender, age, and previous AR experience. There is no specific order to walk the route. Therefore, to keep each mural free of crowds, the participants were divided into two subgroups of five people and two subgroups of six.

Each subgroup was led through the art route to explore the five murals, following a different sequence. The participants explored each mural for five to ten minutes and then proceeded to the next mural. At the end of the tour, they were asked to complete the SUS and UEQ questionnaires. The entire process, from recruitment to the end of experience (after completing both questionnaires), took around 90 min. Finally, the participants received a snack as a token of our appreciation for supporting this study. This space was used by the researchers to talk with the participants to learn about their experience in a more informal way.

---

[3] https://www.ueq-online.org/

5   Results

5.1   Usability

To identify the application's usability, we followed the procedure explained on the official usability website (link provided in the second footnote). This value is a percentage transformation that indicates the overall usability of a specific product. Accordingly, our application's usability was found to be 84.43, which corresponds to "good usability" [3]. The minimum score was 62.50 and the maximum was 92.50, with a total standard deviation of 5.88. Table 1 presents the mean score, the standard deviation, and the coefficient of variation for the overall SUS and for learnability and usability subcomponents. It is important to note that values in Table 1 are derived from the Likert scale and not the percentage transformation. The results indicate no statistical differences between the learnability and usability scores ($t(20) = 0.24, p = 0.94$).

Table 1. SUS questionnaire results

Scale	Mean	Standard deviation	Coefficient of variation
SUS	3.38	0.24	0.07
Learnability	3.41	0.49	0.14
Usability	3.37	0.23	0.07

Additionally, we analyzed the effects by age and gender of the participants. The results in Fig. 4 show slightly higher scores for users over 45, both in the overall and learnability scores; however, there are no statistically significant differences. Regarding usability, users under 30 scored slightly higher but without statistically significant differences. It is important to note that the confidence intervals for users older than 45 years are wider than those for other age groups for learnability and usability, indicating significant variability in scores. On the other hand, the narrower confidence interval in the group of users under 30 indicates a low variability in the scores.

Similarly, the results in Fig. 5 show slightly higher scores for female users for learnability and male users for usability; however, in both cases, there are no statistically significant differences. The confidence intervals are wider for female users for learnability and usability, indicating more significant variability in their results.

5.2   User Experience

We evaluated the UEQ using the data analysis tools provided by the UEQ website. Figure 6 shows the average score for each of the six categories. Each item is scaled from -3 to $+3$. According to the guidelines, values between -0.8 and 0.8 represent a neutral evaluation of the corresponding scale, values > 0.8 represent a positive evaluation, and values <-0.8 represent a negative evaluation [28].

The scales of the UEQ distinguish pragmatic and hedonic qualities. Pragmatic quality refers to task-related quality aspects such as perspicuity, efficiency, and dependability.

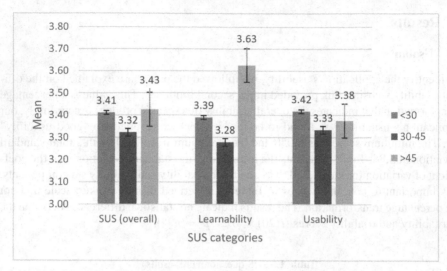

Fig. 4. SUS questionnaire results by the age of the users

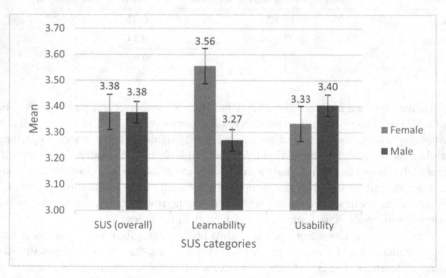

Fig. 5. SUS questionnaire results by gender of the users

On the other hand, hedonic quality refers to the non-task-related quality aspects, such as stimulation and originality. As depicted in Fig. 6, all aspects of the application obtained positive values for both qualities. Overall, pragmatic quality obtained a score of 2.03, while hedonic quality scored 2.56. Finally, we evaluated Cronbach's Alpha-Coefficient (α) to identify each scale's consistency. Alpha values greater than 0.7 have been accepted as sufficient consistency [14]. As depicted in Fig. 6, all Alpha-Coefficient values are above 0.7, except for the scale of dependability ($\alpha = 0.11$). This value seems to indicate that the items related to dependability are interpreted differently by the users and suggest the need to deeply explore the items within this scale. An analysis by gender and age indicates that female users and users under 30 tend to give a lower score to issues related to dependability, suggesting that users in those groups do not feel entirely under the control of the application.

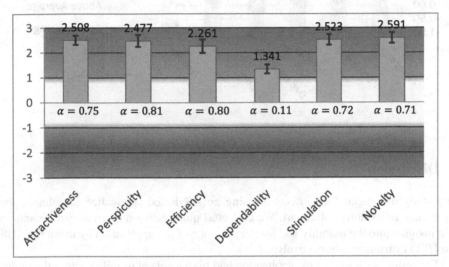

Fig. 6. UEQ questionnaire results

On the other hand, the benchmark shows how good the product is compared to the products in the benchmark data set [29]. This data set includes over 450 product evaluations with the UEQ. The benchmark classifies a product into five categories: excellent, good, above average, below average, and bad.

As seen in Fig. 7, all aspects fall into the excellent category apart from dependability. This indicates that as for attractiveness, perspicuity, efficiency, stimulation, and novelty, the application stands in the range of the 10% best results. As for dependability, the application stands in the range of 50% best results.

The UEQ does not provide an overall score for user experience; however, it offers an extension that allows producing a key performance indicator (KPI) used for indicating a standard overall user experience score. This is done by adding six questions to the questionnaire to specifically ask the contestants to evaluate attractiveness, perspicuity, efficiency, dependability, stimulation, and novelty. We performed such analysis and found an overall user experience score of $2.08(SD = 0.18)$, which corresponds to excellent.

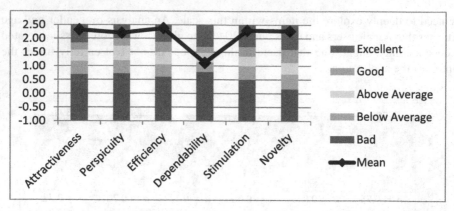

Fig. 7. Benchmark graph for our AR-based application

6   Discussion

This study investigated the effects of using an AR-based application to enhance the experience of exploring street art. We collected quantitative data from participants to gain insights into the usability and user experience of the application by using the SUS and UEQ instruments, respectively.

The results indicate that the application had high levels of usability across the scales of learnability and usability. The overall score of 84.43 suggests that users found the application easy to use, navigate, and understand. This high result is promising since, as stated in previous studies [9, 25, 32], high levels of usability lead to user satisfaction, motivation, and ultimately, learning gains. Additionally, we analyzed the scores by classifying the users by age and gender. The results indicate no statistically significant differences among the different subgroups. This analysis is important considering that usability has been found an issue among older users of AR [9]. Therefore, our findings are positive, since they imply that this application can be used by any type of user regardless of their age. Moreover, previous studies have noted that some AR applications may be scored lower by female users [4, 22], thus worsening gender issues. Our results indicate no gender differences, which implies that gender gaps in terms of technology use are not perpetuated.

Regarding user experience, the application also received positive reviews. The overall KPI of 2.08 indicates that user experience was evaluated as being excellent. In that sense, the scales of attractiveness, perspicuity, efficiency, stimulation, and novelty obtained the highest scores, while the scale of dependability yielded the lowest scores. These results are important since, as stated by previous research [26], a good user experience leads to satisfaction, loyalty, and adoption of the application. Similarly, the benchmark analysis indicates above-average scores for all categories compared to similar applications. This result suggests that the application's quality is sufficient to deploy it massively and to be implemented as a tool to promote engagement, learning, and tourism.

The results of the usability and user experience obtained by the proposed application are positive and lead to some implications both from the street art and AR perspectives. First, the project behind the application presented in this study can be used as a digital archive of the artistic route. This will allow different audiences to access the artistic content long after the physical artwork has been removed or destroyed. This not only helps to preserve the artistic value of the work but also provides a platform for artists to showcase their work to a broader audience. Second, the proposed application can be implemented as an inclusion pedagogical tool. The user experience results suggest that this novel application potentially captivates new consumers of art as it sparks interest due to the innovative and engaging forms powered by AR. Third, the application is valuable for promoting urban tourism and cultural heritage. It can help potential visitors better understand of what to expect when they visit and make more informed decisions. The application also provides historical and cultural context for tourist destinations, enriching the user's experience and increasing their appreciation of the location. Consequently, by providing an engaging and interactive experience, users are more likely to share their experience with others, increasing awareness and interest in the location.

7   Conclusion

This study investigated the effects of using an AR-based application to enhance the experience of exploring street art. The application was implemented in the context of a user study that evaluated the application's usability and user experience. The results demonstrate that the application can significantly enhance the user experience. Through the SUS and UEQ questionnaires, the participants reported high levels of engagement, enjoyment, and satisfaction with the application, implying that they would be more likely to explore street art in the future because of using the application. The use of AR provides a unique and innovative way to enhance the experience of exploring street art, offering users an interactive and immersive experience that allows them to engage with the artwork in new and exciting ways. The ability to overlay additional information, such as artist biographies or historical context, also gives users a deeper understanding and appreciation of the artwork they are exploring. Overall, this study's findings suggest that using an AR-based application to explore street art has the potential to increase engagement, enjoyment, and appreciation of this form of public art. As such, it is recommended that further research be conducted in this area to explore the potential of AR technology to enhance the experience of exploring other forms of public art and cultural heritage sites.

Acknowledgement. The authors are deeply grateful to the Universidad Católica de Oriente and Tecnoparque – SENA, for having supported this project.

References

1. Baldini, A.L.: What is street art? Estet. Eur. J. Aesthet. **59**, 1, 1–21 (2022). https://doi.org/10.33134/eeja.234
2. Benyon, D.: Designing User Experience. Pearson (2019)
3. Brooke, J.: SUS: A "Quick and Dirty" usability scale. In: Usability Evaluation in Industry, pp. 4–7. CRC Press (1996)

4. Cabero-Almenara, J., et al.: Adoption of augmented reality technology by university students. Heliyon **5**, 5, e01597 (2019). https://doi.org/10.1016/j.heliyon.2019.e01597
5. Challenor, J., Ma, M.: A review of augmented reality applications for history education and heritage visualisation. Multimodal Technol. Interact. **3**, 2, 1–20 (2019). https://doi.org/10.3390/mti3020039
6. Chin, K.-Y., et al.: Effects of an augmented reality-based mobile system on students' learning achievements and motivation for a liberal arts course. Interact. Learn. Environ. **27**(7), 927–941 (2019). https://doi.org/10.1080/10494820.2018.1504308
7. Clarke, R.E.: Merging spaces: augmented reality, temporary public art, and the reinvention of site. In: Geroimenko, V. (ed.) Augmented Reality Art: From an Emerging Technology to a Novel Creative Medium, pp. 129–156. Springer International Publishing, Cham (2022). https://doi.org/10.1007/978-3-030-96863-2_7
8. Cohen, J.: Quantitative methods in psychology. Psychol. Bull. **112**(1), 155–159 (1992). https://doi.org/10.1037/0033-2909.112.1.155
9. Dey, A., et al.: A systematic review of 10 years of augmented reality usability studies: 2005 to 2014. Front. Robot. AI. **5**, 1–28 (2018)
10. Garzón, J.: An overview of twenty-five years of augmented reality in education. Multimodal Technol. Interact. **5**(7), 1–14 (2021)
11. Garzón, J., Acevedo, J.: Meta-analysis of the impact of Augmented Reality on students' learning effectiveness. Educ. Res. Rev. **27**, 244–260 (2019). https://doi.org/10.1016/j.edurev.2019.04.001
12. Geroimenko, V. (ed.): Augmented Reality Art: From an Emerging Technology to a Novel Creative Medium. Springer, Cham (2022)
13. Geroimenko, Vladimir (ed.): Augmented Reality in Education: A New Technology for Teaching and Learning. Springer International Publishing, Cham (2020)
14. Gliem, J.A., Gliem, R.R.: Calculating, interpreting, and reporting cronbach's alpha reliability coefficient for likert-type scales. In: Midwest Research to Practice Conference in Adult, Continuing, and Community Education, pp. 82–88. Columbus (2003)
15. Goffinski, A.: Making sense of ARt: a methodological framework for the study of augmented reality art. In: Geroimenko, V. (ed.) Augmented Reality Art: From an Emerging Technology to a Novel Creative Medium, pp. 25–43. Springer, Cham (2022). https://doi.org/10.1007/978-3-030-96863-2_2
16. Gong, Z., et al.: Augmented Reality (AR) as a tool for engaging museum experience: a case study on Chinese art pieces. Digital **2**(1), 33–45 (2022). https://doi.org/10.3390/digital2010002
17. Guazzaroni, G., Pillai, A.: Virtual and Augmented Reality in Education, Art, and Museums. IGI Global, Hershey (2019)
18. Gwilt, I., Wilde, J.: Augmented reality graffiti and street art. In: Geroimenko, V. (ed.) Augmented Reality Art. Springer Series on Cultural Computing, pp. 283–295. Springer, Cham, Cairo (2022). https://doi.org/10.1007/978-3-030-96863-2_15
19. International Organization for Standardization [ISO]: ISO 9241-11:2018 Ergonomics of human-system interaction—part 11: Usability: Definitions and concepts (2018)
20. International OrganiZation for StandardiZation [ISO]: ISO 9241-210: 2019 Ergonomics Of Human-System Interaction - Part 210: Human-Centred Design For Interactive Systems (2019)
21. Laugwitz, B., et al.: Construction and evaluation of a user experience questionnaire. Lect. Notes Comput. Sci. **5298**, 63–76 (2008). https://doi.org/10.1007/978-3-540-89350-9_6
22. Lester, S., Hofmann, J.: Some pedagogical observations on using augmented reality in a vocational practicum. Br. J. Educ. Technol. **51**(3), 645–656 (2020). https://doi.org/10.1111/bjet.12901

23. Lewis, J.R.: Measuring perceived usability: the CSUQ, SUS, and UMUX. Int. J. Hum. Comput. Interact. **34**(12), 1148–1156 (2018). https://doi.org/10.1080/10447318.2017.141 8805

24. Lewis, J.R.: The system usability scale: past, present, and future. Int. J. Human-Computer Interact. **34**(7), 577–590 (2018). https://doi.org/10.1080/10447318.2018.1455307

25. Miguel-Alonso, I., et al.: Developing a tutorial for improving usability and user skills in an immersive virtual reality experience. In: Paolis, L.T.D., Arpaia, P., Sacco, M. (eds.) Extended Reality: First International Conference, XR Salento 2022, Lecce, Italy, July 6–8, 2022, Proceedings, Part II, pp. 63–78. Springer Nature Switzerland, Cham (2022). https://doi.org/10.1007/978-3-031-15553-6_5

26. De Paolis, L.T., et al.: Usability, user experience and mental workload in a mobile Augmented Reality application for digital storytelling in cultural heritage. Virtual Real. 1–27 (2022). https://doi.org/10.1007/s10055-022-00712-9

27. Sauro, J., Lewis, J.: Quantifying the user experience: Practical statistics for user research. Morgan Kaufmann (2016)

28. Schrepp, M., et al.: Applying the User Experience Questionnaire (UEQ) in different evaluation scenarios. In: Design, User Experience, and Usability. Theories, Methods, and Tools for Designing the User Experience, pp. 383–392 (2014). https://doi.org/10.1007/978-3-319-07668-3_37

29. Schrepp, M., et al.: Construction of a benchmark for the User Experience Questionnaire (UEQ). Int. J. Interact. Multimed. Artif. Intell. **4**(4), 40–44 (2017). https://doi.org/10.9781/iji mai.2017.445

30. Skwarek, M.: Augmented reality activism. In: Geroimenko, V. (ed.) Augmented Reality Art. Springer Series on Cultural Computing, pp. 3–40 Springer, Cham, Cairo (2018). https://doi.org/10.1007/978-3-319-69932-5_1

31. Vavassori, V.: (Un)placing street art: augmented reality and urban museums. J. MeCCSA Postgrad. Netw. **15**(2), 1–15 (2022)

32. Vlachogianni, P., Tselios, N.: Perceived usability evaluation of educational technology using the System Usability Scale (SUS): a systematic review. J. Res. Technol. Educ. **54**(3), 392–409 (2022). https://doi.org/10.1080/15391523.2020.1867938

Cultural Heritage Applications Based on Augmented Reality: A Literature Review

Anna Chatsiopoulou(✉) [iD] and Panagiotis Michailidis [iD]

Department of Balkan, Slavic and Oriental Studies, University of Macedonia,
Egnatia Street, 156, 54636 Thessaloniki, Greece
{ahatsiopoulou,pmichailidis}@uom.edu.gr

Abstract. The purpose of our article is to study augmented reality (AR) applications for promoting cultural heritage and their use in the educational process. In recent years, significant steps have been taken in the use of augmented reality in promoting and highlighting tangible and intangible cultural heritage around the world, and it is worth looking at the steps which are followed for their creation, how they are assessed by people who used them, and the gaps and shortcomings that appeared. Based on the shortcomings we will be able to better orient ourselves to the kind of digital application that someone who is not so well trained in the field of IT and building complex applications can design. In addition, according to the studies reviewed for this article, there are not many applications that are purely educational in purpose or use serious games, although many recognize that AR technology is refreshing to the learning process, as students of all ages can learn and interact with the app at their own pace.

Keywords: Augmented Reality · Cultural Heritage

1 Introduction

Our paper is about digital applications for the promotion of cultural heritage and their use in the educational process. Digital applications for promoting cultural heritage is a field that has begun to develop in recent years and makes it possible to preserve the cultural heritage that each place has, but at the same time to make it known to the general public [34].

In recent years with the rise of online courses and lectures, it is clear how the field of education is constantly changing and what new demands instructors/teachers/professors are asked to cover. Within them, the culture and cultural heritage of each small group (of a country or a small geographical area, such as Western Macedonia), have an important role and efforts are being made to promote them [33]. The use of digital applications makes more attractive and easier the educational process, as it escapes the narrow confines of the classroom, as we have known it until now. In the past, digital applications have been proposed in general in the field of cultural heritage using augmented reality (AR) technologies as reported by the review papers [32, 34]. However, there are few studies that examine the effect of AR technology to promote cultural heritage through the educational

L. T. De Paolis et al. (Eds.): XR Salento 2023, LNCS 14219, pp. 194–209, 2023.
https://doi.org/10.1007/978-3-031-43404-4_13

process as well as the effect of the integration of other emerging technologies (such as gamification in our case) in the AR cultural heritage applications in learning to create more immersive and interactive experiences for visitors or students.

In this paper, we will study some of the applications that have been made to promote cultural heritage and its advancement in education, with particular emphasis on those that have used augmented reality (AR) technology. The purpose of our study is to systematically outline the current state of AR applications for cultural heritage, in order to understand the motivations and methodologies used in AR design, development and evaluation to identify research gaps and limitations. In this context, our final goal in this paper is to find out how much the AR technology helps the education process and the way that serious games are being used in these applications.

Our paper is organized as follows: Sect. 2 presents the conceptual framework on digital technologies for cultural heritage. Section 3 presents the methodology we followed for the collection of papers and articles on the promotion of cultural heritage through digital applications and the research questions we posed for the writing of this paper. This is followed by Sect. 4 where we record the results of the research questions raised, Sect. 5 where we have the discussion of our findings and in the last section we conclude the paper by presenting the results and our suggestions for further research on digital applications used for cultural heritage.

2 Conceptual Framework

In this section we list the most basic concepts that we find in our research and they concern the technologies used in the applications to highlight the cultural heritage. Generally, the technologies used are immersive technology (or extended reality) and serious gaming. Immersive technology is a general term that includes augmented, virtual and mixed reality technologies. In the following, there are presented relevant definitions for the above technologies.

Augmented Reality (AR). Augmented Reality places and adds simulated elements to existing aspects of the physical world. These digital complements can be video, graphics or data related to one's geographic location and often combine them to enhance users' perception of their location in the reality around them [28]. According to Economou, the Museum of London was one of the first to adopt the application *"Streetmuseum app"*, which uses historical photos from the museum's collections, allowing app users to wander around the city and see, using their smartphone, views of a street or monument of their choice in the past.

Virtual Reality (VR). Virtual Reality has been used in the field of cultural heritage, describing a variety of applications involving visual, 3D environments where the user is "immersed" in an entire simulated world. Foundation of the Hellenic World was one of the first to use virtual reality for cultural heritage purposes and we mention some of its applications: *"The workshop of Pheidias in ancient Olympia"*, *"A journey to ancient Miletus"*, *"An interactive journey through the ancient market of Athens"* [28].

Mixed Reality (MR). Mixed Reality combines user's real-world environment with digitally generated content, where both environments coexist. In mixed reality, virtual objects behave as if they are in the real world, e.g. they are obstructed by physical objects, their lighting is proportional to real light sources in the environment, they sound like they are in the same space. As the user interacts with the real and virtual objects, the virtual objects change in space as they would if they were physical [29]. An example is "Microsoft's HoloLens app", which allows one to place digital objects in the room they are in and can change their position or interact with the digital objects in any possible way [31].

Serious Games. Serious Games, as they often call games designed with educational goals, have been used in different contexts in cultural heritage and designed for different platforms following different philosophies and design approaches. They are designed for both formal learning environments such as the classroom for students of various ages and levels, as well as informal learning environments such as at home, on tourist trips or during heritage visits.

This area features a wide variety of trivia questions, puzzles, mini-games to interactive exhibitions and mobile apps in museums or tourist attractions using some reward mechanism, simulations of past events (such as the Battle in Waterloo) in adventure games and role-playing games that take place in reliable reconstructions or digital representations of real locations [30].

3 Methodology

The interest of our research was initially see the extent of the research that has been done on augmented reality applications to highlight cultural heritage in Greece and more broadly in the rest of the world. We want to see what kind of cultural stock they choose to highlight (artistic form, such as music and songs, architectural form, such as churches, mansions, traditional settlements, etc.) using augmented reality applications.

Then, taking them into consideration, we will identify the research gaps and limitations. Therefore, in this work we will pose the basic and following questions to which we will answer through the retrieval of relevant articles and researches from specific bibliographic databases that we will define next.

Research Question 1: What is the purpose and motivation of augmented reality applications for cultural heritage?

Research Question 2: Which countries are involved in augmented reality applications that have been used to promote cultural heritage?

Research Question 3: What are the current design methodologies for augmented reality applications for cultural heritage?

Research Question 4: What are the current methodologies for developing and implementing augmented reality applications for cultural heritage?

Research Question 5: What are the technical characteristics (device, operating system, monitoring technique, etc.) that are required to run augmented reality applications for cultural heritage?

Research Question 6: What are the current methodologies for evaluating augmented reality applications for cultural heritage?

Research Question 7: What are the conclusions of the researches?

Research Question 8: Are there any research suggestions for future research on developing augmented reality applications?

To retrieve those researches we need, we have looked at the databases *Scopus* and *Web of Science*. The keywords we have been used were: ("augmented reality" OR "AR") AND "cultural heritage" in the topic (that is, title, abstract and keywords).

We chose the specific keywords, as we were interested in seeing articles, reviews and book chapters related to augmented reality and definitely contain the term of "cultural heritage".

In Table 1 we have the results of the research from databases *Scopus* and *Web of Science*. By using the keywords that we mentioned before, we found in the *Scopus* database 1.171 articles of which we retained 1.058, based on language (English language) and file type (article, book chapter, conference paper, review). We followed the same procedure in the Web of Science database and found 358 articles, of which we retained 350, using the same exclusion criteria.

Then, by studying the abstracts of the articles from both databases, we kept 87 articles from *Scopus* and 3 articles from *Web of Science*, which are about applications and the use of augmented reality in cultural heritage issues. Articles from *Web of Science* are much fewer, as most of them are repeated in *Scopus*. For the selection of these articles, we used as a criterion the time period in which they were written (from 1997 to the present) and that they were about applications for mobile devices that use augmented reality technology to promote the cultural heritage of each study. The reason we only focused on augmented reality applications is that we want to see to what extent AR technology helps the educational process in issues (such as cultural heritage) that are not so emphasized compared to others (such as historical issues).

Table 1. Research results in databases Scopus and Web of Science.

Database	Key-words	Articles
Scopus	("augmented reality" OR "AR") AND "cultural heritage"	1.171
	Language: English Document type: Article, Book Chapter, Conference paper, Review Timespan: 1997–2023	1.058
	Criteria: mobile application, cultural heritage	87
Web of Science	("augmented reality" OR "AR") AND "cultural heritage"	358
	Language: English Document type: Article, Book Chapter, Conference paper, Review Article Timespan: 1997–2023	350
	Criteria: mobile application, cultural heritage	3
Sum of articles		90

Of the 90 articles, only 27 were exclusively concerned with the creation of an application related to augmented reality and its use to promote cultural heritage issues for educational purposes.

4 Results

From the study of those 27 papers we tried to answer the research questions posed in Sect. 3. The following subsections present the results per research question.

4.1 Motivation of AR Applications

Regarding the first research question, we observe that the motivations for creating applications related to augmented reality (AR) for cultural heritage mainly concern the promotion of a cultural inventory for public information and tourism development [4, 5, 7]. More specifically, many are using AR technology to promote the cultural heritage of an area that is hard to research [3, 12, 15], such as underwater cultural heritage [3] where they are addressed to specialized tourists (such as divers) but also to non-specialists, in order to highlight both the cultural reserve and to help the development of tourism in coastal areas and islands.

Another option of using AR technology to highlight a cultural resource is to promote a new thinking on the field of education [4, 7, 8]. Specifically, in the study of Hincapie, M., Diaz, C. et al. [8] has been used AR and GPS technology to revive the cultural heritage around Medellin's Cisnero Square (also called "Park of Lights"), studying the positive effects that new technologies have on the process of learning and assimilating new knowledge [8].

Many choose to create applications for mobile devices (phones or tablets), which mix reality with the virtual representation of buildings or routes, as in the case of Flores, N.M. et al. [15], where by using AR technology they designed and virtually constructed the war-damaged and unrepaired buildings on Corregidor Island, Philippines. Something similar happened in the creation of the "Walk1916" application, where they built a mobile walking tour of the Easter Rising sites in Dublin, Ireland [19]. Here, they identified digital surrogates from archival collections, adding audio and textual description of the image seen by the app user, using AR and GPS technology.

But there are also cases, such as the study by Weking A.N., Suyoto S., Santoso A.J. [13], where an AR mobile phone application was created to promote Indonesian traditional food to preserve the tradition against western influences and pass it on to the next generation.

What has been found is that a small percentage of works concern the creation of gamification applications and two articles that we studied stand out. In [5] Koutsabasis, P., Partheniadis, P. et al. present to us the design of a mobile learning game for the promotion and preservation of the industrial production of oil in Lesvos, as an element of cultural heritage. The article of Koutromanos, G., Styliaras, G. [21] talks about the design of a game with AR and GPS technology that presents traditional old buildings (tobacco warehouses) of Agrinio, a city in Western Macedonia, motivating primary school students to explore these buildings from different perspectives: historical, architectural and

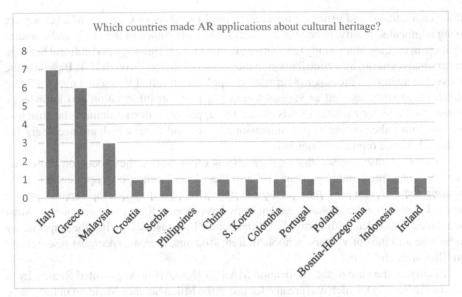

Fig. 1. Country of origin of AR applications

cultural value, as well as their relationship with the economic and cultural development of the city.

4.2 Origin of AR Applications

Regarding the second research question about the regions and countries concerning the AR applications, we notice that most of them have been created in Italy (7 applications), promoting elements and buildings inherited from antiquity and Roman times [1, 4, 6, 23–26]. According to Fig. 1, the next country that has created a big number of applications is Greece, having 6 articles out of the 27 we have studied [3, 5, 16, 17, 21, 27]. The Greek applications refer in their entirety to material cultural heritage [5, 16] and cultural reserve [3, 17, 21, 27], with the aim of promoting it to the general public. Then Malaisia follows with 3 applications and the rest of the countries that mentioned have one application each.

4.3 AR Application Design Methodologies

In design methodologies, the steps followed by most tasks start with requirements analysis, cultural content selection, and development platform selection. More specifically in the paper [8] we see that they start with a review of other applications and works that have been done to promote archaeological sites and at the same time include their own research. They explain that they chose to highlight this specific cultural content, that is, to record the center of Medellin (the Cisneros market) geographically, because it marked an era of change in the life of the city and acted as the backbone of transformation and change in the bourgeoisie. Then, they list the elements that the app they will create should have: characterize and visualize the architectural elements of Cisneros Market Square using augmented reality, to be able to describe the importance of the city's architectural heritage in the case study study) and finally, to propose a technology and cultural heritage experience scenario, as a contribution to the spread of digital through ICT. Based on the above, the authors of the paper [8] created an application called Vitica that uses GPS and augmented reality, as well as various formats to transmit information and knowledge related to the historical sites of this place. The application design defines the structure for presenting the content in two dimensions, space and time, which are necessary for cultural heritage representations [8].

In another case, we see that as they review other works, they focus on those that involve promoting botanic gardens [11] and then describe their own application, high-lighting the different way they set up the app: although they use the separation into themed trails (as other botanic garden apps have done), their trails are about "Must See Trees", "Garden with history", "Birds" and "Biosensors", giving the opportunity to browse all kinds of visitors: schoolchildren, students, tourists, specialist researchers, families with children.

Finally, in the case of the application MARSS (MusAB in Augmented Reality from Science to Society), which was created for use in the Milan Science Museum in Italy, they refer to apps that other museums have developed to showcase some of their exhibits, identifying as a shortcoming that many studies do not have quantitative data on the economic impact of using these apps in museums [1]. Then, they set as the primary goal of the project the creation of a "talking" museum collection, which will lead the visitor to the discovery of astronomy, its history and the role that the "Osservatorio" plays for the city of Milan. They choose the Astronomical Instruments gallery, making an AR application (MARSS) where each astronomical instrument in the exhibit has an AR clip explaining its history and use. The exhibition needed to be modernized and improved and by keeping in mind the basic question "what does an astronomer do", the MARSS project aims to design and develop a digital journey inside the museum allowing different categories of visitors to enjoy the exhibition in an interactive way.

4.4 AR Application Development and Implementation Methodologies

For the creation of 3D models, the development platforms Unity 3D and Vuforia are preferred, which they used to create an interactive 3D book where the user solves puzzles that include historical events, specific words from the legend and other details from the stories [7]. Also, for the creation of 3D models they are also used in the studies [8, 13, 16]. For the creation of maps the Map Box Library and Easy AR [8], as well as Maxon Cinema 4D [4] are used, but also Google maps, where in the study [19] we can see how a map is created with different places marked with a special color and when the user is close to the location, he can select the location to display a fragment of the digital surrogate, seeing the contemporary location along with the digital surrogate, mixing historical figures with the modern setting of the historical site.

More specifically, the applications that used Unity are 11 ([2, 7–9, 11–13, 15–17, 20, 24]), while those that used Vuforia are 5 ([7, 13–16]). Other work has used Easy AR SDK [11], DynaMus [11], where it uses Google and Europeana web services to create 3D objects in the designing of the time travel trip in Bosnia and Herzegovina. Also, in papers [12, 17] and [14] Unreal and AR Markers have been used. Tan, K.L. and Lim, C.K. in paper [20] have been used Adobe Fuse C platform and Mixamo platform in order to give movements in their characters. To design 3D objects, they used Sketch Up [20]. Moving on, we can see that Koutromanos, G., Styliaras, G. in paper [21] used FreshAir Layar Creator to create 3D objects, which were about the depiction of the old tobacco warehouses in the town of Agrinio, while Autocad Map 3D has been used in paper [23] along with ArcGIS online platform by Canciani, M., Chiappetta, F., et al. to depict a 3D map of Villa Andriana in Tivoli, Italy, studying the ruins and ancient paths. Finally, Pietroni, E. used 3D Max to design 3D objects about the city of Matera in Italy [24]. In the rest of the papers, they don't mention exactly what software frameworks they used for AR development.

4.5 Technical Features of AR Applications

The majority of applications that have been created, according to Fig. 2, can be used via smartphone or tablet (with Android), making it easy for everyone to use them. Two applications are only for use by computer [7, 27]. The applications contain GPS geolocation technology, as it helps the user to know exactly where the monument/cultural reserve they are visiting is located, and most of those we studied use it. Also, in combination with QR codes that can be used, the user's location determines the selection of image data that can be consulted [21, 23].

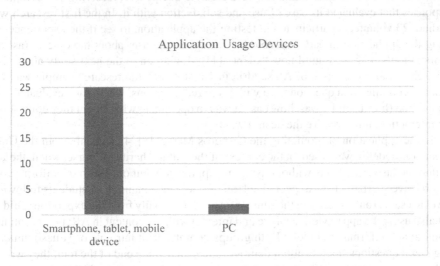

Fig. 2. Devices using the applications

The applications that used GPS are 21 [1–4, 8–12, 14, 15, 17, 19–27], while those that used QR codes are only 3: [2, 9, 14]. The rest of the applications do not use GPS [5–7, 13, 16, 18], since they do not need it, such as application in [5] which is about the industrial oil production in Lesvos, Greece, in [6] is about the designing of a database for the catacombs in Italy and in [7] the application is about an illustrated book of the traditional dance Xi Shi. The application of paper [13] is about the traditional food in Malaysia, while the application of paper [16] talks about the traditional type of watermill in Greece and finally, the application of paper [18] is for restoring digital old objects in their original form, visualizing their actual past state.

4.6 Evaluation Methodologies of AR Applications and Results

From the study of the 27 papers, we noticed that not all of them have progressed to app evaluation methodologies. According to the articles we studied and Fig. 3, we can see that 19 studies have gone into evaluation, of which 3 are technical evaluations and they study whether the application works properly and how users handle it [13, 15, 17], while in the paper [17] have been used both technical evaluation and evaluation from users, but not in a quantitative way. Six applications were not evaluated [2, 3, 7, 23, 25, 26]. Complete evaluations that have results are 5 (as [1, 5, 8, 9, 16]) and they use quantitative research methods such as questionnaires to the applications' users. In these surveys, the interest was focused in addition to the basic demographic data and other parameters, such as the impact of the use of applications for learning new things [1, 8, 9], the promotion of tourism and the new knowledge that one can gain with the help of AR augmented reality on cultural heritage issues [5, 16].

Sample sizes in most surveys were not very large, with the exception of the World Heritage Site AR Tour guide app (protected by UNESCO) Hwaseong Fortress in Suwon of S. Korea [9], where questionnaires were given to 201 people, receiving 169 complete responses that evaluated its ease of use and satisfaction with it. In the first research we studied, 23 volunteers participated in testing the application, to see if the experience of using the application imparts valuable knowledge to the user about the objects (astronomical tools) that were until now "silent" [1]. Moving on to the next study about the Basilica of Saint Catherine of Alexandria in Galatina [4], the research sample was 41 people, who filled in a questionnaire with prepared questions, where they evaluated the application (how useful it was, how easy it was to operate, to what extent they controlled the interaction, how creative the design was).

In the application of promoting the Cisneros Market [8], 48 students from the University of Medellin were used, in the context of the cultural heritage course, where the 22 visited the historical sights without using the application, but only with the information they received verbally from a specialized tour guide. The remaining 26 students followed the exact same route, receiving the same information verbally from the expert tour guide, but also using the app to view, analyze and interact with the content in AR: photos, audio material and information in text. Both groups completed an introductory questionnaire of general questions (mainly about demographics) and at the end of the tour, they wrote a short knowledge test (10 questions) to assess their knowledge of Cisneros Market, without being informed beforehand.

In [10] the application itself collects demographic information about the visitors who used it, which allows us to understand who chooses to use each route in the Lisbon Botanical Gardens, but without giving us the number of visitors. Accordingly, in [11] they tell us that they used questionnaires with closed and open-ended questions for the evaluation, but they do not tell us either the questions or the sample that answered.

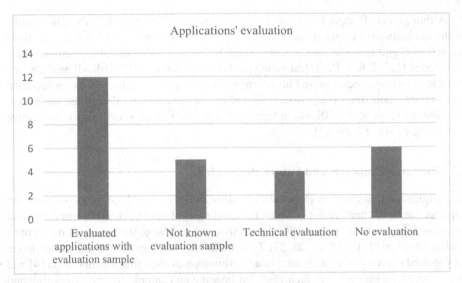

Fig. 3. Applications' evaluation

In the application of paper [14] they state that they used random interviews of 120 museum visitors, while in the application about the Greek type of watermill [16] a sample of 25 people was used with organized visits in groups of 4 people, due to limited devices for the application. At the end of each tour of the site and use of the application, they filled out a questionnaire about their experience and a discussion followed between the researcher (and creator of the application) and the participants.

In application "Walk1916", the walking tour of Easter Rising sites in Dublin [19], the evaluation was done with 15 semi-structured interviews with users of the app to understand how the integration of digital surrogates with mobile technology features affected the participants' perceptions and experience.

Finally, in the application about raising awareness of learning and getting to know historical parts of Malaysia through gamification [20] a sample of 50 people was used, who completed a pre & post-test to evaluate the knowledge they already had, but also the new knowledge they acquired through the game. They also filled out a questionnaire about its use and design. In the research [21] the application was evaluated by only 5 teachers and 21 primary school students. In the oldest application in our research, the digital cultural map of the city of Veria in Greece [27], only 10 users were used to evaluate the usability of the application.

In the remaining applications we notice that they have not proceeded with their evaluation [2, 3, 7, 23, 26], in [25] the application has not been completed, so they do not have an evaluation, while in the surveys [11] and [12] report that questionnaires are provided, without mentioning the sample number. Research [13] was evaluated with a black box testing method that examines the operation of the application, as in researches [17] and [18] where only technical evaluations were done, while in research [15] the evaluation was done by IT experts and tourists, again without mentioning the sample size.

Although not all applications have been evaluated in the same way, from the results of the evaluations we understand that most of those who have used AR applications are satisfied and consider that it really helps to better understand and assimilate new knowledge [1, 2, 5, 8, 9, 19, 21], at young [8, 21] and older ages [12, 16]. AR applications make the learning process more fun and enjoyable [5, 8, 10, 19, 20] and we conclude that they achieve their main goal: awareness and education on cultural heritage issues and monuments [1, 4, 8, 19, 20], while helping the tourism development of the respective area [3, 6, 12–14, 19, 24, 27].

4.7 Research Proposals and Future Research

A key question that emerges from the evaluation (whether it is done by the users of the applications or by their creators) is how the existing applications could be improved and developed into something even better, and this is what most of the applications we have studied focus on [1, 17, 18, 24, 26, 27]. Few are those who propose to use the knowledge they gained to create something new or a continuation of their first attempt, as in [4] and [19] where they propose that their research become an example for the promoting and understanding of other cultural monuments heritage.

More specifically in [4], as future research they wish to create an application enriched with new points of interest for the user and easy access to additional information pages, in order to offer a more complete and structured "study path". But they all the applications come to the common conclusion that the use of AR technology to highlight the cultural heritage and promote education on it, significantly helps to achieve this goal and is done in a more modern and pleasant way.

5 Discussion

In this section we are going to discuss about our findings during our research. It is easily understood that all the applications that were used to enhance the dissemination of knowledge have positive impact on their users. From the applications we have studied 23 of them are being used to enhance the education process, among tourists, students and visitors of the sites. On of them is the application of Hincapie M. et al., which was created to show the revival of cultural heritage in the Medellin's square [8]. This application was also tested by students in context of cultural heritage course, leading us to realize that the use of this application helped them understand better the new knowledge they had to absorb.

However, not many applications include serious games in order to promote the education, only 4 of them use gamification [7, 9, 20] and [21]. In Yan H. et al. research we can observe how they use gamification to promote the myth of Xi Shi (an interactive book, solving puzzles) [7], while Koo S. et al. include gamification activities in their main application, which was designed to highlight the Hwaseong Fortress (S. Korea) as a tourist attraction [9]. Two types of AR construction games are currently available in their application: simple and sandbox. The simple AR construction game is designed for a user to walk through the construction of a monumental structure of the site and let the visitors grasp the architectural and constructional information visually. While the simple construction game is intended for users to follow the construction process as pre-designed, the sandbox AR construction game is intended to build a structure freely within a limited time using various construction materials. Two sandbox construction games are available to play, and seven different types of construction materials are given in each game. To maximize the interaction with the users, the score is calculated and displayed at every step of the construction by computing the similarity with the actual building (pre-designed model). For the sandbox AR construction games, detailed descriptions about the user interface and functions are provided as a tutorial to achieve technology readiness [9].

In the application of Tan K.L. et al. we can see the serious game they created to emphasize historical places in Perak (Malaysia) [20]. The mobile game contains a story mode where it will explain about the goals and objectives of the Exploration Mode. It contains the text which represent the storyline and indicator arrow which link to the next storyline. Also, it contains a storyline in the form of a dialogue where a 2D character called Si Kuntum who will be the user tour guide. Essentially, the module of Clue is to indicate the tasks that the user needs to complete in order to proceed the game while the module of Augmented Reality (Pit Stops) are the most important interfaces that are available in this mobile game. Fundamentally, the module of Clue and Augmented Reality (Pit Stops) is related because the user need to follow the clue in order to arrive at the Pit Stops. There are eleven Augmented Reality interfaces as there are eleven pit stops in Kellies Castle. The app contains a 3D character named William Kellie Smith. This character will appear at each Augmented Reality interfaces to explain some historical info about the places [20].

In Koutromanos G. et al. they have created an educational (serious) game in order for young elementary students to find out about the history, culture and architecture of their city, and especially about old tobacco warehouses in the city of Siatista (Greece) [21]. A mobile device with wireless connectivity, camera and GPS capabilities can access these games from anywhere. When the students are located near the real location in the field, a certain number of "Triggers" are accessible to them. At the location of these "Triggers", which are placed on a map of the physical setting, the students can experience augmented reality visualizations placed over the real environment and digital information such as text, images, video, audio, multiple-choice and open-ended questions. On the other hand, the marker-based part of the augmented reality game "The buildings speak about our city" will use the Layar Creator, which can activate print pages of digital augmented reality content [21].

So, not only there are a few applications that use gamification activities, but they also have not tested them or collected results about their use. Two of them ([20] and [21]) have been tested properly and one of them [20] has collected pre and post-tests about using the application and its design. Having these in mind, we can see that there are some gaps in most of researches concerning the results of using applications. In addition, more emphasis should have been placed on the impact they have on the educational process, while highlighting the respective cultural reserve that has been selected.

Studying their evaluations [9, 20, 21] through questionnaires and mini-tests we can see that indeed those applications have helped users to learn new things about the particular cultural heritage reserve [9, 20]. Moreover, users are encouraged to visit those places and they believe that those applications are easy enough to be used by most of them. However, they have proposed modifications and changes in them, in order to be even more friendly and easy to use [20, 21]. The application [7] has not been evaluated yet.

From the above study of works we find that there are some research gaps. First, there is a small number of studies on AR applications for promoting cultural heritage in Greece and especially for educational purposes. In particular, there are no AR applications around the areas of high cultural interest in Greece, such as for highlighting buildings in the region of Western Macedonia or even for cultural reserves related to the region of Thessaloniki. Secondly, based on this review it was found that the majority of AR applications were developed with platforms and tools (such as Unity, Vuforia, etc.) that required advanced programming knowledge. On the other hand, it has been found that very few applications were developed with platforms (such as Easy AR) that do not require programming knowledge. Therefore, we could further explore the development of AR applications with similar platforms that do not require writing code. This is especially important so that creators or educators who do not have a strong computing background can design and develop AR applications for cultural heritage in a fast way and also, these applications can be easily leveraged in the educational process. Thirdly, there is a limited number of works that have evaluated AR applications integrated in the Greek education system or tourist audience and even fewer that have been reported on World Heritage sites protected by UNESCO [9, 13].

6 Conclusions

In this work, we researched AR applications that were used to highlight cultural heritage (tangible or intangible), with educational purposes or to enhance the touristic element. From our research in the time period 1997–2023, we have come to the conclusion that most applications concern mainly building cultural heritage, whether it belongs to the ancient or the more recent history of these countries, cultural routes within cities or in areas of cities with historical/ cultural nature and fewer are those concerning the intangible cultural heritage. Moreover, we have seen that the use of AR technology for cultural issues is very widespread and those who choose to set up applications to highlight it are technically skilled and create quite complex applications. The biggest deficiency that exists in this area concerns the correct evaluation of these applications, since most of the data that would show us how satisfied users are with each application and how much it helps to promote the cultural stock, as well as according to how helpful they are in the educational process are not published.

Our goal for future research is to create AR applications covering as much as possible the research gaps we mentioned earlier. Specifically, our goal is to create an application which infuses elements of gamification and interactive storytelling into AR experiences with the help of a creator-friendly development platform that will highlight elements of cultural heritage in Greece in an educational way. In addition, the application will be evaluated by a certain number of examinees and the results of the evaluation will be available in order to see to what extent AR technology helps in the learning process in the Greek education system, but also to motivate other researchers to create applications in this direction.

Finally, we must point out that the present review has a limitation in that it was based on articles from the Scopus and Web of Science databases only. Our work could be extended for articles retrieved from Google Scholar to gain even greater insight into the state of AR applications.

References

1. Spadoni, E., Porro, S., Bordegoni, M., Arosio, I., Barbalini, L., Carulli, M.: Augmented reality to engage visitors of science museums through interactive experiences. Heritage **2022**(5), 1370–1394 (2022). https://doi.org/10.3390/heritage5030071
2. Tatic, D.: Mobile presentation of the war history of the city of NIS. In: Digital Presentation and Preservation of Cultural and Scientific Heritage (12), pp. 151–159 (2022). https://doi.org/10.55630/dipp.2022.12.12
3. Manglis, A., Fourkiotou, A., Papadopoulou, D.: A roadmap for the sustainable valorization of accessible underwater cultural heritage sites. Heritage **2021**(4), 4700–4715 (2021). https://doi.org/10.3390/heritage4040259
4. Cisternino, D., et al.: Augmented reality applications to support the promotion of cultural heritage: the case of the basilica of saint catherine of alexandria in Galatina. J. Comput. Cult. Heritage **14**(4), Article 47 (2021). https://doi.org/10.1145/3460657
5. Koutsabasis, P., et al.: Location-based games for cultural heritage: applying the design thinking process. In: CHI Greece 2021: 1st International Conference of the ACM Greek SIGCHI Chapter (CHI Greece 2021). ACM, New York, USA (2021). https://doi.org/10.1145/3489410.3489419
6. Presti, O.L. Carli, M.R.: Italian catacombs and their digital presence for underground heritage sustainability. Sustainability (13) (2021). https://doi.org/10.3390/su132112010
7. Yan, H., Liu, W., Xia, X., Yangying, X., Ssong, T.: Design research of interactive picture books of cultural education based on augmented reality technology, In: The 16th International Conference in Computer Science & Education (ICCSE 2021), pp. 958–962. Lancaster University, UK (2021). https://doi.org/10.1109/ICCSE51940.2021.9569391
8. Hincapie, M., Diaz, C., Zapata-Cardenas, M.-I., Rios, H.J.T., Valencia, D., Guemes-Castorena, D.: Augmented reality mobile apps for cultural heritage reactivation. In: Computers and Electrical Engineering, vol. 93, Elsevier B.V. (2021). https://doi.org/10.1016/j.compeleceng.2021.107281
9. Koo, S., Kim, J., Kim, C., Kim, J., Cha, H.S.: Development of an augmented reality tour guide for a cultural heritage site. ACM J. Comput. Cult. Heritage **12**(4), Article 24 (2019). https://doi.org/10.1145/3317552
10. Postolache, S., et al.: Contributions to the design of mobile applications for visitors of Botanical Gardens. In: CENTERIS - International Conference on ENTERprise Information Systems/ProjMAN - International Conference on Project MANagement/HCist - International Conference on Health and Social Care Information Systems and Technologies 2021, pp. 389–399, Elsevier B.V. (2022). https://doi.org/10.1016/j.procs.2021.12.028
11. Rizvic, S., Boškovic, D., Okanovic, V., Kihic, I.I., Prazina, I., Mijantovic, B.: Time travel to the past of bosnia and herzegovina through virtual and augmented reality. Appl. Sci. **11**, MDPI, Switzerland (2021). https://doi.org/10.3390/app11083711
12. Izani, M., Samad, A., Razak, A.: Augmented reality application based navigating the a famosa fortress site. In: Proceedings of the Third International Conference on Intelligent Sustainable Systems [ICISS 2020] IEEE Xplore, pp. 285–290 (2020). https://doi.org/10.1109/ICISS49785.2020.9316019

13. Weking, A.N., Suyoto S., Santoso A.J.: A development of augmented reality mobile appli-
    cation to promote the traditional indonesian food. Int. J. Interact. Mobile Technol. **14**(9),
    248–257, iJIM, Austria (2020). https://doi.org/10.3991/ijim.v14i09.11179

14. Siang, T.G., Aziz, K.B.A., Ahmad, Z.B., Suhaifi, S.B.: Augmented reality mobile application
    for museum: a technology acceptance study. In: International Conference on Research and
    Innovation in Information Systems, ICRIIS (2019). https://doi.org/10.1109/ICRIIS48246.
    2019.9073457

15. Flores, N.M., et al.: Rebuilding cultural and heritage space of corregidor island using GPS-
    based augmented reality. Int. J. Recent Technol. Eng. **8** (2S11) (2019). https://doi.org/10.
    35940/ijrte.B1345.0982S1119

16. Tzima, S., Smyris, G., Styliaras, G., Bassounas, A.: Digital representations and cultural her-
    itage interactions through the "Greek Type" Watermills Case. In: 9th International Conference
    on Information, Intelligence, Systems and Applications. IEEE Computational Intelligence
    Society, Greece (2018). https://doi.org/10.1109/IISA.2018.8633659

17. Panou, C., Ragia, L., Dimelli, D., Mania, K.: An architecture for mobile outdoors augmented
    reality for cultural heritage. ISPRS Int. J. Geo-Inform. **7**(12), Art. No. 463 (2018). https://doi.
    org/10.3390/ijgi7120463

18. Siekanski, P., Bunsch, E., Sitnik, R.: Seeing the past: An augmented reality application for
    visualization the previous state of cultural heritage locations. In: IS and T International Sym-
    posium on Electronic Imaging Science and Technology, pp. 452–455 (2018). https://doi.org/
    10.2352/ISSN.2470-1173.2018.03.ERVR-452

19. Cushing, A.L., Cowan, B.R.: Walk1916 Exploring non-research user access to and use of
    digital surrogates via a mobile walking tour app. J. Document. **73**(5), 917–933, Emerald
    Publishing Limited, UK (2017). http://www.emeraldinsight.com/0022-0418.htm, https://doi.
    org/10.1108/JD-03-2017-0031

20. Tan, K.L., Lim, C.K.: Digital heritage gamification: an augmented-virtual walkthrough to
    learn and explore historical sites. In: The 2nd International Conference on Applied Science
    and Technology 2017 (ICAST 2017) Conference Proceedings, vol. 1891, Art. No. 020139,
    AIP Publishing, USA (2017). https://doi.org/10.1063/1.5005472

21. Koutromanos, G., Styliaras, G.: "The buildings speak about our city": a location based aug-
    mented reality game. In: IISA 2015 - 6th International Conference on Information, Intelli-
    gence, Systems and Applications, Art. No. 7388031, Ionian University, Greece (2015). https://
    doi.org/10.1109/IISA.2015.7388031

22. Dutra J.P., Ebel I.R.: Cultural hARitage: augmented reality applied on cultural heritage.
    In: Zachmann G., Perret J., Amditis A. (eds.) Conference and Exhibition of the European
    Association of Virtual and Augmented Reality (2014). https://doi.org/10.2312/eurovr.201
    41349

23. Canciani, M., Chiappetta, F., Michelini, M., Pallottino, E., Saccone, M., Scortecci, A.: A
    new GIS-based map of Villa Adriana, a multimedia guide for ancient paths. In: International
    Archives of the Photogrammetry, Remote Sensing and Spatial Information Sciences - ISPRS
    Archives, vol. 40, no. 5, pp. 129–136. ISPRS, Germany (2014). https://doi.org/10.5194/isp
    rsarchives-XL-5-129-2014

24. Pietroni, E.: An augmented experiences in cultural heritage through mobile devices: "Matera
    Tales of a City" Project. In: Proceedings of the 2012 18th International Conference on Virtual
    Systems and Multimedia, VSMM 2012: Virtual Systems in the Information Society, Art. No.
    6365915, pp. 117–124 (2012). https://doi.org/10.1109/VSMM.2012.6365915

25. Renda, G., Gigli, S., Amato, A., Venticinque, S., Di Martino, B., Cappa, F.R.: Mobile devices for the visit of "Anfiteatro Campano" in santa maria capua vetere. In: Ioannides, M., Fritsch, D., Leissner, J., Davies, R., Remondino, F., Caffo, R. (eds.) Progress in Cultural Heritage Preservation: 4th International Conference, EuroMed 2012, Limassol, Cyprus, October 29 – November 3, 2012. Proceedings, pp. 281–290. Springer Berlin Heidelberg, Berlin, Heidelberg (2012). https://doi.org/10.1007/978-3-642-34234-9_28

26. Cutrí, G., Naccarato, G., Pantano, E.: Mobile cultural heritage: the case study of locri. In: Pan, Z., Zhang, X., El Rhalibi, A., Woo, W., Li, Y. (eds.) Technologies for E-Learning and Digital Entertainment, pp. 410–420. Springer Berlin Heidelberg, Berlin, Heidelberg (2008). https://doi.org/10.1007/978-3-540-69736-7_44

27. Garoufallou, E., Siatri, R., Balatsoukas, P.: Virtual maps–virtual worlds: testing the usability of a Greek virtual cultural map. J. Am. Soc. Inform. Sci. Technol. **59**(4), 591–601 (2008). https://doi.org/10.1002/asi.20768

28. Economou, M.: Heritage in the digital age. In: A Companion to Heritage Studies (2015). https://doi.org/10.1002/9781118486634.ch15

29. MinnaLearn Home Page. https://courses.minnalearn.com/el/courses/emerging-technologies/extended-reality-vr-ar-mr/introduction-to-extended-reality-ar-vr-and-mr/. Accessed 12 April 2023

30. Mortara M., Catalano C.E., Bellotti F., Fiucci G., Houry-Panchetti M., Petridis P.: Learning cultural heritage by serious games. J. Cult. Heritage **15**, 318–325 (2014). https://doi.org/10.1016/j.culher.2013.04.004

31. Marr B.: What is extended reality technology? a simple explanation for anyone. In: Forbes (2019). https://www.forbes.com/sites/bernardmarr/2019/08/12/what-is-extended-reality-technology-a-simple-explanation-for-anyone/. Accessed 12 April 2023

32. Laamarti, F., Eid, M., El Saddik, A.: An overview of serious games. Int. J. Comput. Games Technol. **2014**, Hindawi Publishing Corporation (2014). https://doi.org/10.1155/2014/358152

33. Khan, I., Melro, A., Amaro, A.C., Oliveira, L.: systematic review on gamification and cultural heritage dissemination. J. Digital Media Interact. **3**(8), 19–41 (2020). https://doi.org/10.34624/jdmi.v3i8.21934

34. Bekele, M.K., Pierdicca, R., Frontoni, E., Malinverni, E.S., Gain, J: A survey of augmented, virtual, and mixed reality for cultural heritage. ACM J. Comput. Cult. Heritage **11**(2), Article 7 (2018). https://doi.org/10.1145/3145534

Enhancing Art Therapy with Virtual Reality and Hand Gesture Recognition: A Case Study in Pottery Modeling

Nicola Capece[1](✉)[ID], Carola Gatto[2][ID], Gilda Manfredi[1][ID], Gabriele Gilio[1][ID], Benito Luigi Nuzzo[2], Lucio Tommaso De Paolis[2][ID], and Ugo Erra[1][ID]

[1] University of Basilicata, 85100 Potenza, Italy
{nicola.capece,gilda.manfredi,gabriele.gilio,ugo.erra}@unibas.it
[2] University of Salento, 73100 Lecce, Italy
{carola.gatto,benitoluigi.nuzzo,lucio.depaolis}@unisalento.it

Abstract. This paper introduces an innovative approach to Virtual Reality (VR)-based art therapy for pottery modeling using Hand Gesture Recognition (HGR) technology. Traditional pottery modeling methods have limitations in terms of accessibility and cost, making it challenging for individuals with physical or mental health conditions to engage in this therapeutic activity. The paper proposes the use of VR and HGR technologies to provide a more accessible and immersive pottery modeling experience. The VR application simulates the process of modeling and decorating a traditional ceramic vase, providing users with a range of digital tools and materials. The HGR system, based on a neural network, allows users to manipulate virtual pottery with their hands in a natural and intuitive way, providing real-time feedback and guidance. The application offers different modes to accommodate various motor skills and cognitive abilities. The study discusses the therapeutic benefits of VR-based art therapy and the potential of HGR technology in enhancing the immersive and interactive nature of the experience. Overall, the VR-based art therapy program presented in this paper offers a scalable and adaptable solution for individuals with limited access to traditional pottery tools and materials, promoting greater accessibility and personalization in art therapy.

Keywords: art therapy · virtual clay sculpting · immersive virtual environments · gesture-based interaction

1 Introduction

Art therapy is a form of psychotherapy that recognizes the intrinsic relationship between creativity and mental health [1,2]. It aims to provide individuals with a safe and supportive environment where they can express themselves through various art forms, including painting, drawing, sculpting, and pottery modeling. Through the creative process, individuals can explore their emotions [3],

L. T. De Paolis et al. (Eds.): XR Salento 2023, LNCS 14219, pp. 210–226, 2023.
https://doi.org/10.1007/978-3-031-43404-4_14

thoughts, and experiences in a non-verbal and symbolic way, allowing them to gain insight into their inner world and enhance their self-awareness and coping skills. Pottery modeling, in particular, has gained popularity as an activity within art therapy due to its unique tactile and sensory nature. This therapeutic approach involves shaping clay into different forms, allowing individuals to bring their imaginative visions to life. Through the act of creating something tangible and concrete, individuals can experience a profound sense of achievement and mastery, contributing to their overall well-being.

Research has highlighted the diverse therapeutic benefits of pottery modeling, including stress reduction, increased self-esteem, and improved mood [4,5]. Thanks to these characteristics, pottery modeling can be considered a valuable activity for stress management by engaging individuals in a hands-on, absorbing activity that diverts their attention from daily stressors. The sensory engagement provided by handling the clay, coupled with the focused and rhythmic movements required, facilitates relaxation and promotes a sense of calm [3,6]. Compared to other stress management activities, pottery modeling holds unique advantages. While there may be alternative techniques that are less expensive or easier to implement, the specific characteristics of pottery modeling make it a preferred option for many individuals. The hands-on nature of the activity provides a physical and tangible outlet for emotional expression, allowing individuals to externalize their emotions in a non-verbal manner [7]. This can be especially beneficial for individuals who struggle with verbal communication or find it challenging to express their emotions explicitly. Furthermore, pottery modeling encourages a sense of creativity and personal agency. The process of shaping clay into desired forms empowers individuals to manifest their visions and ideas, fostering a profound sense of accomplishment. The tangible outcome of pottery modeling serves as a symbol of their creativity and resilience, promoting increased self-esteem and positive mood.

However, traditional pottery modeling methods require specific tools and materials that may be difficult for individuals to access, especially for those who are unable to leave their homes due to physical or mental health conditions. Pottery modeling typically involves a pottery wheel, which requires physical coordination and strength to operate and may not be readily available to individuals who do not have access to a pottery studio or who have mobility or transportation limitations. Additionally, traditional pottery materials, such as clay, glazes, and kilns, can be costly and require specialized equipment to use safely. Therefore, there is a need for alternative methods of pottery modeling that can provide individuals with the same therapeutic benefits without the limitations of traditional methods. VR and HGR [8] technologies [9,10] provide a potential solution to this problem, allowing individuals to engage in pottery modeling without the need for physical tools or materials. By creating a digital environment that simulates the experience of traditional pottery modeling, VR can provide individuals with access to a range of digital tools and materials, allowing them to create pottery from the comfort of their own homes. Moreover, HGR can enhance the immersive and intuitive nature of the experience, allowing individuals to manipulate virtual pottery with their hands in a natural and intuitive way. This technology can also provide therapists with more accurate and detailed information about client movements and progress, enabling them to provide real-time feedback and guidance [11].

In this paper, we present an innovative approach to VR-based art therapy for pottery modeling, which uses HGR technology. Our application is specifically designed to model and decorate a "Trozzella", a traditional ceramic vase from the Italian region of Puglia. The instruction and techniques used in the program are derived from experimental archaeological studies, ensuring an authentic and culturally meaningful experience for participants. The art therapy activity we defined in this study is divided into three modes: passive, controller-based, and hand gestures. These modes are provided to users to accommodate different levels of motor skills and cognitive abilities. The passive mode allows users to observe the pottery modeling process, the controller-based system provides a smart and interactive solution discussed in this paper by means of VR controllers while the hand gesture modes enable users to actively engage with the virtual pottery wheel and decorating tools. The HGR system used in our application is based on a neural network, which allows for more accurate and precise detection of hand movements. This system recognizes various hand gestures which are essential for pottery modeling. With this technology, users can interact with the virtual pottery wheel and decorating tools more intuitively and naturally. By providing multiple modes and utilizing hand gesture recognition technology, our application allows for a more personalized and adaptable experience. Users can choose the mode that best suits their abilities and preferences, and the HGR system ensures that they can engage with the virtual environment in a way that feels natural and intuitive. Overall, our VR-based art therapy program offers a scalable and adaptable solution that is suitable for individuals with varying levels of motor and cognitive abilities who may not have access to traditional pottery tools and materials. The use of a neural network-based HGR system enhances the sense of immersion and interaction with the virtual environment, making the experience more engaging and potentially more effective as a form of art therapy. By providing an authentic and culturally meaningful experience, we hope to enhance the therapeutic benefits of pottery modeling and promote greater accessibility to art therapy for all.

The remainder of this paper is organized as follows: Section 2 provides a review of the literature on art therapy, VR technology, and HGR technology. Section 3 provides a description of the adopted technologies. Section 4 describes the methodology used in our case study, including the design of the VR-based art therapy application and the use of HGR technology. Section 5 presents the results of our case study, including the feedback we received from participants and the insights we gained about the use of VR and HGR technology in art therapy. Finally, in Sect. 6, we discuss the implications of our findings and future directions for research in this field.

2 Related Work

Art therapy has been widely studied and documented in the literature, with numerous studies demonstrating its efficacy in improving psychological and emotional well-being. Research has shown that art therapy can be effective in reducing symptoms of depression [12], anxiety, post-traumatic stress disorder (PTSD) [13], and other mental health disorders [2]. Pottery modeling, in particular, has been shown to have therapeutic benefits, including stress reduction, increased self-esteem, and improved mood [4,5]. However, traditional pottery modeling methods have limitations, including the need for specialized equipment, the cost of materials, and the physical demands of the activity. VR technology has emerged as a promising tool for enhancing the therapeutic benefits of pottery modeling in art therapy. VR can provide a more accessible and immersive environment for pottery modeling, allowing clients to experience the benefits of the activity without the limitations of traditional methods [14]. Additionally, VR technology can allow therapists to track and analyze client movements, providing a more detailed and accurate assessment of their progress and needs. Previous research has explored the use of VR technology in art therapy, with promising results. An interesting study was conducted by Kaimal et al. [15] on a sample of participants to determine their effectiveness of practicing art therapy sessions. Furthermore, Hacmun et al. [16] explored the potential of art creation in VR for Art Therapy (VRAT) from the perspective of experienced art therapists. After the VR experience, a semi-structured test was conducted to collect key data on their experience as both creators and observers. The results showed that the therapists confirm the substantial value of the new VR medium for art therapy.

Viewing an artistic masterpiece is associated with brain excitation by neural processes that occur quite spontaneously in the observer. This aesthetic experience can even elicit a response in the motor areas of observers. In the neurorehabilitation of stroke patients, art observation has been used to reduce psychological disorders and creative art therapy to improve physical function and cognitive abilities. For instance, Iosa et al. [17] conducted an experiment in which, thanks to VR, some stroke patients had the illusion of painting some art masterpieces, such as Michelangelo's "The Creation of Adam" or Botticelli's "The Birth of Venus," by moving their hand on a virtual canvas. The aim was to measure these patients' improvements in terms of brain activation, thus coming to coin the formula "Michelangelo Effect" to define this improvement in performance when interacting with an artistic stimulus as the Michelangelo effect. In some cases, specific goals were focused on in order to identify the most effective practice in relation to the disorder, for example, in the work of Zeevi et al. [18] VR technology was combined with traditional art therapy to treat adolescents suffering from anxiety and social difficulties. This study showed that this type of technology can lead to a better understanding of adolescents' needs using their perspective and thus to better outcomes.

Hand gesture recognition technology is another promising tool for enhancing the therapeutic benefits of pottery modeling in art therapy. This technology allows clients to manipulate virtual objects with their hands, providing a more natural and intuitive way to interact with the virtual environment [19, 20]. Additionally, hand gesture recognition technology can allow therapists to track and analyze client movements, providing real-time feedback and guidance. Previous research has explored the use of hand gesture recognition technology for therapy purposes. For example, Nasri et al. [21] proposed a 3D game controlled using surface electromyography (sEMG) signals and employs a deep learning-based architecture for real-time gesture recognition. The game experience is primarily designed for rehabilitation [22] exercises and enables individuals with certain disabilities to use inexpensive sEMG sensors to manipulate the game. Another study based on HGR and VR was presented by Ben Abdessalem et al. [23]. They implemented a Zoo Therapy system that provides an immersive experience where patients can interact with animals using hand gestures in a virtual environment. This technology offers patients the sensation of being in a real therapy room and engaging with the animals. To enhance the therapeutic experience, the system includes an intelligent agent that uses electroencephalography to monitor the patients' emotions and direct the animals according to their hand gestures and emotional state. On the same line, Tan et al. [24] presented a human-computer interaction system that utilizes HGR technology in a game-based rehabilitation application. The underlying principle of their project was to aid patients in their rehabilitation process using HGR, while therapists can track patients' progress through the system's results. The studies mentioned are primarily focused on various forms of physical or mental therapies, while our application concentrates more specifically on the art therapy aspects.

3   Background

This study provides a second development of a previous preliminary work [25] aimed at creating an Art Therapy scenario by means of VR technology, to be used for stress reduction therapy of patients admitted to hospital wards. This second phase of development aims to implement the use of Hand Gesture Recognition to allow simple but realistic actions without the use of controllers for interaction. For the realization of the VR application, the following software was used: Blender (2021), open-source software for 3D modeling, and Unity (2021.3.14.f1). The former software was used, primarily, for modeling 3D objects and rendering structures. Unity, a cross-platform graphics engine used for the realization of the entire application, was used for the implementation of the VR application and gesture integration. For the application described here, the Meta Quest 2 Head Mounted Display (HMD) was chosen because it is a stand-alone HMD, which does not need cables or connections to a PC in order to function, and this greatly facilitates operations, especially in a context such as a clinical setting. In this development, we enhance the simulation of clay by utilizing a well-defined Unity asset named Clayxels[1] Clayxels comprises a volumetric toolkit designed to create, animate, and sculpt game assets with clay-like effects during gameplay. The clay simulation is facilitated through a specific Unity game object called the

---

[1] The Clayxels Unity asset: https://www.clayxels.com/.

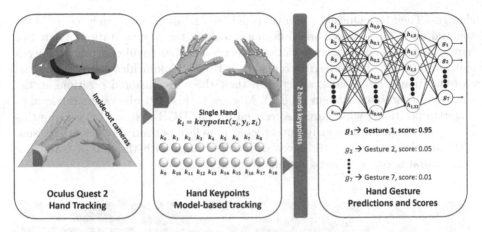

Fig. 1. The figure illustrates the workflow of our HGR system, which involves real-time hand tracking using the Meta Quest device's inside-out cameras. The hand keypoints obtained from the tracking are used as input for our trained FFNN, which generates a list of gesture scores, with the highest score indicating the detected gesture.

ClayContainer, which implements an interface that encapsulates the *ClayObjects* as child elements. The *ClayObjects* represent the actual clay elements and offer various parametric features, such as the "Blend" property, enabling the adjustment of interaction levels with other *ClayObjects*. Additional features include the additive or subtractive effects between *ClayObjects*, as well as options for adjusting the color and thickness of the clays, among others. The *ClayObjects* are constructed using basic primitives like cubes, spheres, cylinders, tori, etc. Different clay primitives can be combined to create the final pot clay. A noteworthy capability of the Clayxel asset is the ability to convert the *ClayContainer* into a mesh through the "freeze" function. This feature proves useful for exporting the clay objects in FBX format using, for example, the *FBX Unity exporter* package, enabling further editing in modeling programs or facilitating 3D printing. For our specific objectives, we define a single *ClayContainer* consisting of a collection of *ClayObjects* with additive behavior, serving as the initial blob (refer to Figs. 5 and 6), which can be manipulated using virtual hands that mimic the movements of the user's real hands via the Meta Quest 2 hand tracking feature [26] and our HGR system (see Sect. 5). The additive behavior of *ClayObjects* implies that each object interacts with the nearest objects within a specific distance, thereby simulating the clay as a cohesive entity. Fig. 1 illustrates the workflow of the hand tracking and HGR system. The user's hand pose, including the knuckles and fingertips, was detected as crucial key points using the inside-out cameras of the Meta Quest device. While Meta Quest 2 offers basic predefined gestures such as Point and Pinch, Pinch, Scroll, and Palm Pinch, these gestures are inadequate for our specific requirements. To effectively interact with clay, shape it, and construct a pot, we defined a set of seven static 2-hand gestures and accurate key point positions to manage collisions with the *ClayObjects* and their positional changes. The Meta Quest 2 platform provides a set of APIs, namely *OVR Skeleton* and *OVR Hand*, which offer information about the representation of real user hands in the VR environment, without the need for handheld controllers. Specifically, the *OVR Skeleton* API comprises a list of 19 knuckles representing the aforementioned key points, along with their three-dimensional positions in the Cartesian coordinate system (x, y, z). Moreover, this API allows the retrieval of fingertip positions, which are also crucial for our HGR system. Leveraging this information, we meticulously constructed a well-organized dataset comprising 1200 samples for each of the seven defined gestures, with the aim of training a deep neural network tailored for our HGR system.

Fig. 2. The figure displays the dataset creation scene in our Unity application, featuring a panel with real images representing a collection of studied gestures. Users can easily select a desired gesture using the Pinch default MetaQuest gesture.

The dataset was constructed using a dedicated Unity VR application that establishes a correspondence between the positions of key points on the user's hands at a given moment and a specific hand gesture. The VR scene, as depicted in Fig. 2, consists of a simple workshop setting with a table hosting a synthetic pottery object. The shape of this object is derived from the pose of the user's hands, mimicking the configuration of a real pottery object (refer to Section 4). For each of the seven gestures in our study, the shape of the real pottery object undergoes modifications, consequently altering the shape of the synthetic pottery object in the virtual scene. To select a desired gesture, the user interacts with a panel displaying photographs of the real pottery objects in VR mode, and the corresponding synthetic pottery object appears in the scene, positioned on the virtual table (see Fig. 3).

By utilizing a Pinch default MetaQuest gesture, the user is able to select the desired hand gesture for registration and initiate a 10-second timer. Within

Start registration in: 9.98s
Selected gesture: 2

Fig. 3. During dataset registration, a 10-second timer prompts the user to accurately position their hands in the selected gesture while referencing a synthetic pottery object.

this time frame, the user is required to position their hands, consequently aligning the tracked key points with the appropriate gesture configuration. Once the timer expires, our application starts the process of recording the positions of key points, storing them in a CSV file along with the corresponding hand gesture label. To introduce variation into the dataset and mitigate potential overfitting issues arising from similar data, users are encouraged to move their hands around the pottery objects and slightly adjust finger positions and hand distances, even within the same gesture category. Key point data is collected at intervals of 0.5 seconds. Each subset of gesture samples encompasses 1200 instances, resulting in a dataset dimension of 8400 samples across the seven defined gestures. After completing the recording of samples for a particular gesture, the user has the option to select another gesture, triggering the appearance of the corresponding synthetic pottery object on the virtual table. By employing the Pinch default MetaQuest gesture, the user can then initiate the recording process for the newly selected gesture. Gesture samples were collected with contributions from three individuals with varying hand sizes. Extensive testing involving multiple individuals has revealed that hand size does not significantly impact the performance of our neural network. A collection of Python scripts was developed utilizing the Tensorflow and Keras libraries (version 2.6.0) to define, train, and evaluate the performance of our neural network. Our neural network architecture follows a feed-forward neural network (FFNN) design, similar to the one detailed in our prior work [19]. As depicted in Fig. 1, this version of the FFNN comprises four layers: one input layer, two hidden layers, and one output layer. The input layer has the same dimension as the key points of a single-hand pose (144, representing a triad of 24 key points for each hand). The first hidden layer consists of 64 neurons, the second hidden layer comprises 32 neurons, and the output layer consists of 7 neurons, corresponding to the number of hand gestures considered.

The activation function ReLU is employed for the two hidden layers, while the softmax activation function is utilized for the output layer. The FFNN model was trained using the Adam optimizer [27] with "sparse categorical cross-entropy" as the loss function. Training was conducted over 3000 epochs, with a batch size of 3, a validation split of 0.3, and the inclusion of the "EarlyStopping" parameter, which monitors the validation loss with a patience of 100 epochs. With this configuration, the FFNN achieves a maximum training accuracy of 0.99 and a maximum validation accuracy of 0.94 after about 1300 epochs. In addition, an eighth gesture, referred to as "gesture none", was considered to handle scenarios where the hand gesture is not recognized, preventing unintentional interactions with the pottery object. This gesture was identified using a threshold function that detects unrecognized gestures with a probability of belonging to the training set below 94%. The trained model was converted into a Tensorflow Lite model, specifically as a *Model.TFLite* file, enabling compatibility with a Unity Tensorflow Lite package from a third-party source (version 2.4.0)[2] Within our VR application, when both user's hands are detected, a method is invoked to retrieve the key points and perform inference using our FFNN for each frame, ultimately determining the recognized gesture. Each gesture corresponds to a distinct action within the VR application, facilitating user interaction with the pottery object as elaborated in Sect. 5.

4   Methodology

The purpose of the task is to virtually model and decorate a "Trozzella", with careful instructions that come from studies of experimental archaeology, that provide important information on the methodology of ancient pottery production. This research starts from the consideration that virtual reality offers new possibilities for artistic expression, self-improvement, and motivation in psychotherapy and neurorehabilitation. As shown in Section 2, there is evidence supporting the therapeutic benefits of art creation in virtual reality, which can be attributed to its playful elements, sense of presence, controlled settings, utilization of user data, and appeal to digital-natives. However, it is important for therapy practitioners, researchers, and software developers to consider challenges such as limited digital literacy, technical constraints of current virtual reality devices, absence of tactile feedback in virtual environments, maintenance issues, interdisciplinary collaboration, and inclusivity factors [28]. This research aimed not only at creating an interactive tool for a VR application for therapeutic purposes but also for the far more ambitious purpose of digitizing an intangible heritage. In the case under consideration, the intangible asset is represented by the sequence of actions that, starting from a block of clay, allows to the creation of a ceramic artifact. This process can still be observed within workshops where clay is worked with traditional non-industrial techniques. Art therapy in VR combines the use of techniques corresponding to painting, drawing, collage, and sculpture; therefore, the virtual elements introduced in the application must

---

[2] Tensorflow lite for Unity: https://github.com/asus4/tf-lite-unity-sample.

emulate the real objects used in the practice of ceramic modeling at the potter's wheel. This goal can be achieved through the creation of a work table equipped with all the tools needed to perform the task. The number of actions and their complexity must be limited so that the user can focus on the therapy without being overwhelmed. In addition, these interactions should take as reference the movements used in reality. For the modeling of the old vase, the work of a craftsman was observed and manual gestures were simplified for use in the application. This study provides a second development of a previous preliminary work [25] aimed at creating an Art Therapy scenario by means of VR technology, to be used for stress reduction therapy of patients admitted to hospital wards. In order to develop this application gradually, we start with an automatic application, in which the user just looks at the action in VR, then we pass to an interaction that makes use of controllers. The third step is the one described in this paper, which is based on hand tracking, by means of gesture recognition, a topic that is still open to investigate [29]. Its development involved training a neural network that can recognize the correct gestures and developing an application that can respond with a certain reaction to each identified gesture. To implement an accurate modeling system that would provide for certain actions based on gesture recognition in the virtual environment, preliminary field study, and research work were carried out in order to track down references in reality. For this, the work of a craftsman was observed in order to select the main hand positions and the most recurring movements that were performed during processing. Images were acquired during a photographic campaign held at the "Salvino De Donatis Ceramiche" Laboratory in Cutrofiano (Lecce). The interaction mode based on hand tracking and gesture recognition for what concerns the tracking of the user's hands in the virtual space is in the prototyping stage. Its development is based on the training of a neural network capable of recognizing the correct gestures and the development of an application capable of responding with a given reaction to each identified gesture. In the course of the photographic acquisition, about a hundred photos were acquired, the analysis of which led to the recognition of seven different positions that the hands of the ceramist take during the modeling of the ceramic artifact. For this paper, we considered the training of the neural network of the seven hand positions identified and shown in Fig. 4. Each position determines a specific deformation of the clay, while the user is working on it.

5   The virtual HGR system

In our VR system, we specifically selected a subset of three hand gestures that represent the primary significant states of the pottery object. The choice of these gestures, as listed in Fig. 4, aims to evaluate the system's usability. By utilizing these particular gestures, our objective is to enhance usability and alleviate the burden on users to remember the complete set of gestures utilized for training our neural network. The remaining gestures will be reserved for future enhancements, intended to elevate the level of difficulty in VR pottery modeling. The procedure

	GESTURE 0	DEFORMATION 0
	Palms down, hands open and thumbs touching	Clay changes from irregular to regular disk
	GESTURE 1	DEFORMATION 1
	Hands closed in upright position, reaching upward	Diameter decreases, disk grows in height
	GESTURE 2	DEFORMATION 2
	Same as position 2, but hands go downward	Clay slopes downward
	GESTURE 3	DEFORMATION 3
	Hands downward vertically, thumb closed toward forefinger	The clay opens up and becomes a hollow disk
	GESTURE 4	DEFORMATION 4
	Hands vertically at a distance	The diameter of the belly of the vessel is defined
	GESTURE 5	DEFORMATION 5
	One hand vertically and the other horizontally	The rim of the pot is formed
	GESTURE 6	DEFORMATION 6
	Forefinger of one hand straight, other hand lowered from top to bottom	The foot of the pot is formed

Fig. 4. This figure provide a schematic representation of the seven hand positions we considered for the implementation

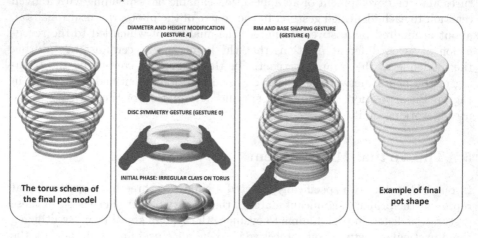

Fig. 5. The figure illustrates the toroidal skeleton of the pottery object and its movements based on user gestures recognized by our HGR system. The Clayxel Unity asset enhances realism and cohesion compared to basic tori.

to simulate pot modeling with hand gestures involves several phases, as shown in Fig. 5. In the initial phase, the pot starts as an irregular disc consisting of a series of concentric tori. Each torus is composed of spherical *ClayObjects*, positioned at fixed intervals from one another (See Fig. 6).

Fig. 6. This depicts the initial state of the clays within the VR scene. Additionally, an example of the "none" gesture is reported.

In the illustrated scenario presented in Fig. 6, the configuration of the user's hands does not correspond to any recognized gesture in our neural network, signifying a gesture denoting a state of none. In the first phase of modeling, a gesture we called "Disc Symmetry Gesture" is employed to transform the clay from an irregular disc into a regular disc, without altering its diameter. As shown in Fig. 7, this gesture allows the user to achieve a more symmetrical shape. The visualization of clay movement is conditioned upon the user accurately executing the aforementioned gesture and the virtual hands coming into contact with tori objects. The size of these tori objects can be adjusted by considering the distance between the metacarpal keypoints of the user's middle fingers. In order to provide feedback to the user regarding the accurate execution of hand gestures, a text label is positioned within the virtual scene, in front of the user's field of view, displaying the recognized gesture.

Moving on to the second phase, a gesture we called "Diameter and Height Modification Gesture" is utilized to modify both the diameter and height of the clay disc. During this phase, the system detects if the user's hands come into contact with any of the tori. If a collision with a torus occurs, the user can adjust the distance of that torus from its initial position by vertically moving their hands while performing Rim and Base Shaping gesture. This modification, as illustrated in Fig. 9, impacts the overall form of the pottery object, enabling alterations in its diameter and height.

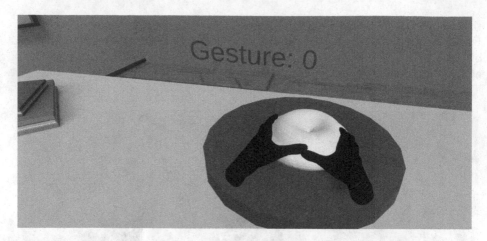

Fig. 7. The "Disc Symmetry Gesture" is employed to transform irregular discs into regular discs. In our VR scene, this particular gesture is denoted as "Gesture 0".

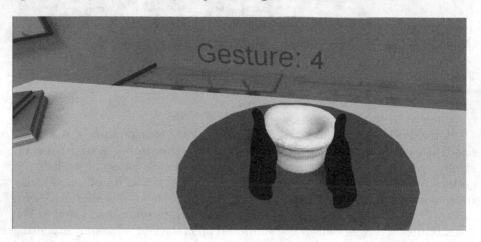

Fig. 8. Diameter and Height Modification Gesture: this refers to the gesture used for modifying the diameter and height of the clay disc, denoted as "Gesture 4" for simplicity.

Lastly, in the third phase of modeling, a gesture we called "Rim and Base Shaping Gesture" is employed to shape the rim and base of the pot (see Fig. 9). By colliding their hands with the tori associated with the pot's rim and base, the user can increase or decrease the diameter of these specific tori. This manipulation helps achieve the desired shape and proportions for the rim and base of the pot. Through the combination of these three gestures, users can simulate the pot modeling process using hand gestures. The system provides real-time feedback and adjustments, allowing for an intuitive and interactive experience in creating the desired pot shape.

Fig. 9. The "Rim and Base Shaping Gesture" is utilized to modify the rim and base of the pot. For simplicity, in our virtual scene, this gesture is referred to as "Gesture 6".

6   Conclusions

Our research has introduced an innovative VR-based art therapy approach for pottery modeling, incorporating HGR technology. Our system focuses on the modeling and decoration of a traditional ceramic vase known as the "Trozzella" from the Italian region of Puglia. The instructions and techniques employed in our application are derived from experimental archaeological studies, ensuring an authentic and culturally significant experience for participants. Our art therapy activity encompasses three modes: passive, controller-based and hand gesture-based. These modes cater to individuals with diverse motor skills and cognitive abilities. The passive mode allows users to observe the pottery modeling process, the controller based system provides a smart and interactive solution by means of VR controllers, while the hand gesture modes enable active engagement with the virtual pottery wheel and decorating tools. Leveraging a neural network-based HGR system, we achieve accurate and precise detection of hand movements, essential for realistic pottery modeling. Users can interact with the virtual environment intuitively and naturally, as the HGR system recognizes a range of hand gestures. Our application provides a personalized and adaptable experience, accommodating users' individual abilities and preferences. This scalability and flexibility make it suitable for individuals who lack access to traditional pottery tools and materials. The integration of HGR technology may enhance the immersive nature of the virtual environment, fostering a deeper sense of engagement and potentially increasing the effectiveness of art therapy.

Through our work, we strive to enhance the therapeutic benefits of pottery modeling, in terms of stress reduction, and promote greater accessibility to art therapy. By offering an authentic and culturally meaningful experience, we aim to foster well-being and emotional growth. Our scalable VR-based art therapy solution may serve as an inclusive platform that empowers individuals with varying motor and cognitive abilities to engage in a creative and therapeutic process. Future work could involve expanding the repertoire of hand gestures incorporated into the VR-based art therapy program. While our current system recognizes a set of essential gestures for pottery modeling, there is room for incorporating additional gestures to enhance the user's creative expression and interaction with the virtual environment. Expanding the range of gestures can enable users to perform more intricate and nuanced actions, such as fine-tuning the shape of the pottery, adding intricate details, or applying different decorative patterns. This can provide a more immersive and realistic experience, allowing users to explore their artistic capabilities and push the boundaries of their creativity within the virtual pottery modeling context. Another potential avenue for future research is to conduct longitudinal studies to assess the long-term effects and benefits of VR-based art therapy, while also examining various aspects such as usability, sentiment, user experience, and learning effectiveness. Our system can serve as a VR serious game [30], enabling researchers to track participants' progress over extended periods. By doing so, valuable insights can be obtained regarding the therapeutic impact and improvements in mental well-being that arise from engaging in VR-based art therapy interventions. Additionally, exploring the integration of collaborative features into the VR-based art therapy program could facilitate group sessions and social interaction. This could involve enabling multiple users to engage in shared virtual spaces, collaborate on pottery projects, and communicate with each other during the art therapy sessions. By fostering social connections and promoting a sense of community, collaborative VR experiences could enhance the therapeutic benefits and provide a supportive environment for individuals undergoing art therapy.

Acknowledgment. This research was supported by the "Casa delle Tecnologie Emergenti di Matera" project.

References

1. Shukla, A., Choudhari, S.G., Gaidhane, A.M., Syed, Z.Q., Gaidhane, A.: Role of art therapy in the promotion of mental health: a critical review. Cureus **14**(8) (2022)
2. Hu, J., Zhang, J., Hu, L., Yu, H., Xu, J.: Art therapy: a complementary treatment for mental disorders. Front. Psychol. **12**, 686005 (2021)
3. Nan, J.K., Hinz, L.D., Lusebrink, V.B.: Chapter 42 - clay art therapy on emotion regulation: research, theoretical underpinnings, and treatment mechanisms. In: Martin, C.R., Hunter, L.A., Patel, V.B., Preedy, V.R., Rajendram, R. (eds.) The Neuroscience of Depression, pp. 431–442. Academic Press (2021). https://doi.org/10.1016/B978-0-12-817933-8.00009-8, https://www.sciencedirect.com/science/article/pii/B9780128179338000098
4. Pérez-Sáez, E., Cabrero-Montes, E.M., Llorente-Cano, M., González-Ingelmo, E.: A pilot study on the impact of a pottery workshop on the well-being of people with dementia. Dementia **19**(6), 2056–2072 (2020)
5. Henley, D.: Clayworks in art therapy: plying the sacred circle. Jessica Kingsley Publishers (2002)

6. Nan, J.K., Ho, R.T.: Effects of clay art therapy on adults outpatients with major depressive disorder: a randomized controlled trial. J. Affect. Disorders **217**, 237–245 (2017)
7. Sholt, M., Gavron, T.: Therapeutic qualities of clay-work in art therapy and psychotherapy: a review. Art Ther. **23**(2), 66–72 (2006)
8. Anwar, S., Sinha, S.K., Vivek, S., Ashank, V.: Hand gesture recognition: a survey. In: Nath, V., Mandal, J.K. (eds.) Nanoelectronics, Circuits and Communication Systems, pp. 365–371. Springer, Singapore (2019). https://doi.org/10.1007/978-981-13-0776-8_33
9. Cheng, H., Yang, L., Liu, Z.: Survey on 3D hand gesture recognition. IEEE Trans. Circuits Syst. Video Technol. **26**(9), 1659–1673 (2016). https://doi.org/10.1109/TCSVT.2015.2469551
10. Jiang, S., Kang, P., Song, X., Lo, B.P., Shull, P.B.: Emerging wearable interfaces and algorithms for hand gesture recognition: a survey. IEEE Rev. Biomed. Eng. **15**, 85–102 (2022). https://doi.org/10.1109/RBME.2021.3078190
11. Pereira, M.F., Prahm, C., Kolbenschlag, J., Oliveira, E., Rodrigues, N.F.: A virtual reality serious game for hand rehabilitation therapy. In: 2020 IEEE 8th International Conference on Serious Games and Applications for Health (SeGAH), pp. 1–7 (2020). https://doi.org/10.1109/SeGAH49190.2020.9201789
12. Blomdahl, C., Gunnarsson, B.A., Guregård, S., Rusner, M., Wijk, H., Björklund, A.: Art therapy for patients with depression: expert opinions on its main aspects for clinical practice. J. Mental Health **25**(6), 527–535 (2016)
13. Chapman, L., Morabito, D., Ladakakos, C., Schreier, H., Knudson, M.M.: The effectiveness of art therapy interventions in reducing post traumatic stress disorder (PTSD) symptoms in pediatric trauma patients. Art Ther. **18**(2), 100–104 (2001)
14. Capece, N., Erra, U., Romaniello, G.: A low-cost full body tracking system in virtual reality based on microsoft kinect. In: De Paolis, L.T., Bourdot, P. (eds.) Augmented Reality, Virtual Reality, and Computer Graphics, pp. 623–635. Springer International Publishing, Cham (2018). https://doi.org/10.1007/978-3-319-95282-6_44
15. Kaimal, G., Carroll-Haskins, K., Berberian, M., Dougherty, A., Carlton, N., Ramakrishnan, A.: Virtual reality in art therapy: a pilot qualitative study of the novel medium and implications for practice. Art Therapy **37**(1), 16–24 (2020). https://doi.org/10.1080/07421656.2019.1659662, publisher Copyright: 2019, AATA Inc
16. Hacmun, I., Regev, D., Salomon, R.: Artistic creation in virtual reality for art therapy: a qualitative study with expert art therapists. Arts Psychother. 72 (2021). https://doi.org/10.1016/j.aip.2020.101745, publisher Copyright: 2020 Elsevier Ltd
17. Iosa, M., et al.: The michelangelo effect: art improves the performance in a virtual reality task developed for upper limb neurorehabilitation. Front. Psychol. 11 (2021). https://doi.org/10.3389/fpsyg.2020.611956, https://www.frontiersin.org/articles/10.3389/fpsyg.2020.611956
18. Shamri Zeevi, L.: Making art therapy virtual: Integrating virtual reality into art therapy with adolescents. Front. Psychol. 12 (2021). https://doi.org/10.3389/fpsyg.2021.584943, https://www.frontiersin.org/articles/10.3389/fpsyg.2021.584943
19. Capece, N., Manfredi, G., Macellaro, V., Carratù, P.: An easy hand gesture recognition system for XR-based collaborative purposes. In: 2022 IEEE International Conference on Metrology for Extended Reality, Artificial Intelligence and Neural Engineering (MetroXRAINE), pp. 121–126. IEEE (2022)

20. Notarangelo, N.M., Manfredi, G., Gilio, G.: A collaborative virtual walkthrough of Matera's Sassi using photogrammetric reconstruction and hand gesture navigation. J. Imaging **9**(4), 88 (2023)

21. Nasri, N., Orts-Escolano, S., Cazorla, M.: An sEMG-controlled 3D game for rehabilitation therapies: real-time time hand gesture recognition using deep learning techniques. Sensors **20**(22), 6451 (2020)

22. Adinolfi, F., et al.: SmartCARE–an ICT platform in the domain of stroke pathology to manage rehabilitation treatment and telemonitoring at home. In: Pietro, G.D., Gallo, L., Howlett, R.J., Jain, L.C. (eds.) Intelligent Interactive Multimedia Systems and Services 2016, pp. 39–49. Springer International Publishing, Cham (2016). https://doi.org/10.1007/978-3-319-39345-2_4

23. Ben Abdessalem, H., Ai, Y., Marulasidda Swamy, K., Frasson, C.: Virtual reality zoo therapy for Alzheimer's disease using real-time gesture recognition. In: GeNeDis 2020: Computational Biology and Bioinformatics, pp. 97–105. Springer (2021). https://doi.org/10.1007/978-3-030-78775-2_12

24. Tan, C.W., Chin, S.W., Lim, W.X.: Game-based human computer interaction using gesture recognition for rehabilitation. In: 2013 IEEE International Conference on Control System, Computing and Engineering, pp. 344–349. IEEE (2013)

25. Gatto, C., Martinez, K., De Paolis, L.T.: Design process of a ceramic modeling application for virtual reality art therapy. In: Extended Reality: First International Conference, XR Salento 2022, Lecce, Italy, July 6–8, 2022, Proceedings, Part I. pp. 92–103. Springer-Verlag, Berlin, Heidelberg (2022). https://doi.org/10.1007/978-3-031-15546-8_7

26. Abdlkarim, D., et al.: A methodological framework to assess the accuracy of virtual reality hand-tracking systems: a case study with the meta quest 2. Behavior Research Methods, pp. 1–12 (2023)

27. Kingma, D.P., Ba, J.: Adam: a method for stochastic optimization. arXiv preprint arXiv:1412.6980 (2014)

28. Hadjipanayi, C., Banakou, D., Michael-Grigoriou, D.: Art as therapy in virtual reality: a scoping review. Front. Virtual Reality 4 (2023). https://doi.org/10.3389/frvir.2023.1065863, https://www.frontiersin.org/articles/10.3389/frvir.2023.1065863

29. Gruosso, M., Capece, N., Erra, U., Angiolillo, F.: A preliminary investigation into a deep learning implementation for hand tracking on mobile devices, pp. 380–385 (2020). https://doi.org/10.1109/AIVR50618.2020.00079, cited by: 5; All Open Access, Green Open Access

30. Mirauda, D., Capece, N., Erra, U.: StreamflowVL: a virtual fieldwork laboratory that supports traditional hydraulics engineering learning. Appl. Sci. **9**(22) (2019). https://doi.org/10.3390/app9224972, https://www.mdpi.com/2076-3417/9/22/4972

Embracing Cultural Heritage Through Virtual Reality: Development, Usability and Enjoyment Evaluation of a VR Environment for the Church of Panagia Aggeloktisti

Louis Nisiotis[1]([✉])[ID], Markos Souropetsis[2][ID], and Eleni A. Kyza[2][ID]

[1] School of Sciences, University of Central Lancashire, Pyla, Cyprus
LNisiotis@uclan.ac.uk
[2] Department of Communication and Internet Studies,
Cyprus University of Technology, Limassol, Cyprus
{Markos.Souropetsis,Eleni.Kyza}@cut.ac.cy

Abstract. The importance of preservation, accessibility and dissemination of Cultural Heritage is universally acknowledged, and the latest technological advancements in visualisation technologies such as Virtual Reality, and Serious VR Games in particular, have been increasingly utilised for innovation and application to support these efforts with great success. This paper presents the development and evaluation of a VR environment focusing on disseminating information on the Byzantine art of Panagia Aggeloktisti church in Cyprus, through an immersive learning scenario requiring users to complete challenges to progress while learning important historical information about the church. The paper presents information on the VR environment development, providing details on the process of capturing, processing and digitising in 3D models the exterior and several artefacts of the church. Two versions of the environment have been developed, featuring Gamified and non-Gamified components. The study presented in this paper compares and evaluates these versions through analysing users perceptions towards usability/playability, enjoyment and visual aesthetics of the environment. A comparative experimental study was conducted and the results revealed that the users' experience was positively perceived regardless of interacting with the gamified elements of the environment or not during their VR experience. The results suggest that the VR environment was perceived usable/playable, enjoyable and with appealing graphics, and is at a stage to be used for public access and further experimentation. The paper also highlights the need for developing and extensively evaluating the efficacy of VR environments to provide immersive, engaging and enjoyable gamified and gaming experiences to embrace cultural heritage.

Keywords: Virtual Reality · Serious Games · Game Based Learning · Digital Cultural Heritage · Computer Graphics

© The Author(s), under exclusive license to Springer Nature Switzerland AG 2023
L. T. De Paolis et al. (Eds.): XR Salento 2023, LNCS 14219, pp. 227–246, 2023.
https://doi.org/10.1007/978-3-031-43404-4_15

1   Introduction

Cultural heritage and our ancestral connections influence and define our lives, our identities and social behaviours. Preserving our cultural ties and ensuring accessibility, availability, and dissemination of history and cultural beliefs is of out-most importance to protect our legacy and progress. Recent technological advancements in hardware, software, and networking capabilities have fostered the digital transformation of the cultural heritage domain, providing opportunities to protect and disseminate open access heritage with significant societal, technological and industrial impact. Extended Reality (XR - the umbrella term encapsulating Augmented, Virtual and Mixed Reality technologies) is one of the emerging technologies that recently attracted considerable research and industrial attention in innovation and application in the field of cultural heritage. Virtual Reality (VR) in particular has been extensively used in cultural heritage, leveraging its capabilities to support high fidelity graphics, visualisations, simulations, and opportunities for developing interactive story telling, fostering the development of interactive experiences that increase presence and immersion to visitors [35]. VR enable the creation of realistic representations of historical locations, buildings, artefacts, events, and phenomena within immersive digital spaces, and a particular type of VR experiences which has been successfully used in cultural heritage is through serious game applications, and recently through VR gaming [28].

This paper presents the development details and evaluation of a VR environment focusing on educating users about the UNESCO protected byzantine art of Panagia Aggeloktisti church in Cyprus, through an immersive gamified learning scenario requiring users to complete a series of learning tasks within a VR world. The paper presents details on the environment design, including the process of capturing, processing and digitising 3D models of the exterior and several artefacts of the church, and the development of gamified components and tasks. The paper also presents the results of an initial evaluation of the environment, focusing on the users' perceptions towards usability/playability, enjoyment, and the visual aesthetics of a Gamified and a non-Gamified version of the VR environment. The aim of this study was to ensure that the current development stage of the environment is usable, enjoyable and visually pleasing regardless of the gamified elements, so to proceed with further empirical evaluations to assess its educational efficacy and relevant technical topics in the future, and for public use.

2   Background and Context

2.1   Digital Cultural Heritage

Cultural heritage and our historical past are closely connected with our lives, beliefs, values, identities and behaviours. Museums, heritage organisations, research institutions and other cultural heritage stakeholders make significant efforts in preserving, safeguarding and disseminating heritage. The use of digital technologies offer tools to support digitisation for storage, reconstruction and representation of tangible and intangible cultural heritage [22]. A fusion of several multi-modal interactive technologies (augmented and virtual reality, mobile phones, tablet devices, sensors and robots among others) are converged with the latest advancements in artificial intelligence, cyber-physical systems, complex computing, computer graphics, and sophisticated software to support the needs of cultural heritage and to enhance the visitors experience through the concept of Digital Cultural Heritage (DCH) [12,15,17,22]. DCH focuses on the digital transformation of historical artefacts, including locations, buildings, traditions, practices, phenomena, cultures and social experiences among a plethora of other tangible and intangible characteristics and attributes of significant historical and cultural importance, supporting transferability, accessibility, and preservability of heritage [7,12,23,24]. To achieve this, the research and application areas in DCH require advanced data capture and processing mechanisms, high fidelity visualization tools and rendering techniques, specialised hardware and advanced technologies. Such sophisticated requirements are now feasible to be developed and applied at scale in DCH, as a result of exponential technological improvements and significant decrease in complexity, costs of ownership and operation of digital technologies. The use of XR is one of the technologies that has been extensively utilised in DCH over the past decade, and its applicability and effectiveness have been studied and established as a successful technological method of providing attractive, engaging and immersive experiences to the users/visitors [2,6,14,17,18,25]. XR offer opportunities to create virtual versions of heritage, enabling users to access and experience famous heritage sites that can be geographically dispersed, inaccessible, or may no longer exist [17,25]. Applications such as Virtual Museums are increasingly developed, enabling navigation in high fidelity immersive spaces, observing and interacting with exhibits, and even communicating with other visitors, formulating new types of immersive, interactive and personalized experiences to the visitors and enhancing the appreciation and understanding of cultural heritage [15,16]. This is developing the concept of 'cultural presence', referring to the feeling of being in the presence of a cultural belief system that visitors develop when visiting a museum or cultural heritage site [4,23]. Further to digital capturing, 3D reconstruction and visualisation capabilities, XR also contributes to the development of interactive story-telling experiences [35] that can enhance the users' feeling of presence and involvement in the immersive experience [21,32]. Cultural heritage institutions, museums and other relevant stakeholders have been early adopters of XR technology to support and enhance the experience of their visitors with great success over the years [1]. Experimentation with VR technology in particular, has led to the emergence of immersive and engaging interactive applications [5] and projects, such as open access heritage though virtual museums and virtual exhibitions, projects focusing on storytelling, visualisation, the promotion and education of cultural heritage, and recently through applications for entertainment purposes.

2.2   Serious Games in Digital Cultural Heritage

The use of Serious Games with the intentions to complete learning objectives and support education, offer opportunities for innovative and engaging game-based learning approaches [27] and have been the focus of extensive research for innovation and application in DCH. Serious games are digital games designed for non-entertainment purposes (i.e., education, training, management, engineering etc.) [34], where the users develop their skills and knowledge by completing tasks and obtaining rewards [8]. Serious games span across a range of genres including puzzles, mini-games, simulations of events, virtual tours, action, adventure and role playing games among others, in single or multiplayer modes [13]. When games are utilised as learning tools, they can increase motivation, support the process of knowledge acquisition and improve learning outcomes, and gamified learning approaches are found to also improve students' attitude, engagement, and performance [27,33]. There is wide range of successful applications in the form of gamification and game-based learning (see comprehensive review in [27]). Translating traditional learning activities into gamified scenarios is a common practice that has been found to increase students motivation and contributing to their cognitive development [26]. Some of the most commonly used elements in gamified applications are reward-based achievements such as points, badges, and leaderboards. The most commonly used elements in game-based learning applications are graphics, points, and levels [27]. In the context of DCH, game-based learning and gamified educational approaches have been drawing significant research attention [11], and have been widely used with great success over the recent years to support documentation, representation and dissemination of DCH [9]. A common serious game design approach is through narrative story telling design and historic scene/setting reproduction [11], and their efficacy and impact in the DCH context has been the focus of extensive research for the past 20 years. However, despite the wide range of research works in this domain, the recent interest in innovation and application of VR in DCH has revealed new and open technological, societal and industrial challenges requiring in-depth exploration to ascertain the affordances and limitations of VR and serious VR games in this domain [3,28].

2.3   VR Gaming in Digital Cultural Heritage

An exponential increase in the use of VR for gaming has been recorded as a result of the significant improvements in hardware and computer graphics, and is considered one of the most interesting technological advancements in the gaming scene [19]. A recent study conducted by [28] identifies a number of VR game genres implemented in DCH, and categorises them in serious games, puzzles, story telling, quests, action, beat-them-up, and multiplayer games. Video games provide new and entertaining ways of experiencing and disseminating heritage, with several examples of serious and entertainment games developed by museums, heritage organisations, research institutions and even entertainment game studios [5]. The literature suggests that there are a plethora of elements that contribute to the enjoyment and satisfaction of video games, such as the usability of the game, its aesthetics and others, and these have been the focus of extensive ongoing research [20]. Successful games are the ones that manage to entertain players and provide them with enjoyable and challenging tasks [19]. Game designers and developers need to ensure that the games are enjoyable to play and also marketable to reach their target audiences [20]. To aid designers, developers and researchers, a plethora of data collection instruments and heuristics have been developed over the years, measuring important areas of the players' gaming experience from multiple perspectives (see overview list in [20]). Understanding the relevant important factors such as usability, enjoyment, immersion, creativity, personal gratification, social connection, and the visual aspect of the game can help game developers to understand their target audience, cater for their playing needs and attract new players [10]. Several methods such as usability testing, heuristics evaluation and play-testing are commonly used to assess video games, helping developers to understand the players' behaviour, attitudes and preferences [20].

2.4 Project Description

The project discussed in this paper presents details on the development and evaluation of a VR environment to support the efforts of promoting and educating people about the Byzantine art of the Church of Panagia Aggeloktisti located in the village of Kiti in Larnaka, Cyprus. In particular, the usability/playability, enjoyment and the visual aspect of the VR environment were evaluated, in preparation for its public use and future experiments. The environment will be used to conduct a series of empirical studies in the future, looking into its efficacy to support DCH education, and other technical considerations.

Panagia Aggeloktisti is an early Christian-Byzantine architecture church renowned for its beautiful decorations spanning across different historical periods. The church is known for its well-preserved 6th-century mosaic depicting the Virgin Mary holding baby Jesus in her arms, and with Archangels Michael and Gabriel on either side. This mosaic is located over the sanctuary apse in a half dome wall structure, is the only survived wall mosaic in Cyprus to date, and is one of the finest and most significant examples of early Christian art. The church also features well-preserved wall paintings from the 11th, 13th and 19th centuries with significant cultural and religious importance. The name "Panagia" means "Virgin Mary" and "Aggeloktisti" translates to "built by angels" in Greek language, according to the local tradition on how the church was constructed. The church is included on UNESCO's Tentative List, highlighting its cultural significance and potential for future world heritage status [29].

To support the efforts of promoting the art history and heritage of the church, the VR environment presented in this paper has been developed, to be used as a vehicle for future experimentation and investigation of topics in the DCH, computer graphics and VR research domains. In preparation of research protocols, the development team has deemed necessary to initially evaluate important usability components of the environment, to determine the extent to which it is at a state which extensive educational research can take place, and to also be used publicly. A comparative research methodology has been devised, and an experiment has been conducted and explained in the sections below.

3   Research Methodology

This study aims to ascertain the extent to which the usability/playability, enjoyment and visual appeal of the VR environment are affected by the implementation of Gamified and non-Gamified elements during an interactive game-based learning activity in VR. Two versions of the VR environment have been developed, the one without gamified elements such as points, time for completion, badges and rewards. The study hypothesizes that the overall playing experience of the users would be positively perceived regardless of the implementation of gamified elements as part of the experience. This would serve as an indicator that both version of the VR environment have reached a development stage where they are usable, enjoyable and visually appealing, to be used for further empirical investigation in the future.

3.1   VR Environment Description

In the VR environment, users immerse and participate in a series of learning activities designed to educate them about the Byzantine art and significance of the church of Panagia Aggeloktisti. This VR environment is designed to have a semi-realistic look and feel influenced by the design and feeling of the interior of the church. Key artefacts of the church such as the wall mosaic and specific paintings have been digitized and featured within the environment (more details in Sect. 3.2).

To connect to the environment and experience the VR world, the users launch the application from the VR headset directly. The environment features an inquiry-based learning approach where the users assume the role of historians attempting to figure out the dating of the mosaic through a collection of evidence. Once the users connects to the environment, a Non-Playing Character (NPC) who is a dedicated learning companion to the user, approaches and provides details on the purpose of the environment and its missions in audio format captioned by text. The gamified activity requires the user to investigate three areas in the church and complete a set of questions before reaching a final area/stage. The user follows the NPC which is responsible for sharing educational and historical information, instructions, and general advice on how to complete each stage to the user throughout the experience. Each area features a different set of educational materials in various multimedia formats, focusing on the historical significance of the mosaic, and general information about the church. After reviewing all materials in each area, the user must answer a question to get access to the next area. The final area features a question that covers all the learning outcomes of the previous areas.

3.2   VR Environment Design and Implementation Details

For the design of the environment, a team of undergraduate students studying Computer Games Development at the University of Central Lancashire, Cyprus (UCLan Cyprus), and the authors of this paper have visited the church multiple times to capture and digitise its exterior and specific key artefacts in display inside the church, including the famous mosaic. Data was captured through drones equipped with high-definition cameras and through high-quality digital single-lens reflex cameras (DSLR). A large volume of photographic data was captured to ensure that enough data will be processed, which was reviewed to ensure that only the best of quality photographs covering the required angles and meet a particular quality threshold would be used, through the process of photogrammetry. The collected data was processed through 3DF Zephyr (www. 3dflow.net) photogrammetry software that uses a range of complex algorithms to process the photographic data of the church, the mosaic, and the other objects, converted them into detailed 3D models (Figs. 1, 2, and 3), to later import them in the VR environment (Fig. 4).

Fig. 1. Point cloud data (left) and 3D generated mesh (right) of the Aggeloktisti church exterior.

The results of the generated 3D models produced meshes with high polygon counts, visual artefacts and issues with textures and shapes. The generated models were processed further using a chain of Computer Aided Design (CAD) software to enhance and optimise their performance by reducing their geometry in ways that keep the original shape and texture quality of the objects intact, but make them efficient for further use in CAD and game engine software. Initially, we have used the Agisoft De-Lighter (www.agisoft.com) software to remove shadows from the textures of the generated models, due to weather and lightning condition changes occurred during the data capture stage. The process of mesh retopology was utilised (Fig. 3) to convert high polygon 3D assets into reduced polygon count models using Instant Meshes software (www.github.com/wjakob/ instant-meshes). UV unwrapping and texture baking process took place using Blender (www.blender.com) to use high detail and quality textures on the newly

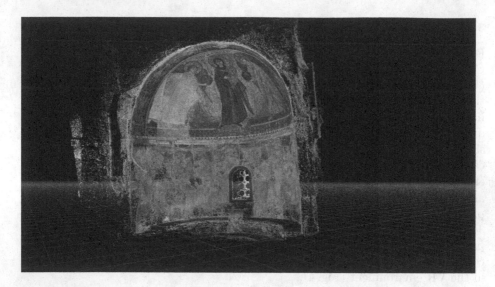

Fig. 2. Example of the generated dense point cloud data of the mosaic.

Fig. 3. Example of mesh retopology and applying high quality texture to the mosaic.

decimated 3D models. The optimised 3D models were then imported into Unreal Engine 4, which was the game engine used to develop the VR environment. This is a widely used game engine developed by Epic Games (www.epicgames.com) which provides advanced rendering engine, programming environment, tools and capabilities for developing high quality games and not only in multiple platforms. The manual process described above, was necessary to ensure that the 3D models would have been optimized enough in terms of size and polygon count to be imported in VR. This helps to improve the loading times and rendering costs of the VR scene, and ensuring high and consistent frame rate counts during the VR experience. To further contribute to this and ensure that the VR environ-

Fig. 4. In-world view of the mosaic.

ment offers a usable and consistent user experience, we have employed a number of optimization techniques to improve graphics rendering and memory management, which are common issues affecting the VR gaming experience. We have used Unreal's forward shading renderer that provides faster rendering passes and supports better performance in VR, and enabled the 4x Multi Sample Anti-Aliasing (MSAA) as suggested by the game engine's best practices guidance [30] to improve the visuals of the VR scene. For the educational aspect of the environment, several learning materials in image format were used, and we have applied texture processing techniques such as varying the level of detail based on distance from the viewer (mip-maps) and texture filtering (triliniear smoothing filtering) to remove visual artefacts. Additional techniques to optimize the VR environment have been implemented using general advise provided by the game engine development team [31] and from the experience of the development team, such as techniques for reducing draw calls, memory management, spatial partitioning and others. For the design of the environment, we have also used 3D models available for public download and reuse for non commercial purposes.

3.3   Environment Functionalities and Mechanics

The environment was developed to target the Meta Quest 2 standalone device, which is one of the worlds' leading consumer ready VR devices. Meta Quest 2 is an all-in-one headset device that can operate either being wired to a computer or completely untethered, and features a hand tracking system through two wireless controllers. The controllers are rendered in the VR environment as the users hands, and the user is using them to interact with the NPC, the learning materials, and the environment during the experience.

In the VR experience, the user must attempt all quiz questions and visit all areas in order to complete the gamified activities. The system features a badge based rewards system, which the user obtains by successfully answering quiz questions. Points are also allocated for each correct question. A feedback system is implemented indicating to users if their answer is correct or not. In either case, the user can progress to the next level/area in the environment. A timer to complete the activities is also provided. The basic gameplay mechanic focus on enabling the user to complete in-world quizzes by interacting with them through their wireless controllers. The user interacts with objects via a blue highlight line (raycast) emitted from the left controller/virtual hand and allow hovering and pressing buttons of the possible answers of each quiz. On the right hand controller, the user can see information about their progress, time available to complete the environment and achieved badges. The user's locomotion in the environment is also facilitated through the wireless controller, and the user rotates around in VR by rotating in the real world. When the NPC is telling a story or giving direct instructions to the user, the user's navigation is temporarily disabled, and the user is only able to rotate around. This was implemented to ensure that the users would pay attention to the NPC when sharing instructions and key information, and to guide the storyline.

To develop the behaviour of the NPC, several tools and scripts have been implemented to enable the NPC to interact with the user, and the VR world (Figs. 5 and 6). The NPC's behaviour is mostly controlled by the behaviour trees and blackboard AI tools provided by Unreal Engine, and with scripted finite state machines AI. Navigation was facilitated through Unreal's NavMesh pathfinding AI functionality, allowing the NPC to navigate in the VR world, as well as through specific scripted actions of reaching goals via waypoints to guide the user throughout the gamified experience. A dialogue tree functional-

Fig. 5. Gameplay example of the user interacting with the NPC.

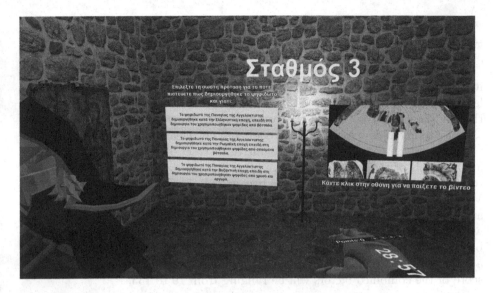

Fig. 6. Gameplay example of the user interacting with quiz and video content.

ity was implemented on the NPC to facilitate communication and interaction with the user. The NPC communicates with the user through pre-recorded audio recordings, which are also captioned to aid the users' understanding. By using the raycasting functionality, the user can interact with the NPC at any time to repeat the last issued instructions.

Two versions of the environment have been developed: 1) a Gamified and a 2) non-Gamified. In the Gamified version of the environment, for each completed area activity, the user is awarded a completion badge and points for each correct answer. Nevertheless, users' progress to the next area during the experience regardless of providing correct or wrong answers. The gamified experience has a countdown timer of 30 min to complete all areas. In the non-Gamified version, the rewards-based functionality and timer have been removed. The user attempts the same quiz questions, and proceeds to the next stage regardless of a correct or wrong answer. In both versions, the status of the answer to quiz questions is highlighted green or red and accompanied by "correct" or "wrong" sound effects accordingly.

3.4   Data Collection Instruments

To collect data for this study, we have used and translated into Greek language the Game User Experience Satisfaction Scale (GUESS) questionnaire developed and validated by [20]. GUESS is a psychometrically validated questionnaire used to evaluate computer games, consisting of 55 questions and organized in 9 factors/subscales namely: including Usability/Playability, Narrative, Play Engrossment, Enjoyment, Creative Freedom, Personal Gratification, Social Connectivity,

Audio Aesthetics, and Visual Aesthetics. The items are rated on a seven-point Likert scale range (1 - Strongly Disagree to 7 - Strongly Agree) and scored by averaging, and also aggregating the results of each subscale, and in total.

For the needs of the study presented in this paper, the factors of Usability/Playability, Enjoyment, and Visual Aesthetics have been adapted, translated and used to directly assess the user experience of the specific factors of the environment. The Usability/Playability factors investigate the ease of which the environment is experienced through having clear goals and objectives in the users mind, and that minimal cognitive distractions from the user interface and controls of the environment have been perceived. Enjoyment factor relates to users perceptions around pleasure because of playing the gamified activities. Visual Aesthetics concern the graphical elements of the environment and their attractiveness. The overall score of each subscale would be considered, together with the overall composite score of all scales. The score to be interpreted should be in a range of 11 to 77 points for Usability/Playability, 5 to 35 points for Enjoyability, and 3 to 21 points for the Visual Aesthetics factor. The total aggregated score of the combined factors will be ranging from 19 to 133.

3.5   Sample and Experimental Procedures

This study was conducted over a period of five weeks and involved the overall participation of 50 undergraduate students from various departments studying at the Cyprus University of Technology. Participants were assigned into two groups, playing the Gamified or non-Gamified version of the VR environment respectively. The Gamified version was played by 12 Male and 13 Female users between 20 and 26 years old ($M = 22$), and the non-Gamified by 7 Male, and 18 Female users between 19 and 23 years old ($M = 21$). The questionnaire was used to measure the users' perceptions of the above mentioned factors through the Gamified and non-Gamified version of the VR environment, and was administered online after the participants exposure with the VR experience. At the end of the experience, their previous experience with VR was qualitatively queried, and have been categorised by the authors of this study into a Likert scale ranging from 1 (No previous Experience with VR) to 5 (Experienced VR User). Participants for both the Gamified ($M = 1.64$, $SD = .5$) and non-Gamified ($M = 1.26$, $SD = .45$) groups had very little experience with VR. In particular, 36% had no previous experience and 64% has very little experience with VR in the Gamified group, with 73% and 26% respectively for the non-Gamified group.

4   Results and Discussion

Before conducting any statistical analyses on the results, the degree of normality of the data distribution for both measurements was tested through Kolmogorov and Smirnov's test for normality. The normality test result for all scales but the non-Gamified Enjoyment scale, have passed the test and fulfilled the normality assumptions. The non-Gamified Enjoyment scale revealed a value ($p = .002$) that violates the test's threshold (p < .05). Visual inspection of the data indicated that the distribution of data was positively skewed, therefore the results must be considered with caution. For all the data analyses employed, parametric tests have been used.

To ensure the validity and reliability of the results reported and interpreted in this paper, a reliability test was conducted on all the scales used in the data collection using the Cronbach's Alpha coefficient. Both the Gamified and non-Gamified scales have been tested and passed the reliability test (Table 1), denoting high internal consistency between the items comprising the scales. The reliability test result confirms the already validated reliability as reported by the original authors of the GUESS scales [20], as well as verifies that translating the scales into Greek language did not invalidate the reliability and validity of the instrument.

Table 1. Reliability results for the Gamified and non-Gamified versions of the VR environment.

	Cronbach's Alpha		N of Items
	Gamified (N25)	Non-Gamified (N25)	
Usability/Playability	.85	.87	11
Enjoyment	.88	.94	5
Visual Aesthetics	.82	.71	3

The data analysis began by investigating the descriptive statistics for both the Gamified and non-Gamified versions of the environment. The average and aggregated results are shown in Table 2 and Table 3 respectively. The descriptive statistics for each individual item comprising the scales are reported in Table 4.

The results for the Usability/Playability factor of the Gamified (M = 5.9, SD = .7) and non-Gamified (M = 5.6, SD = .73) version were very positively rated. These results suggest that both versions of the environment could be played with clear goals and objectives in the user's mind, and that there were minimal cognitive interference and distractions from the user interface (UI) and the controls of the environment that could hinder the playing experience.

Table 2. Descriptive statistics of the average values for the Gamified and non-Gamified Versions of the VR environment.

	Gamified (N25)				Non-Gamified (N25)			
	Mean	SD	Min	Max	Mean	SD	Min	Max
Usability/Playability	5.9	.7	4.18	7	5.6	.73	4.4	6.8
Enjoyment	5.6	1.4	2.20	7	6.2	1	3.2	7
Visual Aesthetics	5.7	1.3	2.33	7	6.2	.8	4.3	7

The results for Enjoyment also revealed high values for the Gamified (M = 5.6, SD = 1.4), and non-Gamified (M = 6.2, SD = .1) version, suggesting that the users perceived high amount of pleasure as a result of playing the gamified activities. Furthermore, the visual aspect, the design and the graphics for both versions of the environment and their attractiveness have also been positively perceived by users (Gamified: M = 5.7, SD = 1.3, non-Gamified: M = 6.2, SD = .8).

The aggregated average results for the Gamified (M = 109.7, SD = 16.9) and non-Gamified (M = 111.2, SD = 13.4) versions were quite high against the maximum achievable score of 133, denoting highly positive experience (Table 3).

Table 3. Descriptive Statistics of the aggregated values for the Gamified and non-Gamified versions of the VR environment.

	Gamified (N25)				Non-Gamified (N25)			
	Mean	SD	Min	Max	Mean	SD	Min	Max
Usability/ Playability	64.8	8	46	77	61.5	8	48	75
Enjoyment	27.8	7.1	11	35	31.1	5.1	16	35
Visual Aesthetics	17.1	3.8	7	21	18.5	2.4	13	21
Aggregated Result	109.7	16.9	64	132	111.2	13.4	85	131

Interestingly, the non-Gamified version of the environment was perceived more positively and with less data dispersion than the Gamified version in terms of Enjoyment, and for the Visual Aesthetics of the environment. To investigate the extent to which the differences between the results for the two groups/versions of the environment were statistically significant, a one-way-ANOVA test was employed using the groups that played the Gamified and non-Gamified version of the VR environment as the dependent variable, and the factors under study as the independent variables. Assumptions for homogeneity of variances were met since the population variances for each group were the same (N = 25 in both groups). The test revealed that the results for Usability/Playability ($F(1, 48) = [2.116]$, $p = 0.152$), Enjoyment ($F(1, 48) = [3.512]$, $p = 0.067$), and Visual Aesthetics ($F(1, 48) = [2.498]$, $p = 0.121$) were not statistically significant.

The results for the individual items comprising each scale were also investigated, to have an in-depth look and evaluation of the user responses from both groups (Table 4). Users found the gamified activities easy to learn how to play, easy to navigate around the UI elements, controls and menus, providing them with the necessary and clear information on how to complete the goals within the environment. However, the lack of gamified elements seemed to have hindered the users' understanding on achieving their objectives in the non-Gamified version of the environment (M = 4.76, SD = 1.59). The same group also perceived the awareness of the next goal after completing a task in the environment relatively low compared to the other items (M = 4.28, SD = 1.4). This may indicate that more structured user feedback to user completed actions on the non-Gamified environment, and more visual clarity on the next task could be implemented.

Clear visual ques and hints such as arrows, signposts, or a task list, to aid the users understanding of what should follow next can be considered for implementation in future iterations of the environment design to support this finding.

Table 4. Descriptive Statistics of All Items Comprising the Factors

Item	Gamified		Non-Gamified	
	Mean	SD	Mean	SD
Playability/Usability				
I think it is easy to learn how to use the environment	6.44	.58	6.00	.86
I find the controls of the environment to be straightforward	6.12	.97	5.52	1.08
I always know how to achieve my goals/objectives in the environment	5.64	1.1	4.76	1.59
I find the environment's interface to be easy to navigate	5.96	.98	5.80	.96
I do not need to go through a lengthy tutorial or read a manual to use the environment	5.88	1.51	5.84	1.14
I find the environment's menus to be user friendly	6.20	.96	6.20	.82
I feel the environment trains me well in all of the controls	5.80	1.12	5.76	1.2
I always know my next goal when I finish an event in the environment	5.40	1.38	4.28	1.4
I feel the environment provides me the necessary information to accomplish a goal within the environment	6.16	.89	5.88	.88
I think the information provided in the environment (e.g., onscreen messages, help) is clear	5.80	1.55	6.24	.83
I feel very confident while interacting with the environment	5.40	1.15	5.24	1.23
Enjoyment				
I think the environment is fun	5.56	1.68	6.44	.92
I enjoy interacting with the environment	5.80	1.55	6.20	1.15
I feel bored while interacting with the environment.*(reversed)	5.16	2.0	6.20	1.12
I am likely to recommend this environment to others	5.84	1.6	6.16	1.11
If given the chance, I want to reuse this environment again	5.48	1.76	6.12	1.42
Visual Aesthetics				
I enjoy the environment's graphics	5.84	1.25	6.04	1.31
I think the graphics of the environment fit the mood or style of the experience	5.60	1.66	6.24	.88
I think the environment is visually appealing	5.64	1.52	6.24	.83

Looking at the environment enjoyability results, the users have enjoyed and found it fun, but some users on the Gamified version of the environment were a little bored during the experience ($M = 5.16$, $SD = 2$). Nevertheless, users indicated that they are very likely to recommend this environment to others, and that they would like to play the gamified activities and the experience again if they had the chance. The graphics of the environment were perceived as enjoyable, relevant to the mood of the environment, and visually appealing.

An ANOVA test was also performed on each individual item comprising each scale as well, without revealing any statistically significant differences between the two groups. These results indicate that the users for both the Gamified and non-Gamified versions have positively perceived the environment's aesthetics, and have enjoyed the experience equally positively. The results were further investigated to identify potential gender differences within and between the two groups, without revealing statistically significant differences. The previous experience of users with VR was also investigated for potential correlations with the measured factors and the items comprising the scales, without revealing any relationships, suggesting that their previous experience did not influence their evaluation perceptions of the environment. Overall, the analysed results indicate that the users' experience was positively perceived regardless of experiencing the gamified elements of the environment or not during the educational experience.

5   Conclusions and Future Work

While the efficacy and applicability of VR in cultural heritage has been established, the field of serious VR gaming needs further studying, and it is important to evaluate the affordances and limitations of such approach to support DCH. New and existing research and application challenges need to be investigated and addressed to support the needs for preservation, reconstruction and dissemination in DCH and to also support and enhance the user experience through immersive interactive ways. Data capture and digitisation tools, optimisation and rendering techniques, interaction methods, NPC behaviour, AI, balance and gameplay, VR hardware and software, are only some of the many areas of ongoing research taking place at academic and industrial levels. Developing and extensively evaluating VR environments, serious games, and VR applications utilising gamified and gaming approaches from multiple perspectives is necessary to innovate and develop novel ways of supporting DCH. The resource intensive and complex computing requirements of VR drive research and innovation, constantly pushing the technological boundaries to the limits, and being responsible for some of the latest revolutionary achievements in the fields of hardware technology, computer graphics, high performance processing, artificial intelligence, user interface and user experience among other software and hardware advancements. Embracing cultural heritage through VR can offer opportunities for engaging the younger generations of visitors who are exposed and used to rich multimedia tools and technologies such as XR, video games and fast networking speeds, promoting heritage and intercultural understanding in fun and innovative ways.

The project presented in this paper describes the development and evaluation of a VR environment designed to support learning about the church of Panagia Aggeloktisti in Cyprus. The paper provides details on the design of the environment and the process of capturing, digitising and optimising 3D models to be used in the environment scene, together with details on the core environment mechanics and gamified elements of the environment. The study presented in this paper was set out to evaluate the users' experience focusing on usability/playabity, enjoyment, and the visual aesthetics of the Gamified and a non-Gamified version of the VR environment. A comparative study was conducted, where users experienced an immersive gamified learning scenario requiring them to complete a series of learning tasks within the VR world. The results of this study indicated that both versions of the environment have been perceived usable and playable, without any major issues hindering the ease in which the environment could be experienced and played. The environment features clear goals and objectives, with minimal cognitive interference or distractions from the environment UI hindering the users' experience. Both versions of the VR environment have been perceived as enjoyable, with high degree of pleasure and delight reported by the users, featuring attractive and visually appealing graphical elements. A key finding that should be considered for future development is the implementation of a comprehensive tutorial level to help the users familiarise with the use of the environment and its functionalities to ease the learning curve. Providing clear guidance and visual ques to help users identify the tasks and challenges within the environment is also deemed necessary based on the results of this study, and should be considered for the future iterations of the environment design.

The purpose of this comparative study was to try out the environment with real users, and evaluate specific aspects of their experience to ensure that the current stage of the environment development is usable, enjoyable and visually pleasing to proceed with further empirical evaluations in the future. Future studies are under preparation including evaluations on the educational efficacy of the VR environment, and technical evaluations. Factors such as presence, engagement and motivation during the VR experience will be assessed, together with engagement and user experience evaluations, as well as investigating issues pertaining VR sickness. Furthermore, additional gaming elements, levels, functionalities and challenges will be implemented to increase re-playability of the gamified activities of the environment.

Acknowledgements. The authors would like to thank the student interns Pavel Telnov and Pascal Schovanez from UCLan Cyprus for their contribution in the development and design of the VR environment, Dr Yiannis Georgiou, Maria Efpraxia and Varnavia Giorgalla from the Cyprus University of Technology for their support during data collection. We would also like to thank the students from the Cyprus University of Technology for their participation in this study. This project is partially funded by the Centre for Cultural Preservation through Creative Practice at UCLan.

References

1. Barsanti, S.G., Caruso, G., Micoli, L., Rodriguez, M.C., Guidi, G., et al.: 3D visualization of cultural heritage artefacts with virtual reality devices. Int. Arch. Photogramm. Remote Sens. Spatial Inf. Sci. **40**(5W7), 165–172 (2015)
2. Carrozzino, M., Bergamasco, M.: Beyond virtual museums: experiencing immersive virtual reality in real museums. J. Cult. Herit. **11**(4), 452–458 (2010). https://doi.org/10.1016/j.culher.2010.04.001. https://www.sciencedirect.com/science/article/pii/S1296207410000543
3. Champion, E.: Culturally significant presence in single-player computer games. J. Comput. Cult. Herit. **13**(4), 1–24 (2020). https://doi.org/10.1145/3414831
4. Champion, E.: Playing with the Past. In: Champion, E. (ed.) Playing with the Past, pp. 129–155. Springer, London (2011). https://doi.org/10.1007/978-1-84996-501-9_6
5. Ferdani, D., Fanini, B., Piccioli, M.C., Carboni, F., Vigliarolo, P.: 3D reconstruction and validation of historical background for immersive VR applications and games: the case study of the forum of Augustus in Rome. J. Cult. Herit. **43**, 129–143 (2020). https://doi.org/10.1016/j.culher.2019.12.004
6. He, Z., Wu, L., Li, X.R.: When art meets tech: the role of augmented reality in enhancing museum experiences and purchase intentions. Tour. Manag. **68**, 127–139 (2018). https://doi.org/10.1016/j.tourman.2018.03.003. https://www.sciencedirect.com/science/article/pii/S0261517718300475
7. Jacobson, J., Holden, L.: Virtual heritage: living in the past. Techné Res. Philos. Technol. **10**(3), 55–61 (2007)
8. Juan, A.A., Loch, B., Daradoumis, T., Ventura, S.: Games and simulation in higher education (2017)
9. Karahan, S., Gül, L.F.: Mapping current trends on gamification of cultural heritage. In: Cordan, Ö., Dinçay, D.A., Yurdakul Toker, Ç., Öksüz, E.B., Semizoğlu, S. (eds.) Game + Design Education. SSDI, vol. 13, pp. 281–293. Springer, Cham (2021). https://doi.org/10.1007/978-3-030-65060-5_23
10. Keebler, J.R., Shelstad, W.J., Smith, D.C., Chaparro, B.S., Phan, M.H.: Validation of the guess-18: a short version of the game user experience satisfaction scale (guess). J. Usability Stud. **16**(1), 49–62 (2020)
11. Malegiannaki, I.: Thanasis Daradoumis: analyzing the educational design, use and effect of spatial games for cultural heritage: a literature review. Comput. Educ. **108**, 1–10 (2017). https://doi.org/10.1016/j.compedu.2017.01.007
12. Markopoulos, E., Markopoulos, P., Liumila, M., Almufti, Y., Romano, C.: Digital cultural strategies within the context of digital humanities economics. In: Ahram, T. (ed.) AHFE 2019. AISC, vol. 973, pp. 283–295. Springer, Cham (2020). https://doi.org/10.1007/978-3-030-20476-1_29
13. Mortara, M., Catalano, C.E., Bellotti, F., Fiucci, G., Houry-Panchetti, M., Petridis, P.: Learning cultural heritage by serious games. J. Cult. Herit. **15**(3), 318–325 (2014). https://doi.org/10.1016/j.culher.2013.04.004. https://www.sciencedirect.com/science/article/pii/S1296207413001349
14. Nisiotis, L., Alboul, L.: Initial evaluation of an intelligent virtual museum prototype powered by AI, XR and robots. In: De Paolis, L.T., Arpaia, P., Bourdot, P. (eds.) AVR 2021. LNCS, vol. 12980, pp. 290–305. Springer, Cham (2021). https://doi.org/10.1007/978-3-030-87595-4_21

15. Nisiotis, L., Alboul, L.: Evaluating presence and technology acceptance of an intelligent reality virtual museum prototype. In: 2022 IEEE 2nd International Conference on Intelligent Reality (ICIR), pp. 1–6 (2022). https://doi.org/10.1109/ICIR55739.2022.00016
16. Nisiotis, L., Alboul, L., Beer, M.: Virtual museums as a new type of cyber-physical-social system. In: De Paolis, L.T., Bourdot, P. (eds.) AVR 2019. LNCS, vol. 11614, pp. 256–263. Springer, Cham (2019). https://doi.org/10.1007/978-3-030-25999-0_22
17. Nisiotis, L., Alboul, L., Beer, M.: A prototype that fuses virtual reality, robots, and social networks to create a new cyber-physical-social eco-society system for cultural heritage. Sustainability **12**(2) (2020). https://doi.org/10.3390/su12020645. https://www.mdpi.com/2071-1050/12/2/645
18. Noh, Z., Sunar, M.S., Pan, Z.: A review on augmented reality for virtual heritage system. In: Chang, M., Kuo, R., Kinshuk, Chen, G.D., Hirose, M. (eds.) Learning by Playing. Game-Based Education System Design and Development. LNCS, vol. 5670, pp. 50–61. Springer, Heidelberg (2009). https://doi.org/10.1007/978-3-642-03364-3_7
19. Pallavicini, F., Pepe, A.: Comparing player experience in video games played in virtual reality or on desktop displays: immersion, flow, and positive emotions. In: Extended Abstracts of the Annual Symposium on Computer-Human Interaction in Play Companion Extended Abstracts, CHI PLAY 2019 Extended Abstracts, pp. 195–210. Association for Computing Machinery, New York (2019). https://doi.org/10.1145/3341215.3355736
20. Phan, M.H., Keebler, J.R., Chaparro, B.S.: The development and validation of the game user experience satisfaction scale (GUESS). Hum. Factors **58**(8), 1217–1247 (2016)
21. Popovici, D.M., Polceanu, M., Popescu, A.: Augmenting user experience in virtual environments through haptic feedback. In: Proceedings of the 7th Balkan Conference on Informatics Conference, BCI 2015. Association for Computing Machinery, New York (2015). https://doi.org/10.1145/2801081.2801100
22. Portalés, C., Rodrigues, J.M.F., Rodrigues Gonçalves, A., Alba, E., Sebastián, J.: Digital cultural heritage. Multimodal Technol. Interact. **2**(3) (2018). https://doi.org/10.3390/mti2030058. https://www.mdpi.com/2414-4088/2/3/58
23. Pujol, L., Champion, E.: Evaluating presence in cultural heritage projects. Int. J. Herit. Stud. **18**(1), 83–102 (2012). https://doi.org/10.1080/13527258.2011.577796
24. Roussou, M.: Virtual heritage: from the research lab to the broad public. Bar Int. Ser. **1075**, 93–100 (2002)
25. Rua, H., Alvito, P.: Living the past: 3D models, virtual reality and game engines as tools for supporting archaeology and the reconstruction of cultural heritage - the case-study of the roman villa of Casal de Freiria. J. Archaeol. Sci. **38**(12), 3296–3308 (2011). https://doi.org/10.1016/j.jas.2011.07.015. https://www.sciencedirect.com/science/article/pii/S0305440311002494
26. Sharp, L.A.: Stealth learning: unexpected learning opportunities through games. J. Instr. Res. **1**, 42–48 (2012). https://doi.org/10.9743/jir.2013.6
27. Subhash, S., Cudney, E.A.: Gamified learning in higher education: a systematic review of the literature. Comput. Hum. Behav. **87**, 192–206 (2018). https://doi.org/10.1016/j.chb.2018.05.028. https://www.sciencedirect.com/science/article/pii/S0747563218302541
28. Theodoropoulos, A., Antoniou, A.: VR games in cultural heritage: a systematic review of the emerging fields of virtual reality and culture games. Appl. Sci. **12**(17) (2022). https://doi.org/10.3390/app12178476

29. UNESCO: Church of panagia aggeloktisti. https://whc.unesco.org/en/tentativelists/5987/

30. UnrealEngine: Forward shading renderer. https://docs.unrealengine.com/4.26/en-US/TestingAndOptimization/PerformanceAndProfiling/ForwardRenderer/

31. UnrealEngine: Reducing draw calls. https://unrealcommunity.wiki/reducing-draw-calls-dtz72780

32. Vi, C.T., Ablart, D., Gatti, E., Velasco, C., Obrist, M.: Not just seeing, but also feeling art: mid-air haptic experiences integrated in a multisensory art exhibition. Int. J. Hum.-Comput. Stud. **108**, 1–14 (2017). https://doi.org/10.1016/j.ijhcs.2017.06.004. https://www.sciencedirect.com/science/article/pii/S1071581917300988

33. Ye, L., Wang, R., Zhao, J.: Enhancing learning performance and motivation of cultural heritage using serious games. J. Educ. Comput. Res. **59**(2), 287–317 (2021). https://doi.org/10.1177/0735633120963828. https://doi.org/10.1177/0735633120963828

34. Zhonggen, Y.: A meta-analysis of use of serious games in education over a decade. Int. J. Comput. Games Technol. **2019** (2019)

35. Škola, F., et al.: Virtual reality with 360-video storytelling in cultural heritage: study of presence, engagement, and immersion. Sensors **20**(20) (2020). https://doi.org/10.3390/s20205851. https://www.mdpi.com/1424-8220/20/20/5851

An Innovative Approach to Shape Information Architecture Related to Ancient Manuscripts, Through Multi-layered Virtual Ecosystems. From Codex4D to DataSpace Project

Eva Pietroni[1]() , Alessandra Chirivì[2] , Bruno Fanini[1] ,
and Alberto Bucciero[2]

[1] Digital Heritage Innovation Lab (DHILab), National Research Council—Institute
of Heritage Science (CNR-ISPC), Rome, Italy
`[email protected]`
[2] Digital Heritage Innovation Lab (DHILab), National Research Council—Institute
of Heritage Science (CNR-ISPC), Lecce, Italy
`https://www.ispc.cnr.it/en/2021/06/16/`
`dhilab-digital-heritage-innovation-lab/`

Abstract. This contribution deals with the theme of ancient
manuscripts and proposes an innovative approach to the construction
of cultural ecosystems and virtual representations capable of integrating
information levels of various kinds: not only textual and iconographic
contents, as it usually happens, but also the form, structure, stratig-
raphy and elements hidden beneath the pictorial layers or beneath the
texts visible on the surface, the constituent materials, the execution techniques, the state of conservation and the storytelling of the cultural context. This multidisciplinary approach results in a multidimensional virtual representation. Starting from the same data set, this cultural model
is differently applied in a plurality of digital environments: 1) a 3D Web
App, developed in the framework of the Codex4D project, conceived for
the scientific visualisation of the manuscript, the analytical exploration
of the virtual model and its information levels; 2) a holographic showcase,
again developed in the context of the Codex4D project, conceived for the
general public of museums and libraries, in which the research data are
translated into a mixed-reality environment adopting a dramaturgical
style; 3) an online digital platform, the DataSpace, mostly oriented to
the scientific community, whose scope is to semantically organize, preserve in the long term, access, share and re-use information and data set
produced by the Institute of Heritage Science, together with the documentation of processes and actions that led to their production. The
contribution develops around these themes: conceptual maps, information architecture, user-experience design, and virtual environments to
increase the knowledge of ancient manuscripts, in relation to various
typologies of users.

© The Author(s), under exclusive license to Springer Nature Switzerland AG 2023
L. T. De Paolis et al. (Eds.): XR Salento 2023, LNCS 14219, pp. 247–267, 2023.
https://doi.org/10.1007/978-3-031-43404-4_16

Keywords: Manuscripts · Virtual ecosystems · Multidisciplinary and multidimensional approach

1 General Context and Contribution to the Research

1.1 Structure of the Paper

The first section of this contribution deals with the state of the art of digital projects and the methodological approach generally applied to the international investigation and valorisation of manuscripts. This general scenario helps to contextualise the potentialities of our proposal. Section 2 is focused on the information architecture we have implemented around the manuscript, in the DataSpace and Codex4D frameworks, both following a multidisciplinary approach and adapted to different contexts of use. In Sect. 3 specific applications are described, developed on this theoretical basis, to create effective user experiences with manuscripts. Conclusions and further perspectives are in Sect. 4.

1.2 The National and International Panorama in the Manuscript Studies and Projects

The many national and international projects for the digitization of illuminated manuscripts and the creation of connected digital libraries have long offered undeniable support to the scientific community, in terms of accessibility to an extremely fragile heritage [5].

Despite the value of digitization campaigns and the creation of thematic networks dedicated to manuscripts, the scientific community wonders how to enhance them and what perspective to adopt, considering the many potentially interested users. It is a particularly numerous and heterogeneous community as the illuminated manuscripts are complex artefacts, containers of texts, ornamental elements and figurative inserts. On the humanities side, the interdisciplinary approach to studying book artefacts has long been adopted and considered indispensable [4, 7] the dialogue with the scientific communities that conduct diagnostic investigations on artefacts is less granted and consolidated, although constantly growing [13, 16].

From the reconstruction of the panorama of the most important initiatives, little general attention emerges for the material representation of the manuscripts in their three-dimensional form, and for the integration of information on several layers, to understand the history of the artefact, its contents, the used techniques, its origin and the conservation history.

Advanced scientific digitization of illustrated and decorated manuscripts should go beyond mere "photographic" reproduction to return information on their making, material characteristics, techniques, and chronology of execution, obtainable from the joint analysis of visible and not visible elements with the naked eye, to be used in digital form, in virtual environments equipped with tools and services designed for different targets. In the general landscape, the

MINIARE project of the Fitzwilliam Museum (Cambridge), and its more recent related initiatives, deserve special mention for the unusual attention paid to the material characteristics of illuminated manuscripts. The project aimed to strengthen the dialogue between the humanities and hard sciences and to increase knowledge of book artefacts thanks to non-invasive complementary diagnostic investigations. The web platform allows you to explore the manuscript and view the heterogeneous data resulting from the conducted investigations (spectra, interpreted data, etc.) using spot points. Starting from these, the user is offered information on the techniques adopted by the illuminators, the materials, as well as the codicological, palaeographic, and historical-artistic description of the volumes[1].

In addition to the MINIARE project, other initiatives demonstrate the gradual consolidation of the dialogue between humanities, experimental sciences, and innovative technologies in the interdisciplinary study of illuminated objects. Among these, there is the ambitious project to digitize the 80,000 manuscripts of the Vatican Apostolic Library [8][2]. For the digitization of book artefacts, the FITS standard was adopted and used by NASA and ESA to acquire information on external elements. In recent years, the library has decided to use MIRADOR[3] and the IIIF framework[4], following the path taken by the most prestigious Museums, Archives, and Libraries [15]. This choice demonstrates the growing sensitivity towards the issues of data interoperability and standardization of viewer functions, beyond the mere care of image quality, which for years has monopolized the attention of scholars. The same protocol is adopted in Italy by the Biblioteca Estense Universitaria in Modena, and in the rest of Europe by other institutions, including the Bodleian Library in Oxford. In general, the state of the art shows a little diffusion of innovative tools and services designed for different targets, despite there being sporadic international initiatives, born around individual manuscripts, that offer innovative technological solutions able to create an immersive, interactive experience: gaming, and 3D modeling, virtual reality. See Using Virtual Reality to Explore 15th Century Illuminated Manuscripts[5], Manuscripts of Lichfield[6] and MUBIL project[7]. So even if the multidisciplinary approach is introduced in some projects, and similarly the practice of annotating the digitised pages, or characterising them semantically, these actions are usually implemented in 2D graphic environments. Moreover, the communication of manuscripts to museums' visitors is still very difficult: they are poorly lit for preservation reasons, they are not intelligible (inaccessible language) and they cannot be browsed. They are mostly considered just for their aesthetical

---

[1] https://www.fitzmuseum.cam.ac.uk/illuminated/footer/credits?back=section/undefined.

[2] https://spotlight.vatlib.it/?tag=Mellon+Project.

[3] https://projectmirador.org/.

[4] https://www.digitale-sammlungen.de/en/p/20aec4c0-dc8a-4e40-84ac-49cfcac9a96c.

[5] https://dornsife.usc.edu/xrlab/neh-vr-exploration-of-illuminated-manuscripts/.

[6] https://lichfield.ou.edu/content/project.

[7] http://mubil.no/avada_portfolio/augmented-book.

appearance, especially if they have beautiful decorations. In a few cases, museums include a 2D digital gallery of the pages that can be browsed, but they are not accompanied by any involving storytelling or engaging tools for exploration.

1.3 DataSpace: Scope, Target

DataSpace was born as a pilot project conducted by the ISPC DHILab with the aim of creating a digital library of Heritage Science datasets that supports ISPC researchers (primarily) in managing their data and scientific processes, within the following areas:

- Storage (ingestion and metadating)
- Information retrieval
- Presentation/Visualization
- Knowledge Discovery
- Cloud based processing

DataSpace is a platform for the sharing, accessing, and long-term conservation of data produced by the Institute of Cultural Heritage Sciences. It allows access to innovative digital tools and services to increase knowledge and enhance the conservation of Cultural Heritage from an interdisciplinary perspective.

DataSpace represents the first step towards the design of a shared and more general platform (DIGILAB), within the European Research Infrastructure for Heritage Science (E-RIHS), that will consist of the core of the research facilities devoted to the study of Heritage by means of integrated Heritage Science and Humanities digital data.

Dataspace provides access to research data, initially generated by HS researchers, curating it according to the FAIR data principles and enabling its interoperability to Virtual Research Environments, where they can access, visualise, interrogate and manipulate such data, to create new Heritage-related knowledge.

DataSpace can also facilitate the exchange of data and their interoperability, promoting the development of open science in the field of heritage science. It will offer virtual access to tools and data supporting multidisciplinary research (i.e. results of scientific measurement, environment for immersive and interactive visualisation of the data set, historical documentation and literature sources, etc.). It guarantees data searchability with advanced tools based on metadata stored in federated repositories. It also grants accessibility of resources through mechanisms of federated identity, delegating access and delivery control to the nodes. Data interoperability is granted by the use of appropriate and shared standards, while re-use is guaranteed by the possibility of data processing through specialised services (i.e., virtual access, scientific visualisation and simulation for digital heritage, collaborative research in immersive and interactive environments accessible on-site o remotely, data georeferencing annotation, analysis etc.) integrated into E-RIHS ecosystem.

The Arches platform was chosen for the implementation of the DataSpace. It is a freely available open-source software platform developed by the Getty

Conservation Institute and the World Monuments Fund. Arches enable the management, discovery, and visualization of cultural heritage data, and can be customized and extended according to specific needs.[8]

1.4 Codex 4D Project: Scope, Target, Case Studies, Results

The project concerns the definition and experimentation of a methodological pipeline to enhance the knowledge of the ancient manuscript, for the digital archiving and for the involvement of a diverse audience in interdisciplinary and cross-cutting experiences, both from an art-historical and a diagnostic-conservative point of view, inside Virtual and mixed reality environments. The aim is to document, on a 3D model, text parts buried in the binding, the sub-surface of illuminations, as well as the characterization of the chemical-physical-biological nature of the materials, through non-invasive and non-destructive analyses. For this reason, a variety of studies, digitisation techniques and diagnostic analyses have been carried out.

The 4D ancient code model is obtained by integrating Structure from Motion (SFM) techniques [12], which use RGB images to process the volumetric model, and IR reflectography and thermography techniques. The latter allows the acquisition of images in the mid-infrared range at various depth levels [6], documenting elements or phenomena under the pictorial final layer, such as gilding preparation, detachments, preparatory drawings, repentance, censorships, fragments of text buried under bindings (Fig. 1).

Fig. 1. 3D model of Ms1474 De Balneis Puteolanis, cc.12v-13r, showing thermal images and RGB textures obtained through SFM techniques. Right in the image: a detail of the illumination in RGB colour and IR, the thermal image shows a small marine creature hidden under the surface, probably a repentance of the artist.

Thermal images are consistently aligned on the 3D model, through a process of orientation of the thermal camera and RGB camera positions.

In some cases, multiband imaging (UV fluorescence, hyperspectral images) is also mapped onto additional visualisation layers of the 3D model.

---

[8] https://www.archesproject.org/.

In addition to the investigation based on "imaging" techniques, microbiological (Next Generation Sequencing, Sanger Sequencing), chemical (High Performance Liquid Chromatograhy, Spectroscopy FTIR), and physical analyses (XRF, RAMAN, UV Fluorescence, Hyperspectral analyses) were conducted on individual points or small areas of the manuscript and its illuminations, to understand the nature of the pigments, inks, binders, preparations, their level of degradation and the general state of health of the artefact (Fig. 2).

The relevant information has been mapped as "annotations" on the virtual multidimensional model, consisting of informative/semantic spots.

The final purpose of the Codex4D project is to create:

1. new approaches in scientific visualization of ancient manuscripts through virtual and mixed reality environments in the web mostly oriented to the expert audience
2. new storytelling and interaction metaphors in museums and libraries through the holographic showcase, using emotional languages, to increase common visitors' curiosity and awareness towards ancient manuscripts
3. improved interaction and sharing processes between research teams

The project will be concluded at the end of 2023; however, the methodological approach has been clearly defined and relevant outcomes for different stakeholders and communities are already available. The entry point of the project is the website: https://codex4d.it/.

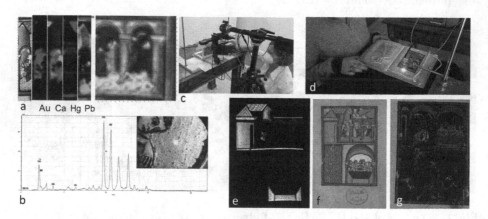

Fig. 2. Analysis on Ms 1474. A) maps of gold, mercury, and lead obtained through XRF analysis; b) Investigation of gilding preparation through XRF; c) XRF instrument moved to Angelica Library in Rome; d) hyperspectral analyses; e) map of the red lake coming from hyperspectral analysis; f) image in false colour IR; g) UV fluorescence. (Color figure online)

In the context of the Codex4D project, after some preliminary tests carried out in Casanatense Library on Ms. 59 Miscellanea, to fix the general methodology on manuscripts composed of several materials (leather, wood, parchment, metal), the project has been developed on three main case studies in the Angelica Library in Rome:

1. Ms 1474 De Balneis Puteolanis[9], a poem by Pietro da Eboli, dated 1258/1266, of which three poses have been acquired in 4D (cc.9v-10r, cc.12v-13r, cc.19v-20r)
2. Ms 1102, Divina Commedia by Dante Alighieri[10], dated 1351/1400, of which two poses have been acquired in 4D (cc.4v-5r, cc.56v-57r)
3. Ms 459 Libro d'Ore [1] a prayer book for secular use, dated at the beginning of the XV century BC, of which three poses have been acquired in 4D (closed book, cc.21v-22r, cc.67v-68r)

All of them are very precious manuscripts, in parchment and with illuminations and gliding.

1.5   Potentialities and Values of the Proposed Approach

The approach we are developing through a series of initiatives and projects stems from the full awareness that the joint analysis of visible and non-visible elements, integrated into multidimensional virtual representations, to be explored and interrogated using innovative tools, can contribute to increasing knowledge of illuminated manuscripts in their extraordinary complexity. The joint interpretation of these elements offers possible useful indications for determining the chronology, reconstructing their history, identifying the production centre, defining the manufacturing techniques, the materials, and the production processes, and revealing the distribution of the operations between the various actors involved. The integration of these elements is based on the synergistic dialogue between scholars of different backgrounds who contribute to increasing the knowledge of the manuscripts and promoting their diffusion with multidimensional virtual representations.

The DataSpace[11] project of the Institute of Cultural Heritage Sciences intends to contribute to strengthening the dialogue between the different communities of Heritage Science, creating a digital semantic platform that allows, among other things, access to data sets, services and innovative tools useful to increase the knowledge, conservation, and use of cultural heritage. In advancing the DataSpace platform, still under development, it was decided to dedicate a case study to some illuminated manuscripts, analysed through complementary and non-invasive diagnostic investigations conducted by the E-RIHS Mobile Laboratories (MOLAB E-RIHS).

Thanks to the MOLAB mobile, instruments can move to the library or museum to carry out diagnostic analyses, thus overcoming the difficulty and risk of moving a precious and delicate object, such as a manuscript, to a digitisation site. The case study has allowed us to address several crucial issues regarding the storage, sharing, processing, and display of different types of digital data. The DataSpace is thus configured to be not a simple archive of data, but rather a

---

[9] https://manus.iccu.sbn.it/opac_SchedaScheda.php?ID=102297.
[10] https://manus.iccu.sbn.it/opac_SchedaScheda.php?ID=102213.
[11] http://dataspace.ispc.cnr.it/.

repository characterized by semantic networks that connect contents, processes, actions and contexts related to the enhancement of informative ecosystems about the manuscript. DataSpace cannot be considered as a final product addressed to the public, but an evolving ecosystem where the stored data set are enriched by metadata, organized and available to be re-used by the scientific communities and creative teams to develop applications.

On the other side, the "Codex4D: four-dimensional journey to the centre of the manuscript" project aims at the creation of digital applications and tools finalised and published to respond to these different requests of the public. The project was started by the Institute of Heritage Science of CNR and the Department of Industrial Engineering of the University of Rome, Tor Vergata in April 2021, thanks to the financial support from Lazio Region.

The project adopts the same interdisciplinary approach, strengthening the dialogue between humanists interested in the study of manuscripts (palaeographers, codicologists, literary historians, art historians, etc.) and researchers specialized in diagnostics for Cultural Heritage.

The peculiarity of the approach and method formalised in the project is to document and represent the manuscript in its characteristics of 1) form and structure, 2) contents and meanings, 3) writing techniques, 4) compositional materials and execution techniques, 5) state of preservation, as well as in its cultural context of origin. This multiplicity of approaches results conceptually in a multi-layered virtual model, i.e. 1) volumetrically explorable from the surface to the stratigraphic levels, and 2) populated with contents pertaining to several disciplines that are interconnected in the information architecture. Communication formats are stylistically diversified, depending on the targets, the contexts of use and the adopted dissemination tools, as we are going to present in the next paragraphs.

2　Information Architecture of the Manuscript

2.1　Information Architecture in the Codex4D Project

In the Codex4D project, the design of the general information architecture considered the needs and desires of the potential users collected through a survey involving both members of the research team and external users. Interviewed people had different geographical origins, gender and age, cultural background, employment, and level of technological literacy. The user needs and desires that emerged from this survey influenced the information architecture and the design of the content. The results that emerged were the subject of a discussion among the scholars of the interdisciplinary research team, made up of humanists (art historians, historians of the illuminated manuscripts, palaeographers, codicologists) researchers in the field of the so-called hard sciences specialized in heritage diagnostics (chemists, physicists, and biologists) and experts in information and communication technologies. This made it possible to define differentiated learning paths and to elaborate and organize multimedia content to be conveyed in different digital environments:

- A website[12] designed for a wide audience provides access to the collection of manuscripts under investigation, which contains descriptions organized in thematic modules to create storytelling that accompanies the user in discovering the codex. The description provides information on the entire codex and not only on the digitized 4D sheets, which are instead explored in depth in the web app and the holographic showcase. The user can also consult a scientifically rigorous narrated glossary in the scrolly telling, but streamlined in content and form, to discover the world of ancient books: the materials used and the stages in the production of the artefacts and illuminations (Fig. 3). The site also offers multimedia insights dedicated to the methodologies adopted to study the contents, materials, execution techniques, and state of conservation. Further insights are reserved for the technologies, hardware, and software tools used for data acquisition and processing. There is also a section dedicated to the work team, reporting, and publications.
- A Web3D application designed and developed to meet the specific needs of the project. It is dedicated to the scientific visualization of the elaborated virtual models. Based on the open-source ATON framework [3], it enables 4D inspection of sheets undergoing diagnostic investigation. The digital environment is a collaborative working space where it's possible to put and visualize many annotations regarding the model and to use analytical tools for exploration. These annotations are organized according to a specific taxonomy that provides different categories and sub-categories created to meet the different users' needs. Categories and subcategories are also useful to organize informative layers, integrate contents coherently and facilitating search functionalities (Fig. 4). The last Category "Musical Annotation" is not currently divided into specific subcategories, which will be added if necessary.

Fig. 3. Codex4D narrated glossary, implemented in the website. It is divided into materials and executive processes of the manuscripts. Each item is told through about 5 sub-items in the scrolly telling.

---

[12] https://codex4d.it.

Categories	Subcategories	
Iconography and Iconology	Description	Characters and Symbols
	Dating and Attribution	Ideological Message
	Style	Sources and Traditions
	Visual Comparisons	Reconsiderations
	Ornamental Elements	Subsequent Modifications
Materials and Execution Techniques	Particularities of Materials	Particularities of Execution Techniques
Structure	Size	Re-use Elements
	Binding	Structure Particularities
	Layout	
Conservation and Restoration	Restoration	Physical Evidence
	Biological Evidence	Theft And Subtraction
	Chemical Evidence	Damage
Text and Writing	Transcription,	Translation
	Particularities of Writing	Notes
	Subsequent Amendments	
Censorship	Text Censures	Damage Censures
Musical Annotation		

Fig. 4. Categories and SubCategories

2.2 Information Architecture in the DataSpace

The design of the platform architecture (Fig. 5) took into account the results of European projects that have been dealing with the same topics for years and the debates still ongoing in the context of similar national and European initiatives (E-RIHS PP now E-RIHS IP, IPERION HS and more). These have brought out the high-level needs of users and the requirements that digital platforms should have.

Fig. 5. DataSpace's Home Page

Starting from this, an extensive survey of software solutions for the management of heterogeneous data in the cultural heritage field was conducted, comparing the main open-source solutions available. In defining the information architecture, we did not start from scratch but from the solution of the Arches platform, which was chosen for the implementation of the project. However, Arches was customized to meet the communities' many needs and different use cases. The logical and semantic organization of information was then partially modified.

The case study on manuscripts is part of the broader and more articulated digital space dedicated to artworks investigated by the MOLAB Laboratories. To manage this data, unlike other case studies, we employed a suite of Resource Models derived from the ongoing development of Arches for Science Fig. 5, a collaborative project within the Arches community. This package encompasses a range of pre-existing Resource Models based on the CIDOC Conceptual Reference Model[13]. These Resource Models are based on the CIDOC Conceptual Reference Model. After the analysis of the data provided by MOLAB, we mapped it with the existing Resource Models (Fig. 6). The models, their relationships, and the thesauri available were therefore modified taking into account our specific needs (Fig. 7).

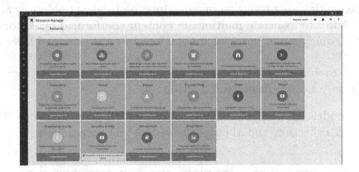

Fig. 6. Resource Models by Arches for Science

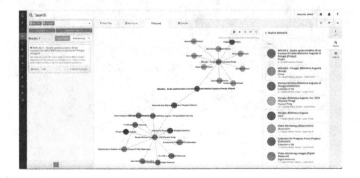

Fig. 7. Relationships between Resource Models

---

[13] https://www.cidoc-crm.org/.

3 Applications Developed on the Ancient Manuscript

3.1 Codex4D Web Application

The presentation and dissemination of interactive 3D content on the Web through common browsers has undergone significant advances in recent years. Such advances allow to create interactive 3D applications or tools that do not require end-user installations and can be consumed on a wide range of devices (smartphones, tablets, museum kiosks, up to immersive VR devices). The open-source ATON framework developed by CNR ISPC [3] allows fast creation and deployment of such applications through several customizable components. Within Codex4D project, we identified specific requirements targeting the creation of a 4D inspection tool for manuscripts' collections, exploiting features and components available in the framework:

- Modular design of the Web3D application to handle multiple manuscripts and related poses
- Simple and easy exploration of the manuscript on mobile and desktop devices
- Responsive user interface (UI)
- Dual profile for the Web3D application: public and editor (through authentication)
- Direct semantic annotations on manuscripts, on localized points or areas and the possibility to associate multimedia content (performed by editors)
- Interactive query and filtering of annotations by categories and layers (public profile)
- Advanced tools for the interactive discovery of hidden layers (e.g.: infrared information), measurements and lighting.

For 3D models of the manuscripts, once created they were uploaded into a cloud-based collection and then published as 3D scenes (see [3], Sect. 3.2)

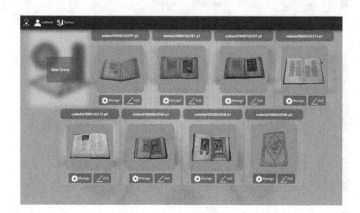

Fig. 8. Published 3D scenes through the ATON framework, corresponding to manuscripts' poses

with each scene corresponding to a manuscript pose (Fig. 8). The web app can thus access directly a selection of scenes (multiple manuscript poses) and allow users to switch between them at runtime. The cloud integration offered a streamlined pipeline for content creators to upload 3D models (manuscript poses, using the glTF standard [14] and multimedia content (e.g. images) to be used in the annotations.

The web-application is designed to consume URL parameters to load specific manuscripts and poses, offering great flexibility for the integration of the interactive presentation into websites or DataSpaces.

Regarding the editor profile, the Web3D app leverages on ATON authentication system, allowing a restricted team to perform persistent modifications on a given manuscript pose (like add, modify or delete semantic annotations) while a large audience (public profile) can explore, inspect and query the virtual object. The editor profile offers two annotation types (basic and free-form) to design semantic shapes right inside the web-app: the first has a spherical shape requiring location and radius, while the second one needs a set of points for the creation of a convex-hull (see [3], section 3.6.5). Once the annotation is completed, a UI form is shown to fill in the title, description, categories, author and a list of media to be presented in the annotation (Fig. 9).

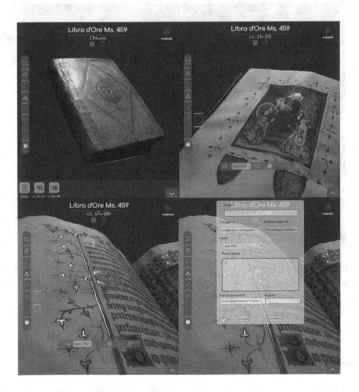

Fig. 9. Editor profile: an authenticated user performs semantic enrichment of manuscript using built-in annotation tools and forms

To allow users to interactively discover hidden layers, like infrared information, a specific tool was developed, based on the interactive lenses approach [17] and more specifically, on a previously developed model for ATON framework [2]. The lens operating in Codex4D web-application allows the discovery of hidden layers on a localized area of the manuscript, through a superficial location and radius. It is possible through the UI to switch among different infrared layers - or other layers - to discover invisible details through a simple and immediate metaphor.

An interactive light is also provided: this allows users to inspect the complexity of the manuscript surface, its details and decorations, with different materials reacting consistently (Fig. 9). This is possible thanks to the adoption of a PBR (Physically-Based Rendering) pipeline for the creation of the 3D models, in particular enriching the base colour (visible layer) with roughness and metalness properties. Annotations can be filtered through a specific interface allowing the user to visualise on the 4D model a selection corresponding to one or more categories of specific interest (Fig. 10, bottom left). Users through the public profile can also query a given annotation showing its content in a side panel (Fig. 10, bottom right).

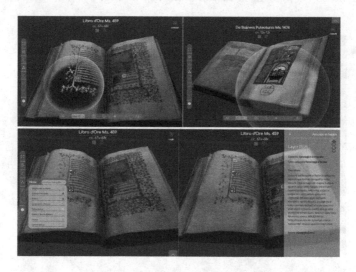

Fig. 10. Top row: interactive discovery of infrared information (multiple layers) on the manuscript using the lens, also inverting the palette; Bottom row: filtering categories and semantic queries.

3.2   Codex4D Holographic Showcase

The holographic showcase, as a mixed reality environment designed for museums, has been conceived and experimented with by CNR ISPC team since 2016 [11]. The hologram is an illusion of reality, and the technique used is based on the Pepper's Ghost projection [9], derived from a theatrical technique that creates an optical illusion for the audience (Fig. 11) The holographic showcase in fact is conceived as a small theatre, provided with lights, scenic design, buttons, sensors, and software to manage multimedia events and interaction.

Fig. 11. Pepper's Ghost projection in XIX centuries theatres and in the modern holographic showcase, on the right the customized for the Codex4D project.

Images or videos are generated interactively by software written specifically for the installation, based on Vvvv[14], a visual programming platform known especially in the field of digital art. Through special perspective studies, the hologram can give the illusion of interacting with real objects on the scene, establishing a relationship between virtual and real content. The purpose of the holographic showcase is thus to recreate through virtual projections the sensory and narrative dimension of the museum's object preserved inside, being a mixed reality environment [10] (Fig. 12 a and c). A totem is positioned in front of the showcase, allowing the user to start the experience. The experience with the holographic showcase engages the user through an alternation of passive and active phases. Passive phases consist in the enjoyment of pre-rendered narrative

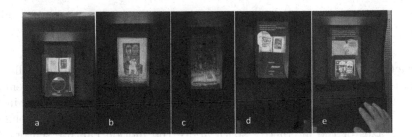

Fig. 12. Codex4D holographic showcase a) real scenography in the showcase; b) the character telling stories; c) sensory dimension with the ground falling down over the manuscript in accordance with the storytelling; d) example of annotation related to the text; e) gesture-based interaction to activate an annotation in IR layer, with magnifying lens.

---

[14] https://visualprogramming.net.

movies regarding the manuscript; active phases require the user to interact using his/her hand, in order to explore contents[15].

Narrative Style. In the holographic showcase, we play with research data, using emotional and poetic language, leading scientific communication to new experimentation scenarios and styles. A purely descriptive and didactic approach would not have been appropriate for this kind of magic experience. A small character, interpreted by an actress shot on a green screen and composed in the virtual scenario, lives in the manuscript, attends all the places, and she knows the people painted in the illuminations. She is as little as the other illuminated figures and she plays actions, using a magnifying lens to explore every detail (Fig. 13). She can tell stories about the meanings of the poem and of the figures, and she encourages the visitor to explore under the surface, to discover an immense and multidimensional world. While the character is three-dimensional, the graphic style of the virtual animations is 2,5D, to create a stylistic connection between the bidimensionality of the manuscript's sheets and the tridimensionality of the holographic showcase (Fig. 12b).

Fig. 13. Dramatized storytelling in Ms459 Libro d'Ore, with character dancing and generating decorations (left) and using revealing IR lens to see under the surface (right)

Interaction. The interaction interface allows the user to select contents directly using the movements of his/her hand, no devices are required. Hand movements are tracked by the *Leap Motion*[16] sensor and work as input of events in the virtual scene. Moving the hand in the air horizontally and vertically, along the X and Y axes of the interactive space above the motion capture sensor, it is possible to explore the manuscript using a magnifying lens to see every detail. Moving the hand along the Z axis of the depth, it is possible to explore the 3D model starting from the RGB surface through three progressive sub-surface IR layers generated by the thermal camera (Fig. 10).

---

[15] https://tube.rsi.cnr.it/w/uSJwd7sKQiY3y8D4TSNfhJ.
[16] www.ultraleap.com.

Using the hand in the same way it is possible to select annotations (Fig. 12e).

In the author's conception, this kind of natural interaction strengthens the sense of magic evoked by the hologram and the visitor's engagement.

The showcases can be accessed by 3–4 people at a time, for a collective experience. One person at a time can lead the system interacting with it, however, the alternation among visitors is easy and immediate.

Annotations. Annotations correspond to very specific points of the model, and they are contextualized and visualised on the RGB or IR layers by means of small spheres. Annotations can be related to the identification of written texts or iconographies, symbolic meanings, translations, structure, materials, state of preservation, and restorations. However, unlike the web app, annotations are divided into categories and cannot be filtered because the experience in the holographic showcase must be simple and short and a selection of 8 annotations in each pose has been chosen. Information provided by each annotation (Fig. 12d)

1) a title; 2) a short written text scrolling automatically; 3) an image, pertinent to the content of the annotation; 4) two or three keywords related to the content of the annotation.

Each annotation has a predefined duration, and it cannot be skipped. At the end of the animation, the model becomes interactive again and another annotation can be selected. This restriction stemmed from the desire not to overcomplicate the interaction for the user because it would have been necessary to introduce another hand gesture to close the annotation at will.

3.3   DataSpace Platform for Illuminated Manuscripts

In implementing DataSpace, we decided to dedicate a case study to an illuminated manuscript analysed by the MOLAB laboratories of E-RIHS. The platform allows storage, processing, and visualizing raw data and interpreted data deriving from instrumental analysis and connecting them with data from the humanistic field.

The manuscript on which we focused is the codex 2792 held in the Augusta Library (ms. 2792). The codex is a Graduale-Kyriale from the end of the 13th century, probably of Spoleto origin. Manuscript 2792 is one of the six illuminated manuscripts of the XIII-XIV century, of the Augusta municipal library of Perugia, on which non-invasive diagnostic investigations were conducted in September 2011. The scientific analyses of the codes were performed by the SMAArt Center of Excellence of the University of Perugia and by the Institute of Molecular Sciences and Technologies of the CNR. Non-invasive integrated analyses were carried out to increase the knowledge relating to the characterization of the materials, the executive techniques, and the assessment of the state of conservation. The techniques used are imaging techniques (visible photography, infrared reflectography, fluorescence, and false colour infrared imaging) and punctual and non-invasive spectroscopic techniques (X-ray fluorescence, infrared spectroscopy, UV-Vis spectroscopy, and X-ray diffraction). We extended Arches' base functionality, which only allowed users to upload their diagnostic data files in a .txt format if they wanted their plots to be rendered, to allow multiple file formats. This way, particular, proprietary formats (e.g. ".mca", ".dpt") are now recognized and plotted accordingly.

The platform allows you to view all the heterogeneous related resources associated with the manuscript, the tab of which contains information about the object (description, size, collection, etc.) (Fig. 14). Related resources can be viewed at the bottom of the sheet or via a map. The manuscript object is therefore accompanied by a series of contents of different types which together provide information on the work in its material and immaterial complexity (Fig. 15).

The digital platform provides some data processing tools useful for the analysis phase, such as the comparative evaluation of different spectra (Fig. 16).

Fig. 14. Different ways to visualize the Related Resources

Fig. 15. Left: Points investigated and spectra XRF (Digital Resources model); Information about the collection (Collection model)

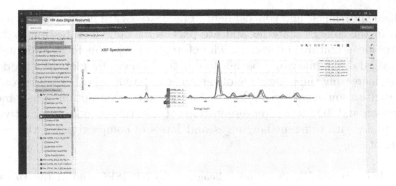

Fig. 16. Comparative analysis of different spectra

4 Conclusions and Next Steps

4.1 Further Perspectives

How and how much the virtual ecosystems designed for CODEX 4D can be expanded within the DataSpace project (new cultural contexts, powerful tools and services), and even more in the DIGILAB platform, are someone issues that we are working on and will be engaged in over the coming months, within the H2IOSC project. One of the pilots expected this. The news digital environments allow the management of heterogeneous research data sets and the sharing, exchange, analysis, and visualization of digital resources, in compliance with the FAIR principles. The principles of Open Science invite consideration of the methodological and technological solutions to be adopted to enable the availability, accessibility, interoperability, and re-use of data.

The Web3D application of Codex4D will be further developed under H2IOSC (Humanities and Cultural Heritage Italian Open Science Cloud) as one of the pilots in WP7. The underneath framework (ATON) will be also further extended in WP6 (servification and remotization), available to researchers and scientific communities as a federated service, thus offering additional integrations - for instance with the DataSpace project. Since the ATON framework also supports Augmented, Mixed and Virtual Reality (see [3]), new directions on immersive web-based presentation and interaction with 4D manuscripts will be indeed explored in future papers.

One of the next tasks will be to complete the study on the usability of the various outputs produced. The users' feedback was collected only for the holographic showcase during the Genoa Science Festival (2022). The study will soon be extended to the WebApp, recently completed and in the final refinement stage, and subsequently to the DataSpace which is under development.

4.2 Conclusions

An ancient codex is a complex object, with a body made up of several materials, it is the fruit of craftsmanship and artistic skills, it may have undergone censorship, dismemberment, and concealment. These stories are imprinted, sometimes hidden, in the codex's material and are part of its value as a testimony to the history of ideas, culture and society. Therefore, the project includes and interconnects several disciplinary approaches under the banner of a global methodology aimed at increasing the knowledge of the ancient manuscript. It goes beyond the simple digitisation of codex contents. It focuses on the conception of new models of narration and 3D virtual representation, of scientific exploration and visualisation tools, with different languages and levels of complexity, for the various contexts of use.

Acknowledgement. We thank all colleagues of CNR ISPC and of the University of Tor Vergata who contributed to the development of contents and to the general conception of the presented projects, the Angelica and Casanatense Libraries in Rome and the Augusta municipal library of Perugia.

References

1. Coccia Desogus, P.: Un libro d'ore francese nella biblioteca angelica di roma. Miniatura, pp. 17–26 (1993–1996). http://opac.regesta-imperii.de/id/1927296
2. Fanini, B., Ferdani, D., Demetrescu, E.: Temporal lensing: an interactive and scalable technique for Web3D/WebXR applications in cultural heritage. Heritage **4**(2), 710–724 (2021). https://doi.org/10.3390/heritage4020040. https://www.mdpi.com/2571-9408/4/2/40
3. Fanini, B., Ferdani, D., Demetrescu, E., Berto, S., d'Annibale, E.: Aton: an open-source framework for creating immersive, collaborative and liquid web-apps for cultural heritage. Appl. Sci. **11**(22) (2021). https://doi.org/10.3390/app112211062. https://www.mdpi.com/2076-3417/11/22/11062
4. Maniaci, M., Orofino, G.: L'officina delle bibbie atlantiche: artigiani, scribi, miniatori. In: Come nasce un manoscritto miniato, pp. 197–212 (2010). http://opac.regesta-imperii.de/id/1597146
5. Maniaci, M., Zamponi, S.: Presentazione del workshop internazionale manuscript digitization and on line accessibility. What's going on? International workshop. Digitalia **IX**, 4–9: 6 (2014)
6. Mercuri, F., et al.: Metastructure of illuminations by infrared thermography. J. Cult. Herit. **31**, 53–62 (2018). https://doi.org/10.1016/j.culher.2017.10.008. https://www.sciencedirect.com/science/article/pii/S1296207417303904
7. Orofino, G.: L'abate desiderio committente di libri: manoscritti miniati a montecassino (1058–1087). In: Il libro miniato e il suo committente, pp. 25–44 (2016). http://opac.regesta-imperii.de/id/2234466
8. Pasini, C.: La digitalizzazione dei manoscritti presso la biblioteca vaticana, in manuscript digitization and on line accessibility. Digitalia **IX**, 10–16: 12 (2014)
9. Pepper, J.H.: True History of the Ghost: And All about Metempsychosis. Cambridge University Press, Cambridge (2012)
10. Pietroni, E., et al.: Beyond the museum's object. Envisioning stories, pp. 10118–10127 (2017). https://doi.org/10.21125/edulearn.2017.0915
11. Pietroni, E., Pagano, A., Fanini, B.: UX designer and software developer at the mirror: assessing sensory immersion and emotional involvement in virtual museums. Stud. Digit. Herit. **2**(1), 13–41 (2018). https://doi.org/10.14434/sdh.v2i1.24634

12. Remondino, F., El-Hakim, S.: Image-based 3D modelling: a review. Photogramm. Rec. **21**, 269–291 (2006). https://doi.org/10.1111/j.1477-9730.2006.00383.x
13. Ricciardi, P.: Manuscripts in the making: art and science. Herit. Sci. **7**(1), 1–3 (2019). https://doi.org/10.1186/s40494-019-0302-x
14. Robinet, F., Arnaud, R., Parisi, T., Cozzi, P.: gLTF: designing an open-standard runtime asset format. In: Engel, W. (ed.) GPU Pro 5, pp. 375–392. CRC Press (2014)
15. Salarelli, A.: International image interoperability framework (IIIF): a panoramic. JLIS.it **8**, 50–66 (2017). https://doi.org/10.4403/jlis.it-12090
16. Stella, P.: The Art & Science of Illuminated Manuscripts: A Handbook (2021)
17. Tominski, C., Gladisch, S., Kister, U., Dachselt, R., Schumann, H.: Interactive lenses for visualization: an extended survey. Comput. Graph. Forum **36**(6), 173–200 (2017). https://doi.org/10.1111/cgf.12871. https://onlinelibrary.wiley.com/doi/abs/10.1111/cgf.12871

Digital Map Based VR Ethnographic Design of Chinese Traditional Hand-Made Paper Culture

YanXiang Zhang$^{(\boxtimes)}$, ChenXiao Zhao, Shixian Ding, WenBin Hu, and Shukun Tang$^{(\boxtimes)}$

Department of Communication of Science and Technology, University of Science and Technology of China, Hefei, Anhui, China
{petrel,sktang}@ustc.edu.cn, {zhaochx2022,sxding, huwb}@mail.ustc.edu.cn

Abstract. Handmade papermaking technology is an important part of Chinese traditional craft culture and a precious intangible cultural heritage. However, on the one hand, this unpopular minority skill is facing the dilemma of disappearing and is in urgent need of recording; on the other hand, the record of handmade paper needs to be presented on a daily basis, which is difficult to achieve by traditional phonetic recording or written recording. Therefore, this paper uses VR ethnography to record, protect and inherit handmade paper culture and integrates VR panoramic photography, VR panoramic video, VR three-dimensional video, and three-dimensional scanning based on web GL to record and display the process and scene of handmade papermaking in many directions and understand the narrative effect of VR ethnography through user feedback. It is found that compared with traditional recording methods, VR ethnography is more three-dimensional and vivid. This paper hopes to provide a reference for the application of VR in protecting and inheriting intangible cultural heritage.

Keywords: VR Ethnography · Digital Map · Intangible Cultural Heritage · Handmade Papermaking

1 Introduction

Traditional handmade papermaking is an intangible cultural heritage of China. It is not only the crystallization of the ancient Chinese people's wisdom but also carries China's history and culture. However, in the current era of industrialization, due to the impact of mechanical papermaking, the living space of this process is shrinking and is on the verge of being lost. The traditional manufacturing technology of Lianshi paper, one of the handmade papermaking techniques, has disappeared from its place of origin for 33 years. The disappearance of Lianshi paper also brings difficulties for the restoration and protection of Chinese traditional paper cultural relics [1]. Therefore, it is necessary to save and record this precious craft and culture. On the one hand, this record may provide some information for the future restoration of the process; on the other hand, it is also a record and inheritance of the culture under the influence of the papermaking process. In addition to the recording function, these materials may provide a reference for follow-up research or derive more diverse cultural forms in later applications.

In previous studies on topics related to culture and folklore, ethnographic research methods were often used to explore organizations and cultures through observation and interviews and recorded in words. However, as Rose said of the materiality's "thereness, that words cannot convey," [2] there are still some limitations in using cultural records of language and writing alone. When visual methods such as photography, image, hyper-media, and video are added to the study of ethnography, this research method is called visual ethnography[3]. In the mid-1970s, visual ethnography gradually rose with the development of technology and equipment. In 1942, Magaret Mead and Gregory Bateson first used photographic images and films to reflect research needs in Bali and New Guinea [4]. Mannay believes that the introduction of visual elements in the process of ethnographic research brings different ways of understanding and makes familiar things unfamiliar, thus looking at things in different ways, which is helpful for researchers to carry out objective and effective research[3].

However, the picture stops the movement, the speed, and the vividness of the rhythm[2],the video lacks the immersive feeling of the scene, and human beings perceive the world in a three-dimensional visual way. Hence, this paper proposes to use VR ethnography to study and record the intangible cultural heritage of handmade paper. VR ethnography introduces VR panoramic photography, VR panoramic video, three-dimensional scanning, and other VR recording methods into ethnography research. The characteristics of VR make it able to carry more and more immersed information in ethnographic records, record more vitality, and facilitate the restoration, inheritance, and development of this intangible cultural heritage and regional culture. With the cross-integration with other technical means or cultural forms based on VR records, more dimensions of cultural inheritance may be developed. The creative side of non-heritage traditional culture may also be explored.

Therefore, the problems to be solved in this paper are as follows:

• Given the intangible cultural heritage of handmade papermaking, how to organize various VR means to carry out ethnographic design?
• What role can VR ethnography play in recording and inheriting intangible cultural heritage? What's the effect?

2 Related Works

There have been many explorations and attempts to apply VR in protecting cultural heritage. Some researchers use 3D modeling to restore and replicate cultural heritage sites. For example, Katsushi Ikeuchi has used computer vision and graphics technology to restore, establish, and preserve the original appearance of a giant Buddha statue [5]. Zi Siang See et al. used photogrammetric techniques at the actual Malacca heritage site to replicate Sultan Hussein Shah's tomb from the 19th century, thereby developing a room-scale VR cultural heritage experience[6]. Similarly, Pongsagon Vichitvejpaisal developed a project that provides users with a highly detailed 3D scan of the Ayutthaya historical park in Thailand, designated as a World Heritage Site. They combined 3D scanning technology with VR technology and virtual tourism experiences to help users experience heritage sites and understand the value of world heritage [7]. The research of Stefan Krumpen et al. focused on providing haptic feedback for VR object detection, allowing experts and the public to experience digital cultural heritage artifacts in a more immersive and interactive way rather than just analyzing them in static images [8]. One type of research uses VR games to enable users to experience culture through interaction, thereby achieving the transmission of culture. For instance, Jing Zhang et al. explored the application of "splashed ink" interaction in the inheritance of Dunhuang murals[9]. However, its limitations lie in only providing users with a partial view of the culture rather than the entire picture. We endeavor to comprehensively record the craftsmanship and culture of handmade paper-making in the form of an ethnographical account, aiming to construct the entire non-material cultural ecosystem under the influence of the technique of handmade paper-making.

In studies on the use of VR technology to protect intangible cultural heritage, various technologies are applied based on the type and content of the intangible cultural heritage. Researchers often use modeling to restore the artist's performance process for the intangible cultural heritage, with performance as the main body. Xiaofei Zhang combined 3D static and 3D dynamic modeling to model the artist's performance process and the scenes and entities needed. According to the image data, Boyan Li used 3D digital modeling technology to restore the "lion dance" performance in Shehuo (Shehuo: a folk acrobatic activity to celebrate festivals in China). 3D scanning technology is used to collect detailed data, such as Li Zhang et al., using laser 3D scanning data acquisition and 3D image acquisition technology based on panoramic photography to collect data on Huishan clay figurines, another intangible cultural heritage in China[10]. These studies show that VR can play a significant role in the active inheritance of intangible cultural heritage. Still, it is worth pointing out that intangible cultural heritage contains more intangible and cultural content than tangible cultural heritage, such as action, behavior, technological process, etc. Using a particular VR technology may only partially restore cultural content and show cultural charm.

Therefore, some researchers, such as E. Selmanovi Cauc, try to combine voiceover narration with 360° video to present the story of the Mostar Bridge's history, architecture, destruction, and reconstruction [11], which gives new inspiration to follow-up researchers.

However, most existing research on VR applications in cultural heritage only uses one VR technology. This paper's innovation is to organize various VR means to record the VR ethnography of the intangible cultural heritage of handmade papermaking.

3 System Design

In manual papermaking technology, the intangible cultural contents that need to be recorded are: the action and behavior of the papermaker, the technological process of papermaking, the physical site, tools and materials, geographical site and cultural site, etc., in the face of the rich and complex content contained in the culture of manual papermaking, it is limited to record in only one way: the recording method of picture and text is one-sided.

The video lacks the immersive feeling of the scene, and the three-dimensional panorama can record the scene in all directions. Still, many papermaking scenes are relatively small, which may not allow people to move the panoramic camera flexibly, which also limits the perspective and position of the recording.

In addition, different ways can play different roles in the recording of intangible cultural heritage, such as in the cultural research site of handmade papermaking; researchers also need to record the size parameters of papermaking tools. At this time, three-dimensional scanning can be used.

Therefore, to record and show the papermaking scene and culture more vividly and deeply, this study adds the recording means of VR panoramic photography, VR panoramic video, VR three-dimensional video, and three-dimensional scanning into the ethnographic investigation and integrates the collected materials based on web GL.

It formed a VR ethnography system (see Fig. 1) that integrates various forms of VR presentation with hot spots, thus realizing a three-dimensional, immersive, and multi-dimensional narrative of the intangible cultural heritage.

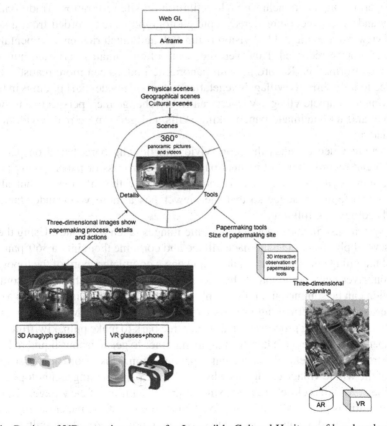

Fig. 1. Design of VR narrative system for Intangible Cultural Heritage of handmade paper.

The integrated design of the VR ethnography system is mainly based on web GL, realized through A-frame, and integrates the three-dimensional image close-up and three-dimensional scanning content into the three-dimensional panorama in the way of a hot spot. We divide the content of handmade paper into three aspects: Scenes, Details, and Tools, and choose the appropriate VR technology to present each aspect. After opening it on the mobile phone, the user can first look around the whole environment of the papermaking site, then click on the hot area representing the stereoscopic image, open the stereoscopic image, and plug the mobile phone into VR devices such as Cardboard to watch, to understand the close-up of each perspective and the technological process of papermaking. Users can then click on the hot spot and view the 3D scanned contents of papermaking tools and scenes interactively through VR or AR mode.

3.1 Scenes

The handmade VR ethnography system is based on 360 panoramic and 360 panoramic videos. The use of QOO CAM 8k resolution camera immersive recording of all angles of the papermaking site to achieve high-definition on-site restoration. Traditional photography and video, including stereoscopic photography, are recorded from a specific point of view. Hence, the field of vision is limited, and much rich environmental information can not be recorded. However, the scene often contains very rich human and geographic information. Recording with panoramic images can more realistically and omnidirectionally show the village's vegetation types and residential buildings in front of us, showing a complete village. Viewers can freely change their perspective to observe the village and its handmade papermaking skills and get a more real, vivid, and rich understanding.

Panoramic video expands the more vivid and flowing parts based on panoramic images. It can record a current manual papermaking process or papermaking process, showing some dynamic fragments, recording not only the information but also the dynamics of life and practice so that the viewer has a more vivid understanding of the local ecology and folklore.

The system also includes aerial panoramic images taken by drones. Using the UAV to take several photos of the handmade village and combine them into a 360°panoramic image of the village in mid-air, such data can keep a complete record of the topography, vegetation, river, and panorama of the current village. Through these data, some new information can be summed up; for example, in manual papermaking, water is a crucial factor because the papermaking process requires a lot of water. Many plants are also used in the papermaking process, such as using tree bark to make pulp, kiwifruit vines to make paper medicine, and the kiwifruit rattan hammer to get a viscous liquid to keep the paper fibers evenly suspended and prevent paper adhesion. This record of 360°suspended images of the whole village can tell us why handmade papermaking technology appears in this village, which is closely related to the natural conditions of the village. The unique natural conditions provided conditions for the emergence of the papermaking industry and then gradually developed into a village's handmade papermaking culture. People and nature influence each other in the cultural practice of handmade papermaking. And together to create a unique and precious cultural practice.

To sum up, 360 panoramic pictures and videos can comprehensively show geographical and cultural scenes, so in the design of the narrative system; they are used as the basis of narration and the carrier of other display means. Users can first understand the overall situation of handmade papermaking culture and then gain an in-depth understanding of the parts and details through other display methods.

3.2 Details

For the details of some actions and processes in manual papermaking, the stereoscopic image technology of VR180 is used in the research. The stereoscopic picture and stereoscopic video are recorded with an insta360 EVO stereoscopic camera. After the user clicks on the hot area of the stereoscopic image, the stereoscopic image can be opened and watched with VR equipment or red and blue glasses. Stereoscopic images can record a dynamic process in the way of stereoscopic vision, and watching them gives people a robust, immersive experience as if they are in the environment. The scene recorded by this means has a three-dimensional depth that can not be provided by traditional recording methods in the past. In addition, stereoscopic images can better record the action flow in papermaking technology, and viewers can more clearly and honestly observe people's movements and behaviors in handmade papermaking villages and, at the same time, get information about space.

Concerning the detailed cultural information about the architectural structure in the papermaking culture, we use a panoramic camera to take a picture in a certain position, then pan the camera, take another panoramic photo, and form two panoramic photos into a three-dimensional panorama. Therefore, the dramatic visual effect with three-dimensional sense can be obtained, which can make up for the lack of three-dimensional sense of simple panoramic recording, and can present the 360-degree stereoscopic visual effect of some static scenes. However, this method only applies to the situation where there are no moving characters in the scene, and ghosting occurs when there is character activity. The following picture shows translation shooting in someone's scene; such a stereo panorama can provide a more realistic perception of the building structure through the fusion of stereo vision and 360 panoramas.

3.3 Tools

Stereoscopic and panoramic images can bring us the feeling of three-dimensional space but can not show the three-dimensional structure. For all kinds of tools used in the manual papermaking process and the survey objects that need to record the size of the paper size, different three-dimensional scanning tools are used in the research process: 3D Scanner pro scanning resolution is not very high, so it is suitable for three-dimensional scene scanning. In contrast, Luma is used to scan small tools. The three-dimensional scanning recording contains information on physical size and spatial structure, which can provide original data for later restoration of handmade paper tools, scenes, etc. As a kind of surveying photography, three-dimensional scanning can record the size and material while scanning and recording the current handmade scene and the elements in the scene. It can present the spatial relationship between the elements.

The three-dimensional scene allows users to observe the various scenes and elements in the handmade papermaking village interactively and from many angles. Users can use iPad pro to output the 3D scanning results into glTF format to realize interactive observation to observe the papermaking site from all angles. They can also enter the AR mode for observation. For small papermaking tools, users can click the link to observe the contents of the Luma scan. However, three-dimensional scanning also has some limitations, it is not suitable for the situation in which the characters in the picture have relatively large movements, and the moving characters will be scanned into incomplete image segments. Therefore, we focus more on recording and restoring the tools, utensils, and their spatial, positional, and size relationships in the scene. We will also find that the result of three-dimensional scanning has its unique artistic beauty in appearance, which can show the spatial sense of some key sites and tools in the handmade papermaking village, like a painting. It contains the space aesthetics that embodies the cultural characteristics of handmade papermaking.

4 System Demonstration

According to the characteristics of different contents in handmade paper culture, we select the most suitable means to record and display them and integrate them with 360 panoramic images and videos through Web GL to form a VR ethnographic narrative system of traditional handmade papermaking culture.

Due to the influence of the natural environment, handmade paper located in different provinces across the country shows different characteristics, forming a variety of handmade paper types, such as Yunnan Province is mainly Dongba paper, while Guizhou Province is mostly leather paper. To show the ethnographic information of handmade paper in all directions, the project builds an interactive handmade paper distribution map based on the Baidu map Javascript API as the system's home page.

After entering the system website, the first thing you can see is the handmade paper dot distribution map. The following picture is a page screenshot of the distribution map (see Fig. 2). As shown in the figure, hot zones are used to label the provinces where there are villages with handmade paper, and the number displayed on the hot zone represents the number of information nodes contained in that point, which the user can click on to interact and go to the next level of the digital map.

The digital map is further zoomed out to the county level as shown in the figure below (see Fig. 3).

With further clicks, the digital map can be zoomed out to the village limits (see Fig. 4 and 5). The upper left corner illustrates the different meanings of the different icons, ▪ stands for human landscape, ▲ on behalf of the paper site, ⬤ indicates paper site, ✚ indicates a research interview, ⬤ indicates an aerial panorama.

At this time, it is possible to see where handmade paper is produced in the village and where it is used, as well as where the research activities took place in the handmade paper village, which will also help subsequent researchers to conduct research and revisit.

By clicking on the icon representing the aerial panorama, one can enter the VR ethnographic digital map constructed based on the 360° panoramic image of the village (see Fig. 6 and 7). The user can drag the mouse to look around the panoramic view of

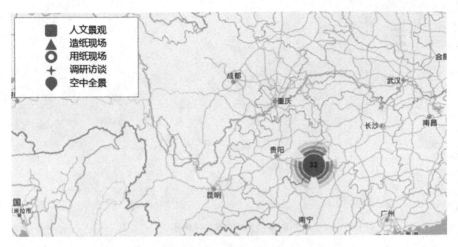

Fig. 2. System screenshot.

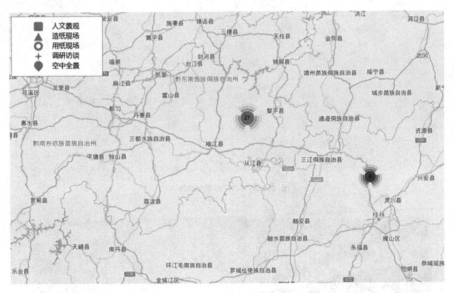

Fig. 3. System screenshot.

the village and see that information about the topography and vegetation of the village is combined with the ethnographic information about the handmade paper.

Clicking on the icon representing the papermaking site, one can see the 360 panoramic image embedded in the system related to the papermaking site. The figure below shows the 360 panoramic view of the inside of the workshop at the papermaking site that opens after clicking on the hotspot representing the papermaking site (see Fig. 8), where users using computers can drag the mouse to look around the papermaking scene. Users using cell phones can switch viewpoints by swiping the screen directly. Since the

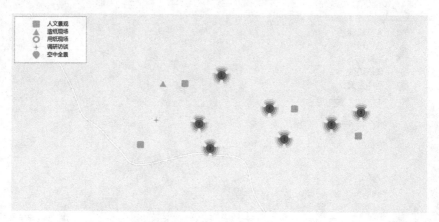

Fig. 4. System screenshot.

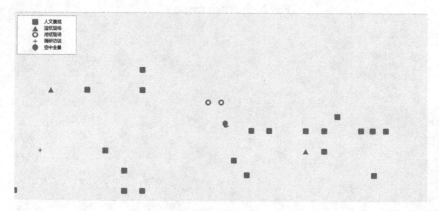

Fig. 5. System screenshot.

Fig. 6. VR ethnographic map based on 360° panoramic images of villages.

Fig. 7. VR ethnographic map based on 360° panoramic images of villages.

papermaking site contains rich ethnographic information, such as papermaking tools, interactive hot zones are also embedded in the panoramic image of the papermaking site.

Fig. 8. 360-degree panoramic image of the papermaking site.

When the user puts the mouse/finger on the papermaking tool, a description of the tool appears as text (see Fig. 9), and by clicking on the hotspot button on the papermaking tool, a picture of the tool can be opened (see Fig. 10).

The user can then enter the glTF scene by clicking on the hot zone button representing the 3D scan to interact with the 3D scan of the papermaking tool (see Fig. 11).

Clicking on the VR button at the bottom right corner of the system screen can be used with a VR device to enter the VR mode for viewing, or if the user is using a computer, it will enter the full-screen mode. Clicking on the hot zone representing stereoscopic images and videos can open the stereoscopic images and videos of the current scene (see Fig. 12 and 13), which can be experienced by computer users with red and blue color separation glasses, and mobile users can use Cardboard or similar devices to view the stereoscopic images.

纸槽是手工纸成型流程——捞纸
的必需设备，不同规格的宣纸选择
相应的纸槽操作。

Fig. 9. Textual introduction to paper-making tools in the system.

Fig. 10. A picture of a papermaking tool.

Fig. 11. Multi-angle interactive observation of the three-dimensional structure of paper slots.

Fig. 12. Panoramic camera stereoscopic recording of handmade paper workshop environment.

Fig. 13. Panoramic camera stereoscopic recording of handmade paper workshop environment.

At the papermaking site, users can watch the three-dimensional image of the papermaking process. Outside the papermaking site, users can choose to watch the panoramic three-dimensional image reflecting the local architectural structure (see Fig. 14); they can also click on the hot zone indicating the humanistic landscape to watch the 360 panoramic photographs and videos documenting the surrounding conditions of the papermaking site. Through the panoramic video, users can see the living footage of the handmade papermaking technology; for example, in the video about the For example, in the record of the riverside scene of the handmade paper village, the panoramic video not only records the ecological environment and humanistic landscape but also records the villagers fetching water from the riverside to process the papermaking raw materials. At the same time, a flock of ducks swims past the water's surface (see Figs. 15 and 16).

Fig. 14. Anaglyph 3d panoramic stereoscopic image of building structure.

Fig. 15. The papermaker was processing raw materials for papermaking by the water.

360 panoramic views of different landscapes in different locations in the village can also record and display rich ethnographic information (see Figs. 17, 18 and 19).

We also made some recordings of the locations where handmade paper was used, such as the panoramic stereoscopic photography that popped up after clicking on an icon representing a paper-use site showing Taoist priests in a village using handmade paper to make Taoist items (see Fig. 20) and another paper-use site where villagers used handmade paper to make handicrafts (see Fig. 21), from which we can combine the geographic locations to gain more intuitive understanding and revelation.

Fig. 16. A flock of ducks swam past the papermaking site, and on the river bank were paper curtains for papermaking.

Fig. 17. A 360 panorama documenting the human landscape.

Fig. 18. A 360 panorama documenting the cultural customs.

Fig. 19. A 360 panorama documenting the cultural customs.

Fig. 20. Panoramic camera stereoscopic recording of the process of paper-cut creation by artists using handmade paper.

Fig. 21. Panoramic camera stereoscopic recording of the process of paper-cut creation by artists using handmade paper.

In addition, the system records information such as the location and interviewees of the ethnographic interviews on a map with a 360 panorama (see Fig. 22) in the hope that this information will help future researchers in their research endeavors.

Fig. 22. A 360 panorama of the interviews

5   User Feedback

Next, to understand the effect of the application of VR ethnography in recording traditional handmade papermaking culture, we randomly recruited ten users through the network. We interviewed them after they experienced VR ethnographic records. When selecting users, we try our best to invite users representing different groups, including but not limited to students, company staff, etc., to ensure cross-departmental evaluation (The user information is shown in Table 1.). We ask users some questions, including but not limited to Q1 how do you evaluate the VR ethnography that records handmade papermaking skills and culture? Q2 What impressed you most? Q3 After the experience, what are your feelings and experiences about the craft and culture of handmade papermaking? Is there any difference between it and before the experience? At the same time, we encourage users to express their experiences and feelings freely, and the final results tend to be saturated.

5.1   A Real, Vivid and Shocking Experience

According to the feedback of users, the recording and presentation of handmade papermaking skills in VR ethnography do bring them a more accurate, vivid and shocking experience than previous flat recordings methods such as text and photos; as user U2 mentioned: *"This has brought me an experience that I have never experienced before, and even if you have not been there, you can see what the village and papermaking tools are like." "The VR way is far more real and shocking than the video, and I feel deeply involved in such a previously unfamiliar cultural scene."*

Table 1. User demographic information.

Users	Gender	Age	Job
U1	Male	19	Undergraduate
U2	Male	27	Company employee
U3	Female	24	Postgraduate
U4	Female	30	Company employee
U5	Male	23	Postgraduate
U6	Male	32	Company employee
U7	Female	20	Undergraduate
U8	Female	22	Postgraduate
U9	Male	21	Undergraduate
U10	Female	26	Company employee

5.2 Impressive Interactions

Several users said that they were impressed by the interactivity of the VR ethnography system for handmade paper, and two users mentioned that the interactivity of the system exceeded that of the museum VR systems they had previously experienced, such as user U3, who said, *"I've seen similar applications to VR museums in the past, but that kind of VR museums are more about the display of the collections, unlike this system that has a very high level of interactivity."*

"This system is particularly rich in content, and it feels like you can tap anywhere on the map to try it out, and you can also watch it with VR glasses." (U10).

5.3 Rich and Interesting Narrative

When collecting user feedback, seven users said that the handmade VR ethnography uses various narrative methods, allowing them to experience the intangible cultural heritage of handmade papermaking from many angles and immersively. As user U7 said: *"This is the first time I know that there are so many VR methods that can be applied to the intangible cultural heritage display, and this is the first time I have had such a rich and interesting experience."*

5.4 Enriched Means of Ethnographic Documentation

The handmade paper VR ethnographic system provides a new means of recording and presenting research results for ethnographic research; as U3 said, *"This is the first time I know that VR can be applied to ethnographic research in this way, in the past, it might be in the form of field notes, and the textual content would be more in traditional ethnographic research, but this system inspired me that since there are textual, photographic, and videos for ethnographic records, then why not VR for ethnographic records?".*

"This kind of map-based VR record can let later researchers know which places were researched, and they can research again or choose new research sites, and it would be better if the content and results of later researchers' research could also be added to the system." (U9).

5.5 Deepen the Overall Understanding of the Intangible Cultural Heritage of Hand-Made Papermaking

Deepen the overall understanding of the intangible cultural heritage of handmade paper-making.VR ethnography has also played a specific role in promoting users' overall understanding of the intangible cultural heritage of handmade papermaking. For example, user U5 said: *"In the past, I may only know the terms' papermaking 'and' intangible cultural heritage,' but there is no corresponding picture in my mind. Now I will feel that this is like this."* And user U1 said: *"It seems to have an overall feeling all of a sudden."*

6 Conclusion and Discussion

This paper is the first to apply a variety of VR means integrally to the recording and display of handmade paper intangible cultural heritage, using different VR means to record different aspects of handmade paper technology and using Web GL to integrate 360 panoramic images, stereoscopic images, and 3D scans of these different types of materials into a digital map-based VR ethnographic system, to protect and pass on the soon-to-be lost intangible cultural heritage of handmade paper. This work can not only provide materials for follow-up research and cultural reproduction and re-creation but also prove from user feedback that VR ethnography is a superior medium for preserving intangible cultural elements and can provide users with a more vivid understanding and feeling, which is also an essential part of intangible cultural heritage inheritance, but may be ignored or can not be realized through technology in the past.

Next, we will improve the system in the following aspects:

- Optimizing VR ethnographic narratives and thinking about how to adopt a more storytelling and interactive approach to pass on traditional handmade paper culture
- Continue to enrich the system by adding new papermaking village sites and information to the system map after field research.
- Beautify the system interface and make the system more aesthetic and artistic while improving the essential functions of the system.

In this paper, we aim to establish a VR ethnographic system of traditional Chinese handmade papermaking culture, make the system a database of intangible cultural heritage with cultural value and provide a reference for the inheritance and protection of intangible cultural heritage.

Acknowledgments. This research is supported by the National Social Science Fund of China (Grant No. 21VJXT019).

References

1. Su, J.: Research on the Protection of the making Technology of Lianshi Paper, Master's thesis, Fudan University (2008)
2. Cheng, Y.E.: Telling stories of the city: walking ethnography, affective materialities, and mobile encounters. Space Cult. **17**(3), 211–223 (2014). https://doi.org/10.1177/120633121 3499468
3. O'Regan, T., Robinson, L., Newton-Hughes, A., Strudwick, R.: A review of visual ethnography: radiography viewed through a different lens. Radiography **25**, S9–S13 (2019). https://doi.org/10.1016/j.radi.2019.06.007
4. Schembri, S., Boyle, M.V.: Visual ethnography: achieving rigorous and authentic interpretations. J. Bus. Res. **66**(9), 1251–1254 (2013). https://doi.org/10.1016/j.jbusres.2012.02.021
5. Ikeuchi, K., Nakazawa, A., Hasegawa, K., Ohishi, T.: The Great Buddha Project: Modeling Cultural Heritage for VR Systems through Observation. Presented at the Proceedings of the 2nd IEEE/ACM International Symposium on Mixed and Augmented Reality (2003)
6. See, Z.S., Santano, D., Sansom, M., Fong, C.H., Thwaites, H.: Tomb of a sultan: a VR digital heritage approach. In: 2018 3rd Digital Heritage International Congress (DigitalHERITAGE) held jointly with 2018 24th International Conference on Virtual Systems & Multimedia (VSMM 2018), 26–30 Oct. 2018, pp. 1–4 (2018). https://doi.org/10.1109/DigitalHeritage.2018.8810083
7. Vichitvejpaisal, P., Porwongsawang, N., Ingpochai, P.: Relive History: VR time travel at the world heritage site. presented at the Proceedings of the 17th International Conference on Virtual-Reality Continuum and its Applications in Industry, Brisbane, QLD, Australia (2019). https://doi.org/10.1145/3359997.3365733
8. Krumpen, S., Klein, R., Weinmann, M.: Towards tangible cultural heritage experiences—enriching VR-based object inspection with haptic feedback. J. Comput. Cult. Heritage **15**(1), 1–17 (2021). https://doi.org/10.1145/3470470
9. Zhang, J., Zou, G., Zhang, G.: ""Meet the Deer King": "Splash-Ink" Interaction in the Innovative VR Game Based on Dunhuang Art and Culture. Presented at the SIGGRAPH Asia 2021 XR, Tokyo, Japan (2021). https://doi.org/10.1145/3478514.3487618
10. Li, B., Cao, Y.: Application of VIRTUAL REALITY TECHNOLOGY IN THE PROTECTION OF INTANGIBLE CULTURAL HERITAGE:—TAKe the "Lion dance" in Shehuo as an example. Presented at the Proceedings of the 2022 7th International Conference on Multimedia Systems and Signal Processing, Shenzhen, China (2022). https://doi.org/10.1145/3545822.3545825
11. Selmanovic, E., et al.: VR Video Storytelling for Intangible Cultural Heritage Preservation (2018)

Immersive Virtual Reality in Cultural Heritage Dissemination: A Comprehensive Application for Novice Users

Bruno Rodriguez-Garcia[1]([✉]) [iD] and Mario Alaguero[2] [iD]

[1] Department of Computer Engineering, Universidad de Burgos, Burgos, Spain
brunorg@ubu.es
[2] Department of History and Geography, Universidad de Burgos, Burgos, Spain
malaguero@ubu.es

Abstract. This paper discusses the increasing relevance of immersive Virtual Reality (iVR) technology in society and its emerging applications, particularly in Cultural Heritage (CH) dissemination. However, the diversification of iVR experiences has led to a need for an application that summarizes the most common types of experiences to familiarize novice users with iVR. To address this need, an iVR application has been developed that presents the four most common types of iVR experiences: Passive, Explorative, Explorative Interaction, and Interactive. The experience includes different reconstructed CH environments and objects showcasing the possibilities for the dissemination of CH using this technology. The application is divided into four levels, and its key design factors are as follows: 1) one type of iVR experience for each level, 2) simple interactions that become more complex as the user progresses, 3) short duration and time-limited progression between levels, 4) development for standalone iVR devices, and 5) different types of reconstructed heritage showcased at each level. The experience was tested in exhibitions and achieved high performance on standalone iVR devices. Usability results are expected to be achieved in the future.

Keywords: Virtual Reality · Cultural Heritage · Head Mounted Display · Virtual Reconstruction · Tutorial

1 Introduction

In recent years, Virtual Reality (VR) has gained significant relevance. This technology has been in development since the 1950s, but it has not been widely adopted by the mainstream audiences until recent years [1]. With the development of technology, VR has evolved into immersive Virtual Reality (iVR), which surrounds the user in large 3D viewing areas such as the Head-Mounted Display (HMD) [2] and the Cave Automatic Virtual Environment (CAVE) [3]. Currently, the affordability and availability of software and hardware technology have contributed to the widespread adoption of iVR, which has opened a wide range of potential applications beyond its initial military and training purposes [4]. One promising application of iVR technology is the dissemination of Cultural Heritage (CH), where diverse experiences have been developed to take advantage of the benefits of iVR [5–7].

L. T. De Paolis et al. (Eds.): XR Salento 2023, LNCS 14219, pp. 287–301, 2023.
https://doi.org/10.1007/978-3-031-43404-4_18

In recent years, iVR has emerged as a technology with significant potential in the fields of heritage dissemination [8], conservation [9], and education [10], due to its unique characteristics. Of these, Flow, Engagement, Immersion, and Presence are among the most important. Flow refers to the sensation of control, while Engagement refers to the connection between the user and the virtual activity. Immersion describes the sensation that the virtual environment replaces the real world, while Presence refers to the feeling of being present in the virtual environment [11].

Within the context of CH reconstruction, Presence is of particular importance, as it is the key factor that enables users to experience the virtual environment as though they were truly present within it [12]. The relevance of Presence in CH reconstruction is particularly significant, as this technology is often used to reconstruct vanished or transformed heritage. Given that virtual environments are used extensively in this context, understanding the impact of Presence on the virtual reconstruction of CH in iVR has been the subject of extensive scientific inquiry, as evidenced by some studies [12–14].

In addition to these features, iVR enables remote visits, which can aid in the preservation of CH by avoiding degradation of delicate elements [15]. Also, remote visits can improve the accessibility of CH, as many heritage sites are inaccessible to people with disabilities [16]. Moreover, iVR is a powerful tool for transmitting information, as its visual nature is much more direct, particularly for non-expert audiences [15], and enhance transmission of spatial information, including the ability to perceive scales and sizes of CH objects [17]. Furthermore, these capabilities have gained even greater significance since the COVID-19 pandemic, which has highlighted the importance of digital tools and demonstrated their effectiveness in the field of CH [18].

All these possibilities of iVR have led to the development of very different types of experiences. It can be mainly found four different types of experiences [19]. They are the following:

- Passive experiences, the user interactivity and movement are very limited, sometimes involving photography or 360° video experiences.
- Explorative experiences, which allows for free exploration of the virtual environment, but no direct interaction.
- Interactive explorative experiences, allow for free exploration and interaction in the virtual environment.
- Interactive experiences, which enable free interaction with the environment, but with restricted movement.

All these experiences differ significantly from one another, mainly due to the size of the environment and the freedom of interactions, resulting in highly diverse iVR experiences. The sum of all possible iVR experiences, coupled with the novelty effect, can create cognitive overload for many users, limiting their performance [20]. This situation highlights the need for the creation of tutorials and experiences that familiarize users and researchers with this technology so that they can understand its possibilities [21].

This paper presents an overview of the conceptualization, design, and implementation of an iVR experience intended to introduce users to the possibilities of iVR through four virtual reconstruction experiences of CH sites and objects. Each of these experiences corresponds to one of the four iVR experience which are presented sequentially to provide users with a comprehensive understanding of the potential of iVR.

The paper is structured as follows: Sect. 2 reviews the related work of iVR experiences involving the virtual reconstruction of heritage sites, with a focus on the four types of experiences. Section 3 explains the design and development of the experience, explaining the design of the experience as a whole and the design of each of its levels. Finally, the conclusions of this paper are presented in Sect. 4.

2   Related Work

This section will provide a summary of some CH reconstruction cases belonging to the four types of iVR experience, sorted by the following order: 1) Passive experience, 2) Explorative experience, 3) Explorative interaction experience and 4) Interactive experience.

Passive experiences are characterized by minimal interaction, often consisting of videos, photographs, or 360° renders. Despite this, many Passive experiences developed for CH reconstruction exhibit significant differences. These differences are mainly due to the use or absence of characters in the reconstruction and the possibility of a guided tour of the environment with various viewpoints. Examples include the virtual reconstruction of the "Villa with Ingresso a protiro" [22–24] which reconstructs a Roman villa located in Italy from the 2nd century. This experience includes many recorded actors and is composed of several 360° viewpoints. A slightly different experience is the reconstruction of the Viking camp in Torksey (UK) from the 9th century [25], which includes digital characters instead of recorded. Finally, another example is the reconstruction of the Presidential Palace in Finland from the 19th century [26]. This experience has also digital characters, but the user moves, but not in a free way, there is a camera that follows a predefined path to show all environment.

Explorative experiences are characterized by having a more or less large environment to freely explore, but there is no possibility of complex interaction with the environment. Considering these characteristics, one of the biggest differences is found in the size of the environments and the passive elements included in them, like panels, infographics, or characters. Some examples of large-scale environments are the reconstruction of the city of Wholverhampton (UK) in the 10th century [27], or the city of Stade (Germany) in the 17th century [28]. However, not all these environments are completely passive, there are also large-scale environments that include external elements such as videos or infographics to be observed by the user, such as the virtual reconstruction of the villa of Briviesca, located in Spain, in the 15th century [29]. This experience includes videos that explain its past and heritage at certain points in the city. There are even smaller environments but with greater vitality and animation, such as the reconstruction of a Neolithic village in Irak that includes a simulation of characters with different routines and behaviors [30].

In Explorative interaction experiences, the complexity of interaction increases, combining exploration with more advanced interactions, such as grabbing objects or some more complex ones that include elaborated games. Therefore, the differences are mainly due to the complexity of the interactions, besides the size. An example of low interaction experience is the reconstruction of Santa Maria d'Agano (Italy) in the 26th century BC where the user can pick up a torch [31]. However, there are also other iVR experiences that are more similar to video games with missions or characters, in which a story is developed with different mechanics in a reconstructed CH environment. Some examples of this type of experience are the reconstruction of "Little Manila" (USA) in the 20th century [32], or the reconstruction of Paestum (Italy) in the 5th century BC [33].

Interactive experiences are characterized by having complex interactions, but limited exploration or absence of movement by the user. This poses two types of differentiated experiences in the field of CH. Those that include a sandbox with different activities to solve, such as the reconstruction of the Roman Theater of Cartagena (Spain) in the 1st century, where users must solve some educational mini-games [34]. Or those in which the developed interaction is an active part of the reconstruction itself, such as the reconstruction of the tennis court of Rennes (France) in the 17th century, where the user can play the sport with digital characters [35].

Table 1 provides an overview of the types of iVR experiences and variations found in cases of CH reconstruction. As can be seen in Table 1, the differences within the experiences are mainly due to the size of the environments, the inclusion of characters and some exclusive differences in the type of experience.

Table 1. Summary of the differences between types of experiences found in the related work.

Type of experience	Size	Characters	Exclusive Differences
Passive	There may be one or more viewpoints	Characters can be recorded, digital or not characters at all	The user can be static, or there may be a guided camera
Explorative	The size of the environment varies depending on the reconstruction	Characters can have complex routines, simple routines, or no characters at all	There may be non-interactive elements such as infographics, panels, or characters
Explorative interaction	The size of the environment varies depending on the reconstruction	Characters can have a high degree of interaction, low, or no characters at all	There can be simple or complex interactions
Interactive experience	The environment is always of small size	Characters can have a high degree of interaction, low, or no characters at all	Interaction may be part of the reconstruction or not

3 Experience Design

In this section, will be summarize the design of the iVR experience. Firstly, the overall design of the experience will be explained. Then, it will be detailed the design of the 4 levels of the experience dedicated to each of the types of iVR experiences set in different virtual reconstruction CH environments.

This experience has been raised to transmit the possibilities of virtual reconstruction of CH in conjunction with iVR to novice users. For this reason, it has been designed to be easy to understand and with the least number of unnecessary stimuli for the user. For this reason, each of the levels seeks to be the simplest type of experience in its category. Therefore, elements such as digital characters to interact with, free navigation between levels or scenarios, vast environments, or complex mechanics more typical of serious games have not been included. In addition, to show the possibilities of virtual reconstruction of CH through this technology, a different type of heritage belonging to different historical periods has been included in each level.

Figure 1 show the design of the application and the elements that have been given consideration in its development. Horizontally, the progress between levels can be seen, and vertically, the characteristics of each level are presented. These characteristics include the type of iVR experience, the type of interaction, the size of the environment, the type of heritage, and the time limit for each level.

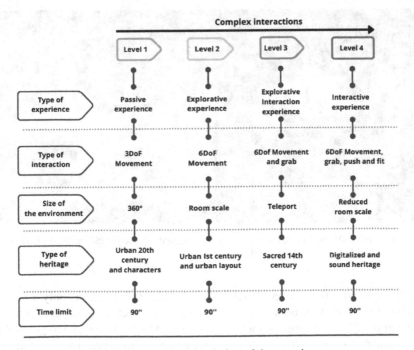

Fig. 1. Summary of the design of the experience.

Firstly, each level has been ordered from least to most interactive (Passive - Explorative - Explorative interaction - Interactive experience). This results in the following types of interactions. The Level 1 is a completely passive 360° scenario, allowing 3DoF move, where the user only to move their head, but not move around de scenario. In the Level 2, the user has 6DoF move, where the user can rotate the point of view and move in all directions [36]. In this level the user and can freely walk in a bounded area of 4 m². In the Level 3, the user can move forward using a teleportation locomotion system (in addition to walking), the locomotion system most used in iVR [37]. The grabbing mechanic is introduced, allowing the user to pick up a glowing torch and light candles with it. In the Level 4, the teleportation locomotion system is removed, and the movement is reduced to 2 m² room scale so that the user can focus on the new mechanics. These include pressing buttons and placing pieces. Additionally, to highlight all these new interactive elements, the entire scenario is in white except for the interactive objects. Figure 2 shows how the interactive elements are highlighted in Level 3, with a halo, and Level 4, with color. This level layout has been designed to promote progressive learning by the user [38]. As the levels progress, the user gains more freedom of movement and possibilities for interaction. In the Level 4, the user's freedom of movement is reduced so they are forced to interact with the environment in new proposed ways. It has been searched to make the interaction with the controls as simple as possible. Therefore, the triggers can only be used to grab objects, and pressing any of the buttons or the joystick will activate the teleportation locomotion system.

Fig. 2. Image from the user's perspective of the highlighted interactive elements in Level 3 (left), with the glow and Level 4 (right), with the color.

Each level ends after one and a half minutes. Each new level has only a few new mechanics, so one this time is sufficient to explore them. After various usage tests, it has been determined that a minute and a half was enough time to explore the possibilities of each scenario. It has been chosen this predetermined time system for the following reasons. One the one hand, a task-based level advancement system could cause the user to feel frustrated if they do not know how to advance to the next level. On the other hand, a free advancement system could cause users to accidentally skip parts of the experience.

To convey the dissemination possibilities of virtual reconstruction of CH, it was decided to include reconstructed heritage of different types and periods. All environments have been reused from previous work of the research group. In the Level 1, an urban environment from the 20th century, the city of Burgos in 192 was reconstructed. Additionally, recorded actors were included in this level to convey some aspects of intangible heritage from that time. In the Level 2, a 1st century urban environment, the Roman city of Legio (now León) Spain, was reconstructed. In this case, to show the urban layout, the user is positioned as a giant who views the city from above. The Level 3 reconstructed a sacred building of the 14th century, the Chapel of San Juan de Acre in Spain. No environment is reconstructed in the Level 4, as the idea of the level is a white stage where the interactive elements stand out. However, sound heritage, such as a 1930s radio with Spanish radio spots or digitized elements like the skull of "Miguelon", a Homo Heidelbergensis fossil found in the Atapuerca site, are included.

Blender was chosen as the 3D modeling software and Unreal Engine 4 as the development engine for this iVR experience. The choice of Blender was based on the development team's previous experience in some reconstructions [10, 39] and its free and open-source model. In addition, the choice of Unreal Engine 4 as the development engine was also based on the team's previous experiences [40, 41], as well as its ease of programming thanks to its visual programming system [42] and the realistic result that can be achieved with this engine [1]. The process of modelling in Blender and programming in Unreal Engine 4 is similar to that described in a previous article by the research group [8]. These two software choices aimed to achieve the highest Level of Detail (LoD) possible to create the best impact on the user [43].

The Oculus Meta Quest 2 has been chosen as the device to run the experience. This device stands out for its affordable price and for being a standalone 6DoF HMD. Standalone HMDs are characterized by not requiring an external computer to run iVR [2], which greatly improve their use by end-users. On the one hand, the absence of wires and computers makes it easier to transport the HMD and eliminates the wire as a potential nuisance for the user. In addition, its low cost facilitates its acquisition. On the other hand, the limited hardware of the device has made the development of the application hard, requiring the optimization of all resources to obtain a visually attractive experience.

Due to the project's requirements, these 4 levels have been carefully designed to be user-friendly and to showcase the possibilities of virtual reconstruction of CH through iVR.

3.1 Level 1: Burgos 1921

Level 1 is developed in the virtual reconstruction of the Main Square of Burgos (Spain) in the year 1921. Figure 3 shows an image of this level from the user's point of view. This scenario serves as an introductory level to the experience. This level is a Passive iVR experience. In this case, a 360° video-based iVR has been chosen. In this experience, the user can only rotate the viewpoint to interact with the environment. Only one 360° point of the virtual reconstruction has been introduced, as a change of environment, even if it is within the reconstruction of Burgos in 1921, could give the user the feeling of advancing to another level. It has been intended to show the simplest possible type of Passive iVR experience, without guided movement, with only one 360° environment to be observed. On the other hand, characters have been introduced in this level. The reason for this design decision is to present to the user the dissemination potential of characters in a virtual reconstruction in the most controlled environment possible, a Passive experience. If they had been introduced in the following levels, users might have approached them to try to interact with them. By including them only in the Passive experience, characters can only be observed, and in this case, they serve the purpose of conveying other heritage information such as clothing or mores of the people of Burgos. The development of this reconstruction is explained in a previous paper of the research group [44]. The reconstruction has been documented through graphic documents such as photographs or building plans and the square has been digitized through 360° photography and photogrammetry to preserve the elements of the city that have not changed in this century. There have been no development issues caused by the limitations of the standalone HMD because the iVR run with a 360° video.

Fig. 3. Image from the user's perspective of the virtual reconstruction of the Main Square of Burgos (Spain) in 1921.

3.2 Level 2: Legio 1st Century

Level 2 takes place in the virtual reconstruction of the city of Legio (Spain) in the 1st century, known as León at currently. Figure 4 shows a user's view of the level. In this level, user interaction is expanded to become an Explorative experience. The environment is of a large size, encompassing the entire city, but the user's movement is limited to 4 m². The size of the environment has been reduced to make the experience more usable. With this limited movement area, the experience can be walked through without the need for a complementary locomotion system such as teleportation system. No extradiegetic elements, such as panels that expand heritage information, have been introduced. This limitation of interactive elements makes this explorative experience as simple as possible. There are characters in the reconstruction populating the city, but they are static being more similar to figures in a model. The archaeological remains of the city were used as historical sources in the reconstruction. Due to the lack of documentation, the user was placed in an elevated position to appreciate the city as a whole and the distribution of the streets, instead of focusing on the details. Due to the technical limitations of the standalone HMD, the model had to be highly optimized. To make it affordable, the original model's geometry was reduced by 64.34%, and ten texture atlases of 4096 × 4096px were used to make the final.fbx file as lightweight as possible, at 29.2mb.

Fig. 4. Image from the user's perspective of the virtual reconstruction of the city of Legio in I^{st} century. The user is located at an elevated viewpoint to better understand the urban layout.

3.3   Level 3: Chapel of San Juan De Acre in 14th Century

Level 3 takes place in the virtual reconstruction of the 14th century Chapel of San Juan de Acre, in Spain. Figure 5 shows a view of the level from the user's perspective. In this level, the iVR experience becomes Explorative interaction, introducing new forms of interaction with the user's controls. The scenario is of medium size, consisting only of the interior of a chapel. However, it is impossible to walk from one end to the other in a normal-sized room. Therefore, the teleportation locomotion system is introduced in this level, which can be activated by pressing the buttons or joysticks of the controller. Additionally, in this level, the user can pick up a torch by squeezing the controller. The torch has a halo of light to make it visually prominent. Both the torch and the candles that can be lit with it are placed in separate points of the environment to force the user to use the teleportation locomotion system. Like in the other levels, it was decided to keep the experience as simple as possible within its category. Therefore, no missions, characters, or complex mechanics were introduced. The only new mechanic is the ability to grab objects and the teleportation locomotion system. The historical sources used in this reconstruction are the archaeological remains of the site and graphical and written documentation. Due to the limitations of the standalone HMD, adaptations had to be made to the original model to make it work correctly. The model was modified to improve the performance of the light, and the number of textures was reduced to six texture atlases to make the final.fbx file as lightweight as possible, 4.05 MB.

Fig. 5. Image from the user's perspective of the virtual reconstruction of the Chapel of San Juan de Acre (Spain) in 14th century.

3.4   Level 4: Workshop

Level 4 takes place in a completely white workshop that houses CH elements in colour. Figure 6 shows a view of the scenario from the user's point of view. In this level, the iVR experience becomes an Interactive experience. The size of the scenario is reduced by 2 m^2 so that the user can interact with the heritage elements on the tables without moving. The system of grabbing objects by squeezing the controller is maintained, but the mechanics of pressing buttons and fitting objects are implemented and the teleport locomotion system is removed. The button of a 1930s radio can be pressed to play a Spanish period advertisement. The mechanics of fitting objects are implemented in a puzzle made up of parts of a mosaic from the Roman villa of La Olmeda that can be observed in Fig. 6. To visually guide the user, images have been placed showing how objects should be arranged, such as in the mosaic puzzle. These interactable elements, along with others that work with the grabbing mechanics, such as the "Miguelon" skull, are in colour to visually stand out for the user [38]. In order to achieve the simplest Interactive experience no characters or elements with complex interactions have been included, being all small simple mini-games. The heritage elements included in this level are partially digitized, such as the mosaic or the skull. To make the environment work correctly, the number of elements in the scenario was reduced, creating a very simple, white environment to run properly on a standalone HMD.

Fig. 6. I Image from the user's perspective of the Level 4. All the elements are in color with except the interactive ones. The background image shows how the puzzle should be solved.

4   Conclusions

iVR technology is becoming increasingly relevant in society. Since its first military and training uses, the technology has expanded into new areas. Among these emerging applications is the dissemination of CH through iVR. However, technological advancements have led to the diversification of iVR experiences, resulting in an increasing number of experience types that are hard to understand for users who do not regularly use iVR. This situation highlights the need for an application that summarizes the most common types of experiences to familiarize novice users with iVR, particularly in the context of dissemination of CH.

For this reason, the development of an iVR experience has been carried out, which presents the 4 most common types of iVR experiences (Passive experience, Explorative experience, Explorative interaction experience, and Interactive experience), showcasing various reconstructed CH environments and elements. The key design factors of this experience are as follows: 1) 4 levels focused on each type of iVR experience, 2) Simple interaction systems that become more complex at each level, 3) Short duration of the experience and time-limited progression between levels, 4) Development of the application for standalone iVR devices to increase usability for users, and 5) Inclusion of different reconstructed CH environments and objects showcasing different possibilities for the dissemination of CH using this technology.

Level 1 presents a Passive experience showcasing the virtual reconstruction of the city of Burgos (Spain) in 1921, including recorded characters. Level 2 provides an Explorative experience of the city of Legio (known as León currently), Spain in the 1st century with limited range of movements. Level 3 showcases an Explorative interaction experience in the medieval Chapel of San Juan de Acre (Spain) in 15th century with a teleportation locomotion system and object gripping. Level 4 offers an Interactive experience with a series of heritage elements, such as digitized objects and sound heritage, introducing new mechanics such as button pressing and fitting pieces.

The development of the application has been successful, achieving high performance on standalone iVR devices. The application has already been tested in museums and exhibitions, and usability results are expected to be achieved in the future.

References

1. Bekele, M.K., Pierdicca, R., Frontoni, E., Malinverni, E.S., Gain, J.: A survey of augmented, virtual, and mixed reality for cultural heritage. J. Comput. Cult. Herit. **11**, 1–36 (2018). https://doi.org/10.1145/3145534
2. Anthes, C., García-Hernández, R.J., Wiedemann, M., Kranzlmüller, D.: State of the art of virtual reality technology. In: IEEE Aerospace Conference Proceedings. IEEE Computer Society (2016). https://doi.org/10.1109/AERO.2016.7500674
3. Bowman, D.A., McMahan, R.P.: Virtual reality: how much immersion is enough? Computer **40**, 36–43 (2007)
4. Banfi, F.: The evolution of interactivity, immersion and interoperability in HBIM: digital model uses, VR and AR for built cultural heritage. ISPRS Int J Geoinf. **10**, 685 (2021). https://doi.org/10.3390/ijgi10100685
5. Theodoropoulos, A., Antoniou, A.: VR games in cultural heritage: a systematic review of the emerging fields of virtual reality and culture games. Appl. Sci. **12**, 8476 (2022). https://doi.org/10.3390/app12178476
6. Marto, A., Gonçalves, A., Melo, M., Bessa, M.: A survey of multisensory VR and AR applications for cultural heritage. Comput. Graph. (Pergamon) **102**, 426–440 (2022). https://doi.org/10.1016/j.cag.2021.10.001
7. DaCosta, B., Kinsell, C.: Serious games in cultural heritage: a review of practices and considerations in the design of location-based games. Educ. Sci. **13**, 47 (2022). https://doi.org/10.3390/educsci13010047
8. Checa, D., Alaguero, M., Bustillo, A.: Industrial heritage seen through the lens of a virtual reality experience. In: De Paolis, L., Bourdot, P., Mongelli, A. (eds.) AVR 2017. LNCS, vol. 10324, pp. 116–130. Springer, Cham (2017). https://doi.org/10.1007/978-3-319-60922-5_9
9. Banfi, F.: BIM orientation: grades of generation and information for different type of analysis and management process. In: The International Archives of the Photogrammetry, Remote Sensing and Spatial Information Sciences, vol. XLII-2/W5, pp. 57–64 (2017). https://doi.org/10.5194/isprs-archives-XLII-2-W5-57-2017
10. Bustillo, A., Alaguero, M., Miguel, I., Saiz, J.M., Iglesias, L.S.: A flexible platform for the creation of 3D semi-immersive environments to teach cultural heritage. Digit. Appl. Archaeol. Cult. Herit. **2**, 248–259 (2015). https://doi.org/10.1016/j.daach.2015.11.002
11. Tcha-Tokey, K., Christmann, O., Loup-Escande, E., Richir, S.: Proposition and validation of a questionnaire to measure the user experience in immersive virtual environments. Int. J. Virtual Real. **16**, 33–48 (2016)
12. Slater, M., et al.: Virtually being Lenin enhances presence and engagement in a scene from the Russian revolution. Front. Robot. AI **5** (2018). https://doi.org/10.3389/frobt.2018.00091

13. Pujol-Tost, L.: "3D·CoD": a new methodology for the design of virtual reality-mediated experiences in digital archeology. Front. Digit. Humanit. **4** (2017). https://doi.org/10.3389/fdigh.2017.00016
14. Pujol-Tost, L.: Cultural presence in virtual archaeology: an exploratory analysis of factors. Presence Teleoper. Virtual Environ. **26**, 247–263 (2017). https://doi.org/10.1162/PRES_a_00296
15. Gabellone, F.: Virtual environments and technological solutions for an enriched viewing of historic and archeological contexts. In: First Olympia Seminar, pp. 223–232 (2015)
16. Njerekai, C.: An application of the virtual reality 360° concept to the Great Zimbabwe monument. J. Herit. Tour. **15**, 567–579 (2019). https://doi.org/10.1080/1743873X.2019.1696808
17. Checa, D., Bustillo, A.: Advantages and limits of virtual reality in learning processes: Briviesca in the fifteenth century. Virtual Real. **24**, 151–161 (2020). https://doi.org/10.1007/s10055-019-00389-7
18. Meegan, E., et al.: Virtual heritage learning environments. In: Ioannides, M., Fink, E., Cantoni, L., Champion, E. (eds.) EuroMed 2020. LNCS, vol. 12642, pp. 427–437. Springer, Cham (2021). https://doi.org/10.1007/978-3-030-73043-7_35
19. Checa, D., Bustillo, A.: A review of immersive virtual reality serious games to enhance learning and training. Multimed Tools Appl. **79**, 5501–5527 (2020). https://doi.org/10.1007/s11042-019-08348-9
20. Wu, H.K., Lee, S.W.Y., Chang, H.Y., Liang, J.C.: Current status, opportunities and challenges of augmented reality in education. Comput. Educ. **62**, 41–49 (2013). https://doi.org/10.1016/j.compedu.2012.10.024
21. Miguel-Alonso, I., Rodriguez-Garcia, B., Checa, D., De Paolis, L.T.: Developing a tutorial for improving usability and user skills in an immersive virtual reality experience. In: De Paolis, L.T., Arpaia, P., Sacco, M. (eds.) XR Salento 2022. LNCS, vol. 13446, pp. 63–78. Springer, Cham (2022). https://doi.org/10.1007/978-3-031-15553-6_5
22. Rizvic, S., Boskovic, D., Bruno, F., Petriaggi, B.D., Sljivo, S., Cozza, M.: Actors in VR storytelling. In: 2019 11th International Conference on Virtual Worlds and Games for Serious Applications, VS-Games 2019 – Proceedings, pp. 1–8 (2019). https://doi.org/10.1109/VS-Games.2019.8864520
23. Škola, F., et al.: Virtual reality with 360-video storytelling in cultural heritage: study of presence, engagement, and immersion. Sensors **20**, 1–17 (2020). https://doi.org/10.3390/s20205851
24. Bruno, F., et al.: Virtual tour in the Sunken "villa con Ingresso a Protiro" within the underwater archaeological park of Baiae. In: ISPRS Annals of the Photogrammetry, Remote Sensing and Spatial Information Sciences, pp. 45–51. Copernicus GmbH (2019). https://doi.org/10.5194/isprs-archives-XLII-2-W10-45-2019
25. Schofield, G., et al.: Viking VR: designing a virtual reality experience for a museum. In: Proceedings of the 2018 Designing Interactive Systems Conference, pp. 805–815. ACM, New York (2018). https://doi.org/10.1145/3196709.3196714
26. Setiawan, P.A.: Delivering cultural heritage and historical events to people through virtual reality. In: IOP Conference Series: Earth and Environmental Science. IOP Publishing Ltd. (2021). https://doi.org/10.1088/1755-1315/729/1/012111
27. Ramsey, E.: Virtual Wolverhampton: recreating the historic city in virtual reality. Archnet-IJAR **11**, 42–57 (2017). https://doi.org/10.26687/archnet-ijar.v11i3.1395
28. Walmsley, A., Kersten, T.P.: Low-cost development of an interactive, immersive virtual reality experience of the historic city model Stade 1620. In: International Archives of the Photogrammetry, Remote Sensing and Spatial Information Sciences - ISPRS Archives, pp. 405–411. International Society for Photogrammetry and Remote Sensing (2019). https://doi.org/10.5194/isprs-archives-XLII-2-W17-405-2019

29. Checa, D., Alaguero, M., Arnaiz, M.A., Bustillo, A.: Briviesca in the 15th c.: a virtual reality environment for teaching purposes. In: De Paolis, L., Mongelli, A. (eds.) AVR 2016. LNCS, vol. 9769, pp. 126–138. Springer, Cham (2016). https://doi.org/10.1007/978-3-319-40651-0_11

30. Trescak, T., Bogdanovych, A.: Case-based planning for large virtual agent societies. In: Proceedings of the ACM Symposium on Virtual Reality Software and Technology, VRST. Association for Computing Machinery (2017). https://doi.org/10.1145/3139131.3139155

31. de Paolis, L.T., Faggiano, F., Gatto, C., Barba, M.C., de Luca, V.: Immersive virtual reality for the fruition of ancient contexts: the case of the archaeological and Naturalistic Park of Santa Maria d'Agnano in Ostuni. Digit. Appl. Archaeol. Cult. Herit. **27**, e00243 (2022). https://doi.org/10.1016/j.daach.2022.e00243

32. Vu, S., et al.: Recreating little manila through a virtual reality serious game. In: 2018 3rd Digital Heritage International Congress (DigitalHERITAGE) held jointly with 2018 24th International Conference on Virtual Systems & Multimedia (VSMM 2018), pp. 1–4 (2018). https://doi.org/10.1109/DigitalHeritage.2018.8810082

33. Pagano, A., Palombini, A., Bozzelli, G., De Nino, M., Cerato, I., Ricciardi, S.: ArkaeVision VR game: user experience research between real and virtual paestum. Appl. Sci. **10** (2020). https://doi.org/10.3390/app10093182

34. Egea-Vivancos, A., Arias-Ferrer, L.: Principles for the design of a history and heritage game based on the evaluation of immersive virtual reality video games. E-Learn. Digit. Media **18**, 383–402 (2020). https://doi.org/10.1177/2042753020980103

35. Gaugne, R., Barreau, J.B., Duc-Martin, P., Esnault, E., Gouranton, V.: Sport heritage in VR: real tennis case study. Front. Virtual Real. **3** (2022). https://doi.org/10.3389/frvir.2022.922415

36. Rossi, S., Viola, I., Toni, L., Cesar, P.: From 3-DoF to 6-DoF: new metrics to analyse users behaviour in immersive applications. J. Latex Class Files **14** (2015). https://doi.org/10.48550/arXiv.2112.09402

37. Prithul, A., Adhanom, I.B., Folmer, E.: Teleportation in virtual reality; a mini-review. Front. Virtual Real. **2** (2021). https://doi.org/10.3389/frvir.2021.730792

38. Miguel-Alonso, I., Rodriguez-Garcia, B., Checa, D., Bustillo, A.: Countering the novelty effect: a tutorial for immersive virtual reality learning environments. Appl. Sci. **13** (2023). https://doi.org/10.3390/app13010593

39. Alaguero, M., Checa, D.: Optimización en proyectos de realidad virtual de bajo presupuesto en la didáctica del patrimonio. Comunicación y Pedagogía: nuevas tecnologías y recursos didácticos **317–318**, 6–9 (2019)

40. Checa, D., Gatto, C., Cisternino, D., De Paolis, L.T., Bustillo, A.: A framework for educational and training immersive virtual reality experiences. In: 7th International Conference on Augmented Reality, Virtual Reality, and Computer Graphics, AVR 2020, pp. 220–228 (2020). https://doi.org/10.1007/978-3-030-58468-9_17

41. Guillen-Sanz, H., Rodríguez-Garcia, B., Martinez, K., Manzanares, M.C.S.: A virtual reality serious game for children with dyslexia: DixGame. In: De Paolis, L.T., Arpaia, P., Sacco, M. (eds.) XR Salento 2022. LNCS, vol. 13446, pp. 34–43. Springer, Cham (2022). https://doi.org/10.1007/978-3-031-15553-6_3

42. Mendoza, M.A.D., De La Hoz Franco, E., Gómez, J.E.G.: Technologies for the preservation of cultural heritage—a systematic review of the literature. Sustainability **15**, 1059 (2023). https://doi.org/10.3390/su15021059

43. Royan, J., Gioia, P., Cavagna, R., Bouville, C.: Network-based visualization of 3D landscapes and city models. IEEE Comput. Graph. Appl. **27**, 70–79 (2007). https://doi.org/10.1109/MCG.2007.155

44. Rodriguez-Garcia, B., Alaguero, M., Guillen-Sanz, H., Miguel-Alonso, I.: Comparing the impact of low-cost 360° cultural heritage videos displayed in 2D screens versus virtual reality headsets. In: De Paolis, L.T., Arpaia, P., Sacco, M. (eds.) XR Salento 2022. LNCS, vol. 13446, pp. 391–404. Springer, Cham (2022). https://doi.org/10.1007/978-3-031-15553-6_27

The Silence of Art: Investigating the Emotional Experience of a Virtual Museum by Facial Expression Analysis

Maurizio Mauri[1], Stefano Triberti[2(✉)], and Daniela Villani[1]

[1] Department of Psychology, Università Cattolica del Sacro Cuore, Milan, Italy
{maurizio.mauri,daniela.villani}@unicatt.it
[2] Department of Human Sciences, Università Telematica Pegaso, Naples, Italy
stefano.triberti@unipegaso.it

Abstract. Art is a fundamental part of human experience. Today the fruition of art is often mediated by new technologies such as virtual environments reproducing museums and expositions, and even more during the COVID-19 pandemic and related safety measures that confined people in their homes for long periods. Different factors can influence involvement/engagement (as a component of sense of presence) and emotions during art fruition in virtual museums. For example, while supporting information enriches real-life art fruition, some literature suggests that art should be accessed in silence. This study aimed at analyzing participants' experience of a virtual museum with or without supporting information (audio guides), by implementing both self-report and facial expressions analysis. Results show that emotions as shown by facial expressions (specifically happiness, anger, confusion) differed between conditions, highlighting a more positive experience for the participants who explored the virtual museum without audio guides. It is possible that audio guides may generate information overload within virtual museums, and that sometimes (especially in art-focused exhibitions, where emotions and deep personal reflection are important), the opportunity to visit in silence should be guaranteed. The discussion gives indications for media design to support immersive and pleasant art fruition experience, as well as future research focused on the involvement/engagement component of sense of presence.

Keywords: Virtual Environment · Emotions · Facial Expressions · Virtual Museums

1 Introduction

Art is a fundamental part of human experience. The fruition of art is associated with notable positive outcomes in terms of well-being and personal growth [1–3]. In the last decades, designers have relied on new technologies to extend the boundaries of opportunities to enjoy art. For example, virtual reality and 360 videos (i.e., computer-generated environments that approximate physical reality and can be accessed through desktop or head-mounted displays) can be used to develop immersive experiences ("virtual museums") that allow the audience to explore art exhibitions from the comfort of their homes

L. T. De Paolis et al. (Eds.): XR Salento 2023, LNCS 14219, pp. 302–312, 2023.
https://doi.org/10.1007/978-3-031-43404-4_19

[4, 5]. A virtual museum can be defined as a is a digital entity that draws on the characteristics of a museum, while maintaining the characteristics of such institutions according to the definition of the International Council of Museums: "a not-for-profit, permanent institution in the service of society that researches, collects, conserves, interprets and exhibits tangible and intangible heritage".

Such technologies have become even more important during the COVID-19 pandemic, where safety measures such as the repeated lockdowns confined people in their homes for relatively extended periods. In this context, people have adapted to explore old and new forms of entertainment and personal enrichment [6, 7], technology-mediated art fruition included [8–10]. According to literature [8, 11], there is still room for improving our understanding of the factors that affect emotions and engagement within technology-mediated art exhibitions.

It is possible that some aspects relevant to engaging art fruition will never be completely reproducible within virtual simulations: as Pelowski and colleagues [12] say in their review, factors such as texture (especially when touching the artwork is allowed), physical presence and immediacy, perceived authenticity, size of the artwork compared to the visitor's body, all concur to the complete fruition experience.

That considered, the research on virtual museums highlights that such experiences could be conducive of intense emotions [8, 13–15] and it is important to understand what factors should be exploited to improve the fruition of virtual cultural heritage. An interesting hypothesis is that the enjoyment of art in museums (physical and virtual) is improved by adding information that supports the audience during the visit. Indeed, for physical museums, many studies highlight the importance of guides that accompany visitors and facilitate learning and understanding [16–19]. For this reason, research on technology-mediated art fruition has often focused on ways to reproduce such addition of information in the exposition experience, in order to enrich learning opportunities: this is literally the main function of Augmented Reality (AR) tools, which superimpose digital objects onto physical ones, for example to link additional information without taking physical space [20] or to show visitors how an ancient artwork was in the past [21].

Research on virtual museums has often explored the possibility to simulate professional guides, meaning virtual agents that could interact with the visitor, however results on their effects in terms of emotions and engagement are relatively limited. Sylaiou and colleagues [13] have shown that the audience felt emotions different in valence and intensity towards virtual agents differently framed in their role (i.e., a curator, a museum guard, another visitor). Another study [22] considered the audience preferences towards virtual guides in terms of appearance and traits and found that a sample of young girls wanted their virtual guides to be smart, friendly and patient as the most important traits to promote engagement. However, virtual agents could be complex to design and also not strictly necessary if the aim is to just add information to a virtual museum. While finding that agent-guides (in this case, robots) lead to more information retained and more enjoyment than audio guides in their sample, Velentza and colleagues [23] commented that guiding tools should be adapted to the specific museum and visitors' intention (e.g., audiences looking for a "serious" experience may prefer less invasive tools). In addition, other studies found that virtual agents generated more social presence in visitors than audio-only guides in a mixed reality exhibition, but there were no differences regarding other effectiveness and engagement parameters [24].

Indeed another possibility is to replicate audio-only guides by inserting spoken narratives within the museum virtual environment. Audio guides in virtual museums are generally considered more effective than panels and information to read [25], which could be annoying or scarcely usable in virtual reality. The utilization of audio guides in virtual museums is supported by literature from the interactive storytelling field, based on the belief that audio narratives would improve sense of presence and interest in the visitors [26–28]. That said, it seems difficult to find research that compared the same virtual art exhibition experience with and without audio narrative. Rzayev and colleagues' [29] participants evaluated more positively a virtual museum in the condition where they were not accompanied. A recent study by Hutchinson and Eardley [30] analyzed art fruition in three conditions, namely no audio guide vs. standard vs. more detailed audio guide: while people in the two audio guide conditions showed better recall of the art and higher engagement at a later time (e.g., talking to others about the pictures they had seen), there were no significant differences across conditions in terms of enjoyment and emotional responses.

Mason and Sayner [31], who explored the multiple meanings of "silence" in museums, noticed that silent spaces may be purposely created inside museums for particular means, for example in order to promote visitor's reflection (e.g., a room that respectfully commemorates a dramatic historical event). Art exhibitions are supposed to be accessed in silence, to the point that they could feature signs that prohibit visitors from laughing or talking loudly [32]. The renowned German art historian Wolfgang Kemp has written about the "efficacy" of silence when enjoying art, in the sense that the audience that would fully experience the beauty of an artwork is expected to find themselves in silent awe in front of it [33]. On this basis, it is interesting to analyze how visitors of a virtual museum would respond emotionally to silent vs. audio-guided exploration. While research that compares properties of virtual tours/virtual museums is rich, to our knowledge this is the first study comparing the experience of an art-based virtual museum with audio guides and in silence, with a focus on engagement and emotional aspects.

Beyond art fruition, this is also an opportunity to analyze complex aspects of immersive experiences and involvement/engagement as components of the sensation of "being there" or the sense of presence. Involvement/engagement can be characterized mostly in emotional terms [34], meaning that one may feel more present in a simulation in a meaningful way, given that properties of the simulation generate emotional responses that could make the experience more pregnant, vivid, and memorable beyond the mere technical features of the virtual environment.

2 Methods

2.1 Experimental Protocol

This study was carried out in the first half of 2021, while the lock-down to cope with the pandemic diffusion of Covid-19 was still applied in the whole country of Italy. 32 students from Università Cattolica of Milan (50% male, mean age: 23 ± 4) were contacted via email and pre-assessed during a phone call. Participants recruited were required to have visited at least one art exhibition in the previous 12 months, to have an internet connection, together with a personal computer equipped with a webcam, with a minimum definition resolution of 1,280 pixels × 720 pixels. Figure 1 illustrates the experimental protocol, completely carried out remotely. The study had between subjects design. Both "Group with no audio" and "Group with audio" have been exposed to the same video, showing a virtual tour of the museum chosen, by means of a 360° video: with or without an audio guide explaining the paintings. The video showed the Mauritshuis museum, located in The Hague (Netherlands), displaying some paintings, with a final focus on painting labeled "Girl with a Pearl Earring" (1665–1666) by Johannes Vermeer. The 360° video has a duration of 2.13 min, enough to raise emotional reactions in the participants, as shown by previous studies [35, 36].

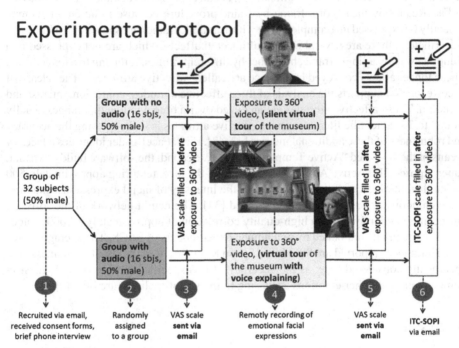

Fig. 1. The figure above illustrates the experimental protocol that enabled to perform the whole research remotely, during COVID-19 lockdown: from "step 1" (recruiting of experimental subjects via e-mail) to "step 6" (self-questionnaires provided always via email).

2.2 Self-reports Measures

Two questionnaires have been used: a) the "Visual Analogue Scale" or "VAS" [37], that measures intensity of 10 emotional states on a scale ranging from 1 (low intensity) to 7 (high intensity), self-reported by participant both before viewing the video stimulus and after watching it; b) to assess engagement, the engagement subscale of the "Sense of Presence Inventory" or "ITC-SOPI" questionnaire [34]. It was decided to administer exclusively the Engagement scale given the nature of the experimental stimuli and the study aims. This scale is characterized by 14 items, with a Likert scale of 5 options (from 1 = "completely disagree", to 5 = "Completely agree").

2.3 Automatic Emotional Facial Expression Analyses

Facial expressions of participants were recorded during the exposure to the two videos, and processed using FaceReader, version 9.0, from Noldus [38, 39]. The software employs a three-layer neural network (i.e., a method of computation and information processes that mimics human brain's neurons) that automatically detects and scans emotional facial expressions [40]. It identifies and categorizes facial expressions from pictures and from videos as basic emotions [41]. Facial expressions of emotions are assessed in FaceReader by means of a frame-by-frame procedure because basic emotions may typically be expressed in a complete way within a single frame (or "snapshot") of the face. Nevertheless, there are several more multifaceted affects, which are not expressed in a complete way by a single frame, but rather by different frames, referring to a longer time. These longer affects conveyed by the face are called "affective attitudes". The release of FaceReader 7.1 supports the analysis of three affective attitudes: confusion, interest and boredom. These affective attitudes are analyzed over a time window that ranges usually from 2 to 5 s. Scientific literature about affective attitudes is still exploring the accuracy and robustness of these additional metrics [42, 43]. First, FaceReader identifies a face, by means of the so-called "Active Template Method". Second, the software builds a virtual, superimposed 3D "Active Appearance Model" of the face, featuring approximately 500 typical landmarks. The third step measures the intensity of facial expressions, enabling basic emotions to be assessed and computed [44]. The neural network of the software has been trained, relying on a high-quality correlation of approximately 10,000 images that were manually annotated by real human expert coders of FACS. The average scores of performances reported are 89% [40, 45] and 87% [46]. Results about "happiness" are specifically considered here, as the accuracy of this specific emotion is the highest in comparison to all other emotions according to the scientific literature [46–49].

3 Results

Regarding the engagement scale, it did not show any significant difference between the two groups, however the no-audio group revealed higher scores. Regarding the emotional evaluation from VAS scale, Table 1 summarizes the results.

Taking into account the emotional facial expressions analyses, Table 2 summarizes the results. All values are expressed in standardized scores, between 0.000 (it indicates that the specific emotion considered is not displayed on the face) and 1.000 (the highest intensity of the emotion considered is conveyed by the face). Three emotional states reveal significant difference between the two groups: a) happiness (two tailed t-test: $p < 0.05$): the higher values of happiness for the no-audio group (M 0.008, SD 0.002) indicate higher positive emotional reactions in comparison to audio one (M 0.002, SD 0.001); b) anger (two tailed t-test: $p < 0.05$): the significant higher level of anger in the audio group (M 0.123, SD 0.062) indicates a more important negative emotional reaction

Table 1. Results from VAS scale, before and after the exposure to the virtual tour of the museum, in the 2 groups (Group with audio, with the voice explaining the paintings; Group no audio, with silence). Mean values across all subjects, with S.D. values in brackets.

Emotions	Before watching the video		After watching the video	
	Group with audio	Group no audio	Group with audio	Group no audio
Surprise	2.44 (1.41)	2.44 (1.37)	4.06 (1.80)	3.25 (1.73)
Relax	4.62 (1.36)	4.63 (1.45)	5.62 (1.02)	5.38 (1.08)
Sad	2.13 (0.71)	3.06 (1.62)	1.44 (0.81)	1.69 (1.35)
Angry	2.06 (1.53)	2.56 1.63)	1.31 (0.60)	1.25 (0.77)
Scared	2.69 (1.66)	2.44 (1.46)	1.13 (0.34)	1.25 (0.77)
Curious	5.50 (1.03)	5.19 (1.64)	4.63 (1.59)	4.94 (1.24)
Confus	2.81 (2.07)	2.75 (1.69)	1.56 (0.96)	1.81 (1.22)
Disapp	1.62 (1.31)	2.44 (1.67)	1.56 (0.89)	1.81 (1.28)
Interested	5.63 (1.31)	5.44 (1.03)	4.94 (1.23)	5.25 (0.77)
Amazed	2.81 (1.68)	2.38 (1.46)	3.94 (0.97)	4.00 (1.36)

when compared with the no-audio group (M 0.023, SD 0.034); c) confusion (two tailed t-test: $p < 0.05$): the audio group scored, on average, higher values (M 0.009, SD 0.002) than the no-audio group (M 0.001; SD 0.001).

Table 2. Results from automatic emotional facial expressions analyses, during the exposure to the virtual tour of the museum, in the 2 groups ("Group with audio", with the voice explaining the paintings; "Group no audio", with silence). Mean values across subject and SD in brackets. Values in bold and with an asterisk indicate significant differences amongst the two groups.

Emotions	Group with audio	Group no audio
Neutral	0.747 (0.105)	0.846 (0.111)
Happy	0.002 (0.001)	**0.008 (0.002)***
Sad	0.078 (0.016)	0.101 (0.019)
Angry	0.123 (0.032)	**0.023 (0.007)***
Surprised	0.053 (0.013)	0.030 (0.014)
Scared	0.013 (0.07)	0.013 (0.06)
Disgusted	0,009 (0.003)	0,011 (0.004)
Boredom	0,079 (0.019)	0,089 (0.020)
Confused	0.009 (0.002)	**0,001 (0.001)***
Interest	0,009 (0.005)	0,033 (0.016)

4 Discussion and Future Directions

This study explored participants' emotions and engagement towards a virtual museum experience with and without audio guide. Emotion-related and engagement questionnaires did not yield significant results. Nevertheless, significant differences emerged when analyzing facial expressions. According to these, participants who had the opportunity to enjoy the virtual art exhibition in silence were happier, less angry and less confused than the other group. This supports the idea that virtual museums may be more effective in terms of emotions/engagement without audio guides; besides being more or less informative, audio guides may be perceived as intrusive, possibly interfering with participants' autonomous exploration and enjoyment. People may prefer to observe art pieces according to their own time and interest, without being distracted by external guidance. This may be related to a form of information overload, which occurs when an individual is presented with more information than s/he has the time or the cognitive ability to process [50–52].

Future research may explore this hypothesis taking into account that the proclivity to information overload has been associated with individuals more than technology's characteristics [52]; so, it may be interesting to assess individual differences related to the fruition of virtual museums with different features. It is also possible that "silence" during a virtual museum visit (meaning the absence of audio guides) would be more important in art-based exhibitions (such as the one evaluated here) than in museums focused on science, history, etc., because silence is considered fundamental for achieving an aesthetic experience [33], while external guidance may be appreciated when the visitor's main interest is to obtain new knowledge. This result is also consistent with a study that found that silent virtual reality (VR) was more effective in eliciting some specific emotional experiences than both VR with music and VR with background sounds [53].

The main limitations of this study should be identified in its small sample and in the usage of a relatively short virtual museum experience. Moreover, the study was conducted online, with low possibility for the researchers to control environmental interference in the experimental procedure; on the other hand, such type of fruition for the virtual museum was considered adequate as it mirrors the way many people enjoy virtual museums in the wild. Another possible limitation is related to specific characteristics of the audio guide; future studies may compare different audio guides (e.g., voices, tone, content) to explore whether specific features would affect visitors' emotions.

Instead, a strength of the study was the usage of facial expressions analysis, which allowed the researchers to collect both implicit and explicit measures of emotional activation and involvement/engagement. Since facial expressions showed significant differences, future research may explore further the utilization of such methods for the analysis of digital means for the enhancement of cultural heritage, for fields ranging from neuromarketing [54] to user experience [35]. Indeed, the involvement/engagement component of sense of presence is somewhat ill defined across the literature. However, according to many sources [37, 55], it comprises emotional activations that give meaning to a mediated experience and concur to the sensation of "being there" – not only in a place, but in a situation or experience, that becomes pregnant, vivid, and memorable thanks to effective emotional design [56]. Taking into consideration the complexity of the involvement/engagement concept, the present study showed that self-report tools and objective measures of emotional arousal may diverge, a result not uncommon in the literature [57, 58]. This is related to the fact that felt responses and automatic activation of facial expressions are governed by different systems (i.e., the first ones are mediated by the subjects' language, culture, and understanding of emotions) [59]. The results of the present study support further research on multiple indexes to analyze the complex components of sense of presence within specific types of experiences mediated by virtual reality.

References

1. Mastandrea, S., Fagioli, S., Biasi, V.: Art and psychological well-being: linking the brain to the aesthetic emotion. Front. Psychol. **10**, 739 (2019)
2. Chatterjee, H.J., Camic, P.M.: The health and well-being potential of museums and art galleries. Arts Health **7**(3), 183–186 (2015)
3. Bennington, R., Backos, A., Harrison, J., Reader, A.E., Carolan, R: Art therapy in art museums: promoting social connectedness and psychological well-being of older adults. Arts Psychother. **49**, 34–43 (2016)
4. Sundar, S.S., Go, E., Kim, H.S., Zhang, B.: Communicating art, virtually! Psychological effects of technological affordances in a virtual museum. Int. J. Hum. Comput. Interact. **31**(6), 385–401 (2015)
5. Styliani, S., Fotis, L., Kostas, K., Petros, P.: Virtual museums, a survey and some issues for consideration. J. Cult. Herit. **10**(4), 520–528 (2009)
6. Durosini, I., Triberti, S., Savioni, L., Pravettoni, G.: In the eye of a quiet storm: a critical incident study on the quarantine experience during the coronavirus pandemic. PLoS ONE **16**(2), e0247121 (2021)
7. Brindha, D., Jayaseelan, R., Kadeswaran, S.: Covid-19 lockdown, entertainment and paid OTT video-streaming platforms: a qualitative study of audience preferences. Mass Commun. Int. J. Commun. Stud. **14**(4), 12–16 (2020)
8. Trupp, M.D., Bignardi, G., Chana, K., Specker, E., Pelowski, M.: Can a brief interaction with online, digital art improve wellbeing? A comparative study of the impact of online art and culture presentations on mood, state-anxiety, subjective wellbeing, and loneliness. Front. Psychol, 2305 (2022)
9. Radermecker, A.-S.: Art and culture in the COVID-19 era: for a consumer-oriented approach. SN Bus. Econ. **1**(1), 1–14 (2020). https://doi.org/10.1007/s43546-020-00003-y
10. Samaroudi, M., Echavarria, K.R., Perry, L.: Heritage in lockdown: digital provision of memory institutions in the UK and US of America during the COVID-19 pandemic. Mus. Manag. Curatorship **35**(4), 337–361 (2020)
11. Bekele, M.K., Pierdicca, R., Frontoni, E., Malinverni, E.S., Gain, J.: A survey of augmented, virtual, and mixed reality for cultural heritage. J. Comput. Cult. Herit. (JOCCH) **11**(2), 1–36 (2018)
12. Pelowski, M., Forster, M., Tinio, P.P., Scholl, M., Leder, H.: Beyond the lab: an examination of key factors influencing interaction with 'real' and museum-based art. Psychol. Aesthet. Creat. Arts **11**(3), 245 (2017)
13. Sylaiou, S., Kasapakis, V., Gavalas, D., Dzardanova, E.: Avatars as storytellers: affective narratives in virtual museums. Pers. Ubiquit. Comput. **24**(6), 829–841 (2020)
14. Beck, J., Rainoldi, M., Egger, R.: Virtual reality in tourism: a state-of-the-art review. Tour. Rev. **74**(3), 586–612 (2019)

15. Alelis, G., Bobrowicz, A., Ang, C.S.: Comparison of engagement and emotional responses of older and younger adults interacting with 3D cultural heritage artefacts on personal devices. Behav. Inf. Technol. **34**(11), 1064–1078 (2015)

16. Schep, M., van Boxtel, C., Noordegraaf, J.: Competent museum guides: defining competencies for use in art and history museums. Mus. Manag. Curatorship **33**(1), 2–24 (2018)

17. Best, K.: Making museum tours better: understanding what a guided tour really is and what a tour guide really does. Mus. Manag. Curatorship **27**(1), 35–52 (2012)

18. Uyen Tran, L., King, H.: The professionalization of museum educators: the case in science museums. Mus. Manag. Curatorship **22**(2), 131–149 (2007)

19. Burnham, R., Kai-Kee, E.: Teaching in the Art Museum: Interpretation as Experience. Getty Publications (2011)

20. Ghouaiel, N., Garbaya, S., Cieutat, J.M., Jessel, J.P.: Mobile augmented reality in museums: towards enhancing visitor's learning experience. Int. J. Virtual Real. **17**(1), 21–31 (2017)

21. Recupero, A., Talamo, A., Triberti, S., Modesti, C.: Bridging museum mission to visitors' experience: activity, meanings, interactions, technology. Front. Psychol. **10**, 2092 (2019)

22. Swartout, W., et al.: Ada and grace: toward realistic and engaging virtual museum guides. In: Allbeck, J., Badler, N., Bickmore, T., Pelachaud, C., Safonova, A. (eds.) IVA 2010. LNCS, vol. 6356, pp. 286–300. Springer, Heidelberg (2010). https://doi.org/10.1007/978-3-642-15892-6_30

23. Velentza, A.M., Heinke, D., Wyatt, J.: Museum robot guides or conventional audio guides? An experimental study. Adv. Robot. **34**(24), 1571–1580 (2020)

24. Rzayev, R., Karaman, G., Henze, N., Schwind, V.: Fostering virtual guide in exhibitions. In: Proceedings of the 21st International Conference on Human-Computer Interaction with Mobile Devices and Services, pp. 1–6 (2019)

25. Carrozzino, M., Colombo, M., Tecchia, F., Evangelista, C., Bergamasco, M.: Comparing different storytelling approaches for virtual guides in digital immersive museums. In: De Paolis, L., Bourdot, P. (eds.) AVR 2018. LNCS, vol. 10851, pp. 292–302. Springer, Cham (2018). https://doi.org/10.1007/978-3-319-95282-6_22

26. Sljivo, S., Bosnia, S.: Audio guided virtual museums. In: Central European Seminar on Computer Graphics (2012)

27. Murphy, D., Pitt, I.: Spatial sound enhancing virtual story telling. In: Balet, O., Subsol, G., Torguet, P. (eds.) ICVS 2001. LNCS, vol. 2197, pp. 20–29. Springer, Heidelberg (2001). https://doi.org/10.1007/3-540-45420-9_3

28. Rizvic, S.: Story guided virtual cultural heritage applications. J. Interact. Humanit. **2**(1), 2 (2014)

29. Rzayev, R., Habler, F., Ugnivenko, P., Henze, N., Schwind, V.: It's not always better when we're together: effects of being accompanied in virtual reality. In: Extended Abstracts of the 2020 CHI Conference on Human Factors in Computing Systems, pp. 1–8, April 2020

30. Hutchinson, R., Eardley, A.F.: Inclusive museum audio guides: 'guided looking' through audio description enhances memorability of artworks for sighted audiences. Mus. Manag. Curatorship **36**(4), 427–446 (2021)

31. Mason, R., Sayner, J.: Bringing museal silence into focus: eight ways of thinking about silence in museums. Int. J. Herit. Stud. **25**(1), 5–20 (2019)

32. van Kessel, E.: The role of silence in the early art museum. In: von Andreas Beyer, H., Le Bon, L. (eds.) Silence. Schweigen, Deutscher Kunstverlag (2015)

33. Kemp, W.: Die Kunst des Schweigens. In: Koebner, T. (Hg.) Laokoon und kein Ende. Der Wettstreit der Künste, München, pp. 96–119 (1989)

34. Lessiter, J., Freeman, J., Keogh, E., Davidoff, J.: A cross-media presence questionnaire: the ITC-sense of presence inventory. Presence Teleoper. Virtual Environ. **10**(3), 282–297 (2001)

35. Mauri, M., Cipresso, P., Balgera, A., Villamira, M., Riva, G.: Why is Facebook so successful? Psychophysiological measures describe a core flow state while using Facebook. Cyberpsychol. Behav. Soc. Netw. **14**(12), 723–731 (2011)
36. Mauri, M., Rancati, G., Gaggioli, A., Riva, G.: Applying implicit association test techniques and facial expression analyses in the comparative evaluation of website user experience. Front. Psychol., 4392 (2021)
37. Gross, J.J., Levenson, R.W.: Emotion elicitation using films. Cognit. Emot. **9**(1), 87–108 (1995)
38. Noldus, L.P.J.J.: FaceReader: Tool for Automated Analysis of Facial Expression: Version 6.0. Noldus Information, Wageningen (2014)
39. Loijens, L., Krips, O.: FaceReader Methodology Note. Noldus Information Technology Inc., Leesburg (2019)
40. Den Uyl, M.J., Van Kuilenburg, H.: The FaceReader: online facial expression recognition. In: Proceedings of Measuring Behavior, Wageningen, vol. 30, pp. 589–590 (2005)
41. Ekman, P.: Universal and cultural differences in facial expression of emotion. In: Nebraska Symposium on Motivation, vol. 19, University of Nebraska Press, Lincoln (1997)
42. Borges, N., Lindblom, L., Clarke, B., Gander, A., Lowe, R.: Classifying confusion: autodetection of communicative misunderstandings using facial action units. In: 8th International Conference on Affective Computing and Intelligent Interaction Workshops and Demos (ACIIW), Cambridge, pp. 401–406. IEEE (2019)
43. Hirt, F., Werlen, E., Moser, I., Bergamin, P.: Measuring emotions during learning: lack of coherence between automated facial emotion recognition and emotional experience. Open Comput. Sci. **9**(1), 308–317 (2019)
44. van Kuilenburg, H., Wiering, M., den Uyl, M.: A model based method for automatic facial expression recognition. In: Gama, J., Camacho, R., Brazdil, P.B., Jorge, A.M., Torgo, L. (eds.) CML 2005. LNCS, vol. 3720, pp. 194–205. Springer, Heidelberg (2005). https://doi.org/10.1007/11564096_22
45. Terzis, V., Moridis, C.N., Economides, A.A.: Measuring instant emotions based on facial expressions during computer-based assessment. Pers. Ubiquit. Comput. **17**, 43–52 (2013)
46. Lewinski, P., den Uyl, T.M., Butler, C.: Automated facial coding: validation of basic emotions and FACS AUs in FaceReader. J. Neurosci. Psychol. Econ. **7**, 227–236 (2014)
47. Lewinski, P., Fransen, M.L., Tan, E.S.: Predicting advertising effectiveness by facial expressions in response to amusing persuasive stimuli. J. Neurosci. Psychol. Econ. **7**, 1–14 (2014)
48. Stöckli, S., Schulte-Mecklenbeck, M., Borer, S., Samson, A.C.: Facial expression analysis with AFFDEX and FACET: a validation study. Behav. Res. Methods **50**, 1446–1460 (2018)
49. Dupré, D., Krumhuber, E.G., Küster, D., McKeown, G.J.: A performance comparison of eight commercially available automatic classifiers for facial affect recognition. PLoS ONE **15**, e0231968 (2020)
50. Farhoomand, A.F., Drury, D.H.: Managerial information overload. Commun. ACM (2002)
51. Näsi, M., Koivusilta, L.: Internet and everyday life: the perceived implications of internet use on memory and ability to concentrate. Cyberpsychol. Behav. Soc. Netw. **16**(2), 88–93 (2013)
52. Karr-Wisniewski, P., Lu, Y.: When more is too much: operationalizing technology overload and exploring its impact on knowledge worker productivity. Comput. Hum. Behav. **26**(5), 1061–1072 (2010)
53. Chirico, A., Gaggioli, A.: Virtual-reality music-based elicitation of awe: when silence is better than thousands sounds. In: Cipresso, P., Serino, S., Villani, D. (eds.) MindCare 2019. LNICST, vol. 288, pp. 1–11. Springer, Cham (2019). https://doi.org/10.1007/978-3-030-25872-6_1
54. Stasi, A., et al.: Neuromarketing empirical approaches and food choice: a systematic review. Food Res. Int. **108**, 650–664 (2018)

55. Triberti, S., Kelders, S.M., Gaggioli, A.: User engagement. In: Kip, H., Kelders, S.M., Sanderman, R., van Gemert-Pijen, L. (eds.) eHealth Research, Theory and Development, pp. 271–289. Routledge (2018)

56. Triberti, S., Chirico, A., La Rocca, G., Riva, G.: Developing emotional design: emotions as cognitive processes and their role in the design of interactive technologies. Front. Psychol. **8**, 1773 (2017)

57. Glenn, C.R., Blumenthal, T.D., Klonsky, E.D., Hajcak, G.: Emotional reactivity in nonsuicidal self-injury: divergence between self-report and startle measures. Int. J. Psychophysiol. **80**(2), 166–170 (2011)

58. Diminich, E.D., Bonanno, G.A.: Faces, feelings, words: divergence across channels of emotional responding in complicated grief. J. Abnorm. Psychol. **123**(2), 350 (2014)

59. Vrana, S.R.: The psychophysiology of disgust: differentiating negative emotional contexts with facial EMG. Psychophysiology **30**(3), 279–286 (1993)

Integrating Fragmented Historical Sites VR Based on Time-Space Clues for Modern History Education

Yanxiang Zhang[✉], Yidan Wang, and Yi Song

University of Science and Technology of China,
Jinzhai Road, Baohe District, Hefei, Anhui, China
petrel@ustc.edu.cn

Abstract. In recent years, VR technology has become a focus in education. Based on constructivist learning theory, gamification learning, and cognitive load theory, the researcher integrates the fragmented VR resources of modern historical relics based on the spatial and temporal relationship of historical events and restores a historical event's spatial and temporal picture through the narrative design in time and space. The VR resources are integrated with historical events' temporal and spatial relationships. The researcher brings an immersive experience to modern history education and provides a new way of thinking for constructing modern history education resources based on new media.

Keywords: Virtual Reality · Time-space · Modern history education · Historical relics

1 Introduction

With educators aiming to improve students' attitudes towards learning and improve the learning experience through ICT, e-learning has become an essential means for students around the globe to learn to acquire knowledge rapidly [1]. Thousands of online courses are available where learners engage in collaborative learning, delivery of assignments, and discussions [2]. The digitization of education has transformed the learning process for learners and has become an essential means of facilitating the process of globalization and promoting scientific innovation [3].

VR technology realizes a 3D reproduction of the natural world employing computers, and virtual simulation, in which the user interacts with the environment and the content, which can lead to partial and complete sensory experiences [4]. VR technology characteristics: immersion and realism make it a potentially important tool in tourism, sports, and medicine [5]. VR technology in education can achieve enough to transform the center of the classroom and develop the learner's subjective initiative. VR technology creates natural learning environments that can experience scenes and events difficult to realize in daily life and the classroom [6]. Users can wear the device and realize the

© The Author(s), under exclusive license to Springer Nature Switzerland AG 2023
L. T. De Paolis et al. (Eds.): XR Salento 2023, LNCS 14219, pp. 313–321, 2023.
https://doi.org/10.1007/978-3-031-43404-4_20

interaction with the environment. However, VR devices have not been widely disseminated, are costly, and many users experience fainting and discomfort when entering the environment [7].

Humanities education can develop students' thinking about values and life goals. Students in higher education need to pay more attention to education in humanities, and humanistic literacy needs to be improved [8]. Modern history courses re-present those essential historical events and characters so that learners can discover the nation's inheritance of humanistic spirit and literacy from these histories. Therefore, modern history education can help students to improve their comprehensive quality ability, including students' thinking and recognizing ability, as well as the cognitive ability of society. Therefore, modern history teaching is crucial in humanities education [9]. Historical sites are of great significance to modern people regarding feeling culture, promoting national spirit, and recognizing the law of historical development. Scholars are also committed to exploring the application of historical sites in other fields [10]. Integrating historical monuments and media technology has also become a concern for educators. In 1998, the Committee of Ministers of the Council of Europe emphasized the importance of cultural heritage education. In its statement No. R (98) 5 to the Member States, the Committee mentioned that "education in the field of heritage is the ideal way of giving meaning to the future through a better understanding of the past" [11]. Historical monuments can be used as a practical base for college and university students in civic and political education, as well as a topic for the conduct of civic and political workers and the subject of academic papers. Organizing students to visit modern historical sites can inspire the spirit of patriotism and cultural preservation and enhance students' attention to culture and history [12]. However, the cost of visiting historical sites offline is high, and the safety of students is difficult to guarantee. Therefore, offline visits to historical sites tend to be rare activities. History educators will present specific historical sites in the classroom with pictures and videos. However, the pictures and videos of the sites presented in the traditional digital classroom do not capture the interest and attention of the students and do not allow them to appreciate the complete picture of the historical sites [13].

According to heritage theorist David Lowenthal (1985), historical knowledge can be gained from three sources: memory, history, and relics. These three sources of knowledge complement each other to learn as much as possible about the past. In order to restore the complete picture of a historical event, the visualization of knowledge becomes more critical, and we cannot wholly restore past events with digital media technology, but we can construct historical culture. According to Mosaker, VR technology is a contemporary "time machine" and an essential tool for visualizing history [14]. The addition of digital technology has led to a greater interest in monuments and a greater interest in visualizing historical knowledge. Scholars such as Peter K. Allen and others have argued as early as 2003 that 3D models of historical sites can be an essential tool for education and are committed to using new methods to maximize the restoration of the complete picture of historical sites [15].

2 Related Work

2.1 Literature Review

In the literature on modern history education in China in recent years, many scholars have explored the benefits of modern history education from different perspectives. From an ideological and moral point of view, heroes and figures in modern history can be role models that encourage students to set up correct values, and students can improve their critical thinking skills by evaluating history and historical figures. Modern history education can improve the public's knowledge of and attention to history, and it is also an important educational program to cultivate the public's emotional identity [16]. Regarding modern history classroom teaching strategies, scholars encourage students to learn by listening, speaking, reading, and writing with multi-sensory participation in the modern history classroom [17].

In the following, we will analyze the literature closely related to our work. The foundation of the Hellenic World is an essential promoter of the application of VR technology in history and culture. FHW researches and transmits history and culture in the context of cultural heritage by exhibiting Greek sites with the latest technology and resources. They have developed two immersive VR systems where only ten or fewer students daily can experience the VR program [18]. Scholars Rasheed et al. found that in areas with historical resources, what is presented in regular history classrooms with pictures and videos can differ from what students visit, leading to a disconnect between the classroom and reality. This shortcoming led to a decline in student interest in history classes. They developed a VR application through panoramic videography. A panoramic view of a historical site was presented in this application. The experiment's final results were that the students who participated in the VR instruction performed significantly better in the test than those who were taught conventionally. Some students reported that using VR equipment made them uncomfortable and scared [19]. One of the main advantages of implementing VR in education is that it provides an immersive and engaging learning experience. VR can take learners to places that are difficult to access, such as historical sites.

VR historical sites respond to the development of the technology and information age, fulfill the national demand for cultural heritage transmission and protection, and are a valuable presentation of the nation's humanities, science, and history. Educators combine VR historical monuments and education, expanding the way of history classroom teaching, increasing the interest and interactivity of the classroom, and students are more able to appreciate the charm and value of historical monuments.

We found some things that could be improved based on the scholars' exploration of VR historical sites and modern history education. The number of existing historical sites is enormous and needs to be more systematic. For learners, the understanding of a period of history needs to be comprehensive and in chronological order. Most of the existing VR historical sites are isolated and not well linked to other sites from the same event. Teaching with fragmented VR monuments would result in poorly constructed knowledge of the historical event and poor student learning outcomes.

2.2 Theoretical Support

In the following, we will give some theories to support the basis of this educational model inquiry, and these theories are also used as the basis of assessment when carrying out the work.

Gamified learning has become an essential trend in the development of educational models in recent years. Its purpose is to improve students' participation and interactivity in the classroom [20]. VR history classroom overcomes the limitations of traditional history classes and learns historical knowledge by simulating the scenes of honest sites. VR sites with a sense of realism can enjoy students' senses and give them an unforgettable learning experience [21].

Cognitive load theory is a theoretical framework for optimizing learners' working memory capacity by managing cognitive load in the learning process. Cognitive load theory categorizes cognitive load into three types: intrinsic, extrinsic, and related. Through the definition of cognitive load, educators need to reduce intrinsic and extrinsic conformity and increase relevant load [22]. VR may impose a cognitive load on learners due to its technological characteristics. In VR modern historical sites education, we need to eliminate unnecessary information in the VR system and simplify the operation to reduce the cognitive load the VR system brings. In addition, to increase the learners' relevant load, it is also necessary to closely integrate the VR system with the learning materials to increase the learning experience. The role of the educator in this model is also vital, active interaction and timely feedback from the learners can make the teacher pay attention to their compliance, and appropriate management and answering of questions can also increase the load of the learners [23].

3 System Design

In our current inquiry, we combine modern history education and VR historical sites, and screen and integrate historical sites distributed in various regions according to the temporal and spatial order of historical events, and apply them to the history classroom. For better learning effect, we connect the fragmented historical relics and historical events, and temporally and spatially make a complete VR modern history navigation (see Fig. 1). Based on the above theory, we need to follow four principles when designing this model: simple interaction, comprehensive display, and prioritized user experience. Based on the consideration of cost and learner acceptance, we put the host body of VR relics on the webpage, the presentation mode is spherical panorama, and the interaction mode is mouse click. We need to contact the producers of the existing VR relics on the web to obtain the copyright, and for the VR relics that have not been developed in the historical events, we need to produce them by ourselves. On the technical level, for the user's spatial experience to be close to the physical spatial characteristics of the actual ruins, we need to conduct field visits to the ruins and image acquisition of the spatial data of the ruins: through photographic and measurement technologies, such as panoramic photography, photogrammetry, and obtaining the copyright of some existing panoramic ruins materials. In order to enhance the historical immersion of the learners, we will add binaural audio to the VR monuments to increase the spatial experience of the learners. We can ask the local residents of the relics to tell a historical story in dialect and insert it into the VR relics; the background music adopts the music that fits the historical events; and we can also add some movie soundtracks to resonate with students [24]. In order to increase the learners' game experience, we set the students' identity as soldiers in the historical events before entering the relic interface.

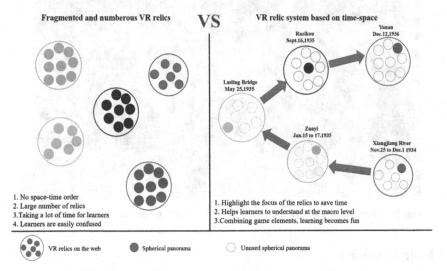

Fig. 1. System design for integrating fragmented VR relics

In order to tell a complete historical story based on VR relics, we need to collect historical relics that appear in historical events. Our key to designing this model is to utilize the VR relics to tell a good story of a historical event and increase students' retention of information as much as possible. In order to save time and cost and reduce students' cognitive load, we will filter out some of the historical relics in our design and focus on the scenes where essential events occurred or have educational significance. In addition, a navigation map is added to the interactive interface of the relics: the navigation routes are based on the spatial and temporal order of the relics that appeared in the historical events. The design of the navigation interface is different from the traditional map navigation style, and historical elements are added to the navigation map to enrich the interaction interface in the VR relic (see Fig. 2).

A complete education of modern history in VR monuments also requires educators to be managers; a digital classroom lacking management will make learning entertaining. The teacher needs to manage the students while they are visiting the VR historical site, monitor the students' concentration on history learning, and be available to answer their questions about their learning and the system's operation. At the end of the class, the teacher needs to test and question the students about the historical events that appeared in the VR classroom. At the same time, the teacher needs to collect the students' comments and questions about the VR classroom after the class and provide timely feedback.

Fig. 2. Navigating the route to the VR historical sites at the Zunyi Conference site

4   User Feedback

We use a crucial modern history event in China, the Long March, to build a VR modern history site education system. The research team completed the production of the system in May 2023. We recruited 30 students taking modern history courses and four modern history teachers as our experimental subjects. Semi-structured interviews were conducted with the participating students and teachers in June.

The researcher selected the conversations of some of the interviewees and analyzed the results of the interviews with the content analysis method as follows:

1. VR Embodied Learning Stimulates Students' Interest in Learning

   Of the 30 students who participated in the experiment, all were very interested in this new way of teaching. Student F said, "It is my first time learning in such a novel way in the classroom, and I feel very interested." The VR technology made students feel more immersed in historical events, and this kind of embodied learning motivated them to learn. Student O stated, "VR historical sites bring me an experience of historical games, which I have never had in a history class." As the theoretical support of this study, the gamification theory, students interact with historical events through VR relics to get multi-sensory engagement in the classroom, which further allows them to experience the fun of learning.

2. VR immersive learning builds students' sense of historical identity

   According to our statistics, 80% of the students think that the traditional, modern history classroom is difficult to bring them the shock of historical events. After this experiment, 28 out of 30 students thought our system made them feel the hardship of the Long March event. Student B said, "I did not feel anything about the ruins in the Long March when I saw them in photos. When I viewed them in this system, I felt how difficult the Long March was." By building up a framework of historical events, this system brings more historical resonance to students than stand-alone relics or separate explanations of historical events. Another student, G, also said, "I was impressed by the relics presented by the system, and the Long March brought me a strong sense of impact." The 3D relics VR presents will be more vivid than ordinary pictures and videos, so presenting historical events will bring shock and resonance to students' minds.

3. Students construct overall cognition of historical events through spatiotemporal clues

This study reduces the external load on students by integrating fragmented VR relics under the guidance of cognitive load theory. We conducted an interview test with students at the end of the experiment about their overall knowledge of the Long March event. The results showed that 25 out of 30 students could retell the Long March event in a complete and organized manner. Student L said, "I think history classes are difficult, and this is the first time I could understand a historical event in its entirety." The historical knowledge learned in ordinary classrooms needs to be more cohesive, and it is difficult for them to construct a historical framework in their minds. Student C said, "What I learned about history before was fragmented, but this VR learning allowed me to make sense of the chronological and spatial order of the Long March events." In our VR system, the key is to give students a historical travel-like experience through spatial and temporal clues. This experience can satisfy students' need to understand historical events completely.

4. Efficient Learning Reduces the Burden of Classwork on Students and Teachers

We selected five students as a comparison group and asked them to browse the general VR relics first and then the relics of our system. We gave them the original links to the VR relics of the Long March event and other VR relics about the Long March on the Internet and asked them to browse and time them. The results showed that the average time spent browsing the general VR relics of the Long March was 1h26min, and the average time spent by students browsing the system was 7min. We know from interviewing the students in the comparison group that, although VR can bring an immersive learning experience to the students if the learning is not systematized, it will only add to their external and internal cognitive load, which is not helpful to the learning effect. K, a student who participated in the comparison group, said, "After browsing the VR system, I quickly figured out the whole event." Systematized VR relics can make learning more efficient, and students are happy to participate in this kind of learning that produces results quickly. Student M said, "I didn't realize that I could learn about a historical event with a few clicks of the mouse, and I was able to memorize the place and time of the event in a short period of time." For teachers, the learning system also reduces the burden of lesson planning. Several teachers said that VR relics are great educational tools, but due to the sheer number of online relics, they would need help applying them in class. Teacher A said, "If relics and historical event frameworks can be presented quickly through a VR system, it can make classroom learning efficient." The students accomplished this event efficiently in a very short learning time, precisely what this system is trying to achieve.

5 Discussion

Based on the test results and students' feedback, we learned that these VR relics of history education will stimulate students' interest in learning history, and the learning effect is better than in traditional history classrooms. There are still some things that could be improved in this study; firstly, students' immersive experience and learning effect may be inferior in this system compared with the classroom using VR equipment. In addition, not all historical events can be taught with VR relics, historical events have complexity, and the location of the events is difficult to quantify, which leads to the scope of its application only in a part of historical events with relics, so the scope of application of this model needs to be further explored and improved. The system is mainly used in modern history education; the key to modern history education is to cultivate students' humanistic literacy; we are still determining whether the system can improve learners' humanistic literacy in a short time. The education of VR modern historical relics adapts to the needs of classroom digitization and learner's subjectivization; due to the high cost of its use, VR technology is still a " luxury." Virtual Reality technology also needs continuous breakthroughs and innovations for more applications and lower costs in the field of education. VR education of modern historical legacy is a multidisciplinary linkage education model in which educators must optimize it by actively interacting with students and continuously discovering and solving problems.

Acknowledgments. The research was sponsored by The National Social Science Fund of China, project number: 21VSZ1242;

The New Liberal Arts Fund of the University of Science and Technology of China, project number: FSSF-A-230311;

The Center for Marxism and Contemporary Chinese Studies, University of Science and Technology of China, project number: 2021YJZX007YB;

The Institute of Party Building and Ideological and Political Work of the University of Science and Technology of China (2021–2022).

References

1. Kamińska, D., et al.: Virtual reality and its applications in education: survey. Information 10(10), 318 (2019)
2. Zhang, D., et al.: Instructional video in e-learning: assessing the impact of interactive video on learning effectiveness. Inf. Manag. 43(1), 15–27 (2006)
3. Castillo, H.G.C.: The triple helix model as a means for university-business linkage. Natl. J. Adm. 1(1), 85–94 (2010)
4. Rojas-Sánchez, M.A., Palos-Sánchez, P.R., Folgado-Fernández, J.A.: Systematic literature review and bibliometric analysis on virtual reality and education. Educ. Inf. Technol. 28(1), 155–192 (2023)
5. Baidoo-Anu, D., Ansah, L.O.: Education in the era of generative artificial intelligence (AI): understanding the potential benefits of ChatGPT in promoting teaching and learning. SSRN 4337484 (2023)
6. Guttentag, D.A.: Virtual reality: applications and implications for tourism. Tour. Manag. 31(5), 637–651 (2010)

7. Virtual LEGOs: Incorporating Minecraft into the art education curriculum. Alexandra Overby, Brian L. Jones. Art Educ. (1) (2015)

8. Basu, A., Johnsen, K.: Ubiquitous virtual reality 'To-Go'. In: 2014 IEEE Virtual Reality (VR). IEEE (2014)

9. 鲁勇 中国近代史教育对高校人文教育的促进启示. 现代商贸工业 44(07), 156–158 (2023)

10. 董悦 中国近代史教育在高职院校人文素质教育中的作用研究. 辽宁省交通高等专科学校学报 17(04), 61–63 (2015)

11. 王孝俊 简论历史教育在大学生人文素质培养中的作用. 中国德育 (04), 35–38 (2006)

12. Veltman, K.H.: Challenges for ICT/UCT applications in cultural heritage. In: Carreras, C. (ed.) ICT and Heritage (2005). Online dossie

13. 赵振工 利用当地历史资源提高学生历史素养. 天津教育 653(20), 31–33 (2021)

14. Mosaker, L.: Visualising historical knowledge using virtual reality technology. Digit. Creat. 12(1), 15–25 (2001)

15. Allen, P.K., Troccoli, A., Smith, B., Murray, S., Stamos, I., Leordeanu, M.: New methods for digital modeling of historic sites. IEEE Comput. Graph. Appl. 23(6), 32–41 (2003)

16. 王秀绒 试论中国近代史教学中的思想道德教育. 大学教育 1(06), 62–63 (2012)

17. 智日勤 近代史教育与民族精神培育. 科教导刊(中旬刊) 95(16), 81+83 (2011)

18. Roussou, M.: Immersive interactive virtual reality in the museum. In: Proceedings of TiLE (Trends in Leisure Entertainment) (2001)

19. Rasheed, F., Onkar, P., Narula, M.: Immersive virtual reality to enhance the spatial awareness of students. In: Proceedings of the 7th Indian Conference on Human-Computer Interaction, pp. 154–160 (2015)

20. Marougkas, A., et al.: Virtual reality in education: a review of learning theories, approaches and methodologies for the last decade. Electronics 12(13), 2832 (2023)

21. Akman, E., Çakır, R.: Pupils' opinions on an educational virtual reality game in terms of flow experience. Int. J. Emerg. Technol. Learn. 14(15) (2019)

22. Parmar, D., et al.: A comparative evaluation of viewing metaphors on psychophysical skills education in an interactive virtual environment. Virtual Real. 20, 141–157 (2016)

23. Sweller, J.: Cognitive Load Theory. Psychology of Learning and Motivation, vol. 55, pp. 37–76. Academic Press (2011)

24. Schrier, K.L.: Revolutionizing History Education: Using Augmented Reality Games to Teach Histories. Massachusetts Institute of Technology, Department of Comparative Media Studies (2005)

The Application of "Panoramic VR Fusion Animation Reproduction" of Historical Sites in Modern History Education Under the Multimodal Learning Theory

Yanxiang Zhang[✉] and Ke Wang

University of Science and Technology of China, Jinzhai Road, Baohe District, Hefei, Anhui, China
petrel@ustc.edu.cn

Abstract. Historical relics are an essential carrier of historical education, providing evidence for historical facts. There are many historical relics from modern history that still exist today, but they are distributed in different regions, making it costly to visit them personally. Through VR technology, historical relics can be viewed without having to be physically present, and VR is widely used in VR historical patriotic education. Although many historical relics have VR recordings, they only provide a 360° physical space restoration. Matching animation scenes to 360° panoramic photos can integrate animated scenes into real space, presenting a more intuitive, vivid, and immersive reproduction of historical events. In this study, a representative scene from the "Pursuing the Long March Memories" of the Communist Youth League Central Committee's "Panoramic VR Animation Re-enactment" was selected, and four groups of 360° panoramic VR photo scenes were matched. Through Emotiv Epoc X monitoring of the viewer's brain waves of θ waves, α waves, and β waves. Exploring the cognitive effects of the "panoramic VR fusion animation" learning model on learning in history education under the multimodal learning theory. It was found that when viewers watched panoramic films with animation effects, their brainwave data showed a more active state. This could better stimulate thinking, focus attention, and reduce fatigue, indicating the feasibility of using panoramic VR with animated re-enactment integration for learning and cognitive effects in history. This research extends and enriches the model of multimodal learning in VR.

Keywords: VR · Historical Relics · Brainwave

1 Research Background

Historic sites are essential carriers of history education, reflecting historical events and facts visually, leading us into history, feeling history, and allowing us to understand the past better and grasp today. As a significant historical period, many historical relics have survived. These historical relics are not only buildings, relics, and sites but also evidence of history and historical and cultural heritage [1]. Visiting these historical sites plays a

L. T. De Paolis et al. (Eds.): XR Salento 2023, LNCS 14219, pp. 322–338, 2023.
https://doi.org/10.1007/978-3-031-43404-4_21

vital role in citizens' patriotic consciousness and emotional identity of national concepts, and we can better understand the political, economic, cultural, and social background of the society at that time so that we can better understand historical events and facts, cultivate citizens' love for the motherland and national pride, and form correct historical concepts and cultural self-confidence [2].

Many historical sites are located in different geographical areas, and the time, energy, and financial costs of visiting these historical sites are high [3]. To overcome these difficulties, VR technology is gradually being widely used in historical site preservation and history education [4].

With VR technology, we can view historical sites without having to be physically present, enhancing our perception of historical events and facts; for example, specific VR devices such as Oculus Quest and HTC Vive Focus series independent VR headsets and mobile VR headsets such as Samsung Gear VR are used to watch and learn some historical sites with a sense of being present. VR historical site presentation technology can simulate the live environment, allowing us to immerse ourselves in the character- istics of historical events and buildings and visit historical sites with three-dimensional panoramic views through VR technology, such as visiting various national museums and strolling through some well-known historical, scenic spots, to understand the back- ground of historical events and knowledge of related cultural relics [5]. Moreover, VR technology not only provides a realistic visiting experience but can also provide learners with a multidimensional learning approach, where learners can independently choose different perspectives to observe historical building features or use VR technology to reconstruct the historical backgrounds of yesteryear, travel through time, and understand historical rituals and culture [6]. Through VR technology, learners are not only closely exposed to history but also enhance learner engagement and improve learning efficiency.

Although VR technology can record the primary forms of historical sites and present 3D models in various ways, many VR presentations are limited to 360° restoration of physical space only. Such presentations make it difficult for learners to gain a sense of historical events and lack intuitive, vivid, and immersive feelings and experiences to truly understand the occurrence of events, people, and so on [7].

Inspired by the multimodal learning theory, in order to improve the effectiveness of the use of VR historical sites, it is necessary to change the boring learning situation caused by the use of a single modality in history education in the past, and make some improvements and innovations to it. This study tries to introduce new media modalities to improve the effect of history learning [8].

To enhance the use of VR historical sites, some improvements and innovations need to be made. One practical and innovative way to create a more immersive and interactive learning experience of historical and cultural heritage is to combine VR technology with other technologies for 360° panoramic moving match mover technologies such as Imagineer Systems Mocha VR, which can accurately match objects in virtual scenes with objects in real space matches, making the integration of animated scenes and realistic scenes more natural and realistic [9]. Mobile matching for panoramic VR can seamlessly integrate the simulated presentation of historical figures and events into VR images, presenting an intuitive, vivid, and immersive recreation of historical scenes. As shown in Fig. 1, this method can help people better understand historical events and scenes, reproduce human history more realistically, and realize the multidimensional expansion of VR reproduction history from space to time, characters, events, and interactions.

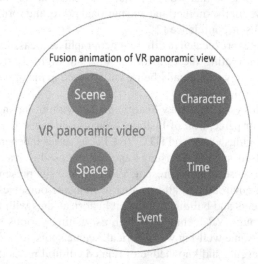

Fig. 1. Multidimensional Elements of Panoramic VR Fusion Animation.

Panoramic VR fusion animation simulation of historical education VR film " Pursuing the Long March Memories" is launched by the Central Committee of the Communist Youth League of China featuring "panoramic VR fusion animation simulation" VR film, which allows viewers to personally experience and feel the magnificent journey of the Long March of the Chinese Workers and Peasants Red Army. The VR film is divided into ten chapters, presenting various scenes of the 25,000-mile Long March through virtual reality technology, including physical scenes of historical relics such as meadows, river valleys, mountains, and forest areas, and seamlessly integrating animated images of historical figures and events into the panoramic VR screen based on mobile match mover technology. Through the panoramic VR mode of "Pursuing the Long March Memories," viewers can immerse themselves in the magnificent scenery of standing on a cliff overlooking the march of the Long March team or walk into the guerrilla trenches on the Grassland to feel the spirit of the arduous Long March. At the same time, "Pursuing the Long March Memories" is also equipped with professional audio effects, bringing the audience ultimately into the historical scene and comprehending the inner meaning and value of the Long March spirit.

2   Literature Review

In recent years, with the rapid development of VR technology, the application of 360-degree VR technology in historical education has attracted increasing attention. For instance, Song et al. (2020) studied how to use 360-degree VR technology to provide interactive historical exhibitions. Using VR technology, users can intuitively understand historical relics and scenes and engage in interactive operations, effectively improving user participation and learning effects [10]. Yu et al. (2018) proposed a teaching design model that uses 360-degree VR technology to improve history teaching. The model divides students into three learning stages: perceptual recognition, experiential cognition, and abstract cognition. Presenting historical scenes through 360-degree VR technology enhances student involvement and interest [11]. Swafford and Drechsler (2017) studied how to use VR technology to protect historical heritage. They proposed a new virtual reality system that uses 360-degree VR technology to present historical buildings and scenes, which helps maintain and restore historical relics and provides better resources and tools for researchers and educators [12]. Jang and Kim (2018) used Vatican's Borgia Apartment as an example and presented it in a VR scene. They use 360-degree VR technology to allow users to tour a virtual scene and understand its history, helping to improve students' understanding and interest in history [13]. Morris et al. (2019) used 360-degree video technology to support history teaching to provide teachers with a more vivid and intuitive resource to teach history. Presenting historical scenes and events through 360-degree video technology enhances students' visual experience and interaction and promotes their understanding and interest in history [14].

Previously, the application of VR technology to historical relics in historical education mainly focused on recording and reproduction, and this application model often lacks the presentation of historical figures and events, making it difficult for people to establish a sense of immersion and cognition about historical figures and events. However, there is a lack of research on the educational effect of novel VR content, such as panoramic VR fusion animation simulation.

Multimodal learning usually includes visual-verbal modality, visual-audio modality, visual-depth modality, visual-motor modality, etc. The application of VR for history education can provide users with a more integrated and enriched sensory experience through the combination of multimodal learning modalities to better immerse them in the virtual reality environment [15].

In the process of historical development, the trend of single learning modality to multimodal evolution is often reflected. Exploring multimodal learning as applied to history education, the following three modalities may exist in VR history education. The first is a traditional VR panoramic movie, the second is a VR movie matched with related animation videos but independent of each other, and the third is a VR movie in which the animation related to the theme is deeply integrated through mobile matching technology. In contrast, the first independent VR film does not have the advantage of multimodal learning; the second mode is not strictly multimodal integration, the animation and VR experience is isolated and fragmented, multimodality is interrupted; while the third mode by adding animation effects in the traditional VR film to make the presentation content more vivid, is the simultaneous role of multiple senses of the immersive and embodied contact, can mobilize and utilize multiple sensory modalities. Mobilize and utilize multiple sensory modalities to achieve the effect of $1 + 1 > 2$ for history learning [16]. The learning mode of panoramic VR fused with animation has few related studies and reports, so the object of our study is more novel.

In this paper, we will take the VR movie "Pursuing the Long March Memories" featuring "panoramic VR fused with animation simulation" as a case study, and explore the cognitive effect of the "panoramic VR fused with animation" learning mode in history education under the theory of multimodal learning, with a view to enhancing people's understanding of the role of this new VR multimodal learning mode in history education. In order to improve people's understanding of the role of this new VR multimodal learning mode in history education, and further expand and enrich the application of multimodal learning in VR.

3   Research Methodology

Based on the three modalities of VR application to history education described above, the first traditional mode and the third mature multimodal learning mode, i.e., the traditional VR panoramic movie and the panoramic VR fusion animation, were selected for comparison, to test the perceived effect of multimodal learning scenarios on history learning.

Experimental Environment: For this study, we selected representative scenes from the VR interactive work "Pursuing the Long March Memories" and gathered matching 360-degree panoramic VR photo scenes. Viewers watched the video and its comparison group by manipulating the panoramic mode. We used the Emotiv Epoc X device to monitor the average values of viewers' brainwave theta waves, alpha waves, and beta waves to conduct a comparative analysis of the cognitive validity of VR.

For this study, we selected four representative scenes from "Pursuing the Long March Memories": Luding Bridge, Taiping Ferry, the Grassland Pass, and the Meeting Point

Control Film				
Scene	Luding Bridge	Taiping Ferry	Crossing of the Grassland	The Huishimen Gate
360° panoramic images				
"Pursuing the Long March Memories"				
Animation feature	Highly restore the scene of Luding Bridge, reproduce the Red Army soldiers to deal with the rapids, and pressure waves, hiding under the scene details.	Restore the orderly command of the Red Army, the blood boat close-up, and the use of 3D technology to present historical figures such as Zhu De, Liu Bocheng, and other images vividly.	Vividly restore the tragic scenes of Red Army soldiers falling to the ground, unable to move forward, helping each other, and trudging horses in the rainstorm, presenting a more three-dimensional and rich historical scene.	Multiple perspectives and scenes have been set up, including soldiers waving flags in the meeting hall upstairs, allowing the images of critical revolutionary leaders such as Mao Zedong, Zhou Enlai, and Zhu De to be integrated into the VR scenes.

Fig. 2. An overview of the four groups of scenes selected

Gate, as shown in Fig. 2. These four scenes are indispensable landmarks in the history of the Chinese Workers' and Peasants' Red Army's Long March.

Luding Bridge: Luding Bridge is located in Luding County, Sichuan Province. It was a virtual battlefield for the Chinese Workers' and Peasants' Red Army during the Long March. In May 1935, when the Red Army arrived at Luding Bridge, it encountered a heavy siege. However, with the close cooperation of the entire army, they ultimately broke through the enemy's defense and achieved victory, marking the departure of the Chinese Workers' and Peasants' Red Army from Sichuan [17].

The fragment of Luding Bridge in "Pursuing the Long March Memories" is shown in Fig. 3, and the 360° panoramic image segment is shown in Fig. 4.

Regarding the VR animation features of Luding Bridge in "Pursuing the Long March Memories," there are several aspects:

Realistic perspective: The VR animation scene highly reproduces the on-site situation of Luding Bridge, enabling users to experience the arduous journey of the Red Army soldiers crossing Luding Bridge and the Jinsha River in a virtual environment. At the same time, the perspective of the VR animation is also very realistic, allowing users to freely observe various scenes and details of soldiers fighting as they control their movements, enhancing interactivity and immersion.

Situation restoration: The VR animation includes scenes such as crossing the Luding Bridge, attacking and defending the Luding Bridge and the Red Army taking the Luding Bridge under heavy gunfire, restoring the authenticity of historical events. For example, in the scene of crossing the Luding Bridge, the VR animation accurately depicts the details of Red Army soldiers coping with rapid currents and waves and hiding underneath the bridge, enhancing the authenticity of history.

Fig. 3. Selected Clip of Luding Bridge from "Pursuing the Long March Memories."

Taiping Ferry: Taiping Ferry, located in Sichuan's Daxian County, is a famous crossing in the Long March of the Chinese Workers and Peasants Red Army. On June 14, 1935, the Red Army crossed the river at Taiping Ferry, escaped the encirclement and pursuit of Chiang Kai-shek's army, and fought the historically famous Taiping Battle here [18].

Fig. 4. Selected panoramic 360° image of the Luding Bridge.

The segment of Taiping Ferry in "Pursuing the Long March Memories" is shown in Fig. 5, and the 360° panoramic picture segment is shown in Fig. 6.

In VR "Pursuing the Long March Memories," the VR animation features for the selected Taiping Ferry mainly include the following aspects:

Animation restoration of historical facts: In the Taiping crossing scene, the animation restores the process of the Red Army's crossing, the road across the river is long and dangerous, and the clip adds a close-up scene of the Red Army's orderly command, courageous advance, and blood crossing despite sacrifice, allowing the audience to feel more deeply the Red Army's departure to the sun and the rampant enemy, increasing the battle tension and cruelty of the historical event and reproducing the Red Army's fighting spirit of the four crossings of the Red River.

3D technology presents historical figures: VR animation uses 3D technology to present historical figures such as Zhu De, Liu Bo Cheng, Ye Ting, and Peng De Huai in a vivid and very realistic way, reproducing historical figures in VR animation and inspiring viewers' remembrance and memories of historical figures.

Fig. 5. Selecting the footage of Taiping Ferry of "Pursuing the Long March Memories"

Fig. 6. Selected panoramic 360° image of Taiping Ferry

Perilous crossing of the Grassland: Perilous crossing of the Grassland, located near Xichang City in Sichuan Province, is a hazardous section of the Long March of the Chinese Workers and Peasants Red Army. While passing through the Grassland, the Red Army faced many difficulties, such as bad weather, lack of food and grass, and challenging pace. However, the Red Army commanders held the indomitable spirit and inflexible will and finally succeeded in passing through the Grassland. This is also an important symbol in the history of the Long March of the Chinese Workers and Peasants Red Army [19].

The footage of crossing the Grassland is shown in Fig. 7 in "Pursuing the Long March Memories," the 360° panoramic picture segment is shown in Fig. 8.

In the VR "Pursuing the Long March Memories," the VR animation features for the selected perilous crossing of the Grassland mainly include the following aspects: the atmosphere of the problematic Long March is reproduced: through the VR animation form, some Red Army soldiers wearing uniforms are presented in the picture, they stride forward, against the fierce wind, sweeping around vigilantly with their guns, covered

Fig. 7. Selecting the footage of "Pursuing the Long March Memories"

with mud and water. This way of presentation allows the audience to feel the hardship of the white terror and the harsh reality of the Red Army soldiers running through the grass at that time.

Vivid restoration of historical facts: The film restores historical phenomena as real-istically and vividly as possible through VR animation, such as the scene of Red Army soldiers helping each other in the dangerous swampy meadow, the sad sacrificial scene of Red Army soldiers falling on the grass and unable to move forward, and the vigilant attitude of soldiers holding horses while trudging through the storm. These animation effects cleverly combine static grass and real vivid historical situations, presenting the audience with a more three-dimensional, rich history of the dangerous crossing of the grass.

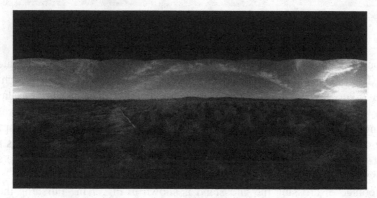

Fig. 8. Select the panoramic 360° image of the dangerous crossing of the Grassland.

Huishimen: Located in the southwest of Langzhong City, Sichuan Province, Huishi-men is a magnificent pass on the Red Army's Long March and where Mao Zedong, Zhou Enlai, Zhu De, and others met. Upon arriving at the rendezvous gate, Mao Zedong famously called out, "Our ranks are invincible, despite this exhaustion!" which also marked a new stage in the victory of the Long March of the Chinese Workers and Peasants Red Army [20].

The segment of Huishimen Gate in "Pursuing the Long March Memories" is shown in Fig. 9, and the segment of the 360° panoramic picture is shown in Fig. 10.

In VR "Pursuing the Long March Memories," the VR animation features for the selected rendezvous gate mainly include the following aspects:

Multiscene rendering atmosphere: VR animation for the critical moment of the ren-dezvous gate set up several perspectives and scenes; for example, in the rendezvous, upstairs gathered the excited soldiers waving flags, downstairs celebrating the victory, shouting and cheering people, the audience can immerse themselves in the joy and excitement of the people at that time, the animation set up by these stars and fires gradu-ally coalesce and grow the process, so that the audience can more deeply appreciate The animation sets up the process of the gradual coalescence of these stars and fires, allowing the audience to more deeply appreciate the joy and difficulty of the Long March victory.

3D technology presents historical figures: the historical figures of VR animation apply 3D technology to present a very high degree of realism so that the images of Mao Zedong, Zhou Enlai, Zhu De, and other critical revolutionary leaders are seamlessly integrated into the VR scenes. Users roam in the virtual scene of the meeting gate, strengthening their perception of historical figures and bringing the audience into the present moment of critical historical events, immerse themselves in the scene and genuinely feel the warm atmosphere of people's mood at that time and the power of unremitting pursuit of faith.

Fig. 9. Selecting the footage of the Huishimen Gate of "Pursuing the Long March Memories"

Fig. 10. Selecting 360° panoramic images of the Huishimen Gate

Experimental process: Three test subjects were recruited for this study, downloaded the EmotivPRO software, plugged the U disk end of the Emotiv Epoc X instrument into the computer, soaked the 16 induction felts with saline, and put them into the card position of the instrument, then put the instrument on the test subject's head, opened the EmotivPRO software, adjusted the position of the 16 induction felts according to the software prompts, and when the device showed the real-time dynamics of the test subject's brain waves at different sensing locations, entered the account number to start data acquisition. The Emotiv Epoc X device was used to collect the EEG alpha, beta, and theta wave data of the test subjects watching different groups of movies and to maintain a quiet environment in a closed room while watching the movies. The test subjects manipulated the mouse to watch the images, and their brain waves were recorded in EmotivPRO software. After the experiment, it was found that the fluctuations of α-wave, β-wave, and theta-wave EEG data of each group were consistent, and the average value was taken for data analysis.

4 Research Results

The fluctuations of EEG alpha, beta, and theta wave data presented by the EmotivPRO software of the three test subjects were consistent. The mean value of the theta wave of the selected fragment images of VR "Pursuing the Long March Memories" was lower than that of the panoramic 360° images, and the mean value of the alpha and beta waves of the selected fragment images of VR "Pursuing the Long March Memories" was higher than that of the panoramic 360° images. The following is a set of data averages for the detailed analysis of the brain wave data and presentation results.

Luting Bridge
Panoramic 360° images: theta waves many times to 10, once as high as 30, alpha and beta waves mean values 1–2, as shown in Fig. 11;

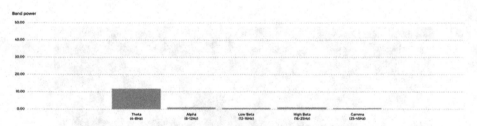

Fig. 11. Brainwave data chart for the Luding Bridge VR panoramic 360° images.

VR animation of "Pursuing the Long March Memories": theta waves below 10, beta waves mean value 2–4, as shown in Fig. 12;

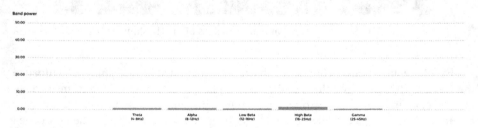

Fig. 12. Brainwave data chart for the Luding Bridge VR animation of "Pursuing the Long March Memories."

Taiping Ferry
Panoramic 360° images: theta waves mean 5, alpha waves many times to 15, beta waves mean 1–2, as shown in Fig. 13;

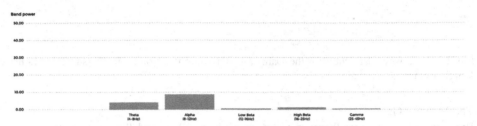

Fig. 13. Brainwave data chart for the Taiping Ferry Panoramic 360° image.

VR "Pursuing the Long March Memories" animation: theta wave mean value 3, alpha wave many times to 15, beta wave mean value 2–3, as shown in Fig. 14;

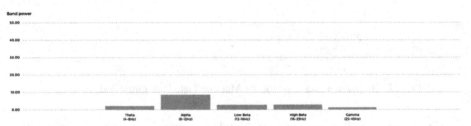

Fig. 14. Brainwave data chart for the Taiping Ferry VR "Pursuing the Long March Memories" animation.

Dangerous Crossing the Grass
Panoramic 360° images: theta waves reach 10 many times, once as high as 20; alpha and beta waves fluctuate less, occasionally reaching 3, as shown in Fig. 15;

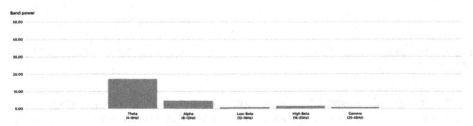

Fig. 15. Brainwave data chart for the Dangerous Crossing the Grass Panoramic 360° images.

VR "Pursuing the Long March Memories" animation: θ waves below 10, Low and High β waves to 5 many times, mean value 2–3, as shown in Fig. 16;

Fig. 16. Brainwave data chart for the Dangerous Crossing the Grass VR "Pursuing the Long March Memories" animation.

The Meeting Gate
Panoramic 360° image: θ waves twice as high as 20, α and β waves floating less, occasionally reaching 3, as shown in Fig. 17;

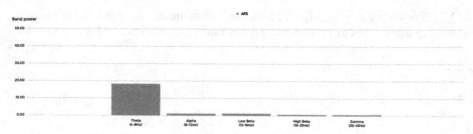

Fig. 17. Brainwave data chart for the Meeting Gate Panoramic 360° images.

VR animation of "Pursuing the Long March Memories": θ waves were below 10, α and β waves reached 5 several times, as shown in Fig. 18;

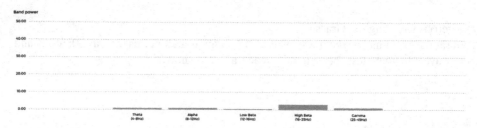

Fig. 18. Brainwave data chart for the Meeting Gate VR animation of "Pursuing the Long March Memories."

According to the image data, θ waves were generally higher when viewers watched the panoramic 360° images, with mean values above 10 and peaks reaching 30. α and β waves floated less and had smaller values, with mean values of 1–2. Viewers had lower θ waves, with mean values below 10, and α and β waves floated more, with mean values of 2–4, when they watched the VR "Pursuing the Long March Memories."

Brain waves are electrical activity generated in the cortical regions of the human brain, usually detected by EEG, and include theta, alpha, and beta waves [21].

Theta waves are brain waves generated by the brain with a frequency between 4 and 8 Hz. It is usually seen in light sleep, a relaxed state, and a hypnagogic state. In these states, the brain is in a relatively relaxed state, with slower thinking and less concentration but with some ability to associate and think creatively. Theta waves can help people reduce symptoms of anxiety, stress, and fatigue and promote physical relaxation [22].

Alpha waves are waves produced by the brain with a frequency between 8 and 14 Hz. It usually occurs during relaxed states, sitting quietly with eyes closed and doing deep relaxation exercises. In these states, the brain is in a relatively relaxed state, but the mind is more precise and able to focus. Alpha waves can help people relieve stress and anxiety and promote physical relaxation and mental balance [23].

Beta waves are waves produced by the brain with a frequency between 14 and 30 Hz. It usually occurs in states of high cognitive load, such as concentrated attention, thinking, analysis, and calculation. In these states, the brain is in relative arousal, with quick thinking and concentration. Beta waves can help people improve their cognitive abilities and enhance their work efficiency and learning ability. However, beta waves may also lead to stress and anxiety in a state of prolonged and sustained excitement [24].

According to the experimental data, when the viewer watches the panoramic 360° films, the θ wave is generally high, α wave and β wave value is low; when the viewer watching "Pursuing the Long March Memories," the θ wave is low, α wave and β wave mean value is high, combined with the different states represented by different brain waves described above, it can be found that The high theta wave means that the viewer has the better cognitive ability, improve work efficiency and learning ability when watching the history education film, so that he can better understand and absorb the history education knowledge, while the high α wave and β wave mean that the viewer's body and mind are in a relaxed rest and light sleep state when watching the history education film, and the cognitive and learning state is poor.

Therefore, for panoramic 360° films, when watching VR of historical sites with animation effects and multidimensional presentation of space, scenes, time, people, and events, it is more able to mobilize thinking, focus attention, reduce drowsiness, and enhance perception, cognition, and learning ability for historical events; when watching VR films without animation effects, which only achieve spatial and scene presentation, it is easier to when watching VR movies without animation effects, which only present space and scenes, it is easier to feel drowsy and have weaker concentration. The above EEG values illustrate the feasibility of the learning and cognitive effects of panoramic VR incorporating animation to reproduce history. The feasibility of the cognitive learning effect of the panoramic VR fusion animation reproduction of history was verified under EEG monitoring. Most traditional history courses use static text, images, and other multimedia languages, which often produce a sense of sleepiness and low learning efficiency among students. The new model of panoramic VR technology incorporating animation to recreate history not only presents the appearance of historical events but also allows students to closely observe every detail and angle of historical events, enhancing the interactivity and participation of learning and allowing students to understand and understand historical events more deeply.

Compared with VR panoramic films that merely reproduce static scenes, panoramic VR fusion animation can help students feel the heaviness and importance of historical events more intuitively and improve their awareness and motivation to learn about them. Panoramic VR fusion animation can reproduce historical events more intuitively and vividly and enhance users' participation and immersion through richer animation effects and interactive devices, making it easier for learners to understand and remember relevant knowledge, thus improving learning cognitive effects. In contrast, VR panoramic photos can only provide static scenes, which may have significant differences in visual perception and cannot accurately restore the whole process of historical events [25].

According to the experimental results, among the three modalities of VR applied to history education described above, the multimodal learning mode of panoramic VR fused with animation resulted in a better perception of the effect of history learning and a higher learning effect among the testers, which provides a new mode of validation as well as the possibility of exploring more modalities for multimodal learning. By integrating data from multiple sensory modalities, the history learning experience can be enriched and the understanding of historical events and culture can be enhanced, while providing more information and perspectives for historiographic research [26].

In the future, some research could attempt to elicit more modalities into the VR domain so that more modalities can act on history learning at the same time, further extending and enriching the application of multimodal learning in VR.

5   Analysis of Results

The viewers' brain wave data showed a more active state when watching the panoramic film with animation effect in VR, "Pursuing the Long March Memories," which is more capable of mobilizing thinking, concentrating attention, and reducing drowsiness compared with the VR panoramic pictures that can only present the physical environment, indicating that the VR reproduction of historical relics has a better communication effect when presenting the multidimensional expansion of space, scene, time, people and events, i.e., the panoramic VR fusion animation reproduction of history is feasible for learning cognitive effect.

Regarding space and scenes, the presentation of VR "Pursuing the Long March Memories" in terms of space mainly relies on the spatial mapping of VR technology to reproduce various areas in the Long March, including landmarks such as the mountains, streams, and bridges of Luding Bridge. The technology of VR allows viewers to achieve a 360-degree panoramic view, as well as a more substantial, more three-dimensional observation effect in specific scenes while creating a similar sense of reality for people and things [27].

In terms of time, VR "Pursuing the Long March Memories" can help viewers travel through time and space and immerse themselves in the backward flow of history. VR presentation allows viewers to experience simulated marches, battles, military operations, etc., restoring the light and the strange in the course of the Long March and allowing viewers to understand better the historical background of the Long March and the events that occurred during the Long March.

In terms of characters, VR "Pursuing the Long March Memories" uses virtual character technology to recreate the Red Army soldiers, revolutionary leaders, and other characters from the Long March. Through the presentation of virtual characters, viewers can learn about the historical figures at that time, observe from multiple angles, gain a deeper understanding of the characters' character, words, and deeds, recognize the environment and dangers that the characters faced during the Long March, and further comprehend the great spirit of the revolutionary forefathers who fought for the nation and humanity.

In terms of events, the presentation of VR "Pursuing the Long March Memories" can simulate a series of historical events that occurred during the Long March and provide the audience with participation and experience. For the coverage of a series of historical events, including the Luding Bridge incident, VR adopts a digital approach to restore the historical situation, allowing the audience to participate and experience first-hand, find some clues in the historical scenes, and reflect on the truth and importance of history [28].

Acknowledgments. The research was sponsored by The National Social Science Fund of China, project number: 21VSZ1242;

The New Liberal Arts Fund of the University of Science and Technology of China, project number: FSSF-A-230311;

The Center for Marxism and Contemporary Chinese Studies, University of Science and Technology of China, project number: 2021YJZX007YB;

The Institute of Party Building and Ideological and Political Work of the University of Science and Technology of China (2021–2022).

References

1. Tang, S.F.: Innovative path study on the integration of tourism, science and technology and education based on "Princess Wencheng's historical and cultural resources." Tibet Sci. Technol. **02**, 32–35 (2023). (in Chinese)
2. Zhang, Y.: The Significance of historical sites as carriers of historical education. J. Cult. Tour. Res. **14**(2), 56–64 (2021)
3. Mudička, Š., Kello, J.: Augmented reality in the dynamic world of virtual tourism. IOP Conf. Ser. Earth Environ. Sci. (1) (2021). https://doi.org/10.1088/1755-1315/942/1/012031
4. Zhao, W., Su, L., Dou, F.: Designing virtual reality based 3D modeling and interaction technologies for museums. Heliyon (6) (2023). https://doi.org/10.1016/J.HELIYON.2023.E16486
5. Li, H.: The Application of VR technology in historical site visits. Int. J. Virtual Real. Augment. Real. **3**(2), 45–56 (2019)
6. Ke, H.: Virtual reality technology for historical site learning: a review. Educ. Technol. Res. Dev. **68**(5), 2386–2408 (2020)
7. Wang, J.: The limitations of VR technology in historical site learning: a critique. Int. J. Emerg. Technol. Learn. **16**(3), 277–289 (2021)
8. Mou, Z.J.: Multimodal learning analytics: a new growth point for learning analytics research. Res. Electrochem. Educ. (05), 27–32+51 (2020). (in Chinese). https://doi.org/10.13811/j.cnki.eer.2020.05.004
9. Li, Y.: The application of match mover technology in VR historical site learning. J. Educ. Technol. Dev. Exch. **11**(2), 23–30 (2018)
10. Song, Y., Yang, L., Zhang, X., Tang, Y.: Using 360-degree virtual reality technology to provide interactive historical exhibitions. Int. J. Emerg. Technol. Learn. **15**(22), 4–16 (2020)

11. Yu, Z., Li, P., Wang, X.: A teaching design model based on 360-degree virtual reality technology for improving historical education. Educ. Technol. Res. Dev. **66**(6), 1579–1594 (2018)
12. Swafford, J., Drechsler, M.: Protecting cultural heritage: utilizing virtual reality to enhance cultural resource management. J. Archaeol. Sci. Rep. **12**, 292–301 (2017)
13. Jang, Y., Kim, Y.: Virtual reality in art education: a case study of the Borgia apartment in the Vatican. J. Educ. Technol. Soc. **21**(3), 119–130 (2018)
14. Morris, R., Bell, F., Cohen, J.: Using 360-degree video to support history teaching: a case study. Educ. Media Int. **56**(2), 112–126 (2019)
15. Baltrusaitis, T., Ahuja, C., Morency, L.P.: Multimodal machine learning: a survey and taxonomy. IEEE Trans. Pattern Anal. Mach. Intell. **PP**(99), 1 (2017)
16. Di Mitri, D., Schneider, J., Specht, M., Drachsler, H.: From signals to knowledge: a conceptual model for multimodal learning analytics. J. Comput. Assist. Learn. **34**(4), 338–349 (2018)
17. Wang, H.: Red spirit inheritance from Luding Bridge. Talent **14**, 13–15 (2021). (in Chinese)
18. Meng, D.-F., Yu, Y.-X.: Research on the types of red cultural resources and their protection in Sidu Chishui. In: Imago Wenchuang, no. 11, pp. 107–110 (2022). (in Chinese). https://doi.org/10.20024/j.cnki.cn42-1911/i.2022.11.034
19. Xinyuan, W.: The Red Army's Long March on the way through snowy mountains and grasslands for ideal belief education. J. Party Sch. CPC Shijiazhuang Munic. Comm. **07**, 28–31 (2016). (in Chinese). https://doi.org/10.13736/j.cnki.zgsjzswdxxb.2016.0080
20. Guo, X.: Tracing the footprints of the Long March of the Red Army No. 6 Into Huining Huishi City. Lit. Hist. Mon. **12**, 25–33 (2016). (in Chinese)
21. Sanei, S., Chambers, J.A. (eds.): EEG Signal Processing. Wiley, Hoboken (2013)
22. Addante, R.J., Mairy, Y., Rosemarie, V., Constance, G., Raechel, M.: Boosting brain waves improves memory. Front. Young Minds (2021). https://doi.org/10.3389/FRYM.2021.605677
23. Azhari, A., Susanto, A., Pranolo, A., Mao, Y.: Neural network classification of brainwave alpha signals in cognitive activities. Knowl. Eng. Data Sci. **2**(2), 47 (2019)
24. Niedermeyer, E.: The average EEG of the waking adult. In: Electroencephalography: Basic Principles, Clinical Applications, and Related Fields, pp. 117–154 (1997)
25. Liu, M., Huang, D., Zhao, X.: Immersive virtual reality in history education: a comparative study of low-cost VR and high-end VR. Sustainability **11**(17), 4761 (2019)
26. Liu, Q., Li, X.-J., Xie, K., Chang, Y.B., Zheng, X.X.: Development and prospects of empirical research on multimodal learning analytics. Res. Electrochem. Educ. (01), 71–78+85 (2022). (in Chinese). https://doi.org/10.13811/j.cnki.eer.2022.01.009
27. Yu, X., Zhu, Y.F.: Strategy of digital development of red history resources based on VR technology. J. Tianjin Sino-Ger. Univ. Appl. Sci. **03**, 59–64 (2023). https://doi.org/10.16350/j.cnki.cn12-1442/g4.2023.03.013.(inChinese)
28. Barbatsis, K., Economou, D., Papamagkana, I., Loukas, D.: 3D environments with games characteristics for teaching history: the VRLerna case study. In: ACM International Conference on Design of Communication; SIGDOC 2011. Informatics Teacher Regional Directorate of Primary and Secondary Education of Central Macedonia Greece; School of Electronics and Computer Science University of Westminster W1W 6UW, United Kingdom; Department of History and Archaeology Aristotle University (2012)

CaldanAugmenty – Augmented Reality and Serious Game App for Urban Cultural Heritage Learning

Irene Capecchi[1]([✉]), Iacopo Bernetti[1], Tommaso Borghini[2], and Alessio Caporali[2]

[1] Department of Agriculture, Food, Environment and Forestry (DAGRI),
University of Florence, Piazzale delle Cascine 18, Florence, Italy
{irene.capecchi,iacopo.bernetti}@unifi.it
[2] Department of Architecture, University of Florence, via della Mattonaia 14, Florence, Italy
{tommaso.borghini,alessio.caporali}@unifi.it

Abstract. This research presents CaldanAugmenty, a GPS-enabled geolocalised augmented reality (AR) application. Applied to the historic village of Caldana, the application uses serious gaming elements to create an interactive treasure hunt that offers users an enriching journey through the local history and architecture of the region.

CaldanAugmenty features a unique collection of 3D animated historical characters that bring the village's heritage to life. In the treasure hunt, players must find these characters by exploring the physical landscape of Caldana; these characters appear within the AR interface at various points of interest. These characters delve into the local history and architectural heritage of the village and challenge users with intriguing questions that provide elements for localization of the treasures.

CaldanAugmenty incorporates the village's hidden treasures into the virtual gameplay. These treasures are located in four real underground passages that are physically inaccessible for security reasons. The application incorporates these dungeons into a 'virtual tour' function, complete with immersive photo spheres. As users discover treasures during their virtual exploration, these are manifested in AR at the entrances to the real dungeons.

The effectiveness of the application as an interactive educational tool was evaluated using a comprehensive questionnaire administered to 79 middle school students. The questionnaire was designed to assess the dimensions of intrinsic motivation, ease of use and intention to use the application in the future. Preliminary results suggest that CaldanAugmenty is a highly engaging tool to facilitate learning about local history and heritage, with the majority of students expressing a high intention to continue using the application.

Keywords: Augmented reality · GPS · Serious game · Urban cultural heritage

1 Introduction

Cultural heritage can be defined as the legacy of physical artifacts (cultural goods) and intangible attributes of a group or society inherited from the past. Culture can promote economic growth (cultural tourism, crafts, food, etc.) and environmental sustainability

L. T. De Paolis et al. (Eds.): XR Salento 2023, LNCS 14219, pp. 339–349, 2023.
https://doi.org/10.1007/978-3-031-43404-4_22

(preservation of cultural and natural heritage). For this reason, it is essential to preserve cultural identities around the world because they can accelerate the transition to a more sustainable future. UNESCO [1] issued the Historic Urban Landscape Recommendation to recognize the living character of cities. This document expands the concept of cultural heritage; it takes into consideration the dynamic character of cities, recognizing them as living entities, not just expressions of their past. In short, cultural heritage is a permanent categorical construction that takes into account the past and the present.

There are already published works on the need to engage the public with cultural heritage using virtual reality (VR) or augmented reality (AR) experiences [2, 3]. There is also work [4, 5] examining how museums seek to engage and bridge the distance between the user and their cultural heritage, reinforcing the importance museums already place on building relationships between users, objects, and institutions.

At the time of this writing, there is enough literature examining how institutions are making use of AR, or the impact of experiences especially in museum visitation.

First, AR is enhancing the heritage and museum user experience by making it more engaging. This is based on articles in which immersive technologies seem to keep people's attention [6] and increase engagement. Second, AR allows the user to better remember the information conveyed. This is based on articles written on AR in teaching and learning [7] that conclude that AR improves users' retention of information. Therefore, this study aims to contribute to the field of museums and cultural heritage by analyzing the use, potential benefits, and constraints of AR outside the museum space.

Another important tool for the enhancement of cultural sites are serious games (SG), i.e., games designed for educational purposes; SG are applied in cultural sites through trivia, puzzles and mini-games for participation in interactive exhibitions, mobile applications and simulations of past events. The combination of Augmented Reality (AR) and digital cultural content has produced examples of cultural heritage recovery and revitalization around the world. Through AR, the user perceives the information of the visited place in a more real and interactive way [8]. Another interesting technological development for the revitalization of cultural sites is the combination of AR and Global Positioning System (GPS), which integrated have the ability to enhance the user's perception of reality by providing historical and architectural information related to specific places organized on a route [9].

To the authors' knowledge, there are currently few applications that combine GPS AR and SG for urban heritage revitalization, and these are generally aimed toward adult tourists [9] rather than young people.

The present research focused on evaluating the impact of a GPS and AR-based application for the promotion of visits to small historic villages aimed specifically at the alpha generation (AG) (those born after 2010). Visiting scientific, cultural and natural heritage tourist sites, such as museums, is an integral part of most Western childhood education [10], and AG represents a culturally and racially diverse demographic group of technology-savvy children. Therefore, the aim of this work is to test the hypothesis of whether the use of AR applications can increase the motivation of the AG to visit urban heritage centers by changing the way a technological present relates to the historical and architectural evidence of the past.

The rest of the paper has been divided into the following sections. Section 2 describes the study area and the design of the GPS+AR+SG application. Section 3 presents the questionnaire that is employed in the evaluation; finally, Sect. 4 presents the concluding remarks.

Learning methods can be distinguished between student-centered and teacher-centered methods [11]. Constructivism is a learning paradigm that is part of the student-centered methods and is based on the assumption that the subject constructs knowledge from his or her own experiences; knowledge is thus a dynamic quality built around discovery [12].

The use of games is the most natural way to achieve high levels of interactivity. Games are activities designed to engage users in an environment where they can learn with a learner-centered approach to education. The use of games in learning is widely demonstrated in the literature because they influence and increase learner engagement and motivation to learn in a more conscious and lifelong way [13].

2   Materials and Methods

The SG GPS-AR implementation process is divided into the following phases

1. Selection of the study area. The characteristics of the study area should be: (i) allow the implementation of appropriate storytelling; (ii) facilitate the use of the application by younger generations; (iii) allow transferability to other urban heritage sites.
2. Definition of the storyboard. In this phase, the cultural information to be provided, the village locations that will make up the route and the historical characters that will interact with the children were identified. The information was then organised into a series of screens that made up the SG storyboard.
3. Application design and development. In these stages of the application we create the 3D model and then develop the interactions.
4. Evaluation. Structuring and carrying out the questionnaire to determine the effectiveness of the application.

2.1   Study Area

The study area is the renaissance village of Caldana in Tuscany, Italy (Fig. 1). We have been chosen a small village for the development of this GPS-AR application compared to a big city, in order to understand if new technologies can help to make the educational offer of a lesser known artistic, urban and architectural heritage more attractive. In particular, the Caldana neighborhood was chosen because of its small and protected size that allows for safe experimentation and on the entire urban context.

The Renaissance village of Caldana in the province of Grosseto is an outstanding choice for an augmented reality (AR) application aimed at promoting urban cultural heritage. This stems from its rich cultural and architectural heritage, intricate urban design, compelling history, and potential for educational engagement. Caldana's unique urban organization, historical structures, and detailed design provide an ample educational material and engaging physical context. This can be enhanced by AR, offering an immersive way to narrate the town's history and architectural evolution. Moreover,

AR can be a powerful educational tool, especially for younger audiences, to kindle interest in history, architecture, and urban planning, demonstrating the importance of cultural preservation. Lastly, the accessibility provided by an AR application can expose this somewhat remote village to a global audience, fostering awareness of its cultural significance and making its rich heritage more accessible.

In addition, Caldana has urbanistic peculiarities: it is a Renaissance fortified village that is built above the walls, has a unified urban structure, and more has a labyrinth dungeon that cover much of the outer village. The dungeons for security reasons are not accessible, but they remain an immense heritage of the village that can be discovered and enjoyed thanks to these technologies. All these features, both functional and aesthetic, have made it the village of choice.

Fig. 1. Study area.

2.2 Storyboard Definition

The storyboard of the SG is based on the history of the three characters who built the village: marquis Marcello Agostini, who was commissioned by Cosimo I de Medici Grand Duke of Tuscany to build the village, his son Ippolito and his architect Lorenzo Pomarelli. The game is structured as a treasure hunt divided into the following steps (Fig. 2).

1. An introductory phase, where students find the initial game menu with 7 items, start game, continue game, characters, treasure map, locations, final prize, thanks. Items number 3, 4, 5 and 6 in the menu are locked because they will be unlocked upon completion of the related steps (Fig. 2.1a). On the second game screen (Fig. 2.1b) the participant must choose his or her virtual assistant, from two archaeological explorers: Maya and Jack. In the third game screen (Fig. 2.1c) explains or purpose of the game: *"Caldana is an ancient fortified village, within it are hidden treasures that few people know about. You will have to go on a real treasure hunt! If you find all the clues and solve the riddles, the entrances to Caldana's dungeons will be revealed. Now your phone is a time machine and you can talk to the ghosts of Marcello Agostini, his*

son Ippolito and architect Lorenzo Pomarelli. Look for them in the village and they will tell you the story of Caldana. Listen to them well, because their clues will be invaluable. You must also have patience and perseverance; ghosts are hard to find and tend to disappear suddenly to reappear not far away."

2. A Tutorial phase, where students can learn how to use app during the 3 historical characters (Marcello Agostini, Ippolito Agostini, and Lorenzo Pomarelli) introduce themselves in AR summarizing their role in the history of the village of Caldana (Fig. 2.2.)

3. Game phase, the first map displayed is the clues map, which through lens-shaped icons indicates points of historical interest (Fig. 2.3a). Participants by clicking on one of the lenses can, thanks to their virtual assistant, know the name of the place where they have to go to view the character in AR with GPS target; once the character is found (Fig. 2.3b), it tells historical information about the place and asks a simple question that the student has to answer (Fig. 2.3c). For each correct answer the user receives a reward a door or key randomly. The doors are displayed in the second map the treasure map (Fig. 2.3d) The user can through a swipe interaction change maps and decide whether to continue with the clues map, and continue looking for the lenses, or to start opening the entrances to the dungeons, assuming they have enough keys. The dungeons are actually not accessible to the public for security reasons; by virtually opening the door they are reproduced on the smartphone through 360-degree images that form non-immersive virtual tours (Fig. 2.3e). Hidden within each dungeon is a hotspot that activates the display of virtual treasures in AR in front of the entrance door (Fig. 2.3f). The virtual treasures are also related to the history of Caldana village and the use of the cellars in the past.

4. The final phase, completed the game the student has access to the entire menu unlocked (Fig. 2.4a). Within the *"Premio Finale"* final prize item, the students can scan the virtual identity card (Fig. 2.4b) to have the final prize, the Agostini family medal (Fig. 2.4c), appear in augmented reality. In addition, the user can take home all the information collected. In the *"Personaggi"* that is the characters section, the biography of the historical characters is given via a short textual description, and it is also possible to make the characters appear in AR any place thanks to floor recognition (Fig. 2.4f). In the *"Luoghi"*, although place item, it has a map summary (Fig. 2.4d) of the places visited with a textual description and a slideshow of images for each place (Fig. 2.4e). In *"Mappa del Tesoro"* that is the treasure map section (Fig. 2.4g), users can visit the dungeons at any time and view the prizes in floor recognition.

3 Evaluation

3.1 The Questionnaire

The evaluation of the AR application was aimed at measuring children's motivation to visit urban cultural heritage. The learning motivation scale was originated from the two dimensions of the Intrinsic Motivation Inventory (IMI), namely interest/fun and value/utility. Part of the content was modified from the measure proposed by the Museum Play Motivation Questionnaire of Bossavits [14] and Li Ye et al. [15]. Using a five-point

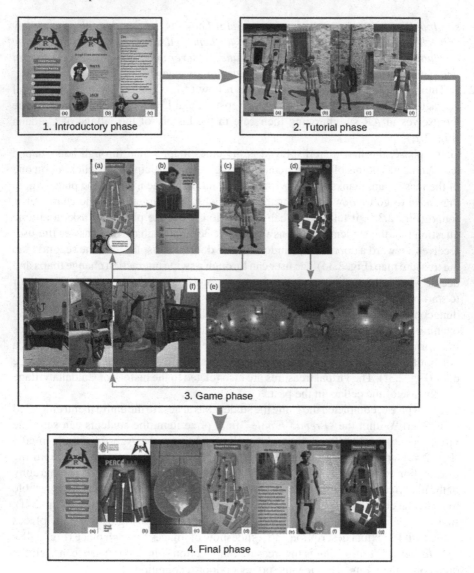

Fig. 2. Storyboard.

Likert to investigate students' motivational changes after play. In addition to the two scales of primary motivation and motivational change, the usability of the AR application was also assessed based on the dimensions proposed by Sang Min Ko et al. [16].

The items are distributed in the three dimensions of primary motivation (10 items), usability (15 items) and motivational change (5 items). Among them, the primary motivation theme was used to assess participants' attitudes toward cultural heritage and visits to historic cities before the experiment. The usability theme was used to assess the AR application experience of using the serious games in terms of User-informations,

User-Cognitive and User-interaction. The theme of change in motivation was used to re-evaluate participants' attitudes toward their willingness to visit urban cultural heritage after the experiment. The contents of the scale are shown in Table 1. All questions in the scale have been accurately translated into Italian to ensure that participants can understand and answer them correctly.

Table 1. Scales and items used to evaluate AR application.

Dimension	Sub-dimension	
Usability	User information	1. The app was easy to use (Default) 2. The initial screens and menus of the App were understandable (Language familiarity) 3. The map of Caldana was easy to understand (Spatial familiarity) 4. The screens of the App were aesthetically beautiful (2D Enjoyment) 5. The assistants (Jack and Maya) were pleasant (2D Enjoyment) 6. The 3D characters of Caldana were aesthetically beautiful (3D Enjoyment)
	User cognitive	7. It was easy to Fig. out what I needed to do to continue the game (Predictability) 8. It was easy to answer questions (Learnability) 9. The information given by the characters was helpful in answering the questions (Consistency) 10. The rewards were fun and satisfying (Award consistency)
	User interaction	11. It was easy to find the characters in different places around the country (Spatial Interaction) 12. App buttons were easy to use (2D interaction) 13. The voice and movements of the 3D characters were realistic and engaging (Human interaction) 14. The screen of my smartphone/tablet was adequate to use augmented reality (Device efficiency) 15. Audio was easy to hear (Audio efficiency)
Primary motivation		1. I like historical countries and like to have information about them 2. I often visit countries and cities of art 3. I liked Caldana 4. When I am on vacation, I am happy if my parents take me to visit countries and art cities 5. It is nice to visit countries and art cities on school trips 6. When I visit a country or an art city, I don't want to have explanations 7. I like to visit a country or an art city by listening to explanations from a tour guide 8. I like to visit a country or an art city by listening to explanations from my school teacher 9. I like to watch documentaries about countries and art cities on television 10. I like to read books about countries and art cities

(continued)

I. Capecchi et al.

Table 1. (*continued*)

Dimension	Sub-dimension	
Motivation change		1. Augmented reality helped me understand the history of Caldana
		2. I would like to find augmented reality applications in other cities
		3. I would recommend the augmented reality experience in Caldana to my friends who were not here today
		4. I would like to have more augmented reality experiences similar to this one at school
		5. I would like to have more augmented reality experiences similar to this one with my parents and/or friends

3.2 Results

We recruited experimental subjects from the second- and third-year courses of a middle school. A total of 79 middle school students participated in the study: 50.6% female and 49.4% male, with an age range of 12 to 16 years and a mean of 13.08 years and a standard deviation of 0.01.

Figure 3 displays the frequency distributions of the Likert scales used to assess the questionnaire items. The items concerning the usability of the GPS-AR-SG application received consistently positive evaluations, with over 70% overall positive ratings. Evaluations of the motivation for alpha generation towards urban heritage varied. The items related to the motivation to visit cities of art (items 16 to 20) received the highest evaluations, ranging from 71% (item 17: I enjoy visiting cities of art) to 81% (item 19: I like it when my parents take me to visit countries and cities of art). Conversely, the items related to the motivation to acquire knowledge from traditional sources of information (items 21 to 25) garnered limited interest, with generally low ratings throughout. The highest positive response rate was only 60% for item 22 (I enjoy visiting a country or art city while listening to a tour guide), while the lowest positive response rate was 38% for item 25 (I enjoy reading books about countries and art cities).

The Cronbach's alpha coefficient for the entire questionnaire was determined to be 0.93, indicating a high level of reliability. The coefficient alphas for the four dimensions ranged from 0.71 to 0.87 (user information: 0.87, user cognitive: 0.71, user interaction: 0.79, motivation: 0.76, and intention to use: 0.80), which suggests acceptable reliability for research purposes.

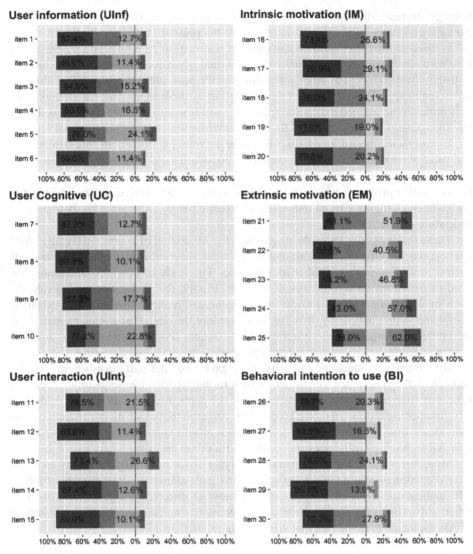

Fig. 3. Results

4 Conclusion and Future Developments

The findings obtained from the experimental study conducted with secondary school students, utilizing the Serious Game-Augmented reality application in the village of Caldana, have provided substantial evidence to support our approach. Specifically, our hypothesis has been validated, demonstrating that the utilization of these emerging technologies within the dynamic and lived spaces of a historical city extends beyond being mere tools for documentation, intervention, representation, and transmission of urban heritage. Instead, they have the potential to bring about transformative shifts in our personal connection with the past in relation to the present.

In essence, the selection of certain physical remnants as cultural heritage, when coupled with virtual and augmented representations and educational games, has the capacity to foster novel connections among the realms of the past, present, and future within the urban landscape. This implies that the integration of these innovative technologies not only enriches our understanding and appreciation of historical contexts but also reshapes our engagement and perception of the urban environment on a deeply personal level.

By embracing these digital tools, we open up avenues for reimagining the significance and value of heritage, transcending traditional boundaries and facilitating dynamic interactions between individuals and their urban surroundings. This transformative potential offers exciting prospects for the preservation, interpretation, and revitalization of urban heritage, encouraging a more immersive and participatory experience for both present and future generations.

These findings offer valuable insights into the utilization of augmented reality (AR) applications for urban heritage among the younger generation. However, there are still several areas that warrant further investigation. The study has certain limitations that need to be addressed through future research. Firstly, the application was developed for a small historical city, allowing for an augmented reality experience that could be completed within half a day. It is crucial to explore the design and implementation of storyboards in larger and more intricate cities, where serious game (SG) experiences may require longer visits spanning multiple days.

Due to privacy concerns, the software responses of the participants could not be recorded as they interacted with the app on their mobile phones. Consequently, it becomes necessary to investigate the learning aspect of the application and its impact. Additionally, broadening the demographic scope of the research to include older generations and individuals from diverse geographical locations would enhance our understanding of how AR technology influences engagement with urban heritage.

Moreover, conducting a comparative analysis of various design elements and user interface features would yield more specific insights, aiding the development of future AR applications. By evaluating the effectiveness of different design choices, we can refine and optimize the user experience, thereby improving the overall quality and impact of AR applications in the realm of urban heritage.

References

1. UNESCO: Recommendation on the Historic Urban Landscape, Including a Glossary of Definitions (2011)
2. He, Z., Wu, L., Li, X.R.: When art meets tech: the role of augmented reality in enhancing museum experiences and purchase intentions. Tour. Manag. **68**, 127–139 (2018)
3. Carrozzino, M., Bergamasco, M.: Beyond virtual museums: experiencing immersive virtual reality in real museums. J. Cult. Herit. **11**(4), 452–458 (2010)
4. Katz, M.: Augmented reality is transforming museums. Wired (2018). Dostupnona. https://www.wired.com/story/augmented-reality-art-museums

5. García Münzer, M.: How can augmented reality improve the user experience of digital products and engagement with cultural heritage outside the museum space? In: IOP Conference Series: Materials Science and Engineering, vol. 949, p. 012040. IOP Publishing, November 2020

6. Biocca, F., Tang, A., Owen, C., Xiao, F.: Attention funnel: omnidirectional 3D cursor for mobile augmented reality platforms. In: Proceedings of the SIGCHI Conference on Human Factors in Computing Systems, pp. 1115–1122, April 2006

7. Dunleavy, M., Dede, C.: Augmented reality teaching and learning. In: Handbook of Research on Educational Communications and Technology, pp. 735–745 (2014)

8. Mortara, M., Catalano, C.E., Bellotti, F., Fiucci, G., Houry-Panchetti, M., Petridis, P.: Learning cultural heritage by serious games. J. Cult. Herit. **15**(3), 318–325 (2014)

9. Hincapié, M., Díaz, C., Zapata-Cárdenas, M.I., Rios, H.D.J.T., Valencia, D., Güemes-Castorena, D.: Augmented reality mobile apps for cultural heritage reactivation. Comput. Electr. Eng. **93**, 107281 (2021)

10. Sutcliffe, K., Kim, S.: Understanding children's engagement with interpretation at a cultural heritage museum. J. Herit. Tour. **9**(4), 332–348 (2014)

11. Norman, D.A., Spohrer, J.C.: Learner-centered education. Commun. ACM **39**(4), 24–27 (1996)

12. Dewey, J.: Democracy and Education: An Introduction to the Philosophy of Education. Macmillan (1923)

13. Landers, R.N.: Developing a theory of gamified learning: linking serious games and gamification of learning. Simul. Gaming **45**(6), 752–768 (2014). https://doi.org/10.1177/104687 8114563660

14. Bossavit, B., Pina, A., Sanchez-Gil, I., Urtasun, A.: Educational games to enhance museum visits for schools. J. Educ. Technol. Soc. **21**(4), 171–186 (2018)

15. Ye, L., Wang, R., Zhao, J.: Enhancing learning performance and motivation of cultural heritage using serious games. J. Educ. Comput. Res. **59**(2), 287–317 (2021)

16. Ko, S.M., Chang, W.S., Ji, Y.G.: Usability principles for augmented reality applications in a smartphone environment. Int. J. Hum. Comput. Interact. **29**(8), 501–515 (2013)

eXtended Reality in Health and Medicine

Cycling in Immersive VR: Motivation and Affects in Post-COVID Patients

Marta Mondellini[1]([✉]) [iD], Sebastian Rutkowski[2] [iD], and Vera Colombo[1] [iD]

[1] Institute of Intelligent Industrial Technologies and Systems for Advanced Manufacturing – STIIMA, Via Previati 1/A, 23900 Lecco, Italy
{marta.mondellini,vera.colombo}@stiima.cnr.it
[2] Faculty of Physical Education and Physiotherapy, Opole University of Technology, Opole, Poland

Abstract. The present work reports preliminary results in a group of post-COVID patients participating in a pulmonary rehabilitation program with an Immersive Virtual Reality system. 22 participants performed endurance training for 3 weeks, cycling in an Immersive Virtual Park while wearing a Head-Mounted Display. Motivation, positive and negative emotions, and flow status are assessed at the beginning (t0) and end (t1) of the rehabilitation program. All the variables related to motivation (Intrinsic Motivation, Identified Regulation, and External Regulation) obtain higher average scores after the rehabilitation program (respectively, $p = 0.003$, $p = 0.006$, $p = 0.015$), showing that the experience is perceived as fun, motivating, and as a choice and not an obligation. Similarly, the flow state increases with the experience ($p = 0.024$). At the same time, amotivation decreases during the 3 weeks of treatment ($p < 0.001$). During the PR program, no difference emerges between positive and negative affects, but positive affects are reported more often than negative ones. These preliminary results suggest that training with the Immersive Virtual Park is perceived as a highly positive experience and can support the patient's motivation for long-term rehabilitation.

Keywords: Human Factor · Motivation · Virtual Reality · Pulmonary Rehabilitation

1 Introduction

Long COVID, or post-COVID syndrome, has recently emerged as a new chronic respiratory condition characterized by various symptoms, including generalized chest and muscle pain, fatigue, shortness of breath, and cognitive dysfunction [27]. Pulmonary rehabilitation (PR) is a multidomain intervention including physical training as a cornerstone, and already proven effective in improving exercise capacity, reducing dyspnea, and recovering a good quality of life for individuals with chronic respiratory diseases [22]. PR interventions designed for other types of patients with respiratory deficits have also been used for individuals with long-COVID with respiratory symptoms and/or impaired physical functions [3,23]. Such programs mainly include physical training in the hospital or at home. Endurance training, performed on a cycle-ergometer or a treadmill, aims to improve cardiorespiratory fitness and strengthen leg muscles.

Despite its proven benefits, rehabilitation is often not perceived as motivating and necessary for one's health but rather as a task and a duty imposed from the outside. This negatively influences the effectiveness of the rehabilitative intervention because patients abandon it, do not correctly follow the exact indications of the therapists, or, as in the large majority of chronic patients, do not adhere to the prescribed treatment once they return home. Conversely, patients with higher motivation perceive rehabilitation protocols as more important, engage more, and are more likely to achieve an optimal health-related quality of life) [24]. Therefore, it is necessary to design pulmonary rehabilitation programs specifically for long-COVID patients and devise solutions that intrinsically motivate patients to rehabilitation, which should elicit positive emotions and offer an overall positive experience.

In this direction, virtual reality (VR) technology offers promising opportunities to improve traditional rehabilitation programs. The ability to simulate an environment in which to interact, use gamification techniques and provide feedback to participants is among the features that make VR promising in supporting the motivational aspects of rehabilitation patients [17].

To date, few specific works on motivation and how it fluctuates with the rehabilitation experience seem to exist. Since motivation is a crucial issue for chronic respiratory patients, we believe it is necessary to consider it more often and to evaluate it in a more structured way. In such a scenario, the present study intends to evaluate the motivation, the positive and negative emotions, and the state of flow, experienced by individuals with post-COVID performing a 3-week endurance training program in immersive VR.

2   Related Works

Lately, the problem of encouraging patients to practice rehabilitation appropriately has been addressed by offering to patients exercises with digital or virtual gaming experiences [14]. Exergaming has been shown to be effective in aiding exercise motivation, and it has been applied in many rehabilitation contexts due to its ability to combine physical activity with game-inspired design mechanics [34]. In the last 10 years, most studies have evaluated the effectiveness of commercial devices and games in pulmonary rehabilitation. For example, LeGear and colleagues [21] measured the clinical effectiveness of using the Nintendo Wii in 10 COPD patients by comparing it to traditional training. Again, Albores [1] evaluated 20 clinically stable COPD patients after 12 weeks of home training with the same instrument. The conclusions suggest an efficacy similar but not superior to traditional training; unfortunately, as far as the authors know, the motivation aspect is not sufficiently considered, and results are based almost exclusively on clinical efficacy. A recent study by our research group assessed the user experience and the state of flow over a complete 3-week PR program in which patients performed the endurance exercise while simulating a bicycle ride in a virtual park and showed promising results in terms of long-term engagement [6]. The use of VR in pulmonary rehabilitation is rapidly growing with promising results regarding patients' acceptability and satisfaction [4, 8, 34]. A few examples also focus specifically on patients with post-COVID syndrome [7, 19, 29, 33]. For example, Jung investigated if a remotely supervised VR-based pulmonary rehabilitation improves pulmonary rehabilitation compliance among COPD patients [16]; the study reports qualitative and quantitative data. The authors conclude that a VR program can improve patient compliance, engagement, satisfaction, and feelings of safety, among other things.

Virtual reality offers immersive scenarios that capture attention, engage in the task [13, 26], and can distract the patient from the negative feelings of fatigue [5, 31]. Among other works, 20 patients were enrolled in a study [30] where the authors measured dyspnea in long-term post-COVID-19 patients with mild cognitive impairment during exercise with and without a VR system. In their analyses, dyspnea was lower during exercise with RV than without RV.

As already said, in research, the motivation and the positive emotional state of the participants are often not evaluated, while other psychological variables such as anxiety [2] and depression are rather considered [11, 18, 23].

Few research explored the compliance and motivation of participants in immersive PR programs [16, 25]. However, the motivation was not explicitly evaluated, and no baseline for this aspect was considered. It could be assumed that the participants were already highly motivated by agreeing to be part of the experimental group. More in the perspective of a long-term evaluation, [14] proposed an aerobic exercise in an immersive VR environment representing a park to patients with COPD, and evaluated motivation to train throughout the rehabilitation program. Although participants' motivation was high, it did not differ from that reported in traditional therapy. In this case, however, it must be said that the clinical sample consisted of only three participants.

In conclusion, in a field of emerging interest such as that of virtual reality for pulmonary rehabilitation, it is necessary to continue studying how the rehabilitation experience influences the motivational aspect, how it is correlated with the characteristics of the virtual system itself, and how it interacts with other psychological variables. This study intends to be a further step in this direction.

3   Methods

This study is part of a larger project approved by the Opole Medical Chamber Bioethics Commission in Opole (Approval number: No. 343, November 25, 2021), registered in ClinicalTrials.gov (NCT05244135) and was performed in accordance with the guidelines of the Declaration of Helsinki.

3.1   Participants

This study is conducted among patients with post-acute sequelae of COVID-19 (PASC) symptoms who participate in inpatient pulmonary rehabilitation at the Glucholazy Specialty Hospital in Poland. Patients are excluded if they cannot perform exercise independently, they have musculoskeletal/neurological pathologies, have active pneumonia or heart disease, have artery bypass grafting, coronary angioplasty, diabetes mellitus, lung cancer, cognitive deficit, or Mini-Mental State Examination < 24). All participants sign the written informed consent.

3.2   Equipment

Participants carry out the rehabilitation exercise by using the immersive Virtual Park, an immersive VR cycling system developed by the research group CNR-STIIMA that simulates a bicycle ride in a park. The necessary equipment, represented in Fig. 1), includes: a cycle-ergometer with an embedded pulse-oximeter (COSMED ergoline 4), a head-mounted display (HTC Vive Pro full kit), a heart rate band (Polar H7), and a VR application developed in Unity specifically for the project. The VR application, running on a Windows OS VR-ready laptop, handles all the connected devices: it controls the workload of the ergometer to implement the endurance training program defined by the clinicians, transforms the speed data to move the virtual bicycle along a predefined path in the park, receives the physiological data, and renders the virtual environment displayed in the HMD. The scenario represents a naturalistic scenario with graphical and audio elements conveying the pleasant and relaxing sensations of a bicycle ride. The user can explore the all-around scenario by turning his/her head while proceeding along the path by following a predefined trajectory. The reader is referred to XX for more details on all the functionalities of the immersive Virtual Park.

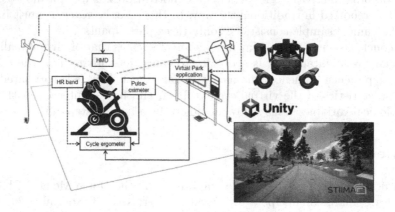

Fig. 1. The Immersive Virtual Park system.

3.3   Study Protocol

The protocol consists of 3 weeks of endurance training with the immersive Virtual Park. The exercise intensity (training heart rate and workload) is defined for each patient based on his/her baseline condition. For each session, the workload increases every 4 min by steps of 10 W for a maximum duration of 24 min. The sequence of workloads is automatically adjusted by the VR application according to the performance obtained in the previous session. The aim is to reach at the end of each session the training heart rate, defined as a percentage of the heart rate obtained in a baseline test of exercise capacity. Participants are asked to maintain a cycling speed between 50 and 70 RPM. A therapist supervises the whole session to monitor the patient's physiological response and assist in case of need.

3.4   Measures

Questionnaires to measure motivation, emotions, and flow are proposed to participants at the beginning (T0) and the end (T1) of the rehabilitation program.

The Situational Motivation Scale (SIMS) [12] is chosen for assessing motivation. This scale was created based on the Deci and Ryan self-determination theory [10], whereby it is assumed that human behavior is driven by different types of motivation and that the different kinds of motivation differ precisely for varying levels of self-determination. The scale evaluates four aspects:

- Intrinsic Motivation, namely the level of pleasure and satisfaction given by the activity itself, in which the level of self-determination is maximum;
- External Regulation: the behavior is perceived as an obligation to achieve a reward or avoid a punishment;
- Identified Regulation, in which the aim is the same of external regulation, but the behavior is perceived as chosen (however, the motivation is extrinsic because subjects act to obtain something);
- Amotivation, namely the lack of the sense of purpose.

The scale consists of 16 items in total (4 per subscale); the subject expresses the degree of agreement for each sentence on a scale from 1 to 7.

The short flow state scale (SFSS) [15] is completed by the participants. Flow is a well-known psychological construct that describes the experience of deep absorption in a task. The questionnaire consists of 9 items, based on the 9 key flow variables, namely: challenge-skill balance, action-awareness merging, clear goals, unambiguous feedback, concentration on the task at hand, sense of control, loss of self-consciousness, time transformation, and autotelic experience. Participants must rate their degree of agreement with each sentence on a 5-point Likert scale.

Finally, the International Positive and Negative Affect Schedule Short Form (I-PANAS-SF) [32] is proposed to assess positive and negative emotions after the immersive experience. Ten emotions, of which 5 are positive (determined, attentive, alert, inspired, active) and 5 negative (afraid, nervous, upset, ashamed, hostile), compose the questionnaire. Participants indicate how much they feel a certain way on a scale from 1 to 5.

All questionnaires are translated into Polish and filled in by patients via MS form.

3.5 Statistical Analysis

Given the size of the sample, non-parametric statistics are used. However, the distribution of the curves of the variables is observed to understand the phenomena better. The reliability of the scales is evaluated using the alpha and omega coefficients. For each variable at both times, T0 and T1, descriptive analyzes are run to observe the scores. The Wilcoxon paired-samples test is performed on the variables to evaluate score differences between T0 and T1. Simple and partial Spearman correlations are run to evaluate the relationships between variables at T0 and T1 separately. Statistical analyzes are performed with IBM SPSS v.28 statistical software.

4 Results

4.1 Participants

Twenty-three patients with post-acute sequelae of COVID-19 participate in the hospital-based pulmonary rehabilitation program and completed the subjective experience assessments at the beginning and the end of the training. One subject is an outlier in both the SFSS and I-PANAS-SF scores. For this reason, we exclude him/her from the statistical analyses. Therefore, the final sample consists of 22 participants.

The group is composed of 16 females and 6 males. The other characteristics of the participants are shown in Table 1.

Table 1. Participants' characteristics.

	Min.	Max.	Mean	St. Dev.
Age	41	69	60.05	6.04
Weight	60	127	85.14	17.45
Height	152	190	168.41	8.80
BMI	22.31	38.86	29.83	4.41

4.2 Reliability of the Scales

All the scales used demonstrate excellent reliability. In particular, as regards the SIMS at T0, the scales obtains $\alpha = 0.89$ and $\omega = 0.89$ (intrinsic motivation-IM), $\alpha = 0.92$ and $\omega = 0.92$ (identified regulation-IR), $\alpha = 0.89$ and $\omega = 0.90$

(external regulation-ER), $\alpha = 0.93$ and $\omega = 0.93$ (amotivation-A). The same scales at T1 obtains $\alpha = 0.75$ and $\omega = 0.75$ (intrinsic motivation), $\alpha = 0.82$ and $\omega = 0.85$ (identified regulation), $\alpha = 0.88$ and $\omega = 0.86$ (external regulation), and finally $\alpha = 0.88$ and $\omega = 0.90$ (amotivation).

Regarding the flow, the scale obtains $\alpha = 0.93$ and $\omega = 0.93$ at the beginning of the rehabilitation program, and $\alpha = 0.86$ and $\omega = 0.86$ at the end.

Positive affect subscale obtains $\alpha = 0.80$ and $\omega = 0.81$ at T0, and $\alpha = 0.83$ and $\omega = 0.84$ at T1; Negative affect subscale $\alpha = 0.89$ and $\omega = 0.93$ (T0), and $\alpha = 0.84$ and $\omega = 0.85$ (T1).

4.3 Motivation

The motivation-related variables (SIMS) have a normal distribution, with kurtosis and skewness smaller than $|2|$.

Means and standard deviations of the four subscales in T0 and T1 are reported in Table 2. The pre-post means are represented in Fig. 2; the possible range goes from a minimum of 1 to a maximum of 7.

Table 2. Means and standard deviations (in the brackets) of SIMS.

Subscale	T0	T1	Z	sig
Intrinsic Motivation	5.50 (1.22)	6.24 (0.87)	−2.924	0.003
Identified Regulation	5.95 (0.84)	6.65 (0.51)	−2.753	0.006
External Regulation	5.61 (0.96)	6.23 (1.02)	−2.422	0.015
Amotivation	3.68 (1.60)	2.22 (1.41)	−3.532	< 0.001

The difference between the two evaluation times is statistically significant for all 4 variables. Respective Z values and significance are shown in Table 2; regarding this, the first three comparisons (IM, IR, ER) are based on negative ranks, while the last comparison is on positive ranks.

4.4 Positive and Negative Affects

Positive and negative emotion scores have a normal distribution. The total score for positive and negative affects is the sum of the five items' scores. As regards T0, the average score of positive emotions is 13.09 ± 4.61, while for negative ones it is 7.27 ± 2.91, as shown in Fig. 3. Similarly, at T1 the two variables obtain 13.09 ± 4.58 e 7.27 ± 2.60 (PA and NA respectively). No difference between the scores in the two different moments of evaluation results.

4.5 Flow

The scores of Flow have normal distributions at T0 and T1. Average scores, reported in Fig. 4, are 4.18 ± 0.71 at T0, and 4.58 ± 0.5 at T1. The difference between the two scores is statistically significant, with $Z = -2.25$ (based on negative ranks), and $p = 0.024$.

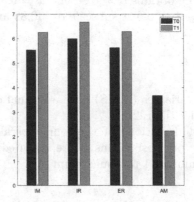

Fig. 2. Pre-post scores of Situational Motivation Scale (IM = intrinsic motivation, IR = identified regulation, ER = external regulation, AM = amotivation).

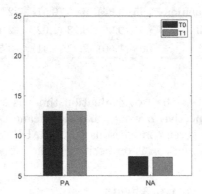

Fig. 3. Pre-post scores of International Positive and Negative Affect Schedule Short Form (PA = positive affects, NA = negative affects).

4.6 Correlations Between Variables

T0. Concerning T0, correlations between Intrinsic Motivation and Identified Regulation ($\rho = 0.82$, $p < 0.001$), between Intrinsic Motivation and External Regulation ($\rho = 0.86$, $p < 0.001$), and between Identified Regulation and External Regulation ($\rho = 0.79$, $p < 0.001$) emerge. These correlations do not persist running partial correlations.

Furthermore, flow correlates with the first three SIMS scales (Intrinsic Motivation: $\rho = 0.75$, $p < 0.001$; Identified Regulation $\rho = 0.67$, $p < 0.001$; External Regulation $\rho = 0.81$, $p < 0.001$), but only with simple correlations.

Finally, positive emotions and negative emotions are correlated, with $\rho = 0.50$ and $p = 0.019$; this result remains with partial correlation ($\rho = 0.54$ and $p = 0.026$). Observing partial correlation, a reverse relation between flow and positive emotion appears ($\rho = -0.54$ and $p = 0.024$).

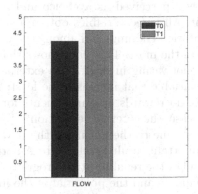

Fig. 4. Pre-post scores of Short Flow State Scale.

T1. In T1, the correlations between the first three SIMS variables appear again: Intrinsic Motivation and Identified Regulation ($\rho = 0.63$, $p = 0.002$), between Intrinsic Motivation and External Regulation ($\rho = 0.60$, $p = 0.003$), and between Identified Regulation and External Regulation ($\rho = 0.80$, $p < 0.001$). Again, these correlations do not remain running partial correlations.

Intrinsic motivation also correlates with positive ($\rho = -0.42$, $p = 0.049$) and negative ($\rho = -0.45$, $p = 0.034$) emotions, but only with simple correlations. Furthermore, there is a strong relationship between flow and intrinsic motivation ($\rho = 0.92$, $p < 0.001$), which remains even when performing the partial correlations ($\rho = 0.85$, $p < 0.001$).

Identified Regulation correlates also with Amotivation ($\rho = -0.63$, $p = 0.002$), Flow ($\rho = 0.68$, $p < 0.001$), and Positive Affects ($\rho = -0.45$, $p = 0.035$), but only with simple correlations.

External Regulation correlates with Amotivation ($\rho = -0.61$, $p = 0.002$), Flow ($\rho = 0.71$, $p < 0.001$), and Positive Affects ($\rho = -0.63$, $p < 0.002$); in this second case, the relation persists with partial correlation, with $\rho = -0.53$ and $p = 0.029$.

Flow correlates negatively with Amotivation ($\rho = -0.45$, $p = 0.035$), Positive Affects ($\rho = -0.56$, $p = 0.006$), and Negative Affects ($\rho = -0.59$, $p = 0.004$), but no partial correlations emerge.

The two scales of PANAS correlate also in this case, with $\rho = 0.76$, $p < 0.001$ with simple, and $\rho = 0.72$, $p < 0.001$ with partial correlations.

5   Discussion

First, the collected results all have a normal distribution; thus, means and deviations are effectively descriptive indices of the sample.

One significant result of the present work is related to motivation. First, the first three variables (Intrinsic Motivation, Identified Regulation, and External Regulation) obtain high average scores. The highest score is of Identified Regulation, demonstrating that actually, the action of participating in the pulmonary rehabilitation program was perceived as a choice and not as an obligation in order to obtain a benefit. All three variables obtain a statistically higher score at the end of the rehabilitation training, and among these, intrinsic motivation is the variable that increases the most. This data shows that participants perceive the activity as fun and motivating in itself. The external regulation, although greater than T1, is the variable that increases the least; this is understandable since there were actually no rewards or punishments for the participants, and probably, in this specific case, the external regulation is perceived as very similar to the identified regulation due to the nature of the reward, namely improving one's health. Another important result is related to Amotivation; already low in T0, it decreases at the end of the rehabilitation program. This demonstrates the satisfaction of the participants and the potential of the immersive Virtual Park system to motivate them to exercise regularly.

Instead, no difference between T0 and T1 in positive and negative emotions appears; however, it can be taken into consideration that the positive states obtain higher scores than the negative ones, and they also have a higher standard deviation, an index of greater individual variability.

The Flow state gets high scores and increases significantly from T0 to T1. This result is extremely positive for the context of rehabilitation. It indicates that the proposed VR system is engaging even if used often and over a relatively long time, and therefore that the positive impact is not only due to the participant's novelty or curiosity.

Regarding the correlations, it can be seen that the first three SIMS variables are positively correlated; this complies with the basic theory in [10] that adjacent subscales along the self-determination continuum correlate more positively. In [12]'s work, motivation correlates positively with external regulation, but in this specific case, penalties or rewards to be avoided and acquired do not really exist, and the reward is more connected to feeling good and, therefore, could be placed more on the pole of the continuum more self-determining.

Since no partial correlations between SIMS variables are found, it is possible that there are latent factors when all the four sub-scales are considered together, for example, perceived skills [12] or contextual factors (namely, the way in which the activity was proposed, or if there was any interference during the sessions, etc.). The Amotivation variable correlates negatively with the other scales in T1 but not in T0; again, it can be considered that external factors may influence the link between the variables differently in the two evaluation times.

The results indicate that the flow correlates positively (both at T0 and T1) with the motivation scales, in accordance with [9]. It is interesting that at T1 (and at T1 only), the correlation between the two variables also persists when partializing the joint effects of the other variables; this fact may indicate that the concept of flow and/or intrinsic motivation is perceived in a different and perhaps more aware way at the end of the rehabilitation program.

Finally, flow and positive emotions correlate negatively in both assessment times. Although it is not a strong correlation, this data is not theoretically understood and does not agree with other works, for example, [28]. This result suggests that it is necessary to study the construct validity of the PANAS in this sample in more detail to exclude that the negative correlation is due to the weak validity of the scale. Furthermore, the positive correlation between positive and negative affects, usually present but negative, may support the hypothesis of the weak construct validity. Another hypothesis may be that the experience evokes mixed emotions [20] and that, therefore, there is a concurrence of positive and negative aspects. For example, it is possible that a subject who reports high alertness also has a higher degree of upset.

6   Conclusion and Future Works

This paper presents preliminary results on the effects of immersive cycling training on motivation and affects in a group of individuals with long-COVID. Participants used the immersive Virtual Park for performing endurance training on a cycle-ergometer for 3 weeks. The human factors evaluation was performed before and after the rehabilitation period.

Our data suggest that exercising with the immersive Virtual Park is intrinsically motivating and is an experience accompanied by a high level of flow. These characteristics not only remain but actually increase over time. This is a very important result to improve treatment compliance and help patients improve over time.

There are some limitations of the present study that indicate future directions to take. First, these results need to be confirmed by a study with a larger sample size so that the positive effect of VR training can be confidently generalized. Secondly, the results suggest that other variables, not considered in the present time, could better explain how the activity of cycling in the immersive Virtual Park impacts on the human factor. One of these variables could be perceived competence, but expectations with respect to training, different in T0 and T1, and personal attitudes could also be taken into account. Qualitative assessments could be combined with quantitative ones to better understand the subjective world of patients, especially at the end of the pulmonary rehabilitation program, through interviews or focus groups.

The different correlations between T0 and T1, especially regarding the relationship between intrinsic motivation and flow, could be better understood by evaluating if one of the two constructs, or both, are perceived differently at the beginning and at the end of the program. In this regard, with a larger sample, confirmatory factor analyses could be carried out on the quantitative data. Furthermore, the results suggest that PANAS may lack construct validity in our sample; in the future, evaluating this possibility and proposing alternatives to measure patients' emotions will be appropriate.

Another aspect that will be interesting to investigate is the relationship between physiological data and psychological data. Thanks to the integration of sensors to collect biometric data, such as heart rate variability or skin conductance, the correlations with the subjective experience reported by the patient could be analyzed.

Our results, though preliminary, make a step forward to investigate the use of immersive VR to support aerobic exercise in individuals with respiratory diseases. In particular, this work provides interesting insights into the motivational aspects associated with the use of this technology with this target population, specifically post-COVID patients. Thanks to the modularity and scalability of VR and the Virtual Park system, such results could be further extended to other contexts of use - e.g., for continuity of care - and target groups with similar needs - e.g., chronic obstructive pulmonary diseases - towards the implementation of PR programs that are able to motivate patients over a long period of time.

Acknowledgements. The authors would like to thank the personnel of the Glucholazy Specialty Hospital in Poland for conducting the study.

References

1. Albores, J., Marolda, C., Haggerty, M., Gerstenhaber, B., ZuWallack, R.: The use of a home exercise program based on a computer system in patients with chronic obstructive pulmonary disease. J. Cardiopulm. Rehabil. Prev. **33**(1), 47–52 (2013)
2. Bashir, Z., Misquith, C., Shahab, A., Has, P., Bukhari, S.: The impact of virtual reality on anxiety and functional capacity in cardiac rehabilitation: a systematic review and meta-analysis. Curr. Probl. Cardiol. 101628 (2023)
3. Chen, H., Shi, H., Liu, X., Sun, T., Wu, J., Liu, Z.: Effect of pulmonary rehabilitation for patients with post-COVID-19: a systematic review and meta-analysis. Front. Med. **9**, 837420 (2022)
4. Colombo, V., Aliverti, A., Sacco, M.: Virtual reality for COPD rehabilitation: a technological perspective. Pulmonology **28**(2), 119–133 (2022)
5. Colombo, V., Bocca, G., Mondellini, M., Sacco, M., Aliverti, A.: Evaluating the effects of virtual reality on perceived effort during cycling: preliminary results on healthy young adults. In: 2022 IEEE International Symposium on Medical Measurements and Applications (MeMeA), pp. 1–6. IEEE (2022)
6. Colombo, V., Mondellini, M., Fumagalli, A., Aliverti, A., Sacco, M.: A virtual reality-based endurance training program for copd patients: acceptability and user experience. Disabil. Rehabil. Assist. Technol. 1–10 (2023)
7. Colombo, V., et al.: Rehabilitation of post-COVID patients: a virtual reality home-based intervention including cardio-respiratory fitness training. In: De Paolis, L.T., Arpaia, P., Sacco, M. (eds.) Extended Reality, pp. 3–17. Springer, Cham (2022). https://doi.org/10.1007/978-3-031-15546-8_1
8. Condon, C., Lam, W.T., Mosley, C., Gough, S.: A systematic review and meta-analysis of the effectiveness of virtual reality as an exercise intervention for individuals with a respiratory condition. Adv. Simul. **5**, 1–17 (2020)
9. Csikszentmihalyi, M., Nakamura, J.: The dynamics of intrinsic motivation: a study of adolescents. In: Csikszentmihalyi, M. (ed.) Flow and the Foundations of Positive Psychology, pp. 175–197. Springer, Dordrecht (2014). https://doi.org/10.1007/978-94-017-9088-8_12

10. Deci, E.L., Ryan, R.M.: Intrinsic motivation and self-determination in human behavior. Perspectives in Social Psychology (1985)
11. Grosbois, J.M., Gephine, S., Le Rouzic, O., Chenivesse, C.: Feasibility, safety and effectiveness of remote pulmonary rehabilitation during COVID-19 pandemic. Respir. Med. Res. **80**, 100846 (2021)
12. Guay, F., Vallerand, R.J., Blanchard, C.: On the assessment of situational intrinsic and extrinsic motivation: the situational motivation scale (SIMS). Motiv. Emot. **24**, 175–213 (2000)
13. Herne, R., Shiratuddin, M.F., Rai, S., Blacker, D., Laga, H.: Improving engagement of stroke survivors using desktop virtual reality-based serious games for upper limb rehabilitation: a multiple case study. IEEE Access **10**, 46354–46371 (2022)
14. Høeg, E.R., Bruun-Pedersen, J.R., Serafin, S.: Virtual reality-based high-intensity interval training for pulmonary rehabilitation: a feasibility and acceptability study. In: 2021 IEEE Conference on Virtual Reality and 3D User Interfaces Abstracts and Workshops (VRW), pp. 242–249. IEEE (2021)
15. Jackson, S.A., Martin, A.J., Eklund, R.C.: Long and short measures of flow: the construct validity of the FSS-2, DFS-2, and new brief counterparts. J. Sport Exerc. Psychol. **30**(5), 561–587 (2008)
16. Jung, T., Moorhouse, N., Shi, X., Amin, M.F.: A virtual reality-supported intervention for pulmonary rehabilitation of patients with chronic obstructive pulmonary disease: mixed methods study. J. Med. Internet Res. **22**(7), e14178 (2020)
17. Kern, F., Winter, C., Gall, D., Käthner, I., Pauli, P., Latoschik, M.E.: Immersive virtual reality and gamification within procedurally generated environments to increase motivation during gait rehabilitation. In: 2019 IEEE Conference on Virtual Reality and 3D User Interfaces (VR), pp. 500–509. IEEE (2019)
18. Kiper, P., et al.: Effects of immersive virtual therapy as a method supporting recovery of depressive symptoms in post-stroke rehabilitation: randomized controlled trial. Clin. Interv. Aging 1673–1685 (2022)
19. Kolbe, L., Jaywant, A., Gupta, A., Vanderlind, W.M., Jabbour, G.: Use of virtual reality in the inpatient rehabilitation of COVID-19 patients. Gen. Hosp. Psychiatry **71**, 76–81 (2021)
20. Larsen, J.T., Hershfield, H., Stastny, B.J., Hester, N., et al.: On the relationship between positive and negative affect: their correlation and their co-occurrence. Emotion **17**(2), 323 (2017)
21. LeGear, T., LeGear, M., Preradovic, D., Wilson, G., Kirkham, A., Camp, P.G.: Does a Nintendo Wii exercise program provide similar exercise demands as a traditional pulmonary rehabilitation program in adults with COPD? Clin. Respir. J. **10**(3), 303–310 (2016)
22. Li, W., Pu, Y., Meng, A., Zhi, X., Xu, G.: Effectiveness of pulmonary rehabilitation in elderly patients with COPD: a systematic review and meta-analysis of randomized controlled trials. Int. J. Nurs. Pract. **25**(5), e12745 (2019)
23. Liu, K., Zhang, W., Yang, Y., Zhang, J., Li, Y., Chen, Y.: Respiratory rehabilitation in elderly patients with COVID-19: a randomized controlled study. Complement. Ther. Clin. Pract. **39**, 101166 (2020)
24. Maclean, N., Pound, P., Wolfe, C., Rudd, A.: Qualitative analysis of stroke patients' motivation for rehabilitation. BMJ **321**(7268), 1051–1054 (2000)
25. Moorhouse, N., Jung, T., Shi, X., Amin, F., Newsham, J., McCall, S.: Pulmonary rehabilitation in virtual reality for COPD patients. In: tom Dieck, M.C., Jung, T. (eds.) Augmented Reality and Virtual Reality. PI, pp. 277–290. Springer, Cham (2019). https://doi.org/10.1007/978-3-030-06246-0_20

26. Pedroli, E., et al.: Characteristics, usability, and users experience of a system combining cognitive and physical therapy in a virtual environment: positive bike. Sensors **18**(7), 2343 (2018)

27. Rajan, S., et al.: In the wake of the pandemic. Preparing for long COVID. Policy Brief **39** (2021)

28. Rogatko, T.P.: The influence of flow on positive affect in college students. J. Happiness Stud. **10**, 133–148 (2009)

29. Silva, T.D.D., et al.: Comparison between conventional intervention and non-immersive virtual reality in the rehabilitation of individuals in an inpatient unit for the treatment of COVID-19: a study protocol for a randomized controlled crossover trial. Front. Psychol. **12**, 622618 (2021)

30. Stavrou, V.T., et al.: Breathlessness and exercise with virtual reality system in long-post-coronavirus disease 2019 patients. Front. Public Health **11**, 1115393 (2023)

31. Stewart, T.H., et al.: Actual vs. perceived exertion during active virtual reality game exercise. Front. Rehabil. Sci. **3**, 887740 (2022)

32. Thompson, E.R.: Development and validation of an internationally reliable short-form of the positive and negative affect schedule (PANAS). J. Cross Cult. Psychol. **38**(2), 227–242 (2007)

33. Vlake, J.H., Van Bommel, J., Hellemons, M.E., Wils, E.J., Gommers, D., Van Genderen, M.E.: Intensive care unit-specific virtual reality for psychological recovery after ICU treatment for COVID-19; a brief case report. Front. Med. 1143 (2021)

34. Wang, Y.Q., et al.: Active video games as an adjunct to pulmonary rehabilitation of patients with chronic obstructive pulmonary disease: a systematic review and meta-analysis. Am. J. Phys. Med. Rehabil. **99**(5), 372–380 (2020)

A Cheap and Powerful Stereo Endoscope Lab Mock-Up for Robotic Surgery to Implement and Test Machine Vision and Augmented Reality Prototypes

A. R. Mendicino[1]([✉]), E. Bani[1], M. Caretto[2], F. Cutolo[1], T. Simoncini[2], and V. Ferrari[1]

[1] Department of Information Engineering, EndoCAS Center for Computer Assisted Surgery,
University of Pisa, Pisa, PI, Italy
antonella.mendicino@endocas.unipi.it, vincenzo.ferrari@unipi.it
[2] Department of Clinical and Experimental Medicine, University of Pisa, Pisa, PI, Italy
tommaso.simoncini@unipi.it

Abstract. Robotic surgery has reached a very high level of advancement, in particular, Da Vinci Xi robotic system allows the execution of surgical tasks of the highest precision. It offers advantages in terms of reduced blood loss, reduced postoperative hospital stay, and less postoperative pain. The disadvantage the surgeon has found is progressive tactile loss, a long training curve and very high cost. This can be overcome by using Augmented Reality and trying to combine the advantages of this technology. In AR-based applications, the key challenge is to ensure the highest degree of realism in blending computer-generated elements with the surgical scene. To implement new AR protocols and be able to perform pre-clinical tests without having to use the complex and expensive robotic vision system, it was decided to design a stereo endoscope laboratory mock-up (SELM), which reproduces the Da Vinci vision tool, so as to be able to have the instrument in any bioengineering laboratory. This paper presents our new vision system, that has stereoscopic vision, 5.5 mm diameter camera, 1280×720 resolution, 7–40 cm depth of field, 80° angle of view, and real-time imaging up to 30 fps. These data compared with the technical characteristics of the endoscope present in the Da Vinci Xi robotic system makes it possible to state that the use of this endoscope can replace in terms of visual quality, the endoscope of the Da Vinci and thus the development time of new robotic techniques and AR is less, compared to the classical realization of in vitro tests to be performed in robotic operating rooms.

Keywords: Da Vinci robot · Augmented Reality · Stereoscopic Endoscope · New Endoscope

1 Introduction

The greatest surgical innovation of the past three decades is the advent of minimally invasive surgery (MIS). This revolution has fundamentally changed surgical practice by combining multiple technological developments. Cameras and high-definition micro

L. T. De Paolis et al. (Eds.): XR Salento 2023, LNCS 14219, pp. 367–378, 2023.
https://doi.org/10.1007/978-3-031-43404-4_24

instruments, which enter the human body through small incisions, replace the surgeon's eyes and hands. The benefits are several: reduced surgical trauma and incision-related complications, reduced hospital stay, earlier return to daily activities and improved cosmetic outcome. Expertise in MIS requires intensive work and continuous training as it is technically challenging due to unnatural vision and absence of tactile perception [1]. This type of surgery usually involves preoperative planning, in which a virtual patient model is created from biomedical images of the real patient. In addition, this 3D model could also be fused with real-time patient images, providing an intraoperative navigation tool that highlights the target, i.e., the various anatomical structures. This process of fusing real image and virtual image is referred to as Augmented Reality. The surgeon's abilities are enhanced: the augmented surgical eye can see through transparency, through virtual and augmented reality, and the enhanced surgeon's hand is provided by robotic technologies that offer improved tele handling. Tele-operated robots, including the Da Vinci Xi, are operated by the surgeon, seated at the console observing the surgical field through a stereoscopic endoscope that provides a magnified, high-resolution view. The surgical instruments are guided by haptic interfaces that replicate and filter hand movements, that is, they possess the same degrees of freedom as the human hand and filter out its natural tremor. To date, more than 5,000 da Vinci surgical systems have been implemented worldwide, performing more than 7 million surgical procedures in different anatomical regions [2]. Urology, gynecology, and general surgery represent the main application areas in which the da Vinci surgical system has been used, although many other surgical areas have also developed robotic approaches, such as in thoracic and transoral surgery [3]. In addition to clinical research, the da Vinci Surgical System has also facilitated many engineering publications and stimulated innovation in surgical robotics technology. In the early years since the clinical introduction of the robot, such engineering research focused mainly on developing algorithms that used system data, video or kinematic information, or external sensors added to the main robotic platform. However, few laboratories had da Vinci surgical systems for research use. Most platforms were dedicated to clinical use, and kinematic information was accessible through an application programming interface, which required a research collaboration agreement with ISI. This inevitably limited the number of academic or industrial researchers able to contribute to the advancement of the field. Research, at present, has focused on six fields: automation, training, skill evaluation and gesture recognition, hardware implementation and integration, systems simulation and modeling, and image and vision, and in this paper, we will address the latter field of study.

The Da Vinci robot, specifically Da Vinci Xi, is a teleoperated robot consisting of a master unit and a slave unit. We have the master console displaced from the slave unit, where the surgeon operates via joysticks controlling the slave unit (Fig. 1).

Viewing of the surgical field, in the Da Vinci Xi robotic system, is done through the master station, where the physician through his or her own eyes immerses himself in the surgical scene captured by a stereoscopic endoscope. This unit is high-definition 3D for optimal immersion of the surgeon in the scene; the depth perspective is provided by two independent-vision-channels, which are the two cameras of the endoscope reported on two viewers in the master unit (stereovision). The surgeon looks through a binocular viewer embedded in the console. The position of the surgeon's eye relative to

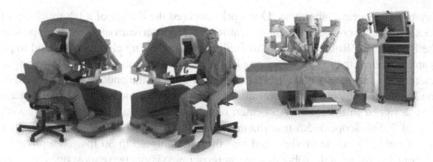

Fig. 1. Da Vinci robot system, including master and slave units.

the hands roughly mirrors that of the endoscope relative to the instrument. The surgical scenario before the operator's eyes is consistent, to some degree of approximation, with the position of the hands relative to it [4]. The disadvantage the surgeon has found is progressive tactile loss, a long training curve and very high cost. Advances in technology allow us to combine the benefits of robotic surgery with extended reality (XR) systems. XR refers to all real and virtual combined environments generated using computers and wearables, such as Virtual Reality (VR), Augmented Reality (AR), and Mixed Reality (MR) technologies. The classification of XR technologies can be considered a virtuality continuum where applications may cross definition boundaries depending on the use [5]. For our work, we focus on Augmented Reality, and we try to combine the advantages of this technology. In AR-based applications, the key challenge is to ensure the highest degree of realism in blending computer-generated elements with the surgical scene. They have the potential to support surgeons with navigation and orientation before, during, and after surgery. Medical AR applications will enable more advanced preoperative imaging studies, allowing physicians and surgeons to examine a holographic view of patients' internal anatomy segmented by CT, MRI and ultrasound data. In addition to visual feedback, AR systems can integrate haptic devices (tactile or vibratory feedback tools) to allow surgeons to feel the texture of tumors or otherwise explore a patient's condition through touch, without having to perform open surgery. In addition, an AR system combined with reliable and consistent force feedback could make more difficult surgeries totally minimally invasive [6]. A new challenge is to improve surgical training by creating surgical simulators capable of replicating surgical tasks in the laboratory. Simulators are also useful to teach new techniques to experts. Finally, simulators can also help develop non-technical competencies, including teamwork and communication. In recent years, the field of surgical simulation has made a lot of progress. Today, not only VR surgical simulators but also surgical simulators based on AR and MR have been developed [7]. Sophisticated techniques and algorithms have allowed surgeons to conduct correct surgical procedures, intraoperative control and postoperative tracking. AR is beneficial for preoperative surgical preparation, providing useful outcome predictions and intraoperative navigation to minimize possible risks. To implement new AR protocols and be able to perform pre-clinical tests without having to use the complex and expensive robotic vision system, it was decided to design a stereo endoscope laboratory mock-up, which reproduces the Da Vinci vision tool, to be able to have the instrument in any bioengineering laboratory. Our work involved the design of a lab mock-up of a stereoscopic endoscope capable of replicating the characteristics of the endoscope found in the Da Vinci Xi Robotic System, to facilitate and speed up clinical trials and to possess an instrument in the bioengineering laboratory that is economical, space-saving and efficient. An attempt was made to meet the guidelines of the endoscope characteristics of the Da Vinci Xi by evaluating the various endoscopes for industrial use in the market. SELM designed in the EndoCAS center, has these main features: stereoscopic vision (union of 2 endoscopes), 5.5 mm diameter camera, 1280×720 resolution, 7–40 cm depth of field, 80° angle of view, and real-time imaging up to 30 fps. To replicate the endoscope hardware of the robot that has stereoscopic vision, two endoscopes were used joined by a 60-cm-long aluminum cylinder and locked inside with clamps and hot glue, so that the vision of the two cameras is oriented in the same way and the views are consistent. We called it cheap, because the total cost is about $100. The result is promising and will soon be used in vitro tests in place of the Da Vinci endoscope.

2 Materials and Methods

This section describes the methods that were used to obtain our results. Section 2.1 describes the hardware of the endoscope of system Da Vinci Xi Sect. 2.2 describes the hardware of the endoscope SELM. Section 2.3 describes the test of calibration of both systems.

2.1 Hardware of Robotic System Da Vinci Xi

The da Vinci console provides immersive stereoscopic viewing. The surgeon, inserting his/her head into the hood, obtains a stereoscopic view of the operating field through the binoculars. The console hood serves to block peripheral vision, providing a fully immersive experience. The Da Vinci stereoscopic visualization system is composed of a 3D endoscope with two separate optic channels, connected to a pair of charge-coupled device (CCD) chip cameras (Fig. 2). The optic channels have a distance of 6 mm between axes, resulting in retinal disparity (different image in each retina), which thereby creates a true stereoscopic image [4]. This image considerably helps surgeons in orientation and manipulation in complex operative landscapes. Images after noise filtering are displayed through high-resolution monitors, mounted in front of the eyes and providing a stereoscopic view. The endoscope can be oriented with a gradation of 0 and 30° and has the feature of image magnification between 6x and 10x. The resolution of the image projected on the surgeon's console is 1280×1024 (SXGA standard).

In addition, the camera lens is designed to provide automatic focus on the surgical field when the distance between the arm and the tissue is 34 ± 5 mm. This automatic image focusing is very practical and timesaving [8].

To know the parameters of the Da Vinci endoscope's cameras, the calibration was performed, explained within Sect. 3.1.1. Once specifications such as baseline, angle of view, lens diameter were obtained, the search for an industrial endoscope capable of similar characteristics began.

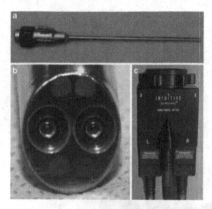

Fig. 2. Stereo Endoscope of Da Vinci Xi system.

2.2 Hardware of Our Stereo Endoscope

In order to faithfully realize or at least, to have a stereo endoscope capable of producing images like those of the Da Vinci Xi Robotic System, we searched for an endoscope for industrial use with the characteristics like those of the robot.

The search involved choosing among different types of industrial endoscopes and fell on the DEPSTECH USB 720P endoscope (Fig. 3) with the following characteristics [9]:

- **3-in-1 Interface Design:** This endoscope camera adopts USB/Micro USB/Type-C interfaces with wide compatibility and application range. Compatible with Windows & Mac OS & Android devices.
- **Upgraded Snake Cable:** Semi-rigid cable can bend and hold its shape to access a variety of closed places to meet different needs, such as curved holes or pipes.
- **720P HD Inspection Camera:** Endoscope camera with 1280 × 720P, 5.5 mm lens helps to inspect narrow places, giving you a super clear world and seeing every detail exactly. Equipped with 3 useful accessories (side mirror, magnet, and hook), which makes your job easier.
- **Other Features:** Built-in 6 brightness adjustable LED lights, allowing you to work easily in dark environments. And the waterproof endoscope camera can detect the underwater environment effectively.
- **Long Focal Range:** DEPSTECH expand the focus range of the USB endoscope up to 7 cm from 40 cm, so the images and the videos from the camera will have broader sharp views.

The stereo endoscope is reproduced by joining two of these endoscopes together, evaluating the proper position of the camera by viewing what they both take on a computer screen. Then they were inserted into a cylindrical tube so that it would be stable during use and reproduce a stereo endoscope with two cameras (Fig. 4). It was chosen to place the proximal part to the camera inside an aluminum cylinder to give stability, locking the two wires with clamps and the tips of the two endoscopes and the base of the cylinder with hot glue to prevent rotation and changes in the view of the endoscopes. The

Fig. 3. Depstech Usb 720p.

total cost is 100$, because the individual endoscope costs about 37$ and the cylindrical tube costs about 20$.

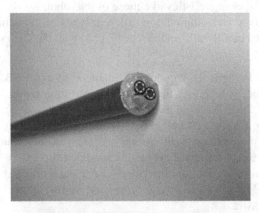

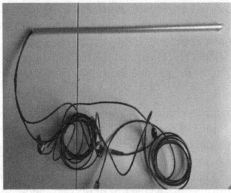

Fig. 4. The tip of our stereo endoscopic system and the entire cylindrical tube that cover cables.

3 Results

3.1 Camera Calibration

Camera calibration, which involves estimating intrinsic and extrinsic camera parameters, is the essential first procedure. Plane-based camera calibration methods can be applied, such as the well-known method of Zhang, which requires the camera to observe a planar calibration pattern in some unknown orientation. Initially correspondences are found between the points of the 3D world (corners of a given chessboard) and the corresponding points of the 2D image [10, 11]. For this purpose, in this work, we have used a calibration model of the 4×5 chessboard (implemented in the MATLAB toolbox (Fig. 5a) for camera calibration) by acquiring the dedicated calibration grid from 20 different positions (Fig. 5b).

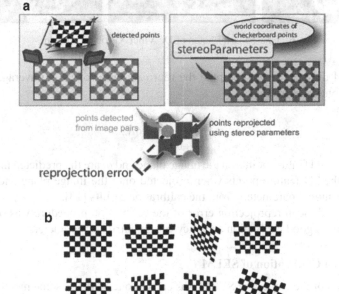

Fig. 5. a) MATLAB Toolbox; b) Chessboard used for calibration.

3.1.1 Camera Calibration of Da Vinci Xi System

Calibration of the camera of the Da Vinci endoscope, at one of the robotic surgical rooms at Cisanello Hospital, was carried out using the method just described, already done in other works [10, 11].

Here, we report some of the calibration photos of the right and left camera, respectively (Fig. 6).

Fig. 6. Chessboard Photos of Da Vinci Xi robotic system.

Expressed differently, we compute the reprojection error as the average norm of point correspondence errors:

$$e = \frac{1}{N} \sum_{i=0}^{N-1} |p_i - q_i|_2$$

p_i are the observed feature points on the image plane and q_i are the predicted image plane locations of the 3D feature points when projected onto the image plane and distorted using the lens model parameters from the calibration results [13].

The obtained mean reprojection error of the calibration procedure was of 0.16 px, which indicates a good calibration accuracy for the intrinsic parameters.

3.1.2 Camera Calibration of SELM

The calibration of the camera of SELM was carried out, with the same methodology.

Here, we report some of the calibration photos of the right and left camera, respectively (Fig. 7).

The obtained mean reprojection error of the calibration procedure was of 0.7 px. One possible reason why the reprojection error is higher than that of the Da Vinci is that the endoscope used, commercialized in the industrial and non-medical market, does not have an advanced brightness control in the technical specifications.

As can be seen from the graph below, the calibration was carried out under the same conditions, at the same distance, with the same grid and framing it correctly in the centre of the image. (Fig. 8a, 8b):

3.2 Comparison of Two Stereo Endoscopes

After a description of the specifications and calibration of both endoscopes under consideration, a comparison of the two can be made. The endoscope of the Da Vinci Xi

Fig. 7. Chessboard Photos of Da Vinci Xi robotic system

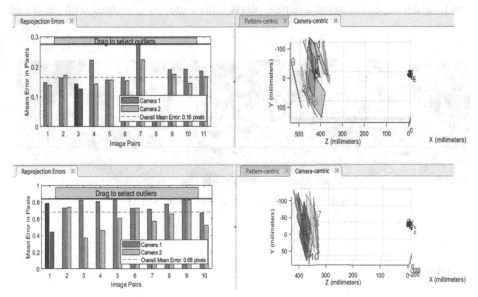

Fig. 8. a) Reprojection Errors Graph of Da Vinci Xi; b) Reprojection Errors Graph of our stereo endoscope

and SELM has a stereoscopic viewing, thanks to the presence of two camera and two optical channels, the Da Vinci Xi has the stereocamera baseline measures 6 mm, while that of SELM about 4 mm. The diameter of the cameras is similar, it is about 4 mm for the Da Vinci Xi, while for our endoscope it is 5.5 mm. The angle of view, after an accurate measurement, for the Da Vinci Xi is 84°, while for our endoscope 80°. Another important parameter to evaluate is the focal length, to be able to use SELM for different types of in vitro tests, for ours it is 7–40 cm, like that of the Da Vinci which is capable of 6x and 10x magnify.

Here is a summary table of the compared parameters.

	Da Vinci Xi	SELM
Stereoscopic Viewing	✓	✓
Stereocamera Baseline	6 mm	4 mm
Endoscope Diameter	12 mm	14 mm
Angle of View	84°	80°
Depth of Field	6–35 cm	7–40 cm

In the Figure (Fig. 9) below, there is an example of Augmented Reality implemented with SELM, in which it is possible to see the stereoscopic vision. Using algorithms developed in MATLAB, it was possible to use the new SELM endoscope to recreate the virtual scenario, recreating the stereoscopic view of the Da Vinci. The right and left cameras present inside the endoscope provide two images on which the virtual content, which in this case represents a female pelvis with a uterus, is merged with excellent accuracy.

Fig. 9. A trial of augmented reality with SELM

4   Discussion

Robotic surgery, over the last few years, has achieved important goals in terms of technological advancement. In particular, the Da Vinci robotic system allows the execution of very high precision surgical tasks. The disadvantage encountered by the surgeon is a progressive tactile loss, a training curve, the volumetric size of the robotic system and the very high cost. To overcome this, robotic technology can be merged with Augmented Reality. AR has proven to be a new technology that can quickly reduce the learning curve for users and improve the performance of this activity. In AR-based applications, the main challenge is to ensure the maximum degree of realism in merging computer-generated elements with the surgical scene [14]. As AR is a premature technology for surgery, the aim of many publications included in the survey is to demonstrate whether using AR in specific robotic assisted surgery (RAS) procedures is feasible. The concept of AR-integrated RAS is shown to be feasible in partial nephrectomy, cholecystectomy, TECAB, radiofrequency ablation, radical prostatectomy, mandibular angle split osteotomy, thyroidectomy, lung segmentectomy, cochlear implant procedure, and transoral surgery [15]. Possible robotic surgical applications can be simplified using Augmented Reality paradigms. Examples, objects of current studies, are total and partial kidney nephrectomies and different gynaecological surgical tasks. At the basis of these studies, in addition to a strict collection of anatomical information by the surgeon, a pre-planning with biomedical images (CT, MRI) is defined, then a virtual content is developed, which can facilitate the surgeon's actions during the surgery. Thus, having in the laboratory, an image receiving system, like that in robotic operating rooms, makes it possible to proceed with tests and simulations more quickly. Therefore, to speed up the programming of preclinical tests or facilitate the implementation of AR paradigms, without owning the entire robotic system or having to go inside hospital structures, it was decided to design a lab mock-up stereoscopic endoscope, replicating the Da Vinci Xi vision tool to have it in any bioengineering laboratory. SELM has stereoscopic view, 5.5 mm diameter camera, 1280×720 resolution, 7–40 cm depth of field, 80° angle of view, 30 fps. These data compared with the technical characteristics of the present endoscope in the Da Vinci Xi robotic system and combining this with the results of the calibrations carried out for both endoscopes, means that it is possible to state that the use of this endoscope can replace the Da Vinci endoscope in terms of visual quality and this it would lead to a reduction in the development time of new robotic and AR techniques, since the tests could be carried out in one's own laboratories, avoiding having to go to robotic operating rooms. It is also an endoscope capable of being implemented with a low cost, but which achieves very attractive results.

5 Conclusions

In this study, we presented the design and construction of a stereoscopic endoscope with USB or Type C connection, with the technical characteristics that reflect the endoscope used in the DaVinci Robotic System. This work makes the realization of in vitro tests in bioengineering laboratories more accessible and faster, while maintaining the same qualitative result of a robotic system present in the operating room.

Acknowledgment. We acknowledge the support of the European Union by the Next Generation EU project ECS00000017 'Ecosistema dell'Innovazione' Tuscany Health Ecosystem (THE, PNRR, Spoke 9: Robotics and Automation for Health), and the Italian Ministry of Education and Research (MUR) in the framework of the FoReLab and CrossLab projects (Departments of Excellence).

References

1. Robotic Surgery. https://www.forbesindia.com/article/brand-connect/robotic-surgery/705 51/1
2. D'Ettorre, C., et al.: Accelerating surgical robotics research: a review of 10 years with the da Vinci research kit. IEEE Robot. Autom. Mag. **28**(4), 56–78 (2021)
3. Da Vinci intuitive surgical – Procedures, da Vinci Surgery (2020). https://www.davincisu rgery.com/. Accessed 10 Aug 2020

4. Freschi, C., et al.: Technical review of the da Vinci surgical telemanipulator. Int. J. Med. Robot. Comput. Assist. Surg. **9**(4), 396–406 (2013)
5. Venkatesan, M., et al.: Virtual and augmented reality for biomedical applications. Cell Rep. Med. **2**(7) (2021)
6. Samset, E., et al.: Augmented reality in surgical procedures. In: Human Vision and Electronic Imaging XIII, vol. 6806, p. 68060K. International Society for Optics and Photonics, February 2008
7. Lungu, A.J., Swinkels, W., Claesen, L., Tu, P., Egger, J., Chen, X.: A review on the applications of virtual reality, augmented reality and mixed reality in surgical simulation: an extension to different kinds of surgery. Expert Rev. Med. Dev. **18**(1), 47–62 (2021)
8. Specifications for the da Vinci Xi Robotic Surgery system. https://www.wbhealth.gov.in/upl oaded_files/notice/UROLOGY/Da%20vinci%20Xi%20robotic%20surgery%20set.pdf
9. 720P USB Endoscope, 5.5mm Type-C Snake Inspection Camera 16.5ft. https://depstech.com/en-eu/collections/usb-endoscopes/products/usb-endoscope-86t-1mp
10. Mamone, V., et al.: Low-computational cost stitching method in a three-eyed endoscope. J. Healthc. Eng. **2019**, 5613931 (2019). https://doi.org/10.1155/2019/56139318.
11. Ferrari, V., et al.: Augmented reality visualization of deformable tubular structures for surgical simulation. Int. J. Med. Robot. Comput. Assist. Surg. (2015)
12. Chen, D., et al.: A 3D stereo system to assist surgical treatment of prostate cancer. In: Workshop of International Conference on Medical Image Computing and Computer Assisted Intervention, pp. 9–17 (2008)
13. The Retroprojection Error? https://www.camcalib.io/post/what-is-the-reprojection-error
14. Hu, X., Baena, F.R.y., Cutolo, F.: Head-mounted augmented reality platform for markerless orthopaedic navigation. IEEE J. Biomed. Health Inform. **26**(2), 910–921 (2022). https://doi.org/10.1109/JBHI.2021.3088442
15. Qian, L., Wu, J.Y., DiMaio, S.P., Navab, N., Kazanzides, P.: A review of augmented reality in robotic-assisted surgery. IEEE Trans. Med. Robot. Bionics **2**(1), 1–16 (2020). https://doi.org/10.1109/TMRB.2019.2957061

Augmented Reality in Orthognathic Surgery: A Multi-Modality Tracking Approach to Assess the Temporomandibular Joint Motion

Laura Cercenelli[1]([✉]), Nicolas Emiliani[1], Chiara Gulotta[2], Mirko Bevini[3], Giovanni Badiali[2,3], and Emanuela Marcelli[1]

[1] Laboratory of Bioengineering – eDIMES Lab, Department of Medical and Surgical Sciences (DIMEC), University of Bologna, Bologna, Italy
{laura.cercenelli,nicolas.emiliani2,emanuela.marcelli}@unibo.it
[2] Department of Biomedical and Neuromotor Sciences (DIBINEM), University of Bologna, Bologna, Italy
chiara.gulotta@studio.unibo.it, giovanni.badiali@unibo.it
[3] Oral and Maxillofacial Surgery Unit, IRCCS Azienda Ospedaliero Universitaria di Bologna, Bologna, Italy
mbevini.27@gmail.com

Abstract. Augmented Reality (AR) is a rapidly emerging technology finding growing applications in various surgery domains. In this study, we develop and test the feasibility of a novel AR application for Microsoft HoloLens2 Head Mounted Display (HMD) to support surgeons in the clinical evaluation of temporomandibular joint (TMJ) alterations that may require surgery. The application implements a multi-modality tracking based on the combination of a marker-less and a marker-based approach to simultaneously track the fixed part of the joint and the moving mandible. The AR application was tested on a volunteer performing the TMJ task, i.e. the opening and closing of the mouth. During the task, video recordings were taken from the HoloLens cameras to derive the trajectories as well as the horizontal and vertical excursions of the jaw movements. The AR-derived TMJ movements were then compared with standard kinesiographic acquisitions. The results demonstrated the feasibility of the proposed AR application in superimposing the 3D visualization of the joint to the patient's head, thus facilitating the diagnostic evaluation for the surgeon. The AR-derived trajectories were consistent with the kinesiography curves. Future improvements are needed to reduce the encumbrance of the tracker and to provide additional visual cues for the surgeon. The presented methodology can be easily transferred to other surgical applications which require simultaneous tracking of two anatomical parts, such as the case of bone repositioning to a pre-planned target location in maxillofacial and orthopedic surgery.

Keywords: Augmented reality · 3D technologies · HoloLens · orthognathic surgery · tracking technology · diagnosis

L. T. De Paolis et al. (Eds.): XR Salento 2023, LNCS 14219, pp. 379–394, 2023.
https://doi.org/10.1007/978-3-031-43404-4_25

1   Introduction

Augmented Reality (AR) preserves and detects the real view by enriching it with computer-generated elements that can be added to the surrounding natural environment. In surgery, AR represents a cutting-edge technology that improves the user's perceptual and comprehensive ability by projecting additional relevant information about patient anatomy and surgical planning directly onto the surgical field. Over the past decade, with the advent of high-detailed medical imaging, numerous surgical specialties have integrated AR into their surgical workflow namely, neurosurgery [1, 2], orthopedics surgery [3, 4], maxillofacial surgery [5–9], urology [10–13], ophthalmology [14], cardiovascular surgery [15] and spinal surgery [16, 17].

Especially, see-through head-mounted displays (HMDs) are promising technologies since they offer a direct projection of virtually augmented entities in the surgeon's field of view, a hands-free interaction, and 3D viewing capacity via stereoscopic rendering.

As emerged by recent reviews [18, 19], the HoloLens HMD is one of the most widely experienced devices in medical AR research in the last five years for supporting healthcare professionals in tasks such as diagnosis, treatment planning, and treatment execution.

The most ambitious research goal is to use AR technology for surgical navigation. However, technical challenges still remain to be addressed prior to the widespread adoption of these systems in the operating room to safely guide the surgical act with sufficient accuracy and comfort for the surgeon. Indeed, the accuracy of AR systems has been previously demonstrated in the order of 2–5 mm in phantom models for commercial headsets like Microsoft HoloLens [20–24], while an improved accuracy has been reported for wearable AR platforms specifically designed for high-precision surgical tasks [16, 25–28]. At the current state of technology, the use of general-purpose HMDs like HoloLens is very promising as tools for 3D visualizations in preoperative planning or in surgical simulation, which are low-risk scenarios compared to that of intraoperative guidance, not requiring sub-millimeter precision [19].

In the field of orthognathic surgery, some diagnostic procedures, preparatory to possible intervention, are routinely carried out simply through clinical examination by the surgeon. Specifically, the temporomandibular joint (TMJ), which articulates the mandible to the glenoid fossa of the temporal bone through the mandibular condyles, is fundamental to ensure the correct mandible movements, including chewing and speaking, therefore it is of great interest in the diagnostic phase, as well as in the post-surgery evaluation. In the routine clinical examination, the surgeon observes the interincisive line while the patient opens and closes the mouth, and makes a direct palpation of the TMJ, without counting on any type of imaging showing the underlying joint.

In some cases, the temporomandibular joint disorders are quantitively evaluated by jaw kinesiography which consists of an electronic system designed to trace and record the mandibular movement in three dimensions [29], thus typically providing the joint trajectories in both frontal and sagittal view. However, such instrumental analysis is not widely adopted in the clinical routine.

The aim of this paper is to develop and test the feasibility of a novel AR application for Microsoft HoloLens2 HMD to support the maxillofacial surgeons in the clinical evaluation of temporomandibular joint in patients who may be candidates for orthognathic surgery. The application exploits a multi-modality tracking, i.e. which combines two different tracking modalities to allow the simultaneous tracking of the fixed part of the joint, i.e. the glenoid fossa of the temporal bone, and the moving part, i.e. the mandibular condyles. We extracted the joint trajectories as perceived from the AR views by post-processing the video recordings captured by HoloLens cameras, and we compared them to the trajectories obtained from the kinesiography recordings.

2 Related Works

AR systems proposed for diagnostic purposes and surgical navigation need to match virtual information with the real world, and some require to track an anatomical moving part or surgical tools in real-time. Hence, registration and tracking techniques play a crucial role. A recent review [30] gives a clear overview of the registration and tracking techniques used in AR surgical navigation systems. Tracking methods can be mainly divided into tracking with integrated cameras and external tracking.

The first category refers to that several AR devices incorporate cameras into their tracking process. These cameras are used to track surface features or markers in the surgical environment for either marker-less tracking or marker-based tracking. For marker-based tracking, small planar markers are commonly created using libraries, such as Vuforia, AprilTags, and ArUco. Several studies incorporated such markers for creating AR navigation applications [31–33], while some others proposed their own custom-designed markers [34, 35]. For marker-less tracking, a real object is tracked in real-time without markers attached to it using the images captured by the cameras integrated into the AR device. Example of using marker-less registration and tracking methods in AR surgical navigation systems can be found in [36, 37].

In the case of external tracking, custom devices, such as visible light tracking (Micron tracker) or infrared tracking (NDI Polaris), are used as external tracking in the operating room [38, 39]. Another option is the point cloud tracking method (Intel RealSense sensor) that can capture the patient's surface in real-time and can be used for marker-less tracking [40].

In some cases, a combination of integrated and external tracking methods has been proposed to maximize the performance of the AR navigation system [41, 42].

Focusing specifically on AR applications for diagnostics, Teatini et al. [43] reported a MR tool able to provide better understanding of the pathological anatomy for orthopaedic hip and pelvic diagnostics by showing dynamic holograms which follow the movements of the patient to diagnose anomalies in the hip joint, and surgical instrument navigation. Their tracking approach is based on using HoloLens (integrated cameras) in combination with an external optical tracking system.

In our work we proposed an AR tool applied to diagnostic-surgical field, in which the tracking is essentially based on integrated cameras of HoloLens, but with a combined marker-less and marker-based approach.

3   Materials and Methods

In the following sections we present the development steps of the AR application, and the experimental phase. The AR application was designed to provide both a frontal and a sagittal view, thus allowing a comprehensive exploration of TMJ movement in the 3D space.

3.1   Anatomical 3D Modeling and Virtual Content Preparation

The study involved a volunteer, having a computed tomography (CT) scan of the midface available, and it was approved by Bioethics Committee of the University of Bologna (protocol n. 0025237, 02 February 2023).

The skull, the mandible, and the head skin of the volunteer were segmented from CT scan using Mimics Medical 25.0 (Materialise, Leuven, Belgium). Three-dimensional (3D) meshes were then generated from all the segmented masks and saved in Standard Tessellation Language (STL) format (Fig. 1).

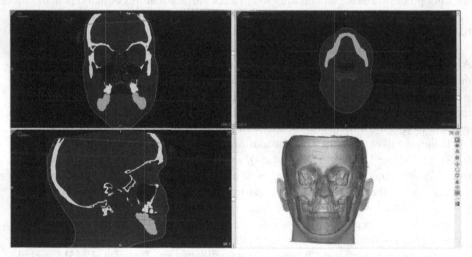

Fig. 1. Anatomical 3D modeling prepared for the AR application starting from the volunteer's CT scan.

The skull model was cut using 3-Matic design software (Materialise, Leuven, Belgium), so that only the glenoid fossa, i.e. the depression in the temporal bone that articulates with the mandible, was left (Fig. 2). The STL file of the mandible was duplicated and the copy was symmetrically cut in a way to separate the left and the right branch. This latter was used as virtual content to be displayed in the sagittal AR view (right side) so that to avoid the perspective overlap of the contralateral ramus if using the whole mandible. Some virtual spherical markers were added both on the fixed glenoid fossa and the moving mandible to have some reference points to follow in the reconstruction of the TMJ trajectories from video recordings captured during the AR view (Fig. 2).

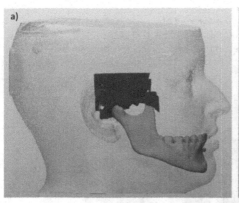
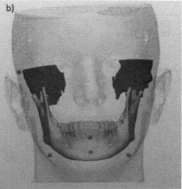

Fig. 2. The virtual content to be displayed in augmented reality for the sagittal (a) and frontal (b) views: the glenoid fossa in the temporal bone (blue), the mandible (green) with the spherical markers for trajectory reconstruction (pink). (Color figure online)

3.2 AR App and Multi-modality Tracking

The AR scenes were built using Unity3D v2019.4.21f1 (Unity Technologies, San Francisco, CA, USA). All virtual models of interest (i.e. the glenoid fossa, the mandible, the head skin) were imported into Unity3D software extended with the Vuforia Engine Software Development Kit (PTC Inc., Boston, MA, USA). Vuforia Engine uses feature tracking and matching concept of computer vision to track and detect objects and images in the real world and based on their orientation it renders the corresponding virtual objects on those.

For the presented AR application, it is required to simultaneously recognize and track two different anatomical parts involved in the TMJ, i.e., the fixed glenoid fossa and the moving mandible. So, a multi-modality tracking approach was implemented, by combining two different tracking modalities. For the glenoid fossa, which represents the fixed component of the joint, a marker-less Vuforia Engine tracking modality ("Model Target"), based on object recognition by its shape, was used. For tracking the moving mandible, a marker-based tracking was implemented, by leveraging the Vuforia Engine "Image Target" tracking mode (Fig. 3). Details on these tracking modalities were reported in the following paragraphs.

Working with this multi-modality tracking approach, the movement of the mandible can be tracked continuously, and its position can be displayed to the surgeon wearing the HoloLens 2 device in relation to the fixed glenoid fossa.

Two different AR applications were created and tested: one for the frontal view and one for the sagittal view, in order to replicate the main views investigated during the clinical observation and in the kinesiography examination. Moreover, interactable user interface toggles (check boxes) were added to turn on/off the rendering of each virtual structure during the AR view.

Model Target (Marker-Less Tracking). This is one of the Vuforia Object Tracking methods. It allows to recognize objects in the real world based on their shape using pre-existing 3D models, such as a 3D CAD (computer-assisted design) model or a 3D scan

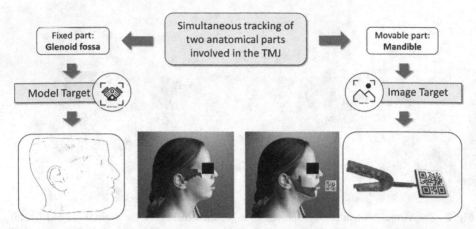

Fig. 3. Scheme of the multi-modality tracking approach experimented to assess the temporomandibular joint motion.

of the object. The object has to be geometrically rigid and to present not shiny surface features. To implement this marker-less tracking method, it is required to generate a Model Target using the Model Target Generator (MTG) application. The MTG takes as input a 3D model representing the object to be tracked, draws an image showing an approximation of the object's 3D shape and allows for setting up the distance and viewing angle the object should be recognized from ("Guide View"). Then, it is required that the user holds the AR display at these angle and distance relative to the real object (i.e. the set Guide View), to initialize the tracking. The Model Target tracking also works if the object is not well textured or its appearance varies – e.g. different colors or textures.

Image Target (Marker-Based Tracking). This is the most commonly used Vuforia Engine tracking method based on the recognition and tracking of a pre-defined image (Image Target) that provides sufficient details to be detected, typically a QR-code pattern. The Vuforia Engine detects and tracks the image by comparing extracted natural features from the camera image against the known Image Target previously selected in terms of tracking performance and then stored in a cloud database. The selected Image Target can be downloaded from the database as a package suitable for integration in the Unity app.

For the study, the 3D model of the volunteer's head skin was used as Model Target to track the subject's head, to allow the virtual-to-real registration of the glenoid fossa, which is the fixed part of the TMJ. Two Guide Views were generated for the Model Target to implement both the frontal and sagittal AR views.

For the Image Target tracking a dedicated tracker was designed.

3.3   Tracker Design and Fabrication

The reconstructed mandible was used to design a patient-specific dental splint fitting the lower arch teeth of the subject. The splint was provided with a holder that can be univocally connected to the marker used for tracking the movable mandible.

To implement Image Target tracking we used a flat marker ($40 \times 40 \times 3$ mm) with a binary QR-code pattern. It was necessary to provide two versions of the tracker, one with the QR-code having an orientation parallel to the frontal plane, one with an orientation parallel to the sagittal plane. This ensures to have the Image Target constantly pointing towards the front camera when the surgeon looks at the subject from the two perspectives (Fig. 4).

The splint with the holder was then produced with stereolitography 3D printer (Form3B, FormLabs, Somerville, MA, USA) using a biocompatible resin (Surgical guide, FormLabs, Somerville, MA, USA), while the flat markers were produced as textured objects using Polyjet 3D printing technology (J720 Dental 3D printer (Stratasys Ltd., Eden Prairie, MN), and then securely connected to the holder through a pin-hole mechanical joint.

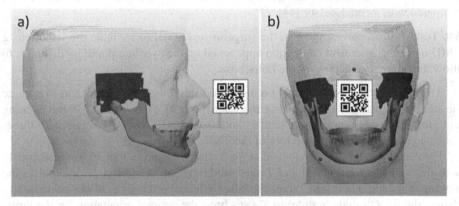

Fig. 4. The designed tracker anchored to the subject's teeth and provided with the flat Image Target with two different orientations to ensure to be easily detected in both sagittal (a) and frontal (b) views.

3.4 Experiments

To evaluate the feasibility of the developed AR app based on the multi-modality tracking approach, a pilot study was conducted on a volunteer.

Kinesiographic Recordings. A commercially available kinesiography (KG) device (K7 Myotronics Kynesiograph, Harari MS, Milan, Italy) was used for measuring and recording the mandibular function on the volunteer. All KG assessments were made by a specialist who had expertise in the use of such devices. During the examination, the subject was seated on a chair, with her trunk perpendicular to the floor and head upright. The KG recordings were made with the use of a magnet temporarily positioned on the subject's buccal mucosa under the mandibular central incisors to monitor the location of the mandible against a sensor array suspended in front of the face by a lightweight frame placed on the bridge of the nose and connected behind the head by straps. Following the indications of the specialist, the volunteer performed the opening and closing jaw movements (that we call "TMJ task"). The frame registered in real-time the magnetic field variations during the movement of the magnet in the three space directions, and with these coordinates, graphic representation of TMJ trajectories along the frontal and the sagittal view were provided. From these trajectories the maximum mouth opening and the maximum lateral deviations from the mid-sagittal plane during jaw opening (in millimetres) can be extracted.

Experimental AR Device. For testing the developed AR application, we used the Microsoft HoloLens 2 device, one of the most relevant commercially available Optical See-Through (OST) HMDs. It consists of a high-definition, stereoscopic, optical HMD with a set of grayscale, RGB, and depth cameras which identify the surrounding geometries. Moreover, it includes sensor fusion algorithms which recognize hand gestures and voice commands. It represents an upgrade in terms of hardware (enhanced field of view (52°), reduced weight (566 g) and improved battery life (3 h)) and software, compared with its predecessor [44].

AR Test. Before starting the test, the surgeon was asked to calibrate the HoloLens 2 HMD using the Microsoft calibration app, based on the user interpupillary distance, to allow the optimal perception of the holograms.

The volunteer was asked to put on the dental splint with the tracker and to execute the same TMJ task performed during the kinesiography examination, i.e. the opening and closing of the mouth. Both sagittal and frontal AR views were tested to three-dimensionally evaluate the trajectory of the TMJ.

For each view, the surgeon looked at the volunteer in order to track simultaneously both the subject's head via Model Target modality, and the QR-code, integral to the moving mandible, via Image Target modality. Changing the view, it was necessary to change the flat QR-code in order to always have the optimal orientation for the target image with respect to the HoloLens camera. During the procedure the surgeon can press toggle buttons to turn on/off the rendering of the virtual elements.

The AR views perceived by the surgeon, with the glenoid fossa and the corresponding moving mandibular condyles directly superimposed on the patient's face, were reported in Fig. 5.

3.5 Trajectories Reconstruction from AR View

In addition to the direct superimposition of the underlying TMJ of interest on the subject's face, we also tried to extract quantitative information on the trajectories of the moving mandible with respect to the fixed glenoid fossa. These trajectories were reconstructed from the video recordings captured by the HoloLens cameras during the AR view. The video frames were imported in Matlab App-Designer (R2019b, MathWorks, Natick, MA, USA). A script was created to recognize in each video frame the virtual spherical markers positioned on the moving mandible and the ones positioned on the glenoid fossa and forehead as references (Fig. 2). A complete joint closing/opening cycle in which tracking of both the fixed glenoid fossa and the moving mandible remained stable and reliable was selected for video recording analysis. The displacement of mandible markers from one frame to another was computed, and plots of the mandible trajectory,

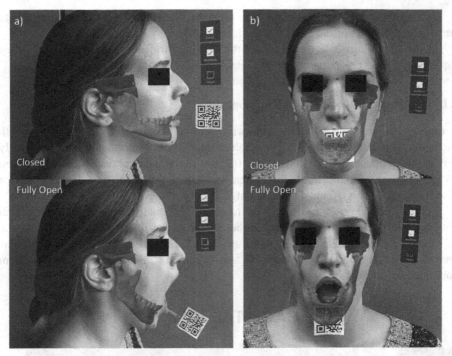

Fig. 5. The sagittal (a) and frontal (b) AR views experienced by the surgeon during the test. The fixed glenoid fossa (in blue) is registered via the Model Target tracking based on the volunteer's head skin model. The moving mandible (in green) is detected and tracked via the flat Image Target anchored to a dental splint. (Color figure online)

as described by the spherical markers during the TMJ tasks, were obtained for both the frontal and sagittal views. The reference markers on the glenoid fossa and forehead were also followed in the video frames to possibly correct errors due to a misalignment in the virtual-to-real registration during the TMJ tasks.

4   Results

The developed AR application demonstrated to be able to track and display in overlay on the subject the anatomical structures of interest for evaluating the TMJ kinematics.

The marker-less Model Target tracking worked efficiently in recognizing the subject's head shape, and the AR markers on the dental splint were almost immediately detected in both the sagittal and frontal applications. The surgeon visually confirmed a correct registration based on the good alignment of the virtual skin's head model with the actual subject's head shape, and the AR markers silhouette with the actual AR markers mounted on the tracker.

The subject considered acceptable the presence of the tracker anchored to the teeth during the execution of the task.

In the following sections we report the obtained trajectories from the AR video captures and their comparison with the kinesiography recordings.

4.1 Comparative Results with Kinesiography

For the sagittal view, the AR-derived trajectories of the opening and closing of the mouth showed a good match with the kinesiographic signals, both qualitatively and quantitively (Fig. 6). We obtained a deviation of only 0.2 mm for the vertical displacement between the closed mouth and the mouth fully open, and a deviation of 0.7 mm for the posterior extension, i.e. the horizontal displacement (Table 1).

For the frontal view, the AR-derived trajectory was qualitatively comparable to that obtained with the kinesiography, but a higher deviation was found for both the horizontal (2.1 mm) and vertical displacement (6.5 mm) (Fig. 7, Table 1). Specifically, the AR view underestimates the vertical displacement and slightly also the horizontal displacement compared to kinesiography.

SAGITTAL View

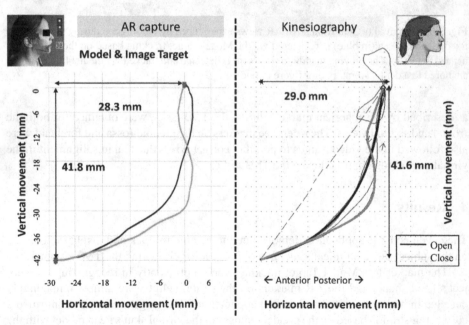

Fig. 6. Comparison between the mandible trajectories derived from AR view and the ones obtained by kynesiography, in the sagittal view.

FRONTAL View

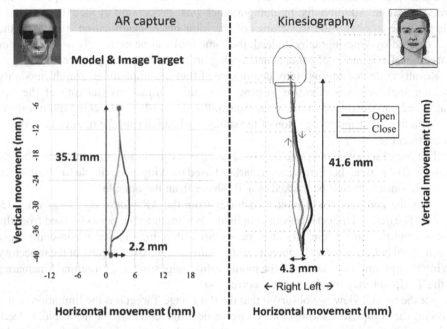

Fig. 7. Comparison between the mandible trajectories derived from AR view and the ones obtained by kynesiography, in the frontal view.

Table 1. Horizontal and vertical displacements (from closed to fully open mouth), obtained for both Sagittal and Frontal views.

	SAGITTAL View		FRONTAL View	
	Horizontal displacement [mm]	Vertical displacement [mm]	Horizontal displacement [mm]	Vertical displacement [mm]
Kinesiography	29.0	41.6	4.3	41.6
AR capture	28.3	41.8	2.2	35.1

5 Discussion

5.1 Results Discussion and Study Limitations

In this study we investigate the feasibility of using a novel AR application for Microsoft HoloLens 2 to help the surgeon in the diagnosis of possible alterations of TMJ requiring surgical interventions. Advantage over the standard clinical examination and kinesiography is that the surgeon is provided with a sort of "x-ray" view of the underlying anatomical structures involved in the joint, by simply looking at the patient performing the opening and closing of the mouth. Therefore, the AR view can offer a diagnostic contribution to the clinical evaluation provided by the only natural visual inspection and direct palpation. Additionally, by doing a quick post-processing of the AR recordings it is possible to obtain the trajectories of the joint under examination, similar to the ones derived by kinesiography. Indeed, the same tool can be extremely useful also for post-surgical evaluation of patients undergoing orthognathic surgery procedures.

Results collected in this study demonstrated that the implemented multi-modality tracking approach was effective in providing the simultaneous tracking of the two anatomical parts involved in the joint. Indeed, the marker-based tracking did not interfere with the 3D shape recognition of the subject 's head during the marker-less Model Target tracking.

The use of a marker-less tracking is advantageous since it avoids any encumbering tracker on the patient, but in this case a marker-based tracking is inevitable for the moving mandible since it cannot be tracked as a 3D shape from the outside.

Also, the computation of joint trajectories from the AR video recordings was successful. The derived trajectories were qualitatively similar to the ones obtained from the kinesiographic exam. From a clinical perspective, they highlighted a non-completely symmetrical behavior between opening and closing (i.e., no overlapping of the trajectory during the opening and closing of the mouth), this suggesting a sub-optimal kinematics of the TMJ, that may require surgical correction.

For the frontal view, we observed that the flat Image Target has the limitation of not allowing the complete tracking of the entire vertical movement of the mandible. Indeed, at the position of the maximum opening of the mouth, the AR marker surface with the QR-code no longer appears in a frontal view with respect to the HoloLens camera, so tracking is lost. This explains why the frontal vertical excursion is underestimated. To overcome this limitation, the option of replacing the flat Image Target with a cuboid Multi Target, which uses multiple image targets assigned to each face of a cube, will be experimented in future studies. Indeed, Multi Target functions in such a way that all faces of the cuboid can be tracked at the same time because they have a shared pre-defined pose relative to Multi Target's origin. This should ensure to have the target image visible throughout the entire vertical excursion of the joint, also without requiring to change the tracker orientation when passing from sagittal to frontal view.

As we previously reported for a phantom study [20, 24], also in this case we observed that, especially for the marker-less Model Target tracking, the registration accuracy is quite sensitive to ambient light conditions. So, it was necessary to make several attempts, optimizing the light conditions, before obtaining an acceptable and stable registration of virtual-to-real head of the subject.

Another limitation is the latency in tracking the moving mandible, i.e. the delay between when a pose of the mandible changes and the AR display changes in response. Indeed, a too fast opening/closing of the mouth causes a loss of tracking of the moving mandible, therefore errors in virtual-to-real registration and consequent unreliable AR-derived movements. For this reason, it was necessary to ask the subject to perform the TMJ task quite slowly.

5.2 Future Directions

The presented AR application will certainly be tested and evaluated on other subjects, also including patients with evident alterations of TMJ kinematics.

The design of the tracker should be optimized in order to make it fully visible throughout the entire excursion of the joint.

Moreover, it could also be useful to integrate the AR application with additional visual cues that may further help the surgeon in the diagnosis process. For example, a video recording of the physiological movement of the TMJ in the frontal and sagittal view can be projected in the right up angle on the HoloLens field of view. In this way, the surgeon during the AR-assisted clinical examination can use it as reference.

An interesting feature of the presented methodology consists in that it can be transferred to specific surgical tasks requiring the simultaneous tracking of two objects. As for example, in orthognathic surgery the repositioning of bone parts, such as the jaw, following a predefined preoperative plan after it has been cut, is a quite common task. In this case the marker-less tracking through the facial 3D shape can be used to project on the patient the target jaw position, e.g. by displaying a cubic volume that circumscribes the jaw part in its planned position. The cut jaw can be tracked in real-time with the marker-based mode using a tracker anchored to the teeth as in the present application. The cut jaw can be also displayed circumscribed in a virtual cubic volume which identifies it in the 3D space. The surgeon wearing the HMD looks at the patient, tracks via Model Target his/her head and views the planned target volume for repositioning, superimposed on the patient. Looking at the cut jaw, via the marker-based tracking, the surgeons can track in real-time the resected bone part. The repositioning task is to superimpose under AR guidance the virtual cubic volume associated with the movable cut jaw to the virtual cubic target volume projected onto the patient.

Similar approaches can be thought for bone repositioning tasks in other surgical fields, like orthopedic surgery.

6 Conclusion

In this study, we developed an AR application for Microsoft HoloLens 2 based on a multi-modality tracking to assist the surgeon in the diagnosis of possible TMJ alterations. We evaluated the methodology in an experimental scenario, taking as reference the standard kinesiography examination for quantitative assessments. The combination of the marker-less Model Target tracking with the marked-based tracking exploiting the anchorage to the subject's teeth seemed to be a promising solution. It can be easily introduced in the clinical practice in the near future, even if some aspects for the tracker still have to be improved. Compared to kinesiography and standard clinical examination, the proposed AR application offers the advantage to directly see-through the anatomy of the patient, having a direct visualization of the joint at work, superimposed on the patient's face.

The reported experience can represent an inspiration for future developments of AR applications in which similar multi-modality tracking approaches are required to simultaneously track two anatomical parts, such as the case of intraoperative bone repositioning in maxillofacial and/or orthopedic surgery.

References

1. Cannizzaro, D., et al.: Augmented reality in neurosurgery, state of art and future projections: a systematic review. Front Surg. **9**, 864792 (2022). https://doi.org/10.3389/fsurg.2022.864792
2. Dadario, N.B., Quinoa, T., Khatri, D., Boockvar, J., Langer, D., D'Amico, R.S.: Examining the benefits of extended reality in neurosurgery: a systematic review. J. Clin. Neurosci. **94**, 41–53 (2021). https://doi.org/10.1016/j.jocn.2021.09.037
3. Hunter Matthews, J., Shields, J.S.: The clinical application of augmented reality in orthopaedics: where do we stand? Curr. Rev. Musculoskel. Med. **14**(5), 316–319 (2021). https://doi.org/10.1007/s12178-021-09713-8
4. Jud, Lukas, et al.: Applicability of augmented reality in orthopedic surgery – a systematic review. BMC Musculoskel. Disord. **21**(1), 103 (2020). https://doi.org/10.1186/s12891-020-3110-2
5. Badiali, G., et al.: Review on augmented reality in oral and cranio-maxillofacial surgery: toward "Surgery-Specific" head-up displays. IEEE Access **8**, 59015–59028 (2020). https://doi.org/10.1109/ACCESS.2020.2973298
6. Benmahdjoub, M., van Walsum, T., van Twisk, P., Wolvius, E.B.: Augmented reality in craniomaxillofacial surgery: added value and proposed recommendations through a systematic review of the literature. Int. J. Oral Maxillofacial Surg. **50**(7), 969–978 (2021). https://doi.org/10.1016/j.ijom.2020.11.015
7. Ceccariglia, F., Cercenelli, L., Badiali, G., Marcelli, E., Tarsitano, A.: Application of augmented reality to maxillary resections: a three-dimensional approach to maxillofacial oncologic surgery. J. Pers. Med. **12**(12), 2047 (2022). https://doi.org/10.3390/jpm12122047
8. Battaglia, S., et al.: Augmented reality-assisted periosteum pedicled flap harvesting for head and neck reconstruction: an anatomical and clinical viability study of a galeo-pericranial flap. J Clin Med **9**(7), E2211 (2020). https://doi.org/10.3390/jcm9072211
9. Battaglia, S., et al.: Combination of CAD/CAM and augmented reality in free fibula bone harvest. Plast. Reconstr. Surg. Glob. Open **7**(11), e2510 (2019). https://doi.org/10.1097/GOX.0000000000002510
10. Reis, G., et al.: Mixed reality applications in urology: requirements and future potential. Ann. Med. Surg. (Lond.) **66**, 102394 (2021). https://doi.org/10.1016/j.amsu.2021.102394
11. Schiavina, Riccardo, et al.: Real-time augmented reality three-dimensional guided robotic radical prostatectomy: preliminary experience and evaluation of the impact on surgical planning. Eur. Urol. Focus **7**(6), 1260–1267 (2021). https://doi.org/10.1016/j.euf.2020.08.004
12. Schiavina, R., et al.: Augmented reality to guide selective clamping and tumor dissection during robot-assisted partial nephrectomy: a preliminary experience. Clin. Genitourin Cancer **19**(3), e149–e155 (2021). https://doi.org/10.1016/j.clgc.2020.09.005
13. Bianchi, L., et al.: The use of augmented reality to guide the intraoperative frozen section during robot-assisted radical prostatectomy. Eur. Urol. **80**(4), 480–488 (2021). https://doi.org/10.1016/j.eururo.2021.06.020
14. Li, T., et al.: Augmented reality in ophthalmology: applications and challenges. Front Med. (Lausanne) **8**, 733241 (2021). https://doi.org/10.3389/fmed.2021.733241
15. Lareyre, F., Chaudhuri, A., Adam, C., Carrier, M., Mialhe, C., Raffort, J.: Applications of head-mounted displays and smart glasses in vascular surgery. Ann. Vasc. Surg. **75**, 497–512 (2021). https://doi.org/10.1016/j.avsg.2021.02.033
16. Molina, C.A., Sciubba, D.M., Greenberg, J.K., Khan, M., Witham, T.: Clinical accuracy, technical precision, and workflow of the first in human use of an augmented-reality head-mounted display stereotactic navigation system for spine surgery. Oper. Neurosurg. **20**(3), 300–309 (2021). https://doi.org/10.1093/ons/opaa398

17. McCloskey, K., Turlip, R., Ahmad, H.S., Ghenbot, Y.G., Chauhan, D., Yoon, J.W.: Virtual and augmented reality in spine surgery: a systematic review. World Neurosurg. **173**, 96–107 (2023). https://doi.org/10.1016/j.wneu.2023.02.068

18. Doughty, M., Ghugre, N.R., Wright, G.A.: Augmenting performance: a systematic review of optical see-through head-mounted displays in surgery. J. Imaging **8**(7), 203 (2022). https://doi.org/10.3390/jimaging8070203

19. Gsaxner, C., et al.: The HoloLens in medicine: a systematic review and taxonomy. Med. Image Anal. **85**, 102757 (2023). https://doi.org/10.1016/j.media.2023.102757

20. Cercenelli, L., et al.: Augmented reality to assist skin paddle harvesting in osteomyocutaneous fibular flap reconstructive surgery: a pilot evaluation on a 3D-printed leg phantom. Front. Oncol. **11**, 804748 (2022). https://doi.org/10.3389/fonc.2021.804748

21. Puxun, T., Gao, Y., Lungu, A.J., Li, D., Wang, H., Chen, X.: Augmented reality based navigation for distal interlocking of intramedullary nails utilizing Microsoft HoloLens 2. Comput. Biol. Med. **133**, 104402 (2021). https://doi.org/10.1016/j.compbiomed.2021.104402

22. Zhou, Z., Jiang, S., Yang, Z., Bin, X., Jiang, B.: Surgical navigation system for brachytherapy based on mixed reality using a novel stereo registration method. Virt. Real. **25**(4), 975–984 (2021). https://doi.org/10.1007/s10055-021-00503-8

23. Uhl, C., Hatzl, J., Meisenbacher, K., Zimmer, L., Hartmann, N., Böckler, D.: Mixed-reality-assisted puncture of the common femoral artery in a phantom model. J. Imaging **8**(2), 47 (2022). https://doi.org/10.3390/jimaging8020047

24. Ruggiero, F., et al.: Preclinical application of augmented reality in pediatric craniofacial surgery: an accuracy study. J. Clin. Med. **12**(7), 2693 (2023). https://doi.org/10.3390/jcm12072693

25. Cercenelli, L., et al.: The wearable VOSTARS system for augmented reality-guided surgery: preclinical phantom evaluation for high-precision maxillofacial tasks. J. Clin. Med. **9**(11), E3562 (2020). https://doi.org/10.3390/jcm9113562

26. Condino, S., et al.: Wearable augmented reality platform for aiding complex 3D trajectory tracing. Sensors (Basel) **20**(6), E1612 (2020). https://doi.org/10.3390/s20061612

27. Carbone, M., et al.: Architecture of a hybrid video/optical see-through head-mounted display-based augmented reality surgical navigation platform. Information **13**(2), 81 (2022). https://doi.org/10.3390/info13020081

28. Badiali, G., et al.: The vostars project: a new wearable hybrid video and optical see-through augmented reality surgical system for maxillofacial surgery. Int. J. Oral Maxillofacial Surg. **48**, 153 (2019). https://doi.org/10.1016/j.ijom.2019.03.472

29. Venturi, G., et al.: Use of kinesiography to assess mandibular function following segmental resection and microvascular reconstruction. J Craniofac Surg **31**(8), 2256–2259 (2020). https://doi.org/10.1097/SCS.0000000000006774

30. Ma, L., Huang, T., Wang, J., Liao, H.: Visualization, registration and tracking techniques for augmented reality guided surgery: a review. Phys Med Biol **68**(4), 04TR02 (2023). https://doi.org/10.1088/1361-6560/acaf23

31. Liebmann, F., et al.: Pedicle screw navigation using surface digitization on the Microsoft HoloLens. Int. J. Cars **14**(7), 1157–1165 (2019). https://doi.org/10.1007/s11548-019-01973-7

32. Frantz, T., Jansen, B., Duerinck, J., Vandemeulebroucke, J.: Augmenting Microsoft's HoloLens with vuforia tracking for neuronavigation. Healthc Technol. Lett. **5**(5), 221–225 (2018). https://doi.org/10.1049/htl.2018.5079

33. Luzon, J.A., Stimec, B.V., Bakka, A.O., Edwin, B., Ignjatovic, D.: Value of the surgeon's sightline on hologram registration and targeting in mixed reality. Int. J. Cars **15**(12), 2027–2039 (2020). https://doi.org/10.1007/s11548-020-02263-3

34. Zhou, Z., Yang, Z., Jiang, S., Zhuo, J., Zhu, T., Ma, S.: Augmented reality surgical navigation system based on the spatial drift compensation method for glioma resection surgery. Med. Phys. **49**(6), 3963–3979 (2022). https://doi.org/10.1002/mp.15650

35. Dibble, C.F., Molina, C.A.: Device profile of the XVision-spine (XVS) augmented-reality surgical navigation system: overview of its safety and efficacy. Expert Rev. Med. Dev. **18**(1), 1–8 (2021). https://doi.org/10.1080/17434440.2021.1865795

36. Gu, W., Shah, K., Knopf, J., Navab, N., Unberath, M.: Feasibility of image-based augmented reality guidance of total shoulder arthroplasty using microsoft HoloLens 1. Comput. Methods Biomech. Biomed. Eng. Imaging Vis. **9**(3), 261–270 (2021). https://doi.org/10.1080/216 81163.2020.1835556

37. Pepe, A., et al.: A marker-less registration approach for mixed reality-aided maxillofacial surgery: a pilot evaluation. J. Digit Imaging **32**(6), 1008–1018 (2019). https://doi.org/10. 1007/s10278-019-00272-6

38. Guo, N., Wang, T., Yang, B., Hu, L., Liu, H., Wang, Y.: An online calibration method for microsoft hololens. IEEE Access **7**, 101795–101803 (2019). https://doi.org/10.1109/ACC ESS.2019.2930701

39. Chan, H.H.L., et al.: An integrated augmented reality surgical navigation platform using multi-modality imaging for guidance. PLOS ONE **16**(4), e0250558 (2021). https://doi.org/ 10.1371/journal.pone.0250558

40. Hu, X., Baena, F.R., Cutolo, F.: Head-mounted augmented reality platform for markerless orthopaedic navigation. IEEE J. Biomed. Health Inf. **26**(2), 910–921 (2022). https://doi.org/ 10.1109/JBHI.2021.3088442

41. Gao, Y., Liu, K., Lin, L., Wang, X., Xie, L.: Use of augmented reality navigation to optimise the surgical management of craniofacial fibrous dysplasia. Brit. J. Oral Maxillofacial Surg. **60**(2), 162–167 (2022). https://doi.org/10.1016/j.bjoms.2021.03.011

42. El-Hariri, H., Pandey, P., Hodgson, A.J., Garbi, R.: Augmented reality visualisation for orthopaedic surgical guidance with pre- and intra-operative multimodal image data fusion. Healthcare Technol. Lett. **5**(5), 189–193 (2018). https://doi.org/10.1049/htl.2018.5061

43. Teatini, A., Kumar, R.P., Elle, O.J., Wiig, O.: Mixed reality as a novel tool for diagnostic and surgical navigation in orthopaedics. Int. J. Comput. Assist. Radiol. Surg. **16**(3), 407–414 (2021). https://doi.org/10.1007/s11548-020-02302-z

44. Palumbo, A.: Microsoft HoloLens 2 in medical and healthcare context: state of the art and future prospects. Sensors (Basel) **22**(20), 7709 (2022). https://doi.org/10.3390/s22207709

Enhancing Visualization of Surgical Tool Through Integrated Motion Tracking System

A. Kavitha[1]($\boxtimes$), S. Pravin Kumar[1], G. Darsana[1], and G. Sudhir[2]

[1] Department of Biomedical Engineering, Center for Healthcare Technologies,
Sri Sivasubramaniya Nadar College of Engineering, Kalavakkam, Tamil Nadu, India
kavithaa@ssn.edu.in
[2] Sri Ramachandra Medical College, Chennai, Tamil Nadu, India

Abstract. Spinal surgeries come up with various intra-operative complications and this demands a flawless tool tracking procedure of the surgical tool. Computerized navigation improves the accuracy of invasive surgical tool placement during spine surgery. This paper reports a navigation technology with minimal infrastructural requirement that supports surgical operations with a real-time non-obstructive view of the surgical field enabling the surgeon to see three-dimensional (3D) structures of medical images. Proposed system employs Hololens hardware with the integrated motion tracking system for visualization and image analysis. Results show that the spatial error of the overlaid virtual tool is 0.01 units can be achieved using this integrated system.

Keywords: Surgical Tool tracking · Hololens · Vuforia engine · Unity 3D

1 Introduction

Image guided surgery (IGS), is a computer-assisted navigation system employed in operating rooms. Has become increasingly common in surgical operations, particularly in neurosurgery, traumatology, and orthopaedics. In circumstances of minimally invasive surgery (MIS), visualisation in IGS may be accomplished through a smaller and narrower dissection [1]. Image guided navigation, which allows for a larger region of bone and soft tissue visualisation through a smaller area of surgical dissection, can be a tremendous help to MIS surgeons during spinal surgery.

For neurosurgical interventions alone 13.8 million patients undergo complicated surgical procedures worldwide every year [2]. In spine and brain surgeries the anatomical structures under surgical margins are highly intricate demanding extremely sophisticated and skilled surgical standards. Due to these limitations, the development of intraoperative navigation systems is especially beneficial since they can enhance patient outcomes by lowering postoperative morbidity, extending patient survival, and enhancing postoperative quality of life by minimizing neurological abnormalities.

With the advent of extended reality, it is now becoming increasingly possible to employ real and virtual world interactions in a seemingly natural environment. This requires tracking of real-world objects to place the virtual objects as overlays on the

L. T. De Paolis et al. (Eds.): XR Salento 2023, LNCS 14219, pp. 395–404, 2023.
https://doi.org/10.1007/978-3-031-43404-4_26

required positions. The various tracking systems include mechanical, acoustic, optical and electromagnetic tracking systems. The mechanical trackers make use of the linkages to track the real time positions. Whereas optical systems employ cameras and markers for tracking. Acoustic systems make use of ultrasound sensors with the transmitted and received ultrasound signals to estimate the real time positions of the objects. Among the various tracking systems available, optical trackers are highly practical and relatively accurate to submillimeter levels [4–6]. The markers are normally attached to the surgical tool that is being tracked in optical systems. The infrared (IR) markers can be active emitting the IR or passive reflecting the IR, based on the requirements.

The integrated hardware and software systems are employed in real-time of the surgical tools in the intraoperative procedures and also for the surgical planning. The surgeon can see the relative positions of the tools that are being used with respect to the anatomical structures. This allows them to ensure that they operate within the safer surgical margins, and not injuring the neighboring delicate structures [7].

It has been shown that accuracy in minimally invasive spinal surgical procedures such as pedicle screw placement has been improved by the computer assisted navigation techniques. It also minimizes radiation risks to both patients and medical team by reducing the frequent intraoperative imaging [8]. Employing an Augmented reality (AR) based system that integrates a Microsoft HoloLens device with a three-dimensional (3D) point tracking module [3, 9–13] is shown to be effective in tele surgery and surgical training.

The proposed system makes use of HoloLens hardware with the integrated motion tracking system for visualization and image analysis to track the positioning of the virtual surgical tool. An infra-red marker tracking using the Microsoft HoloLens head-mounted display is employed. HoloLens can map the environment, register the surgical tool, and track the infrared markers in the system.

2   Materials and Methods

Image registration and Modeling: During the surgery, the internal anatomical data must be registered in the real scene using the preoperative CT or MRI scan data in DICOM format. For testing purposes, we have used a spine model mannequin (Fig. 1). The CT scan data is imported to 3D slicer software for segmenting the spine region (Fig. 2) and then exported in FBX format (Fig. 3) compatible with Microsoft HoloLens2 for further virtual projection of the anatomical data.

Development of Augmented reality environment: The designed Preoperative 3D model of the spine has to be projected as an overlaid operative guidance above the mannequin. For this purpose, an augmented reality environment of the 3D anatomical model was created using Unity3D Software, Vuforia, and Microsoft Mixed Reality (MRTK) SDK. The developed AR environment is imported via Holography remote sensing application into the head mount display (Hololens2) based on augmented vision.

Initially, the Vuforia method, which uses the Vuforia engine, was employed. The engine provides plugins and licenses to use in the Unity software, and it also provides the database to upload the preferred image as a marker. After creating a sample scene in Unity 3D, the Vuforia engine installed as a plugin is conventionally used to handle the ARcamera and the Image Target (markers- uploaded as predefined assets linked to a

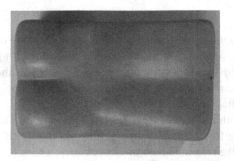

Fig. 1. Spine model mannequin

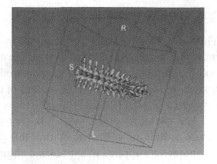

Fig. 2. Segmentation using 3D slicer

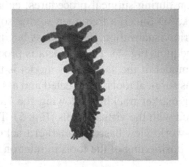

Fig. 3. 3D file format in FBX

license) as its GameObjects. Unity 3D play mode then allows visualizing the AR overlay on the recognized markers. The marker has been printed. To build the application for hololens2 in Unity3D the platform was switched to Universal Windows. By selecting the target device as Hololens, and the architecture as ARM64 (hololens2) the application has been built and the path has been specified for the Visual Studio Solution. The Visual Studio Solution helps to configure hololens2 for the deployment of the unity-built application via remote machine using its IP address and it has been visualized in Hololens2. Object tracking has been done using the infrared markers.

2.1 Hardware

The Hololens2 headset was used to collect tracking data for the proposed system. It incorporates an array of sensors, such as an inbuilt IR emitter and sensor, to facilitate tracking and perception in an augmented reality environment. Unlike traditional high-end optical trackers, Hololens2 offers a more accessible and cost-effective solution for tracking. The tracking technology of Hololens2 allows for real-time detection and accurate positioning of the markers, enabling precise alignment of virtual assets, such as surgical tools, with the real-world environment. The inbuilt IR emitter and sensor of Hololens2 were used to detect and track the passive IR markers placed in the physical space.

2.2 Software

The software system for surgical tool tracking consists of several components. One or multiple cameras are used to capture the movement of markers within a defined tracking volume. These cameras feed the captured images to a system unit, which processes the images and calculates the 3D positions of the markers. The markers, uniquely identifiable for each tool, will be fixed onto the tools that require tracking.

The workflow of the system begins with the input of patient DICOM data into an image computing platform. Within this platform, image segmentation and registration techniques are applied to extract and align the relevant anatomical structures. The resulting volumetric data is then utilized in the modeling process to create 3D computer models. This facilitates the overlaying of surgical tools and the creation of surgical resection planes in a three-dimensional environment. This integrated approach enables precise navigation and visualization during surgical procedures, enhancing surgical accuracy and outcomes. In this work, 3D Slicer, a free open-source software has been used for segmentation and volumetric visualization. The process begins with the acquisition of CT data of the spine mannequin (Fig. 4). The CT data is processed using 3D Slicer to generate a volumetric 3D model of the spine. This model is then imported into Unity, where virtual assets, such as surgical tools, are created and associated with the 3D spine model. Vuforia is used for marker tracking, allowing the Hololens headset to detect and track markers associated with the virtual assets (Fig. 5). The Hololens overlays the virtual assets onto the real-world view based on marker tracking information, enabling real-time visualization and positioning of the tools in relation to the spine model.

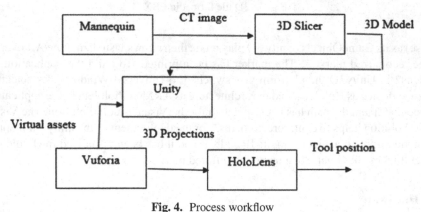

Fig. 4. Process workflow

To calculate the positional error in the virtual scalpel position placement in the context of surgical tool tracking using Unity3D, Vuforia, and the Microsoft Mixed Reality Toolkit (MRTK) SDK, the following steps are followed:

1. **Set up the AR environment**: Create an AR scene in Unity3D using the Vuforia engine. Import the necessary assets, including the 3D models of the surgical tools and the markers used for tracking. Set up the Vuforia configuration and image targets to detect and track the passive IR markers in real-time.

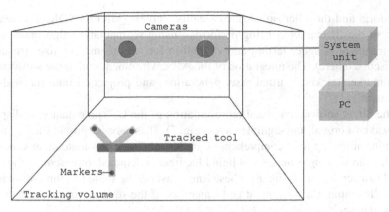

Fig. 5. Schematic diagram of infra-red optical tracking system

2. **Track the surgical tools**: Use Vuforia's image target tracking to detect and track the passive IR markers.
3. **Obtain the virtual scalpel position**: Use the MRTK SDK to generate virtual assets, such as the virtual scalpel, based on the tracked marker positions. Calculate the position and orientation of the virtual scalpel relative to the marker positions.
4. **Project the virtual assets**: Send the generated virtual assets back to Hololens2 for projection onto the real-world environment. The virtual scalpel will be superimposed on the surgical tool in the real scene, aligning with the marker positions.
5. **Calculate positional error**: Compare the position of the virtual scalpel with the real-world position of the markers obtained from the IR emitter and sensor of the Hololens2. Calculate the positional error by measuring the Euclidean distance between the virtual projected positions.

Estimating positional errors on a non-linear surface like a mannequin can be challenging. Non-linear surfaces introduce complexities in accurately measuring and quantifying positional errors due to the lack of a simple reference frame. On a non-linear surface, the positional error can vary depending on the location and orientation of the markers. The deformations and curvatures of the surface can affect the accuracy of the marker tracking system.

To mitigate this challenge, a 6 × 6 uniformly spaced linearized grid with a grid spacing of 3 cm is used for analysis.

3 Results and Discussion

The technical viability of surgical tool motion tracking is investigated using a phantom model (Fig. 6). For tracking the surgical tool, image-based and IR markers can be employed. This work reports the initial evaluation being done using image-based markers. However, retroreflective (Infrared) IR markers are proposed for real time tracking of the position of the surgical tool on a spinal phantom. The proposed AR environment, has to be imported via the Holography remote sensing application into the Hololens2 head-mounted display, utilizes augmented vision and the Unity3D software integrated with Vuforia and the Microsoft Mixed Reality Toolkit (MRTK) SDK. The real time tracking of the IR marker is being performed using segmentation algorithms and the AR environment is under testing and validation for various marker sizes (results not being discussed here). The integration of the AR environment with these software tools enables marker tracking, virtual asset generation, and projection onto the real-world environment.

In the Slicer software, a visual representation of the CT spine dataset is displayed, showing axial, coronal, and sagittal images (Fig. 7). These images provide different views of the spine, allowing for a comprehensive understanding of its anatomical structures.

Within the viewing pane, a set of light blue lines is depicted, representing the marker attached to a surgical tool (Fig. 8). These lines traverse the spine in a three-dimensional manner, illustrating the movement and trajectory of the surgical tool in relation to the CT spine dataset.

By overlaying the marker's path onto the CT spine images, the user can visually track and analyze the tool's motion in real-time. This visualization enhances the understanding of how the surgical tool interacts with the spine's structures and aids in surgical planning, simulation, or assessment of the tool's positioning during a procedure.

The axial, coronal, and sagittal images, together with the moving marker representation, provide valuable insights into the spatial relationship between the surgical tool and the CT spine dataset, assisting in accurate surgical guidance and facilitating better decision-making during spine-related procedures.

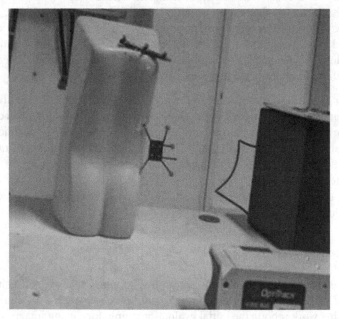

Fig. 6. Proposed system with Spine mannequin attached with the IR reflective markers.

This work reports use of printed markers in place of IR markers for preliminary results and comparison. Figure 9 illustrates the setup and measurement process for

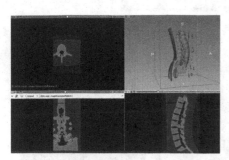

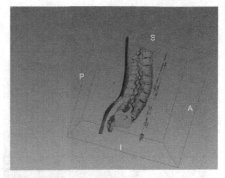

Fig. 7. Slicer displays axial, coronal, sagittal images of CT Spine dataset.

Fig. 8. Light blue lines representing surgical tool marker moving across the spine in 3D Viewing pane.

estimating tool position on a linearized surface using a 6 × 6 grid and marker placement. The grid consists of uniformly spaced linearized points 3 cm apart. The markers were moved one grid point to the next and the corresponding tool transformation values were measured. The grid provides a reference frame for measuring positional errors. The markers' positions are tracked using the marker tracking system, and their locations are compared to the corresponding positions on the grid. The positional differences between the measured marker positions and the expected positions on the grid were calculated.

Table 1 presents the tool position measurements obtained over the grid. The first two rows are shown as example readings, while similar results were obtained for all other grid points. The measurements provide an insight into the accuracy of the tool's positioning on the non-linear surface.

For both X and Y axes, the maximum error observed across the measurements is 0.01 units, indicating the largest deviation from the expected position. On average, the X-axis error is calculated to be 0.0016 units, representing the average deviation across all the readings whereas the Y-axis error is calculated to be 0.0025 units.

The low average errors suggest that the tracking system and marker placement techniques were successful in achieving accurate tool positioning.

It is important to note that the presented study focused on a specific tool and a particular linearized surface representation. This measurement process can be extended to evaluate angular variations, curved distances, and can be applied to different types of surgical tools. It will provide valuable information about the precision and accuracy of the tool positioning, assisting in improving surgical procedures, optimizing tracking systems, and ensuring reliable and precise tool placement in complex surgical scenarios.

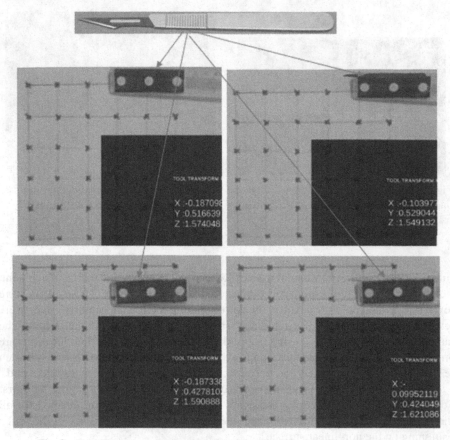

Fig. 9. Grid Placement, Marker Configuration, and Tool Position Measurement

Table 1. Tool position measurements over the grid

X Y Z positions	Column 1	Column 2	Column 3	Column 4	Column 5	Column 6
Row 1	0.51	0.44	0.35	0.27	0.18	0.10
	0.51	0.52	0.52	0.52	0.52	0.52
	1.49	1.51	1.52	1.54	1.57	1.55
Row 2	0.52	0.44	0.36	0.27	0.18	0.10
	0.42	0.41	0.39	0.41	0.42	0.42
	1.52	1.55	1.55	1.58	1.59	1.62
......	....	....	....	....	....	....
Average X-axis positional error	0.0016 units		**Maximum X-axis positional error**		0.01 units	
Average Y-axis positional error	0.0025 units		**Maximum Y-axis positional error**		0.01 units	

4 Conclusion

The system proposes that the recorded surgical tool position can be accurately mapped into the actual tool position, so the method could be implemented in tracking surgical tools in real time for surgical planning and navigation. The applicability and generalizability of the findings to different tool types and non-linear surfaces should be further investigated through additional experiments and evaluations. By employing this grid-based measurement technique, the positional accuracy and errors can be quantitatively assessed, enabling a better understanding of the tool's positioning accuracy and potential deviations from the expected placement on the non-linear surface. This information is crucial for ensuring precision and reliability in surgical procedures and guiding improvements in the tracking system and tool placement techniques. With this approach intraoperative complications can be reduced, and fatigue of surgeons can be brought down.

Acknowledgements. This research work is supported by the SERB-POWER Grant (FILE No. SPG/2021/001684) from Science and Engineering Research Board (SERB), New Delhi, India. The authors would like to acknowledge Mr. Vishu of Machenn Innovations for the technical assistance provided.

References

1. Fan, Z., Ma, L., Liao, Z., Zhang, X., Liao, H.: Three-dimensional image-guided techniques for minimally invasive surgery. In: Handbook of Robotic and Image-Guided Surgery, pp. 575–584. Elsevier (2020)
2. Dewan, M.C., et al.: Global neurosurgery: the current capacity and deficit in the provision of essential neurosurgical care: executive summary of the global neurosurgery initiative at the program in global surgery and social change. J. Neurosurg. **130**(4), 1055–1064 (2018)
3. Glossop, N.D.: Advantages of optical compared with electromagnetic tracking. JBJS **91**(Supplement_1), 23–28 (2009)
4. Wiles, A.D., Thompson, D.G., Frantz, D.D.: Accuracy assessment and interpretation for optical tracking systems. In: Medical Imaging 2004: Visualization, Image-Guided Procedures, and Display, vol. 5367, pp. 421–432. SPIE (2004)
5. Nafis, C., Jensen, V., Beauregard, L., Anderson, P.: Method for estimating dynamic EM tracking accuracy of surgical navigation tools. In: Medical Imaging 2006: Visualization, Image-Guided Procedures, and Display, vol. 6141, pp. 152–167. SPIE (2006)
6. Welch, G., Foxlin, E.: Motion tracking: No silver bullet, but a respectable arsenal. IEEE Comput. Graph. Appl. **22**(6), 24–38 (2002)
7. Grunert, P., Darabi, K., Espinosa, J., Filippi, R.: Computer-aided navigation in neurosurgery. Neurosurg. Rev. **26**, 73–99 (2003)
8. Rainer Wirtz, W.S., et al.: The benefit of neuronavigation for neurosurgery analyzed by its impact on glioblastoma surgery. Neurol. Res. **22**(4), 354–360 (2000)
9. Liu, P., et al.: A wearable augmented reality navigation system for surgical telementoring based on Microsoft HoloLens. Ann. Biomed. Eng. **49**, 287–298 (2021)
10. Pieper, S., Halle, M., Kikinis, R.: 3D slicer. In: 2004 2nd IEEE International Symposium on Biomedical Imaging: Nano to Macro (IEEE Cat No. 04EX821), pp. 632–635. IEEE (2004)

11. Lasso, A., Heffter, T., Rankin, A., Pinter, C., Ungi, T., Fichtinger, G.: PLUS: open-source toolkit for ultrasound-guided intervention systems. IEEE Trans. Biomed. Eng. **61**(10), 2527–2537 (2014)
12. Tokuda, J., et al.: OpenIGTLink: an open network protocol for image-guided therapy environments. Int. J. Med. Rob. Comput. Assist. Surg. **5**(4), 423–434 (2009)
13. Kunz, C., et al.: Infrared marker tracking with the HoloLens for neurosurgical interventions. Curr. Direct. Biomed. Eng. **6**(1) (2020)

Realter: An Immersive Simulator to Support Low-Vision Rehabilitation

Mattia Barbieri[1,2]([✉]) [iD], Giulia A. Albanese[1] [iD], Elisabetta Capris[3],
Andrea Canessa[2] [iD], Silvio P. Sabatini[2] [iD], and Giulio Sandini[1] [iD]

[1] Department of Robotics, Brain and Cognitive Sciences, Istituto Italiano di Tecnologia,
Genova, Italy
mattia.barbieri@iit.it
[2] Department of Informatics, Bioengineering, Robotics and Systems Engineering (DIBRIS),
University of Genoa, Genoa, Italy
[3] Istituto David Chiossone per Ciechi e Ipovedenti, Genoa, Italy

Abstract. The project REALTER (wearable egocentric altered reality simulator)
exploits immersive technologies and extended reality (XR) environments to support low-vision rehabilitation, by offering an immersive simulator of low-vision
conditions. Perceiving and navigating the world as low-vision individuals has the
potential of being a useful tool for ophthalmologists and visual rehabilitators to
increase empathy with the assisted population and to improve the existing therapeutic techniques. Additionally, by analyzing ocular movements acquired during
experimental sessions with healthy-sighted individuals in a condition of simulated low vision, researchers may collect quantitative data to extend the state of
the art in understanding the behavioral changes of low-vision persons. The project
involved the implementation of an immersive system by using commercial device
tools currently available on the market. The hardware consists of an immersive
virtual reality (VR) headset with an integrated eye tracker and a pair of external
cameras, to provide gaze-contingent altered/extended reality (XR) content by a
pass-through modality. The software can realistically simulate several low-vision
conditions, such as age-related macular degeneration, glaucoma, and hemianopsia,
and simultaneously acquire eye and head movements for data analysis.

Keywords: Extended Reality (XR) · gaze-contingency · low-vision
rehabilitation

1 Introduction

In 2014 the number of visually impaired persons (VIPs) worldwide was estimated to be
285 million, of whom 39 million were totally blind and 19 million were children below
the age of 15 [1]. Many persons who are registered as blind nevertheless retain some
residual vision and are said to have "low vision". In most cases, low vision concerns
damage – or in some cases loss – of the peripheral or central vision. The specific form of
visual impairment varies according to the individual medical condition, but often low-
vision people experience an extreme loss of high spatial frequencies perception and a

reduction of the field of view (FOV). Depending on the specific pathological conditions, this loss affects the central area of the FOV (maculopathy), the peripheral area (tubular vision), or half of the vertical FOV (hemianopsia). Individuals affected by maculopathy show symptoms as a distorted vision in the form of metamorphopsia in addition to the appearance of a dark-grey spot [2]; tubular vision, also known as "tunnel vision", is the loss of peripheral vision with retention of central vision, resulting in a constricted circular tunnel-like FOV [3]; hemianopsia is a loss of vision or blindness (anopsia) in half the visual field, usually on one side of the vertical midline [4]. The acquisition of rehabilitation techniques requires a strong immersion in the reality of daily life to understand how patients experience their low vision condition. If simulating absolute blindness is achievable with empirical methods, simulating low vision is much more complicated but fundamental for the accurate training of the rehabilitation operator. This is even more complicated given the wide variety of low-vision symptoms, which makes it hard for rehabilitators to figure out how their patients perceive the environment. This difficulty inevitably causes "gaps" in rehabilitators' training path. Past attempts to simulate visual impairments using immersive technology such as virtual reality (VR) and augmented reality (AR) have already been made. Jones et al., [5] developed gaze-contingent simulations of visual impairment presented using head-mounted displays (HMD). They concluded that the simulator could replicate and objectively quantify some of the key everyday difficulties associated with visual impairments. Starting from the advantages described by Jones, our research project aims to create an immersive extended reality (XR) experience in order to simulate the effects of low vision for rehabilitators of VIPs. Differently from Jones et al. which explored both VR and AR with emphasis on glaucoma, we focused on an AR approach. Specifically, we addressed the idea of measuring visually guided behavior in a real environment in the presence of several low-vision disabilities (see Sect. 3) and the possibility of simulating low vision conditions monocularly or binocularly. In this paper, we introduce this eye-contingent, binocular simulation, in which the view of the real world is altered in real-time in a controlled and personalized way, and we refer to it as *alTered Reality* (TR).

2   Project Requirements

The project was conducted in collaboration with ophthalmologists from the *Chiossone Institute for Blind and Low-Vision Individuals* in Genoa.

The *Chiossone Institute* is familiar with the training of ophthalmologists based on "analogic" tool simulating low-vision conditions, such as spectacles with semi-transparent lenses to simulate a loss in acuity, or cardboard masks covering part of the field of view. The objective of the project REALTER is to make the training more effective, efficient, and intuitive, improving the empathy level of the rehabilitators towards the people they assist. To achieve this goal, the project investigates how to replace these tools with TR immersive simulation and improve the realism of the simulation by exploiting eye-movement contingency. Starting from the need for assessing the best rehabilitation strategy according to the specific pathology, REALTER project adopted TR for altering normal sight and rendering the perception of several low-vision conditions.

In the current state of the art, XR is defined as an umbrella term to group all immersive technologies as virtual reality (VR), augmented reality (AR), and mixed reality (MR) [6].

The peculiarity of immersive technologies is the ability to elicit a sense of immersion and presence. Immersion intended as a physical phenomenon is a unique feature of immersive technologies, (immersion as a mental phenomenon is proper of other media) and it is achieved when a user interprets visual, auditory, and haptic cues to gather information and navigates and controls objects in the synthetic environment [7]. On the other hand, presence is defined as a person's subjective sensation of being in a scene depicted by a medium, usually of virtual nature [8].

According to Azuma et al. [9], "The basic goal of an AR system is to enhance the user's perception of and interaction with the real world through supplementing the real world with 3D virtual objects that appear to coexist in the same space as the real world". REALTER required interaction with the real world, altered by simulated low-vision diseases. For this reason, we employed a peculiar form of AR in which the real world is not augmented, but altered by computer graphics, in order to resemble the reality of low-vision individuals. Most AR head-mounted displays (HMD) adopt optical see-through (OST) displays to allow the users to see the real world with their own eyes through a transparent lens. Differently, REALTER employs stereoscopic video see-through (VST) HMDs, in which the user's visual perception of the 3D world is mediated by two different optical systems, i.e. the acquiring camera and the visualization display [10]. Indeed, OSTs are unable to display image effects in the proper way due to the incapacity of displaying black or opaque contents [11]. In the low-vision rehabilitation scenario, where accuracy and realness of simulations are required at the highest level, OST limitations cannot be ignored. For these reasons, even if both technologies are currently used for augmented reality applications [12], HMD with pass-through cameras was chosen instead of OST for the current study.

To realistically simulate low-vision conditions and meet the *Chiossone Institute* needs, we identified the following hardware and software requirements:

1. An *immersive portable system* able to acquire images from the real world and display content in real-time and in an immersive way.
2. An *eye tracker* to record users' ocular movements and enable the gaze-contingent paradigm as human-computer interaction.
3. A *software able to acquire and process images* of the real world in real-time, to alter reality to simulate low vision effects through the gaze-contingent paradigm.
4. *Gaze-contingent paradigm* to update the position of the disabilities according to the current subject's fixation point.
5. *Binocular image processing* to simulate realistically low-vision conditions. Since low-vision conditions affect each eye differently, we managed to render images to the left and right eye separately.
6. *Ocular movements data* storage to conduct quantitative analysis, such as the detection and characterization of saccadic eye movements and fixations.

3 Research, Design, and Measurements

3.1 User Research

Thanks to a close partnership with ophthalmologists and rehabilitators of the *Chiossone Institute for Blind and Low-Vision Individuals*, the project design followed a user-centered design approach divided into three stages:

1. **Identification stage**: involving ophthalmologists' background knowledge to understand the effects of low-vision disabilities. The ophthalmologists identified the
   low-vision diseases more widespread and difficult to empathize with. Binocular
   maculopathy, tubular vision, and hemianopsia were chosen for the simulator (Fig. 1).
2. **Simulation stage**: By implementing shader graphics and 2D images overlapping the
   images acquired through the cameras, it was possible to recreate an altered reality
   that resembles the point of view of several low-vision individuals. All simulations
   used the gaze-contingent paradigm.
3. **Evaluation stage**: Every low-vision simulation was qualitatively evaluated by ophthalmologists wearing the immersive system, in order to approve or edit the realness
   of the simulation in terms of appearance and behaviors (Fig. 2).

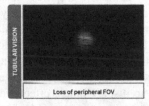

Fig. 1. The three groups of low vision disabilities are currently implemented in REALTER
portfolio. Loss of central FOV (left), loss of peripheral FOV (center), loss of half FOV (right).

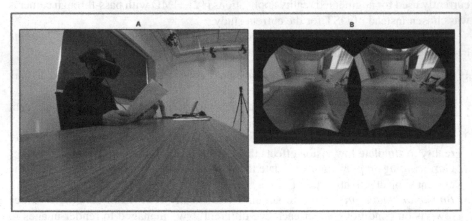

Fig. 2. Evaluation stage with Chiossone Institute's ophthalmologists. **Panel A**: frame extract from
video recorded with an external camera. **Panel B**: immersive experience recorded from headset.

3.2   Immersive System Design

From the hardware perspective, at the current state REALTER is composed of:

- **HTC Vive Pro Eye**: an immersive VST HMD. This headset is equipped with a dual
  3.5-inch screen size with resolution 2880 × 1600 pixels, which is split into two

displays with resolutions 1440 × 1600 pixels per eye and pixels density equal to 615 pixels per inch (PPI). HTC Vive Pro Eye is able to reproduce contents with a refresh rate of 90 Hz and diagonal FOV of 110° and requires a connection with a computer and two external base stations. The device is also equipped with an integrated Tobii eye tracker with an estimated accuracy of 0.5°–1.1° and a sampling frequency of 120 Hz. SteamVR Tracking, G-sensor, gyroscope, proximity, inter-pupillary distance (IPD) sensor, are also included in the headset to track head movements and rotations. HTC Vive Pro Eye, as XR headset, ensures the possibility to exploit the altered world through a totally immersive experience.

- **Stereolabs Zed Mini**: external cameras to provide high resolution images of the real world. Adopting Zed Mini as replacement of the embedded HTC Vive Pro Eye AR cameras improved the maximal spatial resolution (from 480p to 720p), at the expense of field of view (from 96° to 90° in horizontal FOV; from 80° to 60° in vertical FOV). Despite the loss of FOV, the replacement of cameras for AR allows a higher visual acuity and reduces the motion sickness effects.
- **HP VR Backpack G2**: wearable computer wired to HMD and cameras. PC uses Windows 10 as operating system, Intel Core i7-8850H as processor, NVIDIA GeForce RTX 2080 with 8 GB dedicated GDDR6 as graphic card, and Mini DisplayPort 1.4, USB Type-C Thunderbolt 3 enabled with DisplayPort 1.2, DisplayPort 1.2 on HP Z VR Backpack Dock as video outputs. By deploying a wearable PC, it is possible to make the system portable (Fig. 3).

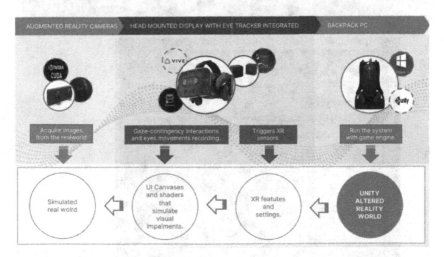

Fig. 3. The REALTER architecture.

The software was developed in Unity game engine with C# as programming language (version 2021.3.3f1). The system requires the installation of ZED SDK 3.7.0, Cuda 11.6.1, SR Runtime, SteamVR 2.7.3. Unity game engine also requires several SDKs: OpenVR through importing in project SteamVR v1.14.15, ZED SDK v3.7, and SRanipal v1.3.6.

The eye tracker integrated in the HMD allows the storage of data about subjects' ocular movements and the design of gaze-contingent simulations. Since most low-vision diseases affect the same part of the retina while the eyes are moving, a gaze-contingent paradigm is required to update the position of the disability according to the subject's fixation point (Fig. 4, Panel A shows fixation points). By combining gaze information from SRanipal and head movements from SteamVR, it is possible to integrate a gaze-contingent paradigm. To simulate low-vision diseases in AR, 2D images and 3D game objects rendered with shaders are overlaid onto real-world images captured by Zed Mini cameras. Each visual condition required specific techniques to be implemented.

The computer keyboard was chosen as a tool for interacting with the interface: by pressing the keyboard button is possible to trigger low-vision disabilities and functionalities, such as start/stop storing data or launch eye calibration. All instructions are stored in a specific menu (Fig. 4, Panel B).

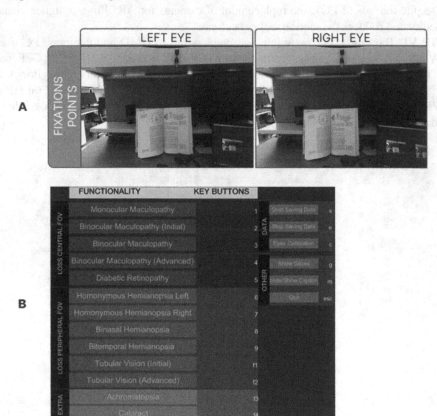

Fig. 4. REALTER functionalities. Panel A: Fixation points (blue left eye, orange right eye). Panel B: main menu. (Color figure online)

3.3 Gaze-Contingent Simulations

3.3.1 Maculopathy

Maculopathy can affect one or both eyes. For this reason, REALTER is equipped with a simulation of both monocular and binocular maculopathy (BM).

- **Monocular maculopathy:** the right eye is affected by a form of maculopathy that manifests itself as an image distortion and blur effect at the center of both eyes FOV (Fig. 5, Panel A).
- **Early-stage BM:** both eyes are affected by a form of maculopathy that manifests itself as an image distortion and blur effect at the center of both eyes FOV (Fig. 5, Panel E).
- **Medium-stage BM:** both eyes are affected by a dark-grey spot at the center of the FOV and a warping distortion at the spot edge (Fig. 5, Panel C).
- **Advanced-stage BM:** both eyes are affected by a dark-grey spot at the center of the FOV and a warping distortion at the spot edge. All the background is rendered with a blurred effect and a yellow-based filter effect. (Fig. 5, Panel B).
- **Multiple maculopathy:** both eyes are affected by multiple dark-grey spots all over the FOV. The background is rendered with a blurred effect and color loss (Fig. 5, Panel D).

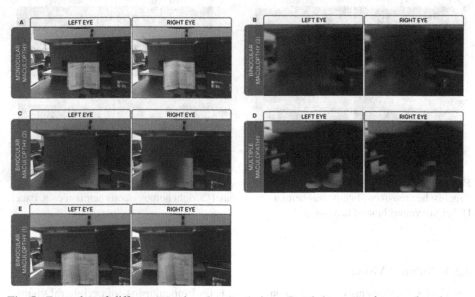

Fig. 5. Examples of different maculopathy simulations. Panel A: monocular maculopathy on the right eye. Panel B: advanced status of binocular maculopathy. Panel C: common binocular maculopathy that simulates age-related macular degeneration. Panel D: multiple maculopathy that simulates an advanced status of diabetic retinopathy. Panel E: early-stage binocular maculopathy.

3.3.2 Hemianopsia

Since, during the identification stage of the design process, it has emerged that hemi-anopsia affecting one eye is quite rare, all the simulations of hemianopsia involved both eyes. Namely, REALTER simulates homonymous and heteronymous hemianopsia. All hemianopsia are simulated by a 3D object in front of the camera's FOV, rendered with a shader that blurred the specific image portion.

- **Homonymous Hemianopsia Left**: both eyes are affected by the loss of the left half of the field of view. (Fig. 6, Panel A).
- **Homonymous Hemianopsia Right**: both eyes are affected by the loss of the right half of the field of view. (Fig. 6, Panel C).
- **Heteronymous Bitemporal Hemianopsia**: the left eye is affected by the loss of the left field of view; the right eye is affected by the loss of the right field of view. Namely, individuals affected by this form of hemianopsia suffer from loss of FOV close to the temples (Fig. 6, Panel B).
- **Heteronymous Binasal Hemianopsia**: the left eye is affected by the loss of the right field of view; the right eye is affected by the loss of the left field of view. Namely, individuals affected by this form of hemianopsia suffer from loss of FOV close to the nose (Fig. 6, Panel D).

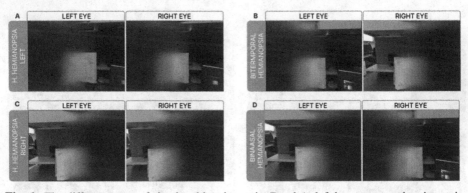

Fig. 6. The different types of simulated hemianopsia. Panel A: left homonymous hemianopsia. Panel B: heteronymous bitemporal hemianopsia. Panel C: right homonymous hemianopsia. Panel D: heteronymous binasal hemianopsia.

3.3.3 Tubular Vision

REALTER implements two types of simulations for binocular loss of peripheral vision. Both simulations are obtained by overlapping a virtual object in front of the cameras:

- **Early-stage tubular vision**: both eyes are affected by a peripheral loss that manifests itself as a blurred effect. The left eye is affected by the loss of the left peripheral FOV; the right eye is affected by the loss of the right peripheral FOV (Fig. 7, Panel A).
- **Advanced-stage tubular vision**: both eyes are affected by a significant loss of peripheral FOV. The FOV lost is perceived as totally dark grey (Fig. 7, Panel B).

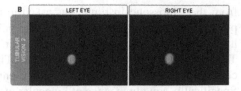

Fig. 7. The two simulated conditions of tubular vision. Panel A: tubular vision at an initial stage. Panel B: tubular vision at an advanced stage.

3.4 Data Acquisition and Storage

Time information is obtained by either the timestamps from SDK SRanipal or Time.fixedTime from Unity Engine. Since the employed version of SRanipal has not been improved from a timestamp bug as reported by Imaoka et al. [15], we preferred to use the time data from Unity.

Eye movement data from both the left and right eye were read from VerboseData in the struct data of ViveSR.anipal.Eye.EyeDatav2 as Imaoka et al. already validated: validity of eye data, eyes openness, pupil diameter ([mm]), pupil position (normalized vector between −1 and 1), gaze origin ([mm]), and gaze direction (normalized vector between −1 and 1). The possibility to store ocular data is a core feature of the system to get quantitative measurements. Gaze origin and gaze direction information enable to quantify distinctive features of ocular movement such as saccades and fixations. Investigating eye movements for each simulated low-vision disability, in terms of occurrence, duration, and amplitude could be relevant to understand how low-vision conditions affect the performed eye movements. For example, when reading a text, a healthy-sighted individual alternates fast horizontal linear saccades and long fixations [13]. During the same task, in the condition of simulated or real binocular maculopathy, we expect a different behavior, such as a higher number of nonlinear saccades, and shorter periods of fixations [14]. Basically, we aim to underline the differences in ocular behaviors between all simulated low vision conditions and healthy sight. When making comparisons, it's important to take into account the limited resolution of the cameras used in the developed system. Therefore, it would be more appropriate to consider the condition of vision through the cameras without any simulated low-vision conditions as the "healthy sight" condition.

Moreover, head data can be stored from Unity.Engine.XR in the struct data of InputTracking.GetLocalPosition(XRNode.CenterEye). Head data are crucial to quantify and describe how low-vision disabilities affect head kinematics in VIPs and the behavioral strategies they apply to compensate for their disability.

All data listed above can be stored in a.xlsx file for processing.

3.5 Preliminary Results

Although a quantitative evaluation of REALTER is currently missing, in this section, we present some preliminary results collected during the validation stage of the immersive system. To assess qualitatively the different low-vision conditions, an ophthalmologist from the Chiossone Institute was asked to perform a reading test. Being in a sitting position and keeping the head fixed, the ophthalmologist was asked to read a text in his mother tongue on an A4 format paper written in Times New Roman 72 (font). The test was performed wearing the REALTER system under three different low-vision conditions (one for each macrofamily presented in 3.3) and in a healthy-sight condition. Specifically, a medium stage of binocular maculopathy (Fig. 5, Panel C), homonymous hemianopsia right (Fig. 6, Panel A), and advanced-stage tubular vision (Fig. 7, Panel B) have been chosen as low-vision conditions. In the healthy-sight condition, the subject wore the system, but no visual warp has been applied. The focus of the test was to achieve preliminary knowledge about the different behaviors of the oculomotor system in the four different visual conditions, particularly in terms of saccades' number and magnitude, and scanpaths. To detect saccades, we used REMoDNaV [15], and existing software able to recognize and detect ocular movements from eye tracker data. In addition, plotting the fixation points in the visual scene, we extracted a scanpath of ocular movements.

The preliminary results showed significant alteration in the oculomotor system from healthy sight to low-vision conditions (Fig. 8). In particular, the healthy-sight condition showed linear saccades which follow the distribution of the words on the paper surface. Contrarily, the path of binocular maculopathy was unstable, with several and wide saccades in different directions. Saccades in homonymous hemianopsia were more linear than in binocular maculopathy, and mainly restricted in the healthy side of the FOV. The amplitude of saccades was still higher than in the healthy-sight condition. Finally, tubular vision was overall the closest to healthy sight, both in terms of scanpath and in the properties of the saccades detected.

Starting from these results, future work will include the quantitative validation of the immersive system in a more comprehensive experimental session. Specifically, the focus will be to assess the real potential of REALTER to induce, in healthy sight subjects under simulated low-vision conditions, the same alteration detected in subjects affected by binocular maculopathy, homonymous hemianopsia, and tubular vision.

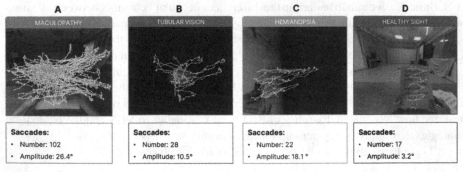

Fig. 8. Preliminary test results. Panel A: binocular maculopathy outcome. Scanpath (above); saccades detection (below). Panel B: tubular vision outcome. Scanpath (above); saccades detection (below). Panel C: homonymous hemianopsia outcome. Scanpath (above); saccades detection (below). Panel D: Healthy sight outcome. Scanpath (above); saccades detection (below).

4 Conclusions

The presented work involved the development of a system able to arouse a sense of immersion and presence in order to let users experience the condition of disability brought by several different low-vision impairments. Thanks to the active involvement of the ophthalmologists from Chiossone Institute, it was possible to develop an exhaustive simulator of low-vision conditions based on a peculiar form for XR that we called TR. Several user tests conducted on ophthalmologists validated the system as a simulation tool for low-vision conditions. What is currently missing is the quantitative assessment of the validity of REALTER as a system able to reproduce with high accuracy ocular movements performed by low-vision individuals. In order to do this, future perspectives will consist of 1) a collection of experimental data from healthy-sighted subjects in simulated low-vision conditions during the performance of daily activities such as reading a text, navigating the space, and manipulating objects; 2) the interpretation of the data collected under different simulated low-vision conditions and the comparison between them and with the behaviors of visually-impaired people with an equivalent level of disability.

Nonetheless, there are some limitations inherent in the hardware components that must be appointed. Previous studies consider 250 Hz as the threshold to separate eye trackers with low-speed sampling frequency from high-speed sampling frequency [16]. With its sampling frequency of 120 Hz, HTC Vive Pro Eye belongs to the first category. Despite HTC Vive Pro Eye as a tool to assess saccadic movement in VR was already explored with optimal results from Imaoka et el [16], employing this type of eye tracker brings some limitations when considering eye movements different from fixations or saccades. Eye trackers employed in the research field to detect microsaccades have a minimum sampling frequency of 200 Hz [17]. Analogously, eye tremors present an average frequency of 90 Hz: since according to the Nyquist-Shannon theorem a sampling frequency at least twice as large as the frequency of the recorded movement is needed, eye trackers required a sampling frequency of 180 Hz to detect tremors [17].

However, there are a number of commercial eye-tracking tools with frequencies lower than 250 Hz employed for measurements in the research field and not only as instruments for human-computer interaction or gaming [18]. HTC Vive Pro Eye belongs to this group, and it is intended for measuring slower eye movements such as those in the range of speed of saccades or fixations. In the future, the replacement of the Tobii eye tracker with another one with a sampling frequency higher than 250 Hz should be considered.

Acknowledgment. The project REALTER has been funded by Regione Liguria through FILSE SpA in the framework of POR 2014–2020 (Asse 1 "RICERCA E INNOVAZIONE (OT1)" - Azione 1.2.4) and was conducted in collaboration with Chiossone Institute for Blind and Low Vision Individuals, the Electronic Design Laboratory (EDL) of Istituto Italiano di Tecnologia (IIT), GGallery Srl, SIGLA Srl, FOS S.r.l. ETT SpA.

References

1. Gori, M., Cappagli, G., Tonelli, A., Baud-Bovy, G., Finocchietti, S.: Devices for visually impaired people: High technological devices with low user acceptance and no adaptability for children. Neurosci. Biobehav. Rev. **69**, 79–88 (2016)
2. Apte, R.S.: Age-related macular degeneration. New Engl. J. Med. **385**(6), 539–547 (2021). https://doi.org/10.1056/NEJMcp2102061. PMC 9369215. PMID 34347954. S2CID 236926930
3. Medicine Net. https://www.medicinenet.com/tunnel_vision/definition.htm. Accessed 04 Apr 2023
4. Hemianopia (Hemianopsia) Archived 16 May 2017 at the Wayback Machine. https://helpfo rvisionloss.com/. Accessed 04 Apr 2023
5. Jones, P.R., Somoskeöy, T., Chow-Wing-Bom, H., Crabb, D.P.: Seeing other perspectives: evaluating the use of virtual and augmented reality to simulate visual impairments (OpenVisSim). NPJ Dig. Med. **3**(1), 32 (2020)
6. Casini, M.: Extended reality for smart building operation and maintenance: a review. Energies **15**(10), 3785 (2022). https://doi.org/10.3390/en15103785.ISSN1996-1073
7. Suh, A., Prophet, J.: The state of immersive technology research: a literature analysis. Comput. Hum. Behav. **86**, 77–90 (2018)
8. Thornson, C.A., Goldiez, B.F., Le, H.: Predicting presence: constructing the tendency toward presence inventory. Int. J. Hum Comput Stud. **67**(1), 62–78 (2009)
9. Azuma, R., Baillot, Y., Behringer, R., Feiner, S., Julier, S., MacIntyre, B.: Recent advances in augmented reality. IEEE Comput. Graph. Appl. **21**(6), 3447 (2001)
10. Cattari, N., Cutolo, F., D'amato, R., Fontana, U., Ferrari, V.: Toed-in vs parallel displays in video see-through head-mounted displays for close-up view. IEEE Access **7**, 159698–159711 (2019)
11. Konttori, U.: Merge real and virtual content–like never before (2021)
12. Rolland, J.P., Fuchs, H.: Optical versus video see-through head-mounted displays in medical visualization. Presence **9**(3), 287–309 (2000)
13. Abati, S., Giacomelli, G., Volpe, R.: Argomenti di ipovisione: supplemento, vol. 1, pp. 80–84 (2001)
14. Verghese, P., Vullings, C., Shanidze, N.: Eye movements in macular degeneration. Ann. Rev. Vision Sci. **7**, 773–791 (2021)
15. Dar, A.H., Wagner, A.S., Hanke, M.: REMoDNaV: robust eye-movement classification for dynamic stimulation. Behav. Res. Methods **53**(1), 399–414 (2021)
16. Imaoka, Y., Flury, A., De Bruin, E.D.: Assessing saccadic eye movements with head-mounted display virtual reality technology. Front. Psych. **11**, 572938 (2020)
17. Holmqvist, K., et al.: Eye tracking: a comprehensive guide to methods and measures. OUP Oxford (2011)
18. Gibaldi, A., Sabatini, S.P.: The saccade main sequence revised: a fast and repeatable tool for oculomotor analysis. Behav. Res. Methods **53**, 167–187 (2021)

Emotions and "Sense of Presence" in the Psycho-Verse: Psychological Support for Breast Cancer Survivors in the Metaverse

Ilaria Durosini[1]([envelope]) [iD], Milija Strika[1,2] [iD], Silvia Francesca Maria Pizzoli[3] [iD], and Gabriella Pravettoni[1,2] [iD]

[1] Department of Oncology and Hemato-Oncology, University of Milan, Milan, Italy
ilaria.durosini@unimi.it
[2] Applied Research Division for Cognitive and Psychological Science, IEO, European Institute of Oncology IRCCS, Milan, Italy
[3] Psychology Faculty, Università Cattolica del Sacro Cuore, Milan, Italy

Abstract. Breast Cancer survivors often struggle with psychological sequelae after cancer diagnosis and treatments. eHealth and virtual interventions have been increasingly employed and investigated to enhance patients' well-being and psychological support. Among the possible approaches that might yield benefits in breast cancer survivors' support, the use of the Metaverse, which provides virtual environments in which users can interact with others through avatars, has been rarely investigated. The present study assesses the impact and benefits on the emotional experience of a virtual psychological support group carried out in the Metaverse. Specifically, six breast cancer survivors were included in a support group supervised by two psycho-oncologists and were asked to discuss and share relevant and emotional topics of their experience. Emotional dimensions and emotion intensity were assessed before and after the intervention, and the sense of presence was assessed after the experience. Results showed benefits for participants in terms of enhanced control over emotions and decreased intensity of negative emotions (fear and sadness). Furthermore, the experience in the Metaverse was characterized by a good level of engagement in the activities and virtual environment. Results from this preliminary study will allow us to better understand the possible emotional benefits related to the use of new immersive environments for psychological purposes.

Keywords: Metaverse · Emotions · Sense of Presence · Breast Cancer Survivors · Psychological Support

1 Introduction

Receiving a diagnosis of breast cancer (BC) is generally related not only to physical health consequences but also to significant psychological challenges that might affect everyday life and personal activities. The psychological consequences of cancer can be severe and persist over time - also after successful oncological treatments. Emotional

L. T. De Paolis et al. (Eds.): XR Salento 2023, LNCS 14219, pp. 417–426, 2023.
https://doi.org/10.1007/978-3-031-43404-4_28

well-being, social functioning, and quality of life may be impacted, and the cancer journey may be related to long-term psychological side effects [1–3]. Symptoms related to depression, anxiety, and distress may persist for a long time and may reduce the personal ability of patients to return to a "normal" life after the diagnosis [4].

For these reasons, it is paramount to support people who received an oncological diagnosis to improve their well-being and quality of life, helping them in the promotion of personal strengths and abilities. Over the years, some psychological interventions have been proposed to help people to empower their resources and improve their emotional management [5–7]. For example, the use of collaborative, empathic, and supportive techniques might be helpful for the assessment of patients' questions about their lives, helping them to find a progressive understanding of their inner world [8], sustaining their self-curiosity [9–11]. The involvement and the adherence to psychological intervention often require patients' intrinsic motivation and notable attention to some dynamic psychological factors [1]. Taking attention to these aspects could help the promotion of a better commitment and engagement to some activities and adherence to the treatment plan [12].

Alongside traditional psychological and psychotherapy pathways, in recent years, new technologies are increasingly being adopted to support patients over their cancer journey. This represents an alternative therapy delivery modality that provides emotional support despite geographical distances and physical limitations [13–15]. For example, internet-based psychotherapy could be a valuable resource to help BC survivors overcome psychological issues related to their cancer journey. Different forms of internet-based psychotherapy include videoconferencing, web chat, virtual reality (VR), and avatars. Generally, BC survivors tend to have positive attitudes towards internet-based or digital interventions [16, 17].

The literature highlighted that people with a history of cancer tend to appreciate those communication technologies that still assign a central role to their relationship with psychotherapists within the psychological sessions (such as Virtual Reality). Thanks to the high resolution, these virtual technologies allow the creation of clinical situations closer to equivalent real ones [18]. Patients have the possibility to stay in immersive environments similar to real-life, eliciting in participants a vivid "sense of presence" [19]. The sense of presence is considered the feeling of "being there" within an environment [20, 21] and is positively associated with the intensity of emotions experienced by participants who lived the virtual experience [22, 23]. By having a digital identity connected to their physical body, people can use various perspectives to interact with virtual objects and the environment, making them feel as if they are in that space [24]. This feeling is called presence or telepresence, creating the illusion of not being mediated by technology. This illusion means that users overlook the technological medium facilitating their communication and behave as though it does not exist. Furthermore, communication with others can enhance this sense of presence [24].

A new immersive virtual environment similar to VR that serves as an alternate reality for its users is the Metaverse [26, 27]. The Metaverse allows participants to experience novel means of communication through an avatar that acts in a digital 3D environment that mimics real-life experiences [28]. It is expected that the Metaverse will impact some areas related to health, such as medicine and clinical psychology, allowing the treatment of different kinds of problems and reducing the gap between the virtual and the real words [29]. In the medical area, the Metaverse can be used as a virtual environment in which physicians and patients may communicate throughout the clinical journey [30] or as a virtual university where professors can instruct medical students [31]. Concerning the psychological area, the Metaverse can act as an occasion to support the communication between the psychotherapist and the patients. Using a digital avatar allows one to stay in a group of people who lived similar life experiences to promote a collaborative environment. The user can stay in front of a screen and interact with others in a new immersive way, protecting their anonymity and experiencing a sense of presence. This could be useful, especially with patients who experienced an intense experience in their life, such as receiving an oncological diagnosis, which can be difficult to share with other people due to fears or shame related to one's diagnosis and one's experiences. Especially in the oncological area, some people tend to "wear a mask" and hide their disease and emotions [1]. The use of a virtual environment with an avatar that protects their identity may allow survivors to have an initial occasion to talk with people who lived similar life experiences and, also thanks to the help of a psychotherapist, get rid of the burden of hiding the disease and make their personal voices heard.

To our knowledge, today the possible emotional benefits related to using Metaverse as a means of psychological support have not yet been largely explored. For this reason, this study aims to preliminary test the emotional benefits related to the use of a Metaverse as a psychological support tool by conducting virtual psychological group sessions with BC survivors and expert psychotherapists. Specifically, the Metaverse will be used as a virtual context in which women who lived similar experiences of cancer can talk about specific aspects of their cancer journey, creating a collaborative and empathic context. Changes in their emotions and in the perception of their sense of presence will be explored.

2   Method

2.1   Participants

Six women with a history of cancer participated in this study (Table 1). All of them were recruited through announcements at an Italian association and social networks (e.g., Facebook, Instagram). Participants need to receive in the past an oncological diagnosis and need to speak and understand Italian to be enrolled in this study.

The involved participants have an age range between 44 and 59 years old ($M_{age} = 52.00$; $SD_{age} = 5.73$), and the majority of them were higher educated (50% of participants obtained a post-university degree).

Women involved in the study received the oncological diagnosis between 1997 and 2021. All women were diagnosed with breast cancer, and two received more than one cancer diagnosis over the years. In addition, three participants were actually under hormonal therapy.

All the participants voluntarily participated in this study, were not compensated for their participation, and were not paid for the psychological session. The study was conducted in accordance with the Declaration of Helsinki.

Table 1. Descriptive statistics of participants

Participants	Age	Level of Education	Oncological diagnosis	Year of diagnosis
Participant #1	44	High school degree	Breast cancer and Hodgkin's lymphoma	2018
Participant #2	47	Post-university degree	Breast cancer	2021
Participant #3	52	University degree	Breast cancer	2019
Participant #4	53	Post-university degree	Breast cancer	2019
Participant #5	57	Post-university degree	Breast cancer	2013 and 2018
Participant #6	59	University degree	Breast cancer, thyroid cancer, and ovarian cancer	1997, 2020, and 2022

2.2 Procedure

All the participants who declared an interest in participating in this study received a detailed description of the study procedure and were invited to read and sign an informed consent. Women have the possibility to take part in a group psychological session in the Metaverse with two expert psycho-oncologists with extensive experience in the oncological field.

Before the psychological support group, one researcher meets the participants to describe the Metaverse environment and allow familiarization of participants with the virtual world. The virtual environment selected for this study is neutral (appearing like a room), allowing an easy conversation between participants and a non-specific emotional state. All elements that could result as unusual or unlikely were removed from the Metaverse. The participants can enter the virtual environment through a personal avatar (choosing from some avatars already available on the platform) and through a real or imaginary proper name. Interestingly, some participants decided to enter the Metaverse with an imagery proper name (37%). These women decided to use a fake name to protect their anonymity and feel freer to talk about specific topics related to their personal history of cancer.

The psychological support groups in the Metaverse were conducted in March and April and involved an average of 4 participants for each group. The session lasts around 2 h. During the session, women can talk about their history of cancer and related emotions sustained by the perception of group belonging. The psychologist helped the creation of an empathic, supportive, and collaborative environment [8] and focused the dialogue around some crucial aspects generally related to the oncological journey - social support, body appearance, and intimate relationships. In order to promote the dialogue in the groups, some evocative images related to the selected topics were shown to participants. These images were used to lead women to talk about some aspects of their illness experiences and reflect their emotions in the groups.

Before and after the psychological group session in the Metaverse, participants were invited to complete some self-report questionnaires that assessed their psychological and emotional state and their sense of presence in the Metaverse.

2.3 Measures

Participants were asked to complete a battery of online questionnaires presented with the Qualtrics platform before and after the psychological support group conducted in the Metaverse. Specifically, participants were required to fulfill socio-demographic ad-hoc questionnaires and self-reported questionnaires on perceived psychological states and personal emotions.

Before and after the group in the Metaverse, women were presented with the Self-Assessment Manikin (SAM) [32], a 9-point three visual item scale to rate three dimensions of the emotional experience. Specifically, the questionnaire assesses the pleasantness of the emotional state (*SAM_valence*), the perceived level of psychophysiological activation (*SAM_arousal*), and the perceived control over the emotional state (*SAM_dominance*).

Subsequently, participants were invited to rate the extent to which they experienced seven emotions. The explored emotions included both positive (*happiness* and *sense of amusement*) and negative (*anger, disgust, fear, sadness*, and *irritation*) emotions, rated on a 7-point Likert scale.

Lastly, after the session in the Metaverse, a questionnaire on the perceived sense of presence, the ITC-Sense of Presence Inventory (ITC-SOPI) [33] was administered. This questionnaire is composed of 42-items and explores, through a 5-point Likert scale, four dimensions related to the sense of presence: the *sense of physical space*, the *engagement*, the *ecological validity*, and the *negative effect*.

3 Data Analysis

Descriptive statistics were performed on all the variables of interest.

Given the small sample size, non-parametric analyses were carried out in this study. Specifically, we performed the Wilcoxon signed-rank test to assess the paired difference before and after the psychological experience in the Metaverse in the emotions experienced by participants (as assessed by the SAM and the ad hoc scales on seven specific emotions' intensity). The sense of presence in the Metaverse was also assessed and was considered a measure of involvement in the virtual experience.

Furthermore, to explore if the sense of presence might have an impact on the emotions experienced by women before and after the psychological experience, we performed a Kruskal–Wallis H test for ranks. These analyses allow us to check if there were differences in the emotional experience or in the intensity of emotions between those who experience a high or low sense of engagement (the cut-off was established on the basis of the median of the sample).

4 Results

Overall, mean scores on all the subscales of the ITC-SOPI questionnaire pointed out that participants perceived a fair level of ecological realism in the Metaverse and during the psychological group (*Ecological Validity*: $M = 16.33$, $SD = 5.37$, Range $= 11$–25) and experienced a good level of engagement in the activities and virtual environment

(*Engagement*: $M = 42,83, SD = 9.26$, Range $= 31–57$). The physical space was perceived as realistic (*Physical Space*: $M = 48.33$, $SD = 18.58$, Range $= 26–73$). Concerning the unpleasant aspects of the experience, participants reported a medium degree of discomfort during the experience in the Metaverse (*Negative effect* scale yielded a $M = 14.6, SD = 3.13$, Range $= 10–18$).

The Wilcoxon Signed Rank test was used to compare the features of the emotional experience (SAM) and emotions levels of participants before and after the psychological intervention in the Metaverse (Table 2). As regards the dimensions of the global emotional experience, participants reported greater control over emotional state after the virtual support group (*SAM_dominance*; $z = -2.00, p < .05$). No significant results emerged on the dimensions of the pleasantness and activation related to the emotional state (valence and arousal dimensions respectively).

Concerning the intensity of the specific emotions, overall results showed that participants experienced a significant decrease in the intensity of negative emotions after the virtual support group. Specifically, breast cancer survivors involved in this study tend to perceive a lower level of fear and sadness after the psychological support group in the Metaverse (*Fear*: $z = -2.26, p < .05$; *Sadness*: $z = -1.89, p = .05$), compared to the initial data collection. Even if not statistically significant, a similar trend emerged for the intensity of irritation experienced by participants during the Metaverse session.

Finally, the Kruskal–Wallis H test for ranks on participants divided according to high or low sense of engagement in the Metaverse, yielded non significant results both on the emotion dimensions (*Valence*: H (1) $= .05, p = .82$; *Arousal*: H (1) $= 1.34, p = .25$; *Dominance*: H (1) $= .05, p = .81$) and the intensity of the seven specific emotions (*Anger*: H (1) $= .07, p = .79$; *Disgust*: H (1) $= .07, p = .80$; *Fear*: H (1) $= .89, p = .35$; *Sadness*: H (1) $= .00, p = .9$; *Irritation*: H (1) $= .81, p = .37$; *Happiness*: H (1) $= .05, p = .82$; *Sense of amusement*: H (1) $= 2.6, p = .1$).

5   Discussion and Conclusion

Living with a cancer diagnosis could greatly impact physical and emotional levels, also after successful treatment. From a psychological point of view, fear of cancer recurrence, distress, and negative emotions could impact cancer survivors' general quality of life and hinder their return to everyday life. Psychological support or group psychotherapy could represent an occasion to allow people with similar life experiences to talk about their personal histories and explore new ways to manage their personal emotions [2].

New technologies are nowadays used for psychological purposes, in order to promote emotional well-being and help patients to manage their inner world. For example, different kinds of Internet-based delivery of psychotherapy through videoconferencing, virtual reality, chatbots, and avatars can be used for health purposes. Recent research highlighted that breast cancer survivors tend to perceive the tools for internet-based psychotherapy that include direct audio and video interaction with the psychotherapist as useful, effective, reassuring, and reliable [16]. Allowing patients to maintain communication with the therapist similar to the real world regarding non-verbal cues and taking turns in conversation could represent a crucial element. In addition, immersive scenarios can increase the sense of presence, or the illusion of patients of "being there" and elicit strong emotional responses [18, 21].

Table 2. Wilcoxon Signed-Ranks Test on SAM scale and ad-hoc items on emotions intensity

Variables	M (pre, post)	SD (pre, post)	z	p
SAM_Valence	Mpre = 5.83 Mpost = 6.33	SDpre = 2.14 SDpost = 2.42	−1.73	.83
SAM_Arousal	Mpre = 7.17 Mpost = 8.00	SDpre = 1.83 SDpost = 1.26	−1.89	.06
SAM_Dominance	Mpre = 5.17 Mpost = 3.00	SDpre = 2.79 SDpost = 1.26	−2.00	.04*
Happiness	Mpre = 4.00 Mpost = 5.00	SDpre = 2.28 SDpost = 2.10	−1.60	.11
Sense of amusement	Mpre = 3.70 Mpost = 3.83	SDpre = 1.75 SDpost = 2.49	−.28	.78
Anger	Mpre = 3.50 Mpost = 2.67	SDpre = 2.81 SDpost = 2.66	−1.63	.10
Disgust	Mpre = 2.67 Mpost = 1.67	SDpre = 2.11 SDpost = 1.21	−1,07	.28
Fear	Mpre = 4.17 Mpost = 2.17	SDpre = 2.31 SDpost = 1.94	−2.26	.02*
Sadness	Mpre = 3.83 Mpost = 3.00	SDpre = 2.31 SDpost = 2.28	−1.89	.05*
Irritation	Mpre = 3.83 Mpost = 2.50	SDpre = 2.49 SDpost = 1.90	−1.84	.06

Note. $*p < .05$

More recently, a new immersive virtual environment similar to Virtual Reality that serves as an alternate reality for its users is used for health purposes. This virtual tool, the Metaverse, allows participants to experience novel means of communication through an anonymous avatar that acts in a digital 3D environment that mimics real-life experiences. In this study, the Metaverse is used as a tool to conduct group psychological support with women who experienced a breast cancer diagnosis in their life. The session was supervised by expert psychotherapists and aimed to promote a collaborative and empathic context in which participants could talk about some aspects generally related to an oncological diagnosis and related emotions. Towards this end, we used a pre-post quantitative methodology investigating the changes in emotions experienced by participants before and after the intervention and their sense of presence within the virtual environment. Preliminary results of this study showed that participants tend to perceive the Metaverse as realistic, experiencing a good level of engagement in the proposed psychological activities and the virtual environment. This allows participants to experience greater control over their emotional state (dominance dimension) and to feel a significant decrease in the intensity of negative emotions, such as fear and sadness, after the virtual support group.

It is possible that the use of a virtual environment that allows a group interaction with an anonymous avatar could allow participants to experience a realistic group support experience. Talk about personal experiences related to their oncological diagnosis, speaking freely about their illness. This could allow them to take off the "mask" they are wearing for time and experience emotional support, thanks to the comparison with a group of people who lived similar life experiences [1]. This aspect could contribute to emotional change, experiencing less fear and sadness after the virtual experience in the Metaverse. In the current state, both anonymity and the virtual means of delivering presence and realistic experience may have contributed to participants' positive experiences. The specific therapeutic elements of the intervention should be further explored in future studies.

Future research could further analyze patients' experiences related to their emotional well-being and personal experiences lived in the Metaverse. The small number of participants limited the possibility of generalizing our results. A-priori power analysis (with power $1-\beta$ set at .80 and α equal to .05) highlighted that a sample size of 34 participants will be adequate to avoid the risk of incurring Type II errors [34]. Additionally, different results might emerge considering participants with different age ranges, maybe because younger age can shape resilience to cancer experience or familiarity with the technology. Studies with more ecological and real-life scenarios might also be planned to check differences in behaviors and experiences in settings where privacy is granted in different ways, for instance, with fake names or masking the participants. Future studies with enlarged sample sizes and control groups are needed to test these preliminary results and to tailor the interventions according to participants' specific needs related to age or cancer stage. However, this study could represent an important starting point for further research in which the Metaverse is used for psychological purposes for different patients.

Acknowledgements. I.D. was supported by Fondazione Umberto Veronesi. M.S. is a Ph.D. student within the European School of Molecular Medicine (SEMM).

References

1. Durosini, I., Savioni, L., Triberti, S., Guiddi, P.: Pravettoni, G: the motivation journey: a grounded theory study on female cancer survivors' experience of a psychological intervention for quality of life. Int. J. Environ. Res. Publ. Health **18**(3), 950 (2021)
2. Durosini, I., Triberti, S., Savioni, L., Sebri, V., Pravettoni, G.: The role of emotion-related abilities in the quality of life of breast cancer survivors: a systematic review. Int. J. Environ. Res. Public Health **19**(19), 12704 (2022)
3. Oliveri, S., et al.: PTSD symptom clusters associated with short- and long-term adjustment in early diagnosed breast cancer patients. Ecancermedicalscience **13** (2019)
4. Stein, K.D., Syrjala, K.L., Andrykowski, M.A.: Physical and psychological long-term and late effects of cancer. Cancer **112**(11 Suppl), 2577–2592 (2022)
5. Gudenkauf, L.M., Ehlers, S.L.: Psychosocial interventions in breast cancer survivorship care. Breast **38**, 1–6 (2018)
6. Han, J., Liu, J.E., Su, Y.L., Qiu, H.: Effect of a group-based acceptance and commitment therapy (ACT) intervention on illness cognition in breast cancer patients. J. Contextual Behav. Sci. **14**, 73–81 (2019)

7. Durosini, I., Triberti, S., Ongaro, G., Pravettoni, G.: Validation of the Italian version of the brief emotional intelligence scale (BEIS-10). Psychol. Rep. **124**(5), 2356–2376 (2021)
8. Durosini, I., Aschieri, F.: Therapeutic assessment efficacy: a meta-analysis. Psychol. Assess. **33**(10), 962 (2021)
9. Aschieri, F., Durosini, I., Smith, J.D.: Self-curiosity: definition and measurement. Self Identity **19**(1), 105–115 (2020)
10. Aschieri, F., Durosini, I.: Development of the self-curiosity attitude-interest scale. Test., Psychometrics, Methodol. Appl. Psychol. **22**(3), 326–346 (2015)
11. Aschieri, F., Durosini, I., Locatelli, M., Gennari, M., Smith, J.D.: Factor structure invariance and discriminant validity of the self-curiosity attitude-interest scale. TPM: Test., Psychometrics, Methodol. Appl. Psychol. **23**(2) (2016)
12. Yussof, I., Mohd Tahir, N.A., Hatah, E., Mohamed Shah, N.: Factors influencing five-year adherence to adjuvant endocrine therapy in breast cancer patients: a systematic review. Breast (Edinburgh, Scotland) **62**, 22–35 (2022)
13. Durosini, I., Triberti, S., Savioni, L., Pravettoni, G.: In the eye of a quiet storm: a critical incident study on the quarantine experience during the coronavirus pandemic. PLoS ONE **16**(2), e0247121 (2021)
14. Dickinson, R., Hall, S., Sinclair, J.E., Bond, C., Murchie, P.: Using technology to deliver cancer follow-up: a systematic review. BMC Cancer **14**, 311 (2014)
15. Akechi, T., et al.: Smartphone psychotherapy reduces fear of cancer recurrence among breast cancer survivors: a fully decentralized randomized controlled clinical trial (J-SUPPORT 1703 study). J. Clin. Oncol. **41**(5), 1069–1078 (2023)
16. Durosini, I., Triberti, S., Pravettoni, G.: Breast cancer survivors' attitudes towards internet-based psychotherapy. Annu. Rev. Cybertherapy Telemed. **18**, 201 (2020)
17. Pizzoli, S.F.M., et al.: Comparison of relaxation techniques in virtual reality for breast cancer patients. In: IEEE 5th Experiment International Conference (exp. at'19), pp. 348–351 (2019)
18. Parsons, T.D.: Virtual reality for enhanced ecological validity and experimental control in the clinical, affective and social neurosciences. Front. Hum. Neurosci. **9**, 1–19 (2015)
19. Triberti, S., Riva, G.: Being present in action: a theoretical model about the "interlocking" between intentions and environmental affordances. Front. Psychol. **6**, 1–8 (2016)
20. Riva, G., Waterworth, J.A.: Presence and the self: a cognitive neuroscience approach. Presence Conn. **3** (2003)
21. Riva, G., Waterworth, J.A., Waterworth, E.L.: The layers of presence: a bio-cultural approach to understanding presence in natural and mediated environments. Cyberpsychol. Behav. **7**(4), 402–416 (2004)
22. Baños, R.M., Botella, C., Alcañiz, M., Liaño, V., Guerrero, B., Rey, B.: Immersion and emotion: their impact on the sense of presence. Cyberpsychol. Behav. **7**(6), 734–741 (2004)
23. Diemer, J., Alpers, G.W., Peperkorn, H.M., Shiban, Y., Mühlberger, A.: The impact of perception and presence on emotional reactions: a review of research in virtual reality. Front. Psychol. **6**, 1–26 (2015)
24. Dwivedi, Y.K., et al.: Metaverse beyond the hype: Multidisciplinary perspectives on emerging challenges, opportunities, and agenda for research, practice and policy. Int. J. Inf. Manag. **66**, 102542 (2022)
25. Lombard, M., Ditton, T.: At the heart of it all: the concept of presence. J. Comput.-Mediated Commun. **3**(2), JCMC321 (1997)
26. Mystakidis, S.: Metaverse. Encyclopedia, MDPI AG **2**(1), 486–497 (2022)
27. Sparkes, M.: What is a metaverse (2021)
28. Wiederhold, B.K.: Ready (or Not) player one: initial musings on the metaverse. Cyberpsychol. Behav. Soc. Netw. **25**(1), 1–2 (2022)
29. Cerasa, A., Gaggioli, A., Marino, F., Riva, G., Pioggia, G.: The promise of the metaverse in mental health: the new era of MEDverse. Heliyon **8**(11), e11762 (2022)

30. Yang, D., et al.: Expert consensus on the metaverse in medicine. Clin. eHealth **5**, 1–9 (2022)
31. Mesko, B.: The promise of the metaverse in cardiovascular health. Eur. Heart J. **43**(28), 2647–2649 (2022)
32. Bradley, M.M., Lang, P.J.: Measuring emotion: the self-assessment manikin and the semantic differential. J. Behav. Ther. Exp. Psychiatry **25**, 49–59 (1994)
33. Lessiter, J., Freeman, J., Keogh, E., Davidoff, J.: a cross-media presence questionnaire: the ITC-sense of presence inventory. Presence **10**, 282–297 (2021)
34. Faul, F., Erdfelder, E., Lang, A.G., Buchner, A.: G*Power 3: a flexible statistical power analysis program for the social, behavioral, and biomedical sciences. Behav. Res. Methods **39**, 175–191 (2007)

Detection of Stress Stimuli in Learning Contexts of iVR Environments

José Miguel Ramírez-Sanz⬛, Helia Marina Peña-Alonso⬛,
Ana Serrano-Mamolar⬛, Álvar Arnaiz-González$^{(\boxtimes)}$⬛, and Andrés Bustillo⬛

Universidad de Burgos, 09001 Burgos, Spain
alvarag@ubu.es

Abstract. The use of eye-tracking in immersive Virtual Reality (iVR) is becoming an important tool for improving the learning outcomes. Nevertheless, the best Machine Learning (ML) technologies for the exploitation of eye-tracking data is yet unclear. Actually, one of the main drawbacks of some ML technologies, such as classifiers, is the scarce labeled data for training models, being the process of data annotation time-consuming and expensive. This paper presents a complete experimentation where different ML algorithms were tested, both supervised and semi-supervised, for trying to identify the stressors/distractors present in iVR learning experiences simulating the operation of a bridge crane. Results shown that the use of semi-supervised techniques can improve the performance of the Machine Learning methods making possible the identification of stressful situations in iVR environments. The use of semi-supervised learning techniques makes possible training ML algorithms without the need of great amount of labeled data which makes the data exploitation cheaper and easier.

Keywords: Machine Learning · Semi-supervised learning · Inmersive Virtual Reality · Game-based Learning · Eye-tracking · Stress

1 Introduction

Over the last 10 years, the number of applications in immersive Virtual Reality (iVR) has increase significantly [11]. Concurrently, the development of different sensors for biometric measurements is allowing their integration into these applications, which facilitates understanding in detail how the user is interacting and

This work was supported by the Junta de Castilla y León under project BU055P20 (JCyL/FEDER, UE), the Ministry of Science and Innovation of Spain under project PID2020-119894GB-I00, co-financed through European Union FEDER funds. This work is part of the project Humanaid (TED2021-129485B-C43) funded by MCIN/AEI/10.13039/501100011033 and the European Union "NextGenerationEU"/PRTR. We also acknowledge European Union NextGenerationEU/PRTR funds for the Margarita Salas 2022–2024 Grant awarded by Universidad de Burgos. It also was supported through the Consejería de Educación of the Junta de Castilla y León and the European Social Fund through a pre-doctoral grant (EDU/875/2021).

L. T. De Paolis et al. (Eds.): XR Salento 2023, LNCS 14219, pp. 427–440, 2023.
https://doi.org/10.1007/978-3-031-43404-4_29

reacting in the virtual world [16,30]. Unfortunately, the processing and analysis of the massive datasets produced by these sensors have become a bottleneck in achieving added value from these sensors for iVR experiences.

There is strong evidence coming from previous research showing that stress influences learning performance [13]. Numerous studies have analyzed the relationship between the learner's stress, cognitive behavior, learning performance, and intrinsic behavioral characteristics [2,24]. In the field of education and training, iVR experiences have already demonstrated their effectiveness [6] in improving learning rates. However, as with any other type of learning experience, the effectiveness and efficiency of learning in iVR are limited by user's stress factors [25]. The solution to this limitation seems to lie in the use of biometric sensors that can identify stress levels and modify the iVR experience to reduce them to levels that do not affect learning [7]. It is, therefore, necessary to identify the most efficient techniques capable of processing data from these sensors and classifying whether the educational experience is taking place in a situation of significant stress or not.

For this purpose, data mining and Machine Learning (ML) techniques can play a fundamental role. Such techniques are particularly adapted to the automatic extraction of complex patterns hidden in massive datasets [8]. Therefore, they seem particularly appropriate for this task. Among these techniques, there is a family of algorithms, the semi-supervised classifiers, that have demonstrated their special effectiveness when part of the training data is unlabeled, that is: it is not classified [28]. In the case of detecting stress situations in iVR educational or training experiences, this is particularly common [18,23], as while there are objective stress factors (lack of time, obstacles in task execution, task difficulty level, etc.), they do not affect different users in the same way. Thus, the use of semi-supervised techniques to classify stress levels in educational and learning experiences seems to be an optimal strategy for improving the efficiency of Machine Learning techniques in this task.

This research aims to produce the groundwork on the use Semi-Supervised Learning (SSL) applied to stressful stimuli detection in iVR environments. To make it possible in a low intrusive manner user data is collected from the eye-tracking device already integrated in common iVR head-mounted displays. To this end, several supervised and semi-supervised classifiers have been compared using eye-tracking recordings. These recording were gathered in an iVR learning tool with novice trainees operating a bridge crane.

The rest of the paper is organized as follows: firstly, a brief introduction to semi-supervised learning approaches is presented in Sect. 2; secondly, Sect. 3 explains the dataset acquisition; then, Sect. 4 details the Machine Learning experimentation and results obtained; finally, Sect. 5 compares these results with previous works and Sect. 6 gathers the main conclusions and the future research work.

2   Semi-supervised Learning

Machine Learning algorithms usually fall in one of the two big categories, based on the information that the instances/examples has. When instances have a feature/attribute of interest (i.e. a label) the task is called supervised learning, whereas when there is no any label of interest to learn, it is commonly known as unsupervised learning. In between, a recently novel approach emerged when there are only a few instances with label and many more without class, this is called semi-supervised learning (SSL) [28]. SSL methods learn from a small set of labeled instances and a (usually large) set of unlabeled instances, exploiting the underlying information present on the unlabeled data for improving the classification.

The applications of semi-supervised learning are varied and increasingly frequent. This approach finds utility in various domains, including industrial problems [21], medical issues [5], image detection [1], natural language processing [17], fraud detection [19], among others.

SSL methods are usually divided into transductive and inductive methods [28]. Transductive methods are graph-based methods that can only predict the unlabeled data available on the training phase. On the other hand, inductive methods can predict the label of new data that was not been seen during the training phase. Inductive methods are more commonly used and can be further divided into wrapper methods, unsupervised pre-processing, and intrinsically semi-supervised techniques.

There have been several SSL algorithms introduced to date. However, only wrapper SSL algorithms have been considered within the scope of this work. The basic principle of these methods is to train a model using only the labeled data and then pseudo-labels are generated for the unlabeled data using the trained model iteratively.

The process followed by wrapper methods to create pseudo-labels begins with training one or more base estimators using only the labeled data. Subsequently, these methods make attempts to predict the unlabeled data, selectively incorporating the predictions that gain the highest level of trust from the algorithm into the labeled data as pseudo-labels.

There are multiple types of wrapper SSL methods, primarily distinguished by the number of base estimators and the views of the dataset that the base estimators uses, and typically fall into one of three categories: Self-Training, Co-Training, and Boosting. Hereinafter the SSL algorithms used in the experimentation of this work are explained.

One of the simplest wrapper SSL method is Self-Training, which employs a single supervised base estimator for training and prediction [27,29]. Co-Training can be understood as an ensemble-based[1] adaptation of Self-Training [3]. In Co-Training, there exist two or more base estimators that may share the same

---

[1] Broadly speaking, in ML community an ensemble is an algorithm (meta-model) that is composed by several algorithms (base models/estimators) that work together [14]. The decisions made by an ensemble depend on the predictions of the base models.

view (single view) or have different views (multi-view) of the dataset. These base estimators are trained and make predictions, typically by voting or selecting the highest mean confidence.

Democratic Co-Learning is a Co-Training method where three or more base estimators share the same view of the data. This is a special method since the instances to be labeled as pseudo-labels must satisfy both the voting criterion and the sum of confidences criterion [31].

Tri-Training is one of the most popular Co-Training methods. As its name suggests, Tri-Training uses three base estimators with different views of the dataset [32].

Another Co-Training method is Co-Forest, which is the SSL adaptation of the popular Random Forest classifier [4]. In Co-Forest, during each train-predict iteration, every tree receives the pseudo-labels generated by the other trees [15].

3   Materials and Dataset Description

In this research, the abilities of novice trainees to operate a bridge crane under ideal conditions and with external factors that can induce stress and affect performance were analyzed. For this purpose, different environments were created in which the task to be performed was always the same, consisting of moving the hook of a bridge crane towards a barrel in an initial position, hooking it and completing the proposed route in the shortest possible time, trying not to knock down any cone [6] (Fig. 1).

Data collection was performed over three sessions conducted in consecutive weeks. The first session aimed to familiarize participants with the iVR environment. Thus, this session consisted of the completion of a tutorial and thus avoid the novelty effect in the rest of the sessions [20]. They then completed the standard iVR experience exercise, which consists of operating the bridge crane to transport the load along a circuit of cones without the load falling down or knocking over any cones. This same standard exercise is repeated throughout the sessions in order to improve the participants' ability in controlling the overhead crane. One week later, in the second session, the participants were proposed to perform five exercises, of which the first, third and fifth were standard exercises. However, in the second and fourth exercises, stressors were included. Thus, in the second exercise, the user controlling the overhead crane had to follow strict safety procedures while other operators walked around the factory, while the fourth exercise included the sound of a factory bell that could be stressful for the operator's performance. Finally, a third session was conducted with another five exercises. As in the previous session, while the first, third and fifth exercises followed the standard pattern, stressors were added to the second and fourth exercises. In this case, in the second, lighting conditions were degraded and in the fourth, distracting and potentially stressful noises were added. At the end of the experience, participants responded to a satisfaction survey in order to gather information on the impact of the stressors on each participant.

(a) Standard tutorial.

(b) Low lighting condition.

(c) People walking condition.

(d) Timer condition.

Fig. 1. Snapshots of the iVR simulator with the different visual conditions.

Table 1. Summary of the experiences performed on data collection. Exercises highlighted with an asterisk are those identified with stressful conditions.

Session	Exercise	Type of Exercise
1	1	Tutorial (standard)
2	2	Standard
	3*	People walking condition
	4	Standard
	5*	Timer condition
	6	Standard
3	7	Standard
	8*	Low lighting condition
	9	Standard
	10*	Noise condition
	11	Standard

In summary, over the three sessions conducted with the participants, they performed a total of 11 exercises, of which 1 was the tutorial as a preparatory exercise, and of the remaining 10, 4 exercises included stressors and 6 did not as it can be also seen in Table 1. This means that the final dataset has a ratio of positive/negative instances of 40/60%. A dataset was built as a result of the experiences, including two types of data: 1) data related to the exercises themselves and 2) data related to the trainee's performance. Regarding the exercises-related, the attributes selected were: trainee identifier; time spent to perform the task; collision failures; and number of times that two buttons were pressed simultaneously on the crane control. Regarding trainee performance data, it consisted of 15 entries or attributes within the iVR environment related to the position and rotation of: the crane, the load, and the trainee's head. In addition, 10 inputs were extracted from the eye-tracking system: gaze focus position; distance between the trainee and the focal point; eye opening; and pupil position. Those latter inputs were time series acquired 120 Hz. The original dataset has been previously presented in detail in [26]. In this case, the variable used as the label of the dataset and therefore as the output to be predicted by the models is the type of exercise, which defines whether it is an exercise with stressors (labeled as 1) or without stressors (labeled as 0).

4 Data Analysis and Results

Once the dataset was collected, a standard Machine Learning process was carried out in the following three stages:

- Feature extraction: each experience is a time-series which contains data from different attributes gathered from the eye-tracking device. From this series a feature extraction process was performed using the tsfresh library [9].
- Models training: 8 ML algorithms were used both supervised (3) and semi-supervised (5), with different combinations that results in 14 models.
- Models evaluation: to assess the performance of the different ML algorithms by using different metrics.

4.1 Feature Extraction

As it was previously mentioned, tsfresh library [9] was used in order to obtain features from the time-series. This Python package is a fast and standardized ML library for automatic time series feature extraction and selection on basis of the FRESH algorithm [10]. From each of the 25 parameters collected by the eyetracker, the minimal version of tsfresh extracts 9 features that includes parametric measures of distribution such as mean, median, variance and standard deviation, resulting in a total of 225 features in the final dataset.

4.2 Models and Parameters

During the experimentation[2] both supervised and semi-supervised algorithms were used. All the experiments were launched in Python 3 by using sklearn [22] and sslearn [12] libraries. The algorithms used and their parameters are listed below:

---

[2] The source code for the Machine Learning experimentation can be publicly accessed from the following link: https://github.com/Josemi/StressDetection_iVR.

- Supervised learning:
  - Decision Tree classifier (DT) with the default parameters.
  - k-Nearest Neighbors (kNN) with the number of neighbors set to three ($k = 3$).
  - Gaussian Naïve Bayes (NB) with the default parameters.
- Semi-supervised learning:
  - Self-Training with three different SL classifiers: DT, NB, and kNN.
  - Co-Training with three different SL classifiers: DT, NB, and kNN. The features were split into two disjoint subsets of equal size to simulate the two different independent views that Co-Training requires for training.
  - Tri-Training with the parameters proposed in the original paper [32], i.e. DT as base classifier.
  - Democratic Co-Learning with the parameters proposed in the original paper [31], i.e. the SL classifiers DT, NB, and kNN.
  - Co-Forest with the parameters proposed in the original paper [15], i.e. number of trees equal to 7.

4.3 Experimental Methodology

All the experiments were launched with repeated k-fold cross-validation, a common practice in ML community. The k value was set to 5 what means that the original dataset was split into five groups of approximately equal size, using four of them (k-1) to train the model and the one out for testing. This process is repeated k times using a different group as test for each validation. This procedure ensures that every single instance/example is used at least once for training and avoid overfitting. Finally, the whole process is repeated five times in order to reduce error variability, i.e. 5×5-fold cross-validation.

The metric used for evaluating the performance of the different classifiers was accuracy that is computed as follows:

$$accuracy = \frac{\#correctly\_classified\_instances}{\#total\_instances}$$

With the aim to assess the classification capabilities of the SSL for different percentage of labeled instances, the experiments were launched from 10% to 90% in steps of 10% (random label elimination was used).

4.4 Results

The results of the set of experiments performed for each of the tested algorithms are described bellow. As indicated above, three different Self-Training and Co-Training algorithms were launched (one for each of the supervised classifiers that was also tested alone: kNN, DT, and NB). Then, from the results obtained from those experiments, the best Self-Training and Co-Training configuration is inferred in order to compare them with the rest of algorithms. Table 2 shows the accuracy results for Self-Training while Table 3 shows the results for Co-Training. The best results for each column (i.e. percentage of labeled instances) have been highlighted in bold. As the results show, the best configuration for both Self-Training and Co-Training was the one using Decision Tree as base classifier, achieving the best results for most of the configurations.

Table 2. Results of accuracy for the Self-Training models with the different base classifiers: Decision Tree (DT), Naïve Bayes (NB), and k-Nearest Neighbors (kNN). The best result for each column is highlighted in bold.

Algorithm	Percentage of labeled instances								
	10 %	20%	30%	40%	50%	60%	70%	80%	90%
Self-Training (DT)	69.89	**75.49**	**80.15**	**82.41**	**84.24**	**85.46**	**86.78**	**87.50**	89.21
Self-Training (NB)	59.71	59.38	59.96	67.52	66.40	66.48	69.87	70.37	72.47
Self-Training (kNN)	**70.29**	72.73	71.83	72.79	71.83	71.48	72.44	71.91	71.77

Table 3. Results of accuracy for the Co-Training models with the different base classifiers: Decision Tree (DT), Naïve Bayes (NB), and k-Nearest Neighbors (kNN). The best result for each column is highlighted in bold.

Algorithm	Percentage of labeled instances								
	10 %	20%	30%	40%	50%	60%	70%	80%	90%
Co-Training (DT)	**73.89**	**79.62**	**83.58**	**85.09**	**86.11**	**86.89**	**88.14**	**89.59**	**90.12**
Co-Training (NB)	59.85	57.95	60.80	66.24	68.14	66.94	69.47	71.35	72.32
Co-Training (kNN)	67.85	70.49	72.30	71.39	71.48	71.63	72.15	70.58	71.04

Thus, these configurations of Self-Training and Co-Training using Decision-Tree as base algorithm were then compared with the rest of algorithms (both SL and SSL) in the general Table 4. Looking at the Table 4 it can be seen that, as it

Table 4. Results of accuracy for all the algorithms tested in the research including both the supervised (the top three methods) and semi-supervised learning. The best result for each column is highlighted in bold.

Algorithm	Percentage of labeled instances								
	10%	20%	30%	40%	50%	60%	70%	80%	**90%**
Decision Tree	69.63	75.20	79.92	82.94	83.34	85.93	88.14	88.08	90.64
k-Nearest Neighbors	67.94	69.25	70.26	71.22	70.87	71.20	71.71	71.89	71.57
Gaussian NB	63.25	61.71	65.00	68.30	68.84	66.80	71.24	70.31	71.05
Self-Training (DT)	69.89	75.49	80.15	82.41	84.24	85.46	86.78	87.50	89.21
Co-Training (DT)	**73.89**	**79.62**	**83.58**	**85.09**	86.11	**86.89**	88.14	89.59	90.12
Tri-Training	70.41	76.54	79.83	82.01	85.12	86.42	88.08	89.30	90.09
Democratic co	67.08	67.96	71.89	78.55	80.72	80.46	83.31	86.14	88.26
Co-Forest	73.81	78.14	81.45	84.51	**86.28**	86.80	**89.60**	**90.84**	**90.81**

was expected, all the algorithms (both SL and SSL) improve their performance as the percentage of labeled instances increases. It is worth noting that for all the percentages of labeled instances SSL algorithms performed the best, being Co-Training and Co-Forest the best ones. More specifically, with low labeled ratios Co-Training outperformed the rest of the SSL methods and as percentage of labeled instances increases Co-Forest performed the best. Nevertheless, the differences between Co-Training and Co-Forest were really small (around 1%) in any of the cases.

Results of Table 4 are depicted on a plot in Fig. 2. The percentage of labeled instances is represented on the horizontal axis while the accuracy is represented on the y axis. Supervised learning classifiers are represented on dashed lines in order to differentiate them from their SSL counterparts.

5   Discussion

Taking into account the results presented in the previous section, several discussions can be made.

Firstly, the DT algorithm outperforms all other supervised algorithms in absolute terms. While up to now mainly supervised algorithms have been tested for stress detection in iVR learning experiences [26], this result opens a promising approach to improve the accuracy of ML models applied to iVR environments. Additionally, DT shows more prominent evolution as the percentage of labeled data increases compared to the rest of SL models. A noteworthy observation can be made regarding the evolution of the other two supervised models, k-Nearest Neighbors and Naïve Bayes. This result also outlines the difference in human

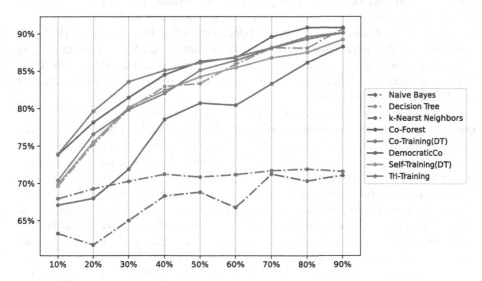

Fig. 2. Accuracy results of the classifiers evaluated as the percentage of labeled instances increases.

behavior expected in iVR environments [20], in this case in the response to stressors, because a more homogeneous response would assure a higher accuracy of k-Nearest Neighbors models. Besides, the differences between learning patterns of different users will reinforce the low accuracy of k-Nearest Neighbors models and outline the importance of finding better models for iVR learning environments, like DT models. It can be observed that despite the addition of more labeled data, the results obtained do not show significant improvement or even remain stable. This phenomenon may be attributed to the fact that these models achieve a reasonable performance with a small amount of labeled data, making further improvement challenging even with additional information. Moreover, no fine-tuning parameter selection was performed which may also contribute to their poor performance.

Secondly, focusing on SSL models, several findings have been made. It has been determined that DT, in addition to being the best supervised learning model on its own, serves as the optimal base estimator for Self-Training and Co-Training (as well as Co-Forest that also uses it inside the ensemble). Upon looking at the results of all SSL models, it is evident that two models outperform the others. The first is Co-Training with DT, which exhibits superior performance at low labeled proportions. The second is Co-Forest, which demonstrates the best results at higher labeled proportions. Nonetheless the differences between Co-Training and Co-Forest are not significant.

Regarding the other SSL alternatives, i.e. Self-Training, Tri-Training, and Democratic Co-Learning, they are performing worse. The reason behind the bad performance of Democratic Co-Learning can be explained because it was used with the classifiers that authors proposed in the original paper (i.e., DT, kNN, and NB) and two out of three of these classifiers have demonstrated an extremely bad performance in this problem. Tri-Training uses DT inside, as well as Self-Training, which may explain that its performance was similar.

In the light of these results, it has been proven the high potential that SSL methods can offer even with really low labeled datasets, like iVR environments data were labelling is a costly task [20]. Co-Training achieved around 4–5% improvement on low labeled ratios. This improvement decreases as the number of labeled instances increases.

It is important to acknowledge that the current work serves as a Preliminary investigation for stress assessment. While the findings obtained from this research provide valuable insights, it is essential to recognize the limitations and areas for improvement in future iterations. One noteworthy limitation of this study is the utilization of non-standardized tests for stress assessment. Although the selected methods have demonstrated effectiveness in prior research, the absence of widely accepted and validated stress users' assessment protocols may introduce variability and potential biases into the results. To enhance the reliability and comparability of the findings, future versions of this work will incorporate more standardized stress assessment tests that have undergone rigorous testing and validation within the scientific community. Moreover, to improve the generalizability of the outcomes, a leave-n-subjects out strategy could be implemented during cross-validation. This strategy involves systematically excluding a subset of participants from the training and validation process, ensuring that the model's performance is evaluated on unseen data. By implementing this approach, the generalizability of the developed stress assessment model can be enhanced, being less likely to have data-leaks from train set to test set. Addressing the aforementioned limitations will contribute to the advancement of this research and provide a more robust foundation for subsequent investigations on detecting stress stimuli in learning context of iVR environments.

6   Conclusions and Future Work

Today, one of the main challenges of iVR-based learning systems is to be able to adapt them to the user. This adaptation is only possible if the system is able to recognize the wide variety of users' special needs but also being able to detect external adverse conditions that may condition this learning process. In this work we have focused on the latter, and more specifically on those events that can generate stress to the user.

Equally important in this context when we want to apply Machine Learning techniques for pattern recognition in iVR systems, is the lack of training data for model building, due to the high cost and time-consuming of data collection. Therefore, semi-supervised learning approaches are presented as a good alternative in this field to the traditionally (and more common) used supervised methods.

The present work has therefore addressed the problem of detecting stressful environments in iVR learning context while comparing the semi-supervised approach with the supervised one. To this end, an iVR environment and validation experience was designed. The experience was composed of several exercises, all performing the same simple task for the operation of a bridge crane while exposing the user to different perturbations to generate a dataset. The dataset includes gaze tracking data of the user while exposed to different environmental conditions which in this work are summarized in situations with or without stressors. Gaze tracking data was collected by means of the device integrated in the iVR head mounted display, in a non-intrusive manner and thus decreasing the influence on the user's stress state.

Within the experiments, three commonly used supervised algorithms (Decision Tree, k-Nearest Neighbors, and Gaussian Naïve Bayes) have been compared against five popular semi-supervised algorithms (Self-Training, Co-Training, Tri-Training, Democratic Co-Learning, and Co-Forest). The results indicate that all semi-supervised learning algorithms outperform all supervised algorithms except the Decision Tree, which in some cases ties with some of the semi-supervised algorithms. With only 10% of the labeled data, the semi-supervised Co-Training algorithm is able to detect the presence or absence of stressors with 73.89% of accuracy, which is the maximum obtained. As the percentage of labeled data increases, the semi-supervised Co-Forest algorithm becomes the best classifier with up to 90.81% of accuracy when using 90% of the labeled instances.

The results therefore demonstrate the feasibility of applying SSL algorithms for the detection of stressful environments in an iVR learning context from non-intrusively collected gaze tracking data. It should be outlined that the aim of this research is not to find a reliable and robust solution for these classification tasks, but it is a first approach that will provide a baseline for future improvements on the use of semi-supervised algorithms in iVR learning environments and thus overcome an extended problem of lack of data.

In this work, as a first approximation to the solution, the default parameters of the algorithm have been used, so there is still room for improvement in accuracy. Future studies could focus on exploring which hyperparameters are those for which each classifier performs better by applying fine-tuning hyperparameter selection techniques. Additionally, regarding the Tri-Training algorithms applied, although in this work only the classifiers proposed in the original work [32] have been used, others could be explored, and this is something that could be explored in the next stages of this work. Future studies may also focus on exploring the use of this same dataset for user identification, so that the iVR experience can be tailored to the user's needs. Ideally, these findings should be replicated extending the dataset so that the classes (presence or absence of stressors) are more balanced, or considering to use balancing techniques.

References

1. Balcan, M.F., et al.: Person identification in webcam images: an application of semi-supervised learning. In: ICML 2005 Workshop on Learning with Partially Classified Training Data, vol. 2 (2005)
2. Beilock, S.L., Ramirez, G.: Chapter five - on the interplay of emotion and cognitive control: implications for enhancing academic achievement. In: Psychology of Learning and Motivation, vol. 55, pp. 137–169. Academic Press (2011). https://doi.org/10.1016/B978-0-12-387691-1.00005-3. https://www.sciencedirect.com/science/article/pii/B9780123876911000053
3. Blum, A., Mitchell, T.: Combining labeled and unlabeled data with co-training. In: Proceedings of the Eleventh Annual Conference on Computational Learning Theory, pp. 92–100 (1998)
4. Breiman, L.: Random forests. Mach. Learn. **45**, 5–32 (2001)
5. Chebli, A., Djebbar, A., Marouani, H.F.: Semi-supervised learning for medical application: a survey. In: 2018 International Conference on Applied Smart Systems (ICASS), pp. 1–9. IEEE (2018)
6. Checa, D., Bustillo, A.: A review of immersive virtual reality serious games to enhance learning and training. Multimedia Tools Appl. **79**, 5501–5527 (2020)
7. Chiossi, F., Welsch, R., Villa, S., Chuang, L., Mayer, S.: Virtual reality adaptation using electrodermal activity to support the user experience. Big Data Cogn. Comput. **6**(2), 55 (2022)
8. Cho, D., et al.: Detection of stress levels from biosignals measured in virtual reality environments using a kernel-based extreme learning machine. Sensors **17**(10), 2435 (2017)
9. Christ, M., Braun, N., Neuffer, J., Kempa-Liehr, A.W.: Time series FeatuRe extraction on basis of scalable hypothesis tests (tsfresh - a python package). Neurocomputing **307**, 72–77 (2018). https://doi.org/10.1016/j.neucom.2018.03.067

10. Christ, M., Kempa-Liehr, A.W., Feindt, M.: Distributed and parallel time series feature extraction for industrial big data applications. arXiv preprint arXiv:1610.07717 (2016)
11. Dincelli, E., Yayla, A.: Immersive virtual reality in the age of the metaverse: a hybrid-narrative review based on the technology affordance perspective. J. Strat. Inf. Syst. **31**(2), 101717 (2022)
12. Garrido-Labrador, J.L.: jlgarridol/sslearn: v1.0.3.1 (2023). https://doi.org/10.5281/zenodo.7781117
13. Joëls, M., Pu, Z., Wiegert, O., Oitzl, M.S., Krugers, H.J.: Learning under stress: how does it work? Trends Cogn. Sci. **10**(4), 152–158 (2006). https://doi.org/10.1016/j.tics.2006.02.002.   https://www.sciencedirect.com/science/article/pii/S1364661306000453
14. Kuncheva, L.I.: Combining Pattern Classifiers: Methods and Algorithms. John Wiley & Sons, Hoboken (2014)
15. Li, M., Zhou, Z.H.: Improve computer-aided diagnosis with machine learning techniques using undiagnosed samples. IEEE Trans. Syst. Man Cybern.-Part A: Syst. Hum. **37**(6), 1088–1098 (2007)
16. Liang, B., Lin, Y.: Using physiological and behavioral measurements in a picture-based road hazard perception experiment to classify risky and safe drivers. Transp. Res. Part F: Traffic Psychol. Behav. **58**, 93–105 (2018)
17. Liang, P.: Semi-supervised learning for natural language. Ph.D. thesis, Massachusetts Institute of Technology (2005)
18. Livieris, I.E., Drakopoulou, K., Tampakas, V.T., Mikropoulos, T.A., Pintelas, P.: Predicting secondary school students' performance utilizing a semi-supervised learning approach. J. Educ. Comput. Res. **57**(2), 448–470 (2019)
19. Melo-Acosta, G.E., Duitama-Munoz, F., Arias-Londono, J.D.: Fraud detection in big data using supervised and semi-supervised learning techniques. In: 2017 IEEE Colombian Conference on Communications and Computing (COLCOM), pp. 1–6. IEEE (2017)
20. Miguel-Alonso, I., Rodriguez-Garcia, B., Checa, D., Bustillo, A.: Countering the novelty effect: a tutorial for immersive virtual reality learning environments. Appl. Sci. **13**(1) (2023). https://doi.org/10.3390/app13010593. https://www.mdpi.com/2076-3417/13/1/593
21. Okaro, I.A., Jayasinghe, S., Sutcliffe, C., Black, K., Paoletti, P., Green, P.L.: Automatic fault detection for laser powder-bed fusion using semi-supervised machine learning. Addit. Manuf. **27**, 42–53 (2019). https://doi.org/10.1016/j.addma.2019.01.006
22. Pedregosa, F., et al.: Scikit-learn: machine learning in python. J. Mach. Learn. Res. **12**, 2825–2830 (2011)
23. Plunk, A., Amat, A.Z., Tauseef, M., Peters, R.A., Sarkar, N.: Semi-supervised behavior labeling using multimodal data during virtual teamwork-based collaborative activities. Sensors **23**(7), 3524 (2023). https://doi.org/10.3390/s23073524
24. Sandi, C.: Stress and cognition. Wiley Interdisc. Rev. Cogn. Sci. **4**(3), 245–261 (2013)
25. Schwabe, L., Hermans, E.J., Joëls, M., Roozendaal, B.: Mechanisms of memory under stress. Neuron **110**(9), 1450–1467 (2022). https://doi.org/10.1016/j.neuron.2022.02.020
26. Serrano-Mamolar, A., Miguel-Alonso, I., Checa, D., Pardo-Aguilar, C.: Towards learner performance evaluation in iVR learning environments using eye-tracking and machine-learning. Comunicar **31**(76), 9–19 (2023)

27. Triguero, I., García, S., Herrera, F.: Self-labeled techniques for semi-supervised learning: taxonomy, software and empirical study. Knowl. Inf. Syst. **42**, 245–284 (2015)
28. Van Engelen, J.E., Hoos, H.H.: A survey on semi-supervised learning. Mach. Learn. **109**(2), 373–440 (2020)
29. Yarowsky, D.: Unsupervised word sense disambiguation rivaling supervised methods. In: 33rd Annual Meeting of the Association for Computational Linguistics, pp. 189–196 (1995)
30. Zhang, Z., Wen, F., Sun, Z., Guo, X., He, T., Lee, C.: Artificial intelligence-enabled sensing technologies in the 5g/internet of things era: from virtual reality/augmented reality to the digital twin. Adv. Intell. Syst. **4**(7), 2100228 (2022). https://doi.org/10.1002/aisy.202100228
31. Zhou, Y., Goldman, S.: Democratic co-learning. In: 16th IEEE International Conference on Tools with Artificial Intelligence, pp. 594–602. IEEE (2004)
32. Zhou, Z.H., Li, M.: Tri-training: exploiting unlabeled data using three classifiers. IEEE Trans. Knowl. Data Eng. **17**(11), 1529–1541 (2005)

Virtual Reality-Based Rehabilitation for Patients with Stroke: Preliminary Results on User Experience

Sara Arlati[1]([✉])(iD), Marta Mondellini[1,2](iD), Eleonora Guanziroli[3](iD),
Mauro Rossini[3](iD), Isabella Martinelli[3], and Franco Molteni[3]

[1] Institute of Intelligent Industrial Technologies and Systems for Advanced
Manufacturing, National Research Council of Italy,
via Previati 1/E, 23900 Lecco, LC, Italy
{sara.arlati,marta.mondellini}@stiima.cnr.it
[2] Catholic University of the Sacred Heart, Largo Agostino Gemelli 1,
20123 Milano, MI, Italy
marta.mondellini@unicatt.it
[3] Villa Beretta Rehabilitation Center, Valduce Hospital,
via N. Sauro 17, 23845 Costa Masnaga, LC, Italy
eleonora.guanziroli@gmail.com, martinelli.isabella@outlook.it,
{mrossini,fmolteni}@valduce.it

Abstract. Stroke is one of the major causes of disability worldwide, and most stroke survivors require rehabilitation to recover motor and cognitive functions. Virtual Reality (VR) has emerged as a promising means to administer rehabilitative interventions due to its potential to provide high engagement and motivation, with positive effects on treatment compliance. In this context, we present the Virtual Supermarket (VSS), i.e., an immersive ecological VR application to retrain upper limb movements and cognitive functions in patients with stroke. The exercise foresees identifying, reaching, and grabbing grocery items on supermarket shelves and paying for them. Currently, we are conducting a study assessing the user experience of patients with sub-acute and chronic stroke undergoing rehabilitation with the VSS over a period of 4 weeks, 3 times a week. Up to now, 9 patients have experienced the supermarket and have answered questionnaires about perceived ease of use, involvement, and cyber-sickness after the first rehabilitation session. The VSS was evaluated satisfactorily, and no side effects emerged. Although preliminary, these outcomes are encouraging, and we expect the positive results to be maintained at the end of the rehabilitation period too. Further studies will be needed to investigate better clinical improvements that the VSS may lead to.

Keywords: Immersive technology · Motor recovery · Cognitive training · Chronic stroke

1   Introduction

Stroke is one of the major causes of death and disability worldwide [35]. In the European Union, 1.1 million people worldwide suffer from a stroke yearly [10]. Although stroke mortality has decreased in recent years, the number of people living with neurological impairments following a stroke has dramatically increased [9,42].

Stroke can indeed cause cognitive and sensorimotor deficits, which may impact the individual's capability to carry out activities of daily living (ADLs) autonomously [11]. Nonetheless, it is also true that impairments following stroke may be recovered thanks to appropriate rehabilitative interventions. Literature has shown that long-lasting, challenging, intensive, and skill-oriented training could effectively promote the recovery of functions by stimulating neuroplasticity [18,25].

Given the need to provide high-dose interventions to promote recovery, Virtual Reality (VR) has emerged as a promising solution due to its characteristics of being engaging and motivating [15,19]. Moreover, it has other potential benefits: VR can provide an ecological scenario to train in, which may ease the transfer of the acquired abilities to daily life [28]; it allows the creation of a controllable and safe environment in which it is also possible to integrate feedback to evaluate the performance, increasing patients' awareness throughout the rehabilitation sessions [33], and sensors to monitor physiological parameters [24].

Despite these advantages, VR may have some drawbacks, e.g., it may induce *cybersickness* and be perceived as unfamiliar or intimidating, especially to older adults [12,22].

Starting from these considerations, this work presents an immersive VR application developed to retrain upper limb and cognitive functions in post-stroke patients; the study assesses patients' user experience while undergoing rehabilitative treatment with immersive VR. Such a study aims to evaluate the acceptance of VR technology in post-stroke patients and verify its appropriateness to administer rehabilitative interventions.

2   Related Work

There is extensive work on using VR for neuromotor and cognitive rehabilitation in stroke, and many systematic reviews and meta-analyses can be traced in the literature. Up-to-date, there is evidence that VR could improve upper limb functions and cognitive deficits and, in general, reduce disability, either used alone or as an addition to standard therapy [4,16,24,26].

More recently, given the potential of immersive VR to engage and motivate even more the user, also this technology has been explored for stroke rehabilitation, and preliminary outcomes showed that it could be promising and effective [36].

Despite positive outcomes, however, open questions and challenges remain at technical and clinical levels [5]. The heterogeneity of the interventions, in terms of administered exercise, frequency, and length of the training, does not allow for drawing conclusions regarding the optimum for each patient [5]. Moreover, the issue of scarce acceptance of the technology cannot be neglected: the weight of the device, the potential risk of trips and falls, the presence of a cable, and the arousal of cybersickness are all aspects that should be taken into consideration when designing and proposing a new VR-based treatment [31].

In the context of VR-based cognitive training, few years ago, our research group developed an HTC Vive-based virtual supermarket (*VSM*) to train visuospatial abilities in older adults with cognitive decline [6]. The proposed tasks foresaw walking around a supermarket aisle to collect the grocery items presented on a list, placing them in a cart, and paying for them. The rationale underlying the choice of the scenario was the possibility of experiencing an ADL [7] and making the older adults feel more confident while performing the task. The VSM application was assessed in three user-experience studies, two enrolling young healthy adults and one older adults with cognitive deficits. In all cases, it was considered acceptable and enjoyable [6,30,32].

Starting from this experience, considering the need for post-stroke patients to train their cognitive abilities, we revised the VSM to make it suitable and meaningful for this population too.

3   The Virtual Supermarket

The virtual supermarket for stroke patients (*VSS*) has been developed using Unity and deployed for Oculus Rift 2.0. It foresees two different scenarios dedicated, respectively, to grocery items' picking (Fig. 1) and payment (Fig. 2). With respect to the previous versions [6,32], two main novelties have been introduced. First, all the tasks can be carried out while staying seated to avoid any risk of tripping or falling, making the VSS accessible for patients with motor or balance issues too. This feature also allows retraining the upper limb functionalities by performing a task-related training of the reaching movement, i.e., a goal-directed, functional movement that is carried out in a natural environment [39].

Second, a series of features have been added to allow the therapist to customize the difficulty of the training throughout the rehabilitative path. This was made to make the VSS available to patients with different cognitive levels and to increase the complexity of the exercises throughout the sessions avoiding repetitiveness and, thus, boredom. Such features are:

- the number of items on the shelves (9 or 15);
- the number of target items (i.e., items to be picked from the shelves) on the shopping list (from 1 to 8);
- categorization of items (yes/no); if categorization is disabled, the items on the shopping list appear with their name. Otherwise, a category of items is displayed (e.g., dairy products, dishware, vegetables), and the patient is required to pick all the items corresponding to such categories;
- background noise (yes/no) sets whether a distracting sound reproducing supermarket noise (beeps, unintelligible voices, etc.) is on or off;
- the visibility of the shopping list, which can be either displayed or hidden.

Fig. 1. A screenshot of the aisle environment. To complete the shopping, the button "end shopping" [*termina spesa*] has to be clicked. The other buttons are available to the therapist only to change the visibility of the list [*visibilità lista*], to enable/disable the background noise [*rumore di fondo*], and to replay the list items [*leggi lista*].

Fig. 2. A screenshot of the cash register. To complete the payment, the button "end payment" [*termina pagamento*] has to be clicked. The other buttons are available to the therapist only to change the visibility of the amount to pay [*visibilità importo*], and to enable/disable the background noise [*rumore di fondo*].

After setting these parameters, the application is loaded; as mentioned, the first scene is a supermarket aisle. The patient is seated in front of a shelf unit on which the target grocery items are placed, together with distractors. A shopping basket is placed on the right or on the left side of the patient, depending on the arm he/she had to train (this is set in each patient profile). The shopping list is placed on the top of the basket. To grab the target items, patients had to use the Oculus controller, press the grip button on its side, and transport the item in/over the basket. When the patient thinks to have concluded the shopping, they can move on to the payment by clicking the "end shopping" button (using a ray interactor [1], visible in Fig. 2).

The payment scenario foresees a cash register; the amount to pay is generated randomly, and the patient must pay the correct amount by selecting banknotes and coins. Also in this case, the interaction occurs via a laser ray, and the patient has to confirm when he/she believes to have finished.

During the two tasks, the therapist can intervene via buttons displayed on the PC monitor that are invisible to the patients. In particular, the therapist can: enable/disable the background noise, hide/show the list or the amount to pay, and replay - via text-to-speech - the items on the list (only in the aisle scene).

Feedback about the performances is given to the patient at the end of each task (item grabbing and payment) via a panel displaying the time taken, the errors committed, and the omissions or the amount of money still to pay.

4 Evaluation of the User Experience

The study is an interventional study that aims to assess the user experience of patients undergoing a motor and cognitive rehabilitation program with the VSS (as described in Sect. 3) over a period of 4 weeks. This study complies with the Declaration of Helsinki. The trial protocol has been approved by the Insubria Ethical Committee (ref. no. 70, 01/12/2020).

4.1 Methods

Participants. The study participants are enrolled among the stroke patients in the post-acute (time from the stroke longer than 15 days) or chronic phase (6 months) treated in the rehabilitation clinic Villa Beretta (Costa Masnaga, LC, Italy). The inclusion criteria for this study are the following: age $\geq$ 18; clinical stability; absence of pain (assessed with VAS pain scale), postural instability (Berg Balance Scale), muscle hyperactivity (Modified Ashworth Scale < 3), and impairments that prevent the accomplishment of the reaching task; Mini-Mental State Examination (MMSE) $\geq$ 20 or an equivalent cognitive level assessed via task-oriented tests. Exclusion criteria are a history of seizure or motion sickness; severe visual deficits. The estimated sample size is 30.

Study Protocol. The study lasts 4 weeks for each participant and foresees a training session 3 times a week for a total of 12 sessions. Each session lasts 20 min, in which the tasks of doing the shopping and paying for it are repeated recursively. A therapist constantly supervises the sessions and can intervene during the experience to increase or decrease the level of complexity arbitrarily.

At the baseline, patients are assessed to verify inclusion and exclusion criteria (t0-PRE). Then, the therapist explains the features and the tasks to perform in the supermarket and helps them wear and adjust the straps of the head-mounted display. During the first trial, the difficulty of the exercise is set at the lowest level possible. After 20 min of exercise, patients are asked to fill in a battery of self-administered questionnaires evaluating their user experience (Sect. 4.1) (t0-POST).

The same clinical scales questionnaires are administered again to all patients before and after the last (twelfth) session at t1-PRE and t1-POST, respectively.

Outcomes. The user experience is evaluated by assessing the perceived ease of use of the system, involvement, and cybersickness. The first variable is assessed by the corresponding subscale (*Perceived Ease of Use*, PEOU) of the questionnaire proposed in the Technology Acceptance Model 3 [41]; it consists of 4 items assessed on a 7-point Likert scale.

The general engagement of the patients is measured using some items from the *Involvement* subscale of the Presence Questionnaire [45]. Such items are related to how involving the visual aspects of the virtual environment were, and how involved in the experience the participant became; thus, the final scale consists of five items, and the respondent indicates the degree of agreement with each sentence on a Likert scale (1 to 5).

Finally, cybersickness is assessed via the Simulator Sickness Questionnaire (SSQ) [23]; SSQ is composed of 16 symptoms: for each of them, the respondent has to indicate the intensity (*none, slight, moderate, severe*). It provides scores in four categories: nausea (SSQ-N), oculomotor discomfort (SSQ-O), disorientation (SSQ-D), and general factors (SSQ-TS).

Statistical Analysis. Statistical analyses are performed with IBM spss v.28. The one-sample Kolmogorov-Smirnov test is used to verify that the variables are normally distributed. For SSQ and its subscale, the distribution is observed on raw scores. Descriptive statistics are reported for all the variables of interest (means and standard deviations for normal values and median and interquartile ranges for non-normal ones). The reliability of the scales is evaluated with Cronbach's alpha. As reported later in Sect. 4.2, only a few patients have completed t0 at the moment of writing this paper; no one has reached the end of the 4 weeks of treatment. Thus, no comparative statistic test is used at this stage.

4.2 Preliminary Results

Currently, 13 patients have been enrolled in the VSS study and have completed the user experience questionnaire at t0. Their characteristics are reported in Table 1. In the following, we thus present the results of the aforementioned questionnaires (paragraph Sect. 4.1); the complete results will be reported in a later work.

Perceived Ease of Use. PEOU was rated 6.75 (iqr: 1.13) on a scale up to 7. The distribution of the variable at t0 is not normal ($p = 0.002$); the scale was highly reliable ($\alpha = 0.90$).

Table 1. Characteristics of the patients enrolled in the study. M: male, F: female, L: left, R: right, MMSE: Mini-Mental State Examination.

ID	age	gender	time from event	affected side	type	MMSE
1	56	F	1 yr	L	hemorrhagic	25
2	56	M	3 yrs. 2 mths	R	ischemic	30
3	39	M	6 mths	L	ischemic	30
4	46	M	7 mths	L	ischemic	29
5	69	M	7 mths	L	ischemic	25
6	37	M	1 yr	L	hemorrhagic	30
7	56	M	1 mth	L	ischemic	28
8	68	F	1 yr. 3 mths	L	hemorrhagic	28
9	58	M	1 mth	R	ischemic	23
10	58	F	11 mths	R	hemorrhagic	28
11	58	M	6 mths	R	hemorrhagic	28
12	66	F	1 yr. 5 mths	L	hemorrhagic	25

Involvement. Patients rated involvement 3.75 ± 1.04 on a scale up to 5. The scale obtained $\alpha = 0.90$ at t0, showing good reliability. Involvement has a normal distribution ($p = 0.20$).

Cybersickness. SSQ results are reported in Table 2, along with normality and reliability. The SSQ subscales' values are also presented in Fig. 3 in comparison to acceptable values [23].

Table 2. Descriptive statistics and reliability of SSQ subscales. N: nausea, O: oculomotor disturbance, D: disorientation, TS: total score, KS: Kolmogorov-Smirnov.

Scale	KS test	Mean (SD)	Median (iqr)	α
SSQ-N	$p < 0.001$	3.67 (7.33)	0 (2.39)	0.43
SSQ-O	$p = 0.21$	7.95 (11.15)	4.77 (17.06)	0.69
SSQ-D	$p = 0.28$	18.20 (26.89)	13.92 (27.84)	0.77
SSQ-TS	$p = 0.22$	12.37 (16.26)	11.22 (15.90)	0.85

4.3   Discussion

The majority of stroke survivors require rehabilitation to recover motor and cognitive functions and minimize their disability. Although most of the recovery occurs in the acute and sub-acute phases [34], evidence exists that functional capacity can also be regained in the chronic phase [3].

Given its flexibility and motivating characteristics, VR is a good means to provide rehabilitative treatment for extended periods. However, it is essential to assess whether it is suitable for patients with sub-acute and chronic stroke.

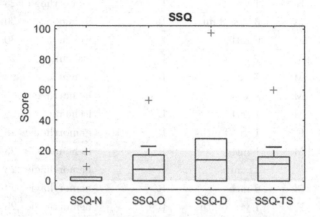

Fig. 3. Boxplots presenting weighted results of SSQ and its subscales (N: nausea, O: oculomotor disturbance, D: disorientation, TS: total score). The green area shows the acceptable values according to [23] (Color figure online).

Although very preliminary, this study's results suggest that an intervention based on the VSS is feasible and acceptable for patients with sub-acute and chronic stroke. Also, patients reported feeling involved in the experience, which is a crucial aspect to consider when trying to promote prolonged adherence to rehabilitative treatments.

PEOU obtained a score of 6.75 out of 7, meaning that the VSS was perceived as intuitive and very easy to use, also in post-stroke patients who may experience cognitive issues and motor deficits, which may impact the handling of the controller. The preliminary tests performed with the VSM and non-vulnerable populations have favored good usability, as they allowed identifying potential sources of complexity [30,32]. For instance, the interaction required for the payment in VSM, which first occurred with two buttons (i.e., pressing the pad to generate the laser ray, and then the trigger to make the selection), was changed as a consequence of healthy adults' feedback [30].

Despite this, the evaluation of the user experience described in this work was essential, as there was no certainty that usability would be positively judged also in the case of VSS, mainly because of two reasons. First, the HMD device and its controllers changed between the two experiments, and the tasks were slightly modified. Second, the population was not only different but potentially more critical in terms of requirements. Indeed, in spite of the high functioning required by the inclusion criteria, some motor or cognitive deficits due to stroke could have influenced the whole experience. The impacts of motor deficits, for instance, were already reported by other research groups: e.g., Huygelier et al.

[21] found that stroke patients with altered hand coordination tended to push more than one button at a time, causing also leaving the game unwillingly. Similarly, although mild to moderate (MMSE $\leq$ 27), we were not aware whether patients' cognitive deficits could have played a role [13].

In our case, however, motor and cognitive disabilities seemed not to play a major role. The PEOU of the VSS was judged as comparable to or better than what was obtained in previous studies involving immersive VR for patients with stroke [21,27,43]. Also, it was slightly higher than what was obtained for the previous version of the supermarket (VSM PEOU was rated 6.37 by older adults with mild cognitive impairment [6]).

Anyhow, it remains difficult to make an appropriate comparison because of both the heterogeneity of the VR applications and included samples, and the complexity of tracing structured usability or ease-of-use assessments in the literature. Tuena et al. [40], who systematically investigated the usability issues of digital applications for older adults in 2020, included only 25 studies. Of these, only 8% of such studies made use of immersive technology, and only 8% were dedicated to stroke.

Regarding involvement, outcomes were also satisfying and comparable to what was obtained in previous experiences with immersive VR, but different applications [8,21,44]. Given this, it will be interesting to evaluate, at t1, whether the engagement of the participants will remain high and, consequently, if immersive VR—and the VSS, in particular—could be a means to promote effective treatment adherence. We expect the increase in the task's difficulty to provide an adequate challenge to support a good user experience and the motivation to train throughout the four weeks of the intervention [14,17].

Finally, regarding adverse effects as measured by the SSQ, the values of all the subscales are mostly in the acceptable range, i.e., <15–20, indicating that drawbacks were slight and infrequent.

The subscale reaching the highest values is *Disorientation*. This agrees with previous findings highlighting that dizziness and vertigo are the most common symptoms in non-navigational environments [43]. Such low values are also in agreement with previous outcomes demonstrating the decrease of motion sickness susceptibility throughout life [2].

Once again, given this evidence and the outcomes obtained with the previous version of the supermarket (VSM) with older [6] and young adults [30,32], this result could be expected. The scores obtained by the age-matched sample for the VSM were the following (median and iqr): SSQ-N = 0(0 − 9.54), SSQ-O = 7.58(0−15.16), SSQ-D = 0(0−27.84), SSQ-TS = 3.74(0−16.83). Although not relevant to cause significant symptoms, the slightly increased values collected in the case of VSS may be induced by some impairments due to the specific pathology consequences, which could eventually worsen some symptoms: e.g., stroke may induce blurred and doubled vision, reduction of the visual field, and neglect, which can impair the perception of the virtual environment through the HMD, causing adverse effects [12] and impacting the user experience negatively [38].

This study has some limitations. Due to the limited sample size and the fact that presented data have been collected after only one session, the obtained results should be interpreted cautiously. Also, they may not be generalizable or reproducible at t1.

Nonetheless, the positive outcomes, together with the good reliability (i.e., Cronbach's $\alpha > 0.7$) of all the evaluated subscales, with the only exception of SSQ-N, are encouraging and boding well for t1 too.

5   Conclusions and Future Work

This work presents the Virtual Supermarket, an immersive VR-based application for training upper limb functions and cognition in patients with sub-acute and chronic stroke.

We are currently conducting a study assessing the user experience of patients undergoing a 4-week period of rehabilitation with the VSS. Preliminary results obtained after the first session are encouraging for the retention of high levels of involvement, which, in turn, can positively influence motivation, performance, and treatment compliance also in the longer period [40].

If results at t1 will also be satisfactory, the VSS will be tested for its therapeutic effectiveness by evaluating more detailed clinical and cognitive outcomes and potentially exploring the neural mechanisms underlying recovery [29].

Moreover, if usability and involvement are also judged adequate for longer trials, the application of the VSS for rehabilitation could also be improved in two ways. First, implementing different interaction methods, which would allow the application to be accessible to patients with more severe motor deficits too. Potential solutions could be the exploitation of hand tracking, to avoid reaching against gravity while holding an additional weight (i.e., the controller), or the implementation of a laser ray-based selection also for grocery items. Second, the VSS could be deployed, with modifications allowing unsupervised use, on a more affordable HMD (e.g., the Meta Quest II) to be considered for the administration of home-based therapies. This solution would provide patients with continuity of care, thus improving rehabilitation outcomes while reducing, at the same time, the economic and social burden of long-term treatments on National Healthcare Systems, patients, and their caregivers [20, 37].

Acknowledgements. This research was supported by Regione Lombardia and Fondazione Cariplo in the framework of the project EMPATIA@Lecco - EMpowerment del PAzienTe In cAsa (Ref. 2016-1428, Decreto Regione Lombardia 6363 del 30/05/2017).

References

1. XR Ray Interactor. https://docs.unity3d.com/Packages/com.unity.xr.interaction. toolkit@2.0/manual/xr-ray-interactor.html. Accessed 21 Apr 2023
2. Allen, R.C., Singer, M.J., McDonald, D.P., Cotton, J.E.: Age differences in a virtual reality entertainment environment: a field study. In: Proceedings of the Human Factors and Ergonomics Society Annual Meeting, vol. 44, pp. 542–545. SAGE Publications Sage CA, Los Angeles, CA (2000)
3. Aprile, I., et al.: Effects of rehabilitation on quality of life in patients with chronic stroke. Brain Inj. 22(6), 451–456 (2008)
4. Aramaki, A.L., Sampaio, R.F., Reis, A.C.S., Cavalcanti, A., et al.: Virtual reality in the rehabilitation of patients with stroke: an integrative review. Arq. Neuropsiquiatr. 77, 268–278 (2019)
5. Arlati, S., Borghetti, D.: XR and neurorehabilitation. In: Roadmapping Extended Reality: Fundamentals and Applications, pp. 257–282 (2022)
6. Arlati, S., et al.: Acceptance and usability of immersive virtual reality in older adults with objective and subjective cognitive decline. J. Alzheimers Dis. 80(3), 1025–1038 (2021)
7. Arlati, S., Zangiacomi, A., Greci, L., di Santo, S.G., Franchini, F., Sacco, M.: Virtual environments for cognitive and physical training in elderly with mild cognitive impairment: a pilot study. In: De Paolis, L.T., Bourdot, P., Mongelli, A. (eds.) AVR 2017. LNCS, vol. 10325, pp. 86–106. Springer, Cham (2017). https://doi.org/10. 1007/978-3-319-60928-7_8
8. Bank, P.J., Cidota, M.A., Ouwehand, P., Lukosch, S.G.: Patient-tailored augmented reality games for assessing upper extremity motor impairments in Parkinson's disease and stroke. J. Med. Syst. 42, 1–11 (2018)
9. Baumann, M., Lurbe-Puerto, K., Alzahouri, K., Aïach, P.: Increased residual disability among post stroke survivors and the repercussions for the lives of informal caregivers. Top. Stroke Rehabil. 18(2), 162–171 (2011)
10. Béjot, Y., Bailly, H., Durier, J., Giroud, M.: Epidemiology of stroke in Europe and trends for the 21st century. La Presse Médicale 45(12), e391–e398 (2016)
11. Broussy, S., et al.: Sequelae and quality of life in patients living at home 1 year after a stroke managed in stroke units. Front. Neurol. 10, 907 (2019)
12. Cobb, S.V., Nichols, S., Ramsey, A., Wilson, J.R.: Virtual reality-induced symptoms and effects (VRISE). Presence Teleoperators Virtual Environ. 8(2), 169–186 (1999)
13. Coldham, G., Cook, D.M.: VR usability from elderly cohorts: preparatory challenges in overcoming technology rejection. In: 2017 National Information Technology Conference (NITC), pp. 131–135. IEEE (2017)
14. Csikszentmihalyi, M., Csikszentmihalyi, M., Abuhamdeh, S., Nakamura, J.: Flow and the Foundations of Positive Psychology: The Collected Works of Mihaly Csikszentmihalyi, pp. 227–238. Springer, Dordrecht (2014)
15. Dias, P., et al.: Using virtual reality to increase motivation in poststroke rehabilitation. IEEE Comput. Graphics Appl. 39(1), 64–70 (2019)
16. Domínguez-Téllez, P., Moral-Muñoz, J.A., Salazar, A., Casado-Fernández, E., Lucena-Antón, D.: Game-based virtual reality interventions to improve upper limb motor function and quality of life after stroke: systematic review and meta-analysis. Games Health J. 9(1), 1–10 (2020)

17. Elor, A., Powell, M., Mahmoodi, E., Teodorescu, M., Kurniawan, S.: Gaming beyond the novelty effect of immersive virtual reality for physical rehabilitation. IEEE Trans. Games **14**(1), 107–115 (2022). https://doi.org/10.1109/TG. 2021.3069445

18. Hao, J., Xie, H., Harp, K., Chen, Z., Siu, K.C.: Effects of virtual reality intervention on neural plasticity in stroke rehabilitation: a systematic review. Arch. Phys. Med. Rehabil. **103**(3), 523–541 (2022)

19. Herne, R., Shiratuddin, M.F., Rai, S., Laga, H., Dixon, J., Blacker, D.: Game design principles influencing stroke survivor engagement for VR-based upper limb rehabilitation: a user experience case study. In: Proceedings of the 31st Australian Conference on Human-Computer-Interaction, pp. 369–375 (2019)

20. Hirschman, K., Shaid, E., McCauley, K., Pauly, M., Naylor, M.: Continuity of care: the transitional care model. Online J. Issues Nurs. **20**(3), 13–27 (2015)

21. Huygelier, H., et al.: An immersive virtual reality game to train spatial attention orientation after stroke: a feasibility study. Appl. Neuropsychol. Adult **29**(5), 915–935 (2022)

22. Ijaz, K., Tran, T.T.M., Kocaballi, A.B., Calvo, R.A., Berkovsky, S., Ahmadpour, N.: Design considerations for immersive virtual reality applications for older adults: a scoping review. Multimodal Technol. Interact. **6**(7), 60 (2022)

23. Kennedy, R.S., Lane, N.E., Berbaum, K.S., Lilienthal, M.G.: Simulator sickness questionnaire: an enhanced method for quantifying simulator sickness. Int. J. Aviat. Psychol. **3**(3), 203–220 (1993)

24. Kim, W.S., et al.: Clinical application of virtual reality for upper limb motor rehabilitation in stroke: review of technologies and clinical evidence. J. Clin. Med. **9**(10), 3369 (2020)

25. Kleim, J.A., Jones, T.A.: Principles of experience-dependent neural plasticity: implications for rehabilitation after brain damage. J. Speech Lang. Hear. Res. **51**(1), S225–S239 (2008)

26. Lee, H.S., Park, Y.J., Park, S.W.: The effects of virtual reality training on function in chronic stroke patients: a systematic review and meta-analysis. BioMed Res. Int. **2019** (2019)

27. Lee, S.H., Jung, H.Y., Yun, S.J., Oh, B.M., Seo, H.G.: Upper extremity rehabilitation using fully immersive virtual reality games with a head mount display: a feasibility study. PM&R **12**(3), 257–262 (2020)

28. Levac, D.E., Huber, M.E., Sternad, D.: Learning and transfer of complex motor skills in virtual reality: a perspective review. J. Neuroeng. Rehabil. **16**, 1–15 (2019)

29. Mazzoleni, S., Puzzolante, L., Zollo, L., Dario, P., Posteraro, F.: Mechanisms of motor recovery in chronic and subacute stroke patients following a robot-aided training. IEEE Trans. Haptics **7**(2), 175–180 (2014). https://doi.org/10.1109/TOH.2013.73

30. Mondellini, M., Arlati, S., Pizzagalli, S., Greci, L., Sacco, M., Ferrigno, G.: Assessment of the usability of an immersive virtual supermarket for the cognitive rehabilitation of elderly patients: a pilot study on young adults. In: 2018 IEEE 6th International Conference on Serious Games and Applications for Health (SeGAH), pp. 1–8. IEEE (2018)

31. Mondellini, M., Colombo, V., Arlati, S., Lawson, G., Cobb, S.: Human Factors and Ergonomics. Roadmapping Extended Reality: Fundamentals and Applications, pp. 229–256 (2022)

32. Mondellini, M., Pizzagalli, S., Greci, L., Sacco, M.: Assessment of an immersive virtual supermarket to train post-stroke patients: a pilot study on healthy people. In: De Paolis, L.T., Bourdot, P. (eds.) AVR 2019. LNCS, vol. 11613, pp. 313–329. Springer, Cham (2019). https://doi.org/10.1007/978-3-030-25965-5_23

33. Mottura, S., Fontana, L., Arlati, S., Zangiacomi, A., Redaelli, C., Sacco, M.: A virtual reality system for strengthening awareness and participation in rehabilitation for post-stroke patients. J. Multimodal User Interfaces 9(4), 341–351 (2015). https://doi.org/10.1007/s12193-015-0184-5

34. Musicco, M., Emberti, L., Nappi, G., Caltagirone, C., Italian Multicenter Study on Outcomes of Rehabilitation of Neurological Patients: Early and long-term outcome of rehabilitation in stroke patients: the role of patient characteristics, time of initiation, and duration of interventions. Arch. Phys. Med. Rehabil. 84(4), 551–558 (2003)

35. Norrving, B., et al.: Action plan for stroke in Europe 2018–2030. Eur. Stroke J. 3(4), 309–336 (2018)

36. Palacios-Navarro, G., Hogan, N.: Head-mounted display-based therapies for adults post-stroke: a systematic review and meta-analysis. Sensors 21(4), 1111 (2021)

37. Seregni, A., et al.: Virtual coaching system for continuity of care and rehabilitation in patients with stroke. Results of the pilot study in the home scenario. Gait Posture 97, 29–30 (2022)

38. Specht, J., Schroeder, H., Krakow, K., Meinhardt, G., Stegmann, B., Meinhardt-Injac, B.: Acceptance of immersive head-mounted display virtual reality in stroke patients. Comput. Hum. Behav. Rep. 4, 100141 (2021)

39. Thielman, G.T., Dean, C.M., Gentile, A.: Rehabilitation of reaching after stroke: task-related training versus progressive resistive exercise. Arch. Phys. Med. Rehabil. 85(10), 1613–1618 (2004)

40. Tuena, C., et al.: Usability issues of clinical and research applications of virtual reality in older people: a systematic review. Front. Hum. Neurosci. 14, 93 (2020)

41. Venkatesh, V., Bala, H.: Technology acceptance model 3 and a research agenda on interventions. Decis. Sci. 39(2), 273–315 (2008)

42. Wafa, H.A., Wolfe, C.D., Emmett, E., Roth, G.A., Johnson, C.O., Wang, Y.: Burden of stroke in Europe: thirty-year projections of incidence, prevalence, deaths, and disability-adjusted life years. Stroke 51(8), 2418–2427 (2020)

43. Weber, L.M., Nilsen, D.M., Gillen, G., Yoon, J., Stein, J.: Immersive virtual reality mirror therapy for upper limb recovery following stroke: a pilot study. Am. J. Phys. Med. Rehabil. 98(9), 783 (2019)

44. Winter, C., Kern, F., Gall, D., Latoschik, M.E., Pauli, P., Käthner, I.: Immersive virtual reality during gait rehabilitation increases walking speed and motivation: a usability evaluation with healthy participants and patients with multiple sclerosis and stroke. J. Neuroeng. Rehabil. 18(1), 68 (2021)

45. Witmer, B.G., Singer, M.J.: Measuring presence in virtual environments: a presence questionnaire. Presence 7(3), 225–240 (1998)

Game Over, Trauma! Empowering Trauma Healing Through Gaming

Giulio Ammannato[1]([✉]) [iD] and Francesca Chiesi[2] [iD]

[1] Istituto dell'Approccio Centrato Sulla Persona, IACP Roma, P.zza Vittorio Emanuele II, 99, 00185 Roma, RM, Italy
giulio.ammannato@iacpedu.org

[2] NEUROFARBA Department, University of Florence, Via di S. Salvi, 12, 50135 Firenze, FI, Italy

Abstract. The purpose of this paper is to propose the development of a serious game centered on psychological trauma that promotes awareness, informs about best treatment practices, instills hope, and provides basic tools to cope with possible symptoms related to trauma. The game will be designed using the Person Centered Approach (PCA) and the five pillars of Trauma Informed Care (TIC) as the theoretical framework. The study will use a mixed-methods pre-post design to evaluate the effectiveness of the game in increasing awareness of psychological trauma and improving players' sense of security. The game is expected to improve player awareness of psychological trauma, to increase their sense of security, and to encourage them to seek professional help when needed. Overall, this study has the potential to contribute to the development of effective interventions for psychological trauma using serious games.

Keywords: Psychological Trauma · Serious Games · Trauma Informed Care

1 Introduction

The aim of the current paper is to describe a project on the development of a serious game focused on psychological trauma, with the objectives of increasing awareness, educating on best treatment practices, providing coping tools, and fostering hope for those who lived this adverse experience. To achieve these goals, the game will be designed using the principles of the Person-Centered Approach (PCA) and the Trauma Informed Care (TIC). All these issues are detailed in the following paragraphs, as a premise to illustrate our serious game for trauma.

1.1 Video Games

Video games have become one of the most popular forms of entertainment worldwide, with a growing number of gamers playing on various platforms such as mobile devices, PCs, consoles, and handheld devices. According to a report by Newzoo, the number of gamers worldwide is estimated to reach 3.3 billion in 2023, up from 2.7 billion in 2020

L. T. De Paolis et al. (Eds.): XR Salento 2023, LNCS 14219, pp. 454–465, 2023.
https://doi.org/10.1007/978-3-031-43404-4_31

(Newzoo, 2021). Regarding gender distribution, there has been a shift towards a more equal distribution of male and female gamers. In 2020, the split was 54% male and 46% female, according to a study by Statista (Statista, 2021a). However, this varies by region and platform. For instance, in Asia, there are more female gamers than male gamers (Newzoo, 2021). The age range of gamers is also quite diverse. According to the same Statista study, the majority of gamers are between the ages of 18 and 34, representing 38% of the global gaming population in 2020. Nevertheless, there is a considerable number of gamers over the age of 35, with the 35–44 age group representing 26% of the gaming population (Statista, 2021b).

The increasing popularity of video games and their diverse player demographics have caught the attention of the scientific community, resulting in a growing body of research examining the impact of video games on individuals and society.

1.1.1 Serious Games

Serious games, also known as educational or instructional games, are games with a different purpose of pure entertainment and have gained increasing attention as a means of promoting learning in various domains. These games are designed with the primary goal of imparting knowledge and skills in an engaging and interactive manner. In recent years, the popularity of serious games has grown due to their potential benefits, which have been studied and documented in academic research.

One of the main advantages of serious games is their ability to enhance learning outcomes (Wouters, Van Nimwegen, Van Oostendorp & Van Der Spek, 2013). Research suggests that serious games can improve learners' knowledge acquisition, retention, and transfer, as well as their problem-solving skills and decision-making abilities. For instance, a study by DeSmet and colleagues found that students who played a serious game on physics concepts performed better on a post-test compared to those who received traditional instruction (DeSmet, Van Ryckeghem, Compernolle, Baranowski, Thompson, Crombez,… & De Bourdeaudhuij, 2014).

Another benefit of serious games is their ability to increase motivation and engagement among learners. Serious games are designed to be fun and challenging, and they offer immediate feedback and rewards to keep players engaged. This can lead to higher levels of motivation, which can improve learning outcomes. A study by Kiili and colleagues found that students who played a serious game on environmental issues reported higher levels of motivation and interest in the topic compared to those who received traditional instruction (Kiili, De Freitas, Arnab & Lainema, 2012).

Serious games also offer a safe and low-risk environment for learners to practice and experiment with new skills and knowledge. They provide opportunities for learners to make mistakes and learn from them without facing real-world consequences. This can lead to increased confidence and competence, which can transfer to real-world settings. For instance, a study by Michael and Chen found that surgical residents who played a serious game on laparoscopic surgery showed improved performance in real-life surgery tasks (Michael & Chen, 2005).

In addition to these benefits, serious games can also be used to promote social and cultural awareness, as well as to support behavioral change. Thus, serious games have been used to promote healthy behaviors, such as physical activity and healthy eating, as well as to raise awareness about social issues, such as poverty and inequality. For instance, a study found that children who played a serious game on healthy eating and physical activity showed improvements in their knowledge, attitudes, and behaviors related to healthy eating (Baranowski, Baranowski, Thompson, Buday, Jago, Griffith,… & Watson, 2011).

Finally, video games show promising potential in enhancing health outcomes, specifically in the domains of psychological therapy and physical therapy (Eichenberg & Schott, 2017; Primack, Carroll, McNamara, Klem, King, Rich, & Nayak, 2012). For example, a meta-analysis of 9 studies found that serious games were effective in reducing symptoms of PTSD, depression, and ADHD (Lau, Smit, Fleming & Riper, 2017). These findings suggest that serious games have the potential to be effective tools for improving mental health and well-being in various populations.

1.2 Psychological Trauma

Psychological trauma is a significant public health issue that affects individuals across the lifespan. It can result from exposure to a variety of adverse experiences, such as abuse, neglect, violence, and disasters. The impact of psychological trauma on individuals can be severe, resulting in symptoms like anxiety, depression, post-traumatic stress disorder (PTSD), and other mental health disorders (Breslau, Davis, Andreski & Peterson, 1991; Kessler, Sonnega, Bromet, Hughes & Nelson, 1995).

Prevalence studies have indicated that a significant proportion of the general population has experienced some form of psychological trauma. For instance, a nationally representative survey conducted in the United States found that approximately 60% of men and 51% of women reported experiencing at least one traumatic event in their lifetime (Kessler et al., 1995). Similarly, a study conducted in the Netherlands found that 71.1% of adults had experienced at least one traumatic event in their lifetime (Knipscheer, Sleijpen, Frank, de Graaf, Kleber, Ten Have & Dückers, 2020). These findings suggest that psychological trauma is a prevalent issue that affects a significant proportion of the population.

Despite the prevalence of psychological trauma, many individuals are not aware of its effects, nor do they have access to tools to help manage their symptoms. This lack of awareness and resources can result in individuals not seeking treatment, which can lead to long-term negative consequences for their mental health and well-being (Bryant et al., 1998; McLean, Clauw, Abelson & Liberzon, 2005).

Therefore, there is a need for effective interventions that can promote awareness and provide tools to help individuals manage their symptoms related to psychological trauma. While traditional therapy approaches, such as cognitive-behavioral therapy, Eye Movement Desensitization and Reprocessing (Lewis, Roberts, Andrew, Starling & Bisson, 2020), and Person Centered Therapy (Joseph, 2015), have been shown to be effective in treating psychological trauma, access to these treatments can be limited by various factors, such as stigma, cost, and geographic location.

1.3 Person Centered Approach

The Person-Centered Approach (PCA), also known as Client-Centered Therapy, is a humanistic psychological theory developed by Carl Rogers in the 1950s. It is grounded in the belief that individuals possess the capacity for self-regulation, self-actualization, and self-awareness and hence the role of the therapist is to facilitate this process through an empathic and non-judgmental relationship. The PCA is characterized by three inter-related theoretical pillars: the person-centered theory of personality, the therapeutic conditions necessary for change, and the process of change.

The first pillar of the PCA is the person-centered theory of personality. This theory posits that each individual has an innate tendency toward growth and self-actualization, a concept derived from Maslow's hierarchy of needs (Maslow, 1943). According to Rogers (1951), individuals are always striving to become their best selves, and they do so by developing an accurate and positive self-concept. The self-concept is the set of beliefs and attitudes an individual has about themselves, including their values, abilities, and personality traits. Rogers argued that when an individual's self-concept is congruent with their actual experience, they experience a state of congruence or psychological health. Conversely, incongruence between the self-concept and actual experience leads to psychological distress and maladjustment.

The second pillar of the PCA is the therapeutic conditions necessary for change. Rogers (1957) identified three core conditions that must be present in the relationship for therapeutic change to occur: empathy, unconditional positive regard, and congruence. Empathy involves the therapist's ability to understand the client's subjective experience and communicate this understanding to the client. Unconditional positive regard refers to the therapist's acceptance and non-judgmental attitude toward the client, regardless of the client's emotions or beliefs. Congruence refers to the therapist's ability to feel his own inner world and the authenticity and genuineness in the therapeutic relationship. These conditions create an environment in which the client feels safe and supported, enabling them to explore their experiences and emotions more deeply and facilitating personal growth and change.

The third pillar of the PCA is the process of change. According to Rogers (1957), therapeutic change occurs when the therapist provides a facilitating environment that allows the client to develop a more accurate and positive self-concept. This process involves the client becoming more aware of their experiences and emotions, accepting and integrating previously denied or disowned aspects of the self, and developing greater self-trust and autonomy. The therapist facilitates this process by providing a non-judgmental, empathic, and accepting environment in which the client can explore and express their feelings and experiences.

Overall, the Person-Centered Approach is a humanistic psychological theory that emphasizes the innate capacity for growth and self-actualization in individuals. It posits that therapeutic change occurs when the therapist provides a facilitating environment characterized by empathy, unconditional positive regard, and congruence. This process leads to greater self-awareness, self-acceptance, and personal growth.

1.4   Trauma-Informed Care

Trauma-informed care (TIC) is an approach to healthcare that recognizes and responds to the pervasive impact of traumatic experiences on individuals' physical, emotional, and psychological health (SAMHSA, 2014). TIC emphasizes the need for healthcare providers to have a comprehensive understanding of trauma and its effects on individuals, families, and communities (Ford & Courtois, 2014). The theoretical pillars of TIC best practices include the neurobiology of trauma, the prevalence and impact of trauma, the principles of safety, trustworthiness, collaboration, choice, and empowerment, and the importance of cultural humility (Harris & Fallot, 2001).

The neurobiology of trauma refers to the changes that occur in the brain as a result of exposure to trauma (Ford & Courtois, 2014). Trauma can result in alterations in the structure and function of the brain, particularly in areas responsible for regulating emotions, cognition, and stress responses (Ford & Courtois, 2014). This can lead to a range of symptoms, including anxiety, depression, hyperarousal, and hypervigilance.

The prevalence and impact of trauma are significant factors in the development of TIC best practices. Trauma is a pervasive issue that affects individuals from all walks of life, with estimates suggesting that up to 70% of adults in the United States have experienced some form of trauma (Felitti, Anda, Nordenberg, Williamson, Spitz, Edwards & Marks, J. S. 1998). Trauma can have long-lasting and wide-ranging effects on physical, emotional, and psychological health, and can increase the risk of developing chronic health conditions (Ford & Courtois, 2014).

The principles of safety, trustworthiness, collaboration, choice, and empowerment are essential components of TIC best practices. Safety refers to creating an environment in which trauma survivors feel physically and emotionally secure. Trustworthiness involves building relationships with patients based on honesty, transparency, and consistency. Collaboration involves working with patients to develop treatment plans that are tailored to their unique needs and goals. Choice and empowerment refer to giving patients a sense of control over their healthcare decisions and supporting their autonomy (SAMHSA, 2014).

Cultural humility is also a critical pillar of TIC best practices (Ranjbar, Erb, Mohammad & Moreno, 2020). This involves acknowledging and respecting the diverse cultural backgrounds, beliefs, and experiences of patients and recognizing the impact of culture on their health and wellbeing (ibid.). Healthcare providers who practice cultural humility strive to be self-aware, open-minded, and respectful in their interactions with patients from different cultural backgrounds (ibid.).

In conclusion, the theoretical pillars of TIC best practices are grounded in a comprehensive understanding of the neurobiology of trauma, the prevalence and impact of trauma, the principles of safety, trustworthiness, collaboration, choice, and empowerment, and the importance of cultural humility. By integrating these pillars into their practice, healthcare providers can create an environment that promotes healing, recovery, and resilience for trauma survivors.

2 Developing a Serious Game for Trauma

To offer an accessible, engaging and interactive way of delivering information and promoting awareness while also providing tools for symptom management, the present project aims to develop a serious game focused on psychological trauma.

The primary objective of the game would be to provide an accessible and effective intervention for individuals affected by psychological trauma. The game is not intended to replace traditional therapy, but rather, to offer a safe space where individuals can become aware of possible traumatic experiences and work on personal safety, a fundamental aspect of treating this disorder. By doing so, the game aims to facilitate the contact between users and expert therapists, if necessary.

Overall, this project seeks to address the lack of awareness and resources for managing symptoms related to psychological trauma, with the aim of promoting greater well-being and improving the lives of those affected by this issue. To achieve this goal, the game will be designed using the Person Centered Approach (PCA) and the pillars of Trauma Informed Care (TIC) as a theoretical framework.

2.1 PCA in a Serious Game

The integration of the pillars of the Person-Centered Approach into the design of a trauma-focused video game has the potential to offer a profound means for individuals to explore and process their emotions and experiences related to trauma. By applying these principles, the game can create a supportive and empowering environment for players.

Drawing upon the Person-Centered Theory of Personality, the game can provide players with the opportunity to create a character that embodies their own identity and lived experiences. As players navigate through the game, they will encounter various environments and interact with diverse characters, each representing different facets of their self-concept. By engaging with these elements, players are encouraged to reflect upon their beliefs and attitudes about themselves, gaining insights into how these beliefs may have been shaped by their past traumas.

The principles of empathy, unconditional positive regard, and congruence can be particularly useful in the design a game about trauma.

Empathy could be incorporated in a serious games by creating realistic and relatable scenarios that simulate the emotional experiences of individuals who have suffered psychological trauma. This can help players develop greater empathy and understanding for individuals who have experienced traumatic events and promote greater emotional awareness and regulation.

Unconditional positive regard could be applied by providing players with a safe and non-judgmental environment to explore and process their emotions. This can involve creating a game that allows players to express themselves in a variety of ways, such as through creative writing, art, or music, without fear of criticism or rejection.

Congruence could be achieved by designing games that promote self-reflection and self-awareness. For example, a game could prompt players to reflect on their own emotions and experiences and provide feedback that encourages them to be more honest and authentic with themselves.

Finally, the game can facilitate the process of change by promoting self-awareness and fostering self-trust and autonomy. Through incorporating activities like journaling or meditation, players are prompted to reflect upon and better understand their trauma-related emotions. The game can also present players with meaningful choices that directly impact the progression and outcomes of the game, allowing them to exercise personal agency and make decisions aligned with their individual needs and preferences.

Incorporating these Person-Centered Approach principles into a serious game has the potential to provide individuals with a safe and supportive environment for exploring and processing their emotions. By promoting empathy, unconditional positive regard, and congruence, these games can help individuals develop greater emotional regulation skills, enhance their coping strategies, and facilitate their healing process.

2.1.1 Existing Games and PCA

While specific games may not explicitly identify themselves as utilizing the Person-Centered Approach (PCA), the principles and values of the PCA can be effectively integrated into the design of serious games, thereby creating experiences that prioritize player agency, personalization, and emotional engagement. Several noteworthy examples of games that embody the spirit of the PCA exist. Below some examples.

The "That Dragon, Cancer" provides players with a deeply emotional narrative that delves into the personal experience of developers Ryan and Amy Green as they navigate their son's battle with cancer. By immersing players in this heartfelt story, the game encourages empathy, reflection, and a greater understanding of the profound impact of illness on individuals and their families.

The "Journey" places emphasis on connection, exploration, and self-discovery. It presents players with a serene and contemplative environment where they embark on a metaphorical journey and encounter other players along the way. By promoting non-verbal communication and cooperation, the game fosters a sense of empathy, shared experiences, and emotional connection.

With its visually stunning design, the "Gris" focuses on the emotional journey of a young girl coping with grief. Through its evocative art style and atmospheric storytelling, it explores themes of resilience, personal growth, and the process of healing. By providing a safe and supportive space for emotional exploration, this game aligns with the principles of the PCA.

2.2 TIC in a Serious Game

One way to incorporate the neurobiology of trauma into a serious game for trauma would be to include educational modules that explain the effects of trauma on the brain and body. These modules could be presented in an interactive and engaging way, such as through mini-games, videos, or quizzes. By providing players with a better understanding of the neurobiology of trauma, the game could help them develop greater self-awareness and emotional regulation skills.

The principles of safety, trustworthiness, collaboration, choice, and empowerment can also be integrated into a serious game for trauma. For example, the game could be designed to provide a safe and supportive environment for trauma survivors to explore and address their experiences. This could be accomplished by including features such as trigger warnings, personalized avatars, and access to supportive resources.

Collaboration and choice could be encouraged by allowing players to make decisions that affect the game's outcome and by providing opportunities for players to collaborate with other players or with virtual characters. Empowerment could be promoted by providing players with a sense of control over their virtual environment and by allowing them to track their progress and achievements.

Finally, cultural humility could be integrated into a serious game for trauma by acknowledging and respecting the diverse cultural backgrounds and experiences of trauma survivors. This could be accomplished by providing players with options to customize their avatar and by including culturally responsive content that is sensitive to the unique experiences of different communities.

2.2.1 Existing Games and TIC

As with PCA, there are currently no specific games that explicitly label themselves as using Trauma-Informed Care (TIC) principles. However, the concepts and values of TIC can be applied in the design of serious games to create experiences that align with trauma-informed approaches. By incorporating elements such as safety, trustworthiness, choice, collaboration, and empowerment, serious games can provide a supportive and healing environment for individuals affected by trauma. While there may not be direct examples of games explicitly implementing TIC, several games demonstrate elements of trauma-informed approaches in their design and content:

"Hellblade: Senua's Sacrifice": This game follows the journey of a Celtic warrior, Senua, as she battles both physical and psychological trauma. It sensitively explores themes of mental health and trauma through its narrative and gameplay. The game incorporates audio and visual techniques to depict Senua's experiences with hallucinations, delusions, and emotional turmoil, aiming to foster empathy and understanding of her psychological challenges.

"Celeste": While not directly focused on trauma, this platforming game explores themes of mental health and personal growth. The protagonist, Madeline, embarks on a treacherous journey to climb a mountain, symbolizing her own internal struggles. The game tackles topics such as anxiety, self-doubt, and resilience, offering players an opportunity to reflect on their own experiences and find inspiration for overcoming obstacles.

"Life is Strange": This episodic adventure game addresses sensitive topics, including trauma, mental health, and the consequences of choices. The game revolves around Max Caulfield, a student who discovers she can rewind time. As she navigates the story, Max encounters characters with various traumatic experiences, and the player's choices can influence the characters' well-being and growth.

While these games may not explicitly adhere to the full spectrum of TIC principles, they incorporate elements that align with trauma-informed approaches. They emphasize empathy, understanding, and exploration of personal challenges, inviting players to engage with characters and themes related to trauma and mental health.

2.3 Serious Games for Trauma and XR Techonologies

The utilization of extended reality (XR) technologies, particularly virtual reality (VR), can significantly enhance the efficacy of the proposed serious game for trauma. VR has demonstrated its effectiveness in treating PTSD through various applications, and its integration into the game can offer unique advantages over traditional VR simulations.

One example of the successful application of VR for treating PTSD is the exposure therapy approach. VR-based exposure therapy allows individuals to confront their traumatic experiences in a controlled and immersive virtual environment. By recreating specific trauma-related scenarios, such as combat situations or natural disasters, VR enables individuals to gradually and safely confront their fears and anxieties. This immersive and interactive nature of VR can evoke emotional responses similar to real-life situations, facilitating emotional processing and desensitization. Some notable titles that effecvielty used this approah are "Virtual Iraq/Afghanistan" and "Bravemind".

In contrast to traditional VR simulations that focus solely on exposure therapy, the serious game for trauma takes a comprehensive approach. By incorporating elements of gameplay, narrative, and interactive challenges, the game can engage players on multiple levels, fostering a deeper sense of involvement and motivation. Through gameplay mechanics, the game can provide a sense of agency and empowerment, allowing players to actively participate in their healing process.

Additionally, the serious game's focus on promoting awareness, informing about best treatment practices, instilling hope, and providing coping tools aligns with the person-centered approach (PCA) and the principles of trauma-informed care (TIC). The game can leverage VR technology to create a safe space where players can explore trauma-related themes, engage with educational content, and practice coping strategies within a supportive and non-threatening virtual environment.

Furthermore, the game's interactive nature allows for personalized experiences and tailored interventions. By incorporating branching narratives, decision-making opportunities, and personalized feedback, the game can adapt to individual player needs and preferences. This personalized approach enhances engagement and relevance, potentially leading to better treatment outcomes.

The game approach in the proposed serious game for trauma offers advantages over traditional VR simulations by combining therapeutic elements with interactive gameplay. By providing a compelling and engaging experience, the game can enhance motivation, sustain attention, and create a sense of enjoyment throughout the therapeutic process. These factors can contribute to increased treatment adherence, longer engagement periods, and improved overall efficacy in addressing psychological trauma.

Collaboration and choice could be encouraged by allowing players to make decisions that affect the game's outcome and by providing opportunities for players to collaborate with other players or with virtual characters. Empowerment could be promoted by providing players with a sense of control over their virtual environment and by allowing them to track their progress and achievements.

In conclusion, the integration of XR technologies, particularly VR, into the serious game for trauma can enhance its efficacy by providing an immersive, interactive, and engaging experience. By incorporating gameplay elements, the game approach has the potential to improve treatment outcomes compared to traditional VR simulations, making it a promising avenue for the development of effective interventions for psychological trauma.

3 Methodology and Expected Results

The proposed study will use a mixed-methods pre-post design to evaluate the effectiveness of the game in increasing awareness of psychological trauma and improving players' sense of security. Participants will be recruited through online advertisements and will be randomly assigned to the experimental group (playing the developed game) and the control group (not playing the developed game).

Data will be collected using both quantitative and qualitative measures. Quantitative data will be collected using a pre- and post-test design, with measures of psychological well-being and awareness of psychological trauma. Qualitative data will be collected through open-ended questions at the end of the study, which will be analyzed using thematic analysis. Deep learning techniques will also be used to analyze data related to game performance, such as time spent playing, in-game choices, and other relevant variables.

Our mixed-methods approach, including both traditional psychological tests and deep learning analysis, will provide a comprehensive evaluation of the game's effectiveness. We anticipate that players may report increased feelings of empowerment, self-efficacy, and hopefulness following gameplay, as well as a reduction in symptoms related to psychological trauma.

4 Conclusion

In conclusion, this video game represents a unique and innovative approach to promoting awareness of psychological trauma and increasing a sense of security. By using the Person Centered Approach and the five pillars of Trauma Informed Care as theoretical frameworks, we would like to create a game that offers both education and empowerment to players. We hope that this game will serve as a useful tool for individuals who have experienced psychological trauma and that it will encourage them to seek professional help when needed. While our project is at an early stage of its development and several refinements steps are required, we believe that our mixed-methods approach will provide a comprehensive evaluation of the game's effectiveness, and we look forward to sharing our results with the scientific community.

References

Baranowski, T., et al.: Video game play, child diet, and physical activity behavior change: a randomized clinical trial. Am. J. Prev. Med. 40(1), 33–38 (2011)

Breslau, N., Davis, G.C., Andreski, P., Peterson, E.: Traumatic events and posttraumatic stress disorder in an urban population of young adults. Arch. Gen. Psychiatry 55(7), 573–579 (1991)

Bryant, R.A., Harvey, A.G., Dang, S.T., Sackville, T., Basten, C.: Treatment of acute stress disorder: a comparison of cognitive-behavioral therapy and supportive counseling. J. Consult. Clin. Psychol. **66**(5), 862–866 (1998)

DeSmet, A., et al.: A meta-analysis of serious digital games for healthy lifestyle promotion. Prev. Med. **69**, 95–107 (2014)

Eichenberg, C., Schott, M.: Serious games for psychotherapy: a systematic review. Games Health J. **6**(3), 127–135 (2017)

Felitti, V.J., et al.: Relationship of childhood abuse and household dysfunction to many of the leading causes of death in adults: the adverse childhood experiences (ACE) study. Am. J. Prev. Med. **14**(4), 245–258 (1998)

Ford, J.D., Courtois, C.A.: Complex PTSD, affect dysregulation, and borderline personality disorder. Borderline Pers. Disord. Emot. Dysregulat. **1**, 1–17 (2014)

Harris, M.E., Fallot, R.D.: Using Trauma Theory to Design Service Systems. Jossey-Bass/Wiley, Hoboken (2001)

Joseph, S.: A person-centered perspective on working with people who have experienced psychological trauma and helping them move forward to posttraumatic growth. Person-Centered Experiential Psychotherapies **14**(3), 178–190 (2015)

Kiili, K., De Freitas, S., Arnab, S., Lainema, T.: The design principles for flow experience in educational games. Procedia Comput. Sci. **15**, 78–91 (2012)

Kessler, R.C., Sonnega, A., Bromet, E., Hughes, M., Nelson, C.B.: Posttraumatic stress disorder in the national comorbidity survey. Arch. Gen. Psychiatry **52**(12), 1048–1060 (1995)

Knipscheer, J., et al.: Prevalence of potentially traumatic events, other life events and subsequent reactions indicative for posttraumatic stress disorder in the Netherlands: a general population study based on the trauma screening questionnaire. Int. J. Environ. Res. Public Health **17**(5), 1725 (2020)

Lau, H.M., Smit, J.H., Fleming, T.M., Riper, H.: Serious games for mental health: are they accessible, feasible, and effective? A systematic review and meta-analysis. Front. Psych. **7**, 209 (2017)

Lewis, C., Roberts, N.P., Andrew, M., Starling, E., Bisson, J.I.: Psychological therapies for post-traumatic stress disorder in adults: Systematic review and meta-analysis. Eur. J. Psychotraumatol. **11**(1), 1729633 (2020)

Maslow, A.H.: A theory of human motivation. Psychol. Rev. **50**(4), 370–396 (1943)

McLean, S.A., Clauw, D.J., Abelson, J.L., Liberzon, I.: The development of persistent pain and psychological morbidity after motor vehicle collision: integrating the potential role of stress response systems into a biopsychosocial model. Psychosom. Med. **67**(5), 783–790 (2005)

Michael, D.R., Chen, S.L.: Serious Games: Games that Educate, Train, and Inform. Muska & Lipman/Premier-Trade (2005)

Newzoo. 2021 Global Games Market Report (2021). https://resources.newzoo.com/hubfs/Reports/2021_Free_Global_Games_Market_Report.pdf?_hsmi=137551623

Primack, B.A., et al.: Role of video games in improving health-related outcomes: a systematic review. Am. J. Prev. Med. **42**(6), 630–638 (2012)

Ranjbar, N., Erb, M., Mohammad, O., Moreno, F.A.: Trauma-informed care and cultural humility in the mental health care of people from minoritized communities. Focus **18**(1), 8–15 (2020)

Rogers, C.: Client-Centered Therapy: Its Current Practice, Implications and Theory. Constable, London (1951). ISBN 1-84119-840-4

Rogers, C.R.: The necessary and sufficient conditions of therapeutic personality change. J. Consult. Clin. Psychol. **21**, 95–103 (1957)

Statista. Distribution of video gamers worldwide as of January 2020, by gender (2021a). https://www.statista.com/statistics/232383/gender-split-of-us-computer-and-video-gamers/

Statista. Age of U.S. video game players in 2020 (2021b). https://www.statista.com/statistics/189582/age-of-us-video-game-players-since-2010/

Substance Abuse and Mental Health Services Administration (SAMHSA). SAMHSA's Concept of Trauma and Guidance for a Trauma-Informed Approach (2014). https://ncsacw.acf.hhs.gov/userfiles/files/SAMHSA_Trauma.pdf

Wouters, P., Van Nimwegen, C., Van Oostendorp, H., Van Der Spek, E.D.: A meta-analysis of the cognitive and motivational effects of serious games. J. Educ. Psychol. **105**(2), 249 (2013)

Angioplasty Surgery Simulator Development: Kazakhstani Experience

Yevgeniya Daineko, Bakhyt Alipova, Madina Ipalakova, Zhiger Bolatov, and Dana Tsoy[✉]

International Information Technology University, Almaty, Kazakhstan
{y.daineko,d.tsoy}@iitu.edu.kz

Abstract. This paper presents the initial stage of the development of an angioplasty simulator. Along with it, the authors explain the reasons for choosing cardiovascular disease treatment procedures and describe the project's work plan. The authors conducted a literature review on the use of extended reality (XR) technologies in various fields of medicine and analyzed the existing virtual simulator market.

The problems and possible disadvantages of the virtual simulations are another object of the authors' attention. The paper emphasizes the importance of paying attention to the nuances of the project to ensure that it successfully achieves its goals.

The main purpose of the project is to provide students with a proper level of knowledge and skills using promising and modern tools such as virtual reality and modern human-computer interaction tools, thereby improving the quality of medical education and practice in Kazakhstan.

This article provides information about the current development of medical simulators in Kazakhstan for coronary angioplasty and the use of XR technologies in medical education that can be useful to researchers, educators, and healthcare professionals around the world.

Keywords: metaverse · surgery simulator · mathematical modelling

1 Introduction

The rapid development of augmented and virtual reality technologies has led to a reduction in the cost of helmets and other compatible devices, which has caused more people to become interested in this area.

The introduction of technology into the daily routine today is experiencing a new stage of development - the complete digitization of life. In this regard, a whole industry has arisen in which virtual reality is not seen as just a separate space for leisure, communication, but also a place for a new way of relationships, including the sale of virtual items for physical money, and the communication of real people through digital avatars [1].

The concept of the metauniverse is defined as a single virtual space in which participants can actively interact with each other, repeating the actions of life in real space, combining social and economic relations [2].

With greater accessibility, XR stack technologies began to conquer new areas of human activity, including medicine. Virtual and augmented reality, having such properties as visibility, game form and interactivity, have already proved themselves in the entertainment industry, education, communications, construction and industry [3]. The next potential area for development is medicine, with technological development, the quality and capabilities of devices have become sufficient for the required level of visualization of medical data, which positively influenced the development of various projects related to this area [4].

One of the most striking and useful uses of VR and AR is the development of modern simulators that allow you to perform various procedures, increasing the level of training of young professionals [5]. In addition, there are new methods of treatment based on the use of individual characteristics of patients [6].

The main cause of death worldwide is diseases of the cardiovascular system [7]. This problem is also relevant for Kazakhstan [8]. At the same time, there is a shortage of professional staff with the necessary experience in performing the most common operation - angioplasty.

Angioplasty is a complex procedure that requires a certain level of training to ensure a high level of safety and effectiveness. To date, the most common way of acquiring the necessary skills is by observing more experienced surgeons, or by learning by doing.

This article describes the work on a project to develop a virtual simulator for angioplasty using mathematical models to simulate the behavior of blood. The project also sheds light on how such a simulation could impact medical education both domestically and internationally.

2 Related Works

The eXtended reality stack has had a significant impact on the development of the industries in which it is used.

Zhen Liu et al. claim Health 4.0 aligns with Industry 4.0 and encourages the application of the latest technologies to healthcare, virtual reality (VR) is a potentially significant component of the Health 4.0 vision [9]. This article was aimed to explore the research of VR in aiding therapy, using mixed research method: bibliometric analysis (a quantitative method) and a qualitative review of the literature. Four major research areas of VR-aided therapy were identified and investigated, i.e., post-traumatic stress disorder (PTSD), anxiety and fear related disorder (A&F), diseases of the nervous system (DNS), and pain management (PM), including related medical conditions, therapies, methods, and outcomes. Based on the results of the bibliographic coupling analysis (BCA) 271 articles total were selected, with the minimum number of citations of an article to five. Also, authors present the 10 most influential terms in virtual reality-aided therapy in Table 1.

In conclusion, the authors note that this study was the first systematic investigation of the research status of VR-aided therapy incorporating articles of two decades

Table 1. The most frequent terms on the theme of VR and therapy

Rank	Term	Occurrences
1	Virtual reality exposure therapy	94
2	Exposure therapy	46
3	Virtual reality therapy	43
4	Test	41
5	PTSD	38
6	Rehabilitation	35
7	Control group	33
8	Anxiety disorder	31
9	Post-traumatic stress disorder	28
10	Phobia	28

(2000 to year 2020), which shows the details of four major research areas, i.e., PTSD, A&F, DNS, and PM, including medical conditions, therapies, methods, and outcomes. And highlights that VR-aided therapy is effective for various medical conditions, and VR has advantages in customization, compliance, cost, accessibility, motivation, and convenience that highlights its potential in Health Care.

Another paper by Raphael Romano Bruno et al. claim VR and AR offer great potential to improve critical care medicine for patients, relatives, and health care providers [10]. VR may help to ameliorate anxiety, stress, fear, and pain for the patient, and it may assist patients in mobilization and rehabilitation and can improve communication between all those involved in the patient's care. Authors summaries background information, current developments, and key considerations that should be considered for future scientific investigations in this field. Thus, the authors studied 54 works and concluded that VR can assist patients, their relatives and health care providers in communication during and after the intensive care unit stay.

The times of the COVID-19 pandemic provoked the growth of the development of the field of telemedicine, such article by authors Lori Uscher-Pines et al. [11] where many psychiatrists have rapidly transitioned to telemedicine. Authors present qualitative study to understand how changes has affected mental health care, including modes of telemedicine psychiatrists used and barriers encountered. At the time of the interviews, all 20 psychiatrists had been using telemedicine for 2–4 weeks and psychiatrists largely perceived the transition positively. As a conclusion, the authors indicate that findings highlight that although psychiatrists expressed some concerns about the quality of these encounters, the transition has been largely positive for both patients and physicians.

Tadatsugu Morimoto et al. [12] also managed to identify the positive impacts of COVID-19, such as the continued spread and adoption of telemedicine services (i.e., tele-education, tele-surgery, tele-rehabilitation) that promote digital transformation. The purpose of their review was describing the accelerators of XR (VR, AR, MR) technology in spine medicine and then to provide a comprehensive review of the use of XR technology in spine medicine, including surgery, consultation, education, and rehabilitation. The authors noted not only the benefits of tele-education with XR HMD, but also the numerous reports on proof of concept and surgical simulation with cadaveric, phantom, and animal models using XR technology such as pedicle screw insertion (cervical, thoracic, thoracolumbar, lumbar), cervical lateral mass screw insertion, vertebral body puncture, vertebroplasty (kyphoplasty), percutaneous sacroiliac screw insertion, percutaneous lumbar discectomy, and facet joint injection. The number of surgical simulations presented in this paper using XR technology hologram in spinal surgery exceeds 34 simulations. In conclusion the authors notes that XR technology in the field of spine medicine has been introduced in areas of education, diagnoses, surgery, and rehabilitation, with remarkable results.

The article of Rakesh Mishra et al. [13] also confirms the prospects for the use of virtual reality technology in the field of surgery. Their review based on 95 references of applications of VR in neurosurgery, in the areas of neurosurgery training, neuronavigation, robotic neurosurgery, pain management, rehabilitation, and consent taking, as well as diagnostic tools. These applications included their utility as a supplement and augment for neuronavigation in the fields of diagnosis for complex vascular interventions, spine deformity correction, resident training, procedural practice, pain management, and rehabilitation of neurosurgical patients. And as the authors point out «The importance of VR and AR, especially in "social distancing" in neurosurgery training, for poor sections, for prevention of medicolegal claims and in pain management and rehabilitation, is promising and warrants further research».

From these works, it can be noted how VR, AR and MR tools are used in medicine in different ways, while demonstrating high potential and efficiency of use. In this connection, it was decided that the use of this direction in the development of the simulator will also create a convenient and useful tool for the development and improvement of medical education, medicine and, as a result, the health of citizens. Due to rich visual features and possibility to provide a person with a fully virtual environment VR was chosen as the most appropriate for the simulator implementation.

3 Methodology

Agile methodology was used while working on the project. Within a project, Agile is used in the form of breaking down all the stages of creating a project into smaller tasks. So, for example, Fig. 1 shows the components that make up the development of the project.

All these components will provide a possibility to extend the simulator working by different scenarios. As the angioplasty itself is percutaneous intervention surgery, the tissues behavior within the human body will not affect the conduction of the operation but it will help to make a more precise interaction between user and a simulator as well apply these features in other scenarios. Developing math model also can spill the light on dependance of the user's condition at different stages of the operation based on personal body and blood characteristics.

As a result of the planning stage, it was decided by the project team that it would contain a component that defines the behavior of tissues, a mathematical model for simulating the behavior of blood, as well as user interaction within the project.

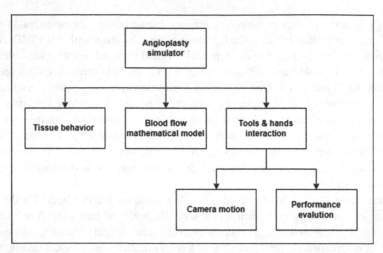

Fig. 1. Project elements in the planning phase

An interventional surgeon was brought in to work on the project, as well as to ensure its medical accuracy.

4 VR Simulator Development

Since cardiovascular diseases in Kazakhstan remain one of the main causes of death, the use of virtual training simulators for cardiac surgeries is a relevant solution for Kazakhstani medicine [14]. The work on the project at the planning stage was divided into several steps that will allow it to be implemented. Now, the developers are facing the following tasks:

- Research and analysis of world experience in the development and implementation of computer training simulators based on various integrated development environments;
- Development of general requirements for a software package using virtual reality technology;
- Development of the camera work algorithm;
- Develop an algorithm for the operation of tools.

The stage of research and determining the world-class development of such projects made it possible to determine the necessary direction of work, as well as draw up a list of requirements for the software being developed. As the work is conducted in a team with practicing endovascular surgeons all the necessary materials and information were given and clarified. The common procedure conduction was defined. In general, coronary angioplasty and stenting operation consist of the following stages:

A doctor takes an x-ray picture of the arteries to install the blockage.

A small catheter is placed into the artery with a tiny balloon through the upper thigh or arm where huge blood vessels are;

Contrast fluid is injected into the artery to ease navigation for the surgeon.

Then the operation takes place, the surgeon may find the blockage and then places the balloon there to inflate it and increase clearance within the artery.

After that, a stent - a small tube made of special non-allergic materials can be placed into this area to prevent re-constriction.

In addition, at this stage, tools for development, selection of equipment were selected. As a result, the Unity game engine version 2021.3.9f1 was chosen as the development environment to ensure the compatibility of the application with the Meta Quest 2 virtual reality helmet.

To make the user experience close to real, video, and photographic material of the operating room, as well as other necessary premises, were obtained. This data became the basis for organizing the application scene, camera views, installations within the virtual space. So, for example, for the procedure, coronography is performed, the results of which are displayed on a separate monitor which is shown in Fig. 2. In addition, the surgeon has access to a monitor with the patient's vital parameters. Fig. 3 contains image of the view on the patient.

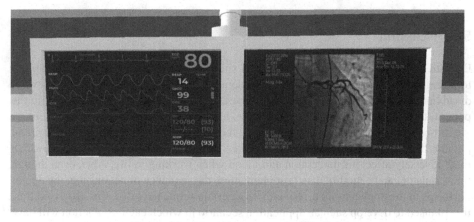

Fig. 2. Monitors in the scene of a simulator

Since the operation is a minimally invasive method of treatment, the issue of the interaction of the surgeon's hands with the instruments becomes more critical. To do this, it was decided to use the Ultraleap controller, which will allow you to determine the speed of movement, the accuracy of the necessary procedures. At the same time, it is planned to use the necessary surgical instruments in the form of conductors, pumps, stents, etc. To track them, a system will be created from a camera and QR codes for each of the items. As a result, when carrying out operations, the user will be able to perform them with his own hands, and not with joysticks, on real equipment, which should also have a positive effect on practical experience.

The next stage of work will involve the development of the math model based on Navier-Stokes for computer simulation of the movement of an inhomogeneous compressible fluid.

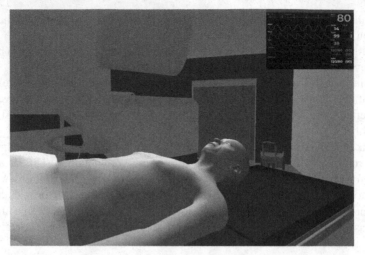

Fig. 3. Patient lying in the operation room.

5 Discussion

Despite all the obvious advantages of such simulators, including visibility, the ability to simulate the necessary case, to study independently, this approach also has several disadvantages that are important to note. These are the lack of live interaction with the patient, the limited scenario of the procedure, as well as the high price of equipment, or the impossibility of acquiring it by educational institutions. When working with a virtual patient, the surgeon's actions may not be taken seriously enough by the surgeon, which may adversely affect his perception and mood when working in life. Also, even though the simulator can be modified and supplemented, the sequence of actions that the doctor performs in the application corresponds to a certain sequence of actions. To avoid this, it is planned to develop such an application scenario in which each user action will have certain consequences and results.

6 Conclusion

An angioplasty simulator in Kazakhstani medical education can be a new step forward if implemented correctly. At the same time, the use of VR will create an immersive effect in the performance of the procedure, which will allow medical students and medical practitioners to find a safe and realistic environment for practicing angioplasty.

In this article, we examined the importance of using new technologies in education and the development of various areas of our activity. A plan for the development of the angioplasty simulator itself was also presented.

The further work of the project participants lies in the creation of a correct model of blood behavior during the operation, as well as the implementation of the functionality of the simulator itself.

Acknowledgement. This research was funded by the Science Committee of the Ministry of Education and Science of the Republic of Kazakhstan (Grant No. AP14871641).

References

1. Yemenici, A.D.: Entrepreneurship in the world of Metaverse: virtual or real? J. Metaverse **2**(2), 71–82 (2022)
2. Ritterbusch, G.D., Teichmann, M.R.: Defining the Metaverse: a systematic literature review. IEEE Access **11**, 12368–12377 (2023). https://doi.org/10.1109/ACCESS.2023.3241809
3. Rauschnabel, P.A., Felix, R., Hinsch, C., Shahab, H., Alt, F.: What is XR? Towards a framework for augmented and virtual reality. Comput. Hum. Behav. **133**, 107289 (2022)
4. Mazurek, J., et al.: Virtual reality in medicine: a brief overview and future research directions. Hum. Mov. **20**(3), 16–22 (2019)
5. Makransky, G., Borre-Gude, S., Mayer, R.E.: Motivational and cognitive benefits of training in immersive virtual reality based on multiple assessments. J. Comput. Assist. Learn. **35**(6), 691–707 (2019)
6. Tian, S., Yang, W., Le Grange, J.M., Wang, P., Huang, W., Ye, Z.: Smart healthcare: making medical care more intelligent. Global Health J. **3**(3), 62–65 (2019)
7. Cardiovascular diseases. https://www.who.int/health-topics/cardiovascular-diseases. Accessed 12 Feb 2023
8. Das, M.: WHO urges immediate action to tackle non-communicable diseases. Lancet Oncol. **23**(11), 1361 (2022)
9. Liu, Z., Ren, L., Xiao, C., Zhang, K., Demian, P.: Virtual reality aided therapy towards health 4.0: a two-decade bibliometric analysis. Int. J. Environ. Res. Public Health **19**(3), 1525 (2022). https://doi.org/10.3390/ijerph19031525. PMID: 35162546; PMCID: PMC8834834
10. Bruno, R.R., et al.: Virtual and augmented reality in critical care medicine: the patient's, clinician's, and researcher's perspective. Crit. Care **26**(1), 326 (2022). https://doi.org/10.1186/s13054-022-04202-x. PMID: 36284350; PMCID: PMC9593998
11. Uscher-Pines, L., Sousa, J., Raja, P., Mehrotra, A., Barnett, M.L., Huskamp, H.A.: Suddenly becoming a "virtual doctor": experiences of psychiatrists transitioning to telemedicine during the COVID-19 pandemic. Psychiatr. Serv. **71**(11), 1143–1150 (2020). https://doi.org/10.1176/appi.ps.202000250. Epub 2020 Sep 16. PMID: 32933411; PMCID: PMC7606640
12. Morimoto, T., et al.: XR (extended reality: virtual reality, augmented reality, mixed reality) technology in spine medicine: status quo and quo Vadis. J. Clin. Med. **11**(2), 470 (2022). https://doi.org/10.3390/jcm11020470. PMID: 35054164; PMCID: PMC8779726
13. Mishra, R., Narayanan, M.D.K., Umana, G.E., Montemurro, N., Chaurasia, B., Deora, H.: Virtual reality in neurosurgery: beyond neurosurgical planning. Int. J. Environ. Res. Public Health **19**(3), 1719 (2022). https://doi.org/10.3390/ijerph19031719. PMID: 35162742; PMCID: PMC8835688
14. Prevalence rate of circulatory system diseases, by sex. https://gender.stat.gov.kz/page/frontend/detail?id=61&slug=-48&cat_id=3&lang=ru. Accessed 12 Feb 2023

eXtended Reality in Industrial Field

Evaluating Telecollaboration Modalities for the Realization of an Industrial Maintenance Operation in a Constrained Environment

Guillaume Klein[✉], Jean-Rémy Chardonnet, Jérémy Plouzeau,
and Frédéric Merienne

Arts Et Métiers Institute of Technology, LISPEN, HESAM Université, 71100
Chalon-Sur-Saône, France
`guillaume.klein@ensam.eu`

Abstract. The continuous improvement of reactivity and resilience of the maintenance teams is one of many industrial companies' priorities, especially in the scope
of urgent interventions. To save valuable time usually lost travelling, it is possible to mobilize a technician near the defective infrastructure, and an experienced
technician to guide him entirely remotely. Teleassistance, or telecollaboration, is a
subject whose interest has grown widely in recent years in line with the evolution
of digital technologies. Our study brings a new eye towards the current state of
the art with an important focus on the industrial aspect of the operation; in terms
of constraints but also of tasks to be realized. We present an interface of telecollaboration specially developed for Android tablets in order to evaluate the quality
of the communication as well as the performance of an industrial maintenance
operation on the operator-assistant format. The raised problematic is related to
the methodology for finding the most optimal methods and formats of communication according to the quality of the available Internet network. The results of
this study intend to provide relevant information on the use of teleassistance in an
industrial environment according to different levels of available Internet speeds,
or different work constraints such as noise or the use of safety equipment. Our
work proves that it is essential to provide some form of audio communication to
the collaborators to ensure the proper execution of the operation; and solutions
are presented in the case where it is impossible to do so, depending on the cause,
whether it is related to the work environment or connectivity.

Keywords: Telecollaboration · Communication · Maintenance

1 Introduction

Many scientific studies address the use of some form of remote intervention in industry
[1–11], such as the use of remotely controlled robots in the nuclear sector [12], collaboration for product design or project review between different teams [13]. Our study
focuses on remote assistance for industrial maintenance, on the operator-assistant format
in synchronous communication.

© The Author(s), under exclusive license to Springer Nature Switzerland AG 2023
L. T. De Paolis et al. (Eds.): XR Salento 2023, LNCS 14219, pp. 477–490, 2023.
https://doi.org/10.1007/978-3-031-43404-4_33

Research on this subject is numerous but generally suffers from at least one of the following two symptoms: the tasks performed are not representative of an industrial maintenance operation or the communication modalities made available do not take into account industrial constraints. If the results show the conditions and modalities according to which communication can be efficient, it seems difficult to transfer these conclusions to a real use case in an industrial context. This paper's main goal is to identify under which circumstances telecollaboration enables a remote assistant to guide an operator on an industrial maintenance task. For industrial usage purposes, this study will focus on telecollaboration using tablets only.

2 State of the Art

Telecollaboration is usually defined as the "remote participation in the realization of a common task". Its purpose is to enable two or more participants to take part in a remote communication enhanced by many sorts of interaction modalities. The availability of these modalities depends on different constraints; may it be hardware or software related, or due to the nature of the task to achieve. Telecollaboration can be used in real time (synchronously), or in delayed time (asynchronously) [6]. Digital interfaces can be varied and different between collaborators (hardware symmetry or asymmetry). The roles of the collaborators can be identical (multiple operators) or different (operator and assistant).

A remote collaboration system relies on two main features. First, the collaborator must have some sort of work environment sharing, like a 3D model of the system on which the task is to be performed. Then, they need to be able to communicate.

Communication. The following communication methods are often employed in scientific studies regarding telecollaboration: audio chat [1, 5, 6, 12] or alternatively a text chat solution, picture exchange [7], drawings [7, 9, 12] and finally spatial markers [6, 7, 9, 12]. Some papers make use of mixed reality tools to further enhance the quality of the communication, for example by representing collaborator's full body avatar, or head and gaze direction [9, 12, 21]. Those modalities require specific hardware to achieve real-time body tracking. Cited work typically address the communication interaction possibilities without any limit regarding hardware usage and invasive equipment; especially for the means of capture and displays (using numerous cameras, body sensors, video projectors, mixed reality interfaces). In this extent, we specifically design our experiment to only rely on the use of one interface: a tablet.

Workspace Sharing. While this work does not aim to study the impact of the choice of the form used to represent the workspace between collaborators, we can expose some technologies that are already used depending on the telecollaboration context. Two main approaches are possible: real time capture of the workspace, or premade models.

Premade models require to have the CAD or 3D model of the system. There is an issue in using those models that are not real-time acquired: it can be difficult to keep track of the system's evolution, most particularly for a real-time intervention. Being able to get a representation of the system on which the operation is to be performed allow the users to always get an up-to-date state version but requires the operator to perform a scan of the system and may need more performances and network bandwidth.

Photogrammetry may give the best result regarding the quality and fidelity of the model, but also takes the most performances and bandwidth [9]. Furthermore, the collaborator must scan the system in a specific manner to ensure a good result. LIDAR scanning is a more lightweight solution and allows to get 3D models in a surprisingly fast time and a quite good quality [10, 12, 20]; it can be performed in real time by a handled device without the help of a server. If the device used does not support LIDAR, one can use an RGB-camera coupled with the right algorithms to try and recreate a 3D model of the scene [7], however, the results are of a lesser quality than with a depth-camera. Finally, if the use case does not allow for the exchange of 3D models, collaborators can share pictures of the system, which can be presented in a more or less structured way to allow them for virtual navigation between pictures [21].

The articles cited before give some interesting results for communication related operation, although the use case on which the experimentation is conducted usually does not take industrial constraints into consideration. Our goal is to provide clues on how to use remote collaboration for the assistance of an <u>industrial maintenance task</u>. To do so, we first need to define those constraints.

Industrial Maintenance. Based on a bibliographical study coupled with an in-situ observation of various maintenance operations, we specify and characterize the industrial use cases for our experimentation using a certain number of criteria: the type of maintenance [14] either preventive or corrective, the frequency of the operation and the execution time. The level of mobility [4] which represents the range of movement of the operator during the maintenance is also evaluated, along with the difficulty of the task and its sensitivity *i.e.* the risk associated in the event of an error occurring during the intervention, whether it is human or material. Subtasks can be categorized according to the standard classification in three levels. The first level represents tasks planned by the manufacturer such as front-end adjustments or replacements of disposable components (like a fuse), the second level requires an identification of defective parts and a certain knowledge to diagnose the system, where the third level involves replacing or changing parts of the system and sometimes altering the initial functioning.

Moreover, performing a maintenance task requires the operators to wear safety equipments; the nature of which varies according to the field of the operation and must be considered to implement the use of telecollaboration, in the same manner as the following specific constraints: work in high places, confined spaces, in a humid atmosphere, heavy load handling.

3 Scientific Issues

The constraints presented in the state of the art are too numerous to be considered all at once. We will then focus our study on two main industrial constraints. First, the need to wear safety equipments and the environment of the operation do not allow the operator to use certain tools for telecollaboration; for example, it is not possible to have an operator wear an augmented reality headset because he must already wear a hard hat. Wearing a glove requires adaptation of touch-sensitive surfaces. Finally, the quality and availability of telecommunication networks (phone, radio, Internet) is not guaranteed, and it is therefore essential to study degraded cases of functioning where the bandwidth is limited. Our work will address the network quality constraint in a simplified way; for instance, parameters like traffic congestion and packet losses will not be considered. The study will focus on the amount of data that may be exchanged in real time; meaning only the bandwidth quality will be a parameter for our experimentation.

3.1 Question

Our study intends to identify the optimal methods and tools for the use of teleassistance in an industrial environment, considering the operational constraints and the different levels of connectivity that are available. The research objective can be formulated as follows:

Evaluation of the quality of the realization of a maintenance task in telecollaboration on the operator-assistant format, according to the industrial conditions and in limited connectivity

The goal of these results is to identify, for an industrial use case, under low connectivity conditions, the optimal telecollaboration methods. Therefore, we adopt the following research question:

To what extent does the use of telecollaboration allow for the assistance of a maintenance operation despite operational constraints and limited connectivity?

3.2 Hypothesis

In order to formulate our research hypotheses, we subdivided the main research question into elementary sub-questions:

- Does telecollaboration on the operator-assistant format allow to realize a maintenance task that the operator could not realize in autonomy?
- If yes, what are the parameters that influence the quality of the task realization on one hand and the communication on the other hand?
- Can a situation of low connectivity compromise the use of telecollaboration? What are the limitations?

We then state the following research hypotheses:

- H0: Telecollaboration allows the remote assistance of an operator for the realization of a maintenance intervention.
- H1: The availability of a diverse number of communication modalities enhances the quality of the communication. This hypothesis has already been proven by the related works, but we want to ensure its validity in an industrial use case.
- H2: The effectiveness of telecollaboration (in terms of execution and communication) depends on the level of available connectivity.

4   Experimentation

4.1   Participants

Pairs of participants take on the role of operator and assistant and must carry out an industrial maintenance operation that the operator does not know. The candidates are chosen among students registered in higher education in industrial maintenance or in engineering school in order to homogenize the profiles and to ensure the basic knowledge in maintenance.

4.2   Setup

The candidates are set in representative conditions of an industrial use case, in separate rooms to simulate distance and prevent natural communication. The following Fig. 1. Presents the setup for the experiment.

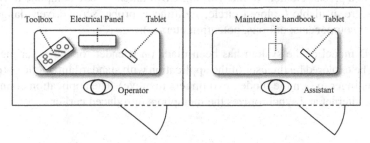

Fig. 1. Experimentation setup

In their respective rooms, the candidates are seated at a table with the necessary equipment for the operation:

- The operator (OP) has on his table a model of an industrial electrical panel (on which he has to perform the maintenance task), the standard intervention tools as well as a tablet on which the telecollaboration application is installed.
- The assistant (AS) has on his table a tablet with the same telecollaboration application, as well as a manual detailing the maintenance procedure.

The maintenance operation that the operator has to perform concerns an industrial electrical cabinet (Fig. 2) allowing to realize a star-delta starting of a three-phase motor. The model presents failures and defects according to three levels of maintenance (standard classification):

- Level I: front panel adjustments and verification of component caliber;
- Level II: verification of the components' normal functioning;
- Level III: replacement of a defective component.

For safety reasons, the operation is carried out without power. The following situation was presented to the candidates in order to reinforce the implication: *After a failure of a*

hydraulic pump, a first quick diagnosis involved the motor control panel. It was removed from the system and taken to the workshop where you will perform an in-depth analysis.
The telecollaboration application (Fig. 2) was developed specifically for the experiment, using Unity (version 2022.2) and running on Samsung Galaxy Tab S7 + 5G (Android 13). This application provides five communication metaphors:

- Audio chat;
- Written chat: useful in the case where audio is not available, or to share a precise information without ambiguity in pronunciation or listening (standard, setting value, name of a component).
- Drawings and plots [7]: a canvas on which it is possible to freehand draw, with a choice of colors and pencil thickness. Can be used for example to share an electrical or kinematic diagram.
- Photos: take a photo with a choice of camera to use, and upload utility and interface to browse all shared photos.
- 3D markers [7]: the user can place a marker by pointing on the 3D model to highlight a zone or a precise element of the working environment or of a component. Different models are available (colored circle, multimeter probe, screwdriver, danger sign, standard components: buttons, potentiometers…).

The 3D model of the system has been made on Blender for the experimentation; and it can be explored by the user of the application with standard interactions (pinch to zoom, one finger to turn the model, two fingers to move). The application connects the tablets via Internet and synchronizes the metaphors introduced earlier.

1   **2**   **3**

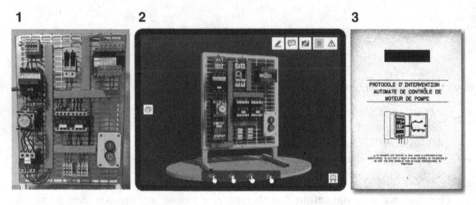

Fig. 2. From left to right: **1.** The electrical panel on which the maintenance operation is to be performed. **2.** The telecollaboration application on the Tab S7 + 5G tablet. **3.** The manual detailing the maintenance procedure.

The assistant is provided with a maintenance manual (Fig. 2) detailing the step-by-step procedure in the clearest possible way. In the case of industrial use, the assistant does not necessarily have such a tool; it is used in our experimentation to simulate the perfect knowledge of the assistant concerning the maintenance operation to be performed. In this regard, the assistant is not allowed to send pictures of the manual to the operator.

4.3 Telecollaboration Scenarios

In conformity with the presented research issue, we want to evaluate the relevance of the use of telecollaboration in an industrial context, depending on the connectivity conditions, *i.e.*, depending on the available bandwidth. Our experimentation takes place in a local network laboratory, where the available bandwidth is maximum. We have therefore designed two telecollaboration scenarios according to the bandwidth requirements of each communication mode.

A preliminary theoretical study allowed us to evaluate the bandwidth needs for each modality. The audio, marker and text needs in terms of data are evaluated theoretically given their implementation in our application. The drawing's weight depends on its complexity, starting at 0KB for no drawing at all going to 100KB or more for a very complex one. This number can be brought down significantly using another way of compressing and synthetizing the data.

The weight of a picture depends on numerous parameters that make it impossible to establish a constant size beforehand; the most influential ones being the subject of the picture and the compression algorithm used, as seen in the following Fig. 3. A picture of the system studied in our experimentation in 480p resolution (720*480 pixels) weighs between 50 and 250KB once compressed in jpeg format. This format has been chosen for its performance in terms of speed and compression rate.

Picture size : 1645 x 2560 pixels

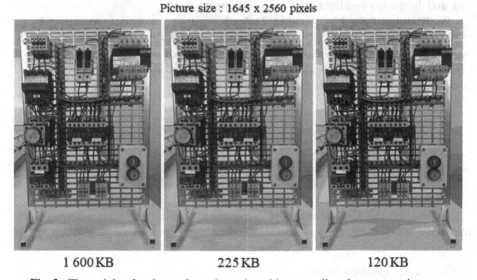

| 1 600 KB | 225 KB | 120 KB |

Fig. 3. The weight of a picture depends on the subject as well as the compression rate.

The results from our preliminary analyses are synthetized in Table 1 below.

These results were then used to define two telecollaboration scenarios presented in the following Table 2. As stated in the introduction, we only address the constraint of low connectivity level only in terms of amount of data that is exchanged in real time.

Table 1. Bandwidth requirement for each communication modality

Modality name	Amount of transmitted data
Audio	200 KB per seconds of audio
Picture	50 KB to 500 KB (depending on quality and subject)
Drawing	10 KB to 100 KB
Marker	12 Bytes
Text	2 Bytes per character

Table 2. Telecollaboration scenarios

Scenario	Name	Available communication modalities	Bandwitdh
S0	Degraded	Text, picture, drawing, marker	50 Ko/s
S1	Nominal	**Audio**, text, picture, drawing, marker	250 Ko/s

4.4 Measures

Numerous metrics have been identified to evaluate the realization of the maintenance task and the quality and fluidity of the communication.

Realization of the Maintenance Task: the metrics concerning the operation are relatively standard [2], [16], [17]. Their purpose is to measure the quality of the intervention: maintenance time, number of errors, number of corrected errors, number of completed tasks. We define a completion rate expressed as a percentage of the total completion and defined by the following relation (1):

$$\tau_{completion} = \frac{N_{accomplished\_tasks} - N_{errors}}{N_{total\_tasks}} \quad (1)$$

The total number of tasks and the number of errors are weighted by coefficients according to the difficulty of the task: level I: coef. 1, level II: coef. 2, level III: coef. 9. The maintenance protocol to be performed is composed of 40 tasks, (I: 7, II: 32; III: 1) for a weighted total of 80 tasks.

Quality of the Communication: we quantify the use of each communication metaphor featured by the application. Moreover, we perform a distinction of the transmitted messages [5] for each scenario:

- OP and AS: question asked;
- OP: proactive or reactive description;
- OP and AS: confirmation;
- AS: proactive or reactive instruction;
- OP and AS: clarification.

This differentiation, especially for proactive/reactive messages, makes it possible to qualify the fluidity of a communication and the impact that each interlocutor brings to the common effort.

We also asked each candidate after the experimentation his level of agreement (5-choice Likert) on four propositions: "my statements were clear for my interlocutor", "the statements of my interlocutor were clear for me", "the application seems to allow me to express myself correctly", "the application seems to allow my interlocutor to express himself correctly". Comparing the perception of the interlocutor's comprehension with one's own perception can reveal the quality of the communication; for instance, in some cases, there is a large dissonance within a pair, which reflects the poor quality of the communication.

Telecollaboration Interface: We proposed a reduced version of the SUS questionnaire to the candidates, composed of 7 items concerning the usability of the application. This allows us to have feedback on the ergonomy of our application, but also to put into perspective some results such as the difficulty or the ease to communicate. The goal is not to have an objective measure of the usability of our telecollaboration system, but rather to get qualitative feedback from the users.

The cognitive load of the candidates was evaluated according to the Nasa TLX questionnaire in order to determine the involvement of the candidates as well as the effects of the communication possibilities on the workload.

5   Results

A total of 22 candidates aged 18 to 22 took part in the experimentation *i.e.*, 11 pairs; 5 for scenario S0, 6 for scenario S1.

The results are clear: none of the pairs deprived of the audio discussion (S0) succeeded in completing the whole operation, despite a much higher average maintenance time: $58(\pm 15)$ minutes for the S0 scenario against $28(\pm 6)$ minutes for the S1 scenario. The S0 pairs ended the experiment by declaring that they had completed the protocol, but tasks were forgotten, and errors were made. S1 pairs almost all passed the experiment completely, except for one group that made an error on a Level II task ($\tau = 98\%$).

The statistical analysis employed is a two-sample t-test; for which we confirm the following assumptions: the observations are independent and the candidates were assigned a scenario randomly. Finally, the normal distribution on such a small sample size is difficult to prove but the two sample t-test is robust against non-normal distribution (in a certain extent) especially in small sample size scenarios. The normal distribution hypothesis is not to be rejected, given the results of the test.

The completion rates are summarized in Fig. 4. The difference in completion rate is highly significant ($p < 0.01$), so is the difference in experimental duration ($p < 0.01$).

Beyond the failure of the S0 pairs to perform the maintenance operation, we observe an augmentation of the mental load with a Task Load Index of $11.4(\pm 1.9)$ against $7.7(\pm 3.3)$ for the S1 pairs ($p < 0.05$). However, further observation by classifying the results by scenario and role, shows a difference of smaller magnitude (Fig. 5).

As for the application and more specifically the usability evaluated through an adapted System Usability Scale, the difference between the two groups is not significant: $14.9(\pm 2.1)$ for S0 and $16.3(\pm 1.9)$ for S1 ($p > 0.3$). However, when classifying the candidates by scenario and role, we observe a slight improvement in usability between the S0 and S1 assistants (Fig. 6).

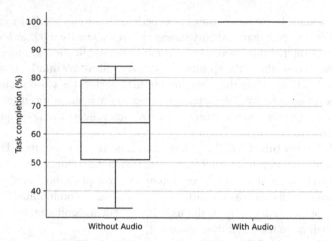

Fig. 4. Task completion for S0 and S1

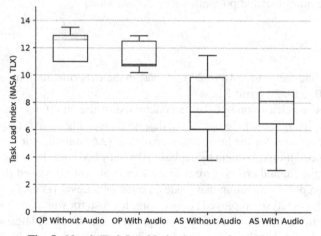

Fig. 5. Nasa's Task Load Index by scenario and by role

The perception of comprehension does not show a significant difference ($p > 0.4$).

Finally, we note a clear improvement in the number of proactive messages: $29\%(\pm4)$ for S0 versus $41\%(\pm5)$ for S1, ($p < 0.01$). The share of reactive messages thus decreased from $18\%(\pm4)$ for S0 and $11\%(\pm2)$ for S1 (Fig. 6).

6 Discussion

In the case where it is possible to make audio communication available in real time, the results show that the operation takes place in very good conditions, and the interlocutors manage to carry out the operation, communicating proactively and smoothly. This validates our hypothesis H0 (Fig. 7).

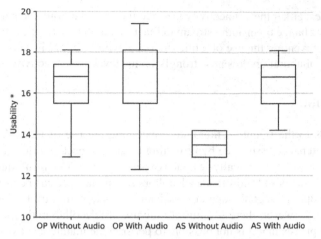

Fig. 6. Adapted SUS by scenario and by role

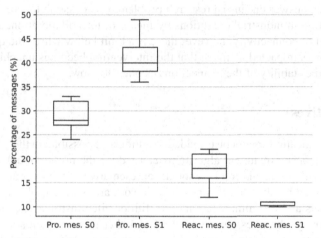

Fig. 7. Percentage of proactive and reactive messages in each scenario

Regarding the telecollaboration interface that we have developed, some interaction metaphors are clearly less used than others (pictures, diagrams). However, these metaphors are essential in some cases. For example, the candidates sent few photos (one per group on average), but they were useful for clearing up ambiguities when the spoken language did not provide a sufficient depiction of the work environment. In this sense, hypothesis H1 is validated insofar as making a larger number of tools available improves the quality of communication.

Finally, our results show that there is indeed a strong link between the telecollaboration interface used and the possibility to perform a maintenance task. It would seem, as it is, that it is not possible to carry out a telecollaboration operation on the operator-assistant format if the collaborators cannot discuss orally. These results are in line with existing work [6] and increase the scope for industrial uses. This impossibility can have two main causes: either the connectivity is too limited and the available bandwidth does not allow the exchange of an audio stream in real time; or the operator evolves in a noisy environment, preventing the use of a microphone. Hypothesis H2 is then validated: the quality of telecollaboration depends strongly on the level of connectivity available.

7   Conclusion

Our work adds to the scientific literature concerning the use of telecollaboration for industrial maintenance assistance by providing a new perspective oriented towards the use case by proposing a specifically designed experimentation. Our results are in line with some previous articles and show that a telecollaboration interface can be used to perform a maintenance operation on the operator-assistant format, but it must be comprehensive and ergonomic. However, there is a limit to the use of telecollaboration: as a matter of fact, our study proves that it is not possible to perform the maintenance operation if the collaborators cannot discuss orally; specific solutions must then be used in case of too weak connectivity.

We can then answer our initial research problem: it is possible to carry out a maintenance operation in industrial conditions by means of telecollaboration, and this with a reduced level of connectivity; however there is a limit below which the quality of the communication is impacted so much that the intervention becomes unachievable if the bandwidth or the stability of the connection becomes too low.

8   Perspectives

If audio communication cannot be provided, solutions are possible: in the case of a noisy environment, acoustic treatment algorithms can reduce the noise enough (to a certain extent) to allow the transmission of a signal representative of the operator's speech. In the case of limited bandwitdth, it is possible to work around the problem: one can use an asynchronous audio communication, with full detailed instructions, and the use of written chat for synchronous communication. Another more elegant solution involves the use of speech recognition technologies: it can be possible to capture the operator's voice, use a speech-to-text algorithm to send the speech as text (which is much less bandwidth intensive) and propose it either in written form or using a text-to-speech algorithm for the interlocutor. This solution may be of great interest in a use case where bandwidth is highly limited and could be the subject of an in-depth study.

The telecollaboration interface can be further enriched compared to the application we have developed. For example, it is possible to display avatars that represent the collaborators, as well as the direction of their gaze in the shared work environment [12, 19]; this allows to bring back some forms of non-verbal communication over the distance.

A very important point to underline is that telecollaboration requires a representation of the workspace, in our case a model designed for this purpose before the experimentation. In an industrial context, it is not always possible to have a 3D model of each of the systems that may undergo a maintenance operation. In this case, there are a certain number of solutions that we would like to study in future works dedicated to the sharing of the work environment, such as 3D scanning (LIDAR) [21], photogrammetry, or more basic solutions such as a set of photos located in space [21].

Acknowledgments. . This work was conducted in the context of a partnership between Arts et Métiers and Suez; therefore, we would like to thank for their investment and their support throughout this project, Ms. LEGOFF Emilie, Mr. PIQUES Julien, Mr. MONNOT Laurent and Mr. BINET Guillaume. We also want to thank L. HUREZ, teacher in industrial maintenance for his availability, help and advices regarding the experimental scenario.

References

1. Johnson, S., Gibson, M., Mutlu, B.: Handheld or Handsfree? Remote collaboration via lightweight head-mounted displays and handheld devices. In: Proceedings of the 18th ACM Conference on Computer Supported Cooperative Work & Social Computing, Vancouver BC Canada, pp. 1825-1836 (2015)
2. Havard, V.: Développement de méthodes et outils basés sur la réalité augmentée et virtuelle pour l'assistance ou l'apprentissage d'opérations dans un contexte industriel. PhD Thesis (2018)
3. Zenati-Henda, N., Bellarbi, A., Benbelkacem, S., Belhocine, M.: Augmented reality system based on hand gestures for remote maintenance. In: 2014 International Conference on Multimedia Computing and Systems (ICMCS), pp. 5-8 (2014)
4. Otmane, S.: Modèles et techniques logicielles pour l'assistance à l'interaction et à la collaboration en réalité mixte. PhD Thesis (2011)
5. Kraut, R.E., Miller, M.D., Siegel, J.: Collaboration in performance of physical tasks: effects on outcomes and communication. In: Computer Supported Cooperative Work'96 (1996)
6. Ladwig, P., Geiger, C.: A literature review on collaboration in mixed reality. In: Auer, M.E., Langmann, R. (eds.) REV 2018. LNNS, vol. 47, pp. 591–600. Springer, Cham (2019). https://doi.org/10.1007/978-3-319-95678-7_65
7. Wolfartsberger, J., Zenisek, J., Wild, N.: Data-driven maintenance: combining predictive maintenance and mixed reality-supported remote assistance. Procedia Manufact. **45**, 307–312 (2020)
8. Alem, L., Li, J.: A study of gestures in a video-mediated collaborative assembly task. In: Advances in Human-Computer Interaction, vol. 2011 (2011)
9. Teo, T., Lawrence, L., Lee, G.A., Billinghurst, M., Adcock, M.: mixed reality remote collaboration combining 360 video and 3D reconstruction. In: Proceedings of the 2019 CHI Conference on Human Factors in Computing Systems (CHI '19) (2019)
10. Adcock, M., Anderson, S., Thomas, B.: RemoteFusion: real time depth camera fusion for remote collaboration on physical tasks. In: 12th ACM SIGGRAPH International Conference on Virtual-Reality Continuum and Its Applications in Industry, NY, USA, pp. 235–242 (2013)
11. Alem, L., Tecchia, F., Huang, W.: Remote tele-assistance system for maintenance operators in mines. In: 11th Underground Coal Operators Conference (2011)
12. Bai, H., Sasikumar, P., Yang, J., Billinghurst, M.: A user study on mixed reality remote collaboration with eye gaze and hand gesture sharing. In: Proceedings of the 2020 CHI Conference on Human Factors in Computing Systems (CHI '20) (2020)
13. Luk, B.L., Liu, K.P., Collie, A.A., Cooke, D.S., Chen, S.: Tele-operated climbing and mobile service robots for remote inspection and maintenance in nuclear industry. In: Industrial Robot, vol. 33, no. 3, pp. 194–204 (2006)

14. Peters, E., Heijligers, B., de Kievith, J., Razafindrakoto, X.: Design for collaboration in mixed reality: technical challenges and solutions. In: 8th International Conference on Games and Virtual Worlds for Serious Applications (VS-GAMES), Barcelona, Spain, pp. 1–7 (2016)
15. Les formes de Maintenance. http://tpmattitude.fr/methodes.html. Accessed 03 Nov 2020
16. Monchy, F., Vernier, J.P. : Maintenance méthodes et organisations 3 e édition (2010)
17. Loizeau, Q., Danglade, F., Ababsa, F., Merienne, F.: Evaluating added value of augmented reality to assist aeronautical maintenance workers - experimentation on on-field use case. In: 16th EuroVR International Conference, Tallinn, Estonia, pp. 1–19 (2019)
18. Marsot, J., Gardeux, F., Govaere, V.: Réalité augmentée et prévention des risques : apports et limites. Hyg. secur. trav. (Paris) **214**, 15–23 (2009)
19. Piumsomboon, T., Day, A., Ens, B., Lee, Y., Lee, G., Billinghurst, M.: Exploring enhancements for remote mixed reality collaboration. In: SIGGRAPH Asia 2017 Mobile Graphics & Interactive Applications on - SA '17. Bangkok, Thailand, pp. 1–5 (2017)
20. Boussaha, M., Vallet, B., Rives, P.: Large scale textured mesh reconstruction from mobile mapping images and Lidar scans. In: ISPRS 2018 - International Society for Photogrammetry and Remote Sensing. Istanbul, Turkey, pp. 49–56 (2018)
21. Nuernberger, B., Turk, M., Höllerer, T.: Evaluating snapping-to-photos virtual travel interfaces for 3D reconstructed visual reality. In: Proceedings of the 23rd ACM Symposium on Virtual Reality Software and Technology. Gothenburg Sweden, pp. 1–11 (2017)

A Comprehensive Approach to the Analysis of VR Training Progress of Industry 4.0 Employees

Adam Gałązkiewicz[(✉)] [ID], Mikołaj Maik[ID], Krzysztof Walczak[ID],
Cyryl Leszczyński, and Julia Głowaczewska

Department of Information Technology,
Poznań University of Economics and Business, Poznań, Poland
{galazkiewicz,maik,walczak}@kti.ue.poznan.pl
https://www.kti.ue.poznan.pl/

Abstract. Innovative workforce training solutions are essential as Industry 4.0 transforms the manufacturing and automation landscape. The Virtual Reality (VR) training system described in this paper uses multiple visualization techniques to track employees' progress. To accommodate a range of user preferences and training objectives, the system makes use of various visualization techniques. PDF printouts offer a concise, portable summary of individual performance metrics, while 2D maps provide an overview of spatial navigation and task completion within the VR environment. 3D scenes allow for a more immersive, interactive visualization of employee progress, allowing users to better understand complex scenarios and relationships. The proposed system seeks to improve user engagement, comprehension, and retention of training outcomes by incorporating these visualization techniques.

Keywords: Visualization · Virtual Reality · Interface · Industry 4.0 · Training

1 Introduction

With the advent of Industry 4.0, there has been a dramatic shift in the realms of manufacturing and automation characterized by an increased focus on digital technology, interconnectedness, and automation [11,16]. Such a profound transformation necessitates a novel approach to workforce training to address the escalating complexity of industrial processes and systems. Virtual Reality (VR) has emerged as an impactful medium for training employees in the context of Industry 4.0, offering an immersive, interactive, and risk-averse setting for skill development [6,18].

A pivotal factor for the effectiveness of VR-based learning systems lies in the proficient monitoring and assessment of user progress [9]. This not only facilitates personalized training tailored to the unique needs of each worker but also generates meaningful feedback that can be leveraged to consistently enhance the training module. In this regard, the employment of visualization techniques for tracking and evaluating user progress within VR has attracted notable interest [2,5].

Most contemporary studies have primarily focused on the use of 3D visualization techniques, which exploit the immersive characteristics of VR to offer detailed, interactive depictions of user behavior and performance [14]. While these techniques offer an impressive level of detail and interactivity, they can also pose complexity and interpretation challenges, especially for those not well-acquainted with VR technology [21]. Moreover, they might not be the most practical or efficient means for providing a quick, broad overview of user progress.

Conversely, 2D visualization techniques provide a straightforward and accessible method for illustrating user data, facilitating an easier understanding of spatial navigation and task accomplishment within the VR setting [10,12]. These techniques effectively summarize individual performance metrics and offer a format that can be easily printed or digitally disseminated for further examination and discussion.

Drawing on these insights, this paper presents a novel VR training system that provides multiple visualization techniques to track and assess employees' progress. To cater to diverse user preferences and training objectives, the system incorporates a variety of visualization techniques. PDF documents, for instance, offer a concise, portable snapshot of individual performance metrics, readily accessible for further discussion and analysis. Complementary, 2D maps deliver a broad overview of spatial navigation and task completion within the VR environment. For a more immersive, interactive visualization of employees' progress, 3D scenes are utilized, allowing users to gain a deeper comprehension of complex scenarios and relationships. By integrating these diverse visualization techniques, the proposed system aims to enhance user engagement, comprehension, and retention of training outcomes. This approach promises to equip Industry 4.0 employees with the skillsets they need to navigate the rapidly evolving landscape of manufacturing and automation.

The remainder of this paper is structured as follows. Section 2 provides a review of related works and offers an analysis of previous research in the fields of VR training and 2D visualization. Section 3 describes the system architecture, while Sect. 4 presents the structure of the processed data, detailing how user interactions in VR training scenarios are recorded and analyzed. Section 5 introduces the Results Analysis Module, discussing its functionality and its role in decoding and presenting training data. Section 6 presents the functionality of the 2D visualization module, detailing how it visually represents the trainee's actions. Section 7 describes the 3D Visualization Module, explaining how it uses a three-dimensional representation of the user's path for a more comprehensive exploration and analysis of training scenarios. Finally, in Sect. 8, conclusions are drawn and directions for future works are discussed.

2   Related Works

The concept of employing VR for training initiatives within the framework of Industry 4.0 has been a subject of considerable research in recent times [1,4,7, 16]. For instance, the works of Gavish et al. [9] underscored the capabilities of VR and Augmented Reality (AR) technologies in enriching the teaching and learning process in industrial environments [15]. This research has mainly focused on the immersive properties of VR and its potential to facilitate effective training.

However, the evaluation of training progress in VR environments is a relatively less explored area [21]. Bowman and McMahan [2] discussed the immersive aspects of VR and how immersion could be quantitatively evaluated. Their work provided valuable insights into the relationship between immersion and user performance, setting the stage for further exploration of evaluation techniques.

The importance of visualization in tracking and evaluating user progress in VR has been underscored by several researchers [20]. Chandler et al. [5] proposed the concept of Immersive Analytics, which aims to leverage VR's immersive capabilities for data analysis and visualization. Their work suggested that immersive visualization could significantly enhance the user's understanding of complex data, thus improving training outcomes [23].

In terms of 2D visualization, Card et al. [3] and Shneiderman [17] have made significant contributions. Card et al. introduced the concept of "information visualization," emphasizing the role of vision in data understanding. Shneiderman, on the other hand, proposed a "task by data type taxonomy" for information visualizations, which serves as a valuable framework for the design of 2D visualization techniques [20].

While these contributions have established a foundation for the application of 2D visualization in VR, there is a continuing need for further research in this field. Specifically, the fusion of 2D visualization techniques with other modalities (like 3D scenes and PDF printouts) for the evaluation of user progress in VR remains a largely unexplored area [23]. This paper aims to fill this gap by proposing a comprehensive visualization that combines PDF documents with 2D and 3D visualizations of users' performance.

3   System Architecture

The VR training system discussed in this paper has been implemented for a Polish power grid operator, Enea Operator Sp. z o.o., to facilitate the safe and efficient training of high-voltage operators in a fully-controlled and adaptable environment [13]. The system incorporates a comprehensive VR Training Application (Fig. 1), which permits the execution of diverse training scenes and scenarios.

Training scenes within the system are representations of specific power infrastructure components, such as power substations. Each training scene comprises a spatial arrangement of 3D models of power infrastructure, constructed from elements sourced from a dedicated training content library [19]. These scenes amalgamate visual aspects with intrinsic interactions—interaction mechanisms that are permanently embedded within the 3D objects. These mechanisms include opening and closing doors or grabbing and moving objects. The development of the training scenes is facilitated by a purpose-built training scene creator, an overlay on the Unity 3D environment, equipped with its own interface.

Each of the training scenes can be coupled with multiple distinct training scenarios used for training specific skills within the training scene. The training scenarios are developed utilizing a specifically-designed semantic scenario editor, a user-friendly desktop application conceived for operation by the training staff [8,22].

Fig. 1. VR Training Application from the perspective of a trainee.

The architecture of the VR training system is organized into several interconnected modules (Fig. 2). At the center of this architecture is the VR Training Application, which captures user positions and user interactions during each training session and feeds these data into the central database. This database subsequently serves as the primary data source for the remaining modules. The Results Analysis Module retrieves user interactions from the database, processing these data to generate valuable insights and reports. In addition, the 2D and 3D Visualization Modules utilize the user positions data stored in the database to create comprehensive visual representations of user movements and actions within the VR training environment. This architecture allows for efficient data processing and presentation of a holistic view of the user's experience and performance in the training program.

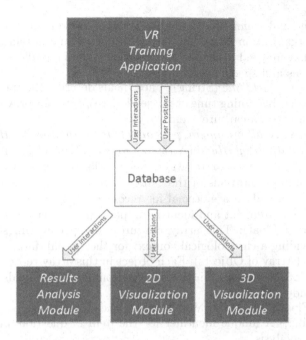

Fig. 2. Overview of the VR training system architecture and module interactions.

4 Structure of the Processed Data

The VR training progress evaluation system makes use of a comprehensive structure of data to capture user interactions during training. These data is then processed and encoded into JSON format, which allows for efficient, machine-readable data exchange. Each field within the data structure plays a specific role in the analysis and interpretation of the user's performance and progress. Below is a detailed breakdown of the data structure, including data types and their respective uses:

- *resultInfo* (Object): This element encapsulates information related to the user and the context of the training scenario. It contains the following fields:
  - *scene* and *scenario* (String): These fields denote the specific training environment and scenario (task sequence) being used. They are critical for segmenting and comparing performance across different tasks and environments.
  - *id* (Integer): A unique identifier for each user, facilitating individual performance tracking and analysis over time.
  - *email*, *firstName*, *lastName*, *username*, *fullName* (String): These fields provide personal information to facilitate communication and personalize the training experience.

- *orgName* and *comments* (Nullable String): These fields may contain the user's organization name and any additional remarks related to the session. They may aid in sorting or categorizing data based on organizational affiliations and specific session notes.
- *sceneName* and *startTime* (String): These fields describe the specific VR environment and the beginning time of the session, respectively, providing a precise context for each data capture event.
- *postionCamera*, *rotationCamera*, *postionLeftHand*, *rotationLeftHand*, *postionRightHand*, *rotationRightHand* (Array of Objects): Each object in these arrays contains *x*, *y*, *z* (and *w* for rotation) fields (Float) representing the spatial coordinates and orientations of the camera and the user's hands at different timestamps. These data are crucial for reconstructing the user's interactions with the VR environment and identifying performance patterns or errors.
- *time* (Array of Float): This array captures the specific timestamps of the session, providing a chronological context for the spatial data.
- *objectStates* (Array of Objects): Each object in this array represents a change in the state of an item within the VR environment. The fields within these objects include:
    - *time* (Float): The timestamp at which the state change occurred.
    - *id* (String): A unique identifier for the item in question, enabling item-specific analysis.
    - *previousState* and *newState* (String): These fields provide a clear before-and-after picture of each state change, facilitating the identification of correct or incorrect actions.
    - *ShouldBeState* (String): This field represents the expected state of the item, serving as a benchmark against which user actions are evaluated.
- *additionalObjectsToRegisterData* (Array of Objects): Each object in this array provides additional data about specific items within the VR environment, including:
    - *gameObjectName* (String): The name of the object, assisting in item-specific analysis.
    - *postionObject* and *rotationObject* (Array of Objects): Each object in these arrays contains *x*, *y*, *z* (and *w* for rotation) fields (Float) representing the spatial coordinates and orientations of the object at different timestamps.
- *analysisSteps* (Array of Objects): Each object in this array represents a step in the analysis of the VR session, including:
    - *name* (String): The name of the analysis step. This provides a high-level description of the task or action sequence that the user is expected to perform at this stage of the training scenario.
    - *time* (Float): The timestamp at which the analysis step was initiated. This provides a chronological context for the actions performed during this step.
    - *actions* (Array of Objects): Each object within this array represents a specific action taken by the user during the analysis step. These actions are essentially sub-tasks or individual actions that the user performs as part of the larger task represented by the analysis step. The fields within these action objects include:

* *name* (String): The name of the action. This provides a description of the specific action that the user is expected to perform.
* *id* (String): A unique identifier for the item in question, enabling item-specific analysis.
* *time* (Float): The timestamp at which the action was performed. This provides a chronological context for the action.
* *objects* (String): A comma-separated list of unique identifiers for the items that are involved in the action. This field is used to track which items the user interacted with during the action.
* *errors* (Array of Strings): This field contains the unique identifiers for any items that were involved in an error during the action. An empty array indicates that no errors were made during the action. This field is crucial for identifying user mistakes and areas for improvement.

5   Results Analysis Module

The Results Analysis Module is a key component of the VR training system. Its purpose is to decode and present training data in a manner that is comprehensible and beneficial to both trainers and trainees. The primary function of this module is data processing and interpretation. It transforms raw data, which is initially stored in MongoDB in JSON format, into a form that can be readily used. This processed data is then employed to generate PDF reports.

The entire process is facilitated by a software module that runs on Node.js. This module initiates the download of the required file containing the training records from the MongoDB database. These records are then processed to generate a PDF report (Fig. 3). The content of the report is determined by the chosen mode of operation, which can be either *Single Run Analysis*, *Multiple Runs Analysis*, or *User Analysis*.

5.1   Single Run Analysis

The *Single Run Analysis* mode is designed for a detailed examination of individual training sessions. It focuses on the performance of trainees in selected training courses for a particular scenario. This mode of analysis provides a comprehensive breakdown of the trainee's performance in the selected scenario, facilitating the provision of focused feedback and targeted improvements.

A report generated in this mode contains several key metrics. Firstly, it provides the time taken for the scenario execution. Secondly, it lists the number of steps and activities performed correctly and incorrectly, thereby offering a clear picture of the trainee's understanding and skills in applying the training content. The percentage of correctly completed scenario steps is also included, offering a quick summary of the trainee's overall performance. In addition, the report enumerates the mistakes made during the scenario execution, providing valuable insight for future training sessions. Finally, it contains information about the virtual tools and security measures used during the training session.

Detailed step analysis

Step 1: Switching off the 15 kV line

Number of actions in a given step: 5

Action list:
  Action 1. Enable MICOM protection and switch to local control
  Action 2. Turn off the 15kV switch
  Action 3. Turn off the 20kV switch
  Action 4. Disconnect the line disconnector of the 20kV line
  Action 5. Open the disconnector from the system of the 2nd 20kV line

Time of execution of individual actions

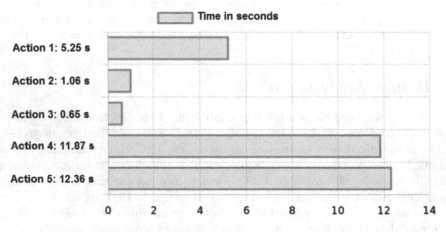

Fig. 3. Excerpt from a PDF file containing data on the training progress of an employee.

5.2   Multiple Runs Analysis

The *Multiple Runs Analysis* mode provides a broader perspective, examining multiple training courses for a selected scenario. This mode of analysis is instrumental in identifying common patterns and trends across different training sessions. It allows for the comparison of performances across different courses, helping to identify areas of strength and weakness across a wider array of training sessions.

The report generated in this mode averages the data from multiple runs of training. It includes the average scenario execution time, offering a benchmark for the expected performance. It also details the average execution times for individual steps and activities, providing an indication of which areas might require additional focus. Furthermore, it provides the average percentage of correctly performed steps and activities, giving an overall measure of performance across the selected courses. The report also lists errors made by users, along with the frequency of their occurrences, which serves as a valuable tool for identifying recurring issues that may need to be addressed in future training sessions.

5.3   User Analysis

The *User Analysis* mode offers a personalized perspective on the training process, focusing on the performance of a selected user across various scenarios. This mode permits a thorough understanding of an individual user's progress and areas for improvement.

The report generated in this mode is highly comprehensive. It starts with the total time of all training sessions completed by the user, indicating the user's dedication and commitment to the training process. It then enumerates the completed training sessions, offering a record of the user's learning journey. Subsequently, it provides information about each training session, allowing for a detailed examination of the user's performance across different scenarios. The report also includes the average scenario execution time, as well as the average execution times of individual scenario steps, providing insights into the user's efficiency and speed in completing tasks. Finally, it lists the errors made by the user along with the frequency of their occurrences, serving as a valuable resource for identifying areas that may require further training or clarification.

6   2D Visualization Module

The 2D Visualization Module can be used to provide a visual representation of the trainee's actions and the path the trainee took to execute them. In the training scenario, every 0.2s, the user's status data are gathered and saved to a JSON file. The parameters used to graph a user's training session are as follows:

- The x, y, and z coordinates of the trainee within the training environment.
- The x, y, and z coordinates for tools the trainee would use during the training session.
- The current progress of the scenario the trainee was supposed to complete. Both successfully completed and failed tasks are included.
- The training site where the session took place.

When a training session ends, regardless of the reason (such as being interrupted by the instructor or trainee or completing all steps successfully), the user is presented with a top-down view of the training site where the session took place (Fig. 4). The map of the training site is slightly modified to ensure visibility without compromising realism (e.g., some roofing is made transparent, so that the objects underneath are visible, and weather effects are toned down).

When the scene loads, the view is centered on an icon representing the trainee. After initializing, the icon begins to move according to the coordinates read from the JSON file - the x and z coordinates from the 3D environment are mapped onto a 2D map so that the movements depicted are spatially accurate. The icons representing tool positions are displayed in the same way. The options for user interaction with the visualization are as follows:

- Pausing, playing, fast-forwarding, and resetting the progress of the trainee on the timeline.

- Manipulating the camera view by clicking and dragging with the mouse cursor, moving the cursor towards the edges of the screen to move the camera in the corresponding direction, or locking the view so that it moves with the trainee centered on the screen.
- Displaying all scenario steps in a side panel, including whether the step has been executed properly, and if so, the exact time of its execution.
- Displaying tooltips with a description of the role of each button.

   To help show the path taken by the trainee, the icon indicating the user's position leaves behind a red trail while traversing from one point to the next. When a step in the training scenario is executed successfully, it leaves a confirmation icon on the map. When the trainee icon reaches the last saved coordinate from the JSON file, the visualization stops and can be reset by clicking the reset button (this also clears the path traced during the visualization).

   It is important to note that though the trainee's path visualization remains spatially accurate, a discrepancy emerges between the time a trainee takes to execute a scenario and the duration of the visualization due to the teleportation capability in the virtual reality environment. This capability allows the trainee to move instantly to a flat surface within their line of sight by simply pointing a controller towards it. In contrast, the visualization maintains a smoother appearance by interpolating the icon's position between subsequent coordinates, instead of instantaneously moving it. The interpolation rate is based on an estimated average speed of a trainee's movement. As a result, the time a trainee spends on a session is typically shorter due to the distances covered by teleportation in the VR environment. The 2D Visualization Module can approximate the scenario's real-world duration, where moving between points requires time.

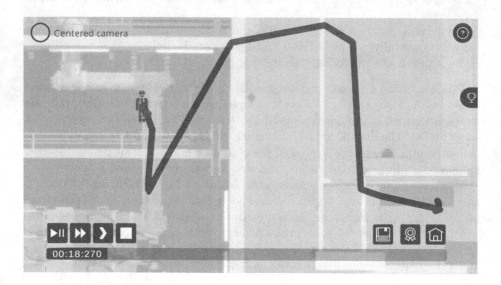

Fig. 4. Visualization of an employee's route progress in 2D.

7   3D Visualization Module

The 3D Visualization Module is designed to provide a more detailed spatial visualization of trainees' behavior. By reconstructing the user's path in a three-dimensional space, it enables comprehensive exploration of the virtual environment and a detailed review of critical actions undertaken during the training exercise (Fig. 5). In contrast to 2D visualization, the 3D Visualization Module provides a more immersive and interactive experience for users, allowing them to examine the training scenario from various perspectives and orientations.

This module utilizes three-dimensional scenes from the training scenario to deliver a clear and informative visualization experience. To ensure maximum visibility and intelligibility, the module omits certain elements, such as roofs and hanging objects, which could potentially obstruct the user's view of the scene. The 3D visualization tool incorporates an orbiting camera feature, which enables users to explore the 3D space from various angles and perspectives.

Fig. 5. Visualization of an employee's route progress in 3D.

The additional level of detail and depth provided by the 3D Visualization Module facilitates a better understanding of the spatial relationships between objects and actions within the virtual environment, ultimately providing more valuable insights for trainees and educators. Moreover, the three-dimensional depiction of the user's path allows for a more thorough and accurate analysis of the user's actions and interactions within the training environment. While the 2D visualization offers an overview of the user's movements, it may not capture the nuances and complexities of the virtual environment, which are crucial for accurate feedback and evaluation.

The 3D Visualization Module's capacity to visualize the user's path in three-dimensional space may increase users' engagement and motivation during the review process. The immersive nature of 3D visualization encourages users to actively explore and analyze their actions, which results in more effective learning and skill development than 2D visualization, which can occasionally feel flat and constrained.

8   Conclusions and Future Works

In this paper, a comprehensive approach to the analysis of the progress of Industry 4.0 employees undergoing VR training has been presented. Methods of managing and interpreting training data have been also detailed, with various modes of analysis used to provide meaningful feedback and insights to trainers and trainees. The significance of visualization in the review and evaluation process has been also discussed, together with the benefits of both 2D and 3D visualization techniques.

The VR training system proposed in this paper has the potential to significantly enhance training outcomes for Industry 4.0 employees. By offering various tools for data interpretation and visualization, the system is intended to enable trainers and trainees to review and understand their performance more effectively. The potential advantages of the 2D and 3D visualization modules might be in offering a comprehensive overview of user actions and fostering a more immersive exploration of the training environment. This approach to VR training evaluation could facilitate better comprehension, engagement, and retention of training outcomes. However, it's important to note that these potential benefits require empirical validation.

There are many areas for future research and development. One direction is the incorporation of machine learning techniques for more sophisticated analysis of training data. This could enable more advanced pattern recognition, prediction of user performance, and personalized feedback. Another avenue of research could be the integration of augmented reality (AR) technologies to complement the VR training experience. AR could provide additional layers of information and interactivity within the training environment, further enhancing user engagement and comprehension. Additionally, future work could focus on optimizing the 3D visualization module to provide more detailed and accurate representations of user actions and interactions within the training environment.

With the continuous development of Industry 4.0, the need for designing innovative and effective training solutions persists as a critical priority. Our proposed approach to analyzing training progress in VR could potentially represent a substantial contribution to this ongoing endeavor.

Acknowledgments. The presented research was co-funded by the National Center for Research and Development under grant number LIDER/55/0287/L-12/20/NCBR/2021.

References

1. Cárdenas-Robledo, L.A., Hernández-Uribe, Ó., Reta, C., Cantoral-Ceballos, J.A.: Extended reality applications in industry 4.0. – a systematic literature review. Telematics Inform. **73**, 101863 (2022). https://doi.org/10.1016/j.tele.2022.101863. https://www.sciencedirect.com/science/article/pii/S073658532200096X
2. Bowman, D.A., McMahan, R.P.: Virtual reality: how much immersion is enough? Computer **40**(7), 36–43 (2007)
3. Card, S.K., Mackinlay, J., Shneiderman, B.: Readings in Information Visualization: Using Vision to Think. Morgan Kaufmann (1999)
4. Carretero, M.P., García, S., Moreno, A., Alcain, N., Elorza, I.: Methodology to create virtual reality assisted training courses within the Industry 4.0 vision. Multimedia Tools Appl. **80**(19), 29699–29717 (2021). https://doi.org/10.1007/s11042-021-11195-2
5. Chandler, T., et al.: Immersive analytics. In: 2015 Big Data Visual Analytics (BDVA), pp. 1–8. IEEE (2015)
6. Chittaro, L.: Improving knowledge retention and perceived control through serious games: a study about assisted emergency evacuation. IEEE Trans. Vis. Comput. Graph., 1–12 (2023). https://doi.org/10.1109/TVCG.2023.3292473
7. Damiani, L., Demartini, M., Guizzi, G., Revetria, R., Tonelli, F.: Augmented and virtual reality applications in industrial systems: a qualitative review towards the industry 4.0 era. IFAC-PapersOnLine **51**(11), 624–630 (2018). https://doi.org/10.1016/j.ifacol.2018.08.388. https://www.sciencedirect.com/science/article/pii/S2405896318315131. 16th IFAC Symposium on Information Control Problems in Manufacturing INCOM 2018
8. Flotyński, J., Walczak, K., Sobociński, P., Gałązkiewicz, A.: Knowledge-based management of virtual training scenarios. Procedia Comput. Sci. **192**, 766–775 (2021)
9. Gavish, N., et al.: Evaluating virtual reality and augmented reality training for industrial maintenance and assembly tasks. Interact. Learn. Environ. **23**(6), 778–798 (2015)
10. Ieronutti, L., Ranon, R., Chittaro, L.: High-level visualization of users' navigation in virtual environments. In: Costabile, M.F., Paternò, F. (eds.) INTERACT 2005. LNCS, vol. 3585, pp. 873–885. Springer, Heidelberg (2005). https://doi.org/10.1007/11555261_69
11. Lasi, H., Fettke, P., Kemper, H.-G., Feld, T., Hoffmann, M.: Industry 4.0. business & information systems engineering **6**(4), 239–242 (2014). https://doi.org/10.1007/s12599-014-0334-4
12. Li, Q., et al.: A visual analytics approach for understanding reasons behind snowballing and comeback in MOBA games. IEEE Trans. Vis. Comput. Graph. **23**, 1–1 (2016). https://doi.org/10.1109/TVCG.2016.2598415
13. Maik, M., Sobociński, P., Walczak, K., Strugała, D., Górski, F., Zawadzki, P.: Flexible photorealistic VR training system for electrical operators. In: Proceedings of the 27th International Conference on 3D Web Technology, pp. 1–9 (2022)
14. Pathmanathan, N., Öney, S., Becher, M., Sedlmair, M., Weiskopf, D., Kurzhals, K.: Been there, seen that: visualization of movement and 3D eye tracking data from real-world environments. Comput. Graph. Forum **42**(3), 385–396 (2023). https://doi.org/10.1111/cgf.14838. https://onlinelibrary.wiley.com/doi/abs/10.1111/cgf.14838

15. Ruddle, R.A., Lessels, S.: The benefits of using a walking interface to navigate virtual environments. ACM Trans. Comput.-Hum. Interact. (TOCHI) **16**(1), 1–18 (2009)
16. Schwab, K.: The Fourth Industrial Revolution. Currency (2017)
17. Shneiderman, B.: The eyes have it: a task by data type taxonomy for information visualizations. In: Proceedings 1996 IEEE Symposium on Visual Languages, pp. 336–343. IEEE (1996)
18. Slater, M., Sanchez-Vives, M.V.: Enhancing our lives with immersive virtual reality. Frontiers Rob. AI **3**, 74 (2016)
19. Strugała, D., Nowak, A., Górski, F., Walczak, K.: Semi-structured visual design of complex industrial 3D training scenes. In: The 25th International Conference on 3D Web Technology, pp. 1–9 (2020)
20. Tory, M., Kirkpatrick, A.E., Atkins, M.S., Moller, T.: Visualization task performance with 2D, 3D, and combination displays. IEEE Trans. Visual Comput. Graphics **12**(1), 2–13 (2005)
21. Tory, M., Moller, T.: Human factors in visualization research. IEEE Trans. Visual Comput. Graphics **10**(1), 72–84 (2004)
22. Walczak, K., et al.: Semantic modeling of virtual reality training scenarios. In: Bourdot, P., Interrante, V., Kopper, R., Olivier, A.-H., Saito, H., Zachmann, G. (eds.) EuroVR 2020. LNCS, vol. 12499, pp. 128–148. Springer, Cham (2020). https://doi.org/10.1007/978-3-030-62655-6_8
23. Yi, J.S., Kang, Y., Stasko, J., Jacko, J.A.: Toward a deeper understanding of the role of interaction in information visualization. IEEE Trans. Visual. Comput. Graph. **13**(6), 1224–1231 (2007)

Extended Reality Product Configuration for Flexible Production Systems: A Case Study

Ilaria Di Blasio[1]([✉]), Julius Emig[1], Elias Niederwieser[1], Dietmar Siegele[1], and Dominik T. Matt[1,2]

[1] Fraunhofer Italia, Via A. Volta 13 A, 39100 Bolzano, Italy
ilaria.diblasio@fraunhofer.it
[2] Free University of Bozen-Bolzano, Piazza Università 5, 39100 Bolzano, Italy

Abstract. Manufacturing companies are increasingly interested in customer-involved product configurators due to their capacity to better meet customers' needs. The capacity of eXtended Reality (XR) product configurators to enhance user experience makes them highly useful for realizing the concept of human-centric design for mass customization. We present a case study of an XR Configuration System (XRCS) compatible with a flexible production system. The aim of this work was the development of an interactive and user-friendly XRCS. The XRCS allows product configurability and customization while considering production and sustainability information. Moreover, it allows to send the final configuration to the production system in real-time. For this purpose, the XRCS has been integrated into the full-scale production demonstrator located at Fraunhofer Italia's Area for Research and iNnovative Applications (ARENA).

Keywords: Extended Reality · Product Configuration · Mass Customization · Smart Manufacturing · Industry 4.0

1 Introduction

The McKinsey Institute [1] reports that 71% of consumers expect companies to deliver customized interactions, and 76% get frustrated when this expectation is not met. Performance and improved customer outcomes are driven by customization. Personalization generates 40% more revenue for businesses with rapid growth than for those with slower growth. The scientific community is concentrating on the implementation of mass customization techniques in contemporary smart manufacturing environments as interest in customization grows more quickly.

Within this context, with the support of the European Regional Development Fund (ERDF) Investment for Growth and Jobs Programme 2014–2020 of the Autonomous Province of Bolzano-Bozen, Fraunhofer Italia developed an infrastructure for promoting, testing, and investigating sustainable, reconfigurable, and customizable production systems. The infrastructure is a full-scale production demonstrator, implementing several technologies from smart production systems and Industry 4.0.

L. T. De Paolis et al. (Eds.): XR Salento 2023, LNCS 14219, pp. 505–516, 2023.
https://doi.org/10.1007/978-3-031-43404-4_35

This paper presents a case study as the outcome of the research activities for developing an eXtended Reality Configuration System (XRCS) which aims at triggering a scheduling management of the production system and fostering product customization. In particular, the research activities address the following challenges: i) to foster mass customization approaches in manufacturing environments by integrating customer-based product configuration with a flexible production system; ii) to allow product configurability and customization taking into consideration production and sustainability information; iii) to create an interactive and user-friendly product configurator by means of XR technology. The XRCS relies on a pre-defined product prototype which aims to conceptualize a product as a combination of standard components. The combination of these components allows for testing different levels of standardization, modularization, and customization, both in product design and in product manufacturing.

The structure of the paper is as follows: Sect. 2 illustrates the state of the art; Sect. 3 illustrates the methodology for addressing the above-mentioned challenges; the resulting XRCS has been described in Sect. 4; and the conclusion and future development of the essay are reported in Sect. 5.

2 State of the Art

2.1 Mass Customization and Smart Manufacturing

The authors of [2] defines the concept of mass customization (MC) in the book "Future Perfect" as the capability of manufacturing tailored products with production costs like those of mass-produced products [3]. Through a selection of predefined features, MC enables each client to configure a product to meet his or her own demands [4, 5]. The implementation of customization capabilities MC has received a growing consideration by the scientific community both in manufacturing and in services delivery [6].

Customization might appear to be an opposition of standardization and modularization, yet in a manufacturing business system, they work in unison. In an effort to find a manufacturing concept that would adequately address the constraints of a global market, [7] pose the following query: what occurs to clients whose tastes differ from what is offered? The authors stress in their study's conclusion that a production concept should be established based on a synergy and synthesis of standardization, modularization, and customization, in accordance with the particular requirements of the market target that is being addressed. The authors of [8] provide empirical evidence on the individual and interactive effects of standardization and innovation in developing MC capability and their joint influence on delivery speed. The authors show that standardization and innovation positively affect MC capability and are complementary in developing MC capability. [9] analyze the direct and indirect impacts of standardization and customization on customer satisfaction and loyalty through service quality through a questionnaire-based survey of 315 customers from three service industries: healthcare, hospitality, and education. The authors highlight that standardization has a higher impact on service quality when compared to customization, and functional quality has a higher impact on customer satisfaction when compared to technical quality. The authors of [10] find that the advantages of service customization include greater perceived control and higher consumer satisfaction. They show that consumers' preference for standardized (vs. customized) service depends on their consumption goal. Specifically, consumers with a hedonic goal tend to prefer customized services, while those with a utilitarian goal tend to prefer standardized services.

The market success of MC Implementations Increases the demand for customization capabilities in manufacturing enterprises. However, MC brings radical changes to the methods used to operate traditional manufacturing enterprises [11, 12]. Manufacturing systems in a mass customization environment should be able to produce small quantities in a highly flexible way and to rapidly reconfigurable [5, 13]. In the past, several concepts for manufacturing system design have been discussed in scientific literature: from flexible manufacturing systems (FMS) [14] to reconfigurable manufacturing systems (RMS) as well as the concept of changeable and agile manufacturing systems [15]. Such manufacturing systems fit the needed requirements for mass customization manufacturing better than a traditional one.

The latest trend in mass customization is digitalization in manufacturing, also known under the term Industry 4.0, and its applied technologies grouped as cyber-physical systems (CPS). The large potential of Industry 4.0 will be a key enabler for further developments in mass customization manufacturing [16, 17]. Intelligent, cognitive, and self-optimizing manufacturing systems can learn and, thereby, perform self-determined changes in production systems [18]. To reach this next level of changeability, it is necessary to equip manufacturing systems with cognitive capabilities to take autonomous decisions in even more complex production processes with a high product variety [19]. The MC becomes a competitive strategy under the condition that the company can quickly respond to the expectations and requirements of its customers, in synergy with other strategies such as Quick Response [20]. According to the authors of [21] this synergy is possible whether a company has a flexible manufacturing system and the possibility of rapid design (in terms of duration), as well as the implementation of new products and processes in their manufacturing. The authors assert that smart design and smart production control are necessary elements of a smart factory of the future that can realize the MC. According to their study, to fulfill the elementary idea of the MC concept, which is supporting each client with individualized products, the application of automated and knowledge-based design systems is invaluable. [22] also highlight limitations of MC, which - according to their study - lacks customer participation in the design phase, limits product combinations among a bunch of predefined alternatives by designers and is not capable of providing personalized services and goods. The authors present a framework for mass personalization production as an evolution of MC based on the concepts of Industry 4.0 to overcome the limits of MC.

2.2 Examples of Product Configuration Systems

Product configurators are becoming increasingly popular among manufacturing companies. A company's competitiveness depends significantly on its ability to provide customized solutions that match customers' requirements [21]. Therefore, manufacturing companies have focused on the development of customer-involved product configurators over the last few years. Many companies, including IKEA, Tesla, Könitz, and MODÚ have already implemented product configurators in their processes. IKEA's web-based configurator allows customers to design room furnishings and visualize them in 3D before making a purchase [23]. Tesla's web-based configurator enables customers to design their car by selecting from a range of possible features and seeing a 3D version of it [24]. Similarly, Könitz's web-based mug configurator offers customers many customization options, including art prints and metallic finishes [25]. The MODÚ smart configurator aims to facilitate the creation of custom furniture from prefabricated boxes and customer inputs so that the design can be tailored to their needs [26].

The eXtended Reality (XR) product configurators become more and more popular among companies involved in product design and manufacturing. XR product configurators using technologies such as Augmented Reality (AR), Virtual Reality (VR), and Mixed Reality (MR) create an interactive and immersive experience that is more appreciated by customers than web-based configurators. According to the authors of [27] customers prefer the XR-based product configurator over the web-based one due to its better performance in product visualization. They analyzed users' experiences of configuring smart respiratory equipment with both a web-page-based configuration system and a VR-based configuration system and found that around 80% of subjects preferred the VR-based system.

Several research studies have been carried out on the application of XR in smart manufacturing. The authors of [28] developed an AR-based system for children's footwear customization that allows customers to define various design features such as color, texture, embroidery, and shape. To facilitate customer integration at the product design phase, an AR-based configurator [29] was developed to provide the end user with the ability to define product features such as product components, colors, and materials and visualize them in the physical environment. The authors of [30] developed an AR-based application for the industry of robotic cell manufacturing that enables customers to visualize robotic cells components as interactive holograms in real time and to customize them. A VR-based city bus configurator [31] was developed to speed up and simplify the selection of an optimal, user-centric product variant in accordance with the manufacturer. Application of VR-based technologies for product visualization and interaction is now widespread worldwide; in fact, an increasing number of companies build their own VR-based configurators [32]. Audi [33] and BMW [34] research and development teams implemented VR-based configurators that allow customers to design their own vehicle models, choose from different colors and materials, take a virtual test drive, and see chosen configurations in a lifelike environment.

XR-based technologies flexibility makes them fit in most manufacturing process phases [35]. Due to that and to their capacity for customer engagement, these technologies have the most potential for realizing the concept of human-centric design for mass customization. According to the authors of [27], XR-based technologies can be a significant milestone for the evolution of product configuration. Moreover, they are the most promising technology to meet manufacturers' demands for providing more customized products and streamlining manufacturing processes.

3   Methodology

The development of an XRCS compatible with a flexible production system is the aim of this study. The XRCS should allow users to input their desired product configuration and initiate production using standard features like selecting and moving components from a library and setting jointing elements. The XRCS should also provide production data such as sustainability metrics, which can be used to suggest optimizations for predefined metrics. Furthermore, to embed the XRCS in a flexible production system, the possibility of sending an abstract production order for the configured product needs to be implemented. So, the XRCS development is based on a three-step approach: (i) definition of the configuration elements; (ii) definition of the XR environment; (iii) definition of the connection to the flexible production system. An overview of the developed XRCS architecture is shown in Fig. 1.

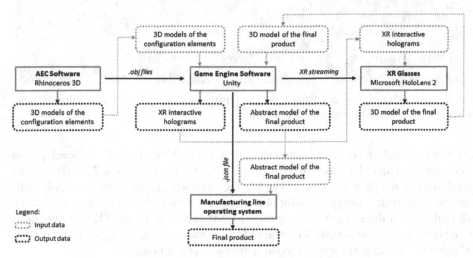

Fig. 1. Extended Reality Configuration System (XRCS) architecture.

3.1 Step 1: Definition of the Configuration Elements

A set of pre-defined standard parts is used to create a combination of standard and customizable elements. Figure 2 shows the standard elements (L-shape, I-shape, i-shape, and r-shape), jointing elements (pins), and an assembly base plate on which the desired product should be configured. These 3D-objects were modelled in a CAD software and represent the starting point for the development of the XRCS and are needed to generate XR interactive holograms.

3.2 Step 2: Definition of the XR Environment

The XRCS runs on a Microsoft Windows 11 workstation, equipped with an Intel Core i7-10810U CPU and an Intel UHD Graphics, and is streamed to Microsoft HoloLens 2 headset via Wi-Fi. This headset features a transparent holographic display, a set of sensors for user movements and surroundings tracking, a custom-built holographic processing unit (HPU 2.0), and the Qualcomm Snapdragon 850 computing platform [36]. Based on these capabilities, the Microsoft HoloLens 2 headset is used to render the XR

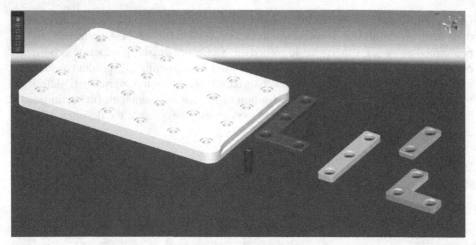

Fig. 2. Screenshot of the pre-defined standard parts (standard elements, jointing element, assembly base plate) for configuring the product.

environment and enable users to interact with it. Unity (Unity Real-Time Development Platform) [37] and Microsoft Mixed Reality Toolkit (MRTK, version 2.8.2.0) [38] are used to create the XR environment. The MRTK facilitates the development of XR applications by providing components for object manipulation and graphical user interfaces. To make use of these components within the XR environment, MRTK was integrated into Unity. In a second step, the following MRTK components are assigned to 3D models of standard and jointing elements to support object interactions:

- *NearInteractionGrabbable* components allow standard elements to be grabbed at close range.
- *ConstraintManager* component constrains object manipulation; standard elements can only be rotated around the vertical axis and cannot be scaled.
- *ObjectManipulator* component enables manipulation of standard elements with an XR-device; enables translation and rotation of standard elements using one or two hands.
- *BoundsControl* component facilitates interaction with standard elements by displaying boundaries and handles for object manipulation.

No MRTK-components are assigned to the assembly base element, since it should not be possible for the user to manipulate its position and orientation. In addition, a toolbar with four buttons was created using the *Button Collections* component of the MRTK. This facilitates the usage of functionalities that are not directly related to object manipulation. The mentioned MRTK-components are crucial for providing a user-friendly and straightforward operation of the XR-Configurator and aim to make the product configuration process as intuitive as possible.

In addition to the MRTK-components, a series of customized functionalities is implemented in order to provide a better user experience. This was done by including C# scripts in the Unity project and calling their methods from inside the previously introduced MRTK-component *ObjectManipulator*. The *ObjectManipulator* component provides an interface for executing custom functions whenever a manipulation of an object is started and ended. This interface was used to include the following custom functionalities:

- Saving the position of an element as soon as the user starts removing it from the storage – The saved position is then used to place a copy of the manipulated element at the original (saved) position in the storage as soon as the user ends the manipulation.
- Translational snapping to predefined grid points on the assembly base – The grid points are chosen to coincide with the position of the pinholes on the assembly base in order to avoid the placement of elements between pinholes and thus product configurations for which it would not be possible to fix the elements with pins.
- Rotation snapping: This functionality snaps elements when the manipulation is ended at the closest 90°-angle (0°, 90°, 180°, 270°).

Analogously, the MRTK *Button Collection* toolbar is modified by adding buttons with the following customized function:

- *Set Layer* button allows to change the vertical offset for snapping, so that standard elements can be placed in different layers.
- *Reset Configuration* button allows to delete all elements, except assembly base and elements in storage.
- *Create Product* button allows to create an abstract representation of the configured product as a *JSON*-file and send it to production line.

The sustainability aspect is considered in terms of a feedback to the user indicating sustainability metrics for the current state of the configuration and then also for the configured product. The idea is to provide relevant information in real-time already during the configuration of a product to assist the user's decision-making.

3.3   Step 3: Definition of the Connection to the Flexible Production System

The *Create Product* button represents the connection between the user and the production line. The abstraction of a configured product is achieved through some basic geometrical checks. All elements that are placed on the assembly base plate are stored in a list. For the elements in this list, a product tree is generated, representing a hierarchical order of elements in order to facilitate the assembly process. Information about each product component such as position, orientation, and element type, is also included in the product tree. Once the configuration process is ended, the abstract representation of the product is sent as a JSON file to the production system.

4   Results

The result of the developed XRCS is shown in Fig. 3. The XRCS is integrated into a flexible and reconfigurable production system developed by Fraunhofer Italia. The full-scale demonstrator, available at Fraunhofer Italia's Area for Research and iNnovative Applications (ARENA), consists of different physical modules such as XRCS, an assembly module, and a quality control module.

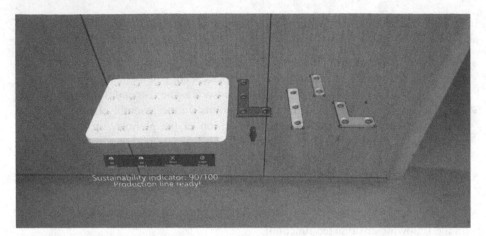

Fig. 3. Screenshot of the developed eXtended Reality Configuration System (XRCS).

Once the XRCS is run on an XR-device, the holograms of the standard elements, the assembly base, and the toolbar are visible. The customer can interact in real-time with the configuration elements in order to reach the desired product.

In particular, the standard elements can be moved freely, rotated, and duplicated by using fingers. The standard elements can be rotated with the hand about the grab point between the thumb and index finger; it should feel as if the object is being held by the hand. Similarly, objects can be moved by grabbing them by the center point, as shown in Fig. 4. The customer can manipulate one standard element at a time and place as many elements as desired on the assembly base due to the fact that a copy of the element is created each time it is grabbed and moved from the storage. Furthermore, once placed on the plate, the element can be rotated or moved again until it reaches the desired position. Instead, the assembly base is fixed and cannot be grabbed or moved by the customer.

A set of pressable buttons allows control of the configuration process. The customer can choose what to do between *Set Layer*, *Reset Configuration*, and *Create Product* by pressing the corresponding button with a finger, as shown in Fig. 5. Standard elements, except pins, can be placed on multiple layers by pressing *Set Layer 1* or *Set layer 2* buttons. Figure 5 shows a product configured by the customer using this function. Furthermore, standard elements can be deleted by pressing the *Reset Configuration* button. So, if the configured product is not the one desired, the customer can reset and start the configuration process again.

Once the configuration process is ended, the customer can send the order directly to the production system by pressing the *Create Product* button. Based on this, the assembly module creates the desired product by assembling the standard components as shown in Fig. 6. The assembly module consists of a robotic arm designed to receive the customer-made product configuration and assemble the final product. Lastly, the quality control module verifies the resulting product's conformity with the one configured by the customer through the XRCS.

The functionalities described above make the XRCS intuitive and easy to use, so that also a non-expert customer can design a product.

Fig. 4. Screenshot of the XRCS with an example of manipulating a standard element.

Fig. 5. Screenshot of the XRCS with an example of a button press and a product configured with standard elements placed on multiple layers.

5 Conclusion and Future Development

In this paper a pilot case study of an eXtended Reality Configuration System (XRCS) compatible with a flexible production system is proposed and described. The XRCS aims to allow customer-based product design and send the final configuration to the production system in real-time. In particular, the developed solution addresses the following challenges: i) to foster mass customization approaches in manufacturing environments

Fig. 6. Robotic assembly module: example of an assembled product.

by integrating customer-based product configuration with a flexible production system; ii) to allow product configurability and customization taking into consideration production and sustainability information; iii) to create an interactive and user-friendly product configurator by means of XR technology. To achieve this goal, the research team developed an XRCS that can be accessed and operated by a user through XR-Glasses such as Microsoft HoloLens 2. Moreover, it has been integrated into the full-scale production demonstrator located at Fraunhofer Italia's Area for Research and iNnovative Applications (ARENA).

The XRCS presented in this essay enables great potential for future developments. The user product configuration experience can be improved by creating a product as a combination of free-form customizable components and not only standard components. Additionally, it can be improved by integrating more advanced sustainability metrics to better support user choices. To make the product configuration experience even more realistic, it can be improved by assigning physics properties to the standard elements (L-shape, I-shape, i-shape, r-shape), jointing elements and assembly base plate, and enabling clash detection. Finally, the number of layers for placing standard elements can be increased to allow more configuration options.

Future development also concerns performing tests with different users to evaluate the quality of the user experience and usability of the XRCS. To facilitate this evaluation, moderated and in person tests will be conducted at Fraunhofer Italia's ARENA. During these tests, users will receive a brief explanation of the XRCS and will be assigned various tasks to complete using the configurator. Furthermore, a questionnaire will be administered to measure effectiveness, efficiency, and satisfaction, among other aspects. Based on the results, necessary improvements and modifications will be implemented to ensure that the XRCS effectively meets users' needs and preferences.

Acknowledgments. The research leading to these results has received funding from the European Regional Development Fund (Fondo Europeo di Sviluppo Regionale FESR Alto Adige 2014–2020) under the Grant Agreement n. EFRE1135 CUP B52F20001530009 (project SMART-Pro).

Author Contributions Statement. Ilaria Di Blasio and Julius Emig contributed equally to the work by drafting the method, implementing, and testing the XRCS. Elias Niederwieser reviewed the manuscript. Dietmar Siegele worked on the method and reviewed the manuscript. Dominik T. Matt supervised the development.

References

1. Arora, N., et al.: The value of getting personalization right—or wrong—is multiplying, McKinsey Insights (2021). https://www.mckinsey.com/business-functions/growth-marketing-and-sales/our-insights/the-value-of-getting-personalization-right-or-wrong-is-multiplying. Accessed 19 Apr 2023
2. Davis, S.M.: From "future perfect": mass customizing. Plan. Rev. **17**(2), 16–21 (1989)
3. Kaplan, A.M.: Toward a parsimonious definition of traditional and electronic mass customization. J. Prod. Innov. Manag. **23**(2), 168–182 (2006)
4. Schreier, M.: The value increment of mass-customized products: an empirical assessment. J. Consum. Behav. **5**(4), 317–327 (2006)
5. Qiao, G.: Flexible manufacturing systems for mass customisation manufacturing. Int. J. Mass Cust. **1**(2–3), 374–393 (2006)
6. Fogliatto, F.S.: The mass customization decade: an updated review of the literature. Int. J. Prod. Econ. **138**(1), 14–25 (2012)
7. Krstić, M.: Unique concept of standardization, modularization and customization of products as a strategy of e-business. Int. Rev. **1**(2), 74–82 (2015)
8. Wang, Z.: Effects of standardization and innovation on mass customization: an empirical investigation. Technovation **48–49**, 79–86 (2016)
9. Kasiri, L.A.: Integration of standardization and customization: impact on service quality, customer satisfaction, and loyalty. J. Retail. Consum. Serv. **35**, 91–97 (2017)
10. Ding, Y.: A re-examination of service standardization versus customization from the consumer's perspective. J. Serv. Mark. **30**(1), 16–28 (2016)
11. Terkaj, W., Tolio, T., Valente, A.: A review on manufacturing flexibility. In: Tolio, T. (ed.) Design of Flexible Production Systems, pp. 41–61. Springer, Heidelberg (2009)
12. Mourtzis, D.: Design and operation of manufacturing networks for mass customisation. CIRP Ann. Manuf. Technol. **62**(1), 467–470 (2013)
13. Thirumalai, S.: Customization of the online purchase process in electronic retailing and customer satisfaction: an online field study. J. Oper. Manag. **29**(5), 477–487 (2011)
14. Wiendahl, H.P.: Changeable manufacturing-classification, design and operation. CIRP Ann. Manuf. Technol. **56**(2), 783–809 (2007)
15. ElMaraghy, H.A., Wiendahl, H.P.: Changeability–an introduction. In: ElMaraghy, H. (ed.) Changeable and Reconfigurable Manufacturing Systems, pp. 3–24. Springer, London (2009)

16. Kull, H.: Intelligent manufacturing technologies. In: Kull, H. (ed.) Mass Customization, pp. 9–20. Apress, Berkeley (2015)
17. Zheng, P.: Smart manufacturing systems for Industry 4.0: conceptual framework, scenarios, and future perspectives. Front. Mech. Eng. **13**, 137–150 (2018)
18. Schmitt, R.: Self-optimising production systems. In: Brecher, C. (ed.) Integrative Production Technology for High-Wage Countries, pp. 697–986. Springer, Heidelberg (2012)
19. Brettel, M.: Enablers for self-optimizing production systems in the context of industrie 4.0. Procedia CIRP **41**, 93–98 (2016)
20. Ko, E.: Impact of business type upon the adoption of quick response technologies. Int. J. Oper. Prod. Manag. **20**(9), 1093–1111 (2000)
21. Zawadzki, P.: Smart product design and production control for effective mass customization in the Industry 4.0 concept. Manage. Prod. Eng. Rev. **3**, 105–112 (2016)
22. Wang, Y.: Industry 4.0: a way from mass customization to mass personalization production. Adv. Manuf. **5**, 311–320 (2017)
23. IKEA Planner. https://www.ikea.com/it/it/planners/?gclsrc=aw.ds&gclid=EAIaIQ obChMIl7_G7YaV_gIV1-F3Ch2dGwQPEAAYASAAEgKIUvD_BwE&gclsrc=aw.ds. Accessed 19 Apr 2023
24. Tesla Homepage. https://www.tesla.com/it_it/model3/design#overview. Accessed 19 Apr 2023
25. Koenitz Configurator. https://www.koenitz.com/en/custom-design/configurator. Accessed 19 Apr 2023
26. Falheiro, M.: Smart configurator to integrate customized furniture design and fabrication. IFAC-PapersOnLine **55**(2), 205–210 (2022)
27. Yuan, L.: VR-based product personalization process for smart products. Procedia Manuf. **11**, 1568–1576 (2017)
28. Yuan Ping, L.: Augmented reality-based design customization of footwear for children. J. Intell. Manuf. **24**(5), 905–917 (2013)
29. Mourtzis, D.: Applications for frugal product customization and design of manufacturing networks. Procedia CIRP **52**, 228–233 (2016)
30. Mourtzis, D.: An augmented reality application for robotic cell customization. Procedia CIRP **90**, 654–659 (2020)
31. Górski, F.: Immersive city bus configurator system for marketing and sales education. Procedia Comput. Sci. **75**, 137–146 (2015)
32. Jiang, M.: Virtual reality boosting automotive development. In: Ma, D., Fan, X., Gausemeier, J., Grafe, M. (eds.) Virtual Reality & Augmented Reality in Industry, pp. 171–180. Springer, Berlin Heidelberg (2011)
33. Audi Homepage. https://www.audi.com/en/innovation/development/holoride-virtual-reality-meets-the-real-world.html. Accessed 19 Apr 2023
34. BMW Homepage. https://www.bmw.co.id/en/topics/offers-and-services/bmw-apps/virtual-and-augmented-reality.html. Accessed 19 Apr 2023
35. Fast-Berglund, A.: Testing and validating Extended Reality (xR) technologies in manufacturing. Procedia Manuf. **25**, 31–38 (2018)
36. Microsoft HoloLens 2, Microsoft 2023. https://www.microsoft.com/en-us/hololens/hardware#document-experiences. Accessed 19 Apr 2023
37. Unity Technologies, Unity Real-Time Development Platform. https://unity.com/. Accessed 19 Apr 2023
38. MRTK Unity Developer Documentation. https://learn.microsoft.com/en-us/windows/mixed-reality/mrtk-unity/mrtk2/?view=mrtkunity-2021-05. Accessed 19 Apr 2023

3D Virtual System of the Automatic Vehicle Painting Process Using the Hardware in the Loop Technique, Oriented to Industrial Automation Training

Luigi O. Freire[1,2]([✉]), Edwin P. Pruna[1], Ivón P. Escobar[1], and Byron P. Corrales[1,2]

[1] Universidad de las Fuerzas Armadas ESPE, Sangolquí, Ecuador
{lofreire,eppruna,ipescobar,bpcorrales}@espe.edu.ec,
{luigi.freire,byron.corrales}@utc.edu.ec
[2] Universidad Técnica de Cotopaxi, Latacunga, Ecuador

Abstract. This project presents a 3D virtual system oriented to the training of Programmable Logic Controllers of the Siemens S7-1200 family through the "Hardware in the Loop" technique of a vehicle painting process; it is divided into three stages: the first one of painting, the second one of immersion in varnish and the third one of drying; the process variables can be seen in a human-machine interface within the virtual environment. In manual mode, the user can manipulate and control the virtual environment through a computer keyboard, while in automatic mode, the user can make an automation proposal through a Grafcet diagram. The application shows a three-dimensional environment with high-level details since the industrial equipment and instrumentation have similar characteristics to the real ones and the user can get involved in the environment and become familiar with each of the elements of the process.

Keywords: 3D virtual process · hardware in the loop · GRAFCET

1 Introduction

An automated industrial process integrates monitoring and control technologies of the process variables, eliminating human intervention, increasing production, efficiency and safety, as well as a product with quality guarantees [1–3]. This requires professionals with theoretical and practical knowledge in the area of industrial automation [4]. The generation of skills, abilities, technical criteria for the selection, installation, operation and manipulation of components such as controllers, sensors and actuators can be achieved through training in process automation [5, 6].

L. T. De Paolis et al. (Eds.): XR Salento 2023, LNCS 14219, pp. 517–530, 2023.
https://doi.org/10.1007/978-3-031-43404-4_36

The automotive industry is one of the fastest growing and the trend is to have efficient processes in the various stages, one of these being the area of vehicle painting which is implementing various automation techniques allowing an increase in the quality of the finished product, reducing waste and labor, since being automated processes can work all year round [7, 8].

The HIL technique together with virtual reality provides the opportunity to obtain virtual industrial environments allowing immersion in a simulated environment, [4] facilitating experimental automation training since it is possible to interact with the programmable logic controller in writing and reading process signals and, unlike a real environment, this allows performance testing by applying different techniques or control methods without production stoppages or economic losses. This presents a great advantage by reducing equipment implementation costs in laboratories [9–11].

In this context, several works have been developed in the field of engineering, specifically in the area of process control applying the HIL technique where it is evident that the realism of the elements of the virtual environment provide the same characteristics as those that exist at the industrial level and this has been gaining strength in recent years [2, 12].

The present work is divided into 5 stages including the introduction, Sect. 2 presents the system structure, Sect. 3 3D virtual environment control modes, Sect. 4 results and finally Sect. 5 conclusions.

2 System Structure

In this stage, the development of a 3D virtual environment of the vehicle painting process is detailed. In the Unity 3D graphic engine, the simulation environment of the operation and functioning of the sensors and actuators is developed by applying the HIL technique, resembling real industrial equipment, allowing automation proposals with the Siemens S7-1200 programmable controller, this structure is developed in the system, as shown in Fig. 1.

2.1 Virtual Environment Modeling

The freely available modeling software Blender allows modeling, rendering and texturing 3D graphics to give the necessary realism to the virtual environment, [4] in this case the vehicle painting process as shown in Fig. 2.

When designing the environment, one of the main parts is the identification of the rotation elements, because the correct configuration and animation of these points will allow a greater realism when simulating, for example, robotic arms, gauges among others, this is shown in Fig. 3.

In the case of using imported models it is necessary to optimize the resources to avoid unnecessary overloading of the computer (Fig. 4).

2.2 Unity 3D Design

To import the design from Blender it should have been previously saved as *.fbx extension, this allows to keep details such as textures among other features and you can add

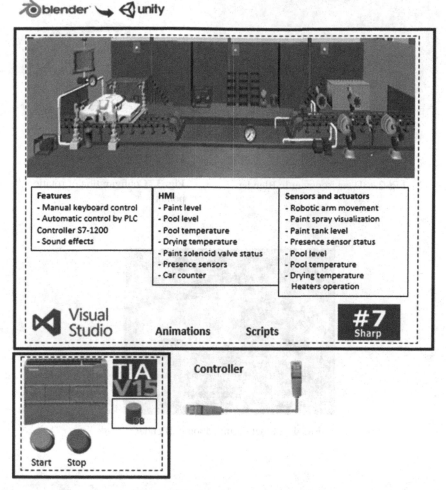

Fig. 1. Virtual environment schematic

other details such as terrain, clouds and other features in order to give more realism as shown in Fig. 5.

2.3 Communication

The communication between the 3D virtual environment and the PLC S7-1200 is done through the Sharp7 library and the TCP/IP communication protocol which relates the Tia Portal variables with the environment variables in Visual Studio. Two buffers are used where Unity3D sends and receives data through a.dll file located in the root of the project with all the scripts, the scheme is shown in Fig. 6.

Fig. 2. 3D environment in Blender

Fig. 3. Configuration of rotation points

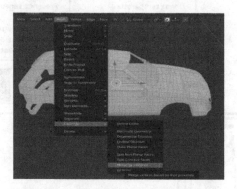

Fig. 4. Model optimization in Blender

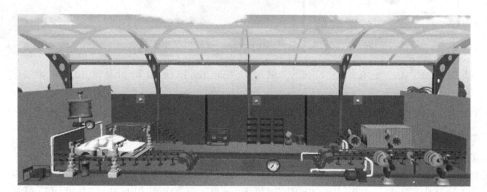

Fig. 5. 3D environment in Unity

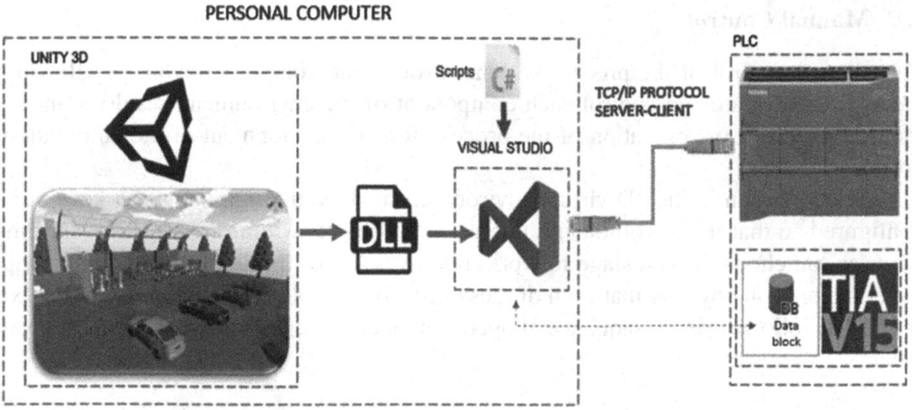

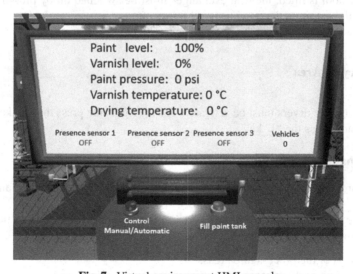

Fig. 6. Communication between the Virtual environment and PLC S7-1200

3 3D Virtual Environment Control Modes

The virtual environment has two control modes: manual and automatic, these will allow the user to become familiar with each of the components of the process such as sensors and actuators prior to the automation proposal.

The process was divided into three stages, the first stage of painting, the second stage of immersion in varnish and the third stage of drying. For this, the paint pressure, varnish temperature and drying temperature must be initially configured in the HMI console as shown in the Fig. 7.

Fig. 7. Virtual environment HMI console

3.1   Manual Control

The manual control of the process is done through the computer keyboard, allowing the user to navigate and control each component of the environment, resulting in the familiarization of the operation of the process for the development of the automation proposal.

The navigation in the 3D virtual environment is done through the arrow keys, it is configured so that it can collide and interact with objects within the scenario, for this the user can choose which stage to work, reading each of the sensors and controlling the actuators conditioning that each of these must be completed to continue to the next stage. The following is the sequence of operation of each stage with the assigned keypad letters.

Stage 1: Painting Area

- The rail that transports the vehicle is activated by pressing the "T" key and the vehicles appear automatically according to the progress of the process.
- For painting, the robotic arms are activated with the "Y" key, provided that the solenoid valve is activated with the letter "U"; if this condition is not met, an error message is displayed on the HMI.

Step 2: Coating Area

- To activate the varnish pool filling pump, press the "O" key.
- Once the pool is filled, the heat exchanger must be switched on by pressing the "I" key, it will heat up to the previously set temperature.
- To empty the varnish from the pool, press the "P" button.

Stage 3: Drying Area

- In this stage the dryers must be activated, for the right side press the "h" key and for the left side press the "J" key.

3.2   Automatic Control

When the process is already known, the next step is the development of the automation proposal.

To make the automation proposal, a basic procedure must be followed that can be applied to any process:

- Subdivision of the process into areas.
- Determination of the sensors and actuators involved in the process.
- Programming in a universal language for PLC (GRAFCET).

Subdivision of the Process into Areas

For the process it is necessary to identify each of the tasks and how they are related to each other allowing to find sub tasks. Figure 8 shows the subdivision of the automatic car painting process.

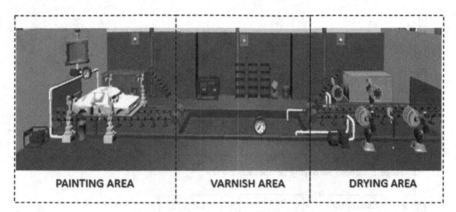

Fig. 8. Subdivision of the process

Determination of the Sensors and Actuators Involved in the Process

Once the process is known, the inputs and outputs (sensors and actuators) of each identified stage are classified and detailed as shown in Fig. 9.

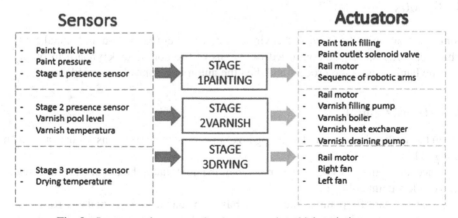

Fig. 9. Sensors and actuators for the automatic vehicle painting process.

Programming in a Universal PLC Language (GRAFCET)
A GRAFCET diagram is created for the process automation, showing the programming sequence to be followed for programming in Tia Portal for the PLC S7-1200 (Fig. 10).

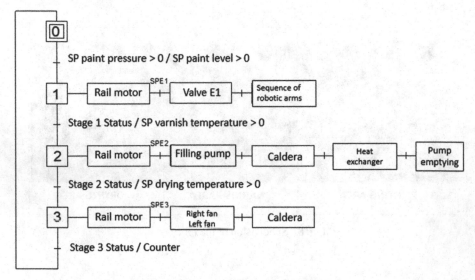

Fig. 10. GRAFCET diagram for automating the vehicle painting process

4 Results

For the validation of the 3D virtual environment, tests were carried out in manual control where the process can be controlled by means of the computer keyboard in order to become familiar with the process and then the automatic control is carried out.

4.1 Manual Control

When the application is started, a dialog box appears with instructions for use, as shown in Fig. 11.

Once the instructions have been reviewed, the next dialog box is displayed to select the vehicle's paint color (Fig. 12).

Once the color for painting the vehicle has been selected, the virtual environment of the process is entered, where the HMI must be used to enter the pressure of the paint to be used, the temperature of the varnish and the drying temperature (Fig. 13).

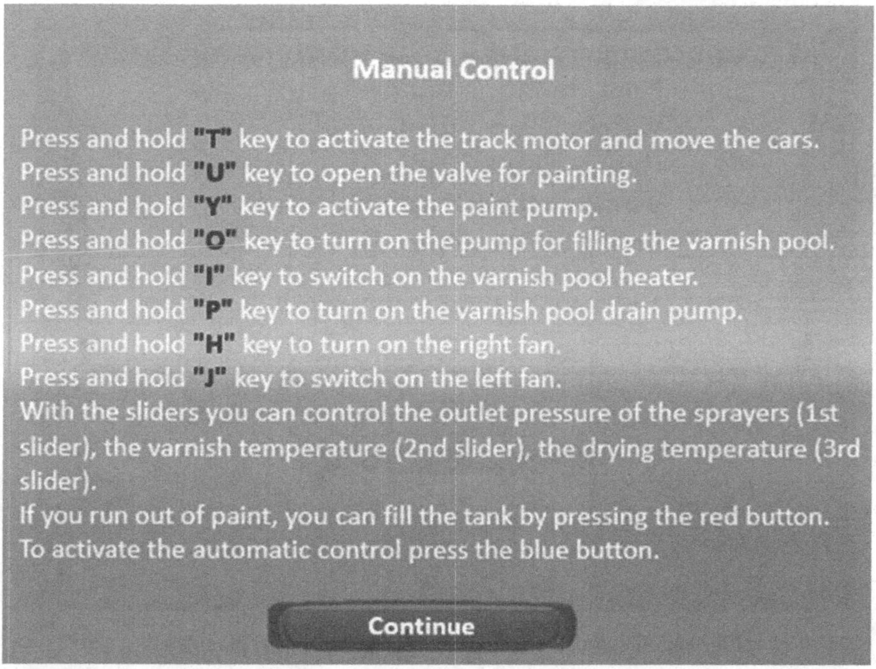

Manual Control
Press and hold "T" key to activate the track motor and move the cars.
Press and hold "U" key to open the valve for painting.
Press and hold "Y" key to activate the paint pump.
Press and hold "O" key to turn on the pump for filling the varnish pool.
Press and hold "I" key to switch on the varnish pool heater.
Press and hold "P" key to turn on the varnish pool drain pump.
Press and hold "H" key to turn on the right fan.
Press and hold "J" key to switch on the left fan.
With the sliders you can control the outlet pressure of the sprayers (1st slider), the varnish temperature (2nd slider), the drying temperature (3rd slider).
If you run out of paint, you can fill the tank by pressing the red button.
To activate the automatic control press the blue button.
Continue

Fig. 11. Manual control dialog box

What color would you like to paint the bodywork?
Continue

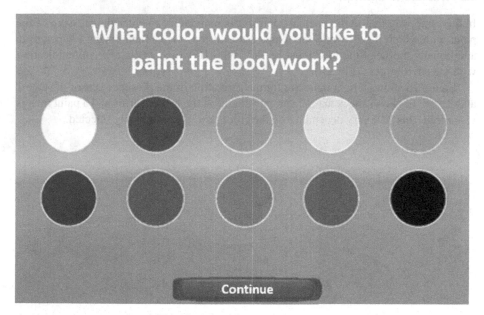

Fig. 12. Manual control dialog box

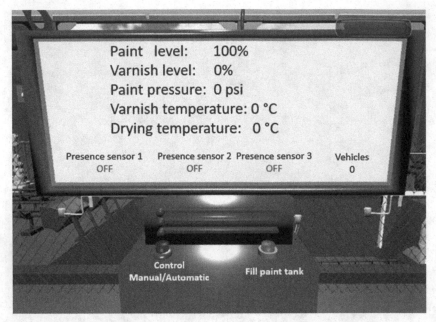

Fig. 13. 3D virtual environment interface of initial parameters

4.2 Automatic Control

In the same way that in the manual control it is mandatory to enter the pressure of the paint with which it will work, the temperature of the varnish and drying temperature, additionally the IP of the PLC must be 192.168.0.10 which will allow communication with the environment (Fig. 14).

Figure 15 shows a light indicator for the activation of the presence sensor of stage 1 and 2, Fig. 16 shows the actuation and movement of the robotic arms and a paint mist is visualized, this will vary depending on the color that was previously selected.

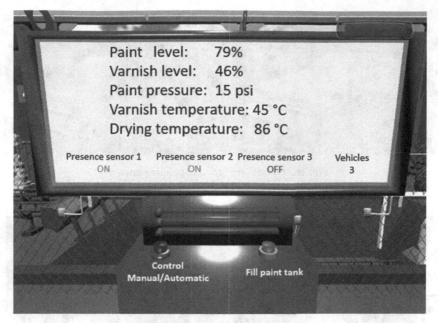

Fig. 14. HMI operation of the virtual environment

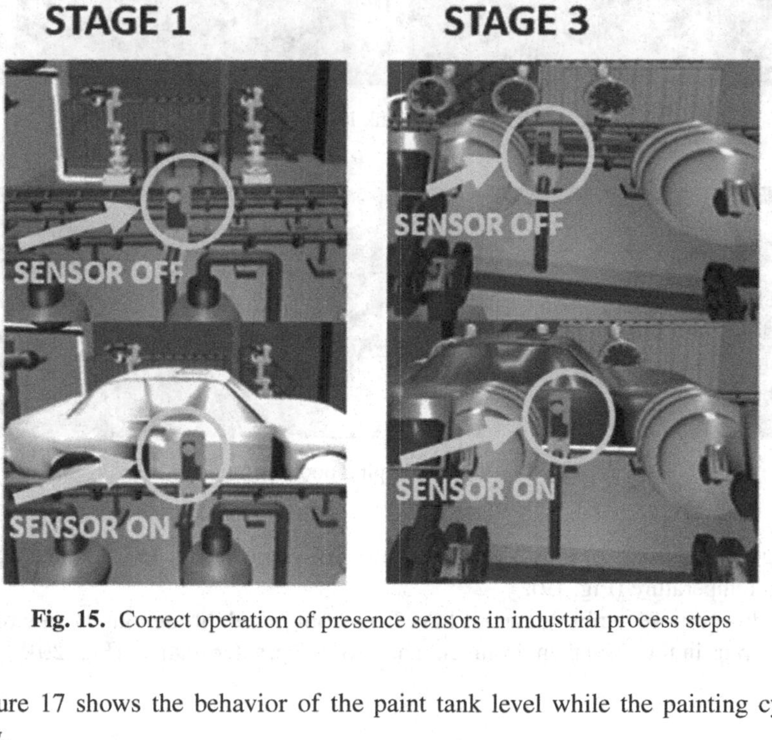

STAGE 1   STAGE 3

Fig. 15. Correct operation of presence sensors in industrial process steps

Figure 17 shows the behavior of the paint tank level while the painting cycle is running.

Fig. 16. Operation of robotic painting arms

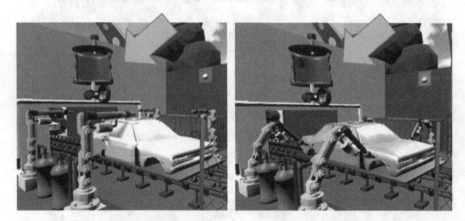

Fig. 17. Paint tank level display

Fig. 18. Varnish dipping pool operation

Stage two consists of immersing the vehicle in varnish (Fig. 18) and heating to the selected temperature (Fig. 19).

For this purpose, ambient sounds have been configured throughout the environment to envelop us in the virtual environment and provide greater realism (Fig. 20).

Fig. 19. Thermometer operation

Fig. 20. Operation of drying fans

5 Conclusions

The development of the 3D virtual environment for vehicle painting generates a user experience similar to the real one, having the option of manual and automatic control allows familiarization with the process to subsequently make a proposal for automation, generating skills in the training of technical personnel at a low cost.

The implementation of Sharp7 as a complement to the Unity3D graphics engine allows communication between the 3D virtual environment of the vehicle painting process and Tia Portal, helping to optimize the HIL technique.

The sensors, actuators and equipment designed in the virtual environment work in real time, as well as the communication with the PLC, generating a reliable system for training in industrial automation.

Acknowledgements. The authors would like to thank the Universidad de las Fuerzas Armadas ESPE for the support for the development of this work, especially the project 2020-PIC-017-CTE "Simulación de proceso industriales, mediante la técnica Hardware in the Loop, para el desarrollo de prácticas en Automatización Industrial".

References

1. Peixoto, D.C.C.: An educational simulation model derived from academic and industrial experiences. In: 2013 IEEE Frontiers in Education Conference (FIE), pp. 691–697 (2013)
2. Aguilar, I.S., Correa, J.L., Pruna, E.P.: 3D virtual system of a liquid filling and packaging process, using the hardware in the loop technique. In: De Paolis, L.T., Arpaia, P., Bourdot, P. (eds.) AVR 2021. LNCS, vol. 12980, pp. 573–587. Springer, Cham (2021). https://doi.org/10.1007/978-3-030-87595-4_42
3. Páez-Logreira, H., Zabala-Campo, V., Zamora-Musa, R.: Análisis y actualización del programa de la asignatura Automatización Industrial en la formación profesional de ingenieros electrónicos. Educación En Ingeniería 11, 39–44 (2016)
4. Rocha, B., Tipan, C., Freire, L.O.: 3D virtual system of an Apple sorting process using hardware-in-the-loop technique. In: Chatterjee, P., Pamucar, D., Yazdani, M., Panchal, D. (eds.) Computational Intelligence for Engineering and Management Applications. LNEE, vol. 984, pp. 675–688. Springer, Cham (2023). https://doi.org/10.1007/978-981-19-8493-8_50
5. Madachy, R.: Software Process Dynamics. Wiley-IEEE Press, New York (2008)
6. Vacacela, S.G., Freire, L.O.: Implementation of a network of wireless weather stations using a protocol stack. In: Reddy, A.N.R., Marla, D., Favorskaya, M.N., Satapathy, S.C. (eds.) Intelligent Manufacturing and Energy Sustainability. SIST, vol. 213, pp. 509–517. Springer, Singapore (2021). https://doi.org/10.1007/978-981-33-4443-3_49
7. Portal Automotriz, 19 October 2021. [En línea]. https://www.portalautomotriz.com/noticias/corporativo-e-industria/durr-crea-un-taller-de-pintura-automatizada-para-vinfast-con. Último acceso: 19 Oct 2021
8. Heijer, B.: Products Finishing, 19 October 2021. [En línea]. https://www.pf-mex.com/articulos/pasos-para-automatizar-su-cabina-de-pintura-con-robots
9. Pruna, E., Jimenez, I., Escobar, I.: Hardware-in-the-loop of a flow plant embedded in FPGA, for process control. In: Reddy, A.N.R., Marla, D., Simic, M., Favorskaya, M.N., Satapathy, S.C. (eds.) Intelligent Manufacturing and Energy Sustainability. SIST, vol. 169, pp. 181–189. Springer, Singapore (2020). https://doi.org/10.1007/978-981-15-1616-0_17
10. Mujber, T.S., Szecsi, T., Hashmi, M.S.J.: Virtual reality applications in manufacturing process simulation. J. Mater. Process. Technol. 155–156, 1834–1838 (2004)
11. Sutherland, I.: The ultimate display. In: Proceedings of IFIPS Congress (2004)
12. Freire, L.O., Bonilla, B.A., Corrales, B.P., Villarroel, J.L.: Hardware in the loop of a level plant embedded in Raspberry. In: Chatterjee, P., Pamucar, D., Yazdani, M., Panchal, D. (eds.) Computational Intelligence for Engineering and Management Applications. LNEE, vol. 984, pp. 635–643. Springer, Singapore (2023). https://doi.org/10.1007/978-981-19-8493-8_47

Author Index